OKLAHOMA
Math

HOUGHTON
MIFFLIN
HARCOURT
School Publishers

www.hmhschool.com

ISBN 13: 978-0-15-385708-9
ISBN 10: 0-15-385708-0

1 2 3 4 5 6 7 8 9 10 1421 17 16 15 14 13 12 11 10 09

OKLAHOMA Math

OKLAHOMA Math

Program Authors

Juli K. Dixon
Associate Professor of
Mathematics Education
University of Central Florida
Orlando, Florida

Matt Larson
Author-in-Residence
K–12 Curriculum Specialist
for Mathematics
Lincoln Public School District
Adjunct Professor, University
of Nebraska-Lincoln
Lincoln, Nebraska
Visiting Adjunct Professor,
Columbia University
New York, New York

Dr. Miriam A. Leiva
Distinguished Professor of
Mathematics Emerita
University of North Carolina
Charlotte, North Carolina

Joyce McLeod
Visiting Professor, Retired
Rollins College
Winter Park, Florida

**HOUGHTON
MIFFLIN
HARCOURT**
School Publishers

www.hmhschool.com

Table of Contents

Unit 1

Whole Numbers and Decimals

Math on Location 1
Get Ready Game: Digit Division 2
Reading and Writing Math 3

CHAPTER 1

Whole Numbers

✓ **Show What You Know** 5
1 Whole Numbers and Place Value 6
2 Add and Subtract Whole Numbers 8
3 Multiply and Divide Whole Numbers 10
4 **Problem Solving Workshop**
   Skill: Interpret the Remainder 14
5 **Algebra** Exponents 16
6 **Algebra** Order of Operations 20
7 **Algebra** Properties 22
   Extra Practice 24
   Wrap Up: Reading and Writing Math 26
   H.O.T. Multistep Problems 27
   Practice for the OCCT 28

Oklahoma Standards

2.2.c 6
2.2.c 8
2.2.c 10
2.2.c 14
2.2.e 16
2.2.e 20
1.4 22

CHAPTER 2 Decimals

✓	Show What You Know	31
1	Decimals and Place Value	32
2	Estimate with Decimals	36
3	Add and Subtract Decimals	40
4	Multiply Decimals	44
5	**Problem Solving Workshop** Strategy: Make a Table	48
6	Divide Decimals by Whole Numbers	52
7	Hands On: Explore Division of Decimals	56
8	Hands On: Divide with Decimals	58
9	Choose a Method	62
	Extra Practice	64
	Wrap Up: Reading and Writing Math	66
	H.O.T. Multistep Problems	67
	Practice for the OCCT	68

Oklahoma Standards

2.1	32
2.2.c	36
2.2.c	40
2.2.b	44
2.2.b	48
2.2.b	52
2.2.b	56
2.2.b	58
2.2.b	62

Unit 1

Performance Assessment	70
Unit Learning Activity	
Geologic Eras	71

THE WORLD ALMANAC FOR KIDS

Money Around the World	72

Standards Quick Check/Challenge

Lesson 1.3	p. 13	**Lesson 2.3**	p. 43
Lesson 1.5	p. 19	**Lesson 2.4**	p. 47
Lesson 2.1	p. 35	**Lesson 2.6**	p. 55
Lesson 2.2	p. 39	**Lesson 2.8**	p. 61

Number Theory and Fractions

Math on Location 75
Get Ready Game: Operation Cover Up 76
Reading and Writing Math 77

CHAPTER 3

Number Theory and Fraction Concepts

✓ **Show What You Know** 79
1 ✋Hands On: Divisibility 80
2 Prime and Composite Numbers 84
3 Prime Factorization 86
4 LCM and GCF 88
5 Understand Fractions 92
6 ✋Hands On: Equivalent Fractions and Simplest Form . . 94
7 Fractions and Mixed Numbers 98
8 Fractions and Decimals. 100
9 ✋Hands On: Fractions, Decimals, and Percents 104
10 Compare and Order Fractions, Decimals, and Percents . 106
11 **Problem Solving Workshop**
Skill: Use a Table 110
Extra Practice 112
Wrap Up: Reading and Writing Math 114
H.O.T. Multistep Problems 115
Practice for the OCCT 116

Oklahoma Standards

2.2.c.	80
1.1.	84
1.1.	86
2.2.a.	88
Maintain Skill	92
2.1.	94
2.1.	98
2.1.	100
2.1.	104
2.1.	106
2.1.	110

CHAPTER 4 Fraction Operations

	Show What You Know	119
1	Estimate Sums and Differences	120
2	Hands On: Add and Subtract Fractions	124
3	Add and Subtract Mixed Numbers	128
4	Record Subtraction with Renaming	132
5	Problem Solving Workshop	
	Skill: Multistep Problems	134
6	Practice Addition and Subtraction	136
7	Estimate Products and Quotients	140
8	Hands On: Multiply Fractions	142
9	Multiply Mixed Numbers	146
10	Hands On: Explore Division of Fractions	148
11	Reciprocals	152
12	Use Reciprocals	154
13	Hands On: Divide Fractions and Mixed Numbers	158
14	Problem Solving Workshop	
	Skill: Choose the Operation	162
	Extra Practice	164
	Wrap Up: Reading and Writing Math	166
	H.O.T. Multistep Problems	167
	Practice for the OCCT	168

Oklahoma Standards

2.2.c.	120
2.2.c.	124
2.2.c.	128
2.2.c.	132
2.2.c.	134
2.2.c.	136
2.2.c.	140
2.2.a.	142
2.2.a.	146
2.2.a.	148
2.2.a.	152
2.2.a.	154
2.2.a.	158
2.2.a.	162

Unit 2

Performance Assessment	170
Unit Learning Activity	
Healthy Eating	171
THE WORLD ALMANAC FOR KIDS	
Counting Votes	172

Unit 3 · Algebra

Math on Location 175
Get Ready Game: Operation Scramble 176
Reading and Writing Math 177

CHAPTER 5 Integers and Rational Numbers

☑ **Show What You Know** 179
1 Understand Integers 180
2 Add Integers. 184
3 Subtract Integers 188
4 ✋Hands On: Multiply Integers 192
5 Divide Integers 196
6 Operations with Integers 198
7 Problem Solving Workshop
  Strategy: Predict and Test 202
8 Rational Numbers. 206
9 Compare and Order Rational Numbers 210
10 Properties of Rational Numbers 212
  Extra Practice 216
  Wrap Up: Reading and Writing Math 218
  🔥H.O.T. Multistep Problems 219
  Practice for the OCCT 220

Oklahoma Standards

2.2.d. 180
2.2.d. 184
2.2.d. 188
2.2.d. 192
2.2.d. 196
2.2.d. 198
2.2.d. 202
2.2.d. 206
2.2.d. 210
2.2.c. 212

CHAPTER 6

Expressions and Equations

✓ **Show What You Know** 223
1 Write Algebraic Expressions 224
2 Evaluate Algebraic Expressions 228
3 Words and Equations 232
4 Solve Addition Equations 234
5 Solve Subtraction Equations 236
6 **Problem Solving Workshop**
   Strategy: Compare Strategies 238
7 Addition and Subtraction Equations 240
8 Solve Multiplication Equations 242
9 Solve Division Equations 246
10 Practice Solving Equations 248
   Extra Practice 250
   Wrap Up: Reading and Writing Math 252
   H.O.T. Multistep Problems 253
   Practice for the OCCT 254

Oklahoma Standards

1.2. 224
1.2. 228
1.2. 232
1.2. 234
1.2. 236
1.2. 238
1.2. 240
1.2. 242
1.2. 246
1.2. 248

Unit 3   Algebra

Math on Location 175
Get Ready Game: Operation Scramble 176
Reading and Writing Math 177

CHAPTER 7   Patterns

  ☑ **Show What You Know** 255
1 Patterns in Sequence 258
2 Number Patterns and Functions 262
3 Geometric Patterns 266
4 **Problem Solving Workshop**
  Strategy: Solve a Simpler Problem 268
  Extra Practice 272
  Wrap Up: Reading and Writing Math 274
  H.O.T. Multistep Problems 275
  Practice for the OCCT 276

Oklahoma Standards

1.1 258
1.1 262
1.1 266
1.1 268

Unit 3

Performance Assessment 278

Unit Learning Activity

Aircraft and Submarines 279

THE WORLD ALMANAC FOR KIDS

The Speed of Sound 280

Standards Quick Check/Challenge			
Lesson 5.1	p. 183	**Lesson 5.10**	p. 215
Lesson 5.2	p. 187	**Lesson 6.1**	p. 227
Lesson 5.3	p. 191	**Lesson 6.2**	p. 231
Lesson 5.4	p. 195	**Lesson 6.8**	p. 245
Lesson 5.6	p. 201	**Lesson 7.1**	p. 261
Lesson 5.8	p. 209	**Lesson 7.2**	p. 265

Unit 4

Geometry and Measurement

Math on Location 283
Get Ready Game: Find the Area 284
Reading and Writing Math 285

CHAPTER 8 Geometry

✓ **Show What You Know** 287
1 Graph on a Coordinate Plane 288
2 Graph Linear Equations 292
3 Similar and Congruent Figures 296
4 Types of Solid Figures 300
5 Hands On: Views of Solid Figures 304
6 Hands On: Models of Solid Figures 308
7 **Problem Solving Workshop**
   Skill: Make Generalizations 310
   Extra Practice 312
   Wrap Up: Reading and Writing Math 314
   H.O.T. Multistep Problems 315
   Practice for the OCCT 316

Oklahoma Standards

3.3 288
3.3 292
3.2 296
3.1 300
3.1 304
3.1 308
3.1 310

CHAPTER 9 Circumference and Measurement

✓ **Show What You Know**	. . . .	319
1	Hands On: Circles	320
2	Hands On: Estimate Circumference.	324
3	Algebra Find Circumference	326
4	Hands On: Area of Circles	330
5	Algebra Area of Circles	332
6	Hands On: Elapsed Time	334
7	Algebra Customary Measurements	336
8	Algebra Metric Measurements	338
9	Hands On: Compare Measurements	340
10	Problem Solving Workshop	
	Strategy: Compare Strategies	342
	Extra Practice	344
	Wrap Up: Reading and Writing Math	346
	H.O.T. Multistep Problems	347
	Practice for the OCCT	348

Oklahoma Standards

4.1.	320
4.1.	324
4.1.	326
4.1.	330
4.1.	332
4.2.	334
4.2.	336
4.2.	338
4.2.	340
4.2.	342

Unit 4

Performance Assessment	. . . .	350
Unit Learning Activity		
Famous Buildings	. . . .	351

THE WORLD ALMANAC FOR KIDS

Quite a Hike!	. . . .	352

Unit 5

Ratio, Proportion, Percent, Data, and Probability

Math on Location 355
Get Ready Game: Rapid Ratios 356
Reading and Writing Math 357

CHAPTER 10 Ratio, Proportion, and Percent

✓ **Show What You Know** 359
1 Ratio and Rates 360
2 ☆**Algebra** Write and Solve Proportions 364
3 ✋Hands On: ☆**Algebra** Ratios and Similar Figures 368
4 **Problem Solving Workshop**
   Strategy: Write an Equation 372
5 ✋Hands On: ☆**Algebra** Scale Drawings 376
6 Proportional Reasoning 380
7 Percent 382
8 Percent, Decimals, and Fractions 384
9 Percent of a Number 388
10 **Problem Solving Workshop**
   Skill: Use a Graph 392
11 Discount and Sales Tax 394
   Extra Practice 398
   Wrap Up: Reading and Writing Math 400
   🌞H.O.T.🌞 Multistep Problems 401
   Practice for the OCCT 402

Oklahoma Standards

2.1. 360
2.1. 364
2.1. 368
1.2. 372
3.2. 376
2.1. 380
2.1. 382
2.1. 384
2.2.c. 388
5.1. 392
2.2.c. 394

CHAPTER 11 Data and Graphs

☑ **Show What You Know** 405
1 Mean, Median, Mode, and Range 406
2 Outliers 410
3 Frequency Tables and Line Plots 414
4 Samples and Surveys 418
5 **Problem Solving Workshop**
   Strategy: Draw a Diagram 420
6 Bar Graphs 424
7 Line Graphs 426
8 Circle Graphs 428
9 Make and Analyze Graphs 430
10 Stem-and-Leaf Plots and Histograms 434
11 Compare Graphs 438
12 Choose an Appropriate Graph 440
13 **Problem Solving Workshop**
   Skill: Draw a Diagram 444
14 Find Unknown Values 446
   Extra Practice 450
   Wrap Up: Reading and Writing Math 452
   H.O.T. Multistep Problems 453
   Practice for the OCCT 454

Oklahoma Standards

5.3	406
5.3	410
5.1	414
5.1	418
5.1	420
5.1	424
5.1	426
5.1	428
5.1	430
5.1	434
5.1	438
5.1	440
5.1	444
5.1	446

Unit 5 Ratio, Proportion, Percent, Data, and Probability

Math on Location 355
Get Ready Game: Rapid Ratios 356
Reading and Writing Math 357

CHAPTER 12 Probability

  ✓ **Show What You Know** 457
1 Theoretical Probability 458
2 Experimental Probability 462
3 Estimate Probability 466
4 Make Predictions 468
5 **Problem Solving Workshop**
   Strategy: Make an Organized List 470
6 Outcome of Compound Events 472
7 ✋Hands On: Explore Independent and
   Dependent Events 476
8 Independent Events 478
9 Dependent Events 480
10 Permutations and Combinations 482
   Extra Practice 486
   Wrap Up: Reading and Writing Math 488
   H.O.T. Multistep Problems 489
   Practice for the OCCT 490

Oklahoma Standards

5.0	458
5.0	462
5.0	466
5.0	468
5.1	470
5.0	472
5.0	476
5.0	478
5.0	480
5.2	482

Unit 5

Performance Assessment 492
Unit Learning Activity
   Board Games 493

THE WORLD ALMANAC FOR KIDS

   Money Around the World 494

Standards Quick Check/Challenge			
Lesson 10.1	p. 363	**Lesson 11.3**	p. 417
Lesson 10.2	p. 367	**Lesson 11.9**	p. 433
Lesson 10.3	p. 371	**Lesson 11.10**	p. 437
Lesson 10.5	p. 379	**Lesson 11.12**	p. 443
Lesson 10.8	p. 387	**Lesson 11.14**	p. 449
Lesson 10.9	p. 391	**Lesson 12.1**	p. 461
Lesson 10.11	p. 397	**Lesson 12.2**	p. 465
Lesson 11.1	p. 409	**Lesson 12.6**	p. 475
Lesson 11.2	p. 413	**Lesson 12.10**	p. 485

Whole Numbers and Decimals

BIG IDEAS!

- Whole number operations are based on base-ten and place-value concepts and basic facts and follow algebraic properties.

- Decimal operations are based on place value and operations with whole numbers.

Math On Location
Online Videos

1

At this contact center, employees take about 2,000,000 customized computer system orders each month.

2

Parts sized precisely to thousandths of an inch move along systems of conveyors in the assembly building.

3

The different parts move on a roller conveyor to where they are divided and sent to different packing areas.

Get Ready Game

Digit Division

Object of the Game Create a division problem with the smallest remainder.

Materials
- 3 sets of 0–9 number tiles
- One number cube labeled with digits 2, 3, 4, 5, 6, and 9

Set Up
Shuffle number tiles. Label a number cube with the digits 2, 3, 4, 5, 6, and 9.

Number of Players 2

How to Play

1 Player 1 picks three number tiles. Player 2 rolls the number cube. Each player makes a dividend from the digits on the number tiles. Players divide by the number on the number cube.

. . . .

2 Players earn points equal to the remainder. If the remainder is 0, the player earns no points.

. . . .

3 Play continues until there are no more number tiles. The points are added, and the player with the lower total wins the game.

Reading
To get the right answer to a mathematics problem, you need to make sure you understand the question.

Problem 1

The Smith and the Jones families both start out on a 1,350-mile trip. On the first day, the Smiths travel 354 miles and the Joneses travel 485 miles. How many miles do the Smiths have to go before they reach their destination?

A 755 miles   **C** 996 miles

B 865 miles   **D** 1,704 miles

Writing
Now it's your turn! Answer Problem 2. Then write about how you solved the problem, step by step.

Problem 2

The Parke County Maple Syrup Fair happens for 6 days each year. If 659 people go on each of the 6 days of the fair, how many total people attended the fair?

A 4,122   **C** 3,295

B 3,954   **D** 3,043

Thinking Through the Problem

- **First, think about the question.** This question asks how many more miles before the Smiths reach their destination.

- **Think about what you know.** You know the whole distance. You know the part of the distance the Smiths have traveled.

- **Think about what you need to do to answer the question.** You need to find the missing part. One way to find a missing part is to subtract. Subtract 354 from 1,350 to get 996. C is the correct answer.

Check your answer.

Whole Numbers

Fun Fact

Kathy Wafler Madison cut the world's longest apple peel on October 16, 1976, in Rochester, New York. It was 172 feet, 4 inches long.

Investigate

The table shows apple production for 5 different states. Explain how you might find a state that produced at least as many pounds of apples as the sum of two other states' production shown in the table.

2005 Apple Production	
State	**Production (pounds)**
Michigan	780,000,000
Pennsylvania	515,000,000
New York	1,040,000,000
California	355,000,000
Washington	5,800,000,000

Technology
Student pages are available in the Student eBook.

✓ Show What You Know

Check your understanding of important skills
needed for success in Chapter 1.

ASSESSMENT
Soar To Success: Math.

▶ Round to the Nearest Hundred and Thousand

Round to the nearest hundred and thousand.

1. 1,367   **2.** 7,560   **3.** 6,405   **4.** 11,742   **5.** 66,899

6. 48,455   **7.** 98,447   **8.** 154,987   **9.** 675,075   **10.** 809,733

▶ Repeated Multiplication

Find the product.

11. $3 \times 3 \times 3$ **12.** $6 \times 6 \times 6$ **13.** $9 \times 9 \times 9$ **14.** $0 \times 0 \times 0 \times 0$

15. $10 \times 10 \times 10$ **16.** $12 \times 12 \times 12$ **17.** $13 \times 13 \times 13$ **18.** $1 \times 1 \times 1$

▶ Use Parentheses

Find the value of the expression.

19. $12 + (4 + 19)$ **20.** $(25 - 2) - 8$ **21.** $(2 \times 10) \times 4$ **22.** $3 \times (4 \times 5)$

23. $(3 \times 2) + (4 \times 1)$ **24.** $(21 \div 7) - (2 \div 1)$ **25.** $(15 - 9) \times (7 + 2)$ **26.** $(20 - 8) \times (3 + 2)$

Vocabulary

Ways to Write a Number	
standard form Use digits only.	416,328
word form Use words only.	four hundred sixteen thousand, three hundred twenty-eight
short word form Use digits and words.	416 thousand, 328
expanded form Show the value of each digit.	$(4 \times 100,000) +$ $(1 \times 10,000) + (6 \times 1,000)$ $+ (3 \times 100) + (2 \times 10) + 8$

Language Tips

Words that look alike in English and
Spanish often have the same meaning.

English	Spanish
add	**sumar**
compare	**comparar**
subtract	**restar**

See **English-Spanish Glossary.**

LESSON 1

★ **2.2.c.** Estimate and find solutions to single and multi-step problems using whole numbers, decimals, fractions, and percents (e.g., 7/8 + 8/9 is about 2, 3.9 + 5.3 is about 9). *also* **2.1.**

Materials
• MathBoard

Whole Numbers and Place Value

Essential Question How is place value used to compare and order whole numbers?

PROBLEM The U.S. Census Bureau projects the world population will reach 7,202,516,136 in 2015. Each digit in a number has a place value. The value of the digit is determined by its position in the number. The value of the digit 7 in 7,202,516,136 is 7 × 1,000,000,000, or 7,000,000,000, since it is in the billions place.

BILLIONS			MILLIONS			THOUSANDS			ONES			← period
Hundreds	Tens	Ones	Hundreds	Tens	Ones	Hundreds	Tens	Ones	Hundreds	Tens	Ones	
		7,	2	0	2,	5	1	6,	1	3	6	

There are different ways to write numbers.

Standard form: 7,202,516,136

Expanded form: 7,000,000,000 + 200,000,000 + 2,000,000 + 500,000 + 10,000 + 6,000 + 100 + 30 + 6

Word form: seven billion, two hundred two million, five hundred sixteen thousand, one hundred thirty-six

Compare. Use < or >.

492,563,710 and 492,538,167

492,5**6**3,710   Start at the left. Compare the digits in the same position.
492,5**3**8,167   The ten-thousands digits are the first that are different.

6 > 3   6 is greater than 3.

So, 492,563,710 > 492,538,167.

Order from least to greatest.

5,293,078; 5,294,278; 5,293,288

Compare every possible pair.
5,293,078 < 5,294,278   5,293,288 < 5,294,278   5,293,078 < 5,293,288

So, the order from least to greatest is
5,293,078; 5,293,288; 5,294,278.

1. Compare. Use < or > for the ⬭.

 5,834,978,201 ⬭ 5,834,798,210   5,834,9̲78,210
                                   5,834,7̲98,201

Write the value of the blue digit.

2. 726,04**3**,791   3. 5,3**9**6,724,209,998   ✓4. 6,2**8**0,049,164   ✓5. 1**4**,807,354,996

6. **Math Talk** **Explain** how you know the value of the digit 6 in the number 2,516,189,073.

Practice and Problem Solving REAL WORLD

Write the value of the blue digit.

7. 42,9**5**6,378,201   8. 39**9**,428,211   9. 4**6**0,278   10. **2**71,326,085

Write in expanded form and word form.

11. 850,309,720   12. 2,507,300,003   13. 9,482,351   14. 600,070,000,000

Compare. Use < or > for each ⬭.

15. 3,920,157 ⬭ 3,902,571   16. 619,358,204 ⬭ 619,305,284   17. 76 billion ⬭ 96 million

Order from least to greatest.

18. 406,320,851; 406,322,700; 406,320,837   19. 9,423,109,634; 9,432,190,634; 9,432,910,643

20. **Write Math** → **What's the Error?** Emma said the U.S. population increased by about 300 thousand between 2004 and 2005. Describe her error, and find the correct answer.

21. Write the names of the states shown in order from least to greatest population in 2005.

22. Which state had the second-greatest population in 2004?

Population Estimates		
	2004	**2005**
U.S.	293,656,842	296,410,371
Illinois	12,712,016	12,763,371
Michigan	10,104,206	10,120,860
New Jersey	8,685,166	8,717,925
New York	19,280,727	19,254,630
Ohio	11,450,143	11,464,042
Pennsylvania	12,394,471	12,429,616

23. Which shows the correct value of the blue digit in 5,4**6**8,279?

     A 6 thousands   **C** 6 ten thousands

     B 6 millions   **D** 6 ten millions

24. Which is six million, four hundred eight thousand, nine hundred six written in standard form?

     A 6,408,609   **C** 6,408,960

     B 6,408,906   **D** 6,480,960

Add and Subtract Whole Numbers

Essential Question How can you use mental math, a calculator, and paper and pencil to find sums and differences; how do you use inverse operations to check the answers?

2.2.c. Estimate and find solutions to single and multi-step problems using whole numbers, decimals, fractions, and percents (e.g., 7/8 + 8/9 is about 2, 3.9 + 5.3 is about 9). *also* **2.2.d.**

Materials
• MathBoard

PROBLEM Two caves in Kentucky are among the longest caves in the United States. How many meters longer is Mammoth Cave than the Fisher Ridge Cave System?

Longest U.S. Caves			
Name	**State**	**Length (mi)**	**Length (m)**
Mammoth Cave	Kentucky	355	571,317
Jewel Cave	South Dakota	125	200,637
Lechuguilla Cave	New Mexico	106	170,252
Fisher Ridge Cave System	Kentucky	98	158,310
Carlsbad Caverns	New Mexico	31	49,729

To solve some problems with whole numbers, you can use mental math. For other problems, paper and pencil or a calculator may be best.

Use mental math to subtract. 571,317 − 158,310

$571,000 - 160,000 = 411,000$ — Look at the thousands. Change 158,000 to 160,000. Subtract.

$317 - 310 = 7$ — Look at the hundreds. Subtract.

$411,000 + 2,000 + 7 = 413,007$ — Since $160,000 - 158,000 = 2,000$, you subtracted 2,000 too much. Add 2,000 and then add 7 to adjust the answer. Add back 2,000 and 7.

So, Mammoth Cave is 413,007 m longer than the Fisher Ridge Cave System.

Add. 170,252 + 49,729

Use paper and pencil.

$$\begin{array}{r} \overset{1}{1}\overset{1}{7}0,252 \\ +\ 49,729 \\ \hline 219,981 \end{array}$$

Check:
$$\begin{array}{r} 219,981 \\ -\ 49,729 \\ \hline 170,252\ \checkmark \end{array}$$

Use a calculator.

170,252 [+] 49,729 [=]

[=] *219,981*

---

1. Look at the table on page 8. What is the difference in miles of the lengths of Mammoth Cave and the Fisher Ridge Cave System?

Use mental math. 98 is almost 100.
Subtract. 355 − 100 = ▓
Add back 2.
So, 355 − 98 = ▓. The difference is ▓ miles.

Find the sum or difference. Estimate or use inverse operations to check.

2. 37 + 95 + 56 + 77   **3.** 963 + 5,554   ✅**4.** 10,002 − 4,663   ✅**5.** 185,000 − 3,342

6. Math Talk **Explain** why you might choose mental math rather than paper and pencil to solve Problem 1.

Practice and Problem Solving REAL WORLD

Find the sum or difference. Estimate or use inverse operations to check.

7. 74,000 − 489   **8.** 516 + 608 + 439   **9.** 32 + 170 + 312   **10.** 3,278 + 9,659

11. 648,601 + 56,724   **12.** 105,007 − 24,672   **13.** 5,552 − 3,706   **14.** 3,455 + 8,045

Real World Data

For 15−18, use the table.

15. Estimate the total vertical distance you would travel if you explored to the bottom and back to the top in both of the U.S. caves.

16. If scientists discovered that the Mexican cave goes 239 ft deeper, what will be the new difference in depth between the Mexican cave and the cave in Georgia?

17. For which two caves might it be easiest to find the difference in depth using mental math? **Explain**.

18. Write Math ▶ What type of number do you get when you add two even numbers? Two odd numbers? An odd and an even number? **Explain**.

Some of World's Deepest Caves		
Cave	**Country**	**Depth (ft)**
Veronja	Georgia	5,610
Systema Huautla	Mexico	4,839
Slovaka Jama	Croatia	4,268
Kazumura	U.S. (Hawaii)	3,612
Lechuguilla	U.S. (New Mexico)	1,567

 OCCT Test Prep

19. Which of the following is the sum of 439,005 and 300,898?

   A 139,022   **C** 740,002

   B 739,903   **D** 741,405

20. Which of the following is the difference of 126,748 and 54,488?

   A 181,236   **C** 90,280

   B 175,248   **D** 72,260

2.2.c. Estimate and find solutions to single and multi-step problems using whole numbers, decimals, fractions, and percents (e.g., 7/8 + 8/9 is about 2, 3.9 + 5.3 is about 9). *also* **2.2.d.**

Materials
• MathBoard

Multiply and Divide Whole Numbers

Essential Question How can you use mental math, a calculator, and paper and pencil to find products and quotients?

PROBLEM Travelers at New Jersey's Newark Liberty Airport can ride the AirTrain monorail from any parking lot to any terminal. Each 6-car train can carry 78 people. If one train makes 99 trips during the day, what is the greatest number of people the train can carry in one day?

Use mental math.

Multiply. 78 × 99

78 × 100 = 7,800   Change 99 to 100. Multiply.

7,800 − 78 = 7,722   Since 100 − 99 = 1, your answer is 1 × 78, or 78, which is too high. Subtract 78 to adjust the product.

So, the train can carry 7,722 people in one day.

Use paper and pencil.

Multiply. 2,286 × 97. Estimate. 2,300 × 100 = 230,000

$$\begin{array}{r} 2,286 \\ \times\ 97 \\ \hline 16002 \\ +205740 \\ \hline 221,742 \end{array}$$

Compare the exact product with your estimate. Since 221,742 is close to the estimate of 230,000, the product is reasonable.

Use a calculator.

Multiply. 2,286 × 97.

You can use this key sequence to find 2,286 × 97.

2,286 97   = 221'742

So, 2,286 × 97 = 221,742.

Remember

Multiplication and division are inverse operations. You can use multiplication to check division and division to check multiplication.

Divide Whole Numbers

Divide large numbers without remainders.

An airport parking lot has 2,800 spaces. If each row has 25 spaces, how many rows are there?

Divide. 2,800 ÷ 25   **Estimate.** 2,500 ÷ 25 = 100

```
        112
   25)2800
     -25↓|
       30|
      -25↓
        50
       -50
         0
```

Compare the exact quotient with your estimate. Since 112 is close to the estimate of 100, the quotient is reasonable.

So, there are 112 rows of parking spaces.

Remember

You can express a remainder with an r, as a fractional part of the divisor, or as a decimal.
26 r1 = $26\frac{1}{5}$ = 26.2

Divide small numbers with remainders.

An AirTrain round-trip takes 18 min. How many round-trips does an AirTrain make in 4 hr? **Hint:** 4 hr = 4 × 60, or 240 min.

Divide. 240 ÷ 18 **Estimate.** 240 ÷ 20 = 12

```
       13r6
   18)240↓
     -18↓
       60
      -54
        6
```

Compare the exact quotient with your estimate. Since 13 r 6 is close to the estimate of 12, the quotient is reasonable.

```
check:    13
         ×18
         104
        +130
         234
        +  6
         240 ✓
```

Multiply the quotient by the divisor.

Add the remainder.

So, the AirTrain makes 13 round-trips in 4 hr.

Divide large numbers with remainders.

Divide. 2,730 ÷ 25

```
       109 r5
   25)2730
     -25↓|
       23|
      - 0↓
       230
      -225
         5
```

Compare the exact quotient with your estimate. Since 109 r 5 is close to the estimate of 100, the quotient is reasonable.

```
check:    109
         × 25
          545
        +2180
         2725
        +   5
         2,730 ✓
```

Multiply the quotient by the divisor.

Add the remainder.

Share and Show

1. Find $29\overline{)986}$. Estimate the quotient to check.

   Hint: $29 \times 3 = 87$.

Find the product or quotient. Check your answer.

2. 672×55 3. $6,114 \div 63$ ✓4. $145 \times 1,113$ ✓5. $3,774 \div 37$

6. **Math Talk** **Explain** why you can use multiplication to check a division problem.

Practice and Problem Solving REAL WORLD

Find the product or quotient. Check your answer.

7. $2,115 \div 72$ 8. $28,536 \div 24$ 9. 522×398 10. $6,758 \times 103$

11. $13\overline{)182}$ 12. 490×48 13. $1,068 \times 22$ 14. $4\overline{)412}$

15. 269×50 16. $9\overline{)3,150}$ 17. $29\overline{)13,266}$ 18. $8,031 \times 539$

Divide. Write the remainder as a fraction.

19. $8\overline{)75}$ 20. $846 \div 36$ 21. $12\overline{)1,150}$ 22. $4,066 \div 20$

Algebra **Find the least whole number that can replace** 🔘 **to make the statement true.**

23. $60 \times$ 🔘 $> 5,519$ 24. 🔘 $\div 9 > 253 + 447$ 25. $2,700 - 312 < 3 \times$ 🔘

26. La Ronde Park in Montreal, Canada, has a monorail that originally carried 12 trains, each with 16 cars. Each car could hold 60 riders. If all the trains ran at once and were full, how many riders were there?

27. **Write Math** ▶ **What's the Question?** A student car wash charged $3 for cars and $5 for vans. The students washed 23 cars and 18 vans. The answer is $21.

★ OCCT Test Prep

28. What is the remainder of $7,756 \div 38$?

   A 3   C 16

   B 4   D 24

29. Mark gave 45 candy corns to 40 of his friends. How many candy corns did Mark have to give to his friends?

   A 85   C 1,640

   B 198   D 1,800

★ Standards Quick Check

Find the product or quotient.

1. 451 × 4

2. 1,500 ÷ 35

3. 174 × 65

4. 254 × 14

5. 368 × 70

6. 984 ÷ 24

Compare. Use < or > for each 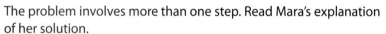 .

7. 14,154 ⬤ 14,145

8. 3,617 ⬤ 36,710

9. 241,766 ⬤ 241,746

Challenge H.O.T.

Writing an explanation helps you think through the steps you need to take to solve a problem. It also helps you understand a math concept or skill.

Small trophies cost $8 each and large trophies cost $15 each. There are two boxes of each size, with 18 trophies in each box. What is the total cost of the trophies?

The problem involves more than one step. Read Mara's explanation of her solution.

The problem asks for the total cost of the small and large trophies. First, multiply the number of boxes of each size by the number of trophies in each box to find the number of small trophies and the number of large trophies.

$$2 \times 18 = 36$$

Next, find the cost of the small trophies and the cost of the large trophies.

$$\$8 \times 36 = \$288 \qquad \$15 \times 36 = \$540$$

Finally, find the total cost of the small and large trophies.

$$\$288 + \$540 = \$828$$

So, the total cost of the trophies is $828.

Write an explanation to show how to solve the problem.

1. John and his dad are watching a soccer game at the stadium. The stadium has 8 sections of seats. John counts 95 seats in half of the section where he is sitting. If all of the sections have the same number of seats, how many seats does the stadium have?

2. Brittany has $535 in a savings account now. She puts at least $107 from her paycheck into her savings account each month. What is the least amount of money she will have in the savings account 6 months from now if she does not take out any money?

Tips

To write an explanation:

- Tell what the problem is in the first sentence.
- Use transition words, such as *first*, *next*, and *finally*, to show the order of your steps.
- Use correct math terms.
- Show all computations.
- State the solution of the problem in the last sentence of your explanation.

★ **2.2.c.** Estimate and find solutions to single and multi-step problems using whole numbers, decimals, fractions, and percents (e.g., 7/8 + 8/9 is about 2, 3.9 + 5.3 is about 9). *also* **2.2.d.**

Materials
• MathBoard

Problem Solving Workshop
Skill: Interpret the Remainder

Essential Question How does the context of a word problem affect how you interpret the remainder of a whole number division problem?

▶ **Use the Skill** REAL WORLD

PROBLEM Memorial Middle School is having a Fun-on-the-Field Day. In planning and running the day, the teachers come across two problems that can be solved by finding quotients.

Ms. Lee decides that she needs 189 bags of trail mix. A box holds 8 bags. How many boxes of trail mix should Ms. Lee buy?

$$\begin{array}{r} 23\ r5 \\ 8\overline{)189} \\ -16 \\ \hline 29 \\ -24 \\ \hline 5 \end{array}$$

The quotient, 23, represents 23 boxes. The remainder represents 5 extra bags that are needed. Since 5 extra bags are needed, increase the quotient by 1.

So, Ms. Lee should buy 24 boxes of trail mix.

For the tug-of-war competition, Coach Martin will cut a 128-ft piece of rope into 18-ft pieces. How many 18-ft pieces will there be?

$$\begin{array}{r} 7\ r2 \\ 18\overline{)128} \\ -126 \\ \hline 2 \end{array}$$

The remainder is not enough for another 18-ft length of rope. Drop the remainder.

So, there will be seven 18-ft pieces of rope.

Solve the problem by interpreting the remainder. Explain your answer.

a. Coach Martin has 208 ribbons to award for 21 events. He needs to award the same number in each event. The remaining ribbons will be saved for next year. What is the maximum number of ribbons that Coach Martin can give out for each event? How many ribbons will be left for next year if Coach Martin gives out that many?

b. The teachers decide that 500 bottles of water will be needed. A case holds 24 bottles. How many cases of water should they buy?

Solve the problem by interpreting the remainder. Explain your answer.

1. The parks department has planned a bus trip for 230 people to a baseball game. Each bus holds 47 people. How many buses will be needed?

   | Number of people | | People in each bus | |

   230 ÷ 47 = ■ r ■

   Think: There must be enough buses to seat everyone.

   So, ■ buses are needed.

2. **What if** each bus held 36 people? How many buses would be needed?

3. Brian took $9.00 to the baseball game to buy baseball cards. Each card costs $0.79. What is the greatest number of cards Brian can buy? How much money will he have left?

4. There are 12 tennis courts at the Tennis Center. The courts can be reserved for 9 A.M., 10:30 A.M., noon, and 1:30 P.M. If 136 people want to play doubles tennis (4 players on each court) as early as possible, how many will have to wait until at least noon to play?

**Real World Data**

For 5–7, use the table.

5. How does the total enrollment for the first four counties shown compare with the enrollment for Kanawha County?

6. Suppose Kanawha County decided that each of its schools should have about the same number of students. About how many students would be in each school if there were 200 schools? **Explain.**

7. **Write Math** Julia has 258 football cards that she wants to share with 4 of her friends. If she divides her cards into 5 equal groups, she'll have some left over. **Explain** how you can determine how many cards Julia will have left over.

West Virginia Counties Public School Enrollment (2008–2009)

County	Enrollment
Pendleton	1,101
Harrison	11,192
Boone	4,622
Ritchie	1,589
Berkeley	17,214
Kanawha	28,465

LESSON 5

2.2.e. Build and recognize models of multiples to develop the concept of exponents and simplify numerical expressions with exponents and parentheses using order of operations.

Vocabulary

base

exponent

Materials

• MathBoard

Math Idea

The zero power of any number, except 0, is defined to be 1.
$4^0 = 1$ $8^0 = 1$ $10^0 = 1$

ALGEBRA:

Exponents

Essential Question How do you evaluate a number in exponent form; what does the exponent tell you?

PROBLEM On July 1, 1925, the airport now known as Cleveland Hopkins International opened in Cleveland, Ohio. More than 100,000 people enjoyed a "flying circus" of planes with lit torches on their wings. Write 100,000 using smaller numbers.

When working with a large number, it is often easier to write the number as the product of repeated equal factors using exponents.

Writing exponents.

Four ways to write 100,000 by using smaller numbers are shown at the right.

$10 \times 10,000$
$10 \times 10 \times 1,000$
$10 \times 10 \times 10 \times 100$
$10 \times 10 \times 10 \times 10 \times 10$

Another way to write 100,000 is by using an exponent. An **exponent** shows how many times a number, called the **base,** is used as a factor.

exponent ↘
$$10^5 = \underbrace{10 \times 10 \times 10 \times 10 \times 10}_{\text{equal factors}} = 100,000$$
base

So, 100,000 can be written as 10^5.

Look at the patterns in the table below.

Exponent Form	Read	Value
$10^1 = 10$	the first power of ten	10
$10^2 = 10 \times 10$	ten squared, or the second power of ten	100
$10^3 = 10 \times 10 \times 10$	ten cubed, or the third power of ten	1,000
$10^4 = 10 \times 10 \times 10 \times 10$	the fourth power of ten	10,000

• Explain how to use the patterns in the table to find the value of 10^6.

Examples

Find the values of 2^1 and 5^2.

$2^1 = 2$ 2 is a factor one time.

$5^2 = 5 \times 5 = 25$ 5 is a factor two times.

Write 64 by using 4 as the base.

$64 = 4 \times 16$ Find the equal factors. Write using a base and exponent.

$= 4 \times 4 \times 4$

$= 4^3$

16

Expanded Form

In January 2007, Cincinnati/Northern Kentucky International Airport recorded 1,186,176 passengers.

You can use powers of 10 or exponents to show numbers in expanded form. The value of each digit in 1,186,176 can be expressed with or without an exponent. For example, the value of 8 can be written as 80,000, as $8 \times 10,000$, or as 8×10^4.

When writing a number in expanded form, you do not need to write the value of a place with a zero digit. For example, $1,003 = (1 \times 10^3) + (3 \times 10^0)$.

Write 1,186,176 in expanded form.

1 **Use powers of 10.**
$1,186,176 = (1 \times 1,000,000) + (1 \times 100,000) + (8 \times 10,000) + (6 \times 1,000) + (1 \times 100) + (7 \times 10) + (6 \times 1)$

· ·

2 **Use exponents.**
$1,186,176 = (1 \times 10^6) + (1 \times 10^5)\ 1\ (8 \times 10^4) + (6 \times 10^3) + (1 \times 10^2) + (7 \times 10^1) + (6 \times 10^0)$

Write $(8 \times 10^4) + (7 \times 10^1) + (9 \times 10^0)$ in standard form.

$8 \times 10^4 = 8 \times 10,000 = 80,000$
$7 \times 10^1 = 7 \times 10 = 70$
$9 \times 10^0 = 9 \times 1 = 9$

$80,000 + 70 + 9 = 80,079$

 Share and Show

1. Copy and complete to write 2^6 using equal factors. Then find the value of 2^6.

$2^6 = 2 \times 2 \times \blacksquare \times \blacksquare \times \blacksquare \times \blacksquare = \blacksquare$

Write as an expression using equal factors. Then find the value.

2. 3^7 **3.** 2^6 **4.** 9^3 **5.** 10^7 ✅**6.** 4^4

Write in exponent form.

7. $3 \times 3 \times 3 \times 3 \times 3 \times 3$ **8.** 5×5 **9.** $7 \times 7 \times 7 \times 7$ ✅**10.** $5 \times 5 \times 5 \times 5 \times 5$

Write in expanded form using powers of 10 and using exponents.

11. 694   **12.** 2,745   **13.** 11,300   **14.** 102,619   **15.** 89,704

16. **Math Talk** **Explain** the difference between 3^4 and 4^3.

Write as an expression using equal factors. Then find the value.

17. 64 **18.** 04 **19.** 40 **20.** 75 **21.** 232

Write in exponent form.

22. $11 \times 11 \times 11 \times 11 \times 11$ **23.** $25 \times 25 \times 25 \times 25$ **24.** $2 \times 2 \times 2 \times 2 \times 2 \times 2 \times 2$

Write in expanded form using powers of 10 and using exponents.

25. 555 **26.** 8,427 **27.** 9,012 **28.** 58,343 **29.** 30,014,000

**Algebra Find the value that will replace ■ to make the statement true.**

30. $3^{■} = 81$ **31.** $10^{■} = 10,000$ **32.** $4^{■} = 64$ **33.** $■^7 = 128$ **34.** $5^{■} = 625$

Compare. Write <, >, or = for each ⬭.

35. 10^2 ⬭ 5^3 **36.** $10,000$ ⬭ 10^5 **37.** 10^0 ⬭ 100^0 **38.** 20^1 ⬭ 20^0 **39.** 2^6 ⬭ 3^6

 Real World Data

For 40–41, use the table.

40. For which data would an estimate of 10^5 be reasonable?

41. Write the number of pounds of mail at Cleveland Hopkins Airport in 2003 in expanded form using exponents.

42. **Explain** the difference between 2^5 and 2×10^5.

Cleveland Hopkins International		
	2003	**2004**
Passengers	9,662,000	10,657,000
Scheduled Departures	107,076	110,751
Freight (lb)	189,371,000	188,998,000
Mail (lb)	17,705,000	12,074,000

★ **OCCT Test Prep** Math Board

43. Which shows $(3 \times 1,000,000) + (4 \times 10,000) + (7 \times 1,000) + (5 \times 1)$ written in standard form?

A 3,475 **C** 3,047,005

B 304,705 **D** 3,470,005

44. Which is 71,012 written in exponential form?

A $(7 \times 10^4) + (1 \times 10^3) + (1 \times 10^1) + (2 \times 10^0)$

B $(7 \times 10^5) + (1 \times 10^3) + (1 \times 10^1) + (2 \times 10^0)$

C $(7 \times 10^3) + (1 \times 10^2) + (1 \times 10^1) + (2 \times 10^0)$

D $(7 \times 10^6) + (1 \times 10^4) + (1 \times 10^2) + (2 \times 10^0)$

GO ONLINE —Technology— Use HMH Mega Math, Ice Station Exploration, *Arctic Algebra,* Levels U, V.

★ Standards Quick Check

Write in exponent form.

1. $10 \times 10 \times 10$

2. $16 \times 16 \times 16 \times 16$

3. 71×71

Write in expanded form using powers of 10 and using exponents.

4. 96

5. 145

6. 5,141

Compare. Use < or > for each ⬭ .

7. 9^4 ⬭ 6^5

8. 13^3 ⬭ 8^4

9. 21^3 ⬭ 20^3

Challenge H.O.T.

Bacteria are everywhere. If the conditions are ideal, a bacterium cell grows slightly, then splits into two "daughter" cells. If the conditions continue to be ideal, the daughter cells will split in 20 min, and there will be 4 cells. This splitting can happen again and again. Scientists who study bacteria try to create the ideal conditions in laboratories.

1. Copy and complete the table.

Cell Division and Multiplication	
Number of Cells	**Time (min)**
$2^1 = 2$	0
$2^2 = 4$	20
$2^3 = \blacksquare$	40
$2^{\blacksquare} = 16$	60
$2^5 = \blacksquare$	80
$2^{\blacksquare} = \blacksquare$	100
$2^7 = 128$	$\blacksquare$

2. Extend your table to find the number of cells after 3 hours. What power of 2 shows the number of cells?

3. Extend your table to find the time it would take to have a total of 4,096 cells.

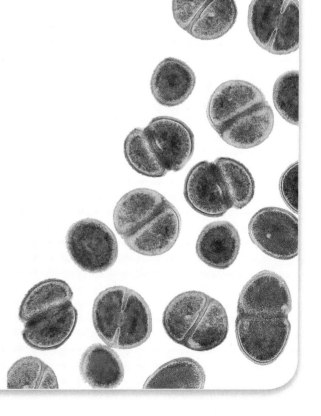

2.2.e. Build and recognize models of multiples to develop the concept of exponents and simplify numerical expressions with exponents and parentheses using order of operations.

Vocabulary

evaluate

numerical expression

order of operations

Materials
• MathBoard

ALGEBRA:

Order of Operations

Essential Question What order should be followed to evaluate expressions that contain more than one operation?

 **Learn**

A **numerical expression** is a mathematical phrase that uses only numbers and operation symbols. Here are some examples.

$(5 - 2) \times 7$ $72 \div 9 + 16$ $2 + 4^3 \div 4$ $5^2 + 13$

For many things you do, you must complete steps in a certain order. For example, when you bake a cake, you may need to crack eggs, beat them, and then add them to the batter.

In mathematics, when you evaluate numerical expressions that have more than one operation, you follow rules called the **order of operations**.

Order of Operations
1. Perform operations in parentheses.
2. Clear exponents.
3. Multiply and divide from left to right.
4. Add and subtract from left to right.

To **evaluate** an expression, find the value of the expression.

Evaluate $3 \times 4 + 3 \times 2$.

A recipe requires 4 c flour and 2 c sugar. If Diego and Heather triple the recipe, how many cups of flour and sugar combined are needed?

Correct	Not Correct
Diego	Heather
$3 \times 4 + 3 \times 2$ First, I multiplied	$3 \times 4 + 3 \times 2$ First, I added.
$12 + 6$ twice. Then I added.	$3 \times 7 \times 2$ Then I multiplied.
18	42

So, 18 c of flour and sugar are needed.

Examples

Evaluate the expression.

$5^2 \times (15 - 8) + 4$	Operate inside parentheses.
$5^2 \times 7 + 4$	Clear the exponent.
$25 \times 7 + 4$	Multiply.
$175 + 4 = 179$	Add.

Evaluate the expression.

$2 + (3^3 - 2^2) \times 2$	Clear the exponents.
$2 + (27 - 4) \times 2$	Operate inside parentheses.
$2 + 23 \times 2$	Multiply.
$2 + 46 = 48$	Add.

Complete each step to evaluate the expression.

1. $4^2 - 2 \times 5$ Clear the exponent.
   $16 - 2 \times 5$ Multiply.
   $16 - 10$ Subtract.
   ▪

2. $(15 - 3)2 \div 9$ Operate inside parentheses.
   $122 \div 9$ Clear exponents.
   $j \div 9$ Divide.
   j

Evaluate the expression.

3. $10 + 6^2 \times 2 \div 9$

④ 4. $10 + (6^2 - 11) \div 5$

⑤ 5. $(10 + 6^2) - 4 \times 10$

6. $3^3 - 2^2 + 4^0 - 3^1$

7. $16 + 18 \div 9 + 3^4 \times 1$

8. $5 + 17 - 10^2 \div 5$

9. **Math Talk** **Explain** how the parentheses make the values of these expressions different: $2^4 - 6 \div 6 - 1$ and $(2^4 - 6) \div (6 - 1)$.

► **Practice and Problem Solving** REAL WORLD

Evaluate the expression.

10. $6 + 24 \div 3 \times 4$

11. $(8^2 + 2^4)^2 \div (4 \times 5^2)$

12. $12 + 21 \div 3 + 2^5 \times 0$

Find the value of ▪ that makes the statement true.

13. $▪^2 + 24 = 10 \times 6$

14. $7 \times ▪ + 2^2 - 3 = 22$

15. $9^2 - 3^0 = ▪ + 4$

Place parentheses in the expression so that it equals the given value.

16. $10^2 - 30 \div 5; 14$

17. $23 + 1^8 \times 5 - 2^2; 32$

18. $3^2 + 5 \div 5 + 2; 2$

For 19–20, write and evaluate an expression to solve.

19. A restaurant has 16 tables for 2 and 14 tables for 4, but 9 chairs are missing from the tables. How many people can be seated at the restaurant?

20. Mr. Wright saved for a new computer for his restaurant. He saved $120 the first week and $50 each week for the next 6 weeks. How much had he saved after 7 weeks?

21. **Write Math** **What's the Error?** Joel wrote $17 - 5 \times 2 = 24$. **Explain** his error.

22. Which is the value of the expression $4 \times 5 + 18 - 4$?

   A 23   **C** 76

   B 34   **D** 88

23. Which is the value of the expression $9^2 + 2^4 \times 4^2 + 24$?

   A 41   **C** 137

   B 106   **D** 361

LESSON 7

★ **1.4.** Write and solve one-step equations with one variable using number sense, the properties or operations, and the properties of inequalities (e.g., $1/3x + 9$).

Vocabulary

variable

Materials

• MathBoard

ALGEBRA:
Properties

Essential Question How do the properties of addition and multiplication help you evaluate expressions?

 **Learn**

Addition and multiplication have similar properties. The properties are shown below with numbers and with variables. A **variable** is a letter or symbol that can stand for one or more numbers.

The Associative Property states that whatever way addends are grouped or factors are grouped does not change the sum or the product.

Associative Property	
Addition	**Multiplication**
$(4 + 7) + 9 = 4 + (7 + 9)$	$(3 \times 5) \times 2 = 3 \times (5 \times 2)$
$(a + b) + c = a + (b + c)$	$(a \times b) \times c = a \times (b \times c)$

The Commutative Property states that if the order of addends or factors is changed, the sum or product stays the same.

Commutative Property	
Addition	**Multiplication**
$8 + 5 = 5 + 8$	$7 \times 6 = 6 \times 7$
$a + b = b + a$	$a \times b = b \times a$

The Distributive Property states that multiplying a sum by a number is the same as multiplying each addend by the number and then adding the products. The Distributive Property also holds true for subtraction.

Distributive Property of Multiplication	
Over Addition	**Over Subtraction**
$8 \times (3 + 5) = (8 \times 3) + (8 \times 5)$	$4 \times (7 - 3) = (4 \times 7) - (4 \times 3)$
$a \times (b + c) = (a \times b) + (a \times c)$	$a \times (b - c) = (a \times b) - (a \times c)$

The Identity Property of Addition states that the sum of zero and any number is that number. The Identity Property of Multiplication states that the product of any number and one is that number.

Identity Property	
Addition	**Multiplication**
$9 + 0 = 9$	$1 \times 10 = 10$
$0 + a = a$	$b \times 1 = b$

1. $36 \times 4 = 4 \times 36$ is an example of the ___?___ Property of Multiplication because changing the order of the factors does not change the product.

Name the property shown.

2. $14 + 10 = 10 + 14$

3. $7 \times (b + 2) = (7 \times b) + (7 \times 2)$

✅ **4.** $c \times 1 = c$

✅ **5.** $4 + (6 + 11) = (4 + 6) + 11$

6. Math Talk Which property is shown by $4 + (5 + 8) = (4 + n) + 8$? **Explain** how you can use the property to find the value of n.

▶ **Practice and Problem Solving** REAL WORLD

Name the property shown.

7. $45 + 75 = 75 + 45$

8. $7 + (18 + 9) = (7 + 18) + 9$

9. $52 \times 1 = 52$

10. $(c \times d) \times f = c \times (d \times f)$

11. $s \times t = t \times s$

12. $(27 + 3) + 0 = 27 + 3$

Find the value of n. Name the property used.

13. $35 \times 24 = 24 \times n$

14. $4 \times (5 \times n) = (4 \times 5) \times 9$

15. $n \times 49 = 49$

16. $63 + 0 = n$

17. $(6 + 5) + 7 = 6 + (n + 7)$

18. $(3 \times 5 + 1) \times 0 = n$

19. Three friends' meals at a restaurant cost \$13, \$14, and \$11. Use parentheses to write two different expressions to show how much they spent in all. Which property does your pair of expressions demonstrate?

20. Sylvia paid for 8 tickets to a concert. Each ticket cost \$18. To find the total cost, she added the product of 8×10 to the product of 8×8, for a total of 144. Which property did Sylvia use?

21. Write Math ▶ **Explain** how the Commutative Property of Multiplication can help you find the product of $25 \times 55 \times 4$.

⭐ **OCCT Test Prep** Math Board

22. Which is the value of f in the expression $75 \times (4 \times f) = (75 \times 4) \times 9$?

    A 4   **C** 36

    B 9   **D** 75

23. What is the value of g? $\frac{8}{9} \times \frac{9}{8} = g$

    A 100   **C** 1

    B 10   **D** 0

⭐ Extra Practice

Set A

Order from least to greatest. (pp. 6–7)

1. 220,351; 220,342; 201,641

2. 1,582,654; 1,582,604; 1,582,650

3. 72,345,100; 72,445,399; 72,445,149

4. 13,313,333; 13,431,345; 13,313,354

5. 118,043,213; 118,443,113; 118,304,913

6. 289,004,356; 299,404,365; 298,444,342

7. 307,420,951; 307,420,972; 307,421,800

8. 619,768,200; 619,678,201; 619,768,202

Set B

Find the sum or difference. Estimate or use inverse operations to check. (pp. 8–9)

1. 6,800 − 379

2. 54 + 55 + 56

3. 64 + 340 + 426

4. 4,531 + 2,719

5. 59,999 − 6,401

6.   513,412
     − 45,665

7. 60,000 − 51,539

8.   165,340
     +   3,361

9.   675,531
     +386,943

10. 3,199 + 4,765

11.   103,462
      − 89,568

12. 17,043 − 8,769

13. One week, 27,305,768 people viewed a television show. The following week, only 19,459,043 viewers tuned in. What is the difference in viewers between the two weeks?

14. A movie made $30,936,133 in three weeks and $4,420,118 the fourth week. How much did the movie make during the four weeks?

Set C

Find the product or quotient. Check the answer. (pp. 10–13)

1. 1,405 × 52

2.   367
     ×144

3. 4,337 × 298

4.   1,118
     ×   429

5. 4,762 × 514

6. 2,660 ÷ 7

7. 17)‾255‾

8. 15)‾1,250‾

9. 19,129 ÷ 37

10. 32,111 ÷ 81

11. 71)‾685,210‾

12. 23)‾14,999‾

13. A railway company has 4 passenger trains. Each train has 8 cars, which hold 48 passengers per car. How many people can the railway move at one time if all the trains run at once and all the cars are full?

14. Kyle drives his truck 429 miles on 33 gallons of gas. How many miles can Kyle drive on 1 gallon of gas?

Go Online Technology
Use HMH Mega Math, Ice Station Exploration, *Arctic Algebra*, Levels Q, R, and X.

Set D

Write as an expression using equal factors. Then find the value. (pp. 16–19)

1. 0^2 **2.** 1^5 **3.** 6^1 **4.** 12^3 **5.** 10^4 **6.** 8^3

7. 72^2 **8.** 13^0 **9.** 2^5 **10.** 5^4 **11.** 16^3 **12.** 4^6

13. An airline catering company sold 4,108,369 packages of pretzels last year. Write this number in expanded form.

14. Chris writes a number in expanded form: $(3 \times 10^5) + (2 \times 10^3) + (6 \times 10^2) + (4 \times 10^1) + (7 \times 10^0)$. Write this number in standard form.

Set E

Evaluate the expression. (pp. 20–21)

1. $9^2 \times 15^0 - 4^2$ **2.** $6^2 + 7 - 3^3$ **3.** $27 + 1^9 \times 7 - 3^2$

4. $12 + 4 \times 16 - (3 \times 7)$ **5.** $(6^2 + 4^3)^2 \div (10^2 \times 2)$ **6.** $14 + (2^4 \times 0) + 16 \div 4^0$

7. $(12^0 \times 7 + 9) \div (5 - 3)^2$ **8.** $5 \times 80 \div 4 + 5^3 - (3 - 2)$

9. At the banquet, there are 8 rectangular tables that seat 6 and 10 round tables that seat 4. The tables are 7 chairs short. Write and evaluate a numerical expression to find the number of people who can sit on chairs.

10. Jacob is installing a tile floor. Each tile is a square with 6-inch sides. Write and evaluate a numerical expression with an exponent to find the area he can cover with a box of 500 tiles.

Set F

Find the value of *n*. Name the property used. (pp. 22–23)

1. $6 + (3 + 45) = (n + 3) + 45$ **2.** $n \times 41 = 41 \times 3$ **3.** $(4 + 7) \times 3 = (4 \times n) + (7 \times 3)$

4. $(7 \times 12) \times 5 = 7 \times (12 \times n)$ **5.** $33 + 14 + n = 14 + 7 + 33$ **6.** $0 + 27 = n$

7. $n \times 52 = 52$ **8.** $17 \times n = 0$ **9.** $(5 \times n) + (5 \times 7) = 5 \times (3 + 7)$

10. Bill is stocking shelves at a grocery store. He is unpacking 4 cartons each with 24 boxes of tissues. Each box has 120 tissues. Write two expressions that show how many tissues are being unpacked. Which property is shown?

11. Ben found the area of his rectangle to be 24 sq in. He said he used the Identity Property of Multiplication to find his result. What must be the dimensions of his rectangle?

Reading & Writing Math

Think about all the ways you have learned to solve addition and subtraction problems.

Copy and complete the table.

Strategy	Good for Addition	Good for Subtraction
Draw a model	yes	yes
Write a number sentence		
Use compatible numbers		
Arrange the numbers in a different order		
Group the numbers differently		

Writing

1. **Draw a model** that represents an addition situation. Write a word problem that the model could represent.

2. Look at your problem and model for Exercise 1. **Write a number sentence** you could use to solve the problem.

3. **Compatible numbers** are numbers that are easy for you to add, subtract, multiply or divide with mental math. Most people think the number pairs whose sum is 10 are compatible. List at least two number pairs that you think are compatible and tell why you chose them.

4. For this number sentence, tell one way you might group the numbers or arrange them in a different order to make an easier problem to solve.

$$2 + 17 + 50 + 33 + 3$$

Reading Look for *James and the Giant Peach* by Roald Dahl in your library.

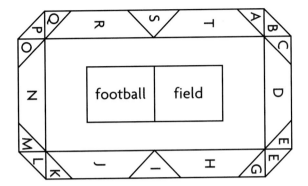 H.O.T. Multistep Problems

1 The diagram shows the football stadium at City College.

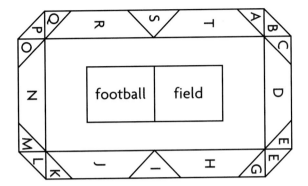

- There are 615 seats in section A. What would be a good estimate for the number of seats in section D? 2.2.c.; 2.2.d.

- At the next football game, 30,000 fans are expected. How can you determine if there will be enough seats?

- The tickets cost $5 or $10. The stadium operators want to take in at least $200,000 on the sale of tickets for a full stadium. How many seats should sell for $10 and how many for $5?

2 You are in charge of renting tables and buying hot dogs and hamburgers to sell at the Fall Fair. You want to have enough food, but not much left over. Use the notes from last year's fair committee to help you plan. 2.2.c.; 2.2.d.

> ### Notes from the Fair
>
> - 475 people ate at the fair.
> - More people bought hamburgers than hot dogs. Some people bought both.
> - Hot dogs: 8 per package
> - Hamburgers: 12 per package
> - Tables seat 10 people.

- Estimate how many people will eat at the fair. You need to seat about half of the people at one time. How many tables should you rent?

- How many packages of hot dogs and hamburgers should you buy? **Explain** why you think these are good estimates.

- This year you decide to order packages of cheese slices so that half of the hamburger orders can have a slice of cheese. Cheese slices come in packages of 24. How many packages of cheese will you need?

Practice for the OCCT

1 Mrs. Forrer bought a new car for $18,898 at Fred's AutoMart. Another car dealership was selling the same car for $20,212. How much did Mrs. Forrer save by buying her car from Fred's AutoMart? ◻ 2.2.c.

A $987   **C** $1,314

B $1,129   **D** $1,413

2 Several middle school track teams from Logan County boarded buses after a track meet. If there were 18 buses and 42 athletes on each bus, how many total athletes were on the buses? ◻ 2.2.c.

A 540

B 756

C 886

D 908

3 The state of West Virginia had a population of 1,793,477 in 1990. In 2000, West Virginia's population was 1,808,344. How many less people lived in West Virginia in 1990 than in 2000? ◻ 2.2.c.

A 14,867

B 18,766

C 22,471

D 48,574

4 In the first week, a movie earned $18,425,937. During the second week the movie earned $24,596,474. How much money did the movie make in its first two weeks? ◻ 2.2.c.

A $6,170,537

B $36,744,598

C $42,974,315

D $43,022,411

5 Each day, Gabriel is allowed to use the computer for 210 minutes. Gabriel uses the computer for 35 days. How many minutes does Gabriel spend on the computer? ◻ 2.2.c.

A 4,510

B 7,350

C 7,555

D 9,450

6 Frank has saved $11,980. Frank wants to know how many new TV's he could buy if each TV costs $849. How many TV's could Frank buy with the money he saved? ◻ 2.2.c.

A 8

B 10

C 14

D 22

7 Which can be used to check the quotient $104 \div 9 = 11$ r5? ◻ 2.2.c.

A $104 - 9 + 5$

B $(9 \times 11) + 5$

C $(9 \times 11) - 5$

D $(5 \times 11) + 9$

8 Which is the correct order of operations to solve the following problem? ◻ 2.2.e.

$$45 \times (9 + 99) - 4 + 6$$

A add, multiply, subtract, add

B multiply, add, add, subtract

C add, add, subtract, multiply

D subtract, add, multiply, add

9 The following chart shows the populations of several states.

State	Population
Kentucky	4,206,074
Indiana	6,345,289
Illinois	12,831,970
Montana	944,632

Which shows the populations ordered from greatest to least? 2.1.

A   Kentucky, Indiana, Illinois, Montana

B   Montana, Kentucky, Indiana, Illinois

C   Illinois, Indiana, Kentucky, Montana

D   Illinois, Kentucky, Indiana, Montana

10 Margaret is helping to set up tables for a local charity event. The convention center can hold 237 tables. Each table can fit 9 people. If all the tables are full, how many people attended the charity event? 2.2.c.

A   983

B   1,450

C   2,073

D   2,133

11 A plane from Indianapolis to Boston has 187 passengers aboard. If each person onboard has luggage that weighs 43 pounds, how many pounds of luggage are on the plane? 2.2.c.

A   8,041

B   7,983

C   6,447

D   4,361

Problem Solving

12 Andy can buy 8 CDs for $40. How many CDs can Andy buy for $70? 2.2.c.

13 Mike saved $3,454 dollars in one year. The next year, Mike saved $1,243. How much money did Mike save over the two years? 2.2.c.

14 Jonathan bought a TV for $1,894. He had $2,453 in his savings account. After he bought the TV, how much money did Jonathan have in his savings account? 2.2.c.

15 Samantha rides her bike 108 miles in a month. If she rode her bike the same distance in each month, how many months would it take her to ride 1,944 miles? 2.2.c.

16 Explain the first step in finding the value of $(3^2 + 7) \times 4$. 2.2.e.

17 Explain how the Commutative Property of Multiplication can help you find $4 \times 37 \times 25$. 1.4.

Decimals

Chapter 2

Investigate

A sprinter is training for a track meet. The graph shows her average times for four sprints of different lengths. She wants to spend between 10 and 15 min of her 60-min training session running sprints. During this time, she must run at least two sprints of each distance, but no more than two 400-m sprints. How many of each sprint could she run?

Fun Fact

The first Olympic race was won by Corubus in 776 b.c. The race, known as the *stadion*, was a 201-yd sprint that was the length of a stadium.

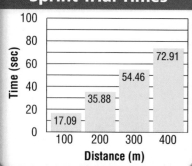

Sprint Trial Times

Time (sec) vs Distance (m)

- 100: 17.09
- 200: 35.88
- 300: 54.46
- 400: 72.91

GO ONLINE
Technology
Student pages are available in the Student eBook.

Check your understanding of important skills needed for success in Chapter 2.

 ASSESSMENT
Soar To Success: Math.

▶ **Add, Subtract, Multiply, and Divide Whole Numbers**

Add or subtract.

1. $24 + 78 + 45$ **2.** $125 - 36 - 25$ **3.** $342 + 65 + 12 + 100$ **4.** $114 - 45$

5. $78 + 302$ **6.** $743 - 289 - 217$ **7.** $507 - 335$ **8.** $445 + 302 + 251$

Multiply.

9. 36×16 **10.** 42×14 **11.** 345×15 **12.** 115×23 **13.** 442×65

14. 45×72 **15.** 150×50 **16.** 100×80 **17.** 720×70 **18.** 709×46

Divide.

19. $512 \div 16$ **20.** $21 \div 7$ **21.** $437 \div 19$ **22.** $900 \div 60$ **23.** $198 \div 9$

24. $72 \div 9$ **25.** $4,140 \div 92$ **26.** $1,958 \div 89$ **27.** $784 \div 8$ **28.** $2,225 \div 25$

Vocabulary

Visualize It!

tenth

one of the equal parts when a whole is divided into 10 equal parts

hundredth

one of the equal parts when a whole is divided into 100 equal parts

thousandth

one of the equal parts when a whole is divided into 1,000 equal parts

Language Tips

Words that look alike in English and Spanish often have the same meaning.

English	Spanish
decimal	decimal
decimal point	punto decimal

See English-Spanish Glossary.

nine thousandths
0.009

★ 2.1. Convert compare, and order decimals, fractions, and percents using a variety of methods.

Materials
• MathBoard

Decimals and Place Value

Essential Question How do you use place value to read and write decimal numbers? To compare and order decimal numbers?

PROBLEM Colin found a 1936 Indian-head nickel. He estimated the diameter of the nickel to be about 1 in. The actual diameter was 0.83 in. What is the value of each digit in 0.83?

Place value helps you understand numbers. The digits and their positions in a number determine the value of the number.

Read the three numbers in the place-value chart. These numbers are part of the decimal system. Look at the first number, 0.83. The digit 0 has a value of 0 ones, the 8 has a value of 8 tenths, and the 3 has a value of 3 hundredths.

Place Value						
Thousands	Hundreds	Tens	Ones		Tenths	Hundredths
			0	.	8	3
		1	4	.	9	
	3	6	1	.	0	2

You use place value when you read and write numbers.

Reading and writing numbers.

1 Standard form: 0.83
Expanded form: 0.8 + 0.03
Word form: *eighty-three hundred*

2 Standard form: 14.9
Expanded form: 10 + 4 + 0.9
Word form: *fourteen and nine tenths*

3 Standard form: 361.02
Expanded form: 300 + 60 + 1 + 0.02
Word form: *three hundred sixty-one and two hundredths*

Math Idea
Knowing the place value of digits will help you read, write, and correctly operate with numbers, including decimals.

Compare and Order

You can compare and order decimals.

Use place value.

Compare 5.92 and 5.9. Use < or >.

Write equivalent decimals.	Compare the tenths.	Compare the hundredths.
Compare the ones.		
5.92	5.92	5.92
5.90	5.90	5.90

So, 5.92 > 5.9 and 5.9 < 5.92.

Use a number line.

The U.S. Mint facility in Philadelphia, PA, the location of the nation's first mint, is currently the only one that engraves the designs of U.S. coins and medals. The table shows the thicknesses of four coins produced by the U.S. Mint. Use a number line to write the thicknesses in order from least to greatest.

Locate each thickness on the number line. Then write the thicknesses in order as they appear from left to right.

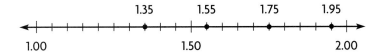

U.S. Coin Thicknesses	
Coin	Thickness (mm)
Penny	1.55
Nickel	1.95
Dime	1.35
Quarter	1.75

So, the thicknesses in order from least to greatest are
1.35 mm, 1.55 mm, 1.75 mm, and 1.95 mm.

The same method can also be used to order two or more decimal numbers.

Order 1.108, 1.02, 1.023, and 1.11 from greatest to least.

Compare the ones. They are the same.

Compare the tenths. 1 > 0. Reorder the numbers.	Compare the hundredths. 1 > 0 and 2 = 2. Reorder the numbers.	Write 1.02 as the equivalent decimal, 1.020. Compare the thousandths. 3 > 0. Reorder the numbers.	
1.108	1.108	1.11	1.11
1.02	1.11	1.108	1.108
1.023	1.02	1.020	1.023
1.11	1.023	1.023	1.02

So, the order from greatest to lease is 1.11, 1.108, 1.023, and 1.02.

1. Write 32.086 and 32.508 in a place-value chart. **Explain** how the chart helps you compare the decimals. Which is greater?

Write the number in expanded form and in word form.

2. 0.802　　　　　**3.** 12.932　　　　　**4.** 48.015　　　　　☑**5.** 7.202

Compare. Write <, >, or = for each ⬭.

6. 1.18 ⬭ 1.17　　　**7.** 0.52 ⬭ 0.54　　　**8.** 0.306 ⬭ 0.31　　　☑**9.** 4.14 ⬭ 4.104

10. Math Talk **Explain** why four and one tenth is greater than four and ninety-nine thousandths.

Practice and Problem Solving REAL WORLD

Write the number in expanded form and in word form.

11. 8.61　　　　　**12.** 0.505　　　　　**13.** 11.327　　　　　**14.** 29.018

Compare. Write <, >, or = for each ⬭.

15. 8.78 ⬭ 8.87　　　**16.** 0.42 ⬭ 0.44　　　**17.** 1.10 ⬭ 1.1

Order from least to greatest.

18. 0.04, 0.104, 0.041, 0.1　　**19.** 56.56, 56.506, 56.056, 56.5　　**20.** 1.05, 10.51, 1.5, 1.15, 1.510

Order from greatest to least.

21. 8.484, 8.469, 8.481, 8.467　　**22.** 1.39, 1.384, 1.209, 1.21　　**23.** 0.07, 0.022, 0.101, 0.008

Real World Data

For 24, use the table.

24. Write the mass of each coin in expanded form and in word form.

25. Write Math ➤ **What's the Error?** Tina wrote 2.2 ≠ 2.20. Lena wrote 2.2 ≠ 2.02. Who wrote a correct statement? **Explain.** Change the symbol in the other statement to make it true.

Coin Specifications		
Coin	**Mass (g)**	**Diameter (in.)**
Quarter	5.67	0.955
Half-dollar	11.34	1.205
Dollar	8.10	1.043
Gold dollar	8.10	1.043

★ OCCT Test Prep　Math Board

26. Which is a true comparison?

　　A 36.78 > 36.87　　　**C** 78.01 = 78.10

　　B 63.1 < 63.1　　　　**D** 145.21 < 145.24

27. Which is three hundred sixty-four and seventy-eight hundredths written in standard form?

　　A 36.478　　　**C** 364.78

　　B 364.078　　　**D** 3,647.8

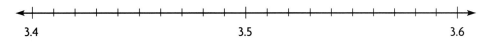
★ Standards Quick Check

For 1–4, copy the number line. Then locate each decimal.

<-|----+----+----+----+----+----+----+----+----+----+----+----+----+----+----|->
3.4   3.5   3.6

1. 3.54 **2.** 3.43 **3.** 3.575 **4.** 3.405

Compare. Write <, >, or = for each ⬭.

5. 0.63 ⬭ 0.601 **6.** 7.207 ⬭ 7.27 **7.** 1.10 ⬭ 1.1

8. 0.03 ⬭ 0.04 **9.** 0.507 ⬭ 0.51 **10.** 0.37 ⬭ 0.4

Challenge H.O.T.

Expanded Form as a Sum of Products

Another way to represent a number is to use a type of expanded form that shows the number as a sum of products.

> **Write 548.2 in expanded form as a sum of products.**
>
> $548.2 = 500 + 40 + 8 + 0.2$
> $= (5 \times 100) + (4 \times 10) + (8 \times 1) + (2 \times 0.1)$
>
> So, $548.2 = (5 \times 100) + (4 \times 10) + (8 \times 1) + (2 \times 0.1)$.

Write each number in expanded form as a sum of products.

1. 51.6 **2.** 678.32

3. 7.29 **4.** 0.847

5. 13.504 **6.** 7.29

★ **2.2.c.** Estimate and find solutions to single and multi-step problems using whole numbers, decimals, fractions, and percents (e.g., 7/8 + 8/9 is about 2, 3.9 + 5.3 is about 9).

Materials
• MathBoard

Estimate with Decimals

Essential Question In what situation should an overestimate be used? In what situation should an underestimate be used?

PROBLEM For his tenth birthday, Ryan, his younger sister, his father, and his grandmother plan to visit the state aquarium. About how much will the four tickets cost if Ryan's grandmother is a senior citizen?

To estimate with decimals, use the same methods you use with whole numbers.

State Aquarium Tickets	
Children under 12	$7.20
Adults	$10.75
Senior Citizens	$5.80

Estimate.

7.20 + 7.20 + 10.75 + 5.80

$$
\begin{array}{rcl}
7.20 & \rightarrow & 7.00 \\
7.20 & \rightarrow & 7.00 \\
10.75 & \rightarrow & 11.00 \\
+\ 5.80 & \rightarrow & +\ 6.00 \\
\hline
 & & 31.00
\end{array}
$$

Round to the nearest whole dollar.

So, the four tickets will cost about $31.00.

Estimate using clustering.

38.3 + 41.7 + 37.6

38.3 + 41.7 + 37.6

↓   ↓   ↓   The three addends cluster around 40.

40   40   40

3 × 40 = 120   So, multiply 40 by 3.

So, 38.3 + 41.7 + 37.6 ≈ 120.

Remember

The symbol ≈ means "is approximately equal to."

Estimate using rounding.

178.39 − 101.56

$$
\begin{array}{rcl}
178.39 & \rightarrow & 180 \\
-101.56 & \rightarrow & -100 \\
\hline
 & & 80
\end{array}
$$

Round to the nearest ten.

So, 178.39 − 101.56 ≈ 80.

Estimate Products and Quotients

Similar methods can be used to estimate products and quotients.

Estimate product using rounding.	Estimate quotient using compatible numbers.
$18.53 × 37.5 $18.55 → $20 Round to the × 37.5 → × 40 nearest ten. $800	152.4 ÷ 5.3 15 and 5 are compatible numbers, so use 150 and 5. $\overset{30}{5.3\overline{)152.4}}$ → $\overset{30}{5\overline{)150}}$

So, 18.53 × 37.5 ≈ 800.   So, 152.4 ÷ 5.3 ≈ 30.

Examples

Ryan wants to buy a pair of socks for $4.59, a T-shirt for $12.99, and a board game for $15.29. If he has $40.00 to spend, will he have enough money?

Estimate. 4.59 + 12.99 + 15.29

4.59	→	5.00
12.99	→	13.00	Round to the nearest
+15.29	→	+15.00	whole dollar.
		33.00

With Ryan's estimate of $33, he will have enough money.

A marine biologist at the aquarium has 243.46 mL of a solution in a container. She needs to pour the solution into small tubes, each containing 6.19 mL of the solution. About how many tubes will she need?

Estimate. 243.46 ÷ 6.19

$\overset{40}{6.19\overline{)243.46}}$ → $\overset{40}{6\overline{)240}}$

So, the marine biologist will need about 40 tubes.

 Share and Show Math Board

1. Estimate the quotient 346.78 ÷ 4.82 by using the compatible numbers 350 and 5.

2. Estimate the product 63.7 × 8.2 by using the rounded factors 60 and 8.

Estimate.

3. 19.6 + 22.7

4. 131.84 ÷ 9.8

5. 82.79 × 28.13

✓6. 41.52 × 37.95

7. 918.4 × 10.6

8. 67.8 + 66.1 + 71.1

9. 137.49 − 72.4

✓10. 358.2 ÷ 8.5

11. **Math Talk** **Explain** how to estimate the sum of 15.89, 14.22, and 14.77.

▶ Practice and Problem Solving · REAL WORLD

Estimate.

12. $5.7 + 9.4 + 19.74$　　**13.** $79.5 \div 9.2$　　**14.** 3.27×45.189　　**15.** $9.89 + 38.2$

16. $\$167.50 + \$81.75$　　**17.** $\$256.08 - \$96.25$　　**18.** $237.91 \div 5.86$　　**19.** $249.91 \div 4.86$

20.　　19.909
　　　$\times\ \ \ 6.84$

21.　　$\$92.04$
　　　$\$89.7$
　　$+\$88.63$

22.　　0.74
　　　0.8
　　$+1.639$

23.　　21.7
　　　$\times\ \ 9.4$

Estimate to compare. Write $<$ or $>$ for each ⬭.

24. 5.35×8.54 ⬭ 48　　**25.** 35 ⬭ $91.42 \div 2.8$　　**26.** 300 ⬭ 41.39×6.898

Real World Data

For 27–29, use the table.

27. Kyle is in charge of two fish tanks at the aquarium. The species in these tanks are fed brine shrimp, bloodworms, and vitamin pellets. About how many ounces of food and vitamins does Kyle feed the fish in Tank A each day? in Tank B?

Daily Feeding for Fish Tanks		
Food	**Tank A**	**Tank B**
Brine shrimp	14.6 oz	4.9 oz
Bloodworms	25.3 oz	5.1 oz
Vitamin pellets	18.5 oz	9.5 oz

28. Kyle needs to buy a week's worth of food and vitamin supplies for his two tanks. About how much of each item should he buy?

29. Fidelia has three fish tanks. She put 1.79 oz of fish food into the first tank, 1.80 oz into the second tank, and 1.08 oz into the third tank. Order the amounts of fish food used from least to greatest. About how many ounces of fish food did she use in all three tanks?

30. **Write Math** ▶ **Explain** how the method of estimation used can affect how close an estimate is to the exact answer. Use examples to support your reasoning.

OCCT Test Prep

31. Which is the best estimate for $452.15 \div 54.42$?

　　A 6　　　　**C** 16

　　B 9　　　　**D** 18

32. Which is the best estimate for 374.15×12.16?

　　A 389　　　**C** 3,280

　　B 2,850　　**D** 4,500

Technology
Use HMH Mega Math, Fraction Action,
Number Line Mine, Level R.

⭐ Standards Quick Check

Estimate.

1. 347.51 + 19.45

2. 6.51 × 74.6

3. 371.2 − 112.9 − 23.45

4. 31.7 × 4.08

5. 277.45 ÷ 37.9

6. 8.48 + 5.60 + 2.13

Estimate to compare. Write < or > for each ⬭.

7. 14.95 + 748.2 ⬭ 750

8. 69.84 ÷ 6.52 ⬭ 5

9. 36.10 + 14.49 ⬭ 540

Challenge H.O.T.

Front-End Estimation

Another way to estimate a decimal sum is to use front-end estimation. When you use front-end estimation, you add or subtract the whole-number values of each decimal.)

Use front-end estimation.

8.**89**	→	Add the whole-number parts only. The
32.**95**	→	whole-number values of the decimals
+ 6.**34**	→	are less than the actual numbers, so the
		sum is an underestimate.

The exact sum is a little greater than 46.

Adjusting for the decimal part of the number allows you to estimate a range for the sum.

0.89	→	1.00	Round the decimals to 0, 0.5, or 1. Find
0.95	→	1.00	the sum. Then add the whole-number
+ 0.34	→	+ 0.50	estimate and the adjusted estimate.
		2.50	

The sum of the estimates is greater than the actual numbers, so 48.50 is an overestimate. The estimated range for the sum is from 46 to 48.50.

Estimate a range for each sum.

1. 12.75 + 23.42 + 15.66

2. 31.15 + 9.48 + 26.79

3. 101.82 + 54.38 + 99.99

4. 67.72 + 0.0408 + 3.21 + 16.65

★ **2.2.c.** Estimate and find solutions to single and multi-step problems using whole numbers, decimals, fractions, and percents (e.g., 7/8 + 8/9 is about 2, 3.9 + 5.3 is about 9).

Materials
• MathBoard

Add and Subtract Decimals

Essential Question How can estimation help you align decimal points correctly before adding or subtracting decimals?

PROBLEM Amanda and three of her friends volunteer at the local animal shelter. One of their jobs is to weigh the puppies and kittens each week and chart their growth. Amanda's favorite puppy weighed 1.32 lb last month. It weighs 2.56 lb this week. How much weight has the puppy gained?

You can add and subtract decimals the same way you add and subtract whole numbers. First, align the decimal points and place the decimal point in the answer.

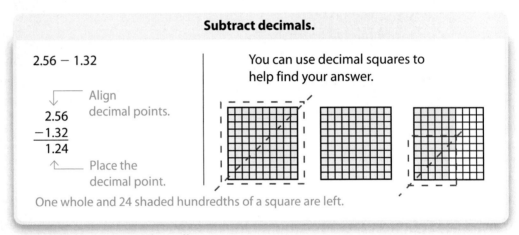

Subtract decimals.

2.56 − 1.32

    2.56   Align decimal points.
  − 1.32
    1.24   Place the decimal point.

You can use decimal squares to help find your answer.

One whole and 24 shaded hundredths of a square are left.

So, the puppy gained 1.24 lb.

You can add zeros to the right of a decimal without changing its value. Use zeros to make all decimals have the same number of decimal places.

Examples

1.5 + 9 + 0.47

      1.50   Align the decimal points.
      9.00   Use zeros as placeholders.
    + 0.47   Place the decimal point. Add.
    ─────
     10.97

Remember

In a whole number, the decimal point is to the right of the ones digit.

168.7 + 89.883

    168.700   Align the decimal points.
  + 89.883   Use zeros as placeholders.
  ─────────   Place the decimal point. Add.
    258.583

Estimate to Check

You can use estimation to check an answer for reasonableness.

By the end of August, Eddie had saved $62.75 to donate to the animal shelter. He saved $23.25 in September and $18.60 in October. How much money did Eddie save in all?

Estimate.

$$
\begin{array}{rcl}
\$62.75 & \rightarrow & \$63 \\
\$23.25 & \rightarrow & \$23 \\
+\ \$18.60 & \rightarrow & +\$19 \\
\hline
& & \$105
\end{array}
$$

Round to the nearest dollar.

Find the sum.

$$
\begin{array}{r}
\$62.75 \\
\$23.25 \\
+\ \$18.60 \\
\hline
\$104.60
\end{array}
$$

Align the decimal points. Place the decimal point. Add.

Compare the answer and the estimate. Since $104.60 is close to the estimate, $105, the answer is reasonable. So, Eddie saved $104.60.

Subtract. $30 - 22.083$

Estimate.

$$
\begin{array}{rcl}
30 & \rightarrow & 30 \\
-22.083 & \rightarrow & -22 \\
\hline
& & 8
\end{array}
$$

Round to the nearest whole number.

Find the difference.

$$
\begin{array}{rcl}
30 & & 30.000 \\
-22.083 & \rightarrow & -\ 22.083 \\
\hline
& & 7.917
\end{array}
$$

Align the decimal points. Use zeros as placeholders. Place the decimal point. Subtract.

 Share and Show Math Board

1. Find $3.42 + 1.9$. Describe what is happening in each step.

Step 1
$$
\begin{array}{r}
3.42 \\
+\ 1.90 \\
\hline
.\ 2
\end{array}
$$

Step 2
$$
\begin{array}{r}
\overset{1}{3}.42 \\
+\ 1.90 \\
\hline
.32
\end{array}
$$

Step 3
$$
\begin{array}{r}
\overset{1}{3}.42 \\
+\ 1.90 \\
\hline
5.32
\end{array}
$$

Estimate. Then find the sum or difference.

2. $2.3 + 5.68 + 21.047$ **3.** $33.25 - 21.463$ **4.** $82 - 38.749$ ✓ **5.** $84.9 + 0.463$

Copy the problem. Place the decimal point correctly in the answer.

6. $47.3 - 0.18 = 4712$ **7.** $0.174 + 1.376 + 4.338 = 5888$

8. $26 + 113.79 + 0.42 = 14021$ ✓ **9.** $45.2 - 38.77 = 643$

10. [Math Talk] **Explain** why it is important to align the decimal points when you add or subtract decimals.

Estimate. Then find the sum or difference.

11.   43.53
   + 27.67

12.   17
       3.6
   + 4.049

13. $3.49
      − 2.75

14.   5.07
     − 2.148

15.   3.92
         16
   + 0.085

16. 630.73 − 84.591

17. 341.27 + 53.7 + 8.446 + 9.5

18. 17.4 − 6.823

Copy the problem. Place the decimal point correctly in the answer.

19. 43.46 + 323.5 = 36696

20. $18.75 + $34 + $7.38 = $6013

**Estimate to determine whether the given sum or difference
is reasonable. Write *yes* or *no*.**

21. 17.63 + 142.9 = 160.53

22. $45.33 + $8.51 + $19.75 = $73.59

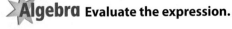 **Evaluate the expression.**

23. 78 − [15 − (4 − 0.1)]

24. 12 × (15 + 8.7 − 3.8 + 0.1)

 **Real World Data**

The graph shows the changing weights of three
kittens at an animal shelter. For 25–26, use the graph.

25. Estimate how much weight Kiki gained between
months 1 and 3. Then find an exact answer.

26. What was the difference between the total weights of
the kittens at Month 1 and Month 2?

27. **What's the Error?** Look at Liam's work below.
Describe his error and find the correct answer.

        60
    − 55.724
        5.724

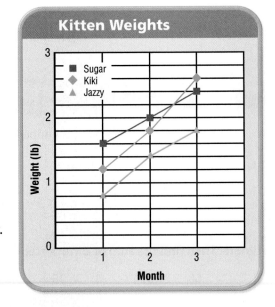

Kitten Weights

■ Sugar
◆ Kiki
▲ Jazzy

Weight (lb)

Month

28. Which is the sum of 75.49 + 163.42?

A 88

C 238.91

B 234.89

D 918.32

29. Which is the difference of 1,773.34 − 568.94?

A 208.64

C 1,570.82

B 1,204.4

D 2,342.28

★Standards Quick Check

Find the sum or difference.

1. $256.4 - 75.07$

2. $41.98 + 13.5 + 27.338$

3. $\$36 + \$2.78 + \$0.35$

4. $24.6 - 8.44$

5. $5.89 - 4.265$

6. $131.56 + 25.305$

Evaluate the expression.

7. $3 \times 18 - (0.7 + 4.8 - 3)$

8. $34.3 - 16 \times (4.5 - 2.5)$

Challenge H.O.T.

Different types of birds lay eggs of different sizes. Small birds lay eggs that are smaller than those that are laid by larger birds. The table shows the average lengths and widths of five different birds' eggs.

Raven

Canada Goose

Robin

Average Dimensions of Bird Eggs

Bird	Length (m)	Width (m)
Canada Goose	0.086	0.058
Hummingbird	0.013	0.013
Raven	0.049	0.033
Robin	0.019	0.015
Turtledove	0.031	0.023

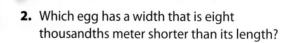

Hummingbird

1. What is the difference in average length between the longest egg and the shortest egg?

2. Which egg has a width that is eight thousandths meter shorter than its length?

3. How many robin eggs, laid end to end, would be about equal in length to two raven eggs? Justify your answer.

4. Which of the eggs is shaped most like a sphere? Justify your answer.

LESSON 4

★ **2.2.b.** Multiply and divide decimals by one- or two-digit multipliers or divisors to solve problems.

Materials
• MathBoard

Multiply Decimals

Essential Question How is the number of decimal places in a product related to the number of decimal places in each factor?

PROBLEM Cameron is vacationing with his family in Canada. He needs to convert his U.S. dollars into Canadian dollars. If each U.S. dollar is worth 1.163 Canadian dollars, how many Canadian dollars will he receive if he exchanges 40 U.S. dollars?

Estimate. $1.163 \times 40 \rightarrow 1 \times 40 = 40$

Since 40 is being multiplied by a number slightly greater than 1, the product should be slightly greater than 40.

$$\begin{array}{r} 1.163 \\ \times\ \ 40 \\ \hline 46.520 \end{array}$$

Multiply as with whole numbers. Since the estimate is slightly greater than 40, place the decimal point after 46.

So, Cameron will receive 46.52 Canadian dollars.

You can use a model or paper and pencil to multiply decimals.

Use a model.

Multiply. 0.6×0.3

Shade 6 of the columns blue to show 0.6.

Shade 3 of the rows yellow to show 0.3.

The green area in which the shading overlaps shows the product, or 0.6 of 0.3.

So, $0.6 \times 0.3 = 0.18$.

You can place the decimal point in a product by estimating or by adding the numbers of decimal places in the factors.

Use paper and pencil.

Multiply. 1.35×6.4 **Estimate.** $1 \times 6 = 6$

$$\begin{array}{r} 1.35 \leftarrow \text{2 decimal places} \\ \times\ \ 6.4 \leftarrow \text{1 decimal place} \\ \hline 540 \\ +\ 8100 \\ \hline 8.640 \leftarrow \text{2 + 1, or 3, decimal places} \end{array}$$

Multiply as with whole numbers. Place the decimal point in the product.

Since the estimate is 6, the answer is reasonable. So, $1.35 \times 6.4 = 8.640$.

44

Zeros as Placeholders

When you multiply decimals, you sometimes have to insert zeros in the answer.

Multiply. 0.084 × 0.096

0.084	← 3 decimal places
× 0.096	← 3 decimal places
504	Multiply as with whole numbers.
+ 7560	The answer must have 6 decimal places,
0.008064	so place two zeros to the left of 8.

So, 0.084 × 0.096 = 0.008064.

Multiply. \$9.70 × 38.5 **Estimate.** \$10 × 40 = \$400

Mr. Friedman works 38.5 hours per week. He earns \$9.70 per hour. How much does he earn in a week?

\$9.70	← 2 decimal places
× 38.5	← 1 decimal place
4850	
77600	Multiply as with whole numbers.
+ 291000	Place the decimal point in the product using
\$373.450	3 decimal places.

Since the estimate is \$400, the answer is reasonable. So, Mr. Friedman earns \$373.45 per week.

Share and Show

Math Board

1. Use the model to find 0.4 × 0.8.

2. Use the model to find 0.8 × 0.3.

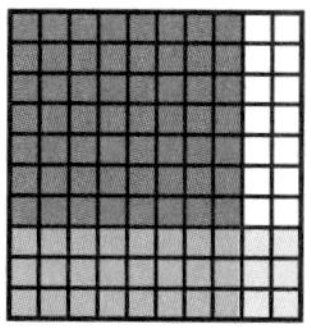

Copy the problem. Place the decimal point in the product.

3. 6.4 × 8 = 512 **4.** 3.1 × 9.1 = 2821 **5.** 28.4 × 2.79 = 79236 ✓**6.** 0.63 × 4.2 = 2646

Estimate. Then find the product.

7. \$15.62 × 4 **8.** 1.25 × 0.6 **9.** 6 × 0.0023 ✓**10.** \$32.05 × 74

11. Math Talk **Explain** how estimation helps you know where to place the decimal point in a product.

Copy the problem. Place the decimal point in the product.

12. $5 \times 7.3 = 365$

13. $8.3 \times 3.2 = 2656$

14. $0.78 \times 0.2 = 156$

15. $19.23 \times 4.9 = 94227$

16. $18 \times 0.59 = 1062$

17. $0.044 \times 15 = 66$

18. $6.88 \times 0.07 = 4816$

19. $9.3 \times 19.5 = 18135$

Estimate. Then find the product.

20. 1.8×5.2

21. 29.14×5.2

22. 0.8×0.7

23. $\$6.95 \times 12$

24. 0.055×1.82

25. 0.88×12.5

26. 9×7.258

27. 250.05×0.9

⭐**Algebra** **Evaluate the expression if $n = 9.4$.**

28. $0.24 \times n$

29. $3.75 \times n$

30. $6.83 \times n$

31. $5.8 \times n$

Real World Data

For 32–33, use the table.

The table shows the major currency exchange rates on a particular day.
The numbers in each row show equivalent amounts of each type of currency.

32. If Tammy exchanges 50 U.S. dollars for euros, how many euros will she receive? Round to the nearest cent.

33. Mr. Jackson needs to exchange his euros for yen. How many yen will he receive if he exchanges 300 euros? Round to the nearest yen.

34. Write Math ► **Explain** how to use a model to show that the product of two decimals less than 1 is less than either of the two factors.

Major Currency Exchange Rates				
Currency	U.S. Dollar	Yen	Euro	Canadian Dollar
U.S. Dollar	1	117.91001	0.74910	1.15720
Yen	0.00848	1	0.00635	0.00981
Euro	1.33494	157.40222	1	1.54479
Canadian Dollar	0.86408	101.90098	0.64728	1

★ **OCCT Test Prep**

35. What is the product of 432.15×3.54?

   A 1,192.11   **C** 1,592.015

   B 1,529.811   **D** 2,543.94

36. Jen makes $15.65 an hour. How much did Jen make if she worked 25.65 hours?

   A $401.42   **C** $362.82

   B $398.62   **D** $41.30

⭐ Standards Quick Check

Find the product.

1. 35.5 × $18.76

2. 0.09 × 0.06

3. 64.3 × 15.7

4. $345 × 5.5

5. 21.095 × 4.8

6. 1,560.9 × 1.2

7. 256.21 × 11.2

8. $845.30 × 7.9

9. 3,427.62 × 9.91

Challenge H.O.T.

Distributive Property

You can use the Distributive Property and mental math to make multiplying money amounts easier.

A library is having a sale. Hardcover books are $3.50 each. How much do 4 hardcover books cost?

Think of $3.50 as $3 + $0.50. Then use the Distributive Property and mental math.

$$4 \times \$3.50 = 4 \times (\$3 + \$0.50)$$
$$= (4 \times \$3) + (4 \times \$0.50)$$
$$= \$12 + \$2.00$$
$$= \$14.00$$

So, 4 hardcover books cost $14.00.

Library Book Sale	
Hardcover	$3.50
Softcover	$1.99
Audiobook	$4.25

Use the table and mental math to solve.

1. How much do 7 hardcover books cost?

2. How much do 5 audiobooks cost?

3. How much do 6 softcover books cost? (Hint: Think of $1.99 as $2 − $0.01.)

4. How much more do 2 audiobooks cost than 2 hardcover books?

2.2.b. Multiply and divide decimals by one- or two-digit multipliers or divisors to solve problems.

2.2.c. Estimate and find solutions to single and multi-step problems using whole numbers, decimals, fractions, and percents (e.g., 7/8 + 8/9 is about 2, 3.9 + 5.3 is about 9).

Materials
• MathBoard

Problem Solving Workshop
Strategy: Make a Table

Essential Question What are three different types of tables that can help you solve problems?

▶ **Learn the Strategy** REAL WORLD

You can use tables to organize different types of data to show relationships between two or more items. A table makes it easy to show tallied data, to compare and order data, and to identify and extend patterns.

You can use a table to show the frequency of data.

Runners' times (in sec)

47.3	46.2	51.7	49.9
50.2	50.8	55.3	48.9
52.1	55.3	54.8	47.5
48.3	51.6	55.2	49.1
54.5	46.8	50.4	52.7

Runners' Times (in sec)		
Interval (in sec)	Tally	Frequency
46.0 – 47.9	IIII	4
48.0 – 49.9	IIII	4
50.0 – 51.9	HHT	5
52.0 – 53.9	II	2
54.0 – 55.9	HHT	5

You can use a table to show data in order.

Batting averages

Chris: 0.362   Al: 0.328

Mario: 0.355   Nicolas: 0.298

Sean: 0.321   Matt: 0.371

Tyrone: 0.338   Corey: 0.314

Tony: 0.325   John: 0.345

Batting Averages			
Player	Average	Player	Average
Matt	0.371	Al	0.328
Chris	0.362	Tony	0.325
Mario	0.355	Sean	0.321
John	0.345	Corey	0.314
Tyrone	0.338	Nicolas	0.298

Math Talk

What are some questions that can be answered by using each of the tables shown above?

You can use a table to look for patterns.

Stephanie earns $7.25 an hour.

Number of hours	1	2	3	4	5	6
Earnings	$7.25	$14.50	$21.75	$29.00	$36.25	$43.50

When making a table to solve a problem, consider the best way to organize the given information. Read the problem carefully to identify what the question is asking you to find. Design the table so that it will help you answer the question.

🔑 UNLOCK the Problem   REAL WORLD

PROBLEM The drama club is having a bake sale. The students are selling brownies, muffins, and cookies. Brownies cost $0.75 each, muffins cost $0.85 each, and cookies cost $0.60 each. Kelsey has $3.00. If she wants to buy only brownies, only muffins, or only cookies, what is the greatest number of each that she can buy?

Read the Problem

What do I need to find?

I need to find the greatest number of each item that Kelsey can buy.

What information do I need to use?

I know that each brownie costs $0.75, each muffin costs $0.85, and each cookie costs $0.60. I also know that Kelsey has $3.00 to spend.

How will I use the information?

I can make a table to show the cost of different numbers of each item.

Solve the Problem

Create a table. The table should have a column for each of the items, along with a column for the numbers 1–5. Fill in the price of 1 of each of the items.

Drama Club Bake Sale

Number	Brownies	Muffins	Cookies
1	$0.75	$0.85	$0.60
2			
3			
4			
5			

Fill in the rest of the chart. To find out how much 2 of each item costs, multiply the price of the item by the number of items you might want to buy. Continue until the chart is completed. For example, you can multiply to find the cost of 2 brownies.

$$\begin{array}{r} \$0.75 \\ \times\ \ \ \ 2 \\ \hline \$1.50 \end{array}$$

Kelsey can buy 4 brownies or 5 cookies for $3.00. Since $3.00 does not appear in the muffins column, find the greatest number that is less than $3.00. Kelsey can buy 3 muffins for $2.55.

Drama Club Bake Sale

Number	Brownies	Muffins	Cookies
1	$0.75	$0.85	$0.60
2	$1.50	$1.70	$1.20
3	$2.25	$2.55	$1.80
4	$3.00	$3.40	$2.40
5	$3.75	$4.25	$3.00

So, Kelsey can buy 4 brownies, 3 muffins, or 5 cookies.

1. The drama club reduced the price of each item by $0.15 during the last half hour of the bake sale. The original prices were: $0.75 for a brownie, $0.85 for a muffin, and $0.60 for a cookie. If Kelsey had waited until the items were marked down, how many of each item could she have bought for $3.00?

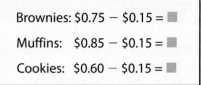

Brownies: $0.75 − $0.15 = ▪

Muffins: $0.85 − $0.15 = ▪

Cookies: $0.60 − $0.15 = ▪

   First, calculate the reduced price of each item.

   Next, make a table to show the costs of different numbers of each item.

   Finally, use your table to find the number of each item Kelsey could have bought for $3.00.

2. **What if** the prices had been reduced by $0.25 instead of $0.15? How many of each item could Kelsey have bought?

3. Sam and Carol will bake cookies and brownies for a bake sale. Each batch of cookies requires 2.5 c of flour. Each batch of brownies requires 1.5 c of flour. Sam and Carol have exactly 12.5 c of flour. How many whole batches of cookies and brownies can they make if they want to use all of the flour and make at least one batch of each?

On Your Own

Make a table to solve.

4. The drama club members sold packages of 3 cookies for $1.60 per package and packages of 2 brownies for $1.50 per package. If Adam wanted to buy only cookies or only brownies for his friends, what was the greatest number of each he could buy with $5.00?

5. Baker's Best Bakery sells cake donuts for $0.70 each and muffins for $0.84 each. Mr. Gleason wants to spend the same amount on cake donuts as on muffins. If he can spend no more than $10.00, how many of each item can he buy?

6. Monica scored 10, 20, or 30 points on each round of a computer game. Her total score after 5 rounds was 90 points. How many different combinations of 10, 20, or 30 points could Monica have scored? List the combinations.

7. The diagram shows the number of squares in each row of a game board that Rosa is designing. If the pattern continues, how many squares will be in Row 8?

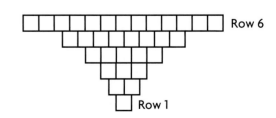

Row 6

Row 1

8. Dan orders pies from a baker to sell at his deli. The baker charges $5.50 for apple pies and $7.00 for blueberry pies. Dan placed a pie order that cost $94.50. If he ordered 7 apple pies, how many blueberry pies did Dan order?

 **Real World Data**

For 9–11, use the graph.

9. Betty's Bakery sold 6 dozen fewer bagels on Sunday than it sold on Saturday. However, it sold the same numbers of plain and sesame bagels as it sold on Saturday. What is the greatest number of pumpernickel bagels that could have been sold on Sunday if at least 9 dozen of each of the other two varieties were sold?

10. At Betty's Bakery, a single bagel costs $0.60, but a half-dozen bagels cost $3.30, and a dozen bagels cost $6.00. What is the least amount of money the bakery could have made selling plain bagels this past Saturday? What is the greatest amount?

11. **Write Math** ▸ The bakery's record for income from bagel sales in one day was $750. If all bagels sold for $0.60 each on Saturday, did the bakery break its record? **Explain** how you know.

12. **Open-Ended** At a bake sale, chocolate chip cookies sell for $0.80 each and oatmeal cookies sell for $0.60 each. Yolanda wants to spend $6.20. What is one way she can spend all of her money?

Choose a Strategy

- Make a Table
- Draw a Diagram or Picture
- Make a Model or Act It Out
- Find a Pattern
- Make a Table or Graph
- Predict and Test
- Work Backwards
- Solve a Simpler Problem
- Write an Equation
- Use Logical Reasoning

Dozens of Bagels Sold on Saturday

Whole Wheat 13.25
Pumpernickel 15
Plain 32.5
Poppy 18.25
Sesame 21.5

 PROBLEM

The Booster Club runs a snack bar during games. It sells hot dogs for $1.25 and hamburgers for $1.75. It also sells chips and water.

13. During one game, the club made twice as much money from selling hot dogs as it did from selling hamburgers. If fewer than 90 hot dogs were sold, what is the greatest number of hamburgers that could have been sold?

14. A bottle of water and 3 bags of baked chips cost $2.50. A bottle of water and 5 bags of baked chips cost $3.80. How much does a bottle of water cost? How much does a bag of baked chips cost?

⭐ **2.2.b.** Multiply and divide decimals by one- or two-digit multipliers or divisors to solve problems.

Materials
• MathBoard

Divide Decimals by Whole Numbers

Essential Question How can estimation help you know when to use a zero as a placeholder in decimal division?

PROBLEM Cliff earned $3.48 interest on his savings account for a 3-month period. What was the average amount of interest Cliff earned per month on his savings account?

You can use a model, paper and pencil, or a calculator to divide a decimal by a whole number.

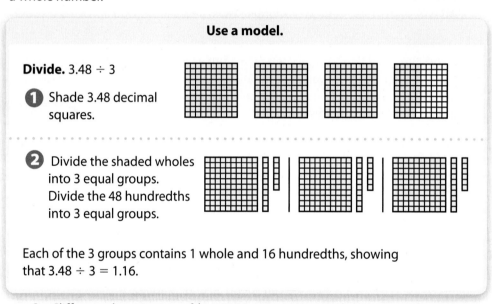

Use a model.

Divide. 3.48 ÷ 3

1 Shade 3.48 decimal squares.

2 Divide the shaded wholes into 3 equal groups. Divide the 48 hundredths into 3 equal groups.

Each of the 3 groups contains 1 whole and 16 hundredths, showing that 3.48 ÷ 3 = 1.16.

So, Cliff earned an average of $1.16 in interest per month.

Divide. 19.75 ÷ 5   **Estimate.** 20 ÷ 5 = 4

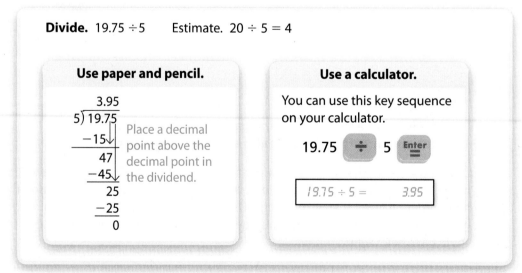

Use paper and pencil.

```
      3.95
  5) 19.75
   −15↓
      47          Place a decimal
   −45↓           point above the
      25          decimal point in
   −25            the dividend.
       0
```

Use a calculator.

You can use this key sequence on your calculator.

19.75 ÷ 5 Enter/=

`19.75 ÷ 5 =        3.95`

Since the estimate is 4, the answer is reasonable. So, 19.75 ÷ 5 = 3.95.

Zeros as Placeholders

Sometimes you have to place zeros in the quotient when dividing decimals.

Examples

Divide. 3.88 ÷ 4   **Estimate.** 4 ÷ 4 = 1

```
      0.97
  4) 3.88
    -0↓
      38
    -36↓
      28
    -28
       0
```

Divide. Since the dividend, 3, is less than the divisor, 4, place a 0 in the ones place in the quotient.

Place a decimal point above the decimal point in the dividend.

So, 3.88 ÷ 4 = 0.97. Since the estimate is 1, the answer is reasonable.

Note that once you place the decimal point in the quotient, decimal division is performed in the same way as whole-number division.

Divide. 42.063 ÷ 7   **Estimate.** 42 ÷ 7 = 6

```
      6.009
  7) 42.063
    -42
      00
     -0
      06
     -0
      63
    -63
       0
```

Place a decimal point above the decimal point in the dividend.

Since 7 > 0 and 7 > 6, place zeros in the tenths and hundredths places in the quotient.

```
    6.009
      ×7
  42.063 3
```

Since multiplication and division are inverse operations, use multiplication to check your answer.

So, 42.063 ÷ 7 = 6.009. Since the estimate is 6, the answer is reasonable.

Share and Show

1. Jan divided 2.48 decimal squares into 4 equal groups. What decimal names each group? What is the quotient? What is 2.48 ÷ 4?

Copy the quotient and correctly place the decimal point.

2. $\dfrac{079}{9)7.11}$ 3. $\dfrac{629}{6)37.74}$ 4. $\dfrac{027}{18)4.86}$ 5. $\dfrac{0267}{4)1.068}$ 6. $\dfrac{204}{6)12.24}$

Estimate. Then find the quotient.

7. 22.8 ÷ 6   8. 7)$17.15   9. 325.8 ÷ 9   10. 3)8.451   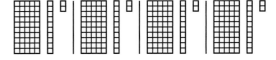11. 12)60.84

12. Math Talk **Explain** how estimation helps you to place the decimal point in a quotient.

Copy the quotient and correctly place the decimal point.

13.
$$\frac{0006}{18)0.108}$$

14.
$$\frac{8405}{14)117.67}$$

15.
$$\frac{0054}{17)0.918}$$

16.
$$\frac{0093}{42)3.906}$$

17.
$$\frac{819}{36)294.84}$$

Estimate. Then find the quotient.

18. $7.6 \div 19$

19. $35)\overline{1.505}$

20. $\$197.12 \div 28$

21. $37.6 \div 8$

22. $6)\overline{\$21.24}$

23. $461.7 \div 19$

24. $4)\overline{7.172}$

25. $\$137.10 \div 15$

26. $28.63 \div 7$

27. $23)\overline{359.26}$

28. Beverly earned $9.36 interest on her savings account for a 12-month period. What was the average amount of interest Beverly earned per month on her savings account?

29. Mrs. Nash deposited $50 per month in her savings account for 3 months. Then she increased her monthly deposit to $75 for the next 2 months. What was the average amount of her deposit per month?

30. Reasoning Ken's dad deposited a total of $225 into his savings account for the first five months of the year. If he deposited $105 into the account in the sixth month, what was the average amount deposited into the account each month?

Real World Data

For 31–32, use the table.

31. What is the average growth per year for girls from age 8 to age 12?

32. Between ages 8 and 14, who experiences greater average growth per year, girls or boys? How much greater? Round averages to the nearest hundredth.

Average Height (in.)				
	Age 8	Age 10	Age 12	Age 14
Girls	50.75	55.50	60.50	62.50
Boys	51.00	55.25	59.00	65.20

33. ≡FAST FACT Bamboo is one of the fastest-growing plants on Earth. In Japan, a bamboo plant grew 45.6 in. in 1 day! What was the average growth of this plant per hour?

34. **Write Math** Divide 366 by 3. Then divide 3.66 by 3. How are the quotients the same? How are they different?

 OCCT Test Prep — Math Board

35. A family-pack of tickets for the amusement park contains 24 tickets and costs $27.60. What is the cost of each ticket?

   A $0.87   **C** $1.15

   B $1.05   **D** $11.50

36. Jack grew an average of 16.8 in. over a 6-year period from age 10 to age 16. What was Jack's average growth per year?

   A 1.4 in.   **C** 3.1 in.

   B 2.8 in.   **D** 22.8 in.

★ Standards Quick Check

Find the quotient.

1. 15.95 ÷ 25

2. 110.85 ÷ 3

3. 59.04 ÷ 6

4. 3.6 ÷ 8

5. 3.45 ÷ 15

6. 60.25 ÷ 5

7. 155.1 ÷ 11

8. 729.12 ÷ 28

9. 2,351.68 ÷ 16

Challenge H.O.T.

Rounding to the Nearest Cent

When you divide a money amount by a whole number, be sure to round the quotient to the nearest cent.

The School Store is having a sale on school supplies. Notebooks are on sale at 5 for $12.99. At this price, what is the price of one notebook?

Divide. $12.99 ÷ 5

```
      2.598
  5 ) 12.990
     −10
      29
     −25
      49
     −45
      40
     −40
       0
```

When there is a remainder, place a zero after the last digit of the dividend and continue to divide.

School Store Sale

Notebooks: 5 for $12.99

Pens: 4 for $4.14

Organizers: 3 for $14.69

Folders: 12 for $2.15 or 18 for $2.99

Round 2.598 to the nearest hundredth, or cent.
So, the price of one notebook is $2.60.

Solve.

1. How much greater is the cost of one organizer than the cost of 18 folders?

2. What is the cost of 6 organizers, 1 notebook, and 4 pens?

3. Before the sale, one pen cost $1.29. How much do you save if you buy one pen at the sale price?

4. How much do you save per folder if you buy 18 folders instead of 12?

LESSON 7

★ **2.2.b.** Multiply and divide decimals by one- or two-digit multipliers or divisors to solve problems.

Materials
• MathBoard
• decimal squares

Explore Division of Decimals

Essential Question In what ways can decimal squares help you find the quotient of two decimal numbers?

PROBLEM Michael lives in Michigan, the top blueberry-producing state. One morning, Michael harvests 3.2 lb of blueberries. If blueberries are stored in containers that hold 1.6 lb of blueberries each, how many containers will he need?

You can make a model to find the number of groups of 1.6 that are in 3.2.

Make a model.

Divide. 3.2 ÷ 1.6

Shade 3.2 decimal squares.

Divide the shaded wholes and hundredths into equal groups of 1.6.

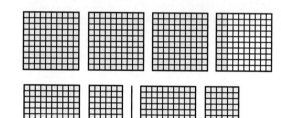

There are 2 equal groups of 1.6, so the model shows the quotient is 2. 3.2 ÷ 1.6 = 2.

So, Michael will need 2 containers.

Look at the model above. The shaded 3 whole squares and 2 tenths represent the dividend, the shaded whole square and 6 tenths in each group represent the divisor, and the 2 equal groups represent the quotient.

1. The model shows 1.25 ÷ 0.25. What quotient does it show? **Explain.**

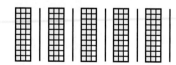

Use a model to find the quotient.

2. 4.5 ÷ 9   3. 2 ÷ 0.4   ✓4. 7.8 ÷ 1.3   ✓5. 3 ÷ 0.75

6. **Math Talk** **Explain** how to use decimal squares to find 6.5 ÷ 1.3.

56

Use a model to find the quotient.

7. 9.3 ÷ 3.1   **8.** 7.5 ÷ 1.5   **9.** 2.1 ÷ 0.7   **10.** 0.52 ÷ 0.13

11. 4.14 ÷ 1.38   **12.** 4.04 ÷ 1.01   **13.** 3 ÷ 1.5   **14.** 2.8 ÷ 0.7

Identify the dividend, divisor, and quotient shown by the model.

15. 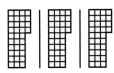   **16.**

 Algebra Use the model to find the value of *n*.

17. 2.64 ÷ *n* = 2   **18.** *n* ÷ 0.27 = 4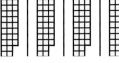

19. At Abner's Farm, blueberries are stored in buckets that hold 2.4 lb of blueberries each. How many buckets are needed for 9.6 lb of blueberries? Draw a model of your work.

20. Mr. Abner sells blueberries in cartons that hold 0.5 pt each. How many cartons are needed for 3 qt of blueberries?

21. Mr. Abner harvests 3.2 lb of blueberries each morning for 6 days and places them in buckets that hold 2.4 lb of blueberries each. How many buckets does Mr. Abner need?

22. **Write Math** ▶ **What's the Question?** Look at the model. The answer is 2.

 OCCT Test Prep

23. The cost of 4 bags of pretzels is shared equally among 6 friends. Each bag costs $1.86. How much is each friend's share?

    A $0.62   **C** $1.86

    B $1.24   **D** $7.44

24. Which is the quotient shown by the model?

    A 4   **C** 2

    B 2.6   **D** 1.3

★ **2.2.b.** Multiply and divide decimals by one- or two-digit multipliers or divisors to solve problems.

Materials
• MathBoard
• decimal squares

Divide with Decimals

Essential Question When dividing by a decimal divisor, how do you rewrite the dividend before dividing?

You can use patterns to help you divide a decimal by a decimal.

HANDS ON

Patterns in decimal division.

• Use a calculator to find the first three quotients in each set.

• Look for a pattern. Try to predict the last quotient in each set.

Set A	Set B
0.28 ÷ 0.04 = ▪	0.874 ÷ 0.038 = ▪
2.8 ÷ 0.4 = ▪	8.74 ÷ 0.38 = ▪
28 ÷ 4 = ▪	87.4 ÷ 3.8 = ▪
280 ÷ 40 = ▪	874 ÷ 38 = ▪

• Describe the pattern that helped you predict the last quotient in each set.

Math Idea

The decimal point moves one place to the right for each power of ten a number is multiplied by. Multiplying the divisor and dividend by the same power often does not affect the quotient.

Decimal division.

To divide two decimals, first multiply the divisor and the dividend by the least power of ten that makes the divisor a whole number.

$$0.6\overline{)45.18} \rightarrow 6\overline{)451.8}$$ THINK: $0.6 \times 10 = 6$ $45.18 \times 10 = 451.8$

Example

Divide. 27.2 ÷ 0.8

$0.8\overline{)27.2}$

$8\overline{)272}$

Make the divisor a whole number by multiplying the divisor and dividend by 10.

$0.8 \times 10 = 8$ $27.2 \times 10 = 272$

Divide.

$$\begin{array}{r} 34 \\ 8\overline{)272} \\ -24 \\ \hline 32 \\ -32 \\ \hline 0 \end{array}$$

So, 27.2 ÷ 0.8 = 34.

When the dividend is greater than the divisor, you may need to add a zero to the right of the dividend so that you can move the decimal point.

Divide. 37.8 ÷ 0.14

```
0.14)37.80
```

Make the divisor a whole number by multiplying the divisor and dividend by 100.

```
     270
14)3,780
   −28
     98
    −98
     00
    − 0
      0
```

0.14 × 100 = 14   37.8 × 100 = 3,780
Divide.

Since the remainder is zero, the quotient is a whole number. You do not need to put a decimal point in the quotient.

So, 37.8 ÷ 0.14 = 270.

If needed, you can write zeros after the last decimal place in the dividend.

Divide. 1.421 ÷ 0.35

```
0.35)1.421
```

Make the divisor a whole number by multiplying the divisor and the dividend by 100.

```
      4.06
35)142.10
  −140
    21
   −0
    210
   −210
      0
```

0.35 × 100 = 35   1.421 × 100 = 142.1
Place the decimal point in the quotient.
Divide.

Since 21 < 35, place a zero in the quotient. To complete the division, write a zero in the hundredths place of the dividend and divide 210 by 35.

So, 1.421 ÷ 0.35 = 4.06.

ERROR ALERT

Be careful to move the decimal point in the dividend the same number of places that you moved the decimal point in the divisor.

 Share and Show Math Board

1. Copy the problem at the right. Make the divisor a whole number by multiplying the divisor and dividend by 10. Place the decimal point in the quotient.

```
         672
14.8)99.456
```

Rewrite the problem so that the divisor is a whole number.

2. 28.7 ÷ 0.7   **3.** 7.29 ÷ 0.09   **4.** 50.284 ÷ 0.26   ✓ **5.** 300.7 ÷ 1.24

Find the quotient.

6. 1.62 ÷ 0.6   **7.** $10.80 ÷ 1.35   **8.** 0.08)7.24   ✓ **9.** 0.55)24.2

10. **Math Talk** **Explain** how you know how many places to move the decimal point in the divisor and why you need to move the decimal point in the dividend the same number of places as in the divisor.

Practice and Problem Solving › REAL WORLD

Rewrite the problem so that the divisor is a whole number.

11. $3.48 \div 0.4$ **12.** $6.495 \div 0.15$ **13.** $26.4 \div 1.76$ **14.** $300 \div 12.5$

Find the quotient.

15. $2.64 \div 0.2$ **16.** $1.43 \div 1.1$ **17.** $0.3\overline{)3.15}$ **18.** $1.08 \div 0.27$

19. $0.78\overline{)0.234}$ **20.** $469.86 \div 8.2$ **21.** $49.50 \div 0.75$ **22.** $0.38\overline{)13.3}$

Copy the problem. Place the decimal point in the quotient.

23. $3.258 \div 0.3 = 1086$ **24.** $53.07 \div 8.7 = 61$ **25.** $27.489 \div 0.15 = 18326$

26. $544.6 \div 1.75 = 3112$ **27.** $257.16 \div 0.6 = 4286$ **28.** $6.482 \div 0.14 = 463$

 Algebra **Evaluate the expression.**

29. $36.4 + (9.2 - 4.9 \div 7)$ **30.** $16 \div 2.5 - 3.2 \times 0.043$ **31.** $142 \div (42 - 6.5) \times 3.9$

 **Real World Data**

For 32–34, use the table.

32. Chad's average cycling speed the first week was 15.9 mi per hr. About how many hours did he cycle?

33. If Chad swims at an average pace of 2.6 mi per hr, how long will it take him to complete the swimming part of his workout during week 2? Round the answer to the nearest tenth of an hour.

Triathlon Training Schedule			
	Week 1	**Week 2**	**Week 3**
Swimming	3.45 mi	3.62 mi	3.96 mi
Cycling	75.60 mi	84.50 mi	97.20 mi
Running	20.25 mi	22.75 mi	23.25 mi

34. Chad's goal is to complete all his running for week 3 in less than 3 hr 30 min. If he runs at an average pace of 7.1 mi per hr, will he achieve his goal?

35. **Write Math** ▶ **What's the Error?** Mia says $0.275 \div 0.25$ is 11. Describe Mia's error and write the correct quotient.

 OCCT Test Prep

36. Mr. Johnson paid $2.31 for 5.5 lb of onions. How much did he pay per pound?

    A $0.42   **C** $4.20

    B $0.46   **D** $12.71

37. Hassan wants to buy a new graphing calculator. The price is $76.50. If he saves $8.50 each week, in how many weeks will he be able to buy the calculator?

    A 7   **C** 9

    B 8.5   **D** 11.25

⭐ Standards Quick Check

Find the quotient.

1. 50.05 ÷ 5.5

2. 50.22 ÷ 8.1

3. 85.36 ÷ 19.4

4. 394.85 ÷ 26.5

5. 723.61 ÷ 26.9

6. 1,093.47 ÷ 12.7

7. 618.64 ÷ 41.8

8. 3.612 ÷ 0.15

9. 6.25 ÷ 0.05

Challenge H.O.T.

Amoebas are tiny one-celled microorganisms. Their flexible outer membranes enable them to constantly change the shape of their bodies. Amoebas can range in size from 0.01 mm to 5 mm in length. You can study amoebas by using a microscope or by studying photographic enlargements of them.

Jacob has a photograph of an amoeba that has been enlarged 1,000 times. The length of the amoeba in the photo is 60 mm. What is the actual length of the amoeba?

Divide. 60 ÷ 1,000

Look for a pattern.
60 ÷ 1 = 60
60 ÷ 10 = 6.0   ← The decimal point moves 1 place to the left.
60 ÷ 100 = 0.6   ← The decimal point moves 2 places to the left.
60 ÷ 1,000 = 0.06 ← The decimal point moves 3 places to the left.

So, the actual length of the amoeba is 0.06 mm.

The number of zeros in the power of 10 tells you how many places to the left to move the decimal point. A similar pattern exists when multiplying.

Solve. Explain your reasoning.

1. Jacob has a photograph of *Amoeba proteus* that has been enlarged 100 times. In the photo, the amoeba appears to have a length of 70 mm. What is its actual length?

2. *Pelomyxa palustris* is the largest amoeba found in pond water. Some specimens are as large as 4.9 mm in diameter. How wide would this amoeba appear in a photograph enlarged 1,000 times?

★ **2.2.b.** Multiply and divide decimals by one- or two-digit multipliers or divisors to solve problems.

2.2.c. Estimate and find solutions to single and multi-step problems using whole numbers, decimals, fractions, and percents (e.g., 7/8 + 8/9 is about 2, 3.9 + 5.3 is about 9).

Materials
• MathBoard

Choose a Method

Essential Question How does using mental math compare with using pencil and paper to solve problems?

PROBLEM For her woodworking project, Vivian needs 3 wooden dowels. A dowel is a wooden rod used to attach pieces of wood together. Vivian needs to cut a dowel that measures 31.5 in. into 3 equal pieces. What will be the length of each piece?

You can use mental math to solve some decimal problems. For others, it may be more appropriate to use paper and pencil or a calculator.

Use mental math.

THINK: $315 \div 3 = 105$ →   So, $31.5 \div 3 = 10.5$

So, the length of each piece will be 10.5 in.

- What makes this problem easy to solve by using mental math?

For his project, Rafael is building a cabinet. Each shelf is 1.20 m long and 0.43 m wide. What is the area of each shelf?

To find the area, multiply the length by the width.

Use paper and pencil.

Multiply 1.20×0.43.

$$\begin{array}{r} 1.20 \\ \times\ 0.43 \\ \hline 360 \\ 4800 \\ +\ 00000 \\ \hline 0.5160 \end{array}$$

The number of decimal places in the product is the sum of the numbers of decimal places in the factors.

Use a calculator.

Use this key sequence.

1.20 **×** 0.43 **Enter** | *1.20 X 0.43   = 0.516* |

So, the area of each shelf is 0.516 m².

1. Copy and complete to find 0.09 × 0.3 mentally.

   9 × 3 = ■. There must be ■ decimal places in the product.

   So, 0.09 × 0.3 = ■.

Solve. Choose mental math, paper and pencil, or a calculator.

   2. $2.50 × 3   **3.** 8.1 ÷ 0.15   **4.** 7.2 ÷ 0.08   ✓ **5.** 3.04 + 7.04 + 5.04

   6. 5.77 − 1.708   **7.** 42.5 × 5.6   **8.** $36.16 ÷ 4   ✓ **9.** 0.333 × 0.3

10. **Math Talk** **Explain** when you might choose mental math over paper and
    pencil or a calculator to solve a problem.

▶ **Practice and Problem Solving** REAL WORLD

Solve. Choose mental math, paper and pencil, or a calculator.

11. $19.75 − $12.25   **12.** 0.64 × 19   **13.** 5.6 ÷ 0.07   **14.** 0.5 × 0.09

15. 132.678 ÷ 16.2   **16.** 18.36 + 16.64   **17.** $14.25 × 4   **18.** 68.5 ÷ 0.04

⭐**Algebra** **Use mental math to find the value of *n*.**

19. 7.92 ÷ n = 0.0792   **20.** n × $6.08 = $30.40   **21.** 8.26 ÷ n = 4.13

22. Marci wants to put a border around two sides of her rectangular flower garden.
    She has a 24-ft piece of lumber. If the lumber will be cut into pieces that are
    0.75 ft long, how many pieces can she cut from the lumber?

23. Tatiana and Emily buy custom-cut pieces of maple. Each piece costs $0.91
    for each inch of length. Tatiana buys a piece of maple that is 52.25 in. long.
    Emily buys a piece that is 47.75 in. long. How much do they spend in all?

24. **Write Math** ▶ **Explain** the method you would use to find 18.09 ÷ 9.
    How would your method change if the problem were 18.09 ÷ 8?

 OCCT Test Prep

25. Jorge used mental math to find the answer to a
    problem. If the answer is 60, which of the
    following could be the problem?

   A 0.24 ÷ 0.04   **C** 4.2 ÷ 0.07

   B 0.36 ÷ 0.6   **D** 5.4 ÷ 0.9

26. Brian and Tino are making benches for the school
    courtyard. They need 6 pieces of wood for each
    bench. If each piece must be 7.5 ft long, how
    many feet of wood will they need for 4 benches?

   A 75 ft   **C** 240 ft

   B 180 ft   **D** 320 ft

⭐ Extra Practice

Set A

Estimate. (pp. 36–39)

1. $7.6 + 3.2 + 22.8$

2. $\$313.04 - \$74.75$

3. $79.7 + 82.4 + 78.5$

4. $11.2 + 28.98$

5. $\$138.45 + \$51.65$

6. $201.05 - 74.809$

7. $92.8 - 17.2$

8. $0.23 + 1.2 + 0.78$

9.
$$\begin{array}{r} 2.4 \\ 3.8 \\ +0.9 \\ \hline \end{array}$$

10.
$$\begin{array}{r} \$45.00 \\ 7.78 \\ 2.49 \\ + 5.13 \\ \hline \end{array}$$

11.
$$\begin{array}{r} 5.4 \\ 0.7 \\ +11.2 \\ \hline \end{array}$$

12.
$$\begin{array}{r} \$56.13 \\ 5.12 \\ +3.91 \\ \hline \end{array}$$

13. Jeff deposited four checks for $87.99, $120.57, $99.85, and $152.01 into his savings account. Order the amounts from least to greatest. About how much money did Jeff deposit?

14. Jeremy is going to buy some puzzles at the store. The puzzles at the store are on sale for $4.89 each. Estimate the number of puzzles Jeremy can buy if he has $26.75 to spend.

Set B

Estimate. Then find the sum or difference. (pp. 40–43)

1.
$$\begin{array}{r} 63.45 \\ +17.65 \\ \hline \end{array}$$

2.
$$\begin{array}{r} 22 \\ 6.7 \\ + 4.159 \\ \hline \end{array}$$

3.
$$\begin{array}{r} \$5.74 \\ - \$ 2.49 \\ \hline \end{array}$$

4.
$$\begin{array}{r} 9.18 \\ - 2.017 \\ \hline \end{array}$$

5. $452.3 - 74.06$

6. $\$43 + \$6.98 + \$0.55$

7. $14.7 - 3.732$

8. $520.85 - 93.807$

9. $81.21 + 12.8 + 28.4$

10. $17.68 - 3.24$

11. $752.23 + 47.7 + 3.8$

12. $9.2 + 2.8 - 1.08$

Copy the problem. Place the decimal point correctly in the answer.

13. $72.96 + 17 + 32.9 + 4.931 = 127791$

14. $\$3.33 + \$5.79 + \$72 = \$8112$

15. $1,936.79 - 854.925 = 1081865$

16. $68.015 - 59.23 = 8785$

Set C

Estimate. Then find the product. (pp. 44–47)

1. 1.4×3.9

2. $\$32.21 \times 7$

3. 0.7×0.3

4. 9.23×0.79

5. 0.04×0.03

6. $\$255 \times 2.4$

7. 0.018×2.53

8. 0.44×16.2

9. 375.1×0.8

10. 6.018×7.25

11. 118×1.4

12. 15.04×0.056

13. 3.14×1.8

14. 0.14×0.55

15. $\$14.95 \times 0.08$

16. $\$3.29 \times 1.12$

Go ONLINE Technology Use HMH Mega Math, The Number Games, *Buggy Bargains,* Levels E, F, and I.

Set D

Estimate. Then find the quotient. (pp. 52–55)

1. 278.53 ÷ 7 **2.** 53.7 ÷ 6 **3.** 410.34 ÷ 5 **4.** 78.98 ÷ 11

5. 351.22 ÷ 5 **6.** 5)$24.75 **7.** 42)3.276 **8.** 0.552 ÷ 12

9. 25.28 ÷ 8 **10.** 1.665 ÷ 37 **11.** 614.16 ÷ 12 **12.** 69.161 ÷ 23

13. The cost of a medium cheese pizza is shared equally among 4 friends. The pizza costs $9.84. How much will each person pay?

14. A 3-oz bottle of the same perfume costs $110.10. What is the cost of the perfume per ounce?

Set E

Use a model to find the quotient. (pp. 56–57)

1. 4.4 ÷ 2.2 **2.** 7.2 ÷ 0.6 **3.** 5.4 ÷ 1.8 **4.** 4.32 ÷ 2.16

5. 3.04 ÷ 0.38 **6.** 0.51 ÷ 0.17 **7.** 8.1 ÷ 0.9 **8.** 5 ÷ 0.25

9. 4.52 ÷ 1.13 **10.** 7.62 ÷ 3.81 **11.** 7.02 ÷ 1.17 **12.** 0.45 ÷ 0.05

13. Susie has 7.5 lb of strawberries. She also has 7 containers that will each hold 1.25 lb of strawberries. Does Susie have enough containers to hold the 7.5 lb of strawberries?

14. Nancy went to the market and bought 4.8 lb of mushrooms for a recipe. She has containers that will hold 1.2 lb. How many of these containers will it take to hold the mushrooms Nancy bought?

Set F

Find the quotient. (pp. 58–61)

1. 4.38 ÷ 0.3 **2.** 0.42)15.12 **3.** 1.56 ÷ 0.26 **4.** 53.60 ÷ 0.8

5. 619.16 ÷ 9.2 **6.** 10.71 ÷ 2.1 **7.** 0.89)0.356 **8.** 200 ÷ 6.25

9. 0.7)2.59 **10.** 90.9 ÷ 0.9 **11.** 144 ÷ 0.16 **12.** 1.5 ÷ 0.03

13. Chuck earned $596.55 for working 72.75 hr at his part-time job after school. Chuck is paid per hour. How much does Chuck earn per hour?

14. Juanita is training to participate in a walk-a-thon to raise money. Over 10.5 days, she walked a total of 70.875 mi. If Juanita walked the same distance each day, how many miles did she walk a day?

Set G

Solve. Choose mental math, paper and pencil, or a calculator. (pp. 62–63)

1. 48.8 ÷ 4 **2.** 7.5 × 0.95 **3.** 0.07 × 0.3 **4.** 1.02 + 4.02 + 2.04

5. $27.36 ÷ 9 **6.** 0.9 ÷ 0.18 **7.** 75.2 − 7.52 **8.** 3 × 12 × 10

9. 0.6 × 0.07 **10.** 5.65 + 18.44 **11.** 26.6 − 2.66 **12.** 7 × 15 × 20

Reading & Writing **Math**

Vocabulary

A place-value chart shows the place name of each digit of a number.

Copy the place-value chart. Write these numbers in your chart in different colors. Make sure you write the digits in the correct places.

Billions			Millions			Thousands			Ones			Decimals	
hundred billions	ten billions	billions	hundred millions	ten millions	millions	hundred thousands	ten thousands	thousands	hundreds	tens	ones	tenths	hundredths	thousandths

45.301

452.09

34,982.7

0.139

Use the numbers in the place-value chart to answer these questions.

1. Which number has the greatest number of digits?

2. Which number has the least number of digits?

3. Write the word form of the number with a 7 in the tenths place.

4. Write the word form of the number with a 9 in the thousandths place.

Writing Think of a number that comes between the least number in the place-value chart and the number 1. Write that number in the chart. Then explain why your choice of number is correct.

Reading Look for *Exploring Numbers (Math for Fun)* by Andrew King in your library

H.O.T. Multistep Problems

1 Alex wants to buy a saddle for his horse. The saddle costs $300. He has $87.25 saved. In addition to keeping his horse at a stable for free, Alex earns $5.25 an hour grooming horses and cleaning out all the stables. He wants to know how many hours he will have to work before he can buy the saddle.

Alex writes this equation to find the amount of money, m, that he needs to buy the saddle.

2.2.c.

$$m + \$87.25 = \$300$$

- Explain how to use the inverse operation to solve for m. Then solve.

- Alex wrote this expression to figure his earnings: $5.25 + h. What mistake did he make?

- How could you find the number of hours Alex needs to work to buy the saddle? How many hours does he need to work?

- Alex has the chance to work at the stable shop. He can work there 2 hours for every 5 hours he works in the stable. Working in the stable shop pays $9.00 per hour. If Alex decided to do this, how many hours must he work at each job to earn enough to pay for the saddle? Explain your reasoning.

2 More than 100 species of cacti grow in Texas. Some of the cactus plants are used for food. Others grow in the wild or are grown in gardens. Yolanda has a cactus collection on her windowsill. She keeps track of the growth of each cactus in the table.

2.2.c.

Cactus	Height
Club Cholla	11.56 inches
Claret Cup	10.61 inches
Prickly Pear	12.45 inches

- Yolanda estimates the difference in height between the tallest cactus and the shortest cactus in her windowsill garden. Round the cacti to the nearest tenth to show how Yolanda should estimate the difference in height.

- Dolores says that there is a cactus in her backyard that has a height equal to the sum of the heights of Yolanda's cacti. How tall is the cactus in Dolores's backyard? Find an estimated height by rounding the height of each of Yolanda's cacti to the nearest whole number and adding. Then find the exact sum.

- One kind of cactus grows very slowly, averaging only about 0.65 inch per year. Dolores finds this type of cactus near her house. The cactus measures 8.67 inches tall. Dolores estimates last year at this time that cactus was 6.5 inches tall. Is Dolores's estimate reasonable? **Explain** your answer.

Practice for the OCCT

1 What is the value of 0.26 × *n* when *n* = 7.2?
2.2.b.

A   0.0566

B   0.1872

C   0.566

D   1.872

2 Martin bought 4 doughboys from the county fair. He paid $2.55 for each doughboy. About how much money did Martin spend for the doughboys?   2.2.c.

A   about $14

B   about $10

C   about $7

D   about $5

3 Anna bought a package of sequins for $2.89, some craft glue for $4.59, and some felt for $3.29 from the craft store in Anderson. Which is the best estimate for the total of Anna's purchase?
2.2.c.

A $6   C $11

B $7   D $14

4 Abigail went to the Museum of Radio & Technology and bought 6 souvenirs for her family. Each souvenir cost the same amount. If Abigail spent $20.10, how much was each souvenir?
2.2.b.

A $3.35

B $3.65

C $4.15

D $4.60

5 Jason went to a skateboard shop to buy some new wheels for his skateboard. He bought 8 new wheels that each cost $9.40. How much did Jason spend for the new wheels?   2.2.b.

A $20.20

B $72.32

C $75.20

D $80.00

6 The Hagans took a trip during the summer. When they left their home, the odometer in their car read 7,429.6 miles. When they returned from their trip, their odometer read 9,278.3 miles. How many miles did the Hagans travel?   2.2.c.

A   987.4

B   1,848.7

C   2,251.3

D   16,707.9

7 The table shows the amount of money raised by 3 homerooms at a school fair. How much more was the total raised by homerooms 6A and 6C than by homeroom 6B?   2.2.c.

Homeroom	6A	6B	6C
Money Raised	$133.88	$148.59	$122.77

A $14.71

B $108.06

C $137.48

D $159.70

8 What is the value of the expression $c \times 16.83$ when $c = 0.14$? 🔲 2.2.b.

   A   0.8415

   B   2.3562

   C   84.15

   D   235.62

9 One cornfield maze covers 3.3 acres. Another cornfield maze covers 12.6 acres. How many more acres is the large cornfield maze than the smaller cornfield maze? 🔲 2.2.c.

   A   15.9

   B   15.3

   C   11.2

   D   9.3

10 For his baseball game, Jonathan bought 7 bottles of juice. Each bottle of juice costs $2.79. How much money did Jonathan spend on bottles of juice? 🔲 2.2.b.

   A $9.79

   B $14.63

   C $19.53

   D $21.35

11 Denise buys 4 anime comic books for $7.95 each. She hands the cashier two $20 bills. How much change should Denise get back? 🔲 2.2.c.

   A $1.80

   B $8.20

   C $11.80

   D $11.85

Problem Solving

12 You knit a scarf using 4 balls of yarn. The yarn costs a total of $24.88. How much does each ball of yarn cost? 🔲 2.2.b.

13 Martin bought 8 ice cream cones for him and his friends. Each ice cream cone cost $1.89. How much did Martin spent for the ice cream cones? 🔲 2.2.b.

14 What is the value of the expression $t \times 43.98$ when $t = 7.42$? 🔲 2.2.b.

15 Rhea is making strawberry jam. She wants to make 2 batches and needs 4 pounds of strawberries for each batch. If she buys containers of strawberries that weigh 2.46 pounds, 1.87 pounds, and 2.85 pounds, about how much more is needed? Is an estimate or an exact answer needed? **Explain**. 🔲 2.2.c.

16 A video store charges $4.75 to rent a new movie and $3.95 to rent other movies. For a monthly fee of $19.95, you can rent an unlimited number of either type of movie. If you rent two new movies and three others each month, is the monthly fee a better deal? **Explain**. 🔲 2.2.c.

Performance Assessment

Writing Math How do you use place value to compare and order whole numbers?

Wind Energy

Wind energy has been used for centuries to pump water, to grind grain, and to power sailboats. Today, many communities use windmills called wind turbines to generate electricity. Several important wind turbine projects are located in Minnesota.

For 1–8, use the table.

1. Order the locations from greatest number of turbines to least.

2. How many more turbines are there at Lake Benton I than at Lake Benton II?

Wind Turbines in Minnesota	
Location	**Number of Turbines**
Lakota Ridge	15
Lake Benton I	143
Lake Benton II	138

3. There are about 50 times as many wind turbines in California as there are at the three sites in Minnesota combined. About how many wind turbines are there in California?

4. How many times as many turbines are there at Lake Benton II than at Lakota Ridge? Write your answer as a decimal.

Electricity is measured in kilowatt-hours (kWh). The turbines at Lakota Ridge generate 30 million kWh per year. The turbines at Lake Benton II generate 355 million kWh per year.

5. About how many kWh are generated each day at Lake Benton II?

6. About how many kWh are generated each year by each turbine at Lake Benton II?

7. About how many kWh are generated each year by each turbine at Lakota Ridge?

8. About how many kWh are generated each day at Lakota Ridge?

Unit Learning Task

Geologic Eras

Objective: To connect unit lesson concepts using real world data.

We are going to research the Cenozoic Era, the Mesozoic Era, and Paleozoic Era of the geologic time scale.

Copy this outline to record the information you research for display and class discussion.

1. I am going to research the

_____ Era.

2. I am using the following references:

_____

_____

_____

_____

3. I have found the following data:

Periods: _____

Epochs: _____

Approximate start dates: _____

Organisms that first appeared:

_____

_____

4. Draw a sketch of your planned classroom display.

5. What information did you find on the connection between half-life dating and the development of the geologic time scale.

_____

_____

6. What are some applications of the geologic time scale?

_____

_____

THE **WORLD** **ALMANAC** FOR KIDS

At the Top of the World

Tall and Taller

The location of the world's tallest building keeps changing. No, the building doesn't move, but people are always designing and constructing newer, taller buildings.

Taipei 101, in Taipei, Taiwan, was completed in 2005. With a height of 1,671 ft, it became the tallest building in the world. But taller buildings are already under construction.

Taipei 101, in Taipei, Taiwan

FACT·ACTIVITY

These heights do not include antennas or decorative features of the buildings.

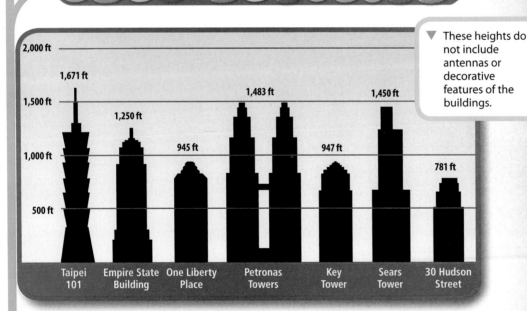

| | 1,671 ft | 1,250 ft | 945 ft | 1,483 ft | | 947 ft | 1,450 ft | 781 ft |

Taipei 101 · Empire State Building · One Liberty Place · Petronas Towers · Key Tower · Sears Tower · 30 Hudson Street

The graph shows seven buildings. Use the information given to answer the questions.

1 Order the buildings from tallest to shortest.

2 What is the difference, in feet, between the two tallest buildings in the graph?

3 **Write Math** ➤ A student estimates that the Petronas Towers are about twice the height of 30 Hudson Street. Do you agree? **Explain.**

Tall Buildings, Low Ceilings

When it was built in 1931, the Empire State Building was the tallest building in the world.

75 years later, it was still in the top ten !

In 1931, the tallest building in the world was 100 stories (floors) tall. Sixty-seven years later the new tallest building was only 88 stories tall. How is this possible? Did the first building shrink? Did people count incorrectly? Read on to find out.

FACT·ACTIVITY

1 Use the data for the Petronas Towers and the Empire State Building to answer the questions.

▶ What is the average number of feet per story in each building? Round the answer to the nearest tenth.

▶ What does this tell you about each building?

▶ Should building height be measured in feet or stories? Why?

2 Design a new skyscraper.

▶ Find the height and the number of stories for your skyscraper.

▶ Find the average number of feet per story in your building. Round the answer to the nearest tenth.

▶ Find the average number of feet per story for your building. **Explain** how to compare this number to the average number of feet per story for the Petronas Towers and the Empire State Building.

The Petronas Towers in Kuala Lumpur, Malaysia, are each 88 stories and 1,483 ft tall.

The Empire State Building is 102 stories and 1,250 ft tall.

Number Theory and Fractions

BIG IDEAS!

- The study of number theory builds understanding of factors and multiples, prime and composite numbers, and divisibility rules; fractions and mixed numbers can be expressed in equivalent forms and can be compared.

- Addition and subtraction of fractions and mixed numbers is based on understanding equivalent fractions; multiplication of fractions involves finding part of a part of a whole; division of fractions is related to repeated subtraction and can be shown with models.

Math On Location
Online Videos

Careful measuring of ingredients using fractions and mixed numbers results in delicious foods.

Herb rolls are cut from dough and placed on baking trays in rows of equal numbers.

Meals that are ready to serve are artfully arranged and decorated with flowers.

Get Ready Game

Operation Cover-Up

Materials
- 1 deck of Operation Cover-Up Cards
- 2 Operation Cover-Up game boards

How to Play   Play in pairs. Each player has a game board. Shuffle the deck of cards and place it face down where both players can reach it. Players should take turns following these steps:

1   Draw two cards from the deck.

2   Decide whether the numbers on the cards make any statements on your board true.

3   Cover a statement with the cards if they make the statement true. If the cards do not make any of the statements true, discard them.

How to Win   Be the first player to cover all six statements on your game board. Or be the player with the most statements covered when all of the cards have been used.

Draw Conclusions

Complete these exercises after playing the game.

1. **WRITING** Is it possible for two cards to make all three statements in the Estimation Squares true? Explain why or why not.

2. **REASONING** Explain why you do not need to calculate exactly to find if a product is between 5000 and 15,000.

Reading & Writing Math

Reading
Before reading a story or article, you can preview it to get an idea of what it's about and how it's organized. You can also preview a math lesson.

Preview Lesson 6 on pages 94–97.
This is what you'll find.

This is an hands on lesson. I'll use the learn section as a reference to complete the problems on the pages.

Lesson 6 Preview

✓ Lesson title: Equivalent Fractions and Simplest Form

✓ Special kind of lesson: Hands On

✓ Essential Question How can you find the simplest form of a fraction in just one step?

✓ Vocabulary (highlighted words): equivalent fractions

✓ Main headings: Learn, Share and Show, Practice and Real World Problem Solving

✓ Special sections: Math Talk, Write Math

✓ Special features: OCCT Test Prep, Standards Quick Check, Challenge

Writing
Use the checklist to preview another lesson. See if the lesson includes the items listed in red type. Then write a sentence or two telling what you think the lesson is about or what you expect to do or to learn.

Number Theory and Fraction Concepts

The scarlet carnation (*Dianthus caryophyllus*) is Ohio's official state flower. It was selected in memory of Ohio's William McKinley, the twenty-fifth President of the United States.

carnation

Investigate

Suppose your class is making seed packets, using the seeds in the table, to raise money to visit a botanical garden. Each packet must have the same number of seeds for a given color with no seeds left over. Find two possible numbers of packets that can be formed and the number of each color contained in one packet.

Seed Collection

Flower Color	Number of Seeds
Pink	336
Purple	288
Red	144
White	96

Technology
Student pages are available in the Student eBook

Check your understanding of important skills needed for success in Chapter 3.

▶ Factors and Multiples

Write the next three multiples.

1. For 3: 3, 6, …   **2.** For 6: 6, 12, …   **3.** For 8: 8, 16, …

4. For 11: 11, 22, …   **5.** For 15: 15, 30, …   **6.** For 21: 21, 42, …

7. For 25: 25, 50, …   **8.** For 29: 29, 58, …   **9.** For 45: 45, 90, …

List the factors of each number.

10. 4   **11.** 9   **12.** 12   **13.** 14   **14.** 15

15. 17   **16.** 20   **17.** 25   **18.** 60   **19.** 72

▶ Model Fractions

Write a fraction for the shaded part.

20.

21.

Vocabulary

Visualize It!

Multiple Ways of Showing the Same Number	
Improper Fraction $\frac{20}{6}$	**Mixed Number** $3\frac{2}{6}$
Mixed Number in Simplest Form $3\frac{1}{3}$	

Language Tips

A prefix is a word part that appears at the beginning of a word. Knowing the meaning of a prefix can help you decode unknown terms. The prefix "-im" means "not". Knowing this can help you determine that impossible means "not possible" or that impolite means "not polite".

In mathematics, an improper fraction is "not in the proper form". An improper fraction has a numerator that is greater than its denominator.

English	Spanish
fraction	**fracción**
prime number	**número primo**

See English-Spanish Glossary.

★ **2.2.c.** Estimate and find solutions to single and multi-step problems using whole numbers, decimals, fractions, and percents (e.g., 7/8 + 8/9 is about 2, 3.9 + 5.3 is about 9).

Materials
• MathBoard

Divisibility

Essential Question What are the divisibility rules for 2, 3, 4, 5, 6, 9, or 10? How can these rules be applied to problem solving situations?

PROBLEM A university marching band is well known for its creative marching formations. For one performance, 180 of the musicians change formation to form lines. All the lines have the same number of musicians. Can the musicians be arranged in 2 lines? In 3 lines? In 4 lines? In 5 lines? In 10 lines?

You can use divisibility rules to help you decide whether a number is divisible by another number. A number is divisible by another number if the quotient is a natural number and the remainder is zero.

Tell whether 180 is divisible by 2, 3, 4, 5, or 10.

Question	Divisibility Test	Conclusion
Is 180 divisible by 2?	The last digit is even.	Since 0 is even, 180 is divisible by 2.
Is 180 divisible by 3?	The sum of the digits is divisible by 3.	$1 + 8 + 0 = 9$ Since 9 is divisible by 3, 180 is divisible by 3.
Is 180 divisible by 4?	The last two digits form a number that is divisible by 4.	$80 \div 4 = 20$ Since 80 is divisible by 4, 180 is divisible by 4.
Is 180 divisible by 5?	The last digit is 0 or 5.	Since the last digit is 0, 180 is divisible by 5.
Is 180 divisible by 10?	The last digit is 0.	Since the last digit is 0, 180 is divisible by 10.

So, 180 musicians can be arranged in lines of 2, 3, 4, 5, or 10.

• If a number is divisible by 10, is it also divisible by 5? Explain.

Example

Tell whether the number is divisible by 2, 3, 4, 5, or 10.

690 is divisible by

2   because the last digit is even.
3   because the sum of the digits is 15.
5   because the last digit is 0.
10   because the last digit is 0.

Divisibility Rules for 6, 8, and 9

You can use what you know about the divisibility rules for 2, 3, and 4 to write divisibility rules for 6, 8, and 9.

Divisibility rules.

Number	2	3	4	5	6	8	9	10
				Divisible By				
312	✓	✓	✓		✓	✓		
3,488	✓		✓			✓		
918	✓	✓			✓		✓	
1,464	✓	✓	✓		✓	✓		
1,881		✓					✓	
1,224	✓	✓	✓		✓	✓	✓	
344	✓		✓			✓		
3,360	✓	✓	✓	✓	✓	✓		✓

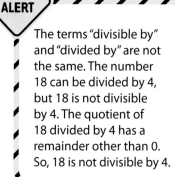

ERROR ALERT

The terms "divisible by" and "divided by" are not the same. The number 18 can be divided by 4, but 18 is not divisible by 4. The quotient of 18 divided by 4 has a remainder other than 0. So, 18 is not divisible by 4.

- Look at the numbers that are divisible by 6. What other divisors do they all have in common? What rule do you think you can use to check for divisibility by 6?

- Look at the last three digits of the numbers that are divisible by 8. Do the last three digits form a number that is divisible by 8? Show your work.

- If a number is divisible by 8, by what other numbers must it also be divisible? Explain.

- Look at the numbers that are divisible by 9. What do you notice about the sums of the digits of these numbers? Explain.

Share and Show Math Board

1. Copy and complete the table to decide whether 2,385 is divisible by 2, 3, 4, 5, 6, 8, 9, or 10.

Last digit?	Last 2 digits?	Last 3 digits?	Sum of digits?
5			

Tell whether the number is divisible by 2, 3, 4, 5, 6, 8, 9, or 10.

2. 45   **3.** 192   **4.** 820   **5.** 7,035   ⊘**6.** 201   ⊘**7.** 916

8. **Math Talk** **Explain** why a number that is divisible by 9 is also divisible by 3.

► **Practice and Problem Solving** REAL WORLD

Tell whether the number is divisible by 2, 3, 4, 5, 6, 8, 9, or 10.

9. 48   **10.** 135   **11.** 320   **12.** 801   **13.** 744   **14.** 596

15. 4,211   **16.** 10,101   **17.** 2,000   **18.** 1,668   **19.** 6,615   **20.** 6,255

Write a four-digit number, with no repeated digits, that fits each description.

21. The number is divisible by 8 and 9.

22. The number is divisible by 3, but not by 9.

23. The number is divisible by 4, but not by 6.

24. The number is divisible by 6, 8, and 10.

25. Four marching bands are from schools with student populations that are divisible by 25. The populations are 750; 2,000; 3,475; and 9,925. Find a divisibility rule for 25, then write three 5-digit numbers that are divisible by 25.

26. A 2-digit number is greater than 30 and divisible by 3, 6, and 9. What might be the number?

27. Alex says that all odd numbers are divisible by 3. Is he correct? Give examples to justify your reasoning.

28. **Reasoning** Why are all multiples of 100 divisible by 4? Use examples to justify your answer.

29. Write Math ► At a national marching band competition, the number of participants is a 5-digit number with no repeated digits. What is a possible number if it is divisible by 4, 6, 9, and 10? By what other numbers must this number be divisible? **Explain.**

 OCCT Test Prep

30. Which number of jelly beans cannot be shared equally among 6 friends?

     A 222   **C** 321

     B 234   **D** 426

31. Which 4-digit number is divisible by 9 but not by 5?

     A 9,840   **C** 8,550

     B 8,793   **D** 6,211

 Technology
Use HMH Mega Math, Ice Station Exploration, *Arctic Algebra,* Levels M and N.

★ Standards Quick Check

Tell whether the number is divisible by 2, 3, 4, 5, 6, 8, 9, or 10.

1. 432

2. 616

3. 875

4. 1,090

5. 3,572

6. 9,999

Write a four-digit number, with no repeated digits, that fits each description.

7. The number is divisible by 2, 4, 5, 8, and 10.

8. The number is divisible by 2, 3, and 6, but not by 9.

H.O.T.

Divisibility Rules and Properties

The divisibility rule for 3 states that if the sum of the digits of a number is divisible by 3, then the number itself is divisible by 3. You can use properties and expanded form to show why 735 is divisible by 3.

$735 = 7 \times 100 + 3 \times 10 + 5$ Write 735 in expanded form.

$735 = 7 \times (99 + 1) + 3 \times (9 + 1) + 5$ Since 99 and 9 are divisible by 3, rewrite 100 as 99 + 1 and 10 as 9 + 1.

$= (7 \times 99) + (7 \times 1) + (3 \times 9) + (3 \times 1) + 5$ Use the Distributive Property.

$= (7 \times 99) + (3 \times 9) + (7 \times 1) + (3 \times 1) + 5$ Use the Commutative Property.

$= (7 \times 99) + (3 \times 9) + 7 + 3 + 5$

Since 99 and 9 are divisible by 3, the sum $(7 \times 99) + (3 \times 9)$ is also divisible by 3. Now check whether the sum of the remaining addends, 7, 3, and 5, is divisible by 3. Since the sum is 15, it is divisible by 3.

Since $(7 \times 99) + (3 \times 9)$ is divisible by 3, and 15 is divisible by 3, then 735 is divisible by 3.

Answer by using properties and expanded form.

1. Explain why 612 is divisible by 3.

2. Explain why 468 is divisible by 9.

Vocabulary

composite number

prime number

Materials
• MathBoard

> ## Math Idea
> The number 1 is neither prime nor composite because it has only 1 factor, 1.

Prime and Composite Numbers

Essential Question How does an understanding of factors and divisbility rules help you decide if a number is prime or composite?

PROBLEM Mrs. Gant's students want to arrange square tables in one large rectangle so a group can sit together. If the students want to choose from several different arrangements, should they use 12 or 13 tables?

Tiles can be used to show the possible arrangements for 12 and 13 tables.

12 tables: ← 3 arrangements

$$1 \times 12 = 12 \qquad 2 \times 6 = 12 \qquad 3 \times 4 = 12$$

13 tables: ← 1 arrangement

$$1 \times 13 = 13$$

More arrangements can be made using 12 tables. So, the students should use 12 tables.

The arrangements above show these factors for 12 and 13.

12: 1, 2, 3, 4, 6, 12   13: 1, 13

A **prime number** is a whole number greater than 1 that has exactly two factors, 1 and itself. Since 13 has only two factors, 1 and 13, it is a prime number.

A **composite number** is a whole number greater than 1 that has more than two factors. Since 12 has six factors, it is a composite number.

Divisibility rules are helpful when looking for factors to determine whether a number is prime or composite.

Tell whether the number is prime or composite.	
45 The sum of the digits is 9. Therefore, since 45 has more factors than 1 and 45, it is not prime. So, 45 is composite.	**37** $37 = 1 \times 37$ Use divisibility rules to look for factors other than 1 and 37. There are no factors other than 1 and 37. So, 37 is prime.

• Which other divisibility rule could you have used to show that 45 is a composite number? Explain.

▶ **Share and Show**

1. Use the rectangular arrays to explain why 15 is a composite number and 11 is a prime number.

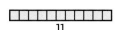
11

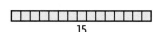
15

15

Tell whether the number is prime, composite, or neither.

2. 30	**3.** 17	**4.** 87	**5.** 26	✓**6.** 61	✓**7.** 55
8. 39	**9.** 23	**10.** 71	**11.** 207	**12.** 47	**13.** 91

14. Math Talk **Explain** why 2 is the only even prime number.

▶ **Practice and Problem Solving** REAL WORLD

Tell whether the number is prime, composite, or neither.

15. 1	**16.** 82	**17.** 73	**18.** 109	**19.** 49	**20.** 51

⭐**Algebra** **Given that *a* and *b* are prime, complete each statement with always, sometimes, or never. Explain your reasoning or give examples.**

21. $a + b$ is ___?___ prime.   22. $a - b$ is ___?___ prime.

23. To prepare for an exam, Jeb studied for 3 hr each day for a week and Amelia studied for 2 hr each day for 5 days. What is the total number of hours they studied? Is the number prime or composite?

24. The Math Club set up a display for Parent Appreciation Week to describe twin primes. Twin primes are prime numbers that differ by 2. The first pair of twin primes is 3, 5. What are the next seven pairs of twin primes?

25. Is it possible for a composite number to have fewer than four factors? Justify your answer.

26. **Reasoning** A prime number is an emirp if, when you reverse its digits, you get a different prime number. Make a list of all numbers less than 100 that are emirps.

27. Write Math ▶ **Explain** why 2 and 3 are the only consecutive prime numbers.

⭐ **OCCT Test Prep**

28. Which of the following numbers is not prime?

   A 101   **C** 401

   B 201   **D** 701

29. Which of the following numbers is not composite?

   A 12   **C** 22

   B 15   **D** 37

Vocabulary

prime factorization

Materials
• MathBoard

Remember

An exponent shows how many times a number (called the base) is used as a factor. $2^3 = 2 \times 2 \times 2$

Prime Factorization

Essential Question How can you find the prime factorization of a number by using division? By using factor trees?

 **Learn** REAL WORLD

PROBLEM At the Math Club meeting, Gianna learned that every composite number can be written as a product of prime numbers. Each club member chose a number to write as a product of prime factors. Gianna's number is 180. How can she write 180 as a product of prime factors?

A number written as the product of all of its prime factors is called the **prime factorization** of the number.

Use division.

$180 \div 2 = 90$

$90 \div 2 = 45$

$45 \div 3 = 15$ Repeatedly divide by the least possible prime factor until the quotient is 1.

$15 \div 3 = 5$

$5 \div 5 = 1$

$180 = 2 \times 2 \times 3 \times 3 \times 5$ List, from least to greatest, the prime numbers by which you divided.

Use a factor tree.

Choose any two factors of 180. Continue finding factors until only prime factors are left.

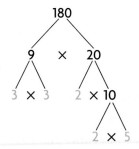

9 and 20 are not prime.

3 and 2 are prime. 10 is not prime.v

2 and 5 are prime.

$180 = 2 \times 2 \times 3 \times 3 \times 5$ List the prime numbers at the end of each factor tree branch.

So, Gianna can write the prime factorization of 180 as $2 \times 2 \times 3 \times 3 \times 5$, or $2^2 \times 3^2 \times 5$.

• Would the prime factorization be different if Gianna chose the factors 6 and 30 for 180? Explain.

Share and Show

1. Copy and complete the factor tree. Write the prime factorization of 40.

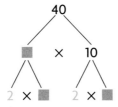

2. Copy and complete the factor tree. Write the prime factorization of 210.

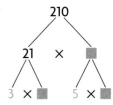

Write the prime factorization of the number as a product of prime factors and in exponent form if possible.

3. 18　　　**4.** 42　　　**5.** 75　　　**6.** 12　　　 **7.** 45　　　 **8.** 165

9. **Math Talk** **Explain** why a prime number cannot be written as a product of prime factors.

Practice and Problem Solving REAL WORLD

Write the prime factorization of the number as a product of prime factors and in exponent form if possible.

10. 27　　　**11.** 68　　　**12.** 104　　　**13.** 225　　　**14.** 306　　　**15.** 76

Write the number whose prime factorization is given.

16. $2^2 \times 5^2$　　　**17.** $2^4 \times 3^2$　　　**18.** $2^2 \times 7 \times 13$　　　**19.** $2^2 \times 5 \times 13$

Algebra **Complete the prime factorization to find the value of *a*.**

20. $99 = 3 \times 3 \times a$　　**21.** $56 = a^3 \times 7$　　**22.** $150 = 2 \times 3 \times a^2$　　**23.** $324 = 2^2 \times a^4$

24. Colleen saved 372 pennies for a Math Club volunteer project. Write 372 as the product of prime factors.

25. The prime factorization of 24 is $2^3 \times 3$. Without dividing or using a diagram, find the prime factorization of 48. **Explain.**

26. What numbers are less than 200 and have the prime factors 2, 3, and 7?

27. **Write Math** **What's the Question?** The answer is $2^3 \times 3^2 \times 7$.

OCCT Test Prep

28. Which of the following is the correct prime factorization of 45?

　A $2^3 \times 3 \times 4$　　C $3^2 \times 5 \times 9$

　B $3^2 \times 5$　　D 5×9

29. Which of the following is the correct prime factorization of 90?

　A $2^3 \times 3 \times 5$　　C $3 \times 5 \times 6$

　B $2 \times 5 \times 9$　　D $2 \times 3^2 \times 5$

LESSON 4

★ **2.2.a.** Multiply and divide fractions and mixed numbers to solve problems using a variety of methods. *also* **2.1.**

Vocabulary

greatest common factor (GCF)

least common multiple (LCM)

Materials

• MathBoard

LCM and GCF

Essential Question How does the greatest common factor (GCF) and the least common multiple (LCM) differ for the same set of numbers?

PROBLEM Biologists test water samples from lakes for pollutants. For one test, equal parts of lake water and pure water are needed. Lake samples are stored in 6-oz test tubes, and pure samples are stored in 8-oz test tubes. All of the water in a test tube must be used. If the test is performed using the least amount of water possible, how many ounces of each type of water will be needed?

You can solve the problem by finding the least common multiple of 6 and 8. The **least common multiple**, or **LCM**, is the smallest number, other than 0, that is a common multiple of two or more numbers.

Use a list.

Multiples of 6: 6, 12, 18, 24, 36, 42, 48, 54, 60, 66, 72, …

Multiples of 8: 8, 16, 24, 32, 40, 48, 56, 64, 72, 80, …

The first three common multiples of 6 and 8 are 24, 48, and 72. The least common multiple, or LCM, is 24.

> **Math Idea**
>
> The factors in the prime factorization of a number are usually listed in order from least to greatest.

Use prime factorization.

$6 = 2 \times 3$
$8 = 2 \times 2 \times 2$, or 2^3 Write the prime factorization of each number.

$2^3 \times 3 = 24$ Write each factor the greatest number of times it appears in any prime factorization. Use exponents if possible. Multiply.

The LCM is 24.

So, the LCM of 6 and 8 is 24.

Example

Find the LCM of 10, 15, and 25.

$10 = 2 \times 5$ Write the prime factorization of each number.

$15 = 3 \times 5$

$25 = 5 \times 5$, or 5^2 Write each factor the greatest number of times it appears in any prime factorization. Use exponents if possible. Multiply.

$2 \times 3 \times 5^2 = 150$

So, the LCM of 10, 15, and 25 is 150.

Greatest Common Factor

The **greatest common factor**, or **GCF**, is the greatest factor that two or more numbers have in common. Since a number is divisible by its factors, the GCF is sometimes called the greatest common divisor, or GCD.

Examples

Jason wants to plant marigolds and dahlias with his tomato plants to keep insects from eating the tomatoes. He wants only one kind of plant in each row, with an equal number of plants in each row. If he has 12 marigolds, 18 dahlias, and 30 tomato plants, how many plants should there be in each row?

Use a list.

To find the number of plants that should be in each row, find the GCF of 12, 18, and 30.

Factors of 12: 1, 2, 3, 4, 6, 12
Factors of 18: 1, 2, 3, 6, 9, 18   Common factors: 1, 2, 3, 6
Factors of 30: 1, 2, 3, 5, 6, 10, 15, 30

Since the common factors are 1, 2, 3, and 6, the GCF of 12, 18, and 30 is 6.

So, there should be 6 plants in each row.

VEGETABLE

NET WT. 100 mg $1.99

SUGAR LUMP
TOMATO

Sweet Flavor

Use prime factorization to find the GCF of 12, 24, and 60.

$12 = 2 \times 2 \times 3$
$24 = 2 \times 2 \times 2 \times 3$
$60 = 2 \times 2 \times 3 \times 5$

Write the prime factorization of each number.

$\downarrow \quad \downarrow \quad \swarrow$
$2 \times 2 \times 3 = 12$

List the common prime factors and find their product.

So, the GCF of 12, 24, and 60 is 12.

Use a ladder diagram to find the GCF of 30 and 75.

3 | 30 | 75
5 | 10 | 25
    2   5

Divide each number by a common factor of the numbers. Keep dividing until the quotients have no common factors.

$3 \times 5 = 15$

Find the product of the divisors.

So, the GCF of 30 and 75 is 15.

 ▶ **Share and Show**

Math Board

1. List the first six multiples of 6 and 9. Circle the common multiples. Then find the least common multiple.

2. List the factors of 18 and 24. Circle the common factors. Then find the greatest common factor.

Find the LCM.

3. 8, 10   **4.** 15, 25   **5.** 2, 3, 4   **6.** 8, 12, 24   ✔**7.** 3, 9, 21

Find the GCF.

8. 16, 20   **9.** 8, 52   **10.** 50, 75   **11.** 6, 18, 30   ✔**12.** 12, 50, 60

13. [Math Talk] **Explain** why the LCM of two prime numbers is their product and the GCF of two prime numbers is 1.

Practice and Problem Solving REAL WORLD

Find the LCM.

14. 8, 14   **15.** 32, 128   **16.** 3, 8, 18   **17.** 18, 21, 36   **18.** 10, 16, 20

Find the GCF.

19. 21, 35   **20.** 200, 215   **21.** 20, 60, 90   **22.** 12, 30, 42   **23.** 18, 36, 54

Real World Data

For 24–25, use the graph. All the water in each test tube must be used.

24. A biologist needs equal amounts of lake water, pure water, and seawater for an experiment. If the biologist uses the least amount of water possible, how many ounces of each type of water are needed?

25. Two water tests are performed using the least possible amount of two types of water. Which combination will require the greatest amount of water: pure water and seawater, lake water and pure water, or lake water and seawater? Justify your answer.

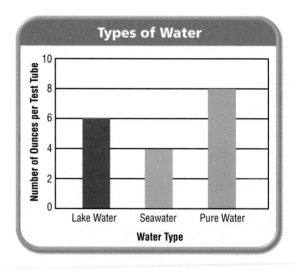

26. **Reasoning** When is the GCF of three numbers the same as one of the numbers? Use an example to explain.

27. [Write Math] ▶ **What's the Error?** Elena says that the LCM of 15 and 20 is 5. Describe her error and write the correct LCM.

 OCCT Test Prep

28. The LCM of three numbers is 90. One of the numbers is 15. Which could be the other two numbers?

   A 6, 8   **B** 18, 30   **C** 2, 10   **D** 30, 50

29. Which is the LCM of 12 and 20?

   A 25   **B** 40   **C** 60   **D** 85

⭐ Standards Quick Check

Find the LCM.

1. 6, 16

2. 8, 96

3. 12, 20

4. 2, 7, 10

5. 4, 27, 36

6. 12, 16, 24

Find the GCF.

7. 15, 28

8. 21, 306

9. 21, 80

10. 6, 50, 60

11. 4, 12, 20

12. 8, 28, 52

Challenge H.O.T.

Identifying Relationships

The table below can be used to identify relationships among numbers, their GCF, and their LCM.

a	b	a × b	GCF	LCM	GCF × LCM
3	7	▨	1	21	▨
5	12	▨	1	▨	▨
5	10	▨	5	▨	▨
9	10	▨	▨	90	▨
6	18	▨	▨	18	▨
9	12	▨	▨	▨	▨

Copy and complete the table. Look for relationships to help you solve the problems.

1. When the GCF of two numbers is 1, what is the LCM?

2. When the GCF of two numbers is one of the numbers, what is the LCM?

3. What is the relationship between the product of two numbers and the product of their GCF and LCM?

★ Maintain Skill

Vocabulary

ratio

Materials

• MathBoard

Understand Fractions

Essential Question When modeling fractions, how are the denominator and the numerator represented?

PROBLEM Archaeologists study the remains of past civilizations by examining artifacts they find as they dig through ancient ruins. A site is divided into equal sections using strings and stakes so the location of each artifact can be tracked. On one such dig, evidence of toys was found in $\frac{3}{5}$ of the sections that were explored. What are some ways you can represent this fraction?

A fraction is a **ratio**, or comparison, of whole numbers. The numerator of a fraction tells the number of parts being used. The denominator tells the number of equal parts in the whole or group.

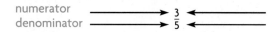

Models can be used to show fractions in different ways.

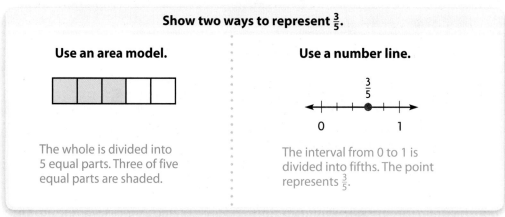

So, you can represent $\frac{3}{5}$ by using an area model or a number line.

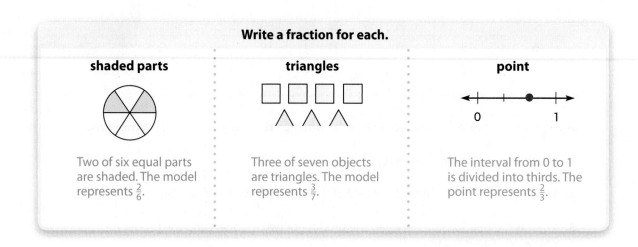

▶ Share and Show

1. Which model shows $\frac{3}{4}$?   **a.**   **b.** ⬜⬜⬜⬜   **c.**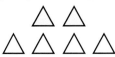

Write a fraction for each.

2. shaded parts

3. point

✓4. green triangles

Draw a model to represent the fraction.

5. $\frac{1}{2}$ **6.** $\frac{4}{6}$ **7.** $\frac{3}{10}$ **✓8.** $\frac{3}{5}$

9. **Math Talk** **Explain** how to draw a number line to show $\frac{6}{10}$.

▶ Practice and Problem Solving REAL WORLD

Write a fraction for each.

10. shaded parts

11. pennies

12. point

Draw a model to represent the fraction.

13. $\frac{1}{3}$ **14.** $\frac{5}{8}$ **15.** $\frac{6}{12}$ **16.** $\frac{5}{6}$

17. **Reasoning** Sarah's class simulates an archaeology dig at two different sites. The class divides each site into 6 equal sections. Each section represents $\frac{1}{6}$ of the site it is in. Draw a model to explain why all the parts may not be the same size.

18. Write a decimal and a fraction to name the shaded parts.

19. **Write Math** ▶ **Explain** why the parts of an area model must be exactly equal in size for the model to accurately represent a fraction.

★ OCCT Test Prep

20. Which fraction names the shaded parts?

A $\frac{2}{6}$ **C** $\frac{2}{8}$

B $\frac{2}{4}$ **D** $\frac{6}{8}$

21. Which fraction names the shaded parts?

A $\frac{2}{3}$ **C** $\frac{4}{8}$

B $\frac{4}{7}$ **D** $\frac{5}{8}$

2.1. Convert compare, and order decimals, fractions, and percents using a variety of methods.

Vocabulary

equivalent fractions

simplest form

Materials
• MathBoard
• fraction bars

Equivalent Fractions and Simplest Form

Essential Question How can you find the simplest form of a fraction in just one step?

PROBLEM A recipe for oatmeal cookies calls for $\frac{3}{4}$ cup of brown sugar. Daniel misplaced his $\frac{3}{4}$-cup and $\frac{1}{4}$-cup measuring cups, so he will use his $\frac{1}{8}$-cup measuring cup. How many times does Daniel need to fill the $\frac{1}{8}$-cup with brown sugar to make the oatmeal cookies?

Equivalent fractions are fractions that name the same amount or part. You can model equivalent fractions to find how many eighths are equivalent to $\frac{3}{4}$.

Finding equivalent fractions.

• Begin with three $\frac{1}{4}$ fraction bars.

• Place $\frac{1}{8}$ fraction bars under the three $\frac{1}{4}$ bars until the lengths are equal.

• How many $\frac{1}{8}$ bars are there?

The model shows that $\frac{3}{4} = \frac{6}{8}$. So, Daniel needs to fill the $\frac{1}{8}$-cup measuring cup six times.

• Use fraction bars. How many twelfths are equivalent to $\frac{3}{4}$?

Complete. $\frac{3}{4} = \frac{\blacksquare}{12}$

Another way to find an equivalent fraction is to multiply or divide. You can multiply the numerator and denominator by the same number, other than 0 or 1. You can also divide a numerator and denominator by a common factor greater than 1.

Examples

$\frac{1}{6} = \frac{\blacksquare}{12}$

To get the denominator 12, multiply the original denominator by 2.

$\frac{1 \times 2}{6 \times 2} = \frac{2}{12}$ To keep the fraction's value the same, also multiply the numerator by 2.

$\frac{4}{12} = \frac{\blacksquare}{3}$

To get the denominator 3, divide the original denominator by 4.

$\frac{4 \div 4}{12 \div 4} = \frac{1}{3}$ To keep the fraction's value the same, also divide the numerator by 4.

• Look at the two examples above. Which operation results in a fraction with more parts than the original fraction? Explain how you know this.

Simplest Form

A fraction is in **simplest form** when the only common factor of the numerator and denominator is 1.

$\frac{17}{24}$ is in simplest form because the only common factor of 17 and 24 is 1.

$\frac{18}{24}$ is not in simplest form because 18 and 24 have the common factor 6.

Write $\frac{24}{36}$ in simplest form.

Use common factors.

24: 1, 2, 3, 4, 6, 8, 12, 24   Find the common
36: 1, 2, 3, 4, 6, 9, 12, 18, 36   factors of 24 and 36.

$\frac{24}{36} = \frac{24 \div 6}{36 \div 6} = \frac{4}{6}$ Divide the numerator and denominator by a common factor other than 1.

$\frac{4}{6} = \frac{4 \div 2}{6 \div 2} = \frac{2}{3}$ Repeat until the fraction is in simplest form.

Use a ladder diagram.

2 | 24/36   Divide the numerator and denominator
2 | 12/18   by a common factor. Repeat until they
3 | 6/9   have no common factors other than 1.
        2/3

$\frac{24}{36} = \frac{2}{3}$ The new numerator is 2 and the new denominator is 3.

So, $\frac{2}{3}$ is the simplest form of $\frac{24}{36}$.

You can find a fraction in simplest form in just one step if you divide by the greatest common factor (GCF).

Write each fraction in simplest form.

$\frac{20}{64}$

20: 1, 2, 4, 5, 10, 20   Find the GCF.
64: 1, 2, 4, 8, 16, 32, 64
GCF = 4

$\frac{20}{64} = \frac{20 \div 4}{64 \div 4} = \frac{5}{16}$ Divide the numerator and denominator by 4.

So, $\frac{5}{16}$ is the simplest form of $\frac{20}{64}$.

$\frac{18}{24}$

18: 1, 2, 3, 6, 9, 18   Find the GCF.
24: 1, 2, 3, 4, 6, 8, 12, 24
GCF = 6

$\frac{18}{24} = \frac{18 \div 6}{24 \div 6} = \frac{3}{4}$ Divide the numerator and denominator by 6.

So, $\frac{3}{4}$ is the simplest form of $\frac{18}{24}$.

> **Share and Show**   Math Board

1. Look at the model. What equivalent fractions does it show?

2. Complete
$\frac{12}{15} = \frac{12 \div 3}{15 \div 3} = \frac{\blacksquare}{\blacksquare}$

Complete.

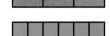

3. $\frac{3}{5} = \frac{\blacksquare}{10}$ 4. $\frac{5}{6} = \frac{\blacksquare}{24}$ 5. $\frac{6}{8} = \frac{\blacksquare}{4}$ 6. $\frac{2}{10} = \frac{\blacksquare}{80}$ 7. $\frac{25}{40} = \frac{\blacksquare}{8}$ ✓8. $\frac{8}{12} = \frac{\blacksquare}{36}$

Write the fraction in simplest form.

9. $\frac{70}{75}$ 10. $\frac{9}{12}$ 11. $\frac{6}{28}$ 12. $\frac{44}{121}$ 13. $\frac{15}{27}$ ✓14. $\frac{18}{54}$

15. **Math Talk** Explain how to find a fraction equivalent to $\frac{12}{15}$.

Complete.

16. $\frac{12}{18} = \frac{\blacksquare}{3}$ **17.** $\frac{15}{51} = \frac{5}{\blacksquare}$ **18.** $\frac{3}{20} = \frac{24}{\blacksquare}$ **19.** $\frac{7}{8} = \frac{\blacksquare}{72}$ **20.** $\frac{\blacksquare}{49} = \frac{4}{7}$ **21.** $\frac{15}{55} = \frac{\blacksquare}{11}$

22. $\frac{3}{\blacksquare} = \frac{18}{24}$ **23.** $\frac{7}{8} = \frac{\blacksquare}{32}$ **24.** $\frac{\blacksquare}{3} = \frac{9}{1}$ **25.** $\frac{66}{75} = \frac{\blacksquare}{25}$ **26.** $\frac{\blacksquare}{6} = \frac{42}{84}$ **27.** $\frac{2}{\blacksquare} = \frac{6}{57}$

Write the fraction in simplest form.

28. $\frac{24}{42}$ **29.** $\frac{18}{30}$ **30.** $\frac{4}{10}$ **31.** $\frac{48}{32}$ **32.** $\frac{45}{20}$ **33.** $\frac{50}{60}$

34. $\frac{10}{65}$ **35.** $\frac{8}{62}$ **36.** $\frac{4^2}{128}$ **37.** $\frac{3^2}{36}$ **38.** $\frac{2^3}{4^2}$ **39.** $\frac{5^2}{10^2}$

For 40–41, write *always, sometimes,* or *never* for each statement.

40. The denominator of an equivalent fraction is less than the denominator of the original fraction.

41. The numerator of a fraction in simplest form is greater than the numerator of an equivalent fraction that is not in simplest form.

 **Real World Data**

For 42–44, use the graph.

42. Which household water use can be written as $\frac{4}{25}$ in simplest form?

43. The fraction for shower use is $\frac{17}{100}$. Is this fraction in simplest form? If not, write it in simplest form. **Explain** your answer.

44. The fractions of which household water uses can be written as equivalent fractions with a denominator of 50?

45. **What's the Question?** Bob has 8 red apples, 6 green apples, and 4 yellow apples. The answer is $\frac{4}{9}$ of the apples.

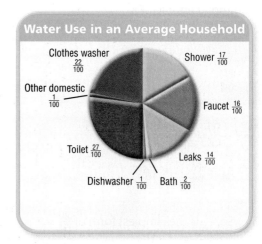

Water Use in an Average Household

Clothes washer $\frac{22}{100}$ Shower $\frac{17}{100}$
Other domestic $\frac{1}{100}$ Faucet $\frac{16}{100}$
Toilet $\frac{27}{100}$ Leaks $\frac{14}{100}$
Dishwasher $\frac{1}{100}$ Bath $\frac{2}{100}$

★ **OCCT Test Prep**

46. Carl saves $\frac{9}{15}$ of his earnings each week. Which of the following is an equivalent fraction for $\frac{9}{15}$?

A $\frac{1}{5}$ **C** $\frac{18}{45}$

B $\frac{5}{3}$ **D** $\frac{3}{5}$

47. A chocolate cake is cut into 16 equal pieces at a birthday party. Four pieces are eaten. Which fraction, in simplest form, represents the amount of cake left?

A $\frac{4}{16}$ **C** $\frac{3}{4}$

B $\frac{1}{3}$ **D** $\frac{12}{16}$

GO ONLINE **Technology**
Use HMH Mega Math Fraction Action, *Fraction Flare Up*, Levels D & E.

⭐ Standards Quick Check

Write the fraction in simplest form.

1. $\frac{60}{65}$

2. $\frac{4}{32}$

3. $\frac{44}{42}$

4. $\frac{3^2}{45}$

5. $\frac{2^3}{8^2}$

6. $\frac{4^3}{2^2}$

H.O.T.

Fractions and Algebra

You can use your knowledge of number relationships and equivalent fractions to find unknown numbers.

Use the clues below to find the values of *a* and *b* for $\frac{4}{5} = \frac{a}{b}$?

Clue 1: Both *a* and *b* are greater than 10 and less than 20.

Based on Clue 1, *a* and *b* can be 11, 12, 13, 14, 15, 16, 17, 18, or 19.

Clue 2: Both *a* and *b* are multiples of 3.

Based on Clues 1 and 2, *a* and *b* can be 12, 15, or 18.

Since $\frac{a}{b}$ has to be equivalent to $\frac{4}{5}$, *a* = 12 and *b* = 15.

Use the clues to find the values of *a* and *b*.

1. $\frac{3}{10} = \frac{a}{b}$

   Clue 1: The sum of the digits of *a* is 9.

   Clue 2: *a* and *b* are two-digit numbers that are less than 65.

2. $\frac{4}{a} = \frac{b}{6}$

   Clue 1: *a* is a multiple of 3 that is less than 30.

   Clue 2: *b* is a prime number.

3. $\frac{5}{7} = \frac{a}{b}$

   Clue 1: *a* and *b* are even numbers that are greater than 10 and less than 30.

   Clue 2: The sum of *a* and *b* is 48.

4. $\frac{a}{9} = \frac{16}{b}$

   Clue 1: The factors of *b* are 1, 2, 3, 4, 6, 9, 12, 18, and 36.

   Clue 2: *a* and *b* are multiples of 4.

2.1. Convert compare, and order decimals, fractions, and percents using a variety of methods.

Fractions and Mixed Numbers

Essential Question How can you represent mixed numbers as fractions and represent certain fractions as mixed numbers?

▶ Learn

A **mixed number**, such as $2\frac{1}{4}$, is a number represented by a whole number greater than 0 and a fraction between 0 and 1. A mixed number can be renamed as a fraction greater than one. Fractions greater than one, such as $\frac{6}{5}$, are sometimes called "improper fractions."

Write $2\frac{1}{4}$ as a fraction.

Use a diagram.

Count the shaded fourths. There are nine fourths, or $\frac{9}{4}$.

. . . .

Use multiplication and addition.

$$2\frac{1}{4} = \frac{(4 \times 2)}{4} + \frac{1}{4} = \frac{8+1}{4} = \frac{9}{4}$$

Multiply the denominator of the fraction part by the whole-number part. Then add the numerator. This sum is the new numerator. Use the same denominator.

So, $2\frac{1}{4} = \frac{9}{4}$

Write $\frac{26}{10}$ as a mixed number in simplest form.

$$\begin{array}{r} 2\ r6 \\ 10)\overline{\ 26} \\ -20 \\ \hline 6 \end{array}$$

$2\frac{6}{10} = 2\frac{3}{5}$

Since $\frac{26}{10}$ can be read as 26 divided by 10, divide the numerator by the denominator.

Use the remainder as the numerator and the divisor as the denominator. Write the fraction in simplest form.

So, $\frac{26}{10} = 2\frac{3}{5}$

▶ Share and Show

Math Board

Vocabulary

mixed number

Materials
• MathBoard

1. Look at the model. Write the modeled number as a mixed number and as a fraction. Then write each in words.

Write the mixed number as a fraction.

2. $6\frac{1}{3}$ **3.** $1\frac{3}{4}$ **4.** $3\frac{2}{5}$ **5.** $1\frac{7}{16}$ ✓**6.** $2\frac{1}{8}$

Write the fraction as a mixed number in simplest form or as a whole number.

7. $\frac{14}{5}$ **8.** $\frac{45}{10}$ **9.** $\frac{56}{8}$ **10.** $\frac{19}{6}$ **11.** $\frac{55}{20}$ ✓ **12.** $\frac{64}{16}$

13. **Math Talk** **Explain** how to use the remainder and divisor when using division to write a fraction as a mixed number.

▶ **Practice and Problem Solving** REAL WORLD

Write the mixed number as a fraction.

14. $4\frac{5}{8}$ **15.** $7\frac{2}{3}$ **16.** $5\frac{5}{6}$ **17.** $11\frac{1}{4}$ **18.** $12\frac{4}{5}$ **19.** $3\frac{7}{10}$

20. $2\frac{1}{2}$ **21.** $8\frac{3}{5}$ **22.** $5\frac{3}{10}$ **23.** $6\frac{3}{8}$ **24.** $3\frac{3}{4}$ **25.** $2\frac{1}{2}$

Write the fraction as a mixed number in simplest form or as a whole number.

26. $\frac{17}{3}$ **27.** $\frac{44}{8}$ **28.** $\frac{45}{12}$ **29.** $\frac{41}{18}$ **30.** $\frac{65}{5}$ **31.** $\frac{85}{25}$

32. $\frac{32}{7}$ **33.** $\frac{60}{4}$ **34.** $\frac{34}{4}$ **35.** $\frac{66}{8}$ **36.** $\frac{23}{3}$ **37.** $\frac{39}{6}$

38. **≡FAST FACT** In a total lunar eclipse, the earth blocks all direct sunlight from reaching the moon. The longest total lunar eclipse in the next 90 years will take place in 2018 and will last $1\frac{11}{15}$ hr. Write $1\frac{11}{15}$ as a fraction, and use the fraction to find how many minutes the eclipse will last.

39. **Write Math** ▶ **What's the Error?** Greg renamed $2\frac{5}{7}$ as $\frac{17}{7}$. Describe his error and write the correct answer.

📊 Real World Data

For 40–41, use the recipe.

40. Lee has only a $\frac{1}{4}$-cup measuring cup to make a peach smoothie refresher. Write the amount of each ingredient, except banana, as a fraction in fourths.

41. Suppose Lee has only a $\frac{1}{8}$-cup measuring cup. Write the amount of peach slices as a fraction in eighths.

Peach Smoothie Refresher
$1\frac{3}{4}$ cups apple juice
1 cup frozen yogurt
$\frac{1}{2}$ banana
1 cup peach yogurt
$1\frac{1}{2}$ cups frozen peach slices

 ★ **OCCT Test Prep** Math Board

42. Which is $\frac{48}{5}$ written as a mixed number?

     A $4\frac{4}{5}$ **C** $7\frac{2}{3}$

     B $5\frac{3}{5}$ **D** $9\frac{3}{5}$

43. John made sixty ounces of mixed fruit. How many pounds of mixed fruit did he use?

     A $3\frac{3}{8}$ pounds   **C** $3\frac{5}{8}$ pounds

     B $3\frac{3}{4}$ pounds   **D** $3\frac{1}{2}$ pounds

★ **2.1.** Convert compare, and order decimals, fractions, and percents using a variety of methods.

Vocabulary

repeating decimal

terminating decimal

Materials
• MathBoard

Fractions and Decimals

Essential Question How do you use division and the greatest common factor (GCF) to write a fraction in simplest form?

PROBLEM The African pygmy hedgehog is a popular pet in North America. The average African pygmy hedgehog weighs between 0.5 lb and 1.25 lb. Write 0.5 as a fraction and 1.25 as a mixed number in simplest form.

Decimal grids can be used to represent decimals, fractions, and mixed numbers.

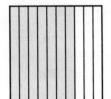

Seven of ten equal parts are shaded.

$\frac{7}{10}$ is shaded.

Seven tenths, or 0.7, is shaded.

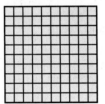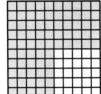

One whole plus three of four equal parts are shaded.

$1\frac{3}{4}$ are shaded.

One and seventy-five hundredths, or 1.75, are shaded.

You can use place value to write a decimal as a fraction or a mixed number.

$0.5 = \frac{5}{10}$ **Think:** 0.5 is "five tenths."

Use division and the GCF, 5, to write $\frac{5}{10}$ in simplest form.

$\frac{5}{10} = \frac{5 \div 5}{10 \div 5} = \frac{1}{2}$

$1.25 = 1\frac{25}{100}$ **Think:** 1.25 is "one and twenty-five hundredths."

Use division and the GCF, 25, to write $1\frac{25}{100}$ in simplest form.

$1\frac{25 \div 25}{100 \div 25} = 1\frac{1}{4}$

So, the average African pygmy hedgehog weighs between $\frac{1}{2}$ lb and $1\frac{1}{4}$ lb.

• How can you use place value to write 0.05 and 0.005 as fractions in simplest form?

A number line can be used to show equivalent fractions as decimals. For example, this number line shows that $\frac{2}{5} = 0.4$ and that $1\frac{1}{2} = 1.5$.

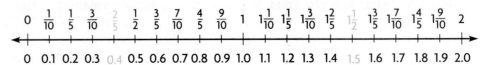

Use division to rename fractions and mixed numbers as decimals.

The average African pygmy hedgehog is about $6\frac{3}{8}$ in. long. Write $6\frac{3}{8}$ as a decimal.

1 Use division to rename the fraction part as a decimal.

$$
\begin{array}{r}
0.375 \\
8\overline{)3.000} \\
-24 \\
\hline
60 \\
-56 \\
\hline
40 \\
-40 \\
\hline
0
\end{array}
$$

2 Then add the whole number to the decimal.

$$6 + 0.375 = 6.375$$

So, $6\frac{3}{8} = 6.375$.

Terminating and Repeating Decimals

A decimal, such as 0.375, that ends when the division produces a remainder of 0, is called a **terminating decimal**.

The decimal form of the fraction $\frac{5}{11}$ does not reach a remainder of zero. This decimal is a **repeating decimal** because it has a pattern of repeating remainders after each division step. This pattern causes one or more digits in the quotient to repeat endlessly.

To write a repeating decimal, show the pattern and then three dots, or draw a bar over the repeating digits.

$$\frac{5}{11} = 0.454545\ldots \qquad \frac{5}{11} = 0.\overline{45}$$

$$
\begin{array}{r}
0.4545 \\
11\overline{)5.0000} \\
-44 \\
\hline
60 \\
-55 \\
\hline
50 \\
-44 \\
\hline
60 \\
-55 \\
\hline
5
\end{array}
$$

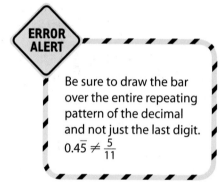

ERROR ALERT

Be sure to draw the bar over the entire repeating pattern of the decimal and not just the last digit.
$0.4\overline{5} \neq \frac{5}{11}$

To write a fraction as a decimal, you can use paper and pencil or a calculator.

Write as a decimal. Tell whether the decimal terminates or repeats.

Use paper and pencil.

$\frac{3}{16} \rightarrow$
$$
\begin{array}{r}
0.1875 \\
16\overline{)3.0000} \\
-16 \\
\hline
140 \\
-128 \\
\hline
120 \\
-112 \\
\hline
80 \\
-80 \\
\hline
0
\end{array}
$$

So, $\frac{3}{16} = 0.1875$. The decimal terminates.

Use a calculator.

$\frac{5}{6} \rightarrow$ [5] [÷] [6] [Enter =]

$5 ÷ 6 = 0.8333333$

So, $\frac{5}{6} = 0.8\overline{3}$. The decimal repeats.

1. The normal body temperature of a hedgehog is ninety-five and five tenths degrees Fahrenheit. Use place value to write this temperature as a mixed number in simplest form.

$$95.5 = 95\frac{5}{\blacksquare} = \blacksquare$$

Write as a fraction or as a mixed number in simplest form.

2. 0.6   **3.** 1.2   **4.** 0.009   **5.** 6.05   ✔**6.** 5.75

Identify a decimal and a fraction in simplest form for each point.

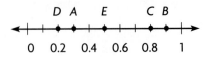

7. Point *A*   **8.** Point *B*   **9.** Point *C*   **10.** Point *D*   ✔**11.** Point *E*

12. **Math Talk** **Explain** how to use place value to change 0.34 to a fraction in simplest form.

▶ **Practice and Problem Solving** REAL WORLD

Write as a fraction or as a mixed number in simplest form.

13. 0.27   **14.** 0.75   **15.** 0.08   **16.** 1.9   **17.** 2.45

Identify a decimal and a fraction or mixed number in simplest form for each point.

18. Point *V*   **19.** Point *W*   **20.** Point *X*   **21.** Point *Y*   **22.** Point *Z*

Write as a decimal. Tell whether the decimal terminates or repeats.

23. $\frac{7}{8}$ **24.** $\frac{2}{3}$ **25.** $\frac{1}{6}$ **26.** $\frac{3}{25}$ **27.** $3\frac{1}{5}$

28. At Eli's pet store, 3 cinnamon, 5 white, and 4 black-and-white hedgehogs were sold in the past week. Eli claims that 0.25 of the hedgehogs sold were black-and-white. Is he correct? **Explain.**

 ★ **OCCT Test Prep**

29. Which is equivalent to a repeating decimal?

     A $\frac{1}{4}$ **C** $\frac{5}{8}$

     B $\frac{2}{5}$ **D** $\frac{4}{9}$

30. Winona's measuring cup is $\frac{5}{18}$ full of water. What is this amount as a decimal?

     A 0.27   **C** 0.28

     B $0.2\overline{7}$ **D** $0.\overline{28}$

⭐ Standards Quick Check

Write as a fraction or mixed number in simplest form.

1. 0.36

2. 2.65

3. 0.04

4. 3.02

5. 0.051

6. 6.42

7. 0.18

8. 1.38

9. 0.087

10. 4.2

11. 10.55

12. 7.25

Challenge H.O.T.

Decimals Between Decimals

Number lines can also be used to explore the numbers that are between other numbers. Locate 0.6 *and* 0.7 on the first number line. What numbers are between 0.6 and 0.7?

The second number line shows that every interval of a tenth can be divided into hundredths. So, 0.68 is one number between 0.6 and 0.7 because it is eight hundredths greater than 0.6 and two hundredths less than 0.7. Remember, you can think of 0.6 as 60 hundredths and 0.7 as 70 hundredths. 0.60 < 0.68 < 0.70.

1. Name three numbers between 0 and 0.1.

2. Name three numbers between 0 and 0.01.

3. Name three numbers between 0.09 and 0.10.

4. How many numbers are there between any two numbers on a number line? **Explain**.

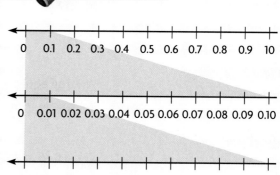

★ **2.1.** Convert compare, and order decimals, fractions, and percents using a variety of methods.

Vocabulary

percent

Materials
• MathBoard
• decimal models

Fractions, Decimals, and Percents

Essential Question How is place value essential in converting among fractions, decimals, and percents?

PROBLEM A class took a survey of girls' names. Thirty percent of the class chose Kayla as the favorite. How do you write 30% as a fraction and as a decimal?

Percent means "per hundred" or "hundredths." The symbol used to write a percent is %. You can use a grid with 100 squares to model percents.

Write percents as decimals and fractions.

Thirty percent means 30 of 100, or $\frac{30}{100}$.

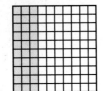

The model for 30% shows 30 of 100 equal parts shaded. It represents $\frac{30}{100}$ and 0.30.

Shade 30 squares of 100 squares.

So, 30% can be written as $\frac{30}{100}$ or 0.30.

You can use place value and equivalent fractions to write a fraction or decimal as a percent.

Write 0.17 as a fraction and as a percent.

Use place value to write the decimal as a fraction.

0.17   **Think:** 0.17 is seventeen hundredths.

$0.17 = \frac{17}{100}$ Percent means "per 100."

So, $0.17 = \frac{17}{100} = 17\%$.

Write $\frac{3}{4}$ as a decimal and as a percent.

Write an equivalent fraction with 100 as the denominator.

$\frac{3}{4} = \frac{3 \times 25}{4 \times 25} = \frac{75}{100}$ **Think:** $\frac{75}{100}$ is seventy-five hundredths.

$\frac{75}{100} = 0.75 = 75\%$ Use place value and the meaning of percent.

So, $\frac{3}{4} = 0.75 = 75\%$.

104

Complete.

1. The model shows ▦ of ▦ equal parts are shaded.

   The model represents the fraction ▦, the decimal ▦, and ▦%.

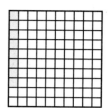

Copy and complete. Write each fraction in simplest form.

	Fraction	Decimal	Percent
2.	▦	▦	63%
4.	$\frac{3}{100}$	▦	▦

	Fraction	Decimal	Percent
✓ 3.	▦	0.05	▦
✓ 5.	$\frac{4}{5}$	▦	▦

6. **Math Talk** Explain how to write $\frac{7}{20}$ as a percent.

▶ **Practice and Problem Solving** REAL WORLD

Copy and complete. Write each fraction in simplest form.

	Fraction	Decimal	Percent
7.	$\frac{7}{10}$	▦	▦
9.	▦	0.10	▦
11.	▦	▦	9%

	Fraction	Decimal	Percent
8.	$\frac{45}{100}$	▦	▦
10.	▦	▦	76%
12.	▦	0.38	▦

 Real World Data

For 13–15, use the table.

13. Which name was popular with $\frac{19}{50}$ of the people surveyed?

14. Which name was popular with 0.3 of the people surveyed?

15. Use decimals and < or > to compare the choices for Puff and Rascal.

16. There are 16 boys and 9 girls in J.T.'s class. Blue is the favorite color of 5 boys and 6 girls. Blue is the favorite color of what percent of the class? Explain.

17. **Write Math** ▶ One third of the students in a class said they had no middle name. Is that fraction more than or less than 30%? Explain.

Favorite Kitten Names

Name	Puff	Ginger	Rascal
Votes	38%	30%	32%

★ **OCCT Test Prep**

18. Which shows 0.45 written as a percent?

    A 4.5%   **B** 45%   **C** 45.5%   **D** 450%

19. Rod got 24 out of 30 questions correct on a math test. What percent of the questions did he get correct?

    A 20%   **B** 30%   **C** 80%   **D** 90%

★ **2.1.** Convert compare, and order decimals, fractions, and percents using a variety of methods.

Materials
• MathBoard

Compare and Order Fractions, Decimals, and Percents

Essential Question How does comparing help to order fractions, mixed numbers, and percents?

PROBLEM Minnesota is one of the top producers of sunflowers. At a festival, prizes were given for the tallest sunflower plants. The winning plants were $5\frac{1}{2}$ ft, $5\frac{2}{3}$ ft, and $5\frac{5}{8}$ ft tall. Order the plant heights from least to greatest.

To compare mixed numbers, compare the whole numbers and then the fractions. You can use common multiples to compare and order fractions and mixed numbers with unlike denominators.

Order fractions.

The whole numbers are the same, so compare the fractions.

$5\frac{1}{2} = 5\frac{12}{24}$ $\qquad$ $5\frac{2}{3} = 5\frac{16}{24}$ $\qquad$ $5\frac{5}{8} = 5\frac{15}{24}$ $\qquad$ Write equivalent fractions.

$5\frac{12}{24} < 5\frac{15}{24} < 5\frac{16}{24}$ $\qquad$ Compare the numerators. Then order the fractions from least to greatest.

So, from least to greatest, the order is $5\frac{1}{2}$ ft, $5\frac{5}{8}$ ft, $5\frac{2}{3}$ ft.

Fractions, Decimals, and Percents

To compare a fraction and a decimal, you can first rewrite the fraction as a decimal. Then compare the decimals.

Use < or > to compare.

Use paper and pencil.	**Use a calculator.**
0.8 ⬤ $\frac{3}{4}$	$\frac{2}{9}$ ⬤ 0.45
Write $\frac{3}{4}$ as a decimal.	
$\begin{array}{r} 0.75 \\ 4\overline{)3.00} \\ -28 \\ \hline 20 \\ -20 \\ \hline 0 \end{array}$	$\frac{2}{9} \rightarrow$ $2 \div 9 = 0.222222$ $\rightarrow \frac{2}{9} = 0.\overline{2}$
$0.80 > 0.75$, so $0.8 > \frac{3}{4}$.	$0.\overline{2} < 0.45$, so $\frac{2}{9} < 0.45$.

When comparing a fraction and a percent, write both the fraction and the percent as decimals.

Compare $\frac{3}{5}$ and 66%. Use < or >.

❶ Write $\frac{3}{5}$ as a decimal.

$$5\overline{)3.0} = 0.6$$

❷ Write 66% as a decimal.

66% = 0.66

❸ Compare the decimals.

0.60 < 0.66

So, $\frac{3}{5}$ < 66%.

You can use a number line to order fractions, decimals, and percents.

Use a number line to order.

Order $\frac{3}{10}$, $\frac{1}{4}$, 0.45, and 10% from least to greatest. Write each fraction or percent as a decimal.

$\frac{3}{10} \rightarrow 10\overline{)3.00} = 0.30$

$\frac{1}{4} \rightarrow 4\overline{)1.00} = 0.25$

$10\% = \frac{10}{100} = 0.10$

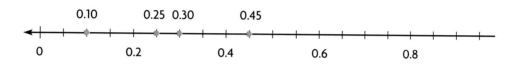

So, from least to greatest, the order is 10%, $\frac{1}{4}$, $\frac{3}{10}$, 0.45.

► Share and Show

1. Use the fraction models to tell which part is greater, $\frac{3}{8}$ or $\frac{3}{5}$.

2. Copy the number line. Write $\frac{3}{4}$ and $\frac{3}{5}$ as decimals and place them on the number line. Then compare the fractions using <, > or =.

Compare. Write <, >, or = for each ⬭.

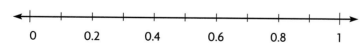

3. $\frac{4}{5}$ ⬭ $\frac{4}{12}$

4. $\frac{5}{18}$ ⬭ $\frac{15}{18}$

5. $\frac{18}{12}$ ⬭ $\frac{12}{8}$

6. $\frac{1}{2}$ ⬭ 62%

✔7. 77% ⬭ $\frac{7}{10}$

Order from least to greatest.

8. 0.22, $\frac{1}{4}$, 20%

9. $1\frac{1}{5}$, 1.15, $1\frac{1}{10}$

10. 3.85, $3\frac{5}{8}$, $2\frac{9}{10}$

✔11. 8%, $\frac{1}{20}$, 0.06

12. **Math Talk** Explain how to use a number line to order $\frac{2}{3}$, $\frac{1}{2}$, and $\frac{11}{12}$ from greatest to least.

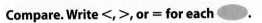
Compare. Write <, >, or = for each ⬭.

13. $\frac{10}{12}$ ⬭ $\frac{11}{12}$ **14.** $\frac{7}{15}$ ⬭ $\frac{7}{10}$ **15.** $\frac{1}{8}$ ⬭ 0.125   **16.** $7\frac{1}{3}$ ⬭ $6\frac{2}{3}$ **17.** 0.9 ⬭ 9%

18. $\frac{6}{7}$ ⬭ $\frac{18}{21}$ **19.** 0.75 ⬭ $\frac{7}{8}$ **20.** $\frac{3}{5}$ ⬭ $\frac{17}{20}$ **21.** $4\frac{8}{9}$ ⬭ $4\frac{9}{10}$ **22.** 35% ⬭ $\frac{3}{10}$

Order from least to greatest.

23. $\frac{1}{2}, \frac{2}{5}, \frac{7}{15}$ **24.** 0.6, $\frac{2}{3}$, 66%   **25.** $1\frac{3}{4}, \frac{5}{7}, 1\frac{3}{5}$ **26.** $\frac{4}{5}, \frac{3}{4}$, 72%, 0.88

27. 65%, 0.59, $\frac{3}{5}$ **28.** 1.20, 125%, $\frac{3}{4}$ **29.** 16%, $\frac{1}{6}$, 0.6   **30.** 5.8, $\frac{5}{8}$, 58%

Order from greatest to least.

31. $\frac{5}{7}, \frac{5}{6}, \frac{5}{12}$ **32.** 89%, $\frac{7}{8}$, 0.9   **33.** $5\frac{1}{2}$, 5.05, $5\frac{5}{9}$ **34.** $\frac{37}{10}, 3\frac{1}{6}, 3\frac{2}{5}, 3\frac{1}{4}$

⭐**Algebra** **Find all possible whole number values for *x* that make the statement true.**

35. $\frac{x}{5} < 0.75$ **36.** $60\% = \frac{3}{x}$ **37.** $\frac{x}{7} < \frac{5}{6}$ **38.** $6\frac{1}{3} > 6\frac{x}{5}$ **39.** $0.84 > x\%$

40. Malia and José each bought 2 lb of sunflower seeds. Each ate some seeds. Malia has $\frac{4}{3}$ lb left, and José has $\frac{7}{5}$ lb left. Write the amounts they have left as mixed numbers. Who ate more sunflower seeds?

41. **Pose a Problem** Look back at Exercise 40. Write a new problem by changing the amounts of sunflower seeds Malia and José have left. Then solve.

42. **Reasoning** Find a fraction that is between $\frac{3}{5}$ and $\frac{4}{5}$. Then find a fraction that is between $\frac{3}{5}$ and your answer. Write all the fractions in order from least to greatest.

43. |Write Math▶ **Explain** how to find which is the lesser number, $\frac{3}{4}$ or $\frac{5}{6}$. Then show the comparison using symbols.

★ **OCCT Test Prep** |Math Board|

44. Which replaces the ⬭ to make the statement $\frac{2}{3} < $ ⬭ $ < 1\frac{1}{8}$ true?

    A $\frac{11}{20}$ **C** $1\frac{1}{3}$

    B $\frac{7}{9}$ **D** $1\frac{1}{5}$

45. Which replaces the ⬭ to make the statement $\frac{4}{5} < $ ⬭ $ < 1\frac{2}{7}$ true?

    A $\frac{1}{5}$ **C** $1\frac{1}{8}$

    B $\frac{3}{6}$ **D** $1\frac{3}{7}$

Compare. Write $<$**,** $>$**, or** $=$ **for each** ⬭**.**

1. 6.25 ⬭ $6\frac{1}{2}$

2. 75% ⬭ 0.30

3. 12.125 ⬭ $12\frac{1}{5}$

4. 20% ⬭ $\frac{2}{10}$

5. 14.45 ⬭ $1\frac{44}{50}$

6. 65% ⬭ $\frac{65}{100}$

Challenge   **H.O.T.**

Using Variables

Remember that a variable is a letter or symbol that can stand for one or more numbers.

Let $x = 35\%$ **and** $y = \frac{3}{5}$**. Tell whether each statement is** *true* **or** *false***.**

$x > \frac{1}{3}$

Replace x with 35%.

$35\% \quad \frac{1}{3}$ Write 35% as a decimal.

$0.35 \quad \frac{1}{3}$ Write $\frac{1}{3}$ as a decimal.

$0.35 > 0.\overline{3}$ ✓

$35\% > \frac{1}{3}$ is true.

$0.62 < y < \frac{1}{2}$

Replace y with $\frac{3}{5}$.

$0.62 \quad \frac{3}{5} \quad \frac{1}{2}$ Write $\frac{3}{5}$ and $\frac{1}{2}$ as decimals.

$0.62 \quad 0.6 \quad 0.5$

Since $0.62 > 0.6$ and $0.6 > 0.5$, $0.62 < y < \frac{1}{2}$ is false.

Let $a = \frac{2}{5}$**,** $b = 66\%$**,** $c = 0.4$**,** $x = 0.28$**,** $y = \frac{3}{4}$**, and** $z = 5\%$**. Tell whether each statement is** *true* **or** *false***.**

1. $y < 0.77$

2. $b > \frac{6}{10}$

3. $\frac{1}{4} < z < 1$

4. $\frac{1}{3} \leq x$

5. $x + c < y$

6. $0.6 < b$

7. $\frac{1}{2} > z$

8. $\frac{5}{8} < a + x < b$

9. $z + b < y$

10. $2c = y + z$

11. $a > y$

12. $x \geq \frac{3}{8}$

13. $\frac{x}{c} < y$

14. $a = c$

15. $2x \leq \frac{1}{2}$

16. $y + c > 1$

Materials
• MathBoard

Problem Solving Workshop
Skill: Use a Table

Essential Question What are some ways to organize a data table to make it easier to compare information?

▶ **Use the Skill** REAL WORLD

PROBLEM In one week, Corning, NY, and Ithaca, NY, received snowfall every day, Monday through Friday. Use the table to find the days when Corning received more snowfall than Ithaca.

The table makes it easy to compare the snowfall amounts measured each day for the two cities.

Use division to change the snowfall amounts in Corning to decimals. Then compare the amounts for the two cities to find the days when Corning received more snowfall than Ithaca.

Corning and Ithaca Snowfall (in inches)		
Day	**Corning**	**Ithaca**
Monday	$4\frac{1}{2}$	4.6
Tuesday	$5\frac{1}{4}$	5.2
Wednesday	$4\frac{5}{8}$	4.5
Thursday	$6\frac{3}{5}$	6.8
Friday	$4\frac{3}{4}$	4.7

Monday: $4\frac{1}{2} = 4.5$ $4.5 < 4.6$

Tuesday: $5\frac{1}{4} = 5.25$ $5.25 > 5.2$

Wednesday: $4\frac{5}{8} = 4.625$ $4.625 > 4.5$

Thursday: $6\frac{3}{5} = 6.6$ $6.6 < 6.8$

Friday: $4\frac{3}{4} = 4.75$ $4.75 > 4.7$

So, Corning received more snowfall than Ithaca on Tuesday, Wednesday, and Friday or $\frac{3}{5}$ of the days.

Use the table and the information below to solve the problems.

The snowfall amounts recorded in Binghamton, NY, on Monday through Friday during the same week were: $4\frac{2}{5}$ in., $5\frac{1}{8}$ in., $4\frac{7}{10}$ in., $6\frac{2}{3}$ in., and $4\frac{4}{5}$ in.

a. On which days did Binghamton receive more snowfall than either Corning or Ithaca?

b. On which days did more snow fall in Ithaca than fell in Binghamton?

c. List the snowfall amounts in the three towns from least to greatest for each day of the week.

Share and Show

1. The normal monthly precipitation for Moline, IL, and Peoria, IL, are shown in the table. During which months is the normal precipitation greater in Moline than in Peoria?

   First, write Peoria's monthly precipitation as decimals.

   Then, compare amounts for Moline and Peoria.

2. **What if** Peoria's precipitation for March were twice Moline's precipitation for April? What would the difference be between the March precipitation for Peoria and Moline?

3. For which months is the difference in precipitation between the cities the least? Write the difference both as a decimal and as a fraction.

Normal Monthly Precipitation in Moline and Peoria (in inches)		
Month	Moline	Peoria
January	1.6	$1\frac{1}{2}$
February	1.5	$1\frac{7}{10}$
March	2.9	$2\frac{4}{5}$
April	3.8	$3\frac{3}{5}$
May	4.3	$4\frac{1}{5}$
June	4.6	$3\frac{4}{5}$

Mixed Applications

4. Zack has exactly $1.25 in his pocket. If he has 11 coins in all, what coins are in his pocket?

5. Write a mixed number that is greater than the sum of 23.67 and 18.45 but less than the difference between 74.06 and 31.88.

 Real World Data

For 6–7, use the table at the right.

6. Identify a relationship between x and y. Then write three other number pairs (x,y) that have the same relationship.

x	1	2	3	4	5	6	7
y	1	4	9	16	25	36	49

7. What if the y-values in the table were changed to 1, 8, 27, 64, 125, 216, and 343? **Explain** how to find y when x = 11.

8. Francesca is baking three cakes for the band's bake sale. She needs 2.5 c of flour for the banana cake, and $\frac{1}{4}$ c more than that for the apple cake. The sponge cake recipe calls for twice as much flour as is needed for the apple cake. What is the total amount of flour that Francesca will need for all three cakes?

9. A minibus will be used to take 160 students and teachers from school to the end-of-year picnic. The minibus holds 36 people. If the bus takes as many people as possible on each trip, how many trips will the minibus have to make? How many people will be left for the last trip?

10. **Write Math** ▶ **What's the Question?** Clarice is making gift bags for her party. Each bag will contain a lip balm, a wristband, and a glitter pen. Lip balms are sold in packs of 8. Wristbands are sold in packs of 12. Glitter pens are sold in packs of 6. The answer is 4 packs of glitter pens.

⭐ Extra Practice

Set A

Tell whether the number is divisible by 2, 3, 4, 5, 6, 8, 9, or 10. (pp. 80–83)

1. 24
2. 48
3. 30
4. 85
5. 56
6. 64

7. 546
8. 284
9. 207
10. 1,428
11. 1,287
12. 3,516

Set B

Tell whether the number is prime, composite, or neither. (pp. 84–85)

1. 0
2. 62
3. 13
4. 333
5. 41
6. 36

7. 221
8. 3
9. 72
10. 417
11. 113
12. 525

13. Julia was able to divide her collection of pencils into four groups of the same number of pencils. Was the total number of pencils in Julia's collection a prime or composite number?

14. Mark has red, green, and blue marbles adding up to a prime number less than 12. He has 3 red marbles and 3 blue marbles. What possible numbers of green marbles can Mark have?

Set C

Write the prime factorization of the number as a product of prime factors and in exponent form if possible. (pp. 86–87)

1. 40
2. 36
3. 135
4. 44
5. 28
6. 360

7. 140
8. 180
9. 99
10. 90
11. 88
12. 440

Set D

Find the LCM. (pp. 88–91)

1. 6, 54
2. 6, 14
3. 28, 42
4. 14, 35
5. 12, 26

6. 21, 63
7. 4, 9
8. 5, 11
9. 10, 15
10. 16, 36

11. 2, 6, 14
12. 4, 10, 25
13. 3, 7, 17
14. 15, 18, 60
15. 8, 9, 10

Find the GCF.

16. 16, 24
17. 8, 16
18. 18, 54
19. 4, 14
20. 84, 108

21. 15, 36
22. 18, 42
23. 18, 30
24. 32, 40
25. 21, 56

26. 12, 24, 32
27. 36, 45, 54
28. 30, 45, 75
29. 21, 35, 84
30. 12, 36, 52

31. Susan is buying supplies for a party. Spoons only come in bags of 4 and forks only come in bags of 3. What is the least number of spoons and the least number of forks Susan can buy so that she has the same number of each?

32. Ms. Collins is buying materials for a drawing class. Erasers only come in packages of 4 and pencils only come in packages of 9. What is the least number of erasers and the least number of pencils she can buy so that she has the same number of each?

Technology
Use HMH Mega Math, Ice Station Exploration, *Arctic Algebra*, Levels O and W.

Set E

Complete. (pp. 94–97)

1. $\frac{3}{15} = \frac{w}{45}$　　**2.** $\frac{34}{42} = \frac{w}{21}$　　**3.** $\frac{22}{25} = \frac{88}{w}$　　**4.** $\frac{56}{84} = \frac{14}{w}$　　**5.** $\frac{w}{18} = \frac{95}{90}$　　**6.** $\frac{100}{w} = \frac{5}{30}$

Write the fraction in simplest form.

7. $\frac{30}{50}$　　**8.** $\frac{12}{21}$　　**9.** $\frac{6}{28}$　　**10.** $\frac{2}{36}$　　**11.** $\frac{16}{100}$　　**12.** $\frac{33}{72}$

Set F

Write the mixed number as a fraction. (pp. 98–99)

1. $4\frac{3}{4}$　　**2.** $5\frac{1}{3}$　　**3.** $2\frac{4}{10}$　　**4.** $3\frac{3}{12}$　　**5.** $6\frac{6}{7}$　　**6.** $7\frac{8}{9}$

7. $\frac{16}{5}$　　**8.** $\frac{88}{4}$　　**9.** $\frac{74}{8}$　　**10.** $\frac{41}{6}$　　**11.** $\frac{95}{25}$　　**12.** $\frac{32}{16}$

Set G

Write as a fraction or mixed number in simplest form. (pp. 100–103)

1. 0.37　　**2.** 0.5　　**3.** 0.06　　**4.** 1.8　　**5.** 2.55　　**6.** 3.026

7. Mrs. Sanchez drives 4.65 miles each day to and from work. Write this number as a mixed number in simplest form.

8. John's backpack weighs 5.65 pounds. Ray's backpack weighs $5\frac{3}{5}$ pounds. Whose backpack weighs more?

Set H

Copy and complete. Write each fraction in simplest form. (pp. 104–105)

	Fraction	Decimal	Percent
1.			7%
3.		0.20	
5.	$\frac{3}{10}$		

	Fraction	Decimal	Percent
2.		0.56	
4.	$\frac{35}{100}$		
6.			96%

Set I

Compare. Write <, >, or = for each ⬭ **.** (pp. 106–109)

1. $\frac{5}{9}$ ⬭ $\frac{5}{7}$　　**2.** $\frac{3}{5}$ ⬭ 0.63　　**3.** $\frac{9}{10}$ ⬭ 95%　　**4.** $3\frac{5}{6}$ ⬭ $3\frac{10}{12}$　　**5.** 33% ⬭ 3.3

Order from least to greastest.

6. 21%, 0.19, $\frac{1}{5}$　　**7.** $1\frac{1}{4}$, 1.22, $1\frac{1}{5}$　　**8.** 4.75, $4\frac{5}{8}$, $3\frac{8}{9}$　　**9.** $\frac{5}{6}$, $\frac{3}{4}$, 80%, 0.78

10. Robert, Sam, and Abe each bought 0.5 pound of raisins. Robert has $\frac{1}{3}$ pound, Sam has 0.35 pound, and Abe has $\frac{2}{5}$ pound left. Order the leftover amounts from greatest to least. Who ate the most raisins?

Reading & Writing **Math**

Vocabulary

Many numbers break down in different ways.

Use the **Word Bank** to match each term with its definition.

1. A _____ is one of two or more numbers that are multiplied to a give a product.

2. A _____ is a whole number that has exactly two factors, 1 and itself.

3. A _____ is a whole number that has more than two factors.

4. The _____ tells how many times the base is a factor.

You can show a number as the product of its prime factors by making a **factor tree.**

	72
Step 1: Write any pair of factors for the number 72.	
Step 2: Write a pair of factors for each number until all the factors are prime numbers.	
Step 3: Write the prime factor of the number. The prime factorization of 72 is $2 \times 2 \times 2 \times 3 \times 3$.	

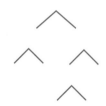

Writing Explain why the number 1 is neither a prime nor a composite number. Use the words in the Word Bank in your explanation.

Reading Check out this book in your library.
On Beyond a Million: An Amazing Math Journey, by David M. Schwartz.

H.O.T. Multistep Problems

1 Anna is making chocolate chip cookies to sell at a bake sale. Here is the recipe that Anna is using. 🔊 2.1.

Chocolate Chip Cookie Recipe	
$1\frac{1}{2}$ cups flour	$\frac{1}{2}$ cup light brown sugar
$\frac{3}{4}$ teaspoon baking soda	1 egg
$\frac{2}{3}$ cup oil	1 cup chocolate chips
$\frac{3}{4}$ cup sugar	
Bake at 375 degrees for 8-10 minutes. Makes 1 batch of cookies (24 cookies).	

- Anna wants to make chocolate chip cookies and she is measuring the flour. She only has a $\frac{1}{4}$ cup measuring cup and a $\frac{1}{3}$ cup measuring cup. Which cup would be the best for her to measure the flour? **Explain.**

- Not including the egg or the baking soda, graph the amount of each ingredient on the number line. Of which ingredient will Ann use the most? Of which ingredient will she use the least? Use the graph to help you decide.

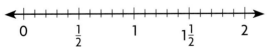

$$0 \qquad \frac{1}{2} \qquad 1 \qquad 1\frac{1}{2} \qquad 2$$

- Anna's chocolate chip cookie recipe makes 1 batch of 24 cookies. Her friend Sean has a recipe for peanut butter cookies that makes 1 batch of 16 cookies. They would like to make the same number of cookies for the school bake sale. How many batches of each kind of cookie do they need to make in order to have the same number of each kind?

2 Mr. Acevedo's class was collecting data to discuss the different heights of the students in their class. Here is the table showing the heights of some of the students in Mr. Acevedo's 6th grade science class. 🔊 2.1.

Name	Height (in inches)
Jane	58.51
Kara	$60\frac{3}{16}$
Raven	58.9
Luis	$61\frac{1}{16}$
Jamal	60.02
Mary	60.3
LaTanya	61.9
Madison	$58\frac{5}{8}$
Lucus	$60\frac{1}{2}$
Peter	$61\frac{7}{8}$

- How many inches taller is Raven than Jane?

- How much taller is Luis than Madison?

- Peter grew 3.2 inches in the past year. Jane grew $3\frac{1}{8}$ inches in the past year. Who grew more?

- Convert all decimals to mixed numbers. Create a new chart that has the students ordered by height from tallest to shortest.

Practice for the OCCT

1 Which point shows $\frac{5}{2}$ on the number line?
🔖 **2.1.**

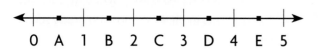

0   A   1   B   2   C   3   D   4   E   5

A   point B

B   point C

C   point D

D   point E

2 Which statement about the mixed number $2\frac{1}{4}$ is true? 🔖 **2.1.**

A $2\frac{1}{4} > 2\frac{1}{3}$

B $2 > 2\frac{1}{4}$

C $2\frac{1}{4} > 2\frac{1}{5}$

D $2\frac{1}{4} < 2\frac{1}{10}$

3 Which of is the least common multiple of the numbers 4, 6, and 9? 🔖 **1.1.**

A   12

B   36

C   48

D   108

4 Miguel bought 6.75 oz of rabbit food at the County Fair. Which is 6.75 written as an improper fraction? 🔖 **2.1.**

A $\frac{675}{100}$

B $\frac{6}{75}$

C $\frac{27}{4}$

D $\frac{29}{5}$

5 Mr. Landis invests $\frac{4}{24}$ of his earnings each month. Which is equivalent to $\frac{4}{24}$? 🔖 **2.1.**

A $\frac{8}{40}$

B $\frac{1}{6}$

C $\frac{1}{4}$

D $\frac{4}{3}$

6 Which list of numbers is ordered from least to greatest? 🔖 **2.1.**

A $\frac{3}{4}, \frac{1}{5}, \frac{2}{3}, \frac{1}{2}$

B $\frac{1}{2}, \frac{1}{3}, \frac{1}{4}, \frac{1}{5}$

C $\frac{2}{7}, \frac{2}{5}, \frac{2}{3}, \frac{7}{8}$

D $\frac{2}{4}, \frac{3}{6}, \frac{4}{8}, \frac{5}{10}$

7 A cake is cut into 12 equal slices at a birthday party. Four of the slices are eaten. Which fraction, in simplest form, represents the portion of the cake that is left? 🔖 **2.1.**

A $\frac{1}{4}$

B $\frac{2}{3}$

C $\frac{4}{12}$

D $\frac{8}{12}$

8 What is the greatest common factor of 64, 48, and 128? 🔖 **2.2.a.**

A   4

B   8

C   12

D   16

9 Kirk went to the store and saw that the couch he wanted was 25% off. What is 25% written as a fraction and as a decimal? 📋 2.1.

A $0.25; \frac{1}{4}$

B $0.25; \frac{25}{10}$

C $25; \frac{25}{100}$

D $0.25; \frac{2.5}{100}$

10 In the election for class president, Marcus received $\frac{5}{12}$ of the votes, Denise received $\frac{1}{4}$ of the votes, and Alonzo received $\frac{1}{3}$ of the votes. Who won the election? 📋 2.1.

A Denise

B Marcus

C Alonzo

D Tim

11 The table shows the distances that 4 bicyclists rode. Who rode the farthest distance? 📋 2.1.

Rider	Suzie	Tom	Nikki	Lisa
Distance (miles)	$\frac{7}{9}$	$\frac{5}{6}$	$\frac{2}{3}$	$\frac{1}{2}$

A Suzie

B Nikki

C Tom

D Lisa

12 The mixed number $8\frac{1}{4}$ is between which pair of numbers on a number line? 📋 2.1.

A $8\frac{1}{6}$ and $8\frac{11}{16}$

B $\frac{58}{7}$ and $\frac{80}{9}$

C $\frac{26}{3}$ and $8\frac{3}{4}$

D $8\frac{7}{8}$ and $9\frac{1}{3}$

Problem Solving

13 What is the least common multiple of 5, 7, and 14? 📋 2.2.a.

14 Carousel horses that move up and down are called jumpers. The Broadway Flying Horses carousel has 28 jumpers out of 40 horses. The carousel at the amusement park has 24 jumpers out of 36 horses. Which carousel has the greater fraction of jumpers? **Explain** how you find your answer. 📋 2.1.

15 The sizes, in inches, of several wrenches are as follows: $\frac{11}{16}, \frac{3}{8}, \frac{3}{4}, \frac{1}{2}, \frac{5}{8}$ and $\frac{7}{16}$. Order the wrenches from least to greatest. **Explain** how you find your answer. 📋 2.1.

16 There are 14 boys and 16 girls in Rebecca's class. Red is the favorite color of 2 boys and 4 girls. Red is the favorite color of what percent of the class? **Explain** how you find your answer. 📋 2.1.

Chapter 4

Fractions Operations

Investigate

Suppose you are making a salad. Your salad bowl can hold 8 c of salad. You start with $3\frac{1}{2}$ c of lettuce.

Look at the table below. What are some combinations of ingredients that will fill the salad bowl to within $\frac{1}{2}$ c of its capacity if the entire amount of each ingredient is used?

Choice of Salad Ingredients
$\frac{11}{4}$ c sliced celery
$\frac{11}{2}$ c cucumber slices
$\frac{1}{4}$ c diced onion
1 c sliced pepper
$\frac{13}{8}$ c tomato slices
$\frac{3}{4}$ c grated carrot
$\frac{3}{8}$ c sliced radish
$\frac{11}{4}$ c croutons

Fun Fact

The Bureau of Labor Statistics projects that nearly 3.6 million Americans will work as chefs, cooks, and food preparation workers in 2014.

GO ONLINE

Technology
Student pages are available in the Student eBook.

Show What You Know

Check your understanding of important skills needed for success in Chapter 4.

ASSESSMENT
Soar To Success: Math.

▶ Equivalent Fractions

Write an equivalent fraction.

1. $\frac{1}{2}$
2. $\frac{4}{6}$
3. $\frac{3}{5}$
4. $\frac{75}{100}$
5. $\frac{3}{9}$

6. $\frac{2}{7}$
7. $\frac{20}{25}$
8. $\frac{15}{20}$
9. $\frac{1}{11}$
10. $\frac{10}{100}$

▶ Simplest Form

Write each fraction in simplest form.

11. $\frac{4}{8}$
12. $\frac{9}{8}$
13. $\frac{24}{32}$
14. $\frac{7}{14}$
15. $\frac{20}{30}$

16. $\frac{4}{16}$
17. $\frac{7}{6}$
18. $\frac{10}{5}$
19. $\frac{6}{8}$
20. $\frac{10}{25}$

▶ Add and Subtract Like Fractions

Find the sum or difference. Write each answer in simplest form.

21. $\frac{2}{3} - \frac{1}{3}$
22. $\frac{1}{8} + \frac{3}{8}$
23. $\frac{5}{6} + \frac{1}{6}$
24. $\frac{6}{7} + \frac{3}{7}$
25. $\frac{15}{16} - \frac{3}{16}$

26. $\frac{8}{18} - \frac{5}{18}$
27. $\frac{3}{4} + \frac{3}{4}$
28. $\frac{5}{9} - \frac{2}{9}$
29. $\frac{5}{12} - \frac{1}{12}$
30. $\frac{17}{32} + \frac{13}{32}$

Vocabulary

Visualize It!

You can multiply to add fractions quickly.

$$\frac{2}{4} + \frac{2}{4} + \frac{2}{4} + \frac{2}{4} = 4 \times \frac{2}{4} = \frac{8}{4} \text{ or } 2$$

Language Tips

Math words that look similar in English and Spanish often have the same meaning.

English	Spanish
estimate	cálculo
reciprocal	reciproco

See **English-Spanish Glossary.**

Estimate Sums and Differences

Essential Question How do you estimate sums and differences of fractions and mixed numbers?

★ **2.2.c.** Estimate and find solutions to single and multi-step problems using whole numbers, decimals, fractions, and percents (e.g., $\frac{7}{8} + \frac{8}{9}$ is about 2, $3.9 + 5.3$ is about 9).

Vocabulary

benchmark

Materials
• MathBoard

▶ **Learn**

Rounding fractions can help you to estimate sums and differences. A **benchmark** is a reference point on a number line that is useful for rounding fractions. Look at the number line. Is $\frac{4}{10}$ closest to 0, $\frac{1}{2}$, or 1?

$$\frac{1}{10} \quad \frac{2}{10} \quad \frac{3}{10} \quad \frac{4}{10} \quad \frac{5}{10} \quad \frac{6}{10} \quad \frac{7}{10} \quad \frac{8}{10} \quad \frac{9}{10}$$

So, $\frac{4}{10}$ is closest to $\frac{1}{2}$.

Also, you can compare the numerator to the denominator.

$\frac{2}{16}$ $\frac{1}{7}$	$\frac{9}{10}$ $\frac{15}{16}$	$\frac{9}{16}$ $\frac{5}{11}$
Each numerator is much less than half the denominator, so the fractions are close to 0.	Each numerator is about the same as the denominator, so the fractions are close to 1.	Each numerator is about half the denominator, so the fractions are close to $\frac{1}{2}$.

Examples

Estimate. $\frac{1}{8} + \frac{15}{16}$

$$\frac{1}{8} \rightarrow 0 \qquad \text{$\frac{1}{8}$ is between 0 and $\frac{1}{2}$, but closer to 0.}$$

$$+\frac{15}{16} \rightarrow +1 \qquad \text{$\frac{15}{16}$ is between $\frac{1}{2}$ and 1, but closer to 1.}$$

$$\overline{\qquad\qquad 1}$$

So, $\frac{1}{8} + \frac{15}{16}$ is about 1.

Estimate. $\frac{7}{8} - \frac{4}{5}$

$$\frac{7}{8} \rightarrow 1$$

$$-\frac{4}{5} \rightarrow -1$$
The numerators are both about the same as the denominators—round both fractions to 1.

$$\overline{\qquad\qquad 0}$$

So, $\frac{7}{8} - \frac{4}{5}$ is about 0.

Mixed Numbers

To estimate sums and differences of mixed numbers, compare each mixed number to the nearest whole number or to the nearest $\frac{1}{2}$.

A marathon runner has a goal to run 20 mi during the first week of training. On Sunday, she ran $8\frac{1}{5}$ mi. On Tuesday, she ran $6\frac{7}{10}$ mi. About how many more miles does she need to run that week to meet her goal?

Estimate. $20 - \left(8\frac{1}{5} + 6\frac{7}{10}\right)$

$20 - \left(8\frac{1}{5} + 6\frac{7}{10}\right)$ $8\frac{1}{5}$ is close to 8, and $6\frac{7}{10}$ is close to 7.

$20 - \left(8 + 7\right)$ Add.

$20 - 15 = 5$ Subtract.

Remember

A mixed number is represented by a whole number and a fraction. $8\frac{3}{5}$ is a mixed number.

So, she needs to run about 5 more miles.

Some situations may require an overestimate or underestimate for the answer. To overestimate the sum of two or more fractions, round some or all of the fractions up. To underestimate the sum of two or more fractions, round some or all of the fractions down.

A figure skater likes to listen to music while he trains. He has only 12 more minutes of memory on his MP3 player. He wants to download 3 songs of $3\frac{2}{10}$ min, $2\frac{3}{4}$ min, and $4\frac{2}{3}$ min. Will all three songs fit on his MP3 player?

Estimate. $3\frac{2}{10} + 2\frac{3}{4} + 4\frac{2}{3}$

To decide whether all three songs will fit, find an overestimate.

$3\frac{2}{10}$ → $3\frac{1}{2}$ $3\frac{2}{10}$ rounds up to $3\frac{1}{2}$.

$2\frac{3}{4}$ → 3 $2\frac{3}{4}$ rounds up to 3.

$+\, 4\frac{2}{3}$ → $+\,5$ $4\frac{2}{3}$ rounds up to 5.
_____

$\qquad\qquad 11\frac{1}{2}$

So, all three songs will fit on his MP3 player.

 Share and Show Math Board

1. Use the number line to tell whether $\frac{1}{3}$ is closest to $0, \frac{1}{2},$ or 1. Write *close to 0, close to $\frac{1}{2}$, or close to 1.*

Estimate the sum or difference.

2. $\frac{6}{7} + \frac{11}{12}$ 3. $\frac{3}{5} - \frac{1}{9}$ ✓4. $9\frac{2}{15} - 3\frac{7}{8}$ ✓5. $5\frac{7}{12} + 1\frac{3}{8}$

6. **Math Talk** **Explain** how to use benchmarks to estimate $4\frac{1}{9} + 4\frac{4}{5}$.

Practice and Problem Solving REAL WORLD

Use the number line to tell whether the fraction is closest to 0, $\frac{1}{2}$, or 1. Write *close to 0*, *close to $\frac{1}{2}$*, or *close to 1*.

Number line: $0 \quad \frac{1}{12} \quad \frac{1}{6} \quad \frac{1}{4} \quad \frac{1}{3} \quad \frac{5}{12} \quad \frac{1}{2} \quad \frac{7}{12} \quad \frac{2}{3} \quad \frac{3}{4} \quad \frac{5}{6} \quad \frac{11}{12} \quad 1$

7. $\frac{7}{12}$ **8.** $\frac{1}{6}$ **9.** $\frac{5}{12}$ **10.** $\frac{5}{6}$

Estimate the sum or difference.

11. $\frac{6}{11} - \frac{1}{6}$ **12.** $\frac{1}{5} + \frac{8}{9}$ **13.** $\frac{6}{13} - \frac{4}{9}$ **14.** $\frac{9}{10} + \frac{1}{5} + \frac{3}{7}$

15. $8\frac{1}{5} + 9\frac{5}{8}$ **16.** $10\frac{1}{5} - 9\frac{4}{7}$ **17.** $7\frac{9}{10} - 5\frac{5}{8}$ **18.** $16\frac{1}{8} + 13\frac{8}{9} + 3\frac{4}{5}$

Estimate to compare. Write < or > for each .

19. $\frac{5}{8} + \frac{7}{12}$ ⬭ 2   **20.** $4\frac{9}{10} - 3\frac{2}{7}$ ⬭ 1   **21.** $12\frac{3}{5} + 4\frac{4}{9}$ ⬭ 15   **22.** $4\frac{1}{12} + 5\frac{1}{6}$ ⬭ 10

 Real World Data

For 23–26, use the graph.

23. Jan and her friends go to the pool several times each week to train in four different swimming styles. Estimate the total number of hours Jan swims in one week.

24. About how many more hours does Ben swim freestyle and backstroke than Darren?

25. Andrea trains for butterfly for $4\frac{1}{5}$ hr each week. About how many more hours does she swim butterfly than Jan?

26. **Write Math** ▶ Ben says he trains for freestyle for a greater amount of time than both Jan and Darren combined. Is this true? **Explain.**

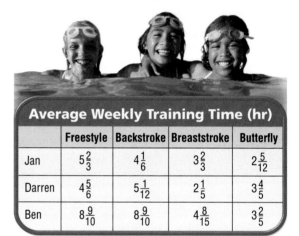

Average Weekly Training Time (hr)

	Freestyle	Backstroke	Breaststroke	Butterfly
Jan	$5\frac{2}{3}$	$4\frac{1}{6}$	$3\frac{2}{3}$	$2\frac{5}{12}$
Darren	$4\frac{5}{6}$	$5\frac{1}{12}$	$2\frac{1}{5}$	$3\frac{4}{5}$
Ben	$8\frac{9}{10}$	$8\frac{9}{10}$	$4\frac{8}{15}$	$3\frac{2}{5}$

 ★ **OCCT Test Prep** Math Board

27. Dr. Driben needs to complete Milo's vet record. What is the best estimate of Milo's new weight?

> **Milo's vet record**
> Prior weight: $15\frac{1}{8}$ lb Weight lost: $2\frac{3}{4}$ lb
> New weight estimation: ▮

A about $2\frac{3}{4}$ lb   **C** about 12 lb

B about 10 lb   **D** about 18 lb

28. Antonio needs to buy 15 lb of chicken for a dinner party. He buys three packages that weigh $2\frac{1}{4}$ lb, $4\frac{7}{8}$ lb, and $3\frac{2}{3}$ lb. About how many more pounds does Antonio need to buy?

A about 2 lb   **C** about 6 lb

B about 4 lb   **D** about 8 lb

⬠ ★ Standards Quick Check

Estimate the sum or difference.

1. $\frac{1}{9} + \frac{9}{11}$

2. $6\frac{4}{15} - \frac{1}{5}$

3. $4\frac{6}{7} + 1\frac{5}{8}$

4. $9\frac{5}{8} - 8\frac{7}{8}$

5. $10\frac{4}{5} - 8\frac{1}{11}$

6. $3\frac{4}{9} + 6\frac{1}{8} + 5\frac{8}{9}$

Challenge H.O.T.

Using a Range to Estimate

You can round fractions and mixed numbers to find a range to estimate a sum or difference.

Estimate. $8\frac{3}{4} + 4\frac{3}{8}$

Since $8\frac{3}{4}$ is between $8\frac{1}{2}$ and 9, find two estimates for the sum.

Estimate 1

$8\frac{3}{4} + 4\frac{3}{8}$
$\downarrow \quad \downarrow$
$8\frac{1}{2} + 4 = 12\frac{1}{2}$

Round down. $8\frac{3}{4}$ is close to $8\frac{1}{2}$ and $4\frac{3}{8}$ is close to 4.

Add.

Estimate 2

$8\frac{3}{4} + 4\frac{3}{8}$
$\downarrow \quad \downarrow$
$9 + 4\frac{1}{2} = 13\frac{1}{2}$

Round up. $8\frac{3}{4}$ is close to 9, and $4\frac{3}{8}$ is close to $4\frac{1}{2}$.

Add.

The estimates are $12\frac{1}{2}$ and $13\frac{1}{2}$.

So, 13, which is between $12\frac{1}{2}$ and $13\frac{1}{2}$, is a good estimate of $8\frac{3}{4} + 4\frac{3}{8}$.

Use a range to estimate each sum or difference.

1. $9\frac{5}{6} + 2\frac{2}{8}$

2. $11\frac{3}{5} + 4\frac{7}{8}$

3. $9 - 4\frac{1}{8}$

4. $8\frac{1}{2} - 2\frac{1}{8}$

5. $13\frac{2}{3} + 17\frac{8}{9}$

6. $17 - 9\frac{1}{5}$

7. $11\frac{1}{2} - 3\frac{1}{6}$

8. $6\frac{3}{4} + 5\frac{2}{5}$

★ **2.2.c.** Estimate and find solutions to single and multi-step problems using whole numbers, decimals, fractions, and percents (e.g., $\frac{7}{8} + \frac{8}{9}$ is about 2, $3.9 + 5.3$ is about 9).

Vocabulary

least common denomintor (LCD)

unlike fractions

Materials
• MathBoard
• fraction bars

Add and Subtract Fractions

Essential Question What do you need to do when adding or subtracting fractions with unlike denominators?

PROBLEM The human body is made of approximately $\frac{3}{5}$ oxygen, $\frac{1}{5}$ carbon, and $\frac{1}{10}$ hydrogen. Find the fraction of the human body that is made up of these elements.

Unlike fractions are fractions with different denominators. You can add and subtract unlike fractions with the help of fraction bars.

Add with unlike denominators.

Add. $\frac{3}{5} + \frac{1}{5} + \frac{1}{10}$ Estimate. $1 + 0 + 0 = 1$

1 First, use mental math to find $\frac{3}{5} + \frac{1}{5}$ $\frac{3}{5} + \frac{1}{5} = \frac{4}{5}$

Then, use fraction bars to model $\frac{4}{5} + \frac{1}{10}$.

2 Find which fraction bars fit exactly across $\frac{4}{5}$ and $\frac{1}{10}$.

$$\frac{4}{5} + \frac{1}{10} = \frac{8}{10} + \frac{1}{10} = \frac{9}{10}$$

Since $\frac{9}{10}$ is close to the estimate of 1, the answer is reasonable.

So, $\frac{9}{10}$ of the human body is made up of oxygen, carbon, and hydrogen.

When subtracting a fraction from a whole number, rename the whole number.

Subtract with unlike denominators.

Subtract. $1 - \frac{3}{8}$ Estimate. $1 - \frac{1}{2} = \frac{1}{2}$

Rename 1 whole using eight $\frac{1}{8}$ bars.

Subtract $\frac{3}{8}$.

$$1 - \frac{3}{8} = \frac{8}{8} - \frac{3}{8} = \frac{5}{8}$$

Since $\frac{5}{8}$ is close to the estimate of $\frac{1}{2}$, the answer is reasonable. So, $1 - \frac{3}{8} = \frac{5}{8}$.

Using Common Denominators

To add or subtract unlike fractions without using models, find equivalent fractions. Equivalent fractions can be written by using a common denominator or the **least common denominator (LCD)**. The LCD is the least common multiple (LCM) of two or more denominators.

Use a common denominator to find $\frac{5}{6} + \frac{4}{9}$.

Estimate. $\frac{5}{6}$ is close to 1, and $\frac{4}{9}$ is close to $\frac{1}{2}$. $1 + \frac{1}{2} = 1\frac{1}{2}$

1
$$\frac{5}{6} = \frac{5 \times 9}{6 \times 9} = \frac{45}{54}$$
$$+\frac{4}{9} = \frac{4 \times 6}{9 \times 6} = +\frac{24}{54}$$

Multiply 6 and 9 to find a common denominator, 54. Use the common denominator to write equivalent fractions.

2
$$\frac{5}{6} = \frac{45}{54}$$
$$+\frac{4}{9} = +\frac{24}{54}$$
$$\frac{69}{54} = \frac{23}{18}$$
$$\text{or } 1\frac{5}{18}$$

Add the numerators. Write the sum over the denominator.

Write the answer as a fraction or as a mixed number.

Compare the answer to your estimate. Since $1\frac{5}{18}$ is close to the estimate of $1\frac{1}{2}$, the answer is reasonable. So, $\frac{5}{6} + \frac{4}{9} = 1\frac{5}{18}$.

Use the LCD to find $\frac{7}{12} - \frac{1}{3}$.

Estimate. $\frac{7}{12}$ is close to $\frac{1}{2}$, and $\frac{1}{3}$ is close to 0. $\frac{1}{2} - 0 = \frac{1}{2}$

1
$$\frac{7}{12} = \frac{7}{12}$$
$$-\frac{1}{3} = \frac{1 \times 4}{3 \times 4} = -\frac{4}{12}$$

The LCD of $\frac{7}{12}$ and $\frac{1}{3}$ is 12. Multiply to write equivalent fractions using the LCD.

2
$$\frac{7}{12} = \frac{7}{12}$$
$$-\frac{1}{3} = -\frac{4}{12}$$
$$\frac{3}{12} = \frac{1}{4}$$

Subtract the numerators.

Write the difference over the denominator. Write the answer in simplest form.

Compare the answer to your estimate. Since $\frac{1}{4}$ is close to the estimate of $\frac{1}{2}$, the answer is reasonable. So, $\frac{7}{12} - \frac{1}{3} = \frac{1}{4}$.

Share and Show Math Board

1. Use the fraction bars to find $\frac{1}{4} + \frac{2}{3}$.

Use a common denominator to write the problem using equivalent fractions.

2. $\frac{5}{8} + \frac{1}{6}$ 3. $\frac{5}{6} + \frac{1}{2}$ 4. $\frac{6}{7} - \frac{1}{2}$ 5. $\frac{7}{9} - \frac{2}{3}$ ✅ 6. $\frac{2}{3} + \frac{5}{12}$

Estimate. Then write the sum or difference in simplest form.

7. $\frac{2}{3} + \frac{1}{12}$ 8. $\frac{11}{18} - \frac{3}{18}$ 9. $\frac{4}{15} + \frac{2}{5}$ 10. $\frac{7}{16} + \frac{3}{4}$ ✅ 11. $\frac{3}{4} - \frac{5}{12}$

12. **Math Talk** Explain how to find $\frac{1}{8} + \frac{5}{6}$.

Use a common denominator to write the problem using equivalent fractions.

13. $\frac{5}{8} + \frac{1}{4}$

14. $\frac{4}{11} - \frac{8}{22}$

15. $\frac{7}{16} + \frac{3}{8}$

16. $\frac{4}{9} + \frac{1}{5}$

17. $\frac{11}{20} - \frac{1}{3}$

Estimate. Then write the sum or difference in simplest form.

18. $\frac{7}{9} + \frac{1}{2}$

19. $\frac{4}{5} - \frac{1}{15}$

20. $\frac{3}{8} - \frac{1}{10}$

21. $\frac{1}{2} + \frac{1}{3}$

22. $\frac{4}{5} - \frac{2}{5}$

23. $\frac{2}{3} - \frac{1}{4}$

24. $\frac{6}{10} + \frac{4}{15}$

25. $\frac{6}{25} + \frac{3}{10}$

26. $\frac{11}{20} + \frac{2}{5} + \frac{1}{2}$

27. $\frac{1}{4} + \frac{1}{3} + \frac{1}{2}$

28. What is the sum of $\frac{2}{7}$ and $\frac{1}{2}$?

29. How much less than $\frac{1}{4}$ is $\frac{1}{6}$?

⭐**Algebra** Use mental math to solve. Write the answer in simplest form.

30. $n + \frac{1}{8} = \frac{7}{8}$

31. $y - \frac{1}{6} = \frac{1}{6}$

32. $m + \frac{1}{3} = \frac{2}{3}$

33. $z - \frac{1}{9} = \frac{6}{9}$

For 34–36, use the diagram.

34. Find the sum of the fractions that are inside the triangle but outside the square.

35. Find the sum of the fractions outside the triangle but inside the square.

36. Find the difference of the fractions inside both the triangle and the square.

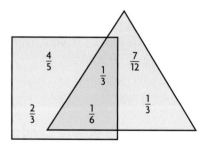

📊 Real World Data

For 37–38, use the table.

37. What fraction of sedimentary rock is not limestone?

38. ≣**FAST FACT** Geologists classify rocks in three main groups: igneous, metamorphic, and sedimentary. The earth's crust is about $\frac{13}{20}$ igneous rock, $\frac{1}{4}$ metamorphic rock, and $\frac{1}{10}$ sedimentary rock. About what fraction of earth's crust is igneous or metamorphic rock?

Type of Sedimentary Rock			
Type	Shale	Sandstone	Limestone
Fraction of Sedimentary Rock	$\frac{3}{5}$	$\frac{1}{4}$	$\frac{3}{20}$

39. **Write Math** **Explain** how to use the LCD to find the sum of $\frac{1}{4}$ and $\frac{5}{6}$ in simplest form.

⭐ **OCCT Test Prep** 🖊️ Math Board

40. Which is the sum, in simplest form, of $\frac{9}{16} + \frac{12}{16}$?

A $\frac{3}{16}$

B $\frac{21}{32}$

C $\frac{31}{32}$

D $\frac{15}{16}$

41. Which is the difference, in simplest form, of $\frac{5}{6} - \frac{3}{8}$?

A $\frac{1}{12}$

B $\frac{11}{24}$

C $\frac{11}{12}$

D $1\frac{5}{54}$

GO ONLINE — **Technology**
Use HMH Mega Math, Fraction Action, *Fraction Flare Up*, Levels G–K.

⭐ Standards Quick Check

Write the sum or difference in simplest form.

1. $\frac{1}{3} + \frac{4}{9}$

2. $\frac{5}{13} - \frac{3}{26}$

3. $\frac{3}{8} + \frac{3}{4}$

4. $\frac{13}{20} - \frac{1}{3}$

5. $\frac{3}{5} + \frac{1}{4}$

6. $1 - \frac{1}{6}$

7. $\frac{5}{8} - \frac{1}{5}$

8. $\frac{2}{5} - \frac{1}{15}$

9. $\frac{5}{7} + \frac{1}{2}$

Challenge H.O.T.

Number Patterns

Number patterns follow rules. If you know a rule for a pattern, you can use it to find the next number. Look at the pattern: $\frac{5}{6}$, $1\frac{1}{3}$, $1\frac{5}{6}$, $2\frac{1}{3}$, ▪.
Find the next number in the pattern.

Find a possible rule.

Since the numbers increase, try addition.

Try adding $\frac{1}{2}$.

$\frac{5}{6} + \frac{1}{2} = \frac{11}{3}$ $1\frac{1}{3} + \frac{1}{2} = 1\frac{5}{6}$ $1\frac{5}{6} + \frac{1}{2} = 2\frac{1}{3}$

A possible rule is **add $\frac{1}{2}$.**

Use the rule to find the next number.

$2\frac{1}{3} + \frac{1}{2} = 2\frac{5}{6}$

So, $2\frac{5}{6}$ is the next number in the pattern.

Write a possible rule. Find the next number in the pattern.

1. $\frac{1}{12}$, $\frac{1}{3}$, $\frac{7}{12}$, $\frac{10}{12}$, ▪

2. 5, $4\frac{1}{4}$, $3\frac{1}{2}$, $2\frac{3}{4}$, ▪

3. $1\frac{2}{3}$, $1\frac{5}{6}$, 2, $2\frac{1}{6}$, ▪

LESSON 3

Add and Subtract Mixed Numbers

Essential Question When you add and subtract mixed numbers, in what situation should you rename a fraction?

2.2.c. Estimate and find solutions to single and multi-step problems using whole numbers, decimals, fractions, and percents (e.g., $\frac{7}{8} + \frac{8}{9}$ is about 2, 3.9 + 5.3 is about 9).

Materials
• MathBoard

PROBLEM At a local amusement park, Valerie spent $2\frac{1}{4}$ min on one roller coaster and $1\frac{3}{8}$ min on another. What is the total amount of time Valerie spent on the roller coasters?

Draw a diagram.

Add. $2\frac{1}{4} + 1\frac{3}{8}$ Estimate. $2 + 1\frac{1}{2} = 3\frac{1}{2}$

Show $2\frac{1}{4} + 1\frac{3}{8}$.

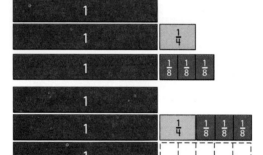

Combine whole numbers. Combine fractions. 8 is a common multiple of 4 and 8. Draw eighths under $\frac{1}{4}$ and $\frac{3}{8}$.

Add fractions. Add whole numbers. Combine as a mixed number.

$2 + 1 = 3$ $\frac{2}{8} + \frac{3}{8} = \frac{5}{8}$

So, Valerie spent $3\frac{5}{8}$ min on the roller coasters.

Use a common denominator.

Add. $3\frac{2}{3} + 2\frac{3}{4}$

$3\frac{2}{3} = 3\frac{8}{12}$

$+ 2\frac{3}{4} = 2\frac{9}{12}$

$\overline{\quad\quad 5\frac{17}{12} = 5 + 1\frac{5}{12} = 6\frac{5}{12}}$

Write equivalent fractions, using the LCD, 12. Add fractions. Add whole numbers.

Rename the fraction as a mixed number. Rewrite the sum.

So, $3\frac{2}{3} + 2\frac{3}{4} = 6\frac{5}{12}$.

Subtract Mixed Numbers

The Kingda Ka, in New Jersey, is the tallest and fastest roller coaster in the world. It reaches the bottom of the longest drop in $3\frac{1}{2}$ sec. The Top Thrill Dragster, in Ohio, has a drop time of $2\frac{1}{4}$ sec. What is the difference in the drop times?

Draw a diagram.

Subtract. $3\frac{1}{2} - 2\frac{1}{4}$

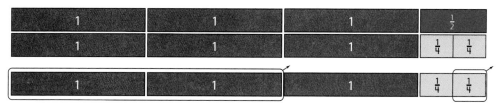

Draw $3\frac{1}{2}$.

4 is a common multiple of 2 and 4. Draw fourths under the $\frac{1}{2}$.

Subtract $2\frac{1}{4}$ from $3\frac{1}{2}$.

$3\frac{1}{2} - 2\frac{1}{4} = 1\frac{1}{4}$. So, the difference in the times is $1\frac{1}{4}$ sec.

Use the LCD.

Subtract. $4\frac{4}{5} - 2\frac{1}{4}$

Estimate. $4\frac{4}{5}$ is close to 5, and $2\frac{1}{4}$ is close to 2. So, the difference is about 3.

$$\begin{aligned} 4\frac{4}{5} &= 4\frac{16}{20} \\ -2\frac{1}{4} &= -2\frac{5}{20} \\ \hline &\quad 2\frac{11}{20} \end{aligned}$$

Write equivalent fractions using the LCD, 20.

Subtract fractions.
Subtract whole numbers.

The answer is reasonable because it is close to the estimate of 3.

So, $4\frac{4}{5} - 2\frac{1}{4} = 2\frac{11}{20}$.

▶ **Share and Show** Math Board

1. Copy the diagram shown. Then use your diagram to record and find the difference.

Draw a diagram to show the sum or difference. Then write the answer in simplest form.

2. $1\frac{5}{6} + 2\frac{1}{3}$ 3. $2\frac{2}{5} + 3\frac{1}{10}$ 4. $3\frac{4}{12} - 3\frac{1}{3}$ 5. $3\frac{1}{3} - 2\frac{1}{4}$ ✅6. $5\frac{4}{5} - 3\frac{3}{10}$

Estimate. Then write the sum or difference in simplest form.

7. $8\frac{7}{8} - 2\frac{1}{8}$ 8. $3\frac{7}{8} + 3\frac{1}{2}$ 9. $10\frac{9}{20} + 8\frac{3}{4}$ 10. $8\frac{1}{3} - 1\frac{2}{15}$ ✅11. $4\frac{1}{6} + 3\frac{1}{4}$

12. **Math Talk** **Explain** how to find $4\frac{5}{8} - 2\frac{1}{4}$.

Draw a diagram to show the sum or difference. Then write the answer in simplest form.

13. $4\frac{1}{2} - 2\frac{1}{5}$ **14.** $9\frac{5}{6} - 1\frac{1}{3}$ **15.** $3\frac{5}{12} + \frac{1}{3}$ **16.** $2\frac{4}{7} - 1\frac{1}{2}$ **17.** $1\frac{1}{3} + 2\frac{1}{6}$

Estimate. Then write the sum or difference in simplest form.

18. $16\frac{3}{4} - 5\frac{1}{3}$ **19.** $30\frac{5}{6} - 21\frac{2}{3}$ **20.** $25\frac{7}{18} + 15\frac{1}{6}$ **21.** $10\frac{9}{20} + 8\frac{3}{4}$ **22.** $4\frac{1}{2} + 3\frac{4}{5}$

23. $12\frac{2}{3} + 6\frac{3}{4}$ **24.** $7\frac{5}{6} - 4\frac{1}{5}$ **25.** $8\frac{3}{8} + 2\frac{1}{3}$ **26.** $4\frac{7}{10} - 1\frac{2}{5}$ **27.** $5\frac{1}{2} - 2\frac{1}{6}$

28. What is the sum of $4\frac{1}{2}$ and $7\frac{1}{6}$?

29. How much greater is $10\frac{3}{4}$ than $8\frac{2}{3}$?

★**Algebra** Find the unknown number, and identify which property of addition you used.

30. $5\frac{1}{2} + \blacksquare = 3\frac{1}{4} + 5\frac{1}{2}$ **31.** $7\frac{1}{8} + 0 = \blacksquare$ **32.** $1\frac{1}{6} + (1\frac{1}{5} + 1\frac{1}{4}) = (1\frac{1}{6} + \blacksquare) + 1\frac{1}{4}$

 Real World Data

For 33–36, use the table.

33. How much faster is the Zaturn roller coaster than the Stealth? **Explain**.

34. How much faster is the Silver Star roller coaster than the Beast? **Explain**.

35. Reasoning Which 2 roller coasters have the least difference in maximum speed?

36. **Write Math** ▶ **What's the Error?** Clinton says that Thunder Dolphin is faster than Zaturn by $\frac{4}{10}$ mi per hr. Describe his error and find the correct answer.

Roller Coaster Speeds	
Roller Coaster	**Maximum Speed (mi per hr)**
Silver Star	$78\frac{9}{10}$
Stealth	$79\frac{1}{2}$
Beast	$64\frac{4}{5}$
Thunder Dolphin	$80\frac{8}{10}$
Zaturn	$80\frac{4}{5}$

37. There are $16\frac{3}{4}$ yards of material on a roll. If $4\frac{2}{3}$ yards are used, how many yards are left on the roll?

A 10 yards   **C** $12\frac{1}{4}$ yards

B $12\frac{1}{12}$ yards   **D** $21\frac{5}{12}$ yards

38. A butcher sold packages of meat weighing $1\frac{1}{4}$ pounds and $5\frac{5}{8}$ pounds. What was the total weight of the meat, in pounds?

A 4 pounds   **C** $6\frac{5}{7}$ pounds

B $4\frac{3}{8}$ pounds   **D** $6\frac{7}{8}$ pounds

Standards Quick Check

Write the sum or difference in simplest form.

1. $5\frac{3}{4} + 6\frac{5}{6}$

2. $7\frac{1}{7} - 4\frac{2}{7}$

3. $7\frac{5}{9} + 3\frac{1}{6}$

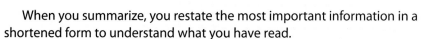

Challenge H.O.T.

Attack the Track

An amusement park in Sandusky, Ohio, offers an amazing 17 roller coaster rides for visitors. Mantis, a 60-mph roller coaster, has entertained more than 13 million riders with 3,900 feet of twisting track since it opened in 1996. Mantis consists of 3 trains with 8 rows per train. Riders don't sit—they stand in rows of 4, for a total of 32 riders per train.

   The operators of Mantis record the number of riders on each train during its run. On the first train, the operators reported that $7\frac{1}{4}$ rows were filled, and on the second train another $5\frac{1}{2}$ rows were filled. On the third train, the operators recorded that $6\frac{1}{2}$ rows were filled. How many more rows were filled in the first train than in the third train?

   When you summarize, you restate the most important information in a shortened form to understand what you have read.

Summary: There are 3 trains with 8 rows per train. Riders stand in rows of 4. A total of $7\frac{1}{4}$ rows were filled on the first train, $5\frac{1}{2}$ rows were filled on the second train, and $6\frac{1}{2}$ rows were filled on the third train.

Summarize the information to solve the problems.

1. Solve the problem above.

2. The park's oldest roller coaster is the Blue Streak. Each of its trains has 4 cars. The train's 24 riders are arranged in 3 rows of 2 riders each. Iron Dragon, another of the park's coasters, has given more than 34 million rides in the past two decades. Each of Iron Dragon's trains has 7 cars, each holding 4 riders. During a count by the operators of both roller coasters, $4\frac{1}{4}$ cars on the train were filled on Iron Dragon and $5\frac{1}{2}$ cars on one train were filled on Blue Streak. How many cars were filled on both the Iron Dragon and Blue Streak trains during the count? Solve the problem.

⭐ **2.2.c.** Estimate and find solutions to single and multi-step problems using whole numbers, decimals, fractions, and percents (e.g., $\frac{7}{8} + \frac{8}{9}$ is about 2, $3.9 + 5.3$ is about 9).

Materials
• MathBoard

Record Subtraction with Renaming

Essential Question How do you subtract mixed numbers with unlike denominators by renaming?

▶ **Learn**

You can use a the LCD to find the difference of two mixed numbers.

Use the LCD.

Find $8\frac{1}{3} - 4\frac{7}{12}$. Estimate. $8\frac{1}{2} - 4\frac{1}{2} = 4$

1 $\quad 8\frac{1}{3} = \quad 8\frac{4}{12}$ $\qquad$ The LCD of $\frac{1}{3}$ and $\frac{7}{12}$

$\quad -4\frac{7}{12} = -4\frac{7}{12}$ $\qquad$ is 12. Write equivalent fractions using the LCD.

- -

2 $\quad 8\frac{1}{3} = \quad 8\frac{4}{12} = \quad 7\frac{16}{12}$ $\qquad$ Since $\frac{7}{12}, \frac{4}{12}$, rename $8\frac{4}{12}$.

$\quad -4\frac{7}{12} = -4\frac{7}{12} = -4\frac{7}{12}$ $\qquad$ $8\frac{4}{12} = 7 + \frac{12}{12} + \frac{4}{12} = 7\frac{16}{12}$.

$\qquad\qquad\qquad\qquad\quad 3\frac{9}{12}$, or $3\frac{3}{4}$ $\qquad$ Subtract and simplify.

So, $8\frac{1}{3} - 4\frac{7}{12} = 3\frac{3}{4}$. The answer is reasonable because it is close to the estimate of 4.

• Is $7\frac{9}{5}$ equivalent to $8\frac{4}{5}$? Explain.

Example

Find $2\frac{1}{2} - 1\frac{5}{6}$.

$\quad 2\frac{1}{2} = \quad 2\frac{3}{6}$

$\quad -1\frac{5}{6} = -1\frac{5}{6}$ $\qquad$ Write an equivalent fraction using the LCD.

$\quad 2\frac{1}{2} = \quad 2\frac{3}{6} = \quad 1\frac{9}{6}$

$\quad -1\frac{5}{6} = -1\frac{5}{6} = -1\frac{5}{6}$ $\qquad$ Since $\frac{5}{6} > \frac{3}{6}$, rename $2\frac{3}{6}$ as $1\frac{9}{6}$.

$\quad 1\frac{9}{6}$

$\quad -1\frac{5}{6}$ $\qquad$ Subtract and simplify.

$\quad\quad \frac{4}{6}$, or $\frac{2}{3}$

So, $2\frac{1}{2} - 1\frac{5}{6} = \frac{4}{6}$, or $\frac{2}{3}$.

Math Idea

Renaming a mixed number decreases the whole-number part by 1 and increases the fraction part by 1.

1. Copy and complete to rename $2\frac{2}{3}$ as $1\frac{5}{3}$. $2\frac{2}{3} = 1 + \blacksquare + \blacksquare = 1\frac{5}{3}$

Estimate. Then write the difference in simplest form.

2. $4\frac{3}{8} - 2\frac{5}{8}$ **3.** $1\frac{3}{4} - \frac{7}{8}$ **4.** $12\frac{1}{9} - 7\frac{1}{3}$ ✓ **5.** $4\frac{1}{2} - 3\frac{4}{5}$ ✓ **6.** $9\frac{1}{6} - 2\frac{3}{4}$

7. **Math Talk** **Explain** how to use renaming to find $3\frac{1}{9} - 2\frac{1}{3}$.

▶ **Practice and Problem Solving** REAL WORLD

Estimate. Then write the difference in simplest form.

8. $2\frac{1}{5} - 1\frac{4}{5}$ **9.** $3\frac{2}{3} - 1\frac{11}{12}$ **10.** $4\frac{1}{4} - 2\frac{1}{3}$ **11.** $11\frac{1}{9} - 3\frac{2}{3}$ **12.** $6 - 3\frac{1}{2}$

13. $4\frac{3}{8} - 3\frac{1}{2}$ **14.** $7\frac{5}{9} - 2\frac{5}{6}$ **15.** $1\frac{1}{5} - \frac{1}{2}$ **16.** $13\frac{1}{6} - 3\frac{4}{5}$ **17.** $7 - 5\frac{2}{3}$

18. What is the difference between $12\frac{2}{5}$ and $5\frac{3}{4}$?   **19.** How much greater is $6\frac{1}{7}$ than $1\frac{11}{14}$?

⭐**Algebra** **Evaluate the expression, in simplest form, for** $c = 2\frac{7}{10}$.

20. $4\frac{3}{5} + c$ **21.** $5\frac{1}{2} - c$ **22.** $4\frac{3}{5} - c$ **23.** $5\frac{1}{2} + c$

📊**Real World Data**

For 24–25 use the table.

24. What is the difference in wall heights at Adventure Land and Rock-a-Wall?

25. Which company's rock wall height is $2\frac{3}{4}$ ft shorter than Rock-a-Wall's?

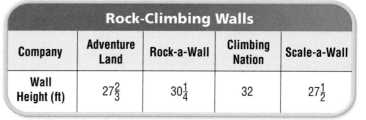

Rock-Climbing Walls				
Company	Adventure Land	Rock-a-Wall	Climbing Nation	Scale-a-Wall
Wall Height (ft)	$27\frac{2}{3}$	$30\frac{1}{4}$	32	$27\frac{1}{2}$

26. **Write Math** ▶ Why do you write equivalent fractions before you rename? Can you rename before you write equivalent fractions? **Explain**.

⭐ **OCCT Test Prep**

27. Which is the difference of $14\frac{2}{5}$ and $8\frac{3}{10}$?

    A $6\frac{1}{10}$ **C** $8\frac{3}{10}$

    B $6\frac{4}{5}$ **D** $22\frac{7}{10}$

28. Tricia works $38\frac{1}{3}$ hr a week. Last week she was sick and was absent $6\frac{3}{4}$ hr. How many hours did she work?

    A $30\frac{3}{4}$ **C** $32\frac{1}{2}$

    B $31\frac{7}{12}$ **D** 46

2.2.c. Estimate and find solutions to single and multi-step problems using whole numbers, decimals, fractions, and percents (e.g., $\frac{7}{8} + \frac{8}{9}$ is about 2, 3.9 + 5.3 is about 9).

Materials
• MathBoard

Problem Solving Workshop
Skill: Multistep Problems

Essential Question What are some useful steps you can use to solve multistep word problems?

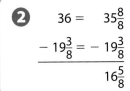 **Use the Skill** REAL WORLD

PROBLEM As part of their study of Native American basket weaving, Lia's class is making wicker baskets. Lia starts with a 36-in. strip of wicker. She cuts an $11\frac{5}{8}$-in. piece and a $7\frac{3}{4}$-in. piece from the strip. Does she have enough wicker left over to cut two $6\frac{1}{2}$-in. pieces?

This problem involves multiple steps. To solve a multistep problem break it down into single steps.

1
$$11\frac{5}{8} = 11\frac{5}{8}$$
$$+ 7\frac{3}{4} = + 7\frac{6}{8}$$
$$\overline{18\frac{11}{8} = 19\frac{3}{8}}$$

Add to find the total amount of wicker pieces that Lia used.

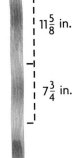

$11\frac{5}{8}$ in.

$7\frac{3}{4}$ in.

2
$$36 = 35\frac{8}{8}$$
$$- 19\frac{3}{8} = - 19\frac{3}{8}$$
$$\overline{16\frac{5}{8}}$$

Subtract to find the amount of the wicker strip that is unused.

3 $6\frac{1}{2} + 6\frac{1}{2} = 13$

Add to find the total length of the needed pieces.

4 $16\frac{5}{8} > 13$

Compare the unused amount of wicker to the total length of the needed pieces.

So, Lia has enough wicker left over to cut two $6\frac{1}{2}$ in. pieces.

a. Could the order of the steps have been different? Explain.

b. Suppose that instead of two $6\frac{1}{2}$-in. pieces, Lia needed three $5\frac{3}{4}$-in. pieces. Would there still be enough wicker left over? Explain.

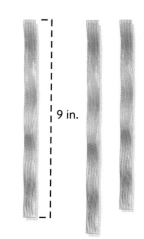

9 in.

1. Jorge made a basket handle using three pieces of wicker. The first piece is 9 in. long and the second piece is $\frac{1}{2}$ in. longer. If the third piece is $\frac{3}{4}$ in. shorter than the second, how much wicker did Jorge use?

Break the problem into single steps.

First, find the length of the second piece of wicker. $9 + \frac{1}{2} = \blacksquare$

Then, find the length of the third piece of wicker.

Finally, find the total length of the 3 pieces of wicker.

2. **What if** the third piece of wicker was $\frac{3}{4}$ in. longer than the second piece? How much wicker would Jorge have used?

3. For a wicker craft project, $\frac{1}{5}$ of the class made baskets and $\frac{2}{3}$ made mats. The rest made bowls. What part of the class made bowls?

4. Mory is buying 6-packs of bottled water for a sporting event. He wants each participant to have 3 bottles. If there are 21 participants, how many 6-packs should Mory buy?

5. Ken chose a number. He multiplied it by 4, added 6, and divided the sum by 2. After he subtracted 4 from the quotient, he got 25. What number did Ken choose?

6. Caitlin has $4\frac{3}{4}$ lb of oven-fire clay. She uses $1\frac{1}{10}$ lb to make a cup, and another 2 lb to make a jar. How many pounds are left?

7. Thelma decides to go to the pet store to buy dog toys and dog food. After spending $\frac{1}{6}$ of her weekly allowance on dog toys and $\frac{1}{3}$ on dog food, she has $9.50 left. What is her weekly allowance?

8. A 50-lb bag of dog food contains meat protein, vitamins, and cereal. In the 50-lb bag, meat protein makes up $19\frac{3}{4}$ lb and vitamins make up $18\frac{7}{8}$ lb. How many pounds of cereal are in the food?

For 9–12, use the circle graph.

9. What fraction of the clients are dogs?

10. What fraction of the clients are short-hair cats?

11. **Reasoning** What fraction of clients are small or miniature dogs? What fraction of clients are long-hair cats? How much greater than the fraction of clients that are long-hair cats is the fraction of clients that are small or miniature dogs?

12. What fraction of the clients are cats?

A-1 Pet Grooming Clients

Large Dogs 90
Long-Hair Cats 55
Short-Hair Cats 80
Miniature Dogs 110
Small Dogs 65

LESSON 6

★ **2.2.c.** Estimate and find solutions to single and multi-step problems using whole numbers, decimals, fractions, and percents (e.g., $\frac{7}{8} + \frac{8}{9}$ is about 2, $3.9 + 5.3$ is about 9).

Materials
• MathBoard

Practice Addition and Subtraction

Essential Question How do you find sums and differences involving fractions and mixed numbers?

PROBLEM The Diaz family spent their vacation cross-country skiing in Medford, Wisconsin. They chose the Beaver Creek Trails, which have a total distance of 4 mi. Yesterday, they skied the $\frac{7}{10}$-mi Tamarack Trail. Today, they skied the $\frac{3}{5}$-mi Pine Trail. If the Diaz family plans to ski all of the Beaver Creek Trails, how many more miles do they have left to ski?

You can subtract the distance they have skied from the total distance.

Find $4 - \left(\frac{7}{10} + \frac{3}{5}\right)$.

Estimate. Both $\frac{7}{10}$ and $\frac{3}{5}$ are close to $\frac{1}{2}$. So, the difference is about $4 - \left(\frac{1}{2} + \frac{1}{2}\right)$, or 3.

Add to find the distance skied so far.

$$\frac{7}{10} = \frac{7}{10}$$

$$+\frac{3}{5} = +\frac{6}{10}$$

$$\frac{13}{10}, \text{ or } 1\frac{3}{10}$$

Write equivalent fractions, using the LCD, 10.

Add.

Rename the fraction as a mixed number in simplest form.

Subtract to find the distance left to ski.

$$4 = 3\frac{10}{10}$$

$$-1\frac{3}{10} = -1\frac{3}{10}$$

$$2\frac{7}{10}$$

Since you are subtracting tenths, rename 4 as $3\frac{10}{10}$.

Subtract fractions. Subtract whole numbers.

The answer is reasonable because it is close to the estimate of 3.

So, the Diaz family members have $2\frac{7}{10}$ mi left to ski.

• **What if** Tamarack Trail was $1\frac{3}{10}$ mi long? How would you expect this to change the answer?

Examples

What is the difference in the average annual snowfall amounts for Fort Wayne and South Bend?

Subtract. $70\frac{3}{10} - 32\frac{2}{5}$ Estimate. $70 - 32\frac{1}{2} = 37\frac{1}{2}$

$$
\begin{array}{r}
70\frac{3}{10} = \quad 70\frac{3}{10} \\
- 32\frac{2}{5} \quad -32\frac{4}{10} \\
\hline
\end{array}
$$

The LCD of $\frac{8}{10}$ and $\frac{2}{5}$ is 10.

Write equivalent fractions, using the LCD, 10.

$$
\begin{array}{r}
70\frac{3}{10} = \quad 70\frac{3}{10} = \quad 69\frac{13}{10} \\
- 32\frac{2}{5} = -32\frac{4}{10} = -32\frac{4}{10} \\
\hline
37\frac{9}{10}
\end{array}
$$

Since $\frac{4}{10} > \frac{3}{10}$, rename $70\frac{3}{10}$.

$70\frac{3}{10} = 69 + \frac{10}{10} + \frac{3}{10} = 69\frac{13}{10}$.

Subtract the fractions. Subtract the whole numbers.

Snowfall Amounts	
Location	**Snow (in.)**
Fort Wayne, IN	$32\frac{2}{5}$
Indianapolis, IN	$23\frac{3}{5}$
Evansville, IN	$14\frac{1}{10}$
South Bend, IN	$70\frac{3}{10}$

So, the difference in the snowfall amounts is $37\frac{9}{10}$ in.

Find $6\frac{1}{2} + 11\frac{7}{16} + 4\frac{7}{8}$.

$$
\begin{array}{r}
6\frac{1}{2} = \quad 6\frac{8}{16} \\
11\frac{7}{16} = \quad 11\frac{7}{16} \\
+ 4\frac{7}{8} = + 4\frac{14}{16} \\
\hline
21\frac{29}{16} = 22\frac{13}{16}
\end{array}
$$

Write equivalent fractions, using the LCD, 16.

Add. Rename $21\frac{29}{16}$ as $22\frac{13}{16}$.

So, $6\frac{1}{2} + 11\frac{7}{16} + 4\frac{7}{8} = 22\frac{13}{16}$.

Find $12\frac{1}{5} - 7\frac{1}{7}$.

$$
\begin{array}{r}
12\frac{1}{5} = \quad 12\frac{7}{35} \\
- 7\frac{1}{7} = - 7\frac{5}{35} \\
\hline
5\frac{2}{35}
\end{array}
$$

Write equivalent fractions, using the LCD, 35.

Subtract.

So, $12\frac{1}{5} - 7\frac{1}{7} = 5\frac{2}{35}$.

Share and Show

Copy and complete the problem. Then find the sum or difference in simplest form.

1. $6\frac{1}{21} = \blacksquare\frac{22}{21}$
$- \frac{1}{3} = -\frac{7}{\blacksquare}$

2. $8\frac{5}{8} = \quad 8\frac{5}{8}$
$+ 5\frac{3}{4} = + 5\frac{\blacksquare}{8}$

3. $10\frac{2}{3} = \blacksquare\frac{4}{6} = \blacksquare\frac{10}{6}$
$- 4\frac{5}{6} = -4\frac{5}{6} = -4\frac{5}{6}$

4. $6 = 5\frac{\blacksquare}{5}$
$- 3\frac{4}{5} = - 3\frac{4}{5}$

Estimate. Then write the sum or difference in simplest form.

5. $\frac{3}{16}$
$+ \frac{5}{8}$

6. $\frac{3}{4}$
$+ \frac{2}{3}$

7. $\frac{4}{5}$
$- \frac{3}{20}$

✅**8.** $\frac{7}{8}$
$- \frac{1}{6}$

9. $3 - (2\frac{1}{6} + \frac{1}{3})$

10. $10\frac{5}{18} + 8\frac{5}{6}$

11. $5\frac{1}{12} - \frac{1}{4}$

✅**12.** $3 - 2\frac{1}{6}$

13. **Math Talk** **Explain** how you know whether renaming is needed to subtract a fraction or mixed number.

Estimate. Then write the sum or difference in simplest form.

14. $\frac{3}{10}$
$+\frac{1}{5}$

15. $\frac{9}{16}$
$-\frac{1}{4}$

16. $\frac{1}{2}$
$+\frac{1}{7}$

17. $\frac{7}{9}$
$-\frac{2}{3}$

18. $4\frac{1}{4}$
$+2\frac{5}{6}$

19. 3
$-1\frac{3}{4}$

20. $6\frac{2}{5}$
$+9\frac{7}{10}$

21. $8\frac{2}{3}$
$-3\frac{4}{5}$

22. $4\frac{3}{4}+2\frac{7}{20}$

23. $2\frac{1}{6}+1\frac{1}{2}$

24. $2\frac{1}{5}-1\frac{1}{20}$

25. $2\frac{3}{5}+5\frac{3}{8}$

26. $8-\left(1\frac{1}{4}+\frac{5}{6}\right)$

27. $7-2\frac{3}{5}$

28. $\frac{3}{5}+\frac{1}{3}+\frac{4}{15}$

29. $6\frac{1}{3}+2\frac{1}{2}+\frac{1}{4}$

30. What number is $\frac{5}{7}$ less than $3\frac{1}{2}$?

31. How much greater than $2\frac{1}{2}$ is $3\frac{5}{12}$?

**Algebra** **Find a possible rule for each pattern. Use the rule to write the next two numbers in the pattern.**

32. $9, 7\frac{3}{4}, 6\frac{1}{2}, 5\frac{1}{4}$, ■, ■

33. $5\frac{3}{8}, 6\frac{3}{4}, 8\frac{1}{8}, 9\frac{1}{2}$, ■, ■

34. $8\frac{1}{6}, 8\frac{11}{12}, 9\frac{2}{3}, 10\frac{5}{12}$, ■, ■

Solve. Then explain how you solved the problem.

35. Danielle spends $3\frac{1}{3}$ hr skiing downhill on Saturday and $4\frac{3}{5}$ hr skiing cross-country on Sunday. How many hours did she spend skiing on the two days?

36. Liam skied $4\frac{1}{3}$ mi on a cross-country trail that ends at a ski lodge. After he skied the first $2\frac{7}{8}$ mi, he passed a farm. How far from the lodge is the farm?

Real World Data

For 37–38, use the table.

37. Mr. Diaz skied two trails. He skied a total of $\frac{9}{10}$ mi. Which two trails did he ski?

38. **Write Math** **What's the Question?** The answer is that Aspen Trail is longer by $\frac{1}{4}$ mi.

 OCCT Test Prep [Math Board]

39. Ben ran $6\frac{3}{4}$ mi on Monday and $3\frac{1}{2}$ mi on Friday. How many total miles did he run?

    A 12 mi   **C** $9\frac{1}{2}$ mi

    B $10\frac{1}{4}$ mi   **D** 8 mi

40. What is the value of n?

$$9\frac{4}{7}=8\frac{n}{7}$$

    A $n=4$ **C** $n=10$

    B $n=9$ **D** $n=11$

⭐ Standards Quick Check

Write the sum or difference in simplest form.

1. $\dfrac{6}{7}$

    $-\dfrac{1}{4}$

2. $10\dfrac{2}{9}$

    $+ 4\dfrac{2}{3}$

3. $7\dfrac{5}{9}$

    $+ 3\dfrac{1}{6}$

4. $5 + 2\dfrac{1}{2}$

5. $2\dfrac{2}{3} + 4\dfrac{3}{8} + \dfrac{1}{2}$

6. $7\dfrac{4}{12} - 6\dfrac{1}{3}$

7. $8\dfrac{4}{9} - 5\dfrac{2}{3}$

8. $7 - 3\dfrac{3}{10}$

9. $12\dfrac{3}{4} - 9\dfrac{1}{6}$

Challenge H.O.T.

Ancient Romans wrote fractions in words rather than by using numerals. For example, the fraction two sevenths would have been represented as *duae septimae*.

However, when ancient Romans needed to do calculations with fractions, they would use the *uncia*, which represented $\dfrac{1}{12}$ of anything. The table shows the ancient Roman representations for some common fractions.

Use the table of Roman names of fractions to solve.

1. Antavius plowed a *triens* of his field in the morning and another *quadrans* of the field in the afternoon. How many *uncia* does he have left to plow?

2. Lucia spilled an *uncia* of the water in the pitcher carrying it from the well. She used a *quadrans* the pitcher to make soup. How many *uncia* the pitcher did Lucia have left?

Fraction	Roman Name
$\dfrac{1}{12}$	uncia
$\dfrac{1}{6}$	sextans
$\dfrac{1}{4}$	quadrans
$\dfrac{1}{3}$	triens
$\dfrac{1}{2}$	semis

Minerva, goddess of ▶ wisdom

LESSON 7

★ **2.2.c.** Estimate and find solutions to single and multi-step problems using whole numbers, decimals, fractions, and percents (e.g., $\frac{7}{8} + \frac{8}{9}$ is about 2, $3.9 + 5.3$ is about 9). *also* **2.2.a.**

Materials
• MathBoard

Estimate Products and Quotients

Essential Question What three methods of estimation are effective when multiplying and dividing fractions and mixed numbers?

PROBLEM Diana wants to put a wallpaper border around her room. She has $2\frac{1}{3}$ rolls of wallpaper border. If each roll is $4\frac{3}{5}$ m long, about how many meters of wallpaper border does she have?

Estimate by rounding.

$2\frac{1}{3} \times 4\frac{3}{5}$ **Think:** $\frac{1}{3}$ rounds to 0, and $\frac{3}{5}$ rounds to 1.

$\downarrow$ $\downarrow$

$2 \times 5 = 10$ Multiply.

So, Diana has about 10 m of wallpaper border.

You can estimate by averaging two estimates.

Estimate by averaging.

Estimate. $20 \div \frac{3}{4}$.

$20 \div \frac{3}{4} \rightarrow 20 \div \frac{1}{2}$ Round the fraction down.

$20 \div \frac{1}{2} = 40$ **Think:** How many $\frac{1}{2}$s are in 20? This is an overestimate.

$20 \div \frac{3}{4} \rightarrow 20 \div 1$ Round the fraction up.

$20 \div 1 = 20$ This is an underestimate. Find the average.

$40 + 20 = 60$ $60 \div 2 = 30$

So, $20 \div \frac{3}{4}$ is about 30.

You can use rounding and compatible numbers to estimate products and quotients.

Use rounding to estimate.

$14 \times \frac{3}{8}$

$14 \times \frac{3}{8}$ $\frac{3}{8}$ rounds to $\frac{1}{2}$.

$14 \times \frac{1}{2} = 7$ **Think:** What is $\frac{1}{2}$ of 14?

So, $14 \div \frac{3}{8}$ is about 7.

Use compatible numbers to estimate.

$14\frac{3}{4} \div 3\frac{9}{10}$

$14\frac{3}{4} \div 3\frac{9}{10}$ Round to the nearest compatible whole numbers.

$\downarrow$ $\downarrow$

$16 \div 4 = 4$ Divide.

So, $14\frac{3}{4} \div 3\frac{9}{10}$ is about 4.

---

1. Estimate by using compatible numbers. $23\frac{4}{5} \div 6\frac{1}{4}$ → $24 \div 6 = $ ■

Estimate the product or quotient.

2. $\frac{7}{8} \times \frac{4}{5}$ 3. $12 \div 3\frac{3}{4}$ 4. $18 \times 1\frac{7}{12}$ ✓5. $13\frac{7}{8} \div 2\frac{1}{3}$ ✓6. $29\frac{7}{9} \times \frac{3}{8}$

7. **Math Talk** **Explain** why you might use compatible numbers to estimate $35\frac{1}{2} \div 6\frac{5}{6}$

▶ **Practice and Problem Solving** REAL WORLD

Estimate the product or quotient.

8. $\frac{13}{16} \div \frac{9}{10}$ 9. $6 \times 2\frac{9}{10}$ 10. $2\frac{1}{3} \times \frac{3}{4}$ 11. $51\frac{5}{6} \div \frac{1}{2}$ 12. $8\frac{1}{5} \times 2\frac{9}{10}$

13. $35\frac{5}{8} \times 1\frac{5}{6}$ 14. $44\frac{1}{4} \div 1\frac{7}{9}$ 15. $46 \times \frac{7}{12}$ 16. $36\frac{2}{9} \div 2\frac{4}{5}$ 17. $71\frac{11}{12} \div 8\frac{3}{4}$

Estimate to compare. Write < or > for each ⬭.

18. $2\frac{1}{4} \times 5\frac{1}{3}$ ⬭ $7\frac{4}{5} \times 1\frac{7}{8}$ 19. $21\frac{3}{10} \div 2\frac{5}{6}$ ⬭ $35\frac{7}{9} \div 3\frac{2}{3}$ 20. $3\frac{2}{7} \times 3\frac{7}{10}$ ⬭ $24\frac{2}{5} \div 2\frac{8}{9}$

21. $29\frac{4}{5} \div 5\frac{1}{6}$ ⬭ $27\frac{8}{9} \div 6\frac{5}{8}$ 22. $15\frac{5}{12} \times 3\frac{3}{4}$ ⬭ $8\frac{9}{10} \times 6\frac{7}{8}$ 23. $55\frac{5}{6} \div 6\frac{7}{10}$ ⬭ $11\frac{5}{7} \times \frac{5}{8}$

24. Estimate the product $1\frac{5}{12} \times 18$ in two ways. Which estimate is closer to the actual product? **Explain**.

📊 Real World Data

For 25–27, use the table.

25. About how many pieces of red fabric will Shane get if he divides all the red fabric into $1\frac{7}{8}$-yd lengths?

26. Lisa needs $6\frac{3}{4}$ times the amount of purple fabric available and 3 times the amount of green fabric available. About how many yards does Lisa need?

27. **Write Math** ▶ Elaine divides the orange fabric into $3\frac{1}{2}$-yd pieces. She estimates that she will have 7 pieces. Is this an overestimate or an underestimate? **Explain**.

Fabric Sale					
	Green	Red	Blue	Purple	Orange
Yards Available	$4\frac{1}{3}$	$19\frac{1}{2}$	$13\frac{2}{3}$	$5\frac{1}{3}$	21

★ **OCCT Test Prep**

28. Which is the most reasonable estimate for $\frac{47}{8} \div \frac{9}{10}$?

    A 3   **B** 6   **C** 9   **D** 12

29. Which is the most reasonable estimate for $7\frac{6}{8} \times 6\frac{1}{9}$?

    A 14   **B** 15   **C** 48   **D** 70

 2.2.a. Multiply and divide fractions and mixed numbers to solve problems using a variety of methods. *also* **2.2.c.**

Materials
- MathBoard
- colored pencils
- paper

Multiply Fractions

Essential Question When a model is used to multiply fractions, what is represented by the sections of the model that are shaded twice?

You can use a model to find a fractional part of a fraction.

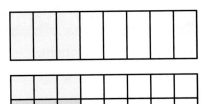

Use a model.

Find $\frac{1}{2}$ of $\frac{3}{8}$, or $\frac{1}{2} \times \frac{3}{8}$.

- Fold a sheet of paper into 8 equal parts. Shade 3 parts to show $\frac{3}{8}$.

- Divide the rectangle in half to show $\frac{1}{2}$ of $\frac{3}{8}$. Shade $\frac{1}{2}$ of the shaded parts.

Of the $2 \times 8 = 16$ parts, $1 \times 3 = 3$ are shaded twice, so $\frac{3}{16}$ of the paper is shaded twice. These parts represent $\frac{1}{2} \times \frac{3}{8}$.

So, $\frac{1}{2} \times \frac{3}{8} = \frac{3}{16}$.

Look at the two factors and the product above. Compare the numerator and the denominator of the product with the numerators and denominators of the factors.

You can use this relationship to multiply fractions without using a model.

$$\frac{\text{numerator} \times \text{numerator}}{\text{denominator} \times \text{denominator}} = \frac{\text{numerator}}{\text{denominator}}$$

$$\uparrow \qquad\qquad \uparrow \qquad\qquad\qquad \uparrow$$
$$\text{factor} \qquad \text{factor} \qquad\qquad \text{product}$$

Example

New York City's Central Park offers a rock-climbing class for children ages 8–17. In one session, $\frac{4}{5}$ of the students are 12 years old. Of the 12-year-old students, $\frac{1}{4}$ are from Brooklyn. What fraction of the students are 12 years old and from Brooklyn?

Find $\frac{1}{4} \times \frac{4}{5}$.

$\frac{1}{4} \times \frac{4}{5} = \frac{1 \times 4}{4 \times 5} = \frac{4}{20}$ Multiply the numerators. Multiply the denominators.

$= \frac{4 \div 4}{20 \div 4} = \frac{1}{5}$ Write the product in simplest form. Divide the numerator and the denominator by the common factor, 4.

So, $\frac{1}{5}$ of the students are 12 years old and from Brooklyn.

Simplify Before Multiplying

When a numerator and a denominator have a common factor, you can simplify before you multiply.

Simplifying before mulitplying.

Find $40 \times \frac{5}{12}$ in simplest form.   Estimate. $40 \times \frac{1}{2} = 20$

$$40 \times \frac{5}{12} = \frac{40}{1} \times \frac{5}{12}$$

Write the whole number as a fraction.

$$= \frac{\overset{20}{\cancel{40}}}{1} \times \frac{5}{\underset{6}{\cancel{12}}}$$

Divide the numerator and denominator by a common factor, 2.
$40 \div 2 = 20$ and $12 \div 2 = 6$.

$$= \frac{20 \times 5}{1 \times 6} = \frac{100}{6}$$

Multiply.

$$= \frac{100}{6} = \frac{50}{3}, \text{ or } 16\frac{2}{3}$$

Write the product as a fraction or a mixed number in simplest form.

The answer is reasonable since $16\frac{2}{3}$ is close to the estimate of 20.
So, $40 \times \frac{5}{12} = 16\frac{2}{3}$.

- **What if** you divided by the GCF in example above? How would that affect your answer?

- Explain how to simplify before multiplying to find $\frac{3}{8} \times \frac{4}{21}$.

Share and Show

1. Use the model to find $\frac{2}{3} \times \frac{3}{4}$.

2. Find $6 \times \frac{3}{8}$.

$$\frac{\overset{3}{\cancel{6}}}{1} \times \frac{3}{\underset{4}{\cancel{8}}} = \frac{\blacksquare}{\blacksquare}, \text{ or } \blacksquare \frac{\blacksquare}{\blacksquare}$$

Use a model to find the product.

3. $\frac{3}{4} \times \frac{1}{4}$ 4. $\frac{1}{3} \times \frac{5}{6}$ 5. $\frac{1}{6} \times \frac{3}{4}$ 6. $\frac{1}{2} \times \frac{3}{5}$ ✓7. $\frac{1}{2} \times \frac{7}{8}$

Find the product. Write it in simplest form.

8. $\frac{3}{8} \times \frac{8}{9}$ 9. $\frac{3}{5} \times \frac{1}{5} \times \frac{1}{3}$ 10. $24 \times \frac{7}{12}$ 11. $\frac{4}{5} \times 9$ ✓12. $\frac{2}{3} \times 27$

13. **Math Talk** **Explain** how to make a model to show $\frac{1}{3} \times \frac{2}{3}$.

Use a model to find the product.

14. $\frac{1}{2} \times \frac{3}{5}$ **15.** $\frac{2}{3} \times \frac{4}{5}$ **16.** $\frac{1}{3} \times \frac{5}{8}$ **17.** $4 \times \frac{1}{5}$ **18.** $\frac{2}{3} \times \frac{3}{8}$

Find the product. Write it in simplest form.

19. $\frac{5}{9} \times \frac{3}{7}$ **20.** $2 \times \frac{1}{8}$ **21.** $\frac{4}{9} \times \frac{4}{5}$ **22.** $\frac{1}{6} \times \frac{2}{3}$ **23.** $\frac{1}{7} \times 30$

24. $\frac{8}{9} \times \frac{2}{3}$ **25.** $\frac{4}{5} \times \frac{5}{6}$ **26.** $5 \times \frac{1}{4}$ **27.** $\frac{1}{12} \times 36$ **28.** $\frac{5}{6} \times \frac{1}{5} \times \frac{2}{5}$

29. $\frac{2}{3} \times 8$ **30.** $\frac{2}{5} \times \frac{4}{7}$ **31.** $\frac{7}{8} \times \frac{4}{21}$ **32.** $\frac{2}{3} \times 5 \times \frac{1}{8}$ **33.** $\frac{1}{2} \times \frac{2}{3} \times \frac{6}{7}$

Compare. Write $<$, $>$, or $=$ for ⬤.

34. $\frac{5}{6} \times 5$ ⬤ 5 **35.** $\frac{1}{6} \times 12$ ⬤ $\frac{1}{3} \times 3$ **36.** $\frac{4}{7} \times \frac{1}{2}$ ⬤ $\frac{1}{7} \times 2$

37. $\frac{5}{8} \times 16$ ⬤ $\frac{3}{4} \times 12$ **38.** $\frac{5}{6} \times \frac{3}{10}$ ⬤ $\frac{2}{5} \times \frac{5}{8}$ **39.** $\frac{1}{4} \times \frac{1}{2}$ ⬤ $\frac{1}{3} \times \frac{1}{2}$

40. On her first try, Danielle climbs $\frac{2}{3}$ of a rock wall's height. Lisa climbs $\frac{3}{4}$ of Danielle's distance. What fraction of the total height does Lisa climb?

41. A group of students comes to the recreation center twice a week. Half of the students live in Brooklyn. Half of the students from Brooklyn are girls, and half of the girls are 11 years old. What fraction of the group are girls who are 11 years old and live in Brooklyn?

42. Pose a Problem Look back at Problem 41. Write a similar problem by changing the fractions and the characteristics of each group, such as age, gender, and home location.

43. Write Math ► Suppose you multiply two fractions less than 1. Is the product greater than or less than the fractions you multiplied? **Explain** by using an example.

★ **OCCT Test Prep** Math Board

44. Which is $\frac{3}{4} \times \frac{8}{9}$?

   A $\frac{4}{9}$ **C** 2

   B $\frac{2}{3}$ **D** 8

45. Destiny finished $\frac{2}{3}$ of a 45-min exercise session. Which is the amount of time she exercised?

   A 15 min   **C** 45 min

   B 30 min   **D** 60 min

GO ONLINE — **Technology** — Use HMH Mega Math, Fraction Action, *Fraction Flare-Up*, Level O.

⭐ Standards Quick Check

Find the product. Write it in simplest form.

1. $\frac{3}{5} \times \frac{3}{4}$

2. $\frac{1}{2} \times \frac{5}{6}$

3. $\frac{1}{3} \times \frac{2}{7}$

4. $\frac{8}{11} \times \frac{11}{20}$

5. $\frac{4}{9} \times \frac{15}{22}$

6. $\frac{7}{16} \times \frac{6}{7}$

7. $\frac{3}{5} \times \frac{3}{8}$

8. $\frac{3}{7} \times \frac{5}{6}$

9. $\frac{4}{9} \times \frac{3}{16}$

Challenge H.O.T.

Changing Recipes

You can make a lot of recipes more healthful by reducing the amounts of fat, sugar, and salt.

Babs has a recipe for muffins that calls for $1\frac{1}{2}$ c of sugar. She wants to use $\frac{1}{2}$ that amount of sugar and use more cinnamon and vanilla. How much sugar will she use?

Multiply $\frac{1}{2}$ and $1\frac{1}{2}$ to find what part of the original amount of sugar to use.

$\frac{1}{2} \times 1\frac{1}{2} = \frac{1}{2} \times \frac{3}{2}$ Write the mixed number as a fraction.

$= \frac{3}{4}$ Multiply.

So, Babs will use $\frac{3}{4}$ c of sugar.

1. Michelle has a recipe that calls for $2\frac{1}{2}$ c of vegetable oil. She wants to use $\frac{2}{3}$ that amount of oil and use applesauce to replace the rest. How much vegetable oil will she use?

2. Tony's recipe for soup calls for $1\frac{1}{4}$ tsp of salt. He wants to use $\frac{1}{2}$ that amount. How many teaspoons of salt will he use?

LESSON 9

★ **2.2.a.** Multiply and divide fractions and mixed numbers to solve problems using a variety of methods. *also* **2.2.c.**

Materials
• MathBoard

Multiply Mixed Numbers

Essential Question What are three steps to remember when multiplying mixed numbers?

PROBLEM A masked lovebird is a small parrot. The male of one pair weighs about $1\frac{3}{4}$ oz. The female can weigh $1\frac{1}{5}$ times as much as a male. About how many ounces can a female masked lovebird weigh?

To multiply mixed numbers, rewrite each mixed number as a fraction.

Multiply mixed numbers.

Find $1\frac{3}{4} \times 1\frac{1}{5}$. Estimate. $2 \times 1 = 2$

$1\frac{3}{4} \times 1\frac{1}{5} = \frac{7}{4} \times \frac{6}{5}$ Write the mixed numbers as fractions.

$= \frac{7}{\overset{}{\underset{2}{4}}} \times \frac{\overset{3}{6}}{5}$ Simplify the fractions. Multiply.

$= \frac{21}{10}$, or $2\frac{1}{10}$ Write the answer as a fraction or mixed number in simplest form.

The answer is reasonable, since it is close to the estimate, 2.
So, the female masked lovebird weighs about $2\frac{1}{10}$ oz.

Examples

Find the product. Write it in simplest form.

$12 \times 2\frac{1}{6}$ Estimate. $12 \times 2 = 24$

$12 \times 2\frac{1}{6} = \frac{12}{1} \times \frac{13}{6}$ Write the whole number and mixed number as fractions.

$= \frac{\overset{2}{12}}{1} \times \frac{13}{\overset{}{\underset{6}{6}}}$ Simplify the fractions. Multiply.

$= \frac{26}{1}$, or 26 Write the product as a whole number.

The answer is reasonable, since it is close to the estimate of 24. So, $12 \times 2\frac{1}{6} = 26$.

You can use partial products to multiply mixed numbers.

$16 \times 4\frac{1}{8}$ Estimate. $16 \times 4 = 64$

$16 \times 4\frac{1}{8} = 16 \times (4 + \frac{1}{8})$ Write the expression by using the Distributive Property.

$= (16 \times 4) + (16 \times \frac{1}{8})$ Multiply 16 by each number.

$= 64 + 2 = 66$ Add.

---

1. Copy and complete to find $2\frac{3}{8} \times 1\frac{2}{7}$.

$$2\frac{3}{8} \times 1\frac{2}{7} = \frac{19}{8} \times \frac{9}{7} = \frac{\blacksquare}{\blacksquare} = \blacksquare \frac{\blacksquare}{\blacksquare}$$

Find the product. Write it in simplest form.

2. $1\frac{1}{8} \times 2\frac{1}{3}$ **3.** $16 \times 2\frac{1}{2}$ **4.** $\frac{3}{4} \times 6\frac{5}{6}$ ✓**5.** $1\frac{2}{7} \times 1\frac{3}{4}$ ✓**6.** $8\frac{1}{3} \times \frac{3}{5}$

7. $\frac{3}{4} \times 1\frac{2}{3}$ **8.** $5\frac{1}{3} \times \frac{3}{4}$ **9.** $2\frac{1}{2} \times 1\frac{1}{5}$ **10.** $1\frac{2}{3} \times 4\frac{1}{2}$ **11.** $1\frac{1}{14} \times 9\frac{1}{3}$

12. **Math Talk** **Explain** how multiplying a mixed number by a whole number is similar to multiplying two mixed numbers.

▶ **Practice and Problem Solving** **REAL WORLD**

Find the product. Write it in simplest form.

13. $4\frac{2}{5} \times 1\frac{1}{2}$ **14.** $12\frac{3}{4} \times 2\frac{2}{3}$ **15.** $2\frac{3}{5} \times 10$ **16.** $3\frac{7}{12} \times 1\frac{4}{5}$ **17.** $3\frac{1}{5} \times 1\frac{5}{6} \times \frac{3}{10}$

18. $3 \times 4\frac{1}{2}$ **19.** $2\frac{3}{8} \times \frac{4}{9}$ **20.** $\frac{1}{3} \times 1\frac{3}{7} \times 1\frac{2}{5}$ **21.** $7\frac{1}{5} \times 2\frac{1}{6}$ **22.** $1\frac{1}{3} \times 1\frac{1}{4} \times 1\frac{1}{5}$

23. $\frac{2}{3} \times 4\frac{1}{5}$ **24.** $5\frac{1}{2} \times 3\frac{1}{3}$ **25.** $1\frac{4}{5} \times \frac{2}{3} \times 1\frac{2}{3}$ **26.** $\frac{1}{15} \times 1\frac{1}{2} \times 7\frac{1}{2}$ **27.** $5\frac{1}{3} \times 3 \times 1\frac{1}{2}$

⭐**Algebra** **Find the value of a.**

28. $a \times 1\frac{3}{8} = 11$ **29.** $1\frac{4}{5} \times \frac{1}{a} = \frac{1}{5}$ **30.** $3\frac{1}{3} \times 1\frac{a}{5} = \frac{10}{3} \times \frac{6}{5} = 4$ **31.** $2\frac{1}{2} \times 3\frac{a}{3} = 8\frac{1}{3}$

32. **≡FAST FACT** In February 2006, a North Island Brown Kiwi, native to New Zealand, hatched at the National Zoo in Washington, D.C. The baby bird weighed $9\frac{3}{4}$ oz. An adult kiwi weighed $8\frac{1}{4}$ times as much as the baby. How many ounces did the adult kiwi weigh?

33. **Reasoning** Use each of the following numbers once to form two multiplication number sentences: $\frac{1}{4}$, $\frac{3}{4}$, $\frac{7}{8}$, $1\frac{7}{8}$, $2\frac{1}{2}$, $3\frac{1}{2}$.

34. **Write Math** **What's the Question?** A bald eagle weighs about $9\frac{9}{10}$ lb. A pigeon's weight is $\frac{1}{9}$ that amount. The answer is $1\frac{1}{10}$ lb.

⭐ **OCCT Test Prep**

35. Maria bought $1\frac{1}{5}$ pound of cherries. Daniel bought $5\frac{3}{4}$ times as many pounds as Maria. How many pounds of cherries did Daniel buy?

   A $\frac{3}{9}$ **C** $6\frac{4}{7}$

   B $5\frac{1}{8}$ **D** $6\frac{9}{10}$

36. A small parakeet weighs $2\frac{2}{5}$ oz. A large parakeet weighs $3\frac{1}{2}$ times as much as the small parakeet. How much does the large parakeet weigh?

   A $5\frac{2}{5}$ **C** $8\frac{2}{5}$

   B $7\frac{4}{9}$ **D** $9\frac{5}{8}$

LESSON 10

2.2.a. Multiply and divide fractions and mixed numbers to solve problems using a variety of methods. *also* **2.2.c.**

Vocabulary

reciprocals

Materials
• MathBoard

Explore Division of Fractions

Essential Question What is another name for the reciprocal?
What is the product of a number and its reciprocal?

▶ **Learn**

Using models will help you understand division of fractions.
You can use fraction circles to find $3 \div \frac{1}{4}$.

 HANDS ON

Draw models.

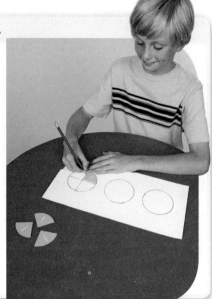

- Trace 3 whole circles on your paper.

- Model $3 \div \frac{1}{4}$ by tracing $\frac{1}{4}$-circle pieces on the 3 circles. One whole equals 4 fourths.

- How many fourths are in 3 wholes? What is $3 \div \frac{1}{4}$?

- Use fraction circles to model $5 \div \frac{1}{3}$, or the number of thirds in 5. Draw a diagram of your model.

HANDS ON

Use models.

Use fraction circles to find $\frac{2}{3} \div \frac{1}{6}$, or the number of sixths in $\frac{2}{3}$.

- Model $\frac{2}{3}$ by using $\frac{1}{3}$-circle pieces.

- Place as many $\frac{1}{6}$-circle pieces as you can on the pieces representing $\frac{2}{3}$.

- How many sixths are in $\frac{2}{3}$? What is $\frac{2}{3} \div \frac{1}{6}$?

- Use fraction circles to model $\frac{3}{4} \div \frac{1}{8}$, or the number of eighths in $\frac{3}{4}$. Draw a diagram of your model.

148

Reciprocals

Two numbers whose product is 1 are **reciprocals**. The reciprocal of a number is sometimes called the multiplicative inverse. You can use reciprocals and inverse operations to write related number sentences.

reciprocals	reciprocals	reciprocals
$\downarrow \quad \downarrow$	$\downarrow \quad \downarrow$	$\downarrow$
$\frac{1}{5} \times 5 = 1$	$4 \times \frac{1}{4} = 1$	$\frac{2}{3} \times \frac{3}{2} = 1$
$1 \div \frac{1}{5} = 5$	$1 \div \frac{1}{4} = 4$	$1 \div \frac{2}{3} = \frac{3}{2}$
$1 \div 5 = \frac{1}{5}$	$1 \div 4 = \frac{1}{4}$	$1 \div \frac{3}{2} = \frac{2}{3}$

Use reciprocals when dividing.

Find $6 \div \frac{1}{3}$.

$1 \div \frac{1}{3} = 3$ **Think** of the reciprocal of $\frac{1}{3}$.

Since $1 \div \frac{1}{3} = 1 \times 3$, $6 \div \frac{1}{3} = 6 \times 3$.

So, $6 \div \frac{1}{3} = 6 \times 3 = 18$. There are 18 thirds in 6 wholes.

- Explain why 1 divided by a fraction between 0 and 1 always has a quotient greater than 1.

Sometimes you can use mental math to divide whole numbers and fractions.

Use mental math when dividing.

$5 \div \frac{1}{6}$

Think $5 \times 6 = 30$

Dividing by $\frac{1}{6}$ is the same as multiplying by 6. There are 30 sixths in 5.

So, $5 \div \frac{1}{6} = 30$.

 **Share and Show**

1. Use the model to find $3 \div \frac{1}{2}$.

2. Complete: If $1 \div \frac{3}{5} = 1 \times \frac{5}{3}$, then $4 \div \frac{3}{5} = 4 \times \blacksquare$.

Write the reciprocal of the number.

3. $\frac{1}{10}$ **4.** 8   **5.** $\frac{4}{9}$ **6.** $\frac{5}{2}$ **7.** $\frac{3}{4}$ ✓**8.** $\frac{1}{7}$

Find the quotient. Write it in simplest form.

9. $\frac{7}{3} \div \frac{1}{3}$ **10.** $\frac{3}{8} \div \frac{3}{5}$ **11.** $9 \div \frac{3}{5}$ **12.** $3 \div \frac{2}{3}$ **13.** $\frac{5}{6} \div \frac{1}{4}$ ✓**14.** $\frac{4}{5} \div \frac{1}{4}$

15. **Math Talk** **Explain** how to use reciprocals and inverse operations to find $\frac{11}{12} \div \frac{1}{4}$.

Write the reciprocal of the number.

16. $\frac{1}{9}$ **17.** 4   **18.** $\frac{5}{8}$ **19.** $\frac{8}{3}$ **20.** 2   **21.** $\frac{3}{7}$

22. $\frac{1}{12}$ **23.** 6   **24.** $\frac{11}{12}$ **25.** $\frac{14}{9}$ **26.** 1   **27.** $\frac{4}{15}$

Find the quotient. Write it in simplest form.

28. $2 \div \frac{1}{8}$ **29.** $\frac{3}{4} \div \frac{3}{5}$ **30.** $\frac{10}{9} \div \frac{1}{3}$ **31.** $7 \div \frac{1}{5}$ **32.** $\frac{5}{6} \div \frac{2}{3}$ **33.** $\frac{7}{10} \div \frac{7}{10}$

34. $\frac{4}{5} \div \frac{2}{3}$ **35.** $4 \div \frac{1}{7}$ **36.** $\frac{5}{8} \div \frac{5}{7}$ **37.** $\frac{14}{15} \div \frac{14}{15}$ **38.** $1 \div \frac{6}{11}$ **39.** $\frac{13}{16} \div \frac{3}{8}$

 Algebra **Use mental math to find each quotient.**

40. $7 \div \frac{1}{2}$ **41.** $5 \div \frac{1}{9}$ **42.** $10 \div \frac{1}{5}$ **43.** $9 \div \frac{1}{10}$ **44.** $8 \div \frac{1}{4}$ **45.** $40 \div \frac{1}{7}$

46. $7 \div \frac{1}{3}$ **47.** $9 \div \frac{1}{8}$ **48.** $8 \div \frac{1}{11}$ **49.** $1 \div \frac{1}{6}$ **50.** $4 \div \frac{1}{15}$ **51.** $5 \div \frac{1}{12}$

Find the value of *n*.

52. if $1 \div \frac{3}{5} = \frac{5}{3}$, then $3 \div \frac{3}{5} = n$ **53.** if $1 \div \frac{1}{3} = 3$, then $2 \div \frac{1}{3} = n$ **54.** if $1 \div \frac{5}{9} = \frac{9}{5}$, then $\frac{1}{3} \div \frac{5}{9} = n$

 Real World Data

For 55–57, use the table.

55. For a science experiment, Mr. Barrows divides all of the salt into equal amounts in small jars. He puts $\frac{1}{8}$ c of salt in each jar. How many jars does Mr. Barrows use?

56. Maria finds that one scoop of sand weighs $\frac{1}{16}$ lb. How many scoops of sand can she get from the class supplies?

57. Each of 10 students needs $\frac{2}{3}$ gal of distilled water. Is there enough water for everyone? **Explain.**

Class Science Supplies	
Items	**Amount**
Salt	$\frac{1}{2}$ c
Sand	$\frac{3}{4}$ lb
Distilled Water	6 gal

58. ⎨**Write Math**⎬ ▶ A quotient may be greater than or less than the dividend when the divisor is a fraction. To support this statement, write an example in which the quotient is greater than the dividend and one in which the dividend is greater than the quotient.

★ **OCCT Test Prep** 📝 Math Board

59. Which of the following has the greatest quotient?

A $3 \div \frac{3}{4}$ **C** $7 \div \frac{7}{8}$

B $11 \div \frac{1}{4}$ **D** $12 \div \frac{1}{2}$

60. Brett has $\frac{3}{2}$ c of rice. If he needs $\frac{1}{4}$ c for each serving, how many servings can he make?

A $4\frac{1}{2}$ **C** $5\frac{1}{2}$

B 5   **D** 6

⭐ Standards Quick Check

Find the quotient. Write it in simplest form.

1. $\frac{3}{8} \div \frac{1}{2}$

2. $\frac{5}{6} \div \frac{2}{3}$

3. $\frac{3}{8} \div \frac{1}{4}$

4. $\frac{6}{7} \div \frac{5}{14}$

5. $\frac{5}{8} \div \frac{15}{16}$

6. $\frac{7}{12} \div \frac{14}{15}$

7. $\frac{5}{6} \div \frac{7}{9}$

8. $\frac{9}{2} \div \frac{3}{2}$

9. $4 \div \frac{3}{10}$

10. $5 \div \frac{2}{3}$

11. $16 \div \frac{1}{4}$

12. $4 \div \frac{2}{3}$

Challenge H.O.T.

Using the LCD to Find Quotients

You can use the least common denominator to find the quotient of fractions. Find $\frac{1}{8} \div \frac{1}{2}$.

First, rename the fractions, using the LCD, 8.

$$\frac{1}{8} \div \frac{1}{2} = \frac{1 \times 1}{8 \times 1} \div \frac{1 \times 4}{2 \times 4} = \frac{1}{8} \div \frac{4}{8}$$

Then divide the numerators and the denominators.

$$\frac{1}{8} \div \frac{4}{8} = \frac{1 \div 4}{8 \div 8} = \frac{\frac{1}{4}}{1} = \frac{1}{4}$$

So, $\frac{1}{8} \div \frac{1}{2} = \frac{1}{4}$.

Use the LCD to find the quotient.

1. $\frac{8}{9} \div \frac{1}{2}$

2. $\frac{3}{4} \div \frac{1}{8}$

3. $\frac{7}{12} \div \frac{2}{3}$

4. $\frac{1}{5} \div \frac{3}{10}$

5. $\frac{3}{4} \div \frac{1}{6}$

6. Does the quotient change if the fractions are renamed with a common denominator other than the LCD? **Explain** by using Problem 2.

LESSON 11

★ **2.2.a.** Multiply and divide fractions and mixed numbers to solve problems using a variety of methods.

Materials
• MathBoard

Reciprocals

Essential Question What is the product of a number and its reciprocal?

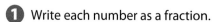

Two numbers whose product is 1 are reciprocals.

$$\frac{1}{3} \times 3 = 1 \qquad \frac{4}{5} \times \frac{5}{4} = 1 \qquad 4 \times \frac{1}{4} = 1$$

↑ ↑   ↑ ↑   ↑ ↑

reciprocals   reciprocals   reciprocals

Writing reciprocals.

1 Write each number as a fraction.

$$\frac{2}{3}$$
$$1\frac{4}{5} = \frac{9}{5}$$
$$7 = \frac{7}{1}$$

· ·

2 **Think:** What other factor will make a product of 1?

$$\frac{2}{3} \times \frac{\blacksquare}{\blacksquare} = 1$$

$$\frac{9}{5} \times \frac{\blacksquare}{\blacksquare} = 1$$

$$\frac{7}{1} \times \frac{\blacksquare}{\blacksquare} = 1$$

· ·

3 Use mental math to find the missing factor.

$$\frac{2}{3} \times \frac{3}{2} = 1$$

$$\frac{9}{5} \times \frac{5}{9} = 1$$

$$\frac{7}{1} \times \frac{1}{7} = 1$$

You can use reciprocals and inverse operations to write related number sentences.

$\frac{2}{3} \times \frac{3}{2} = 1$	→	$1 \div \frac{2}{3} = \frac{3}{2}$ $1 \div \frac{3}{2} = \frac{2}{3}$	Write related number sentences.
$1\frac{4}{5} \times \frac{5}{9} = 1$	→	$1 \div 1\frac{4}{5} = \frac{5}{9}$ $1 \div \frac{5}{9} = 1\frac{4}{5}$	Write related number sentences.
$7 \times \frac{1}{7} = 1$	→	$1 \div 7 = \frac{1}{7}$ $1 \div \frac{1}{7} = 7$	Write related number sentences.

• For $\frac{3}{4} \div \frac{2}{3} = \frac{3}{4} \times \frac{3}{2}$ what do you notice about the divisor in $\frac{3}{4} \div \frac{2}{3}$ and about the second factor in $\frac{3}{4} \times \frac{3}{2}$?

1. Write the reciprocal of $3\frac{1}{2}$.   Think: $3\frac{1}{2} = \frac{7}{2}$ $\frac{7}{2} \times \frac{\blacksquare}{\blacksquare} = 1$

Write the reciprocal of the number.

2. $\frac{1}{2}$ 　　　　**3.** 17 　　　　**4.** $2\frac{5}{8}$ 　　　　**5.** $\frac{4}{9}$ 　　　　✓**6.** $7\frac{1}{3}$

Write related division sentences.

7. $\frac{4}{5} \times 2 = \frac{8}{5}$ 　　**8.** $\frac{2}{3} \times \frac{5}{3} = \frac{10}{9}$ 　　**9.** $\frac{2}{5} \times 2 = \frac{4}{5}$ 　　**10.** $6 \times \frac{8}{9} = \frac{48}{9}$ 　　✓**11.** $\frac{2}{9} \times \frac{3}{8} = \frac{1}{12}$

12. **Math Talk** **Explain** how you can find the reciprocal of any whole number.

Write the reciprocal of the number.

13. $\frac{5}{8}$ 　　**14.** $1\frac{15}{16}$ 　　**15.** $\frac{7}{6}$ 　　**16.** 30 　　**17.** $\frac{1}{3}$

18. $4\frac{1}{6}$ 　　**19.** 24 　　**20.** $\frac{5}{9}$ 　　**21.** $2\frac{4}{5}$ 　　**22.** $8\frac{9}{10}$

Write related division sentences.

23. $\frac{2}{3} \times 8 = \frac{16}{3}$ 　　**24.** $\frac{5}{6} \times \frac{3}{4} = \frac{5}{8}$ 　　**25.** $\frac{1}{3} \times 9 = 3$ 　　**26.** $\frac{8}{9} \times \frac{5}{12} = \frac{10}{27}$ 　　**27.** $\frac{3}{16} \times \frac{8}{9} = \frac{1}{6}$

28. $\frac{1}{5} \times 10 = 2$ 　　**29.** $4 \times \frac{11}{12} = \frac{11}{13}$ 　　**30.** $\frac{5}{7} \times \frac{14}{15} = \frac{2}{3}$ 　　**31.** $\frac{16}{3} \times \frac{3}{7} = \frac{16}{7}$ 　　**32.** $40 \times \frac{5}{2} = 100$

⭐**Algebra** **Find the value of n.**

33. $\frac{9}{28} \times 3\frac{1}{n} = 1$ 　　**34.** $1 \div \frac{4}{7} = \frac{n}{4}$ 　　**35.** $n \times \frac{1}{6} = 1$ 　　**36.** $\frac{4}{3} \times \frac{3}{n} = 1$ 　　**37.** $1 \div 1\frac{1}{4} = \frac{4}{n}$

38. A parade float can travel $\frac{3}{8}$ mi on 1 gal of gas. How many gallons of gas will the float need to travel the 1-mi route?

39. **Write Math** Gus knows that $1 \div \frac{5}{6} = \frac{6}{5}$. **Explain** how he can find the quotients $2 \div \frac{5}{6}$ and $\frac{1}{2} \div \frac{5}{6}$.

40. What is the reciprocal of $\frac{9}{15}$?

　　A 1 　　　　**C** $\frac{9}{15}$

　　B $\frac{3}{5}$ 　　　　**D** $\frac{15}{9}$

41. What is the reciprocal of $\frac{5}{6}$?

　　A 6 　　　　**C** 1

　　B $\frac{6}{5}$ 　　　　**D** $\frac{1}{6}$

Use Reciprocals

Essential Question How do you use reciprocals when dividing fractions?

★ **2.2.a.** Multiply and divide fractions and mixed numbers to solve problems using a variety of methods.

Materials
• MathBoard

Problem Winnie needs pieces of string for her craft project. Each piece must be $\frac{1}{3}$-yd long. How many $\frac{1}{3}$-yd pieces of string can Winnie cut from a piece that is $\frac{3}{4}$-yd long?

Multiply by the reciprocal.

To find the number of $\frac{1}{3}$-yd pieces, find $\frac{3}{4} \div \frac{1}{3}$.

Think: $1 \div \frac{1}{3} = 1 \times \frac{3}{1}$, so $\frac{3}{4} \div \frac{1}{3} = \frac{3}{4} \times \frac{3}{1}$.

$\frac{3}{4} \div \frac{1}{3} = \frac{3}{4} \times \frac{3}{1}$ Use the reciprocal of the divisor to write a multiplication expression.

$= \frac{9}{4}$, or $2\frac{1}{4}$ Multiply.

So, Winnie can cut 2 pieces of string. She will have $\frac{1}{4}$ of a piece left.

• **What if** Winnie needed $\frac{1}{8}$-yd piece of string? How many $\frac{1}{8}$-yd pieces of string could she cut?

To see why you can multiply by the reciprocal to find the quotient, use inverse operations.

Use inverse operations.

$\frac{2}{3} \div \frac{4}{5} = \frac{10}{12}$ Start with a division sentence.

$\frac{2}{3} = \frac{10}{12} \times \frac{4}{5}$ Write a related number sentence using inverse operations.

$\frac{2}{3} \times \frac{5}{4} = \left(\frac{10}{12} \times \frac{4}{5} \right) \times \frac{5}{4}$ Multiply both sides of the equation by the reciprocal of $\frac{4}{5}$, $\frac{5}{4}$.

$\frac{2}{3} \times \frac{5}{4} = \frac{10}{12} \times \left(\frac{4}{5} \times \frac{5}{4} \right)$ Use the Associative Property to group the reciprocals.

$\frac{2}{3} \times \frac{5}{4} = \frac{10}{12} \times 1$ Multiply the reciprocals.

$\frac{2}{3} \times \frac{5}{4} = \frac{10}{12}$

So, $\frac{2}{3} \div \frac{4}{5} = \frac{10}{12}$ is the same as $\frac{2}{3} \times \frac{5}{4} = \frac{10}{12}$.

Divide Whole Numbers and Fractions

You can use reciprocals to divide whole numbers by fractions. Remember, whole numbers can be written as fractions using a denominator of 1.

Examples

> **Toby and his friends are building a backyard fort. They need to cut a 6-ft board into $\frac{1}{4}$-ft pieces. How many $\frac{1}{4}$-ft pieces can they cut?**
>
> To find how many pieces they can cut, find $6 \div \frac{1}{4}$.
>
> $6 \div \frac{1}{4} = \frac{6}{1} \div \frac{1}{4}$ Write the whole number as a fraction.
>
> $\qquad = \frac{6}{1} \times \frac{4}{1}$ Use the reciprocal of the divisor, 4, to write a multiplication expression.
>
> $\qquad = \frac{6}{1} \times \frac{4}{1} = \frac{24}{1}$, or 24   Multiply.

So, they can cut 24 pieces that are $\frac{1}{4}$ ft long.

You can also use reciprocals to divide fractions by whole numbers.

> **Toby has a board that is $\frac{5}{6}$-ft long. He wants to cut the board into 3 equal pieces. How long will each piece be?**
>
> To find the length of each piece, find $\frac{5}{6} \div 3$.
>
> $\frac{5}{6} \div 3 = \frac{5}{6} \div \frac{3}{1}$ Write the whole number as a fraction.
>
> $\qquad = \frac{5}{6} \times \frac{1}{3}$ Use the reciprocal of the divisor, 3, to write a multiplication expression.
>
> $\qquad = \frac{5}{6} \times \frac{1}{3} = \frac{5}{18}$ Multiply.

Math Idea

To divide by a unit fraction, multiply by the denominator of the unit fraction.

So, each piece will be $\frac{5}{18}$ ft long.

 Share and Show

Use the reciprocal of the divisor to write a multiplication expression.

1. $\frac{4}{5} \div \frac{1}{4} = \frac{4}{5} \times \frac{\blacksquare}{1}$ **2.** $\frac{1}{2} \div \frac{3}{8} = \frac{1}{2} \times \frac{\blacksquare}{3}$ **3.** $4 \div \frac{3}{5} = 4 \times \frac{\blacksquare}{\blacksquare}$ ✓ **4.** $6 \div \frac{4}{9} = 6 \times \frac{\blacksquare}{\blacksquare}$

Find the quotient. Write it in simplest form.

5. $\frac{2}{3} \div \frac{5}{12}$ **6.** $\frac{7}{11} \div 2$ **7.** $\frac{2}{5} \div \frac{7}{10}$ **8.** $\frac{11}{12} \div \frac{3}{4}$ ✓ **9.** $\frac{5}{6} \div 6$

10. **Math Talk** Explain how to use a reciprocal to find $\frac{5}{6} \div \frac{4}{7}$.

Use the reciprocal of the divisor to write a multiplication expression.

11. $\frac{2}{9} \div \frac{2}{3}$ **12.** $\frac{5}{8} \div \frac{1}{6}$ **13.** $5 \div \frac{3}{4}$ **14.** $\frac{4}{7} \div \frac{2}{7}$ **15.** $\frac{3}{4} \div \frac{3}{8}$

16. $\frac{1}{5} \div \frac{1}{3}$ **17.** $\frac{3}{8} \div 4$ **18.** $\frac{12}{13} \div \frac{3}{5}$ **19.** $\frac{7}{8} \div \frac{1}{9}$ **20.** $\frac{11}{12} \div \frac{2}{3}$

Find the quotient. Write it in simplest form.

21. $\frac{5}{2} \div \frac{5}{6}$ **22.** $\frac{3}{7} \div \frac{9}{16}$ **23.** $3 \div \frac{8}{3}$ **24.** $\frac{2}{3} \div 4$ **25.** $\frac{1}{2} \div \frac{9}{10}$

26. $\frac{14}{15} \div \frac{2}{7}$ **27.** $\frac{14}{5} \div 2$ **28.** $6 \div \frac{5}{6}$ **29.** $\frac{7}{18} \div \frac{1}{3}$ **30.** $\frac{4}{5} \div \frac{11}{12}$

 **Algebra** **Find the value of the expression. Write it in simplest form.**

31. $\frac{2}{3} \div n$ for $n = \frac{4}{5}$ **32.** $\frac{3}{8} \div n$ for $n = \frac{1}{2}$ **33.** $\frac{9}{10} \div n$ for $n = \frac{3}{5}$

Real World Data

For 34–37, use the table.

34. Kirsten wants to cut ladder rungs from a 6-ft board. How many ladder rungs can she cut?

35. **Pose a Problem** Look back at Problem 34. Write and solve a new problem by changing the length of the board Kirsten is cutting for ladder rungs.

36. Dan paints a design that has 8 equal parts along the entire length of the windowsill. How long is each part of the design?

37. Tim has a board that is $\frac{15}{16}$ yd. How many "Keep Out" signs can he make if the length of the sign is changed to half the original length?

38. **Reasoning** If $\frac{6}{7} \div \frac{n}{4} = \frac{6}{7} \times \frac{n}{4}$, what is the value of n?

39. **Write Math** ▶ **Explain** how to divide the fraction $\frac{1}{2}$ by any whole number.

Tree House Measurements	
Item	**Board Length**
Ladder rung	$\frac{3}{4}$ ft
"Keep Out" sign	$\frac{5}{8}$ yd
Windowsill	$\frac{1}{2}$ yd

40. Which of the following has the greatest quotient?

   A $3 \div \frac{3}{4}$ **C** $11 \div \frac{1}{4}$

   B $7 \div \frac{7}{8}$ **D** $12 \div \frac{1}{2}$

41. Maggy divided $\frac{3}{4}$ pound of flour into 6 bags. Each bag contains the same amount of flour. How many pounds of flour does each bag contain?

   A $\frac{3}{16}$ pound   **C** $\frac{3}{8}$ pound

   B $\frac{1}{8}$ pound   **D** $4\frac{1}{2}$ pounds

★ Standards Quick Check

Use the reciprocal of the divisor to write a multiplication expression.

1. $\frac{2}{7} \div \frac{1}{3}$

2. $6 \div \frac{3}{4}$

3. $\frac{4}{5} \div 8$

4. $\frac{2}{3} \div \frac{1}{6}$

5. $\frac{3}{7} \div \frac{5}{8}$

6. $\frac{2}{3} \div \frac{3}{4}$

7. $\frac{5}{6} \div \frac{7}{8}$

8. $\frac{7}{9} \div \frac{14}{15}$

9. $\frac{4}{5} \div \frac{5}{9}$

Challenge H.O.T.

You can use mental math to divide two fractions that have the same numerators, but not the same denominators.

Find $\frac{3}{8} \div \frac{3}{5}$.

$\frac{3}{8} \div \frac{3}{5} = \frac{3 \div 3}{8 \div 5}$ Divide the numerators and denominators.

$= \frac{3}{3} \div \frac{8}{5}$ Rewrite 3 ÷ 3 as $\frac{3}{3}$ and 8 ÷ 5 as $\frac{8}{5}$.

$= 1 \div \frac{8}{5}$ Notice that the quotient of the numerators, 1, is divided by the quotient of the denominators, $\frac{8}{5}$.

$= 1 \times \frac{5}{8}$ Since the reciprocal of $\frac{8}{5}$ is $\frac{5}{8}$, you can write a related number sentence.

$= \frac{5}{8}$ The answer is the reciprocal of the quotient of the denominators, $\frac{8}{5}$.

So, $\frac{3}{8} \div \frac{3}{5} = \frac{5}{8}$.

Use mental math to find each quotient.

1. $\frac{4}{7} \div \frac{4}{5}$

2. $\frac{2}{3} \div \frac{2}{9}$

3. $\frac{3}{7} \div \frac{3}{4}$

4. $\frac{11}{12} \div \frac{11}{13}$

5. $\frac{3}{10} \div \frac{3}{5}$

6. $\frac{7}{8} \div \frac{7}{12}$

★ **2.2.a.** Multiply and divide fractions and mixed numbers to solve problems using a variety of methods. *also* **2.2.c.**

Materials
• MathBoard
• pattern blocks

Divide Fractions and Mixed Numbers

Essential Question When multiplying mixed numbers, what must you do before multiplying by the reciprocal of the divisor?

PROBLEM During the busiest 7 hours at the train station in New Haven, Connecticut, a train leaves every $\frac{1}{6}$ hr for Grand Central Station in New York, New York. How many trains leave for Grand Central Station in those 7 hours?

You can use multiplication to find the quotient when you divide by a fraction.

Dividing fractions.

Find $7 \div \frac{1}{6}$.

$$7 \div \frac{1}{6} = \frac{7}{1} \div \frac{1}{6}$$ Write the whole number as a fraction.

$$= \frac{7}{1} \times \frac{6}{1}$$ Use the reciprocal of the divisor to write a multiplication problem.

$$= \frac{42}{1}, \text{ or } 42$$ Multiply.

So, 42 trains leave for Grand Central Station in those 7 hours.

Examples

Find $\frac{2}{3} \div \frac{5}{6}$.

$$\frac{2}{3} \div \frac{5}{6} = \frac{2}{3} \times \frac{6}{5}$$ Use the reciprocal of the divisor to write a multiplication problem.

$$= \frac{2}{\cancel{3}_1} \times \frac{\cancel{6}^2}{5}$$ Divide a numerator and a denominator by their GCF, 3.

$$= \frac{4}{5}$$ Multiply.

So, $\frac{2}{3} \div \frac{5}{6} = \frac{4}{5}$.

> **Math Idea**
>
> When you divide by a fraction, multiply by the reciprocal of the divisor to find the quotient.

Find $\frac{7}{8} \div 4$.

$$\frac{7}{8} \div 4 = \frac{7}{8} \div \frac{4}{1}$$ Write the whole number as a fraction.

$$= \frac{7}{8} \times \frac{1}{4}$$ Use the reciprocal of the divisor to write a multiplication problem.

$$= \frac{7}{32}$$ Multiply.

So, $\frac{7}{8} \div 4 = \frac{7}{32}$.

Mixed Numbers

You can use a model to divide mixed numbers.

Use a model.

Find $1\frac{2}{3} \div \frac{1}{6}$, or the number of sixths in $1\frac{2}{3}$.

- Begin with 2 hexagon blocks.
- Show $1\frac{2}{3}$ hexagons by placing rhombus blocks on top.
- Place triangle blocks on the rhombus blocks to show the number of sixths in $1\frac{2}{3}$.
- One whole equals 6 sixths. How many sixths are in $1\frac{2}{3}$?

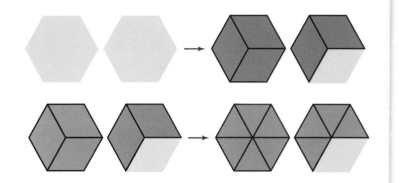

You can divide mixed numbers without making a model.

$10\frac{1}{2} \div 1\frac{1}{6}$

Estimate. $10 \div 1 = 10$

$10\frac{1}{2} \div 1\frac{1}{6} = \frac{21}{2} \div \frac{7}{6}$ Write the mixed numbers as fractions.

$= \frac{21}{2} \times \frac{6}{7}$ Use the reciprocal of the divisor to write a multiplication problem.

$= \frac{\overset{3}{\cancel{21}}}{\underset{1}{\cancel{2}}} \times \frac{\overset{3}{\cancel{6}}}{\underset{1}{\cancel{7}}}$ Simplify.

$= \frac{9}{1}$, or 9   Multiply.

So, $10\frac{1}{2} \div 1\frac{1}{6} = 9$.

$3\frac{1}{3} \div 4$

Estimate. $3 \div 4 = \frac{3}{4}$

$3\frac{1}{3} \div 4 = \frac{10}{3} \div \frac{4}{1}$ Write the numbers as fractions.

$= \frac{10}{3} \times \frac{1}{4}$ Use the reciprocal of the divisor to write a multiplication problem.

$= \frac{\overset{5}{\cancel{10}}}{3} \times \frac{1}{\underset{2}{\cancel{4}}}$ Simplify.

$= \frac{5}{6}$ Multiply.

So, $3\frac{1}{3} \div 4 = \frac{5}{6}$

Share and Show

1. Find $4\frac{1}{3} \div \frac{3}{4}$. $4\frac{1}{3} \div \frac{3}{4} = \frac{13}{3} \div \frac{3}{4} = \frac{13}{3} \times \frac{4}{3} = \frac{\blacksquare}{\blacksquare}$ or $\blacksquare\frac{\blacksquare}{\blacksquare}$

Find the quotient. Write it in simplest form.

2. $\frac{3}{4} \div \frac{5}{6}$ 3. $3 \div \frac{3}{4}$ 4. $3\frac{1}{3} \div 2\frac{1}{2}$ ✓ 5. $\frac{1}{2} \div \frac{3}{4}$ ✓ 6. $7\frac{1}{2} \div 2\frac{1}{2}$

7. **Math Talk** **Explain** why you first write a mixed number as a fraction before using it as a dividend or divisor.

Find the quotient. Write it in simplest form.

8. $\frac{3}{8} \div \frac{3}{5}$ **9.** $\frac{2}{9} \div \frac{4}{5}$ **10.** $5 \div 1\frac{1}{3}$ **11.** $4\frac{1}{2} \div 3$ **12.** $6\frac{3}{4} \div 2$

13. $\frac{4}{5} \div 1\frac{1}{4}$ **14.** $\frac{2}{9} \div \frac{2}{3}$ **15.** $\frac{7}{12} \div 3\frac{1}{2}$ **16.** $2\frac{2}{5} \div \frac{9}{10}$ **17.** $\frac{3}{4} \div \frac{2}{3}$

18. $8 \div 3\frac{1}{2}$ **19.** $2\frac{2}{9} \div 1\frac{3}{7}$ **20.** $1\frac{1}{2} \div 1\frac{1}{4}$ **21.** $8\frac{1}{2} \div 2\frac{1}{8}$ **22.** $5\frac{3}{4} \div 4\frac{1}{2}$

Use mental math to find each quotient.

23. $\frac{4}{9} \div \frac{1}{9}$ **24.** $\frac{11}{4} \div \frac{1}{4}$ **25.** $1\frac{1}{7} \div \frac{1}{7}$ **26.** $1\frac{1}{2} \div 1\frac{1}{2}$ **27.** $2\frac{1}{4} \div \frac{1}{4}$

28. $\frac{12}{5} \div \frac{1}{5}$ **29.** $1\frac{2}{3} \div \frac{1}{3}$ **30.** $2\frac{3}{5} \div \frac{1}{5}$ **31.** $4\frac{1}{8} \div \frac{1}{8}$ **32.** $3\frac{5}{6} \div \frac{1}{6}$

 Algebra Evaluate the expression.

33. $\frac{5}{6} \div n$ if $n = \frac{1}{6}$ **34.** $n \div 2\frac{1}{10}$ if $n = 7$ **35.** $n \div 5$ if $n = 1\frac{2}{3}$ **36.** $4 \div n$ if $n = \frac{3}{4}$

 # Real World Data

For 37–39, use the train schedule.

37. **Reasoning** The 8:06 train from New Haven to Stamford makes 2 stops before Stamford, with equal times between stops. In how many hours will it reach the first stop?

38. On his trip from New Haven to Newark, Hunter went to the snack car every $\frac{3}{4}$ hr. How many times did Hunter visit the snack car?

39. Melissa took a 3-hr train trip. How many times as long as the trip from New Haven to New York was Melissa's trip?

New Haven, Connecticut Saturday Trains Schedule		
Departure Time	**Destination**	**Arrival Time**
8:06 A.M.	Stamford, CT	9:36 A.M.
8:22 A.M.	New York, NY	10:37 A.M.
9:17 A.M.	Newark, NJ	12:17 P.M.

40. **Write Math** **What's the Error?** To find $2\frac{1}{2} \div 2$, Deborah wrote $\frac{2}{5} \times \frac{2}{1}$. Explain her error and correct it.

★ OCCT Test Prep   Math Board

41. Which is the quotient of $1\frac{2}{4} \div \frac{7}{10}$?

A $\frac{3}{10}$ **C** $2\frac{1}{7}$

B 4   **D** $2\frac{7}{28}$

42. A model railroad boxcar in O scale is $12\frac{1}{2}$ in. long. The same boxcar in N scale is $3\frac{1}{8}$ in. long. How many times as great is O scale as compared to N scale?

A $\frac{3}{10}$ **C** $4\frac{1}{3}$

B 4   **D** $16\frac{1}{3}$

⭐ Standards Quick Check

Find the quotient. Write it in simplest form.

1. $4\frac{1}{2} \div \frac{3}{8}$

2. $5\frac{1}{5} \div \frac{2}{5}$

3. $2\frac{1}{3} \div \frac{2}{5}$

4. $14\frac{1}{2} \div \frac{3}{8}$

5. $3\frac{1}{4} \div 1\frac{2}{5}$

6. $8\frac{1}{5} \div 3\frac{1}{3}$

7. $15\frac{1}{3} \div 2\frac{1}{2}$

8. $3\frac{3}{8} \div 1\frac{1}{2}$

9. $4\frac{1}{4} \div 2\frac{3}{4}$

Draw to Explain

One way to explain a solution is to draw a diagram. A diagram helps you visualize and show the information in the problem.

José and three friends had a pizza party. There were $1\frac{1}{5}$ pizzas left over. How can they divide the leftover pizza equally among 4 people?

José drew this diagram to solve the problem.

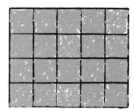 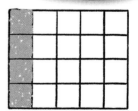

Solve. Draw a diagram to explain.

1. Madison completed a 24-page journal during a trip. She filled $2\frac{2}{3}$ pages every day of her trip. How many days long was her trip

2. Dan has $1\frac{1}{3}$ melons to share among 8 people. If he divides the melons into 8 equal pieces, what part of a whole melon will each person get?

Problem Solving Workshop
Skill: Choose the Operation

Essential Question How can you determine which operation to use when solving problems?

PROBLEM Ricardo makes garden-themed wreaths from old garden hoses. He used $4\frac{1}{8}$-ft, $3\frac{1}{2}$-ft, and $5\frac{3}{8}$-ft lengths of hose to make three wreaths. What is the total length of garden hose that Ricardo used?

This chart will help you decide which operation or combination of operations you can use to solve the problem.

Add	Join groups of equal or different sizes
Subtract	Take away or compare groups
Multiply	Join groups of equal sizes
Divide	Separate into groups of equal size or find how many in each group

The hose lengths are different and you need to find the total length of hose used. So, add the lengths of the hose.

$$4\frac{1}{8} + 3\frac{1}{2} + 5\frac{3}{8} = 4\frac{1}{8} + 3\frac{4}{8} + 5\frac{3}{8}$$

Write equivalent fractions. Add.

$$= 12\frac{8}{8} = 13$$

So, Ricardo used 13 ft of garden hose in all.

Solve. Name the operation or operations used.

a. Marcus makes garden planters by stacking tires to form columns. How many tires with a width of $\frac{3}{4}$ ft are needed to make a planter 3 ft high?

b. Lucy makes floral wreaths from wire coat hangers. One stretched-out hanger is $2\frac{2}{3}$ ft long. If she uses one hanger for each wreath and $1\frac{3}{4}$ ft of flower garland for every foot of wire, how many feet of garland does Lucy use for one wreath?

c. Dan makes stamps from potatoes. He stamps a $2\frac{3}{4}$-in. tall design in the middle of a blank card that is $4\frac{5}{8}$-in. tall. How much space on the card is left above the stamp?

 **Share and Show** Math Board

1. Josh makes picture frames from old CD cases. He glues 3 cases side-by-side to a strip of wood that has a length equal to the total length of the 3 cases. If the length of each CD case is $4\frac{7}{8}$ in., how long is the strip of wood?

   First, decide how the numbers in the problem are related. Three cases, with a length of $4\frac{7}{8}$ in. each, will be placed side-by-side on top of a wood strip of the same length.

   Next, choose the operation and solve. Addition could be used to find the total length. Multiplication could also be used, since each of the 3 cases has the same length.

   $$4\frac{7}{8} + 4\frac{7}{8} + 4\frac{7}{8} = \blacksquare, \ 3 \times 4\frac{7}{8} = \blacksquare$$

2. **What if** Josh made picture frames from 4 CD cases lined up end-to-end? How long would the wooden strip be?

3. Naomi decorates paper towel tubes to make desk organizers. She has cut 5 pieces of tubes. Her first piece is $2\frac{1}{2}$ in. long. If each of the other pieces is $1\frac{1}{2}$ in. longer than the previous piece, how long is the fifth piece?

Mixed Applications

For 4–7, use the table.

4. If Margie hikes the Ohio and Erie Canal Towpath in 10 hr, about how far does she hike in 1 hr?

5. Ron hiked all of the California trails and the Buckeye Trail. Tyler hiked the Canal Towpath. Who hiked farther? How much farther?

6. Compare the moderate California trail and the moderate Ohio trail. Which is longer? How much longer?

7. Dina hikes the moderate and difficult trails in Ohio and hikes one-half of the easy trail. How far does she hike?

8. **Write Math** **Explain** how you decide what operation to use when solving a word problem when no operation sign is given.

9. Anna needs 3 bunches of spinach to make a spinach pie that will serve 6 people. How many bunches of spinach does she need to serve 24 people?

Hiking Trails			
State/Park	Trail	Length (mi)	Difficulty
California: Yosemite National Park	Bridalveil Fall	$\frac{1}{2}$	easy
	Valley Floor Loop	$6\frac{1}{2}$	moderate
	Vernal Fall	$6\frac{1}{2}$	difficult
Ohio: Cuyahoga Valley National Park	Ohio and Erie Canal Towpath	$19\frac{1}{2}$	easy
	Brandywine Gorge	$1\frac{1}{4}$	moderate
	Buckeye Trail (Jaite to Boston)	$5\frac{3}{5}$	difficult

★ Extra Practice

Set A

Estimate the sum or difference. (pp. 120–123)

1. $\frac{4}{11} + \frac{1}{9}$

2. $\frac{7}{8} - \frac{2}{5}$

3. $10\frac{1}{16} - 8\frac{8}{9}$

4. $15\frac{1}{3} + 13\frac{1}{9} + 4\frac{4}{5}$

For 5–6, tell whether an overestimate or an underestimate is needed. Solve.

5. Maggie needs $4\frac{7}{8}$ ft of furry fabric to make 2 stuffed animals for a child at a local children's hospital. How many feet of furry fabric does Maggie need to make the two stuffed animals?

6. Monroe wants his fruit smoothie to contain at least 8 c of ingredients. He combines $3\frac{1}{3}$ c of crushed strawberries, $1\frac{1}{2}$ c of vanilla yogurt, and $2\frac{3}{4}$ c mashed bananas. Estimate the combined ingredients. Will the ingredients meet Monroe's least amount for his smoothie?

Set B

Estimate. Then write the sum or difference in simplest form. (pp. 124–127)

1. $\frac{3}{8} + \frac{1}{4}$

2. $\frac{2}{5} - \frac{1}{15}$

3. $\frac{3}{4} - \frac{2}{5}$

4. $\frac{1}{4} + \frac{1}{6}$

5. $\frac{2}{3} + \frac{3}{4}$

6. $\frac{9}{10} + \frac{1}{3}$

7. $\frac{3}{6} - \frac{1}{8}$

8. $\frac{13}{20} + \frac{3}{5} + \frac{1}{4}$

Set C

Estimate. Then write the sum or difference in simplest form. (pp. 128–131)

1. $12\frac{1}{3} - 7\frac{1}{5}$

2. $5\frac{5}{6} - 3\frac{1}{3}$

3. $9\frac{7}{20} + 5\frac{1}{4}$

4. $5\frac{5}{8} + 3\frac{1}{2}$

5. $5\frac{5}{6} - 3\frac{1}{2}$

6. $12\frac{1}{3} - 9\frac{1}{4}$

7. $32\frac{5}{18} + 4\frac{5}{6}$

8. $3\frac{3}{4} + 7\frac{4}{5}$

9. Each week, Jill spends $9\frac{5}{6}$ hr on homework and $7\frac{1}{3}$ hr practicing guitar. How much longer does Jill spend doing homework?

10. Mr. Sanchez cuts a cable into two pieces. One piece is $3\frac{2}{3}$ ft long, and the other is $6\frac{1}{6}$ ft long. How long was the original cable?

Set D

Estimate. Then write the difference in simplest form. (pp. 132–133)

1. $3\frac{1}{4} - 2\frac{3}{4}$

2. $2\frac{2}{3} - 1\frac{5}{6}$

3. $10\frac{1}{8} - 4\frac{3}{4}$

4. $5\frac{1}{5} - 3\frac{1}{4}$

5. $8 - 4\frac{1}{3}$

6. $5\frac{1}{6} - 4\frac{2}{5}$

7. $1\frac{1}{6} - \frac{2}{3}$

8. $3\frac{3}{8} - 2\frac{1}{2}$

Set E

Estimate. Then write the sum or difference in simplest form. (pp. 136–139)

1. $\frac{1}{10} + \frac{1}{2}$

2. $\frac{13}{16} - \frac{3}{4}$

3. $\frac{1}{2} + \frac{4}{9}$

4. $\frac{7}{8} - \frac{3}{5}$

5. $5\frac{3}{4} + 3\frac{11}{20}$

6. $8\frac{5}{8} - 4\frac{1}{4}$

7. $3\frac{1}{7} - 1\frac{2}{5}$

8. $10 - 3\frac{2}{5}$

9. Louise has $4\frac{1}{2}$ oz of milk. If she uses $\frac{3}{4}$ oz, how many ounces will be left?

10. A farmer bought $14\frac{3}{5}$ lb, $10\frac{1}{6}$ lb, and $15\frac{1}{2}$ lb of grain for his cattle. How much grain did he buy altogether?

GO ONLINE **Technology**
Use HMH Mega Math, Fraction Action, *Fraction Flare-Up,* Levels G–K.

Set F

Estimate the product or quotient. (pp. 140–141)

1. $\frac{7}{8} \div \frac{3}{5}$ **2.** $5 \times 1\frac{9}{10}$ **3.** $3\frac{1}{4} \times \frac{9}{10}$ **4.** $42\frac{1}{4} \div \frac{5}{8}$ **5.** $26\frac{11}{12} \div 8\frac{3}{4}$

6. $\frac{5}{6} \times \frac{4}{5}$ **7.** $3\frac{7}{8} \div 1\frac{9}{10}$ **8.** $16\frac{1}{15} \div 3\frac{7}{8}$ **9.** $12 \times 1\frac{3}{8}$ **10.** $9\frac{11}{12} \times 8\frac{1}{4}$

Set G

Find the product. Write it in simplest form. (pp. 142–145)

1. $15 \times \frac{1}{4}$ **2.** $\frac{1}{5} \times \frac{1}{4}$ **3.** $\frac{4}{5} \times \frac{2}{5}$ **4.** $9 \times \frac{3}{8}$ **5.** $\frac{3}{8} \times \frac{3}{5} \times \frac{3}{4}$

6. $\frac{2}{3} \times \frac{1}{8}$ **7.** $12 \times \frac{3}{4}$ **8.** $\frac{1}{9} \times 36$ **9.** $\frac{5}{9} \times \frac{8}{9}$ **10.** $\frac{9}{10} \times \frac{1}{5} \times \frac{10}{3}$

Set H

Find the product. Write it in simplest form. (pp. 146–147)

1. $2 \times 3\frac{3}{4}$ **2.** $4\frac{1}{2} \times 3$ **3.** $9\frac{2}{3} \times 5\frac{1}{8}$ **4.** $\frac{1}{2} \times 4\frac{1}{3} \times 3\frac{5}{8}$ **5.** $9\frac{1}{3} \times 2\frac{1}{5} \times 1\frac{1}{2}$

6. Mr. Valdez jogs $2\frac{3}{4}$ miles 3 times a week. He has done this for 20 weeks. How many miles has Mr. Valdez jogged?

7. Roberto plays soccer $3\frac{1}{6}$ hours 2 times a week. He has done this for 36 weeks. How many hours has Roberto played soccer?

Set I

Write the reciprocal of the number. (pp. 148–151)

1. $\frac{1}{7}$ **2.** 3 **3.** $\frac{4}{9}$ **4.** 7 **5.** $\frac{10}{9}$

Find the quotient. Write it in simplest form.

6. $8 \div \frac{1}{2}$ **7.** $6 \div \frac{1}{9}$ **8.** $7 \div \frac{1}{3}$ **9.** $15 \div \frac{1}{4}$ **10.** $11 \div \frac{1}{6}$

Set J

Write the reciprocal of the number. (pp. 152–153)

1. $\frac{5}{6}$ **2.** 14 **3.** $3\frac{3}{5}$ **4.** $\frac{2}{9}$ **5.** 9 **6.** $6\frac{2}{3}$

7. $\frac{1}{4}$ **8.** $11\frac{1}{12}$ **9.** $20\frac{1}{2}$ **10.** 16 **11.** $3\frac{1}{3}$ **12.** $\frac{3}{4}$

Set K

Find the quotient. Write it in simplest form. (pp. 158–161)

1. $3\frac{9}{10} \div 4$ **2.** $10 \div 2\frac{1}{2}$ **3.** $3\frac{3}{4} \div 6$ **4.** $\frac{4}{5} \div 2\frac{1}{4}$ **5.** $4\frac{1}{6} \div 2\frac{1}{4}$

6. $5\frac{4}{5} \div 1\frac{1}{6}$ **7.** $1\frac{4}{5} \div 1\frac{1}{2}$ **8.** $6\frac{2}{5} \div 3\frac{1}{6}$ **9.** $1\frac{1}{5} \div 1\frac{1}{4}$ **10.** $12\frac{1}{3} \div 5\frac{1}{2}$

Vocabulary

Use the Word Bank to help you explain how to add **mixed numbers.**

$$3\frac{2}{5} + 5\frac{2}{3}$$

> **Word Bank**
>
> fractions
>
> unlike denominators
>
> equivalent fractions
>
> whole numbers

Step 1: Look at the fractions. The two fractions have _____.
In order to add, the fractions must have a common denominator. The common denominator is _____.

Step 2: Write _____ with the common denominator.

$$3\frac{2}{5} \;=\; 3\frac{\blacksquare}{\blacksquare}$$
$$+\, 5\frac{2}{3} \;=\; +\, 5\frac{\blacksquare}{\blacksquare}$$

Step 3: Add the _____.
Add the _____.

Step 4: Simplify the sum, if possible.

$$3\frac{2}{5} \;=\; 3$$
$$+\, 5\frac{2}{3} \;=\; +\, 5$$

Writing How are improper fractions and mixed numbers alike? How are they different?

Reading Check out this book in your library.
Math Game 1: Rescue Alice from the Evil Math King
by Tori Jung

HOT. Multistep Problems

1 Kara would like to build a fence around her garden. She has a piece of fencing but she is not sure if she has enough. She measures her garden. It is in the shape of a rectangle with a width of $7\frac{5}{8}$ feet and a length of $5\frac{2}{3}$ feet. ◖ 2.2.c.

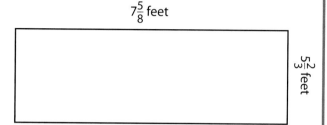

$7\frac{5}{8}$ feet

$5\frac{2}{3}$ feet

- How many feet of fencing does Kara need to go around the whole garden? **Explain** how you found your answer.

- If the piece of fencing she already has is $20\frac{1}{2}$ feet long, how much more fencing does she need to buy to go around the whole garden? **Explain** how you found your answer.

- If Kara decided to build a garden that was twice as large as the one she is planning now, how much fencing will she need total. How much fencing will Kara need to buy if she still has the $20\frac{1}{2}$ feet of fencing?

2 Peter has a photo that is 5 inches long and 7 inches wide. He places the photo in a frame that is $1\frac{3}{4}$ inches wide. He would like to find out how much space that photo will take up on his wall. ◖ 2.2.c.

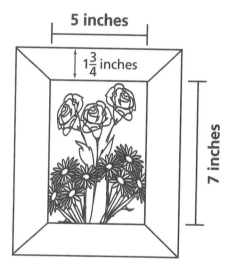

5 inches

$1\frac{3}{4}$ inches

7 inches

- What is the width of the framed photo?

- What is the length of the framed photo?

- If the length and the width of the framed photo doubled, what would the width and the length of the framed photo be?

Practice for the OCCT

1 Julie has $12\frac{4}{5}$ yards of fabric. She uses $3\frac{1}{4}$ yards to make a dress for the Fall Dance. How many yards of fabric does Julie have left? ⌐ **2.2.c.**

   A $8\frac{3}{10}$ yards

   B $9\frac{9}{10}$ yards

   C $9\frac{11}{20}$ yards

   D $11\frac{4}{5}$ yards

2 Maria usually works 40 hours each week. Last week she took $3\frac{1}{5}$ hours of vacation time. How many hours did Maria work last week? ⌐ **2.2.c.**

   A $39\frac{3}{8}$ hours

   B $37\frac{1}{5}$ hours

   C $36\frac{5}{8}$ hours

   D $36\frac{4}{5}$ hours

3 Ruth is training for a marathon. She ran $10\frac{7}{8}$ miles on Saturday and $15\frac{1}{5}$ miles on Sunday. How many miles did Ruth run in all? ⌐ **2.2.c.**

   A $28\frac{1}{8}$

   B $26\frac{3}{40}$

   C 26

   D $25\frac{4}{5}$

4 You make a home movie that contains $\frac{7}{15}$ hour of family trips and $\frac{4}{15}$ hour of birthday parties. If the tape can hold 1 hour of video, how much time is left on the tape? ⌐ **2.2.c.**

   A $\frac{1}{5}$ hour

   B $\frac{4}{15}$ hour

   C $\frac{8}{15}$ hour

   D $\frac{11}{15}$ hour

5 To prepare for a tennis match, Mark ran $\frac{1}{4}$ mile, walked $5\frac{1}{2}$ miles, and then ran $1\frac{1}{4}$ miles. How many total miles did Mark walk and run to get prepared for his tennis match? ⌐ **2.2.c.**

   A 6 miles

   B $6\frac{1}{4}$ miles

   C $6\frac{1}{2}$ miles

   D 7 miles

6 A baker sold loaves of bread weighing $1\frac{2}{3}$ pounds and $1\frac{1}{4}$ pounds. What was the total weight of the bread? ⌐ **2.2.c.**

   A $1\frac{3}{4}$ pounds

   B $2\frac{3}{4}$ pounds

   C $2\frac{11}{12}$ pounds

   D 3 pounds

7 Robert is going to make three different cakes. The table shows how many cups of flour are needed for each cake.

Cake	Flour (in cups)
Double Chocolate	$3\frac{1}{4}$
Angel Food	$2\frac{1}{3}$
Carrot	$2\frac{1}{4}$

How many cups of flour does Robert need to make all three cakes? ⌐ **2.2.c.**

   A 8 cups

   B $7\frac{5}{6}$ cups

   C $7\frac{3}{4}$ cups

   D $5\frac{7}{12}$ cups

8 Steven has $1\frac{2}{3}$ pizzas left over after a party. He divides the pizza equally to send home with 4 friends. How much of a whole pizza does each friend get? 🔖 2.2.a.

A $\frac{5}{12}$

B $\frac{1}{2}$

C $\frac{7}{12}$

D $\frac{2}{3}$

9 Leo needs $\frac{3}{4}$ yd of blue fabric, $\frac{7}{10}$ yd of purple fabric, and $\frac{1}{5}$ yd of white fabric for a sewing project. About how much fabric does Leo need for the sewing project? 🔖 2.2.c.

A about 1 yard

B about $1\frac{1}{4}$ yards

C about 2 yards

D about $3\frac{1}{2}$ yards

10 Mrs. Myers used $1\frac{1}{2}$ cups of flour to make muffins, $4\frac{1}{4}$ cups to make bread, and $\frac{3}{4}$ cup to make gravy. Mrs. Myers had $9\frac{3}{4}$ cups of flour before she started the meal. How much flour does Mrs. Myers have left? 🔖 2.2.c.

A $5\frac{1}{4}$ cups

B $4\frac{2}{4}$ cups

C $3\frac{3}{4}$ cups

D $3\frac{1}{4}$ cups

11 Peter divided $12\frac{1}{4}$ pounds of sand into 6 sandbags. If each sandbag contained the same amount of sand, how many pounds of sand did each sandbag contain? 🔖 2.2.a.

A 2 pounds

B $2\frac{1}{24}$ pounds

C $2\frac{1}{12}$ pounds

D $3\frac{1}{2}$ pounds

Problem Solving

12 In biology class, $\frac{1}{4}$ of the class studied frogs and $\frac{1}{5}$ studied snakes. The rest of the class studied worms. What fraction of the class studied worms? 🔖 2.2.c.

13 The height of a plant is $\frac{17}{28}$ inch. After one week, the plant was $\frac{29}{42}$ inch tall. How much did the plant grow in one week? Mark your answer on a grid. 🔖 2.2.c.

14 You construct a rectangular picture frame out of strips of wood that are $\frac{3}{4}$ inch wide. The dimensions of the outside of the frame are $6\frac{1}{2}$ inches wide by $8\frac{1}{4}$ inches long. Can you fit a picture that is 5 inches wide and 7 inches long in your frame? **Explain**. 🔖 2.2.c.

15 A car is $14\frac{4}{5}$ feet long. Another car is $1\frac{1}{10}$ feet longer. Can the two cars fit end to end in a driveway that is $31\frac{1}{2}$ feet long? If so, how much space is left? If not, how much more space is needed? **Explain** how you solved the problem. 🔖 2.2.c.

Performance Assessment

Writing Math
What steps do you need to take to add or subtract fractions with unlike denominators?

Hiking Trails

Tennessee has more than 40 state parks, with a wide range of activities available at each one. The table below shows information about hiking trails at Dunbar Cave State Natural Area and Cedars of Lebanon State Park.

For 1–4, use the table.

1. How many times as great is the length of Recovery Trail as the length of Short Loop trail?

2. Suppose you hike all three trails at Dunbar. How many miles will you hike in all? **Explain.**

Hiking Trails	
Park/Trail	**Length (mi)**
Dunbar/Lake Trail	$\frac{2}{3}$
Dunbar/Short Loop	$\frac{4}{5}$
Dunbar/Recovery Trail	$1\frac{7}{10}$
Cedars/Cedar Forest Trail	2
Cedars/Dixon Merrit Trail	$\frac{1}{2}$
Cedars/Hidden Springs Trail	5

3. How much longer is the longest trail at Cedars than the longest trail at Dunbar?

4. Over two weeks, Yvette hiked four of the trails. She hiked a total of $8\frac{3}{10}$ mi. On which trails did she hike?

5. In Cedars of Lebanon State Park, a total of 900 acres are used for recreational activities. This represents $\frac{1}{10}$ of the total area of the park. The rest of the park is operated by the state forestry division as a state park. How many acres are **not** used for recreation? **Explain.**

6. **Stretch Your Thinking** The expected winter low temperature in Cedars of Lebanon State Park is 35°F. This is $\frac{7}{18}$ of the expected summer high temperature. What is the expected high temperature during the summer? **Explain.**

Unit Learning Task

Healthy Eating

Objective: To represent fractions and mixed numbers.

1. Discuss what you know about healthy eating and the food pyramid.

2. Find your favorite recipe and make a poster to display the information in the recipe.

3. Show how to convert any mixed numbers to improper fractions on your poster.

4. Does your recipe contain healthy ingredients? **Explain**.

5. How could you modify your recipe so it contains the ingredients that are most healthy? **Explain**.

6. **Explain** how fractions are used in the kitchen.

Counting Votes

George Washington

The Electoral College

When citizens vote for President and Vice President of the United States, they are actually choosing people called electors, who will cast ballots for the President and Vice President in the Electoral College. Today the candidate who gets the most votes from citizens of a particular state generally gets all of that state's electoral votes.

The current total number of electors in the Electoral College is 538. The number of electors each state has equals the number of senators it has in the Senate (2 for each state) plus the numbers of representatives it has in the House of Representatives. States with larger populations have more representatives. Another 3 electors represent the District of Columbia.

FACT·ACTIVITY

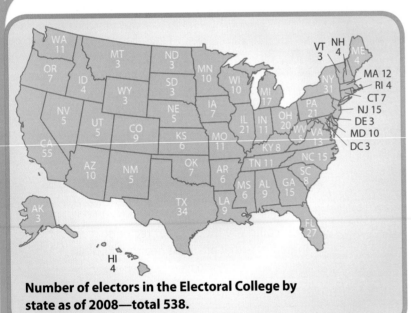

Number of electors in the Electoral College by state as of 2008—total 538.

For 1–4, use the map. Write all fractions in simplest form. Round all decimals to the nearest hundredth.

❶ A candidate must receive a majority (more than half) of the electoral votes to become president. How many electoral votes were needed to win the 2008 election? Write this amount as a fraction and a percent of the total votes.

❷ What fraction of the total number of electors does your state have? What percent of the total does it have?

❸ What is the least number of states or regions a candidate can win and still win the election?

❹ **Pose a Problem** Write a problem like Problem 2 about the number of electors in a state other than your own.

One Vote

ALMANAC Fact

1876 One vote gave Rutherford B. Hayes the presidency of the United States. Although his opponent received more citizens' votes than Hayes, the Electoral College decided in favor of Hayes by a vote of 185 to 184.

Any United States citizen who is 18 years old or older has the right to vote in local, state, and national elections. People vote for the leaders of their cities, counties, states, and country. They also vote to decide important local issues such as whether a new school should be built.

A representative has introduced a bill to eliminate the penny. How would you vote on this issue, which would affect everyone in the United States? The chart below offers some arguments in the debate about pennies.

FACT·ACTIVITY

Conduct a survey of 30 people. Each person should select *Yes* or *No* and a reason for that choice. You may add other reasons, but there should be an equal number of reasons for each choice.

▶ Write a fraction and a decimal for the part of the total number of people who select each option such as *Yes–Reason A* or *No–Reason B*.

▶ Write a fraction and decimal to represent the part of the total number of people who select *Yes* and the part of the total number of people who select *No*.

▶ Write a paragraph analyzing your results. Include a statement that orders the decimals or fractions from greatest to least.

Should the United States Stop Making Pennies?

Yes	No
A Vending machines don't take pennies.	**A** Pennies keep prices down. Without the penny, vendors would raise prices to the next highest nickel.
B Pennies are copper-coated zinc. The price of zinc has increased so much that the penny now costs 1.4 cents to make, according to the United States Mint.	**B** Pennies represent a piece of history and honor President Abraham Lincoln. The Lincoln penny was the first U.S. coin to show a historic figure. Lincoln has been on the penny since 1909, the 100th anniversary of his birth.
C Pennies are too heavy to carry around.	**C** You can cash in rolls of pennies for dollars.

Algebra

BIG IDEAS!

- The number line can be extended to show negative numbers; operations with integers are based on operations with whole numbers; rational numbers build on an understanding of fractions and their opposites and can be compared and ordered on a number line.

- Properties and the concepts of algebra are used to evaluate expressions and solve equations for all four operations.

- Growing and repeating patterns can be generalized with words and symbols.

Math On Location

REAL WORLD

1

The topography of Mars has been studied extensively with scientific explorations.

2

The photographs and data collected from the surface rovers are used to develop and evaluate theories.

3

Scientists use positive and negative rational numbers to describe altitudes and depths.

Get Ready Game

Operation Scramble

$3+4-2\div1=5$

Materials
- 1 deck of *Operation Scramble* cards
- Pencil and paper for each player

How to Play Play in pairs. Shuffle the cards and deal four cards to each player. Players should not show their cards. Turn over the next card and place it face up where both players can see it. The number on this card is the *target number*. Both players should use these steps.

1 Use the numbers on all four cards in your hand and any of the operations $+$, $-$, $\times$, and $\div$ to write an expression that equals the target number. You may use parentheses.

2 The first person to write an expression tells the other person. Both players stop working. Check the work of the player who finished first. If the expression is correct, that player earns one point.

How to Win Be the first player to earn three points.

Draw Conclusions
Complete this exercise after playing the game.

1. **Reasoning** Suppose you have only even numbers on the cards in your hand, and the target number is odd. Give an example of a correct expression and target number that fits this description. Explain how you chose the correct operations to use.

Reading When you read a story, you can look at the illustrations to help you visualize or picture what is happening. To visualize math, it can be helpful to show the information and numbers in a word problem in a different way.

Read the problem.
Use the thermometer to help you visualize the numbers.

Problem 1

Yesterday's temperature was 6 degrees Celsius. The temperature dropped 8 degrees overnight. What is today's temperature?

°Celsius

I can use the thermometer like a number line.

Writing Read Problem 2. Show the information in a different way to solve the problem.

Problem 2

The temperature is ⁻4°C at noon. It rises 5 degrees over the next three hours. By 7:00 P.M., the temperature falls 6 degrees. What is the temperature at 7:00 P.M.?

°Celsius

Integers and Rational Numbers

Investigate

The table shows the 2004–2006 seasonal and 30-year average precipitation amounts at Chicago O'Hare International Airport. Use the data in the table to draw conclusions about four precipitation amounts. Express numbers as positive or negative to represent how much above or below average the amounts are.

Fun Fact

In 2005, northern and western Illinois had one of the area's most severe short-term droughts on record. The period from March to December ranked as the third driest in 112 years.

Chicago O'Hare International Airport 2004–2006 Precipitation (in.)			
Season	2004	2005	2006	1973–2003 Average
Winter	3.43	7.34	5.92	5.59
Spring	10.64	5.00	9.95	9.82
Summer	10.78	5.18	10.70	11.95
Fall	7.39	6.36	13.54	9.00
Total	32.24	23.88	40.11	36.36

GO ONLINE

Technology
Student pages are available in the Student eBook

Show What You Know

Check your understanding of important skills needed for success in Chapter 5.

▶ **Read a Thermometer**

Write the temperature shown by each letter on the thermometer.

1. A
2. B
3. C
4. D

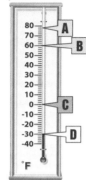

▶ **Missing Factors**

Find the missing factor.

5. $5 \times \blacksquare = 25$ 6. $\blacksquare \times 8 = 48$ 7. $12 \times \blacksquare = 144$ 8. $\blacksquare \times 9 = 63$

9. $\blacksquare \times 11 = 66$ 10. $13 \times \blacksquare = 65$ 11. $\blacksquare \times 24 = 240$ 12. $21 \times \blacksquare = 147$

▶ **Practice Division Facts**

Find the quotient

13. $20 \div 2$ 14. $15 \div 3$ 15. $24 \div 8$ 16. $36 \div 4$ 17. $49 \div 7$

18. $60 \div 5$ 19. $81 \div 9$ 20. $88 \div 11$ 21. $100 \div 5$ 22. $84 \div 12$

Vocabulary

Visualize It!

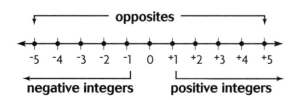

opposites

−5 −4 −3 −2 −1 0 +1 +2 +3 +4 +5

negative integers   positive integers

Language Tips

In Math, every number has an opposite. An opposite in math are two numbers that are equal distance from zero on the number line.

English	Spanish
integer	número entero
negative ntegers	número entero negativo

See **English-Spanish Glossary.**

LESSON 1

★ **2.2.d.** Use the basic operations on integers to solve problems.

Vocabulary

absolute value

integer

negative integers

positive integers

Materials
• MathBoard

Understand Integers

Essential Question How can you use positive and negative counters to add integers?

PROBLEM The highest elevation in the state of Maryland is the top of Backbone Mountain, 3,360 ft above sea level. The lowest elevation in Maryland is the Chesapeake Bay, 174 ft below sea level. How can you use integers to represent these elevations?

Integers include all whole numbers and their opposites. Each integer has an opposite that is the same distance from 0 on a number line but on the opposite side of 0. The opposite of positive 5 ($^+5$) is negative 5 ($^-5$). The opposite of 0 is 0.

Integers greater than 0 are **positive integers**. Write positive integers with or without a positive sign, $^+$. Integers less than 0 are **negative integers**. Write negative integers with a negative sign, $^-$. The integer 0 is neither positive nor negative.

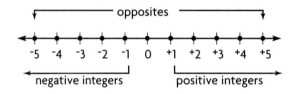

Use integers to represent the situation.

Sea level equals 0 feet. Positive integers represent elevations above sea level. Negative integers represent elevations below sea level.

So, $^+3,360$ or 3,360 represents the highest elevation in Maryland, and $^-174$ represents the lowest elevation in Maryland.

The **absolute value** of an integer is its distance from 0 on a number line.

Look at the opposites $^-2$ and $^+2$. They are both 2 units from 0.

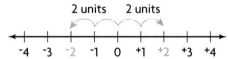

Write: $|^-2| = 2$.   Read: The absolute value of negative two is two.

Write: $|^+2| = 2$.   Read: The absolute value of positive two is two.

So, $|^-3| = 3$.

Find the absolute value of $^-3$.

Look at the number line.
$^-3$ is 3 units from 0.

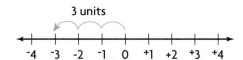

Compare and Order Integers

The coldest January temperature on record for Baltimore, Maryland is ⁻7°F. The coldest February temperature on record is ⁻3°F. Is ⁻7°F colder or warmer than ⁻3°F?

Compare ⁻7°F and ⁻3°F.

You can use a number line to compare temperatures. On a number line, each number is greater than any number to its left and less than any number to its right.

Locate the integers on a number line.

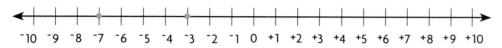

The integer ⁻7 is to the left of ⁻3, which means that ⁻7 is less than ⁻3.

So, ⁻7°F is colder than ⁻3°F.

Compare the integers. Use <, >, or =.

⁺3 and ⁻6

Think about the positions on a number line.

⁺3 is to the right of ⁻6 on the number line.

So, ⁺3 > ⁻6 or ⁻6 < ⁺3.

⁻4 and ⁻9

Think about the positions on a number line.

⁻4 is to the right of ⁻9 on the number line.

So, ⁻4 > ⁻9 or ⁻9 < ⁻4.

• Is a positive integer always greater than a negative integer? Explain.

▶ **Share and Show**

1. Find |⁻4|.
   Think: ⁻4 is 4 units from 0 on the number line.

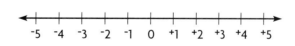

Write the opposite integer.

2. ⁺5   3. ⁻9   4. 0   5. 16   6. |⁻34| ✓7. ⁻23

Write an integer to represent each situation.

8. a gain of 10 yd   9. a cave 3 ft underground   ✓10. a $35 decline in value

11. **Math Talk** **Explain** how to use a number line to compare two integers.

Write the opposite integer.

12. $^{+}20$ **13.** $^{-}10$ **14.** $^{+}62$ **15.** 0 **16.** $^{-}91$ **17.** $^{+}88$

Write an integer to represent each situation.

18. a loss of 5 lb   **19.** a profit of \$100   **20.** a 200-ft increase in altitude

21. a decrease of 10 points   **22.** an increase of 7 cents   **23.** 45 degrees below 0

Compare. Write $<$, $>$, or $=$ for each ⬭.

24. $^{-}8$ ⬭ $^{+}6$ **25.** $^{-}4$ ⬭ $^{-}4$ **26.** $^{-}9$ ⬭ $^{-}7$ **27.** 0 ⬭ 10

28. $^{-}17$ ⬭ $^{-}18$ **29.** $|^{-}24|$ ⬭ $|^{+}21|$ **30.** 16 ⬭ $|^{-}61|$ **31.** $|^{-}95|$ ⬭ $|^{+}95|$

Write the letter that represents the integer on the number line.

32. $^{+}7$ **33.** $^{-}5$

34. $^{-}2$ **35.** $^{+}5$

36. $^{+}1$ **37.** $|^{-}1|$

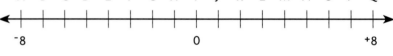

Name the integer that is 1 more.

38. $^{+}7$ **39.** $^{-}3$ **40.** 0 **41.** $^{-}9$ **42.** $^{+}11$ **43.** $|^{+}15|$

44. ≡**FAST FACT** The lowest temperature for the state of Maryland, $^{-}40°F$, was recorded on January 13, 1912. Is this temperature lower or higher than $^{-}38°F$?

45. Reasoning What values can n have if $|n| = 4$?

46. **Write Math** ➤ **What's the Error?** Tom says that $|^{-}9|$ is less than $^{+}8$. Describe his error. What is the correct comparison?

 OCCT Test Prep   Math Board

47. A football team lost 3 yd on the first play of the game. Which integer represents this?

     A $^{-}3$ **C** $^{+}5$

     B $^{+}3$ **D** $^{-}5$

48. Which statement is true?

$$\frac{8}{9} \times \frac{9}{8} = g$$

     A $^{-}6 < ^{-}8$ **C** $^{-}6 > ^{+}8$

     B $^{+}6 > ^{+}8$ **D** $^{-}6 > ^{-}8$

☆Standards Quick Check

Compare. Write <, >, or = for each ⬭ .

1. 2 ⬭ 22

2. 16 ⬭ 0

3. |⁻24| ⬭ |⁺24|

4. ⁺7 ⬭ ⁻6

5. ⁻184 ⬭ ⁺184

6. ⁺105 ⬭ ⁻150

Name the integer that is 1 more.

7. ⁻142

8. ⁺108

9. ⁻42

10. ⁺432

11. ⁻981

12. ⁻1,451

H.O.T.

Scientists categorize the planets Earth, Mercury, Venus, and Mars as terrestrial planets. Terrestrial planets have solid surfaces. Some other planets are made up of gases. The table shows the average surface temperatures of the terrestrial planets.

Average Surface Temperature of Terrestrial Planets

Planet	Temperature (C°)
Earth	15
Mercury	179
Venus	480
Mars	⁻23

Earth Mercury Venus Mars

1. Which terrestrial planet has the greatest average surface temperature?

2. What integer represents the opposite of the average surface temperature of Mercury?

3. What is the absolute value of the average surface temperature of Mars?

4. Compare the average surface temperature of Earth with the average surface temperature of Mars.

★ **2.2.d.** Use the basic operations on integers to solve problems.

Materials
• MathBoard

Remember

Pairs of red and yellow counters equal 0.

Add Integers

Essential Question How do you use number lines or absolute value to add integers?

PROBLEM On the first play of a football game, the home team gained 7 yd. On the second play, it lost 8 yd. How many yards did the home team gain or lose on the first two plays of the game?

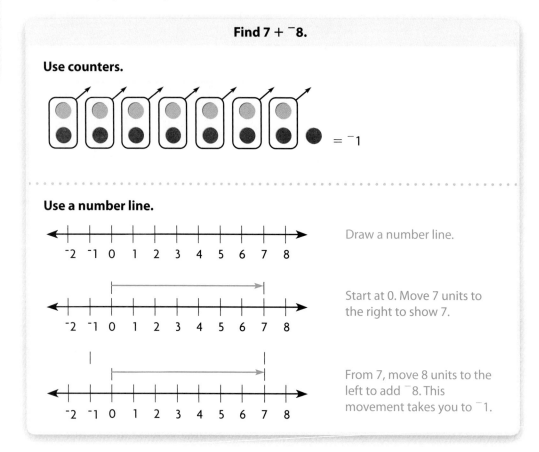

Find 7 + ⁻8.

Use counters.

= ⁻1

Use a number line.

Draw a number line.

Start at 0. Move 7 units to the right to show 7.

From 7, move 8 units to the left to add ⁻8. This movement takes you to ⁻1.

So, the sum of the yards on the two plays is ⁻1. This means that the home team lost 1 yd on the first two plays of the game.

• **What if** the team lost 4 yd on the first play and lost 3 yd on the second play? Use a number line to find the number of yards the team gained or lost in all.

• When integers are added on a number line, when do the arrows point in the same direction? When do the arrows point in different directions?

Use Absolute Value

Adding with the Same Sign

When adding integers with like signs, add the absolute values of the addends. Use the sign of the addends for the sum.

Find ⁻6 + ⁻3.

$$^-6 + {}^-3 = |{}^-6| + |{}^-3| \quad \text{Add the absolute values}$$
$$= 6 + 3 = 9 \quad \text{of the integers.}$$

Use the sign of the original addends. So, ⁻6 + ⁻3 = ⁻9.

Adding with Different Signs

When adding integers with unlike signs, subtract the lesser absolute value from the greater absolute value. Use the sign of the addend with the greater absolute value for the sum.

Find ⁻1 + 5.

$$^-1 + 5 = |5| - |{}^-1| \quad |5| > |{}^-1|, \text{ so subtract}$$
$$= 5 - 1 \quad\quad\; |{}^-1| \text{ from } |5|.$$
$$= 4$$

Use the sign of the addend with the greater absolute value.

$$|5| > |{}^-1| \quad \text{Use the positive sign of}$$
$$\text{the 5. The sum is positive.}$$

So, ⁻1 + 5 = 4.

Find 2 + ⁻8.

$$2 + {}^-8 = |{}^-8| - |2| \quad |{}^-8| > |2|, \text{ so subtract}$$
$$= 8 - 2 \quad\quad\; |2| \text{ from } |{}^-8|.$$
$$= 6$$

Use the sign of the addend with the greater absolute value.

$$|{}^-8| > |2| \quad \text{Use the negative sign of the 8.}$$
$$\text{The sum is negative.}$$

So, 2 + ⁻8 = ⁻6.

Share and Show

1. Use the number line to find ⁻6 + 4.

2. Use the number line to find 6 + ⁻7.

Find the sum.

3. ⁻4 + 5   **4.** ⁻2 + ⁻6   **5.** 3 + 3   **6.** ⁻7 + 1   ✅ **7.** ⁻25 + ⁻12

8. ⁻9 + ⁻6   **9.** ⁻15 + 3   **10.** 16 + ⁻14   **11.** ⁻23 + ⁻9   ✅ **12.** ⁻19 + 24

13. **Math Talk** **Explain** how you determine the sign of the sum of two integers.

Practice and Problem Solving REAL WORLD

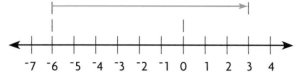

Write the addition problem modeled on the number line.

14.

15.

Find the sum.

16. $^-2 + {}^-1$

17. $4 + 2$

18. $^-5 + 9$

19. $3 + {}^-6$

20. $^-6 + 4$

21. $^-12 + {}^-7$

22. $^-18 + 5$

23. $17 + 12$

24. $22 + {}^-19$

25. $^-48 + 34$

Use mental math to find the value of the variable.

26. $^-4 + t = {}^-14$

27. $y + {}^-3 = 5$

28. $x + 2 = {}^-6$

29. $38 + a = 1$

30. A nationally televised football game usually begins at about 6:00 P.M. on the East Coast. Using the number line at the right, what addition number sentence could you write to show the time on the West Coast at the start of the game?

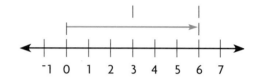

31. Write a situation that this addition sentence could represent.

$$^-16 + 9 = {}^-7$$

32. **Reasoning** Is the sum of a positive integer and $^-7$ greater than or less than $^-7$? **Explain.**

33. At the start of the game, the Wildcats were penalized 5 yd for delaying the game. Then they were penalized 5 yd more for having too many players on the field. After their first play, they gained 12 yd. How many yards had they gained or lost in all?

34. **Write Math** ▶ **What's the Question?** A number line shows a blue arrow beginning at 0 and ending at 5. It also shows a red arrow above the blue arrow beginning at 5 and ending at $^-3$. The answer is $^-3$.

⭐ **OCCT Test Prep** Math Board

35. What is the sum of $^-9$ and $^-3$?

    A $^-12$ **C** 6

    B $^-6$ **D** 12

36. What is the sum of $^-274$ and 182?

    A $^-456$ **C** 92

    B $^-92$ **D** 456

GO ONLINE —Technology— Use HMH Mega Math, Fraction Action, *Number Line Mine,* Level W.

⭐ Standards Quick Check

Find the sum.

1. $9 + {}^-8$

2. $0 + {}^-5$

3. ${}^-10 + {}^-16$

4. ${}^-4 + 16$

5. $15 + {}^-15$

6. ${}^-124 + 18$

Challenge H.O.T.

Using Properties to Simplify Integer Addition

You can use the Commutative and Associative Properties of Addition to simplify the addition of integers.

Commutative Property of Addition

$$
\begin{aligned}
{}^-1 + 3 &= 3 + {}^-1 \quad \text{Change the order of} \\
&= |3| - |{}^-1| \quad \text{the addends.} \\
&= 3 - 1 \\
&= 2
\end{aligned}
$$

Associative Property of Addition

$$
\begin{aligned}
1 + (3 + {}^-1) &= (1 + 3) + {}^-1 \quad \text{Change the} \\
&= 4 + {}^-1 \quad \text{grouping of the} \\
&= |4| - |{}^-1| \quad \text{addends.} \\
&= 4 - 1 \\
&= 3
\end{aligned}
$$

You can use both properties together to simplify problems involving the addition of integers.

Commutative and Associative Properties of Addition

$$
\begin{aligned}
17 + (9 + {}^-17) &= (17 + {}^-17) + 9 \quad \text{Change the order and the} \\
&= 0 + 9 \quad \text{grouping of the addends.} \\
&= 9
\end{aligned}
$$

Use the Commutative and Associative Properties to help find the sum.

1. ${}^-5 + {}^-6 + 5$

2. $(10 + {}^-5) + {}^-2$

3. ${}^-7 + 2 + {}^-13$

4. ${}^-6 + (6 + {}^-8)$

5. $(15 + {}^-3) + 25$

6. ${}^-14 + 19 + {}^-9$

7. ${}^-23 + ({}^-18 + 23)$

8. ${}^-19 + 24$

9. ${}^-36 + 59$

10. ${}^-12 + ({}^-27 + 12)$

11. $(19 + {}^-6) + 11$

12. $(52 + {}^-14) + {}^-16$

★ **2.2.d.** Use the basic operations on integers to solve problems.

Materials
• MathBoard

Subtract Integers

Essential Question How do you use number lines or absolute value to subtract integers?

PROBLEM The temperature in Detroit, Michigan was ⁻2°F in the morning. It increased to 5°F by the afternoon. How much greater was the temperature in the afternoon?

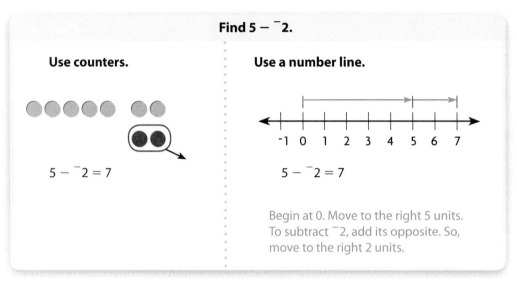

Find 5 − ⁻2.

Use counters.

$5 − {}^{-}2 = 7$

Use a number line.

$5 − {}^{-}2 = 7$

Begin at 0. Move to the right 5 units. To subtract ⁻2, add its opposite. So, move to the right 2 units.

So, the temperature was 7°F greater in the afternoon.

You can find the difference of two integers by adding the opposite of the integer you are subtracting. You can then use the rules for addition of integers.

Find ⁻6 − ⁻3.

$^{-}6 − {}^{-}3 = {}^{-}6 + 3$

$^{-}6 + 3$

$|{}^{-}6| − |{}^{-}3| = 6 − 3 = 3$

$|{}^{-}6| > |3| → {}^{-}6 − {}^{-}3 = {}^{-}3$

Write as an addition problem. Use the rules for addition of integers.

Subtract the lesser absolute value from the greater absolute value.

Use the sign of the addend with the greater absolute value.

So, $^{-}6 − {}^{-}3 = {}^{-}3$.

You can use this key sequence on a calculator.

Examples

The low temperature at the Camelback ski resort in the Pocono Mountains of Pennsylvania was ⁻7°C one day. The high temperature was 4°C. What was the range of temperatures?

Subtract. $4 - {}^-7$

$4 - {}^-7 = 4 + 7$ To subtract ⁻7, add its opposite.
$\phantom{4 - {}^-7} = 11$ Use the rules for addition of integers.

So, $4 - {}^-7 = 11$, which means the range of temperatures was 11°C.

Subtract. $3 - 9$

$3 - 9 = 3 + {}^-9$ Write as an addition problem. Use the rules for addition of integers.
$3 + {}^-9$

$|{}^-9| - |3| = 9 - 3$ Subtract the lesser absolute value from the greater absolute value.
$\phantom{|{}^-9| - |3|} = 6$

$|{}^-9| > |3| \rightarrow 3 - 9 = {}^-6$ Use the sign of the addend with the greater absolute value.

So, $3 - 9 = {}^-6$.

Subtract. ${}^-2 - 5$

${}^-2 - 5 = {}^-2 + 5$ Write as an addition problem. Use the rules for addition of integers.
${}^-2 + 5$

$|{}^-2| - |{}^-5| = 2 + 5$ Add the absolute values of the integers.
$\phantom{|{}^-2| - |{}^-5|} = 7$

${}^-2 + {}^-5 = {}^-7$ Use the sign of the original addends. The sum is negative.

So, ${}^-2 - 5 = {}^-7$.

- How can you check your answers?
- Explain how to find the difference $0 - 3$.

 Share and Show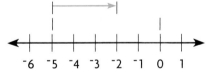

1. Use the number line to find ${}^-5 - {}^-3$.

```
◄──┼──┼──┼──┼──┼──┼──┼──►
   ⁻6  ⁻5  ⁻4  ⁻3  ⁻2  ⁻1  0   1
```

Write the subtraction problem as an addition problem.

2. ${}^-2 - {}^-7$ **3.** ${}^-3 - 8$ **4.** $4 - 19$ **5.** $15 - {}^-11$ ✅ **6.** $23 - {}^-9$

Find the difference.

7. ${}^-1 - 4$ **8.** ${}^-3 - {}^-9$ **9.** $18 - {}^-6$ **10.** ${}^-17 - {}^-12$ ✅ **11.** $13 - 22$

12. **Math Talk** Explain how to use a number line to subtract ${}^-8 - {}^-2$.

Practice and Problem Solving REAL WORLD

Write the subtraction problem as an addition problem.

13. $^-7 - 4$ **14.** $5 - 7$ **15.** $^-8 - ^-1$ **16.** $5 - 11$ **17.** $9 - ^-5$

18. $^-16 - 8$ **19.** $|10| - ^-23$ **20.** $^-24 - |^-37|$ **21.** $|41| - |^-33|$ **22.** $|0| - |^-57|$

Find the difference.

23. $5 - ^-5$ **24.** $^-6 - 5$ **25.** $^-4 - 16$ **26.** $^-12 - ^-7$ **27.** $2 - 17$

28. $0 - ^-36$ **29.** $33 - |^-11|$ **30.** $|^-14| - |^-28|$ **31.** $37 - |^-63|$ **32.** $|^-74| - |^-25|$

Use mental math to find the value of the variable.

33. $3 - a = 2$ **34.** $n - ^-4 = ^-4$ **35.** $7 - ^-6 = s$ **36.** $b - 7 = ^-15$

37. $^-4 - t = ^-13$ **38.** $y - ^-3 = 1$ **39.** $x - 9 = ^-3$ **40.** $1 - x = 5$

Find each output.

41. Rule: Subtract $^-5$.

Input	7	$^-1$	$^-6$
Output			

42. Rule: Subtract 3.

Input	$^-8$	$^-3$	1
Output			

43. Rule: Subtract $^-11$.

Input	0	5	$^-12$
Output			

 Real World Data

For 44–45, use the table.

44. How much greater was the low temperature in Tallahassee, Florida, than in Charlotte, North Carolina?

45. What is the difference between the greatest and least temperatures shown in the table?

46. The temperature on Sunday morning was $^-2$°F. The temperature dropped 7°F by Monday and then rose 5°F by Tuesday. What was the temperature on Tuesday?

47. **Write Math** ▶ **Sense or Nonsense** Maria says that $^-13 - ^-8 = 21$. Does her answer make sense? **Explain.**

Cold Wave of February 1899	
City	**Low Temperature (°F)**
Tallahassee, FL	$^-2$
Washington, DC	$^-15$
Charlotte, NC	$^-5$
Cleveland, OH	$^-16$
Logan, MT	$^-61$

OCCT Test Prep Math Board

48. Which is the difference of $^-14 - ^-6$?

   A $^-20$ **C** 8

   B $^-8$ **D** 20

49. Which is the difference of $^-157 - 65$?

   A $^-222$ **C** 92

   B $^-92$ **D** 222

⭐ Standards Quick Check

Find the difference.

1. ⁻13 − 12

2. ⁻6 − ⁻8

3. 0 − ⁻15

4. 48 − |⁻18|

5. 21 − ⁻16

6. |⁻56| − |⁻42|

Challenge H.O.T.

Windchill is the temperature that the outside temperature feels like when the wind is blowing. The table shows the windchill temperature for a given outside temperature and wind speed.

> Suppose the outside temperature is 10°F and the wind speed is 20 mi per hr. Find the change in windchill if the wind speed increases to 40 mi per hr.
>
> ⁻9 − ⁻15 = ⁻9 + 15 = 6
>
> So, the change is 6°F.

Windchill Temperature

		Outside Temperature (°F)					
		40	30	20	10	0	⁻10
Wind Speed (mi per hr)	5	36	25	13	1	⁻11	⁻22
	10	34	21	9	⁻4	⁻16	⁻28
	15	32	19	6	⁻7	⁻19	⁻32
	20	30	17	4	⁻9	⁻22	⁻35
	25	29	16	3	⁻11	⁻24	⁻37
	30	28	15	1	⁻12	⁻26	⁻39
	35	28	14	0	⁻14	⁻27	⁻41
	40	27	13	⁻1	⁻15	⁻29	⁻43

Use the table to solve.

1. What does an outside temperature of ⁻10°F feel like when the wind speed is 40 mi per hour?

2. Suppose the windchill temperature is ⁻4°F when the wind speed is 10 mi per hr. What is the outside temperature?

3. The outside temperature is 20°F, and the wind speed is 40 mi per hr. How much higher is the outside temperature than the windchill?

4. The outside temperature in the morning and afternoon is 10°F. Find the change in windchill if the wind speed increases from 5 mi per hr in the morning to 30 mi per hr in the afternoon.

2.2.d. Use the basic operations on integers to solve problems.

Materials
- MathBoard
- two-color counters

Multiply Integers

Essential Question How do negative numbers affect multiplication?

Use red and yellow counters to model multiplication of integers. A yellow counter represents 1. A red counter represents ⁻1.

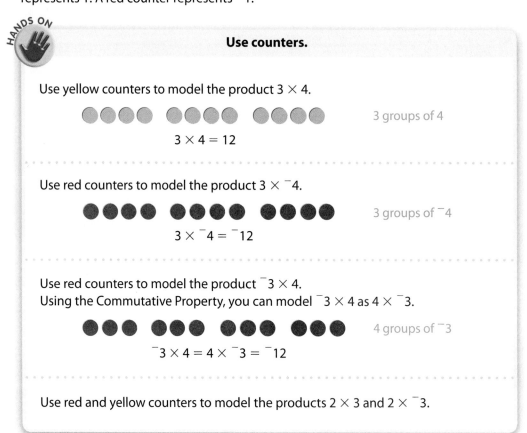

Use counters.

Use yellow counters to model the product 3 × 4.

3 groups of 4

3 × 4 = 12

Use red counters to model the product 3 × ⁻4.

3 groups of ⁻4

3 × ⁻4 = ⁻12

Use red counters to model the product ⁻3 × 4.
Using the Commutative Property, you can model ⁻3 × 4 as 4 × ⁻3.

4 groups of ⁻3

⁻3 × 4 = 4 × ⁻3 = ⁻12

Use red and yellow counters to model the products 2 × 3 and 2 × ⁻3.

- What do you notice about the product of two positive integers? What do you notice about the product of a positive integer and a negative integer?

Use a number line to find 6 × ⁻20.

Many shipwrecks have occurred off the coast of Maine. A British freighter, the *Wandby*, lies 20 ft below sea level. The *Amaretto*, a fishing vessel, lies 6 times as deep as the *Wandby*. At what depth is the *Amaretto*?

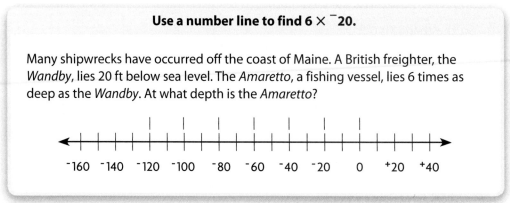

The number line shows that 6 × ⁻20 = ⁻120.
So, the *Amaretto* lies 120 ft below sea level, or at ⁻120.

Multiplication Patterns

Examples

A scuba diver is 3 m below the surface of the water. An underwater vehicle dives 5 times as deep as the scuba diver. How deep is the underwater vehicle?

You can use patterns to find rules for multiplying integers.

Complete the pattern to find $5 \times {}^-3$.

$5 \times 3 = 15$	Study the pattern. As the second factor decreases by 1, the product decreases by 5. Use this rule to complete the pattern.	$5 \times 3 = 15$
$5 \times 2 = 10$		$5 \times 2 = 10$
$5 \times 1 = 5$		$5 \times 1 = 5$
$5 \times 0 = 0$		$5 \times 0 = 0$
$5 \times {}^-1 = {}^-5$		$5 \times {}^-1 = {}^-5$
$5 \times {}^-2 = {}^-10$		$5 \times {}^-2 = {}^-10$
$5 \times {}^-3 = \blacksquare$		$5 \times {}^-3 = {}^-15$

So, the underwater vehicle is 15 m below sea level.

${}^-5 \times 3 = {}^-15$	Study the pattern. As the second factor decreases by 1, the product increases by 5. Use this rule to complete the pattern.	${}^-5 \times 3 = {}^-15$
${}^-5 \times 2 = {}^-10$		${}^-5 \times 2 = {}^-10$
${}^-5 \times 1 = {}^-5$		${}^-5 \times 1 = {}^-5$
${}^-5 \times 0 = 0$		${}^-5 \times 0 = 0$
${}^-5 \times {}^-1 = \blacksquare$		${}^-5 \times {}^-1 = 5$
${}^-5 \times {}^-2 = \blacksquare$		${}^-5 \times {}^-2 = 10$
${}^-5 \times {}^-3 = \blacksquare$		${}^-5 \times {}^-3 = 15$

So, the missing products are 5, 10, and 15.

The two above examples lead to the rules to the right.

> The product of two integers with like signs is positive.
> $5 \times 6 = 30$ ${}^-4 \times {}^-3 = 12$
> The product of two integers with unlike signs is negative.
> $2 \times {}^-3 = {}^-6$ ${}^-7 \times 4 = {}^-28$

 ▶ **Share and Show**   Math Board

1. Use the number line to find $4 \times {}^-2$.

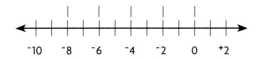

2. Use the counters to find $3 \times {}^-3$.

Find the product.

3. ${}^-3 \times {}^-6$ **4.** 2×12 ✅ **5.** ${}^-19 \times 0$ ✅ **6.** $8 \times {}^-9$

7. Math Talk **Explain** how to determine the sign of a product when you multiply two integers.

Evaluate the expression.

8. $^-8 \times {}^-1$

9. $5 \times {}^-2$

10. $^-7 \times 4$

11. 5×11

12. $0 \times {}^-5$

13. $^-14 \times {}^-7$

14. $10 \times {}^-60$

15. $^-12 \times 12$

16. $^-28 \times 14$

17. $^-47 \times {}^-25$

18. $73 \times |{}^-13|$

19. $|{}^-54 \times {}^-19|$

Use mental math to find the value of the variable.

20. $4 \times c = 12$

21. $^-5 \times n = 35$

22. $8 \times s = {}^-40$

23. $^-9 \times t = {}^-72$

24. $^-12 \times b = {}^-48$

25. $^-14 \times y = 14$

26. $2 \times m = {}^-20$

27. $^-3 \times a = 0$

Evaluate the expression.

28. $^-7 + {}^-8$

29. $^-1 \times 13$

30. $3 \times {}^-9$

31. $^-8 - 6$

32. $16 - 8$

33. $4 - {}^-13$

34. 5×80

35. $-17 + 6$

36. $^-52 + 20$

37. $^-43 \times {}^-13$

38. $32 + 23$

39. $-37 - {}^-18$

40. Show how you could use the Commutative and Associative Properties to help find the product. Then find the product.

$$^-5 \times (13 \times {}^-2)$$

41. Find each output.
Rule: Multiply by $^-5$.

Input	$^-7$	$^-4$	7	11
Output	a	b	c	d

42. What does $0 \times {}^-12$ mean?

43. Look at the diagram at the right. An underwater robot is 30 ft below the surface of the water. A shipwreck is 5 times as deep. How much deeper than the underwater robot is the shipwreck?

44. **Pose a Problem** Look at Problem 43. Write and solve a similar problem.

45. **Write Math** ► **What's the Question?** The answer is the product $^-36$.

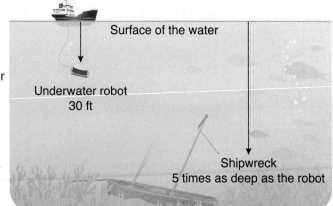

Surface of the water

Underwater robot
30 ft

Shipwreck
5 times as deep as the robot

 OCCT Test Prep

46. Which is the product of $14 \times {}^-8$?

    A 12   **C** $^-112$

    B $^-98$ **D** $^-122$

47. Which is the product of $^-6 \times {}^-11$?

    A $^-66$ **C** 17

    B $^-17$ **D** 66

★ Standards Quick Check

Find the product.

1. $^-4 \times {}^-6$

2. $15 \times {}^-12$

3. $^-9 \times 12$

4. $^-24 \times {}^-5$

5. $18 \times {}^-36$

6. $^-21 \times {}^-17$

H.O.T.

Products of Negative Integers

The sign of the product of any number of positive integers is always positive. However, the sign of the product of negative integers might be either positive $\left(^-3 \times {}^-3 = 9\right)$ or negative $\left(^-3 \times {}^-3 \times {}^-3 = {}^-27\right)$.

Study the pattern in the table.

- What is the sign of the product of 3, 5, or 7 negative integers?

- What is the sign of the product of 4, 6, or 8 negative integers?

- What does this tell you about the sign of the product of an odd number of negative integers? of an even number of negative integers?

$^-2 \times {}^-2 \times {}^-2 = {}^-8$
$^-2 \times {}^-2 \times {}^-2 \times {}^-2 = 16$
$^-2 \times {}^-2 \times {}^-2 \times {}^-2 \times {}^-2 = {}^-32$
$^-2 \times {}^-2 \times {}^-2 \times {}^-2 \times {}^-2 \times {}^-2 = 64$
$^-2 \times {}^-2 \times {}^-2 \times {}^-2 \times {}^-2 \times {}^-2 \times {}^-2 = {}^-128$
$^-2 \times {}^-2 \times {}^-2 \times {}^-2 \times {}^-2 \times {}^-2 \times {}^-2 \times {}^-2 = 256$

- What would be the sign of $^-2 \times {}^-2 \times 2 \times 2$? of $^-2 \times {}^-2 \times 2 \times 2 \times 2$? **Explain**.

So, the product of an odd number of negative integers is negative, and the product of an even number of negative integers is positive.

Find the product.

1. $^-2 \times 1 \times {}^-1$

2. $2 \times {}^-1 \times {}^-2 \times {}^-2$

3. $^-2 \times {}^-3 \times {}^-2 \times 1 \times {}^-3$

4. $^-1 \times 2 \times {}^-3 \times 4 \times {}^-5 \times 6$

5. $7 \times {}^-6 \times 3 \times |{}^-4| \times {}^-8$

6. $13 \times {}^-11 \times |8| \times |0| \times 2$

LESSON 5

2.2.d. Use the basic operations on integers to solve problems.

Materials
• MathBoard

Divide Integers

Essential Question How do negative numbers affect division?

▶ **Learn**

Multiplication and division are inverse operations. To solve a division problem, think about the related multiplication problem.

$63 \div 7 =$ ■   **Think:** What number multiplied by 7 equals 63?

$7 \times 9 = 63$, so $63 \div 7 = 9$.

You can use related multiplication problems to determine the sign of the quotient when dividing integers.

$5 \times 8 = 40$, so $40 \div 5 = 8$. $^-5 \times 8 = ^-40$, so $^-40 \div ^-5 = 8$.

$^-5 \times ^-8 = 40$, so $40 \div ^-5 = ^-8$. $5 \times ^-8 = ^-40$, so $^-40 \div 5 = ^-8$.

Look at the signs of the dividends, divisors, and resulting quotients above.

The following rules apply when dividing integers.

> The quotient of two integers with like signs is positive.
>
> $40 \div 5 = 8$ $^-40 \div ^-5 = 8$
>
> The quotient of two integers with unlike signs is negative.
>
> $40 \div ^-5 = ^-8$ $^-40 \div 5 = ^-8$

Dividing integers.

The table shows the monthly profit or loss for David's dog walking business. What is the average monthly profit or loss?

Monthly Profit and Loss						
Month	Nov	Dec	Jan	Feb	Mar	Apr
Profit or Loss	$^-$$12	$^-$$10	$^-$$5	$7	$^-$$9	$5

$^-12 + ^-10 + ^-5 + 7 + ^-9 + 5 = ^-24$ Find the sum.

$^-24 \div 6 = ^-4$ Divide by the number of months.

So, since the quotient is negative, there is an average monthly loss of $4.

Find the quotient.

$12 \div ^-3$	$^-450 \div ^-50$	$217 \div 7$
$12 \div ^-3 = ^-4$	$^-450 \div ^-50 = 9$	$217 \div 7 = 31$

196

▶ **Share and Show**

1. ⁻3 × ⁻6 = 18, so 18 ÷ ⁻3 = ▓

2. ⁻10 × 4 = ⁻40, so ⁻40 ÷ ⁻10 = ▓

Find the quotient.

3. 36 ÷ ⁻6   **4.** ⁻328 ÷ 8   ✓**5.** ⁻190 ÷ ⁻2   ✓**6.** ⁻222 ÷ ⁻2

7. [Math Talk] **Explain** how to determine the sign of a quotient when you divide integers.

▶ **Practice and Problem Solving** REAL WORLD

Find the quotient.

8. ⁻63 ÷ ⁻7   **9.** 96 ÷ ⁻3   **10.** ⁻30 ÷ 3   **11.** 64 ÷ 8   **12.** 92 ÷ ⁻92

13. 0 ÷ ⁻8   **14.** ⁻75 ÷ ⁻5   **15.** ⁻300 ÷ 6   **16.** 50 ÷ ⁻5   **17.** ⁻252 ÷ 12

Find the product or quotient.

18. ⁻12 × ⁻5   **19.** 20 ÷ ⁻4   **20.** ⁻81 ÷ 9   **21.** 6 × 40

22. ⁻84 ÷ ⁻2   **23.** ⁻35 × ⁻1   **24.** 144 ÷ ⁻3   **25.** ⁻75 × 3

26. ⁻60 × 90   **27.** 300 ÷ 50   **28.** 24 × ⁻12   **29.** ⁻980 ÷ ⁻14

Use mental math to find the value of the variable.

30. $x ÷ 4 = 7$ **31.** $⁻18 ÷ n = ⁻9$ **32.** $s ÷ ⁻5 = ⁻12$ **33.** $⁻48 ÷ b = 1$

34. $\dfrac{⁻40}{t} = ⁻8$ **35.** $\dfrac{⁻y}{9} = 6$ **36.** $\dfrac{c}{3} = ⁻13$ **37.** $\dfrac{⁻60}{a} = 10$

38. Noah's class recorded the outside temperature at 9 A.M. each day for 5 days. The temperatures were ⁻8°F, ⁻7°F, ⁻1°F, ⁻2°F, and ⁻2°F. What was the average temperature at 9 A.M. for the five days?

39. Lisa earns $40 dog walking for 4 days. If her total expenses are $12, what is her average daily profit?

40. **Reasoning** The quotient of ⁻5 ÷ 2 can be written as ⁻2 r ⁻1. How could you write the with a remainder?

41. [Write Math] ▶ Is the quotient of two negative integers greater than or less than quotient of ⁻10 ÷ 7 the integers? **Explain**.

★ **OCCT Test Prep**

42. Which is the quotient 60 ÷ ⁻12?

   A ⁻10   **C** ⁺5

   B ⁺10   **D** ⁻5

43. Which is the quotient ⁻48 ÷ ⁻2?

   A ⁻42   **C** 24

   B ⁻24   **D** 42

Operations with Integers

Essential Question How are addition, subtraction, multiplication, and division related?

PROBLEM The price of Fab Jeans Industries stock was on the decline. It fell $5 in January and $8 in February. By the end of March, the price had declined an additional $14. Evan wants to find out how much the price of the stock changed during the three months, using the expression $^-5 - 8 + {}^-14$.

You can use the rules for integers to find the value of an expression involving combinations of operations with integers.

Evaluate.

$^-5 - 8 + {}^-14$	
$^-5 + {}^-8 + {}^-14$	Write $^-5 - 8$ as an addition expression.
$^-13 + {}^-14$	Add.
$^-27$	

So, the price of Fab Jeans Industries stock dropped $27.

Evaluate the expressions.

$^-24 \div ({}^-6 - 2)$	Perform operations in parentheses. Write as an addition expression.
$^-24 \div ({}^-6 + {}^-2)$	Add.
$^-24 \div {}^-8$	Divide.
3	

$^-3 - {}^-8 \times {}^-14$	Multiply.	$(9 + {}^-5)^2$	Operate inside parentheses.
$^-3 - 112$	Write as an addition expression.	4^2	Clear exponents.
$^-3 + {}^-112$	Add.	16	
$^-115$			

$({}^-22 + 6) \div ({}^-4)^2$	Operate inside parentheses.	$6 \times ({}^-55 \div 5) + 8^2$	Operate inside parentheses.
$^-16 \div (-4)^2$	Clear exponents.	$6 \times {}^-11 + 8^2$	Clear exponents.
$^-16 \div 16$	Divide.	$6 \times {}^-11 + 64$	Multiply.
$^-1$		$^-66 + 64$	Add.
		$^-2$	

2.2.d. Use the basic operations on integers to solve problems.

2.2.e. Build and recognize models of multiples to develop the concept of exponents and simplify numerical expressions with exponents and parentheses using order of operations.

Materials
• MathBoard

ERROR ALERT

When you write a subtraction problem as an addition problem, be sure to add the opposite of the number to be subtracted.

Integer Patterns

A number pattern can repeat the operations of addition, subtraction, multiplication, division, or a combination of these operations.

Find a possible rule. Then find the next two numbers in the pattern.
1, $^-$2, $^-$5, $^-$8, ▨, ▨

Find a possible rule.

Try *subtract 3* because $1 - 3 = {}^-2$.

$^-2 - 3 = {}^-2 + ({}^-3) = {}^-5$

$^-5 - 3 = {}^-5 + ({}^-3) = {}^-8$

A possible rule is to *subtract 3*.

Use the rule.

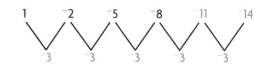

$^-8 - 3 = {}^-8 + {}^-3$ $^-11 - 3 = {}^-11 + {}^-3$

$\quad\quad = {}^-11$ $\quad\quad\quad = {}^-14$

So, $^-11$ and $^-14$ are the next two numbers in the pattern.

You can also use a rule to find missing numbers in a pattern.

Find a possible rule. Then find the missing numbers in the pattern.
$^-$6, ▨, $^-$24, 48, $^-$96, 192, ▨, 768

Find a possible rule.

Try *multiply by $^-2$,* because $^-24 \times {}^-2 = 48$.

$48 \times {}^-2 = {}^-96$

$^-96 \times {}^-2 = 192$

A possible rule is to *multiply by $^-2$*.

Use the rule.

$^-6 \times {}^-2 = 12$

$192 \times {}^-2 = {}^-384$

Check the last number in the pattern.

$^-384 \times {}^-2 = 768$

So, the missing numbers in the pattern are 12 and $^-384$.

▶ Share and Show

Evaluate the expression.

1. $(2 - {}^-7) + 10$

$(2 + 7) + 10$

$9 + 10$

▨

2. $({}^-13 - 3) \div 2^2$

$({}^-13 + {}^-3) \div 2^2$

$^-16 \div 4$

▨

✓3. $({}^-4)^2 + {}^-1 \times {}^-6$

$16 + {}^-1 \times {}^-6$

$16 + 6$

▨

Write a possible rule for each pattern. Then find the missing numbers.

4. $^-7, {}^-11, {}^-15, {}^-19,$ ▨, ▨

✓5. $1, {}^-3, 9, {}^-27,$ ▨, ▨, $729, {}^-2{,}187$

6. **Math Talk** **Explain** how to find a possible rule for a pattern.

Practice and Problem Solving REAL WORLD

Evaluate the expression.

7. $(^-9 - 6) \div {^-5}$ **8.** $(2 - {^-3}) \times 4$ **9.** $^-12 + (^-9 - {^-5})$ **10.** $^-4 \times 6 + 14$

11. $(^-10 - {^-10}) \div 2$ **12.** $(6 - {^-7}) \times {^-8}$ **13.** $^-1 + 8 - {^-6}$ **14.** $8 + (^-10 \times 4)$

15. $(^-18 - 9) \div 3^2$ **16.** $(^-5)^2 + 2 \times {^-8}$ **17.** $^-6 \times {^-4} + 4^2$ **18.** $20 \div (^-2)^2 - 3$

Write a possible rule for each pattern. Then find the missing numbers.

19. $^-5, {^-7}, {^-9}, {^-11}, \blacksquare, \blacksquare$

20. $14, 5, {^-4}, {^-13}, \blacksquare, \blacksquare, {^-40}$

21. $^-2, 6, {^-18}, 54, \blacksquare, 486, \blacksquare$

22. $6, {^-6}, 6, {^-6}, \blacksquare, \blacksquare, 6$

23. $^-11, {^-6}, {^-1}, 4, \blacksquare, 14, \blacksquare$

24. $^-1, {^-4}, {^-16}, {^-64}, \blacksquare, \blacksquare, {^-4,096}$

Compare. Write <, >, or = for each ⬭.

25. $(5 - {^-7}) \times 8$ ⬭ $(6 + {^-3}) \times 9$

26. $^-24 \div (1 - {^-5})$ ⬭ $^-24 \div 4$

27. $(7 - {^-4}) + |^-5|$ ⬭ $(9 + {^-5}) \times 4$

28. $(^-1 \times 7) \div {^-7}$ ⬭ $(7 \div {^-1}) \times {^-1}$

29. Last Tuesday, the high temperature in Gail's city was 3°F greater than twice the number of degrees below zero as the temperature in Daniel's city. If the temperature in Daniel's city was $^-4$°F, what was the high temperature in Gail's city?

30. The temperature dropped 5°F on Monday, 8°F on Tuesday, and then 12°F more on Wednesday. What was the temperature change over the three days?

31. **Reasoning** Write two different rules that can be used to find the next number in the pattern. Then find the next number.
$^-29, {^-18}, {^-7}, 4, \blacksquare$

32. **Pose a Problem** Look at Problem 30. Write a similar problem by changing the daily temperature changes and the number of days.

33. During one week, Built-Up Industries' stock price increased $2 a day for 3 days, and decreased $3 a day for 2 days. By how much did the stock's price change during the week?

34. **Write Math** ► **Explain** how to find the next two integers in the following pattern. Then find the integers. $100,000, {^-10,000}, 1,000, {^-100}, \blacksquare, \blacksquare$

 OCCT Test Prep

35. Which is the value of the expression $(^-7 - {^-11}) \times {^-5}$?

   A $^-90$ **C** 20

   B $^-20$ **D** 90

36. Which is the value of the expression $14 \times (^-16 \div 4)^2$?

   A $^-224$ **C** 56

   B $^-56$ **D** 224

★ Standards Quick Check

Evaluate the expression.

1. $^-10 + (7 - \,^-3)$ **2.** $^-12 + \,^-8 \div 2$ **3.** $(^-25 \times 4) + \,^-50$

Pose a Problem

There are different ways to pose problems. One way is to change the conditions in a problem you are given. For example, you can change the numbers in a problem or exchange known and unknown information. You can also make a problem more open-ended.

Read the problem. Then use all three methods to change it.

Problem *Tammy rides the museum elevator up 6 floors from the ground floor to the art exhibit. Then she rides down 8 floors to the parking garage. How many floors below ground level is the parking garage. Answer: 2 floors*

Change the Numbers
Tammy rides the museum elevator up 3 floors from the ground floor to the art exhibit. Then she rides down 4 floors to the parking garage. How many floors below the ground floor is the parking garage? Answer: 1 floor

Exchange the Known and Unknown Information
Tammy rides the museum elevator from the ground floor up to the art exhibit. Then she rides down 8 floors to the parking garage. The parking garage is 3 floors below the ground floor. How many floors up did Tammy ride to the art exhibit? Answer: 5 floors

Make the Problem More Open-Ended
Tammy rides the museum elevator up 4 floors from the ground floor. Then she rides down to a floor below the ground floor. If there are 4 floors below the ground floor, how many floors down might she have ridden the elevator? Answer: 5, 6, 7, or 8 floors

Use all three methods to change the problem. Then solve.

1. Jason delivers packages to a museum. He enters an elevator 2 floors below the ground floor. He rides up 6 floors to the first delivery, down 3 floors to the second delivery, and up 1 floor to the last delivery. On which floor is Jason's last delivery? Answer: the second floor.

★ 2.2.d. Use the basic operations on integers to solve problems.

Materials
• MathBoard

Problem Solving Workshop
Strategy: Predict and Test

Essential Question How can you use the strategy *predict and test* when working with integers?

▶ **Learn the Strategy** REAL WORLD

You can solve some problems by using number sense to predict a possible answer. You should then test your answer and revise your prediction if necessary.

You can predict and test to find integers with a given sum and difference.

The sum of two negative integers is ⁻7. When the lesser integer is subtracted from the greater integer, the difference is 3. What are the two integers?

Prediction		Test		Result
Greater integer	Lesser integer	Sum	Difference	
−3	−4	⁻3 + ⁻4 = ⁻7	⁻3 − ⁻4 = 1	The difference is too low, so revise.
−1	−6	⁻1 + ⁻6 = ⁻7	⁻1 − ⁻6 = 5	The difference is too high, so revise.
−2	−5	⁻2 + ⁻5 = ⁻7	⁻2 − ⁻5 = 3	correct

You can predict and test to solve some geometry problems.

The perimeter of a rectangle is 40 m. The length is 3 times as great as the width. What are the length and the width of the rectangle?

Prediction		Test	Result
Width	Length	Perimeter $P = 2l + 2w$	
10	3 × 10 = 30	$P = 2(30) + 2(10)$ = 60 + 20 = 80	The perimeter is too high, so revise.
4	3 × 4 = 12	$P = 2(12) + 2(4)$ = 24 + 8 = 32	The perimeter is too low, so revise.
5	3 × 5 = 15	$P = 2(15) + 2(5)$ = 30 + 10 = 40	correct

Math Talk

Explain how the predictions were revised to solve each problem.

UNLOCK the Problem REAL WORLD

PROBLEM Copy the diagram and arrange the additional integers ⁻10, ⁻8, ⁻7, ⁻6, ⁻5, and ⁻4 in the square so that the sum of the integers in each row and each column is ⁻19. Use each integer only once.

⁻12		⁻2
⁻3		

Read the Problem

What do I need to find?

I need to find a way to get the sum of each column and row to equal ⁻19.

What information do I need to use?

I need to use the numbers ⁻10, ⁻8, ⁻7, ⁻6, ⁻5, and ⁻4 only once.

How will I use the information?

I can make a diagram and a chart to try several different numbers to see which arrangement of numbers will get me the answer.

Solve the Problem

Find the values that can be found by calculation. Then predict the other values and their placement in the square.

Since ⁻12 + ⁻2 = ⁻14, use ⁻5 for the first row. ⁻14 + ⁻5 = ⁻19
Since ⁻12 + ⁻3 = ⁻15, use ⁻4 for the first column. ⁻15 + ⁻4 = ⁻19

Second Row

Prediction		Test	Result
Integers		Sums for Row 2	
⁻8	⁻10	⁻4 + ⁻8 + ⁻10 = ⁻22	too low, so revise
⁻7	⁻8	⁻4 + ⁻7 + ⁻8 = ⁻19	correct

Use ⁻7 and ⁻8 for the second row and the remaining numbers, ⁻6 and ⁻10, for the third row.
Now, test the sums of columns 2 and 3.

Prediction

⁻12	⁻5	⁻2
⁻4	⁻7	⁻8
⁻3	⁻6	⁻10

Columns 2 and 3

Prediction		Test	Result
Integers		Sums for Columns 2 and 3	
⁻7	⁻6	⁻5 + ⁻7 + ⁻6 = ⁻18	too high, so revise
⁻8	⁻10	⁻2 + ⁻8 + ⁻10 = ⁻20	too low, so revise

Revision

⁻12	⁻5	⁻2
⁻4	⁻8	⁻7
⁻3	⁻6	⁻10

Exchange ⁻7 and ⁻8 in the second row. Test the sums.

⁻5 + ⁻8 + ⁻6 = ⁻19   ⁻2 + ⁻7 + ⁻10 = ⁻19

Both columns sum to ⁻19, so all rows and columns now sum to ⁻19.

1. Copy the diagram, and arrange the additional integers ⁻6, ⁻7, ⁻8, ⁻10, ⁻11, and ⁻12 in the circles so that the sum of the integers on each side of the triangle is ⁻10. Use each integer only once.

   First, predict and test integers for one side of the triangle.

   Then, if the sum of the integers is ⁻10, predict and test integers for another side of the triangle. If your prediction is incorrect, adjust your prediction and then test it.

   Finally, continue until you have placed all the integers in the circles and the sum of the integers on each side of the triangle is ⁻10.

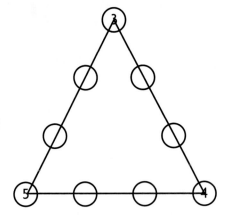

2. What if the integers to be arranged were ⁻6, ⁻2, ⁻1, 0, 2, and 7 and the sum of the integers on each side of the triangle was 8? If you could use each integer only once, what would be the arrangement of the integers?

3. The perimeter of a triangle is 39 in. The length of the second side is 1 in. more than the length of the first side. The length of the third side is 2 in. more than the length of the first side. What is the length of each side?

Predict and test to solve.

4. The Mighty Mathematicians took part in 25 math competitions. They won 9 more competitions than they lost. Two competitions ended in a tie. How many competitions did they win?

5. The perimeter of a rectangle is 32 units. If the width is $\frac{1}{3}$ the length, what are the length and width of the rectangle?

6. The sum of two 4-digit numbers is 5,555. The same 4 digits are used in both numbers without any digits repeating. Find two such numbers.

7. Harry has $37.72 in his toy bank. The number of bills is the same as the number of coins. What are possible numbers of bills and coins in Harry's toy bank?

8. Bev spent $28.25 on two t-shirts at a professional basketball game. One t-shirt cost $5.75 more than the other. How much was each t-shirt?

9. **Write Math** ➤ In Problem 6, how did your first prediction help you make your second prediction?

▶ **Mixed Applications**

Solve.

10. Copy the diagram, and arrange the integers ⁻1 through ⁻19 in the circles so that the sum of the numbers on each line is ⁻30.

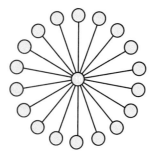

11. If Jack gives one of his pencils to Kim, each student will have the same number of pencils. If Kim gives Jack one of her pencils, Jack will have twice as many as Kim. How many pencils does each student have?

12. Liz, Keith, Olivia, and Alvin are standing in line. Alvin is ahead of Olivia, but he is not first. Liz is behind Alvin. Olivia is last. In what order are the students?

 **Real World Data**

For 13–16, use the number cards.

13. How many different two-digit numbers can you make with the cards?

14. Pose a Problem Make a pattern with the cards. Write a problem to go along with your pattern.

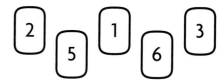

15. Open-Ended Problem Choose four cards. Arrange the numbers on the cards to write a number sentence.

16. If you add 3 to the number on one of the cards, subtract 5 from the sum, and end up with ⁻1, what number was on the card you started with?

☀ **H.O.T.** **PROBLEM**

A magic square is a square array of integers arranged so that the sum of the numbers in any horizontal, vertical, or corner-to-corner diagonal line is always the same.

17. Draw a 3-by-3 square. Arrange any or all of the numbers 1 through 5 so that the sum is 9. Some numbers will repeat.

18. Look at the figure at the right. Copy and complete the 4-by-4 magic square using each of the numbers 1 through 16 only once.

16			13
	10		
		7	
	15		1

LESSON 8

★ **2.2.d.** Use the basic operations on integers to solve problems.

Rational Numbers

Essential Question How do you know if a number is rational or not?

 **Learn**

A **ratio** is a comparison of two numbers, a and b, and can be written as a fraction $\frac{a}{b}$.

A **rational number** is any number that can be written as a ratio $\frac{a}{b}$, where a and b are integers and b is not equal to 0.

> **Write each rational number as a ratio $\frac{a}{b}$.**
>
> $15 = \frac{15}{1}$ | $^-6 = \frac{^-6}{1}$ | $5\frac{1}{4} = \frac{21}{4}$ | $^-3\frac{7}{8} = \frac{^-31}{8}$ | $0.86 = \frac{86}{100}$

• Is $\frac{0}{1}$ a rational number? Is $\frac{0}{1}$ a rational number? Explain.

The **Venn diagram** below shows the relationship among the sets of rational numbers, integers, whole numbers, and natural numbers.

> **Use the Venn diagram to determine in which set or sets each number belongs.**
>
> 68 — The number 68 belongs in the sets of natural numbers, whole numbers, integers, and rational numbers.
>
> $^-9$ — The number $^-9$ belongs in the sets of integers and rational numbers, but not in the sets of whole numbers or natural numbers.
>
> 7.80 — The number 7.80 belongs in the set of rational numbers, but not in the sets of natural numbers, whole numbers, or integers.
>
> $\frac{15}{3}$ — The number $\frac{15}{3}$ is equal to 5, so it belongs in the sets of natural numbers, whole numbers, integers, and rational numbers.
>
> $^-\frac{7}{3}$ — The number $^-\frac{7}{3}$ belongs in the set of rational numbers, but not in the sets of natural numbers, whole numbers, or integers.

> **Rational Numbers**
> Any numbers that can be written as a quotient of two integers $\frac{a}{b}$, where $b \neq 0$
>
> > **Integers**
> > Whole numbers and their opposites
> >
> > > **Whole Numbers**
> > > Zero and natural numbers
> > >
> > > > **Natural Numbers**
> > > > The set of counting numbers 1, 2, 3, 4, 5, . . .

Rational Numbers Between Rational Numbers
Examples

Mari is training for a 7-mi cross-country race. She ran $6\frac{1}{2}$ mi on Monday and plans to run $6\frac{3}{4}$ mi on Wednesday. What distance could she run on Tuesday if she wants to run between $6\frac{1}{2}$ mi and $6\frac{3}{4}$ mi?

You can use a number line to find rational numbers between other rational numbers.

Use the number line to find a distance between $6\frac{1}{2}$ mi and $6\frac{3}{4}$ mi.

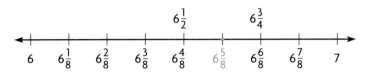

When the number line is marked in eighths, the mark between $6\frac{1}{2}$ and $6\frac{3}{4}$ represents a distance that Mari could run. Other choices are also possible.

So, Mari could run $6\frac{5}{8}$ mi on Tuesday.

You can find a rational number between two rational numbers in decimal form.

Find a rational number between ⁻5.2 and ⁻5.3.

$^-5.2 = {}^-5.20 \quad {}^-5.3 = {}^-5.30$ Add a zero to each decimal.

Use a number line marked in hundredths to find a number between ⁻5.20 and ⁻5.30.

So, ⁻5.23, ⁻5.25, and ⁻5.28 are some of the rational numbers between ⁻5.2 and ⁻5.3.

• Is ⁻2.38 between ⁻2.2 and ⁻2.3? Explain your reasoning.

You can use a common denominator to find a rational number between two rational numbers in fraction form.

Find a rational number between $^-1\frac{3}{4}$ and $^-1\frac{7}{8}$.

$^-1\frac{3}{4} = {}^-1\frac{12}{16} \quad {}^-1\frac{7}{8} = 1\frac{14}{16}$ Use a common denominator to write equivalent fractions.

$^-1\frac{13}{16}$ is between $^-1\frac{12}{16}$ and $^-1\frac{14}{16}$.   Find a rational number between the two other rational numbers.

So, $^-1\frac{13}{16}$ is between $^-1\frac{3}{4}$ and $^-1\frac{7}{8}$.

Write the rational number in the form $\frac{a}{b}$.

1. 0.71   Think: 0.71 is read as "seventy-one hundredths."

2. $^-2\frac{1}{6}$ Think: $2\frac{1}{6}$ is the opposite of $^-2\frac{1}{6}$, so $\frac{13}{6}$ is the opposite of ▉.

3. $^-9$

4. $1\frac{3}{10}$

5. $^-3\frac{7}{8}$

6. $^-0.48$

✓**7.** 12.3

Use the number line to find a rational number between the two given numbers.

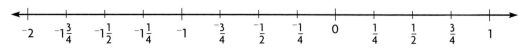

8. $^-1\frac{1}{2}$ and $^-1$

9. 0 and $\frac{1}{2}$

10. $^-\frac{3}{4}$ and $^-\frac{1}{4}$

✓**11.** $^-\frac{1}{4}$ and $\frac{1}{4}$

12. **Math Talk** **Explain** how to use a common denominator to find a rational number between $^-2\frac{1}{3}$ and $^-2\frac{2}{9}$.

► **Practice and Problem Solving** REAL WORLD

Write the rational number in the form $\frac{a}{b}$.

13. $^-14$

14. $^-1\frac{5}{6}$

15. $^-0.39$

16. 2.09

17. $3\frac{7}{12}$

Use the number line to find a rational number between the two given numbers.

18. $^-1.79$ and $^-1.77$

19. $^-1.74$ and $^-1.72$

20. $^-1.7$ and $^-1.72$

21. $^-1.78$ and $^-1.8$

Find a rational number between the two given rational numbers.

22. $\frac{1}{6}$ and $\frac{1}{2}$

23. $2\frac{4}{10}$ and 2.6

24. $^-52.3$ and $^-52\frac{8}{10}$

25. $^-\frac{19}{6}$ and $^-3\frac{5}{6}$

Tell whether the first rational number is between the second and third rational numbers. Write *yes* or *no*.

26. $^-0.74$; $^-0.075$ and $^-0.71$

27. $^-4$; $^-\frac{19}{3}$ and $^-\frac{18}{5}$

28. $\frac{3}{4}$; 0.54 and $\frac{13}{20}$

 OCCT Test Prep

29. Which rational number is between 7.6 and 7.8?

   A 7.07   **C** 7.9

   B 7.7   **D** 8.1

30. Which rational number is between $^-2.3$ and $^-2.6$?

   A 2.5   **C** $^-2.29$

   B 2.4   **D** $^-2.48$

GO **Technology**
ONLINE Use HMH Mega Math, Fraction Action,
Number Line Mine, Levels U, V.

⭐ Standards Quick Check

Find the rational number in the form of $\frac{a}{b}$.

1. $^-2\frac{5}{8}$

2. 3.64

3. $^-23$

4. $^-4\frac{5}{8}$

5. $^-7.91$

6. $^-5\frac{2}{3}$

Challenge H.O.T.

Venn diagrams help scientists show relationships among different types of organisms.

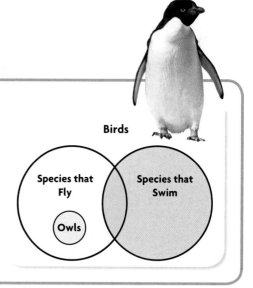

This diagram displays three different ways to categorize birds. The area where the yellow and pink sections overlap represents species of birds that can both fly and swim, such as ducks or geese. Notice that the blue section that represents owls is completely within the yellow section. This means that every species of owl can fly.

Since the blue section does not overlap the pink section, we can conclude that no species of owl can swim.

Birds

Species that Fly

Species that Swim

Owls

Tell the section of the Venn diagram in which each bird belongs.

1. Penguins swim but do not fly.

2. Ducks swim and fly.

LESSON 9

2.2.d. Use the basic operations on integers to solve problems.

Materials
• MathBoard

Math Idea
Grouping rational numbers into positive and negative groups makes it easier to order them.

Compare and Order

Essential Question How can you compare and order rational numbers on a number line?

PROBLEM After a storm passes, mountain climbers observe that the temperature has changed from ⁻5°C to ⁻15°C. Was the temperature greater before or after the storm?

Use a number line to compare ⁻5°C and ⁻15°C.

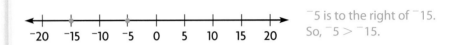

⁻5 is to the right of ⁻15.
So, ⁻5 > ⁻15.

So, the temperature was greater before the storm.

Compare. Use < or >.

$^-3\frac{1}{2}$ ⬤ $^-9\frac{2}{3}$

Think about the positions of the numbers on a number line.

$^-3\frac{1}{2}$ is to the right of $^-9\frac{2}{3}$ on a number line.

So, $^-3\frac{1}{2} > {}^-9\frac{2}{3}$ and $^-9\frac{2}{3} < {}^-3\frac{1}{2}$.

....

⁻5 ⬤ ⁻8.6

Think about the positions of the numbers on a number line.

⁻8.6 is to the left of ⁻5 on a number line.

So, ⁻8.6 < ⁻5 and ⁻5 > ⁻8.6.

Order $6\frac{3}{4}$, ⁻6, and 6.7 from least to greatest.

The only negative number is ⁻6, so it is the least.
Now compare $6\frac{3}{4}$ and 6.7.

$6\frac{3}{4} = 6.75$ 6.7 = 6.70	Write the numbers as decimals with the same number of decimal places.
6.75 > 6.70 6.70 < 6.75	Compare by looking at the place values.
$^-6 < 6.7 < 6\frac{3}{4}$	Order the numbers from least to greatest.

So, from least to greatest, the numbers are ⁻6, 6.7, and $6\frac{3}{4}$.

210

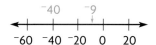
1. Look at the number line. Is $^-40$ greater than or less than $^-9$?

```
         ^-40    ^-9
  ←──┼────┼──┼──┼──┼──→
   ^-60 ^-40 ^-20  0   20
```

Compare. Write $<$, $>$, or $=$ for each ⬭.

2. $^-2$ ⬭ $^-1.5$ **3.** $^-1$ ⬭ $^-1.5$ **4.** $^-3\frac{1}{5}$ ⬭ $^-3$ ✓**5.** 0 ⬭ $^-0.5$ ✓**6.** $^-4$ ⬭ $^-\frac{1}{2}$

7. Math Talk **Explain** how to compare $^-4\frac{2}{5}$ and $^-4.30$.

Practice and Problem Solving

Compare. Write $<$, $>$, or $=$ for each ⬭.

8. $\frac{4}{5}$ ⬭ $\frac{7}{10}$ **9.** $^-0.45$ ⬭ $\frac{-9}{20}$ **10.** $^-2.36$ ⬭ $^-2\frac{1}{3}$ **11.** 3.72 ⬭ 3.27

12. $4.8 + 2.6$ ⬭ $3.7 + 3.9$ **13.** $3\frac{1}{2} \times 4$ ⬭ $2\frac{3}{4} + 11.4$ **14.** $12 \div 4.8$ ⬭ $16 \div 6\frac{2}{5}$

Order from least to greatest.

15. $5, ^-2, 0, ^-2.2$ **16.** $1.8, ^-1.8, 0.8, ^-0.8$ **17.** $\frac{-5}{8}, \frac{-3}{4}, \frac{-1}{2}, \frac{-7}{8}$ **18.** $^-0.3, \frac{1}{5}, 0, \frac{-1}{5}$

⭐**Algebra** **Find a value for *n* so that the set of numbers is in order from least to greatest. Choose an integer value between 1 and 9.**

19. $\frac{-7}{8}, \frac{-5}{8}, \frac{-n}{8}, \frac{-1}{8}$ **20.** $1\frac{1}{n}, 1\frac{1}{6}, 1\frac{1}{5}, 1\frac{1}{3}$ **21.** $\frac{-19}{20}, \frac{-n}{10}, ^-0.88, ^-0.85$

Real World Data

For 22–23, use the table.

22. Compare the record low temperatures for Barrow, Alaska, and Helena, Montana.

23. Between which two cities would a city with a record low temperature of $^-31°$F be placed if the cities were ordered from least to greatest record low temperature?

U.S. Record Low Temperatures	
City, State	Temperatures (°F)
Barrow, Alaska	$^-56$
Phoenix, Arizona	17
Jackson, Mississippi	2
Helena, Montana	$^-42$
Pittsburgh, Pennsylvania	$^-22$

★ OCCT Test Prep

24. Which is a true comparison?

    A $^-9 > ^-6$ **C** $14 < ^-16$

    B $^-4 < ^-2$ **D** $^-14 < ^-16$

25. Greg records the low temperatures in his town for 4 days as $^-4°$F, $3°$F, $^-10°$F, and $^-8°$F. Which temperature is the least?

    A $3°$F   **C** $^-8°$F

    B $^-4°$F   **D** $^-10°$F

LESSON 10

⭐ **2.2.c.** Estimate and find solutions to single and multi-step problems using whole numbers, decimals, fractions, and percents (e.g., 7/8 + 8/9 is about 2, 3.9 + 5.3 is about 9).

2.2.d. Use the basic operations on integers to solve problems.

Materials
• MathBoard

Properties of Rational Numbers

Essential Question How can you use each property for rational numbers?

Using properties of addition and multiplication can help you operate with rational numbers. When you add, subtract, multiply, and divide rational numbers, use the same rules for determining signs as with integers.

Associative Property of Addition

$(^-1\frac{1}{2} + 4) + 2\frac{1}{2}$	Rewrite using the Associative Property.
$^-1\frac{1}{2} + (4 + 2\frac{1}{2})$	Operate inside parentheses.
$^-1\frac{1}{2} + 6\frac{1}{2}$	Use mental math. Add.
5	

So, $(^-1\frac{1}{2} + 4) + 2\frac{1}{2} = 5$.

Associative Property of Multiplication

$(^-1\frac{1}{3} \times 5) \times 3$	Rewrite using the Associative Property.
$^-1\frac{1}{3} \times (5 \times 3)$	Operate inside parentheses.
$^-1\frac{1}{3} \times 15$	Rename as fractions.
$\dfrac{^-4}{\cancel{3}_1} \times \dfrac{\overset{5}{\cancel{15}}}{1}$	Simplify.
$\dfrac{^-20}{1} = ^-20$	Multiply.

So, $(^-1\frac{1}{3} \times 5) \times 3 = ^-20$.

Commutative Property of Addition

| $6.35 + 1.42 + 0.65 = 6.35 + 0.65 + 1.42$ | Rewrite using the Commutative Property of Addition. |
| $= 8.42$ | Add. |

So, $6.35 + 1.42 + 0.65 = 8.42$.

212

Distributive Property

$$^-6 \times 4\tfrac{3}{8} = {}^-6 \times (4 + \tfrac{3}{8})$$

Rename the mixed number as a sum.

$$= ({}^-6 \times 4) + ({}^-6 \times \tfrac{3}{8})$$

Use the Distributive Property.

$$= ({}^-6 \times 4) + (\tfrac{{}^-\cancel{6}^{\,-3}}{1} \times \tfrac{3}{\cancel{8}^{\,4}})$$

Simplify and multiply.

$$= {}^-24 + {}^-\tfrac{9}{4}$$

Write the fraction as a mixed number.

$$= {}^-24 + {}^-2\tfrac{1}{4} = {}^-26\tfrac{1}{4}$$

Add.

So, $^-6 \times 4\tfrac{3}{8} = {}^-26\tfrac{1}{4}$.

ERROR ALERT

Be sure to include the negative sign with the product of a positive rational number and a negative rational number.

Identity Property and Order of Operations

The Identity Properties of Addition and Multiplication apply to rational numbers.

Identity Property of Addition

$$8.47 + 0 = 8.47$$
$$0 + 8.47 = 8.47$$

Identity Property of Multiplication

$$\tfrac{-4}{5} \times 1 = \tfrac{-4}{5}$$
$$1 \times \tfrac{-4}{5} = \tfrac{-4}{5}$$

Apply the rules for the order of operations to evaluate numerical expressions with rational numbers.

Evaluate $^-32 + 4 \times (7.4 - 1.8) \div 0.04$.

$$^-32 + 4 \times (7.4 - 1.8) \div 0.04$$

Operate inside parentheses.

$$^-32 + 4 \times 5.6 \div 0.04$$

Multiply.

$$^-32 + 22.4 \div 0.04$$

Divide.

$$^-32 + 560 = 528$$

Add.

So, $^-32 + 4 \times (7.4 - 1.8) \div 0.04 = 528$.

▶ **Share and Show**   Math Board

1. Copy and complete, using the Commutative Property of Addition.

$$9.46 + 5.39 + 3.54 = 9.46 + \blacksquare + 5.39$$
$$= \blacksquare + 5.39$$
$$= \blacksquare$$

Evaluate each expression.

2. $0.5 + 3.8 + {}^-2.5$

3. $^-7 \times 2\tfrac{3}{7}$

4. $0.35 \times {}^-5.6 \times 1$

5. $12.3 \div 1.5 + {}^-3.4 \times 8.2 - {}^-3$

✔ **6.** $\tfrac{1}{4} + \left({}^-\tfrac{3}{4} + 3\tfrac{1}{3}\right)$

✔ **7.** $\tfrac{4}{5} \times \left(28 \div 5\tfrac{3}{5}\right)$

8. **Math Talk** **Explain** why the Associative Property makes it easier to find the value of $4.48 + 1.23 + 0.02$.

Evaluate each expression.

9. $-\frac{1}{8} + 1\frac{1}{3} + -\frac{5}{8}$

10. $0.5 \times (-6 \times 2.3)$

11. $0 + (4.85 + -3.57)$

12. $\left(-3\frac{2}{5} + 5\right) + 2\frac{2}{5}$

13. $4\frac{4}{5} + 2\frac{1}{3} + 1\frac{1}{5}$

14. $-2\frac{1}{6} \times 4 \times 6$

15. $\frac{1}{5} \times \frac{5}{6} \times \frac{12}{25} + 5\frac{23}{25} \times 1$

16. $-3.8 + 2.5 \times 1.8 \div 3^2$

17. $5\frac{2}{3} \times (3^2 \times 2)$

18. $-3.25 + 6 - 1.75$

19. $\left(-12 \times 3\frac{1}{4}\right) \div -3 + 15$

20. $-18 + 3 \times (4.8 - 1.9) \div 3$

Algebra Find the value of *n*. Name the property used.

21. $1 \times n = 3.08$

22. $0.8 \times 2.75 = (0.8 \times 2) + (0.8 \times n)$

23. $3.2 \times 4.9 \times 5 = 3.2 \times n \times 4.9$

24. $n \times 1 = -4\frac{1}{5}$

25. $-\frac{1}{8} + 2\frac{5}{8} + \left(-\frac{5}{8}\right) = 2\frac{5}{8} + \left(-\frac{1}{8}\right) + n$

26. $\left(3\frac{2}{5} + n\right) + 6\frac{5}{8} = 3\frac{2}{5} + \left(4\frac{3}{8} + 6\frac{5}{8}\right)$

Compare. Write <, >, or = for each ⬭ **.**

27. $-8\frac{6}{7} \times 1$ ⬭ $1 \times -8\frac{6}{7}$

28. $\frac{1}{21} \times 3 + 0$ ⬭ $\left(\frac{2}{7} \times \frac{8}{15}\right) \times \frac{5}{8}$

29. $-90 + 47.6 \div 0.07$ ⬭ $-20 \times -20 \times 1.5$

30. $5.3 + -4 - 1.3$ ⬭ $0.5 \div 3 \times 0.25$

Real World Data

For 31–32, use the expressions in the box.

31. Which property of multiplication could make it easier to evaluate expression B? **Explain**.

32. **Reasoning** Which two expressions have the same value? **Explain** how can you tell without calculating.

> **A** $-2.125 \times (3.2 + 18.3)$
>
> **B** $\left(4.6 \times \frac{8}{9}\right) \times 9$
>
> **C** $5.34 + 3.098 + 0.16$
>
> **D** $3\frac{1}{5} + 18\frac{3}{10} \times -2\frac{1}{8}$

33. Evaluate $8.4 - 15.2 - 6.1$. Would the expression have the same value if you subtracted from right to left instead of from left to right? **Explain**.

34. **Write Math** **What's the Question?** Oliver is given the expression $3\frac{11}{12} - (-9 \div 3) \times \frac{2}{3}$. The answer is to divide -9 by 3.

⭐ OCCT Test Prep 🖊 Math Board

35. Which shows the correct value of the expression $(-12 \div 2.5) + \frac{1}{3} \times (15.8 - 1.4)$?

   A 0   **C** 2.5

   B 2   **D** $2\frac{3}{4}$

36. Which shows the correct value of the expression $\frac{1}{2} \times (-12 + 3\frac{1}{5}) + 4\frac{3}{4}$?

   A $\frac{7}{20}$ **C** $4\frac{3}{4}$

   B $4\frac{2}{5}$ **D** $9\frac{3}{20}$

⭐ Standards Quick Check

Evaluate the expression.

1. $36 \div 3^2 \times (4 - 1.5)$

2. $6.35 + (2.21 + 4.74) \times 3$

3. $14.84 - (8.65 - 3.41) \times 2$

4. $0.5 \times (^-12 \times 8.3)$

5. $^-3\frac{3}{5} + 0.65 - 1\frac{2}{5}$

6. $6 \times 3\frac{2}{3} + (4 - 8) \times \frac{1}{4}$

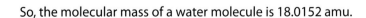

Challenge — H.O.T.

Scientists sometimes need to find the mass of very small pieces of matter, such as molecules. Since each molecule is a group of atoms, the mass of a molecule can be calculated by adding together the masses of all its atoms. Atoms and molecules are measured in atomic mass units (amu).

Atomic Mass			
Atom	Hydrogen (H)	Carbon (C)	Oxygen (O)
Mass (in amu)	1.0079	12.011	15.9994

Find the mass of a water molecule, H_2O.

The 'H_2' means that there $\rightarrow$ H_2O $\leftarrow$ There is no number below 'O',
are 2 hydrogen atoms. so there is only 1 oxygen atom.

The mass of the molecule is the sum of the mass of the atoms.

Mass of 2 hydrogen atoms	+	Mass of 1 oxygen atom	=	Mass of H_2O
2×1.0079	+	15.9994	=	18.0152 Use the atomic mass from the table.

So, the molecular mass of a water molecule is 18.0152 amu.

Use the table to find the mass of the given molecule.

1. carbon dioxide, CO_2

2. propane, C_3H_8

3. glucose, $C_6H_{12}O_6$

★ Extra Practice

Set A

Write an integer to represent each situation. (pp. 180–183)

1. an increase of 5 ft   **2.** a stock drop of $17   **3.** a loss of 21 yards   **4.** a profit of $42

Compare. Write $<$, $>$, or $=$ for each ⬭.

5. $^-3$ ⬭ 6 **6.** 2 ⬭ $^-8$ **7.** 0 ⬭ $|^-15|$ **8.** $|^-31|$ ⬭ $|^+31|$

Set B

Find the sum. (pp. 184–187)

1. $7 + {}^-7$ **2.** $^-8 + {}^-5$ **3.** $^-6 + 16$ **4.** $0 + {}^-32$ **5.** $^-43 + 27$

6. $^-13 + {}^-9$ **7.** $36 + {}^-51$ **8.** $^-25 + 68$ **9.** $^-18 + 0$ **10.** $^-37 + {}^-19$

Set C

Find the difference. (pp. 188–191)

1. $8 - {}^-2$ **2.** $0 - {}^-13$ **3.** $^-26 - {}^-26$ **4.** $^-33 - 51$ **5.** $63 - |^-78|$

6. $13 - {}^-8$ **7.** $9 - 15$ **8.** $^-12 - {}^-12$ **9.** $^-41 - 69$ **10.** $33 - |^-19|$

11. Ethan is taking scuba diving lessons. He dives 32 m below the surface. He then rises 18 m to look at a school of fish. What number represents the location of the school of fish?

12. The temperature on Monday morning was $^-8°$F. The temperature dropped 6°F on Tuesday morning and then rose 15°F on Wednesday morning. What was the temperature on Wednesday morning?

Set D

Find the product. (pp. 192–195)

1. $^-5 \times 6$ **2.** $^-9 \times {}^-7$ **3.** $0 \times {}^-11$ **4.** $^-15 \times 6$ **5.** $^-29 \times {}^-9$

6. Dave's mom rented a trumpet for 10 months at $29.99 a month. How much money will Dave's mom have spent after the 10 months?

7. A fathom is 6 ft. A sunken treasure is 17 fathoms below sea level. How many feet below sea level is the sunken treasure?

Set E

Find the quotient. (pp. 196–197)

1. $36 \div {}^-9$ **2.** $^-125 \div {}^-25$ **3.** $^-320 \div 4$ **4.** $0 \div {}^-256$ **5.** $^-408 \div {}^-17$

6. Greg earns $128 a week mowing lawns for 8 of his neighbors. His total weekly expenses are $32. What is Greg's average profit for each lawn?

7. A stock price dropped 27 points in three days. What was the average drop in points each day?

Set F

Evaluate the expression. (pp. 198–201)

1. $(^-1 - 7) \div {}^-4$ **2.** $(^-10 + {}^-8) - {}^-6$ **3.** $^-7 \times (5 + 18)$

4. $(^-15 - {}^-3) \div 2$ **5.** $64 \div {}^-8 \times {}^-5$ **6.** $^-13 + 6 - {}^-3 \times 2$

GO ONLINE Technology
Use HMH Mega Math, Fraction Action, *Number Line Mine*, Levels W and X.

Set G

Write the rational number in the form $\frac{a}{b}$. (pp. 206–209)

1. 3.14   **2.** $^-2\frac{3}{8}$ **3.** $^-0.741$ **4.** $^-27$ **5.** $4\frac{2}{5}$ **6.** $-\frac{8}{6}$

7. $^-6\frac{3}{5}$ **8.** 5.17   **9.** $^-84$ **10.** $^-0.897$ **11.** $-\frac{11}{5}$ **12.** $3\frac{1}{3}$

Find a rational number between the two given rational numbers.

13. $\frac{4}{5}$ and $\frac{2}{5}$ **14.** $^-1.87$ and $^-1.8$ **15.** 3.6 and $3\frac{1}{5}$ **16.** $-\frac{7}{20}$ and 2.6   **17.** $-\frac{7}{4}$ and $^-1.85$

18. $\frac{6}{7}$ and $\frac{9}{14}$ **19.** $^-7.1$ and $^-7.04$ **20.** $-\frac{17}{2}$ and $^-8$ **21.** $2\frac{4}{5}$ and 2.6   **22.** $^-4\frac{1}{3}$ and $-\frac{8}{3}$

23. At a swim meet, Jackson's first two qualifying trial times were 13.71 sec and 13.83 sec. His final trial time was within the range of the first two trial times. What could have been his time?

24. The change in the price of a gallon of gas in January was $\$^-0.53$ and in March it was $\$^-0.47$. If the change in February was between January's and March's changes, what could have been the change in February?

Set H

Compare. Write <, >, or = for each ◯. (pp. 210–211)

1. $\frac{5}{6}$ ⊖ $\frac{11}{15}$ **2.** $^-0.35$ ⊖ $-\frac{7}{20}$ **3.** 1.68 ⊖ $1\frac{2}{3}$ **4.** $^-98.1$ ⊖ $^-99.8$

5. $^-5.40$ ⊖ $^-5\frac{2}{5}$ **6.** $\frac{1}{5} + 1.6$ ⊖ $\frac{1}{6} + 1.5$ **7.** $5\frac{1}{4} \times 2$ ⊖ $4\frac{1}{2} + 6.2$ **8.** $^-4.5 \div 9$ ⊖ $20\frac{5}{10} - \frac{42}{2}$

Order the rational numbers from least to greatest.

9. $-\frac{3}{5}, -\frac{7}{10}, -\frac{8}{15}, -\frac{17}{20}$ **10.** $^-6.8, ^-4.1, 1, ^-3.7$ **11.** $^-0.2, \frac{1}{4}, 0, -\frac{1}{3}$

12. The average daily temperatures in Montreal, Canada, for three consecutive days were $^-9.8°C$, $^-10.4°C$, and $^-9.75°C$. Order the temperatures from least to greatest.

13. Lucy records the temperatures in her town for five consecutive days as: 37.5°F, 37.1°F, 40.8°F, 39.4°F, and 40.2°F. Which temperature is the second greatest?

Set I

Evaluate each expression. (pp. 212–215)

1. $4.27 + (3.18 + 6.07) - 6$ **2.** $\frac{4}{5} \times (^-5 + 6.25) + 4\frac{3}{4}$ **3.** $-\frac{1}{6} + 2\frac{5}{6} + ^-3\frac{5}{6}$

4. $5\frac{1}{2} + (^-4 \times 2\frac{3}{4}) - (2\frac{4}{5} \div 7)$ **5.** $(^-15 \div 2.5) + 3.6 \times (9.8 - 4.3)$

7. Matthew got an answer of 41 after evaluating the expression below. What was his error and what is the correct answer?

$$4\frac{2}{10} + 4 \times 2 \div 0.4$$

Reading & Writing Math

Vocabulary

You can use a number line to find the **absolute value** of a number,
compare and **order** integers, and add integers.

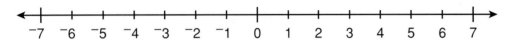

Use the number line to solve the problems.

Find the absolute value of each number.

1. −3   **2.** 6   **3.** 0   **4.** −6

Compare the integers. Write <, >, or = for each ⬭.

5. −4 ⬭ 4   **6.** 5 ⬭ −6   **7.** 3 ⬭ 0   **8.** 0 ⬭ −3

Find the sum.

9. −3 + −2   **10.** 0 + −2   **11.** 4 + −5   **12.** −3 + 3

13. Max owed his brother 3 dollars. Max got 5 dollars for cleaning the basement.
How much money did Max have after he paid his brother back?

Writing Explain how you can use counters to add integers. Explain how you
can use a number line.

Reading Check out this book in your library. *Pythagoras Eagle & the Music of
Spheres* by Anne Carse Nolting

H.O.T. Multistep Problems

1 The chart shows the average low temperatures in January for some different US cities. 📙 2.2.d.

City & State	Temperature (°F)
Cut Bank, MT	-35
Miles City, MT	-30
Kalispell, MT	-25
Greely, NE	-18
Grand Island, NE	-14
Saranack Lake, NY	-36
Massena, NY	-21
Plattsburgh, NY	-21

- How many degrees colder was it in Cut Bank, MT than in Grand Island, NE?

- In McAllen, TX the temperature was 96 degrees higher than in Plattsburgh, NY. What was the temperature in McAllen?

- Suppose the temperature in Massena, NY dropped 8 degrees. What would the new temperature be?

- The wind chill factor in Kalispell, MT made the temperature feel 12 degrees colder. What temperature did it feel like?

2 The chart shows balances of accounts that were overdrawn at the community bank at the end of the month of October. Use the chart to answer the questions. 📙 2.2.d.

Account	Abbott	Bard	Brown	Garcia	Weir
Balance in dollars	-52	-35	-12	-100	-11

- The balance of the Bard account was twice as much the previous month than it was at the end of October. What was the balance the previous month?

- What is the average balance? **Explain** how you found the average.

- Which account balance is closest to the average?

- Which account is overdrawn by $30 less than the average balance? **Explain**.

Practice for the OCCT

1 The elevation of the Dead Sea is 1,310 feet below sea level. What is the elevation of the Dead Sea written as an integer? 2.2.d.

   A ⁺1,310

   B ⁻1,310F

   C ⁺2,620

   D ⁻2,620

2 The average temperatures for three days were ⁻3°F, ⁻5°F, and 1°F. Which shows the temperatures ordered from least to greatest? 2.2.d.

   A 1°F, ⁻3°F, ⁻5°F

   B 1°F, ⁻5°F, ⁻3°F

   C ⁻3°F, ⁻5°F, 1°F

   D ⁻5°F, ⁻3°F, 1°F

3 In the morning the temperature was ⁻6°F. By noon the temperature had risen 11°F. What was the temperature at noon? 2.2.d.

   A ⁻17°F

   B 2°F

   C 5°F

   D 17°F

4 On the first three plays of a football game, the Wildcats gained 15 yards, lost 9 yards, and lost 8 yards. What is the total number of yards gained or lost by the Wildcats on the first three plays? 2.2.d.

   A 32 yards

   B 24 yards

   C 0 yards

   D ⁻2 yards

5 During the first six months of business, a sporting goods store showed its loses as ⁻$3,054. The store lost the same amount each month. What number would the store write down to show how much it lost each month? 2.2.d.

   A ⁻$509

   B ⁻$309

   C $509

   D $309

6 The height of a submarine changed ⁻630 feet over a period of 9 minutes. If the submarine descended at a constant rate, what was the change in height per minute? 2.2.d.

   A ⁻80

   B ⁻70

   C 80

   D 70

7 Which shows the numbers ordered from least to greatest? 2.2.d.

   A 57, 18, ⁻29, ⁻46

   B 57, ⁻46, ⁻29, 18

   C ⁻46, ⁻29, 18, 57

   D ⁻29, ⁻46, 57, 18

8 During one week, Built-Up Industries' stock price increased $2 a day for 2 days, and decreased $3 a day for 3 days. How much did the stock's price change during the week? 2.2.d.

   A ⁻$9

   B ⁻$5

   C $5

   D $9

9 The table shows Jim's score for five computer games. Which shows Jim's scores ordered from greatest to least? 🎓 2.2.d.

Game	1	2	3	4	5
Score	⁻40	41	⁻46	33	⁻41

    A   ⁻40, 41, ⁻46, 33, ⁻41

    B   ⁻46, ⁻40, ⁻41, 41, 33

    C   41, 33, ⁻46, ⁻41, ⁻40

    D   41, 33, ⁻40, ⁻41, ⁻46

10 During the first nine months of the year, a worldwide club showed its total loss of members as ⁻2,718. The club lost the same number of members each month. How many club members did the club lose each month? 🎓 2.2.d.

    A   ⁻404

    B   ⁻302

    C   404

    D   302

11 The lowest point in Louisiana is found in New Orleans. The elevation is 8 feet below sea level. Which point on the number line marks Louisiana's lowest elevation? 🎓 2.2.d.

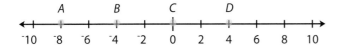

    A   C

    B   A

    C   D

    D   B

Problem Solving

12 At 5 P.M., the air temperature was ⁻5°C. At 10 P.M., the temperature had decreased by 9°. What was the air temperature at 10 P.M.? 🎓 2.2.d.

13 Ken says that ⁻6 + 2 = 8. What is his error? What is the correct sum? 🎓 2.2.d.

14 Julie says that |⁻6| is less than 4. Is Julie correct? **Explain.** 🎓 2.2.d.

15 **Explain** how to use the rules for dividing integers to find the possible signs for the dividend and divisor in ▨72 ÷ ▨8 = 9. 🎓 2.2.d.

16 For what values of a will ⁻2 × (a − 3) be positive? **Explain.** 🎓 2.2.d.

Expressions and Equations

Fun Fact

In any given year, farms in the United States produce more than 76 billion eggs. This is about 256 eggs per year for every American citizen.

Investigate

Suppose you own and run a café. Choose three items from the supply list. Write an algebraic expression that could be used to find the total cost of ordering those items. Then evaluate the expression for five different orders.

Café Supplies		
Items Needed	**Number Ordered**	**Cost per Item**
Coffee filters	3 packages	$3.00
Eggs	2 dozen	$2.00
Bread	5 loaves	$4.00
Cold cereal	4 boxes	$6.00
Milk	2 gallons	$5.00

Technology
Student pages are available in the Student eBook.

Show What You Know

ASSESSMENT
Soar To Success: Math.

▶ Exponents

Find the value.

1. 2^3　　　　**2.** 5^4　　　　**3.** 1^8　　　　**4.** 3^4　　　　**5.** 2^5　　　　**6.** 4^3

7. 5^2　　　　**8.** 6^3　　　　**9.** 6^1　　　　**10.** 7^2　　　　**11.** 10^3　　　　**12.** 3^3

▶ Order of Operations

Evaluate each expression.

13. $2^2 + 4^2$　　　　**14.** $\frac{(4+8)}{6} + 3^2$　　　　**15.** $22 - 6 \div 3$　　　　**16.** $7 + 2 \times 4$

17. $\frac{(14 - 2^2)}{5} \times 2$　　　　**18.** $9^2 \div (20 + 7)$　　　　**19.** $18 - 6 \times 2 + 12$　　　　**20.** $3^3 \div (12 - 9) + 7$

▶ Evaluate Expressions

Evaluate each expression.

21. $x + 4$ for $x = 2$　　　　**22.** $z \div 3$ for $z = 24$　　　　**23.** $g - 6$ for $g = 9$

24. $6 \times a$ for $a = 2$　　　　**25.** $r + 12$ for $r = 8$　　　　**26.** $100 \times k$ for $k = 3$

Vocabulary

Visualize It !

equation

a mathematical sentence with an equal sign

parentheses

grouping symbols that indicate which operations should be performed first

$$\rightarrow (45 + 67) - 28 = 84$$

simplify

to reduce an expression to a simpler form

$$(45 + 67) = 112$$

Language Tips

Math words that look similar in English and Spanish often have the same meaning.

English	Spanish
algebraic expression	expresión algebraic
equation	ecuación

See **English-Spanish Glossary**.

⭐ **1.2.** Write algebraic expressions and simple equations that correspond to a given situation.

Write Algebraic Expressions

Essential Question How do you use numbers and symbols in writing algebraic expressions from words?

PROBLEM Irene's cell phone plan allows 200 text messages each month for a flat rate of $4.99, with $0.10 charged for each text message beyond 200. Write an algebraic expression that gives the amount Irene will have to pay for text messages each month.

An **algebraic expression** is an expression that includes at least one variable.

Write an algebraic expression.

Write a word expression to represent the monthly charge for text messages. Use m to represent the number of text messages over the limit.

$4.99 for the month	plus	$0.10 for each of the m text messages over 200
↓	↓	↓
4.99	+	$0.10 \times m$

So, $4.99 + 0.10m$ represents the monthly cost of Irene's text messages.

Sometimes, you need two or more variables to write an algebraic expression.

Write an algebraic expression using two variables.

A cell phone company charges $0.03 per minute for local calls and $0.12 per minute for long-distance calls. Write an algebraic expression that gives the total cost for local and long-distance calls where a represents minutes of local calls and b represents minutes of long-distance calls.

word expression	algebraic expression
$0.03 per minute for local calls	$0.03a$
$0.12 per minute for long-distance calls	$0.12b$

So, $0.03a + 0.12b$ represents the total cost of local and long-distance calls.

Remember

Multiplication using a variable can be represented in several different ways.

$$8 \times m \quad 8 \cdot m$$
$$8(m) \quad 8m$$

Write an algebraic expression for each word expression.

thirty more than the product of four and some number, x	$4x + 30$
four times the quantity of $x + 30$	$4(x + 30)$
some number, w, divided by 5 times another number, t	$\frac{w}{5t}$

Write an algebraic expression using three variables.

A cell phone company is offering a special deal. For the first month, you pay half the basic monthly service fee plus the charges for text messages and the charges for phone calls. Write an algebraic expression for the total cost for the first month.

Choose your variables. Let b represent the basic monthly service fee, t represent the cost of text messages, and p represent the cost of phone calls.

Write numbers and symbols for the parts of the word expression.

> one-half basic monthly service: $\frac{1}{2}b$
>
> cost of text messages: t
>
> cost of phone calls: p

So, $\frac{1}{2}b + t + p$ represents the total cost for the first month.

- Write an algebraic expression for the total monthly cost if the basic monthly service fee is doubled instead of halved.

You can use algebraic properties to write equivalent algebraic expressions.

Use the properties.

Use the Commutative, Associative, or Distributive Property to write an equivalent algebraic expression.

Property	Expression	Equivalent Expression
Commutative	$3x + 5y$	$5y + 3x$
Associative	$(3x + 5y) + 8z$	$3x + (5y + 8z)$
Distributive	$3(2a + 5b)$	$6a + 15b$

▶ Share and Show

1. Use a fraction bar to write an algebraic expression for x divided by 7.

2. Use an addition symbol to write an algebraic expression for m increased by 14.

Write an algebraic expression for the word expression.

3. g divided by 2.39

4. 2 less than the product of 4 and d

✓ 5. 17 more than x

✓ 6. one-half of some number plus the number squared

7. Math Talk **Explain** how to write an algebraic expression for the following: If you buy 3 shirts, at s dollars each, then you get $5 off the total price.

Practice and Problem Solving REAL WORLD

Write an algebraic expression for the word expression.

8. some number increased by 32

9. $3\frac{1}{2}$ decreased by some number

10. the product of a number and 36

11. length times width times height

12. some number decreased by 45

13. 24 less than two thirds of some number

14. the square of some number which is then divided by 8

15. some number increased by 5, then increased by the same number cubed

Use the indicated property to write an equivalent algebraic expression.

16. Commutative Property
$2x + 4y$

17. Associative Property
$a + (2b + 3c)$

18. Distributive Property
$5(3n + 2m)$

Write a word expression for each algebraic expression.

19. $n - 14$

20. $36 \div 2n$

21. $n + \frac{2}{5} + n^2$

22. $3(n + 1) \div 4$

Solve.

23. A cell phone company charges $0.01 for each extra kilobyte of data usage and $0.05 for each extra text message. Write an algebraic expression that gives the total extra cost where k represents the number of extra kilobytes and t represents the number of extra text messages.

24. On their first month's bill, new customers pay one-fourth off the basic service fee, one-half off the text messaging fee, and an additional $10 off the entire bill. Write an algebraic expression for the total cost for the first month, if s represents the total bill without the discounts.

25. Pose a Problem Look back at Problem 24. Write a similar problem in which new customers get a smaller discount on the cost of data usage and text messages. Choose your own discount.

26. Hazel purchases a new cell phone for $99, and signs up for a plan that will cost $29.99 per month. **Explain** how to write an expression for the total cost of the phone and the monthly plan for a certain number of months.

OCCT Test Prep

27. Which algebraic expression matches the word expression below?

a number, n, divivded by 12

A $12 \div n$ **C** $n \div 12$

B $n \cdot 12$ **D** $12 + n$

28. A camp site costs $15, plus an additional charge of $2.50 for each camper, c. Which algebraic expression could represent the total cost?

A $15 + c$ **C** $15c$

B $15 + 2.50 + c$ **D** $15 + 2.50c$

★ Standards Quick Check

Write an algebraic expression for the word expression.

1. the sum of a number and 109.5

2. 45 divided by a number, *t*

3. 11 less than two times some number, *y*

4. the product of *c* and *d* decreased by 13

Write a Problem

Math is a language of digits, symbols, and words. You use algebra to translate the words to numbers and symbols. You need to understand key words and phrases, know what each variable represents, and know how to follow the order of operations to evaluate expressions.

Mr. Becker asked his students to write a question that can be represented by $7.5y + 6$.

Read the steps that Jenny followed to write her problem.

Key Words and Phrases	Operation
added to, combined, increased by, more than, sum of, together, total of	addition ($+$)
decreased by, difference between/of, fewer than, less, less than, minus, how many more than, how many fewer than, are left	subtraction ($-$)
product of, multiplied by, times	multiplication ($\times$)
per, out of, percent (divide by 100), quotient of, ratio of, shared by, split among, divided among	division ($\div$)

Step 1 The problem could be about buying items that cost $7.50 each and then buying another item that costs $6.00.

Step 2 Think of a situation.

Step 3 Write a problem based on the situation. "Jenny, her little brother, and some friends are going to the movies. The tickets cost $7.50 each for Jenny and her friends and $6.00 for her little brother. Write an expression for the total cost of going to the movies."

Write a problem for each expression.

1. $12(x + 4y)$

2. $12x + 4y$

3. $x(29.5 - 5) + 12.5$

4. $\frac{x + y}{3}$

Evaluate Algebraic Expressions

Essential Question What general steps can you use to evaluate algebraic expressions for different values of the variable(s)?

★ **1.2.** Write algebraic expressions and simple equations that correspond to a given situation.

1.3. Use substitution to simplify and evaluate algebraic expressions (e.g., if $x = 5$ evaluate $3 - 5x$).

▶ Learn

Evaluate $4m - 18 \div 3$ for $m = 7$.	
$4m - 18 \div 3$	
$4 \times 7 - 18 \div 3$	Replace m with 7. Multiply.
$28 - 18 \div 3$	Divide.
$28 - 6$	Subtract.
22	

So, for $m = 7$, the expression $4m - 18 \div 3 = 22$.

- Will evaluating the algebraic expression $4m - 18 \div 3$ for some value of m give the same result as evaluating $(4m - 18) \div 3$? Explain.

You can evaluate an algebraic expression for different values of the variable.

Vocabulary

terms

like terms

Materials
- MathBoard

ERROR ALERT

When squaring a number, be sure to multiply the number by itself and not multiply it by 2.

Evaluate $x^2 + 11$ for $x = 7, 4, {}^-3$ and ${}^-5$.			

$x = 7$		$x = 4$	
$x^2 + 11$		$x^2 + 11$	
$7^2 + 11$	Replace x with 7. Clear the exponent.	$4^2 + 11$	Replace x with 4. Clear the exponent.
$49 + 11$	Add.	$16 + 11$	Add.
60		27	

So, for $x = 7$, $x^2 + 11 = 60$.　　　So, for $x = 4$, $x^2 + 11 = 27$.

$x = {}^-3$		$x = {}^-5$	
$x^2 + 11$		$x^2 + 11$	
$({}^-3)^2 + 11$	Replace x with ${}^-3$. Clear the exponent.	$({}^-5)^2 + 11$	Replace x with ${}^-5$. Clear the exponent.
$9 + 11$	Add.	$25 + 11$	Add.
20		36	

So, for $x = {}^-3$, $x^2 + 11 = 20$.　　　So, for $x = {}^-5$, $x^2 + 11 = 36$.

The parts of an expression that are separated by an addition or subtraction sign are called **terms**. Before you evaluate some algebraic expressions, you can simplify them by combining like terms. **Like terms** have the same variable, raised to the same power.

Algebraic Expression	Like Terms
$3x + 10x + 9$	$3x$ and $10x$
$15y - 8 - 12y$	$15y$ and $12y$
$8z^2 + 17 + 4z + 12z^2$	$8z^2$ and $12z^2$

To make an algebraic expression simpler, combine like terms by adding or subtracting them.

Algebraic Expression	Simplified
$3x + 10x + 9$	$13x + 9$
$15y - 8 - 12y$	$3y - 8$
$8z^2 + 17 + 4z + 12z^2$	$20z^2 + 4z + 7$

If possible, simplify an expression before you evaluate it. Combine like terms, and then evaluate the expression for the given value of the variable.

Evaluate $6y + 12 + 3y$ for $y = 10$.

$6y + 12 + 3y$ $= 6y + 3y + 12$ Use the Commutative Property.
Combine like terms.

$= 9y + 12$

$= 9 \times 10 + 12$ Replace y with 10 and multiply.

$= 90 + 12$ Add.

$= 102$

So, for $y = 10$, $6y + 12 + 3y = 102$.

Combine like terms and evaluate.

A rectangular lot is being made into a skateboard park. The length, l, is 45 yd, and the width, w, is 30 yd. To find the perimeter, the algebraic expression $l + w + l + w$ is being used, where l is the length and w is the width. What is the perimeter of the lot?

$l + w + l + w$ $= l + l + w + w$ Use the Commutative Property.
Combine like terms.

$= 2l + 2w$

$= 2 \times 45 + 2 \times 30$ Replace l with 45 and w with 30 and multiply.

$= 90 + 60$ Add.

$= 150$

So, the perimeter of the lot is 150 yd.

▶ **Share and Show**

1. Evaluate $2y + 4$ for $y = 3$. Replace y with 3, multiply 3 by 2, and then add 4.

2. Evaluate $4g + 21g - 21$ for $g = 2$. Combine like terms, then replace g with 2, multiply, and then subtract 21.

Evaluate the expression for $x = 3, 2, 1,$ and 0.

3. $10 + 5x$

4. $4x - 29$

5. $17 + 4x + x^2$

 6. $0.5x + x^3$

Simplify the expression. Then evaluate the expression for the given value of the variable.

7. $9a + 15a - 6$ for $a = 3$

8. $4x - 12 + 5x$ for $x = 6$

 9. $4c + c + 2c$ for $c = 2$

10. Math Talk Explain how to evaluate the expression $3y - 15 + 8y$ for $y = 12$.

Practice and Problem Solving REAL WORLD

Evaluate the expression for $a = 3, 0, {}^-1,$ and ${}^-3$.

11. $4a$

12. ${}^-6a$

13. $8 - \frac{1}{2}a$

14. $7 + 2a$

15. $(a + 6)^2 - 15$

16. $(a + 1)^3 + 2$

17. $a^2 + 3a - 5$

18. $a^2 + a + 2$

Simplify the expression. Then evaluate the expression for the given value of the variable.

19. $3x + 8x - 11$ for $x = 2$

20. $33n - 15 + 7n$ for $n = 1$

21. $6d + 6d - 6d$ for $d = 6$

22. The tread area of a skateboard wheel can be estimated by using the expression $6.28rw$, where r is the radius and w is the width of the wheel. What is the tread area of a wheel with a radius of 25 mm and a width of 15 mm?

23. The skate park charges $5 admission and a $2 rental fee. To find the total cost for 3 people, the cashier used the expression $a + r + a + r + a + r$ where a is the admission cost and r is the rental cost. What was the total cost for 3 people?

For 24–25, use the cost chart.

The cost chart shows how much a company charges for skateboard wheels. Each pack of 8 wheels costs $50. Shipping costs $7 for any order.

24. Copy and complete the cost chart.

25. **Reasoning** Suppose your skateboard club has a budget of $200 to spend on new wheels this year. How many packs of wheels can you order?

Cost Chart for Skateboard Wheels

Number of Packs	$50 \times n + 7$	Cost
1	$50 \times 1 + 7$	$57
2	$50 \times 2 + 7$	▪
3	▪	▪
4	▪	▪
5	▪	▪

OCCT Test Prep

Math Board

26. Which is the value of the expression $3 + x^2 - 4$ for $x = 5$?

    A 15   **B** 22   **C** 24   **D** 36

27. Which is the value of the expression $3b + c^2$ for $b = 4$ and $c = 5$?

    A 17   **B** 22   **C** 31   **D** 37

 Technology
Use HMH Mega Math, Ice Station Exploration, *Arctic Algebra*, Level I.

⬩★ Standards Quick Check

Evaluate the expression for $x = 10$ and $y = 8$.

1. $6x + 5$

2. $7y - 17.25 + 12y$

3. $12x + 32 - 9x$

4. $3x + 9x - 4$

5. $22y - 19y + 17$

6. $y^2 + 2y + 7$

Challenge H.O.T.

The Distributive Property

You can use the Distributive Property and mental math to evaluate algebraic expressions.

Evaluate lw for $l = 5$ and $w = 68$.

lw	
5×68	Replace l with 5 and w with 68.
$5(60 + 8)$	Think of 68 as $60 + 8$.
$5 \times 60 + 5 \times 8$	Use the Distributive Property and mental math.
$300 + 40$	
340	

So, for $l = 5$ and $w = 68$, $lw = 340$.

Evaluate bh for $b = 3$ and $h = 4.7$.

bh	
3×4.7	Replace b with 3 and h with 4.7.
$3(4 + 0.7)$	Think of 4.7 as $4 + 0.7$.
$3 \times 4 + 3 \times 0.7$	Use the Distributive Property and mental math.
$12 + 2.1$	
14.1	

So, for $b = 3$ and $h = 4.7$, $bh = 14.1$.

Use the Distributive Property and mental math to evaluate each expression.

1. xy for $x = 4$ and $y = 79$

2. rs for $r = 5$ and $s = 37$

3. ma for $m = 3$ and $a = 9.8$

4. The cost for the band to ride a bus is $12 per student. Write an algebraic expression to represent the cost of s students riding the bus. If there are 65 students in the band, how much does it cost to ride the bus?

★ **1.2.** Write algebraic expressions and simple equations that correspond to a given situation.

1.4. Write and solve one-step equations with one variable using number sense, the properties or operations, and the properties of inequalities (e.g., $\frac{1}{3x} + 9$).

Vocabulary

equation

Materials

• MathBoard

Words and Equations

Essential Question What words will help you write equations from word problems?

► **Learn** REAL WORLD

PROBLEM It costs $59.60 to fill up the soccer team's van with gas. Gas costs $2.98 per gallon. Write an equation that could help find the number of gallons the tank holds.

An **equation** is a statement that shows that two quantities are equal. These are examples of equations:

$$8 + 12 = 20 \qquad 15 \times 3 = 45 \qquad a - 3 = 14 \qquad d \div 3 = 7$$

Write an equation.

Use numbers, variables, and operations to translate words into equations.

1 Choose a variable. Let g represent the number of gallons of gas in the tank.

....

2 Know the operation. Divide the total cost by the cost per gallon to find the number of gallons.

....

3 Write using words. Translate the words into an equation.

gallons of gas in van's gas tank	equals	cost to fill up gas tank	divided by	price per gallon
↓	↓	↓	↓	↓
g	=	59.60	÷	2.98

So, an equation is $g = 59.60 \div 2.98$.

Write an equation for a word sentence.

The original amount in Jim's savings account plus the $219.00 he deposited totals $876.54.

Choose a variable. Let a represent the original amount in Jim's savings account.

original amount	plus	$219.00 deposited	totals	$876.54
↓	↓	↓	↓	↓
a	+	219	=	876.54

So, an equation is $a + 219 = 876.54$.

Choose the correct equation for the word sentence.

1. 25 is 13 more than a number.

$$25 = n + 13$$
$$13 = n + 25$$

2. 10 times the number of balloons is 120.

$$10 + n = 120$$
$$10n = 120$$

Write an equation for the word sentence.

3. 6 fewer than a number is $12\frac{2}{3}$.

4. The quotient of 20.7 and a number is 9.

5. Math Talk **Explain** how to translate a word sentence into an equation.

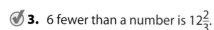 ▶ **Practice and Problem Solving** REAL WORLD

Write an equation for the word sentence.

6. Two-thirds of a number is 18.

7. 56 fewer than g is 40.

8. 18.5 is 75 more than twice a number.

9. 3.67 less than a number equals 46.33.

10. 8 times a number is 62.

11. The quotient of a number and 3 is 16.

Write a word sentence for each equation.

12. $x - 21 = 6$ **13.** $25 = \frac{1}{3}n$ **14.** $15g = 135$ **15.** $w \div 3\frac{1}{3} = \frac{5}{6}$ **16.** $g - 9 = 10$

Real World Data

For 17–18, use the chart.

17. Write an equation you could use to find how many miles a hybrid SUV can travel in the city on 20 gal of gas.

18. A sedan traveled 504 mi on the highway on a full tank of gas. Write an equation you could use to find the number of gallons the tank holds.

Fuel-Efficiency (mi per gal)		
Automobile	mi per gal city	mi per gal highway
Mini van	19	26
SUV	22	26
Hybrid SUV	36	31
Van	14	17
Sedan	20	28

Fuel efficiency is measured in miles per gallon.

19. Write Math ▶ **What's the Error?** Tony is planning a 560-mi trip. He travels 313 mi the first day. He says that the equation $m - 313 = 560$ will help find the number of miles he has left on his trip. Describe his error.

 OCCT Test Prep

20. Which represents the word sentence three times a number, v, is 128?

A $3v + 128$ **C** $128 \div 3v = 3$

B $3v = 128$ **D** $3v - 128 = 4$

21. Which represents the word sentence 12 less than a number, n, is 17?

A $12n = 17$ **C** $n + 12 = 17$

B $\frac{n}{12} = 17$ **D** $n - 12 = 17$

Vocabulary

Subtraction Property of Equality

Materials

• MathBoard

Math Idea

When solving addition equations, subtract the number that is on the same side of the equation as the variable from both sides of the equation.

Solve Addition Equations

Essential Question Why are equations useful?

PROBLEM The world record for a dance marathon is 52 hr. If you have been dancing for 24 hr, how much longer do you have to dance to match the world record?

Solve the problem by using the addition equation $h + 24 = 52$, where h is the number of hours left to dance. To solve an addition equation, use the inverse operation, subtraction.

Subtraction Property of Equality	$7 = 7$
If you subtract the same number from both sides of an equation, the two sides remain equal.	$7 - 3 = 7 - 3$ $4 = 4$

Examples

Solve and check. $h + 24 = 52$

$h + 24 = 52$	Write the equation.
$h + 24 - 24 = 52 - 24$	Use the Subtraction Property of Equality.
$h + 0 = 28$	Use the Identity Property.
$h = 28$	
$h + 24 = 52$	Check your solution.
$28 + 24 \stackrel{?}{=} 52$	Replace h with 28.
$52 = 52 ✓$	The solution checks.

So, you have to dance 28 hr longer.

• Explain the process you would use to solve $n + 13 = 37$.

Solve and check. $10 = 1.5 + x$

$10 = 1.5 + x$	Write the equation.
$10 = x + 1.5$	Use the Commutative Property.
$10 - 1.5 = x + 1.5 - 1.5$	Use the Subtraction Property of Equality.
$8.5 = x + 0$	Use the Identity Property.
$8.5 = x$	
$10 = 1.5 + x$	Check your solution.
$10 \stackrel{?}{=} 1.5 + 8.5$	Replace x with 8.5.
$10 = 10 ✓$	The solution checks.

So, $x = 8.5$.

Solve and check.

1. $x + 8 = 15$
$x + 8 - 8 = 15 - 8$
$x = $ ▩

2. $g + 23 = 20$
$g + 23 - 23 = 20 - 23$
$g = $ ▩

3. $a + 16 = {}^-25$
$a + 16 - ▩ = {}^-25 - ▩$
$a = $ ▩

4. $42 = s + 20$
$42 - ▩ = s + 20 - ▩$
▩ $= s$

5. $b + 7 = 15$

✔ **6.** $y + 6.7 = 9.8$

7. $8\frac{2}{5} = d + 2\frac{2}{5}$

✔ **8.** ${}^-25 = k + 2$

9. Math Talk **Explain** how you get a variable alone on one side of an addition equation.

▶ **Practice and Problem Solving** REAL WORLD

Solve and check.

10. $n + 9 = 25$

11. $y + 11 = 26$

12. $16\frac{1}{2} = x + 4$

13. $4\frac{3}{4} + v = 12\frac{1}{2}$

14. $z + 6.8 = 15$

15. $18.7 + k = 32.2$

16. $p + 13 = {}^-42$

17. ${}^-12 = r + 12$

18. **Reasoning** Which of the numerical values 1, 2, and 3 is the solution of the equation $x + 5 = 7$?

19. What value of k makes the equation $k + 5 = 9$ true?

🖼 Real World Data

For 20–22, use the table at the right. Write an equation and solve.

20. Suppose you jump on a pogo stick 1,600 times in a row. How many more jumps would it take to match the world record?

21. Suppose you want to match the world record for eating ice cream. If you eat 100 g in the first 10 sec, and 98 g in the next 10 sec, how many more grams do you need to eat?

22. Write Math ▶ **What's the Question?** A friend tells you, "I made 3 sets of five hundred jumps each." The answer is 399 more jumps.

World Records		
Name	**Record**	**Amount**
Diego Siu	most ice cream eaten in 30 sec	264g (9.3 oz)
Ashrita Furman	most pogo stick jumps	1,899 jumps
Susan Williams	biggest bubble-gum bubble	58.4 cm wide (23 in.)

  OCCT Test Prep

23. Which is the value of r in the equation $r + 17 = 240$?

    A 223   **C** 193

    B 213   **D** 143

24. Fran is buying an $88 bicycle in two payments. The first payment is $42. Which is the amount of the second payment?

    A $130   **C** $46

    B $100   **D** $2.09

LESSON 5

1.2. Write algebraic expressions and simple equations that correspond to a given situation.

1.4. Write and solve one-step equations with one variable using number sense, the properties or operations, and the properties of inequalities (e.g., $\frac{1}{3x} + 9$).

Vocabulary

Addition Property of Equality

Materials

• MathBoard

Solve Subtraction Equations

Essential Question How do you use the Addition Property of Equality to solve subtraction equations?

PROBLEM A cable station manager at KIDS-TV hired 12 students and did not hire 36 students. How many students applied to work at KIDS-TV?

Solve the problem by using the subtraction equation $s - 36 = 12$, where s is the total number of students who applied. To solve a subtraction equation, use the inverse operation, addition.

Addition Property of Equality	
If you add the same number to both sides of an equation, the two sides remain equal.	$7 = 7$ $7 + 2 = 7 + 2$ $9 = 9$

Examples

Solve and check. $s - 36 = 12$.

$s - 36 = 12$	Write the equation.
$s - 36 + 36 = 12 + 36$	Use the Addition Property of Equality.
$s + 0 = 48$	Use the Identity Property.
$s = 48$	
$s - 36 = 12$	Check your solution.
$48 - 36 \overset{?}{=} 12$	Replace s with 48.
$12 = 12$ ✓	The solution checks.

So, 48 students applied to work at KIDS-TV.

• Explain the process you would use to solve $x - 9 = {}^{-}23$.

Sometimes the variable will be on the right side of the equation.

Solve and check. $6.5 = d - 15.5$.

$6.5 = d - 15.5$	Write the equation.
$6.5 + 15.5 = d - 15.5 + 15.5$	Use the Addition Property of Equality.
$22 = d + 0$	Use the Identity Property.
$22 = d$	
$6.5 = d - 15.5$	Check your solution.
$6.5 \overset{?}{=} 22 - 15.5$	Replace d with 22.
$6.5 = 6.5$	The solution checks.

So, $d = 22$.

Solve and check.

1. $x - 7 = 15$

$x - 7 + 7 = 15 + 7$

$x = \blacksquare$

2. $a - 32 = {}^-49$

$a - 32 + 32 = {}^-49 + 32$

$a = \blacksquare$

3. $78 = w - 39$

$78 + \blacksquare = w - 39 + \blacksquare$

$w = \blacksquare$

4. $9.8 = d - 7.2$

$9.8 + \blacksquare = d - 7.2 + \blacksquare$

$d = \blacksquare$

✔**5.** $y - 4.9 = 9.1$

6. $10 = p - 6\frac{5}{8}$

7. ${}^-52 = s - 14$

✔**8.** $w - 2\frac{3}{5} = 4\frac{2}{5}$

9. Math Talk **Explain** how to use the Addition Property of Equality to solve $x - 15 = 6$.

Solve and check.

10. $n - 26 = 11$

11. $22 = x - 9$

12. $z - \frac{3}{5} = \frac{5}{6}$

13. $a - 9\frac{2}{3} = 15\frac{1}{3}$

14. $y - 3.7 = 13.8$

15. $2.5 = k - 9.9$

16. $p - 22 = {}^-30$

17. ${}^-6 = m - 12$

18. Reasoning Which of the numerical values 19, 20, and 21, is the solution of the equation $x - 12 = 7$?

19. What value of y makes the equation $y - 6 = 10$ true?

 Real World Data

For 20–21, use the bar graph. Write an equation and solve it.

20. The amount of water used for showering is 7.5 gal less than the amount used for washing clothes. How many gallons are used for washing clothes?

21. The amount of water that the average person drinks each week, minus $\frac{1}{5}$ of the water used washing dishes daily, is equal to $\frac{1}{2}$ gal. How much water does the average person drink in a week?

22. Write Math **What's the Error?** Rolando says that the solution of the equation $x - 3 = 12$ is $x = 9$. Find his error and then solve the equation.

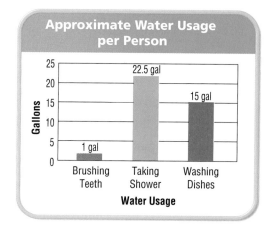

Approximate Water Usage per Person

Brushing Teeth: 1 gal
Taking Shower: 22.5 gal
Washing Dishes: 15 gal

Gallons / Water Usage

23. Which is the solution of $y - 12 = 16$?

A $y = 28$ **C** $y = {}^-4$

B $y = 4$ **D** $y = {}^-28$

24. Which is the solution of $x - 65 = {}^-22$?

A $x = {}^-83$ **C** $x = 43$

B $x = {}^-43$ **D** $x = 83$

LESSON 6

★ 1.2. Write algebraic expressions and simple equations that correspond to a given situation. *also* 1.4.

Materials
• MathBoard

Problem Solving Workshop
Strategy: Compare Strategies

Essential Question When would each strategy be used?

🔑 **UNLOCK the Problem** ⟩ REAL WORLD

PROBLEM Jamal and Lee are selling T-shirts to raise money for volleyball. At the end of the first week, they have sold a total of 79 T-shirts. Jamal has sold one more than twice as many as Lee. How many T-shirts has Lee sold?

Read the Problem

What do I need to find?

I need to find how many T-shirts Lee sold.

What information do I need to use?

I need to use the fact that a total of 79 T-shirts were sold and that Jamal sold one more than twice as many as Lee.

How will I use the information?

I will predict and test and then draw a diagram to find the answer.

Solve the Problem

Predict and Test

Write an equation to describe the situation. Let t represent the number of T-shirts Lee sold and $2t + 1$ represent the number of T-shirts Jamal sold.

$$t + 2t + 1 = 79 \qquad \text{Combine like terms.}$$

$$3t + 1 = 79$$

To predict, substitute numbers for t. To test, see if the result is 79.

Predict (t)	Test ($3t + 1$)	Result
25	76	too low
27	82	too high
26	79	correct

So, Lee sold 26 T-shirts.

Draw a Diagram

Show the relationship between the number of T-shirts Lee sold and the number of T-shirts Jamal sold, which together total 79.

Lee	Jamal		
t	t	t	1
79			

Subtract 1 T-shirt from the total to get 78. Divide 78 by 3 to find the number of T-shirts Lee sold.

$$78 \div 3 = 26$$

Choose a Strategy
- Draw a Diagram
- Predict and Test
- Make a Model or Act It Out
- Make an Organized List
- Find a Pattern
- Make a Table or Graph
- Work Backward
- Solve a Simpler Problem
- Write an Equation
- Use Logical Reasoning

Predict and test or draw a diagram to solve.

1. The boys' and girls' basketball teams have raised $460. The car wash made $10 more than 4 times as much money as the bake sale. How much money did they make from the bake sale?

First, draw a diagram.

Bake Sale	Car Wash				
m	m	m	m	m	10
460					

Then, use the diagram to determine the operations.

Finally, find the money made from the bake sale.

$$(460 - 10) \div 5$$

2. What if the basketball teams had raised $600 and the bake sale had made half as much as the car wash. How much money would they have made from the bake sale?

3. The Lady Hawks lacrosse team played a total of 35 games. They won 3 games more than 3 times the number they lost. How many games did they win?

On Your Own

Solve.

4. Albert and Ryan have 146 football cards altogether. Albert has 4 less than twice the number of cards Ryan has. How many cards does Albert have?

5. During a week of track and field practice, Alvin and Karl ran a total of 36 mi. For every mile that Alvin ran, Karl ran 3 mi. How many miles did each one run?

6. Melinda went to a baseball game and spent a total of $38.45. She bought a program for $5.95, a ticket for $11.50, and some hot dogs for $3.00 each. How many hot dogs did Melinda buy?

7. At the running store, Michael paid $1.49 each for 3 packets of energy bars and $4.97 for a pair of socks. When he left the store, he had $10.56 in his pocket. How much money did Michael start with?

8. Pauline runs in her neighborhood every other day. She swims laps at the pool every third day. If she runs and swims on June 1, what are the next two dates that she will again both run and swim?

9. A package of 4 pens costs $3.00 and a package of 7 pens costs $5.00. What is the greatest number of pens that can be purchased for $33.00?

10. **Write Math** Both Jim and Tamika have savings accounts. Tamika has saved $35 more than 4 times what Jim has saved. Together they have saved a total of $535. How much has Jim saved? **Explain** how to use the problem solving strategy *predict and test* to solve this problem.

Addition and Subtraction Equations

Essential Question How can you use properties of equality and identity to solve addition and subtraction equations?

1.2. Write algebraic expressions and simple equations that correspond to a given situation.

1.4. Write and solve one-step equations with one variable using number sense, the properties or operations, and the properties of inequalities (e.g., $\frac{1}{3x} + 9$).

Materials
• MathBoard

▶ **Learn** REAL WORLD

PROBLEM The Bears scored 59 points in a playoff basketball game. This was 14 points fewer than their opponents, the Panthers, scored. How many points did the Panthers score?

Subtraction Equation

You can solve this problem by writing and solving an equation.

Panthers' score	minus	14 points	equals	Bears' score.
↓	↓	↓	↓	↓
p	−	14	=	59

$$p - 14 = 59 \qquad \text{Write the equation.}$$
$$p - 14 + 14 = 59 + 14 \qquad \text{Use the Addition Property of Equality.}$$
$$p + 0 = 73 \qquad \text{Use the Identity Property.}$$
$$p = 73$$

$$p - 14 = 59 \qquad \text{Check your solution.}$$
$$73 - 14 \stackrel{?}{=} 59 \qquad \text{Replace } p \text{ with 73.}$$
$$59 = 59 \qquad \text{The solution checks.}$$

So, the Panthers scored 73 points.

Math Idea

When using the Addition or Subtraction Property of Equality, remember to add or subtract the same number from each side of an equation so that the two sides remain equal.

Addition Equation

In the championship game, the Eagles won with a score of 67 points, which was 13 points more than the Panthers scored. How many points did the Panthers score?

Panthers' score	plus	13 points	equals	Eagles' score.
↓	↓	↓	↓	↓
p	+	13	=	67

$$p + 13 = 67 \qquad \text{Write the equation.}$$
$$p + 13 - 13 = 67 - 13 \qquad \text{Use the Subtraction Property of Equality.}$$
$$p + 0 = 54 \qquad \text{Use the Identity Property.}$$
$$p = 54$$

$$p + 13 = 67 \qquad \text{Check your solution.}$$
$$54 + 13 \stackrel{?}{=} 67 \qquad \text{Replace } p \text{ with 54.}$$
$$67 = 67 \qquad \text{The solution checks.}$$

So, the Panthers scored 54 points.

▶ **Share and Show**

1. At a track meet, there was a 24-point difference between first place and second place. First place went to the Chavez Middle School track team. The second-place team earned 96 points. How many points did the Chavez team earn?

Chavez score	minus	24	equals	2nd place score
↓	↓	↓	↓	↓
c	$-$	24	$=$	96

$$c - 24 = 96$$
$$c - 24 + 24 = 96 + 24$$
$$c + 0 = \blacksquare$$

Solve and check.

 **2.** $q - 36 = 19$ **3.** $d - 7.25 = 10.75$ **4.** $v + 4\frac{3}{5} = 5\frac{1}{10}$ ✔ **5.** $a + 15 = {}^{-}3$

6. **Math Talk** **Explain** how to decide whether to use an addition equation or a subtraction equation to solve a word problem.

▶ **Practice and Problem Solving** REAL WORLD

Solve and check.

7. $n + 15 = 36$ **8.** $y - 12 = 17$ **9.** $x + 4.7 = 16.5$ **10.** $q + 8 = {}^{-}25$

11. $6 + n = 36$ **12.** ${}^{-}6 = r - 13$ **13.** $z - \frac{2}{3} = \frac{3}{4}$ **14.** $x - 3\frac{3}{8} = 9\frac{5}{12}$

Real World Data

For 15–16, use the table. Write an equation and solve.

Football Scores

Knights 31	Bulls ▢
Tigers 24	Cubs ▢
Hawks 42	Cougars ▢

15. The Bulls lost to the Knights by 15 points. What was the final score for the Bulls?

16. The Tigers beat the Cubs by 7 points. What was the final score for the Cubs?

17. ☰**FAST FACT** The length of a football field is 120 yd. The width of a football field is $66\frac{2}{3}$ yd less than the length. Is the width of a football field greater than 60 yd?

18. **Write Math** **What's the Question?** Lisa and Rodney went to a football game. Lisa spent $8.50 at the concession stand. Rodney spent $3.75 more than Lisa. The answer is $12.25.

★ **OCCT Test Prep** Math Board

19. Jennifer had $36.50 in her bank account. After she spent some money, she had ${}^{-}$$6.45 in her bank account. How much money did Jennifer spend?

  A $16.75   **B** $30.05   **C** $37.05   **D** $42.95

20. Sarah collects money for the track team. She keeps the money in a box. After she put $2.25 in the box, Sarah had a total of $19.75. Which is the original amount of money in the box?

  A $2.25   **B** $17.50   **C** $19.75   **D** $22.00

GO ONLINE **Technology**
Use HMH Mega Math, Ice Station Exploration, *Arctic Algebra, Levels S, Y, Z.*

⭐ **1.2.** Write algebraic expressions and simple equations that correspond to a given situation.

1.4. Write and solve one-step equations with one variable using number sense, the properties or operations, and the properties of inequalities (e.g., $\frac{1}{3}x + 9$).

Vocabulary

Division Property of Equality

Materials

• MathBoard

Solve Multiplication Equations

Essential Question How can you model solving equations such as $3y = 9$ for y?

 **Learn** REAL WORLD

PROBLEM Jake, Melissa, Larry, Beth, and Sal are buying tickets to see a new movie. All tickets are the same price. If the tickets cost $45 altogether, how much does one ticket cost?

number of people	times	price of one ticket	equals	total cost
↓		↓		↓
5	×	n	=	45

Multiplication and division are inverse operations. To solve a multiplication equation, you use the inverse operation, division, to get the variable alone on one side of the equation.

Division Property of Equality	$12 = 12$
When you divide both sides of an equation by the same nonzero number, the two sides remain equal.	$\frac{12}{2} = \frac{12}{2}$
	$6 = 6$

Examples

Solve and check. $5n = 45$

$5n = 45$	Write the equation.
$\frac{5n}{5} = \frac{45}{5}$	Use the Division Property of Equality.
$1 \times n = 9$	$5 \div 5 = 1; 45 \div 5 = 9$
$n = 9$	Use the Identity Property.
$5n = 45$	Check your solution.
$5 \times 9 \overset{?}{=} 45$	Replace n with 9.
$45 = 45$ ✓	The solution checks.

So, the cost of one movie ticket is $9.

Remember

Division can be written using the symbol ÷ or as a fraction. For example, 24 divided by 6 can be written as $24 \div 6$ or as $\frac{24}{6}$.

Solve and check. $2y = 3.2$

$2y = 3.2$	Write the equation.
$\frac{2y}{2} = \frac{3.2}{2}$	Use the Division Property of Equality.
$1 \times y = 1.6$	$2 \div 2 = 1; 3.2 \div 2 = 1.6$
$y = 1.6$	Use the Identity Property.
$2y = 3.2$	Check your solution.
$2 \times 1.6 \overset{?}{=} 3.2$	Replace y with 1.6.
$3.2 = 3.2$ ✓	The solution checks.

So, $y = 1.6$.

Equations with Fractions and Integers

Equations can involve negative integers and fractions.

Examples

Solve and check. $^-3a = ^-24$

$^-3a = ^-24$	Write the equation.
$\dfrac{^-3a}{^-3} = \dfrac{^-24}{^-3}$	Use the Division Property of Equality.
$1 \times a = 8$	$^-3 \div ^-3 = 1;\ ^-24 \div ^-3 = 8$
$a = 8$	Use the Identity Property.
$^-3a = ^-24$	Check your solution.
$^-3 \times 8 \overset{?}{=} ^-24$	Replace a with 8.
$^-24 = ^-24$	The solution checks.

So, $a = 8$.

- Is solving an equation with negative integers different than solving an equation with whole numbers? Explain.

Solve and check. $\dfrac{2}{3} = 4z$

$\dfrac{2}{3} = 4z$	Write the equation.
$\dfrac{2}{3} = \dfrac{4z}{4}$	Use the Division Property of Equality.
$\dfrac{2}{3} \div 4 = 1 \times z$	$4 \div 4 = 1$
$\dfrac{2}{3} \times \dfrac{1}{4} = z$	Multiply by the reciprocal. Use the Identity Property.
$\dfrac{1}{6} = z$	
$\dfrac{2}{3} = 4z$	Check your solution.
$\dfrac{2}{3} \overset{?}{=} 4 \times \dfrac{1}{6}$	Replace z with $\dfrac{1}{6}$.
$\dfrac{2}{3} = \dfrac{2}{3}$ ✓	The solution checks.

So, $z = \dfrac{1}{6}$.

Math Idea

The Division Property of Equality is used to solve multiplication equations because division is the inverse operation of multiplication.

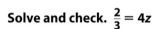 **Share and Show**

Solve and check.

1. $3x = 21$

$\dfrac{3x}{3} = \dfrac{21}{3}$

$x = $ ▨

2. $^-32 = 4y$

$\dfrac{^-32}{4} = \dfrac{4y}{4}$

$y = $ ▨

3. $\dfrac{1}{2}z = 12$

$\dfrac{\frac{1}{2}z}{\frac{1}{2}} = \dfrac{12}{\frac{1}{2}}$

$z = $ ▨

4. $5.6 = 7a$

$\dfrac{5.6}{7} = \dfrac{7a}{7}$

$a = $ ▨

5. $2.8b = 19.6$

$\dfrac{2.8b}{2.8} = \dfrac{19.6}{2.8}$

$b = $ ▨

Solve and check.

6. $7 \cdot x = 63$ ✓ **7.** $12y = 60$ **8.** $^-54 = 9z$ **9.** $1.4 \cdot c = 70$ ✓ **10.** $\frac{2}{5}a = 7$

11. Math Talk **Explain** how the Division Property of Equality is used to solve multiplication equations.

▶ **Practice and Problem Solving** REAL WORLD

Solve and check.

12. $36 = 4x$ **13.** $8y = 32$ **14.** $32 = 4g$ **15.** $38 = 2.5a$ **16.** $3z = 72$

17. $4.25 = 3.4f$ **18.** $12c = 56$ **19.** $^-3b = ^-39$ **20.** $128 = ^-8x$ **21.** $6g = ^-72$

22. $7x = \frac{1}{3}$ **23.** $\frac{2}{5}k = \frac{3}{5}$ **24.** $1.2y = 6.84$ **25.** $18 = 7.5h$ **26.** $2\frac{4}{9} = \frac{5}{6}z$

27. What value of y makes $3y = ^-72$ true?   **28.** What value of x makes $4x = 25$ true?

29. Reasoning Which of the numerical values 2, 4, and 6, is the solution of the equation $3x = 12$?   **30. Reasoning** Which of the numerical values $^-8$, $^-10$, and $^-12$ is the solution of the equation $5x = ^-40$?

Real World Data

For 31–32, use the table. Write an equation and solve.

31. Adult and child tickets are sold at the movie theater. If the total amount of money made in ticket sales for Super Action was $2,176, what was the average cost per ticket?

32. The total amount of money made in ticket sales for all the movies was $8,083.25. What was the average cost per ticket?

33. Beth and her friends buy several buckets of popcorn when they go to see The Amazing Ring. If each bucket costs $5.75 and the total cost of the popcorn is $34.50, how many buckets do they buy?

Cinema 5's Friday Night Ticket Sales	
Movie Title	Tickets Sold
Three Friends	128
Super Action	272
The Big Game	98
Star Journey	347
The Amazing Ring	198

34. Write Math ▶ **What's the Error?** Michael solves the equation $8x = 2$ and gets the solution $x = 16$. **Explain** Michael's error and give the correct solution.

 OCCT Test Prep Math Board

35. Richard earned $399 for 42 hours of work. How much is Richard paid per hour?

    A $0.11   **C** $357

    B $9.50   **D** $16,758

36. Kirsten is paid $295 for cutting yards in her neighborhood. She works for 25 hours. How much is Kirsten paid per hour?

    A $0.45   **C** $11.08

    B $1.18   **D** $11.80

Solve and check.

1. $4z = 64$

2. $\frac{j}{4} = 42.5$

3. $1.6 = \frac{b}{7}$

4. $13 = 6.5v$

5. $2.2 \cdot x = 33$

6. $17f = 54.4$

Theater Seating–Sections

The Orpheum Theatre in San Francisco boasts many historical and decorative features. Since being built in 1926, the theatre has featured vaudeville shows, silent films, movies, musicals, and many other forms of entertainment. The interior of the theatre includes a lobby decorated like a twelfth century Spanish palace, an enormous tapestry covering the stage, and sculptures of lions around the ceiling. It is easy to see why the Orpheum is considered a historical landmark by the city!

Section	Seats Per Section	Rows	Seats Per Row
Middle Left Mezzanine	112	8	x
Back Middle Orchestra	448	y	28
Right Loge	42	3	14

When setting ticket prices at events, one thing to consider is how many seats are in various sections. Look at the data for the Right Loge section of the theater. The number of seats equals the number of rows times the number of seats per row, or $(42 = 3 \times 14)$.

If every row in a section has the same number of seats, you can make the generalization below.

total seats = number of rows $\times$ seats per row

Use generalizations to solve.

1. Write and solve equations to find the values for *x* and *y* in the table.

2. Tickets for the back middle orchestra section cost $50 each. If the theater makes $20,450 from ticket sales in this section, how many tickets were sold?

★ 1.2. Write algebraic expressions and simple equations that correspond to a given situation.

1.4. Write and solve one-step equations with one variable using number sense, the properties or operations, and the properties of inequalities (e.g., $\frac{1}{3x} + 9$).

Vocabulary

Multiplication Property of Equality

Materials
• MathBoard

Solve Division Equations

Essential Question How do you solve division equations by multiplying?

 **Learn** REAL WORLD

PROBLEM Megan buys a box filled with trading cards. She divides the cards into 4 equal piles and gives a pile to each of her friends. If each pile contains 12 cards, how many total cards were in the box when she bought it?

To solve division equations, use the inverse operation, multiplication.

Multiplication Property of Equality	
When you multiply both sides of an equation by the same number, the two sides remain equal.	$8 = 8$ $3 \times 8 = 3 \times 8$ $24 = 24$

Find the total number of cards in the box.

Write an equation.

total cards in box	÷	number of piles		=	12
↓		↓			↓
c	÷	4		=	12

$\frac{c}{4} = 12$	Write the equation.	$\frac{c}{4} = 12$	Check your solution.
$4 \times \frac{c}{4} = 4 \times 12$	Use the Multiplication Property of Equality.	$\frac{48}{4} \stackrel{?}{=} 12$	Replace c with 48.
$\frac{4}{1} \times \frac{c}{4} = 48$			
$\frac{4c}{4} = 48$		$12 = 12$ ✔	The solution checks.
$c = 48$	$4 \div 4 = 1$ and $1 \times c = c$.		

So, there were 48 cards in the box when Megan bought it.

Example

Solve and check. $3.5 = \frac{k}{6}$.

$3.5 = \frac{k}{6}$	Write the equation.	$3.5 = \frac{k}{6}$	Check your solution.
$6 \times 3.5 = 6 \times \frac{k}{6}$	Use the Multiplication Property of Equality.	$3.5 \stackrel{?}{=} \frac{21}{6}$	Replace k with 21.
$21 = \frac{6}{1} \times \frac{k}{6}$			
$21 = \frac{6k}{6}$		$3.5 = 3.5$ ✔	The solution checks.
$21 = k$	$6 \div 6 = 1$ and $1 \times k = k$.		

So, $k = 21$.

246

Solve and check.

1. $\frac{y}{5} = 12$ $\frac{y}{5} = 12$

$5 \times \frac{y}{5} = 5 \times 12$

$y = 5 \times 12$

$y = \blacksquare$

1. $\frac{z}{4} = 2.7$ $\frac{z}{4} = 2.7$

$4 \times \frac{z}{4} = 4 \times 2.7$

$z = 4 \times 2.7$

$z = \blacksquare$

3. $\frac{x}{8} = 2$ **4.** $\frac{a}{4} = {}^{-}15$ **5.** $\frac{m}{20} = \frac{9}{30}$ ✅**6.** $\frac{p}{2} = 27$ ✅**7.** $2.6 = \frac{r}{9}$

8. Math Talk **Explain** why the Multiplication Property of Equality is used to solve division equations.

Practice and Problem Solving REAL WORLD

Solve and check.

9. $\frac{x}{10} = 12$ **10.** $\frac{y}{7} = 8$ **11.** $\frac{m}{4} = 2.5$ **12.** $\frac{n}{3} = 13$ **13.** $6 = \frac{z}{9}$

14. $14 = \frac{b}{4}$ **15.** $\frac{j}{3} = 4.9$ **16.** $2.8 = \frac{p}{9}$ **17.** $\frac{{}^{-}s}{4} = {}^{-}3$ **18.** $14 = \frac{r}{13}$

19. $4.25 = \frac{w}{20}$ **20.** $\frac{d}{12} = {}^{-}6$ **21.** $\frac{h}{6} = \frac{1}{2}$ **22.** $\frac{4}{15} = \frac{g}{30}$ **23.** $\frac{a}{9} = \frac{7}{12}$

24. What number x makes $\frac{x}{3} = 15$ true?   **25.** What number y makes $\frac{y}{12} = \frac{1}{4}$ true?

26. **Reasoning** Which of the numerical values 27, 29, and 31, is the solution of the equation $\frac{x}{3} = 9$?

27. **Reasoning** Which of the numerical values ${}^{-}31$, ${}^{-}33$, and ${}^{-}35$, is the solution of the equation $\frac{a}{5} = {}^{-}7$?

28. Mary has a game that comes with playing tokens. She divides all the tokens between herself and 3 friends. If each player has 15 tokens, how many tokens are in the game?

29. Wanda is selling her trading card collection in batches of 4. By the time she finishes selling 12 batches, she only has 2 cards remaining. How many cards were in Wanda's collection?

30. **Reasoning** In the equation $\frac{48}{x} = 12$, the variable is in the denominator. **Explain** how you would solve the equation.

31. Write Math ▶ **What's the Question?** Mario has a coin collection that he displays in 8 display cases. There are 12 coins in each display case. The answer is 96 coins.

OCCT Test Prep

32. What number x makes $\frac{x}{4} = 20$ true?

A $x = 5$ **B** $x = 6$ **C** $x = 80$ **D** $x = 100$

33. What number a makes $\frac{a}{9} = 10$ true?

A $a = 45$ **B** $a = 80$ **C** $a = 85$ **D** $a = 90$

★ **1.2.** Write algebraic expressions and simple equations that correspond to a given situation.

1.4. Write and solve one-step equations with one variable using number sense, the properties or operations, and the properties of inequalities (e.g., $\frac{1}{3x} + 9$).

Materials
• MathBoard

ERROR ALERT

When solving one-step equations, be sure you are using the correct Property of Equality.

Practice Solving Equations

Essential Question How do you decide which property of equality to use to solve an equation?

PROBLEM Mark charges the same amount for each lawn he mows. Last week, he made $180 for mowing 12 lawns. How much does Mark charge for mowing a lawn?

First choose which type of equation you will use to solve the problem. You know that the total amount of money Mark earned, $180, is the number of lawns he mowed times the dollar amount he charges per lawn. You can use a multiplication equation.

number of lawns	times	amount per lawn	equals	total
↓	↓	↓	↓	↓
12	×	c	=	180

$12c = 180$ Write the equation.

$\dfrac{12c}{12} = \dfrac{180}{12}$ Use the Division Property of Equality.

$c = 15$

$12c = 180$ Check your solution.

$12 \times 15 = 180$ Replace c with 15.

$180 = 180$ ✔   The solution checks.

So, Mark charges $15 for each lawn he mows.

• What division equation could you write to solve this problem?

Example

Louis deposited $152 into his bank account. His balance is now $437. How much was the balance before the deposit?

Since Louis deposited $152, he added it to his balance. Therefore, his balance before the deposit plus $152 gives him a new balance of $437. You can use an addition equation.

balance before deposit	plus	deposit	equals	new balance
↓	↓	↓	↓	↓
b	+	152	=	437

$b + 152 = 437$ Write the equation.

$b + 152 - 152 = 437 - 152$ Use the Subtraction Property of Equality.

$b = 285$

$b + 152 = 437$ Check your solution.

$285 + 152 = 437$ Replace b with 285.

$437 = 437$ ✔   The solution checks.

So, Louis' balance before the deposit was $285.

1. Richard had 71 stickers. After giving a number of stickers away, he now has 54 left. Write and solve an equation to find the number of stickers he gave away

   $n + 54 = 71$
   $n + 54 - 54 = 71 - 54$
   $n = \blacksquare$

Solve and check.

2. $x + 89 = 104$
3. $12y = 90$
4. $64 = \frac{z}{8}$
✓ 5. $r - 46 = 53$
✓ 6. $3a = 9.6$

7. **Math Talk** **Explain** how you decide what kind of equation to use to solve problems.

▶ **Practice and Problem Solving** REAL WORLD

Solve and check.

8. $9x = 153$
9. $35 = y + 19$
10. $m - 87 = 54$
11. $12 = \frac{s}{15}$
12. $\frac{h}{5} = 55.5$

13. $p + 7.8 = 15.2$
14. $8n = {}^-144$
15. $k + \frac{4}{5} = 3\frac{9}{10}$
16. ${}^-53 = t - 61$
17. $\frac{w}{3} = \frac{8}{9}$

Write an equation and solve for 18–22.

18. Helen makes $18 for every lawn she rakes. If she was paid $108 last week, how many lawns did she rake?

19. After Jessica made a $72 withdrawal, her balance was $417. What was her balance before she made the withdrawal?

20. Kendall opens an 18-lb bag of fertilizer. After she spread some fertilizer on the garden, the bag weighed $10\frac{5}{6}$ lb. How many pounds of fertilizer did she use?

21. Forrest has 3 chores to complete for his parents. He divides his time evenly among all 3 so that each chore takes him 20 min. How long does Forrest spend doing all his chores?

22. Marc and April combine their money to buy a rose bush. Marc contributes $10.20. April adds her money to Marc's. Together they buy a rose bush for $16.55 and get $0.15 in change. How much money did April contribute?

23. **Write Math** ▶ **What's the Question?** Melanie walks her dog 4 times around the block in 35 minutes. The answer is $8\frac{3}{4}$ min.

★ **OCCT Test Prep**

24. Which is the value of x in the equation $14x = 91$?

    A 4
    C 7
    B 6.5
    D 8.5

25. Chris mowed 57 lawns during the month of August. He makes $19 per lawn. How much did he make during the month of August?

    A $3
    C $1,003
    B $76
    D $1,083

★ Extra Practice

Set A

Write an algebraic expression for the word expression. (pp. 224–227)

1. twice the sum of c and d

2. ten less than two times y

3. the product of a number and 120

4. 8 times some number, increased by three-fourths

Write a word expression for each algebraic expression.

5. $a - 55$

6. $3n + 70$

7. $7(x - 4)$

8. $2x \div 10$

9. $\frac{1}{2}c - 8$

10. $3 - 0.4b$

11. $6(d + 3)$

12. $25 - y$

13. $11 + \frac{2}{3}x$

14. $\frac{3}{2}a$

Solve.

15. Amanda is working part-time at a shoe store. She is paid $80 per week plus $0.50 for every pair of shoes she sells. Write an expression for her weekly pay.

16. Zoe is giving away her trading cards. She tells 3 friends that she will divide the cards equally among them after giving 20 cards to her sister. Write an expression for the number of cards each friend will get.

Set B

Evaluate the expression for $x = 3, 2, 1,$ and 0. (pp. 228–231)

1. $2x + 15$

2. $239 - x^3$

3. $3x - 25$

4. $6x + x^2$

5. $x^2 + 3x + 5$

6. $28 - x^2$

7. $\frac{1}{2}x + 17$

8. $32 - \frac{1}{4}x$

9. $x^3 + x^2$

10. $0.5x + 4$

Simplify the expression. Then evaluate the expression for the given value of the variable.

11. $3x + 5 + x$, for $x = 7$

12. $5a + 7 + 2a$, for $a = 2$

13. $10b + 5 + 13b$, for $b = 3$

14. $10c - 4 - 2c$, for $c = {}^-2$

15. $3d - 12 + 8d$, for $d = 4$

Set C

Write an equation for the word sentence. (pp. 232–233)

1. One-half of a number is 48.

2. A number decreased by 20 equals 7.

3. The sum of a number and twice that number is 75.

4. Four times a number increased by 6 is 30.5.

5. Twice a number decreased by 3 is 1.

6. Six less than one-third of a number is 29.

7. Two more than the square of a number is 38.

8. Six less than 5 divided by a number is 2.

Write a word sentence for each equation.

9. $5w = 40$

10. $11n = 33$

11. $\frac{x}{5} = 35$

12. $\frac{2}{3}m = 12$

13. $t + 30 = 7$

Technology
Use HMH Mega Math, Ice Station Exploration,
Arctic Algebra, Levels T, AA, and BB.

Set D

Solve and check. (pp. 234–235)

1. $a + 8 = 15$ **2.** $x + 3.5 = 27$ **3.** $92 = 4 + w$ **4.** $4.5 + y = 95$ **5.** $13 + n = 16$

6. $z - \frac{2}{3} = 19\frac{1}{3}$ **7.** $n + 17 = 3$ **8.** $k + 8.7 = 33.2$ **9.** $32.5 = m + 12.9$ **10.** $8 = x + 3$

11. After 4.5 ft of fence was added, the fence had a total length of 10.75 ft. Write and solve an equation to find the original length of the fence.

12. Paul had $220 in the bank before depositing his paycheck. His current balance is $550. Write and solve an equation to find the amount of Paul's paycheck.

Set E

Solve and check. (pp. 236–237)

1. $b - 3 = 2$ **2.** $29 = x - 3$ **3.** $c - 2\frac{3}{4} = 9$ **4.** $16.6 = b - 2.2$ **5.** $15 = x - \frac{1}{3}$

6. $w - 5\frac{4}{5} = 12\frac{9}{10}$ **7.** $y - 12.5 = 17.9$ **8.** $29.1 = x - 13.8$ **9.** $12\frac{1}{4} = z - 19\frac{1}{5}$ **10.** $k - 16 = {}^-42$

11. Christopher used $7\frac{1}{4}$ lb of topsoil for his flower bed. The amount of topsoil Caroline used for her flower bed is $5\frac{1}{2}$ lb more than the amount Christopher used. Write and solve an equation to find the amount of topsoil Caroline used.

12. In an average week, Emily drinks 60 oz of fruit juice. The average amount of fruit juice that Linda drinks each week, less $\frac{4}{5}$ the amount that Emily drinks, is equal to 14.5 oz. Write equations and solve to find the average amount of fruit juice Linda drinks each week.

Set F

Solve and check. (pp. 242–245)

1. $24 = 3x$ **2.** $6y = 36$ **3.** $36 = 1.5b$ **4.** $72 = 8k$

5. $\frac{1}{4} = 2r$ **6.** $105 = {}^-15x$ **7.** ${}^-9v = {}^-108$ **8.** $16 = 6.4h$

9. $4b = 52$ **10.** $4x = \frac{8}{11}$ **11.** $10x = {}^-350$ **12.** $8m = 9.6$

13. Enrique made a total of $625 during the summer painting fences. He painted 25 fences. Write and solve an equation to find how much he was paid per fence.

14. Nine shipping containers hold a total of 36 oil paintings. Write and solve an equation to find the number of oil paintings in each container.

Set G

Solve and check. (pp. 246–247)

1. $\frac{x}{8} = 6$ **2.** $\frac{k}{3} = 2.5$ **3.** $8 = \frac{a}{6}$ **4.** $12 = \frac{c}{7}$

5. $\frac{x}{2} = 3.9$ **6.** $1.8 = \frac{q}{9}$ **7.** $\frac{u}{3} = {}^-4$ **8.** $2.25 = \frac{d}{10}$

9. $\frac{v}{8} = \frac{1}{2}$ **10.** $\frac{1}{15} = \frac{g}{45}$ **11.** $\frac{k}{5} = \frac{16}{20}$ **12.** ${}^-7 = \frac{b}{4}$

Reading & Writing Math

Vocabulary

You use **inverse operations** to solve equations.

The Rand School is having a raffle to raise money for the 5th grade graduation party. To have enough money for the party, they need to sell a total of 750 raffle tickets. They still need to sell 356 tickets. How many tickets have they already sold?

Complete the web to show different ways to solve this problem.

Solving Problems with Equations

Write an addition equation.
$$356 + n = 750$$
What operation will you use to solve the equation?
Solve:

Write a subtraction equation.
$$750 - 356 = n$$
What operation will you use to solve the equation?
Solve:

Which equation was easier to solve?

Writing Write a word problem that can be solved with an addition equation or a subtraction equation. Make a web like the one above for your problem. Solve each equation.

Reading Check out this book in your library. *Math Curse,* by Jon Scieszka

H.O.T. Multistep Problems

1 Before the first meeting of the Woodworking Club, Ms. Hendrix needs to find the number of boxes of supplies she needs to bring. There are 7 students signed up for the club. Each student needs 5 boxes of nails, 3 boxes of screws, and 1 box of tools. She also needs to bring 3 boxes of wood for the group to share. Ms. Hendrix asks Hannah, Jorge, Ira, and Ruth how they would find the total number of boxes she needs to bring. ▄ 1.2.; 1.3.

Hannah writes the expression

$7(5 + 3 + 1) + 3$

Jorge writes the expression

$7 \times 5 + 7 \times 3 + 7 \times 1 + 3$

Ira writes the expression

$7 \times 9 + 3$

Ruth writes the expression

$7 \times 5 + 3 + 1 + 3$

• How many of the students are correct? **Explain** how you know.

• Ms. Hendrix got 5 more students to sign up for the club. Write an expression for the number of boxes she now needs to bring.

• Write an expression for the number of boxes Ms. Hendrix needs to bring if n students sign up for the club.

2 As part of a larger computer program you are building, you need to make a module that will evaluate any numerical expression the user puts into it. ▄ 1.2.; 1.3.

• Write down the steps the computer must go through to evaluate any expression that is put into it.

• Make up your own numerical expression that includes at least three different operations and has part of the expression in parentheses. **Explain** the step the computer will go through to evaluate it.

• Tell how the computer will evaluate the following expression:

$3 \times 0.2 + 9 \div 0.3 - (4^2 - 2^3)$

Practice for the OCCT

1 Last month Karen added quarters, dimes, and nickels to her coin bank. Which expression could be used to find the total amount of dollars she added if *q* is used for the number of quarters she added, *d* for the number of dimes, and *n* for the number of nickels? 🔲 **1.2.**

A $0.25q \cdot 0.10d \cdot 0.05n$

B $0.25q + 0.10d - 0.05n$

C $0.25q - 0.10d + 0.05n$

D $0.25q + 0.10d + 0.05n$

2 The Chens went on a vacation. They started with $1,000. If they spent $125 each day, which expression could be used to show how much money they had after *x* days? 🔲 **1.2.**

A $875x$

B $125x$

C $1,000 - 125x$

D $1,000 + 25x$

3 If the cost of renting a rowboat is $2.25 for each hour, which equation can be used to find *d*, the cost in dollars of the rental for *h* hours? 🔲 **1.2.**

A $d = h + 2.25$

B $d = 2.25h$

C $d = h - 2.25$

D $d = 2.25 \div h$

4 Which shows the result of evaluating the expression $12x - 18 + 3x$ for $x = {}^-2$? 🔲 **1.3.**

A 48

B 3

C $^-36$

D $^-48$

5 Mitch has some change in his backpack. After his friend gave him $0.50, Mitch had $1.25 altogether. Which equation can Mitch use to find the original amount of money, *m*, he had in his backpack? 🔲 **1.2.**

A $1.25 + m = 0.50$

B $1.25 \cdot 0.50 = m$

C $m + 0.50 = 1.25$

D $1.25 = m - 0.50$

6 Which value of *b* makes the following equation true? 🔲 **1.4.**

$$5\frac{1}{2} + b = 20$$

A $b = 4\frac{1}{2}$

B $b = 10\frac{1}{2}$

C $b = 14\frac{1}{2}$

D $b = 14\frac{5}{8}$

7 Doing yard work, Jack earned enough money to pay off an $85.75 loan and still have $15.50 left. Which expression can be used to find out how much money Jack had to begin with? 🔲 **1.2.**

A $x + 85.75 = 15.50$

B $15.50x = 85.75$

C $x - 85.75 = 15.50$

D $\frac{85.75}{x} = 15.50$

8 The actual length of a TV show that airs in a 1 hour time slot is given as $60 - c$ where c is the amount of time, in minutes, of commercials. How long is a show with $\frac{3}{10}$ hour of commercials? ◥ 1.4.

A 42 min

B 32 min

C 22 min

D 18 min

9 You buy a digital video recorder for $99, and the cost per month for the recorder's data service is d dollars. Which expression can be used to find your total cost for 1 year? ◥ 1.2.

A $12d$

B $(99 + 12)d$

C $99 + 12d$

D $99d$

10 A vehicle rental company charges $25 to rent a moving van plus $0.50 for each mile traveled. Which expression represents the total cost of renting a van and driving d miles? ◥ 1.2.

A $25 \times 0.5 + d$

B $25 - 0.5 \cdot d$

C $25 \div 0.5 - d$

D $25 + 0.5d$

11 Vicky drove for 60 miles and then stopped at a rest stop. Then Vicky drove at a constant rate of 55 miles per hour for n hours. Which expression describes the total distance that Vicky drove? ◥ 1.2.

A $115n$

B $60 + 55n$

C $55 + 60n$

D $15n$

Problem Solving

12 You already have t dollars saved, and you plan to save an additional $10.50 per week. How much money will you have after 12 weeks if you already have $42.75 saved? ◥ 1.3.

13 **Explain** the steps you could use to solve the equation below. ◥ 1.4.

$$x + 3.4 = 9.5$$

14 The Desmond family went on vaction. They started with $1,500. They spent $175 each day. Write an expression to represent how much money they had left after n days. How much money do they have left if they had been on vacation for 8 days? **Explain** your answer. ◥ 1.2.

15 Pamela saved $50. Each time she goes to the movie she spends $6.25. Each time she goes ice-skating she spends $6.25. Does the expression $50 - 6.25(x + y)$ describe her saving and spending habits? **Explain**. ◥ 1.2.

Patterns

Investigate

The table below shows some flowers that have a Fibonacci number for their number of petals. The petals on certain types of flowers spiral. In each completed spiral, the number of petals in that spiral is a Fibonacci number. Draw your own flower with petals that spiral. The number of petals should be a Fibonacci number.

Fibonacci Flowers	
Flower	**Number of Petals**
Aster	21
Black-eyed Susan	21
Buttercup	5
Coreopsis	8
Iris	3
Larkspur	5
Lily	3
Pyrethrum	34
Ragwort	13
Wild Rose	5

Fun Fact

On many flowers, the number of petals is a Fibonacci number (1, 1, 2, 3, 5, . . .), which is a number that is part of a famous sequence formed by adding the previous two numbers to get the next number.

GO ONLINE

Technology
Student pages are available in the Student eBook

Show What You Know

Check your understanding of important skills needed for success in Chapter 7.

ASSESSMENT
Soar To Success: Math.

▶ Number Patterns

Write a rule for each pattern and predict the next number.

1. 2, 4, 6, 8, 10, … **2.** 75, 70, 65, 60, … **3.** 68, 66, 64, 62, … **4.** 8, 16, 24, 32, …

5. 225, 250, 275, … **6.** 600, 580, 560, … **7.** 400, 395, 390, … **8.** 25, 100, 175, …

▶ Input/Output Tables

Copy and complete each table.

9.

Input	Output
x	$x - 4$
14	⬜
21	⬜

10.

Input	Output
y	$y + 4.5$
14	⬜
14.5	⬜

11.

Input	Output
c	$c \times 3$
18	⬜
24	⬜

12.

Input	Output
p	$p \times 6$
10	⬜
23	⬜

13.

Input	Output
m	$5m$
4	⬜
6	⬜

14.

Input	Output
a	$2a - 4$
5	⬜
7	⬜

Vocabulary

Visualize It!

function rule

a rule that gives exactly one output value for each input value

function table

a table that matches each input value with a unique output value

Rule: $y = x + 45$

Input (x)	Output (y)
5	50
6	51
7	52
8	53

Language Tips

Looking at the prefixes for the words *input* and *output* will help you know what the words mean. The word *input* means *something that is put in.* The word *output* means *something that is put out.*

Words that look alike in English and Spanish often have the same meaning.

English	Spanish
function	**función**

See **English-Spanish Glossary.**

LESSON **1**

★ **1.1.** Generalize and extend patterns and functions using tables, graphs, and number properties (e.g., number sequences, prime and composite numbers, recursive patterns like the Fibonacci numbers.)

Vocabulary

sequence

term

triangular number

Materials
• MathBoard

Patterns in Sequences

Essential Question How can you write a rule for a pattern?

PROBLEM The pep squad is building a human pyramid. The triangular arrays below show possible formations. So far, the largest human triangular pyramid that they have built has had 10 squad members. What is the next largest triangular pyramid they could build?

A number that can be represented by a triangular array is called a **triangular number**. You can show the pattern for triangular numbers as a number sequence. A **sequence** is an ordered set of numbers. Each number in the sequence is called a **term**.

Model using counters.

Triangular numbers can be modeled using counters. Start with 1 counter. Add 2 more beneath it to model the next triangular number, 3. To build successive triangular numbers, add 1 more counter for each new row.

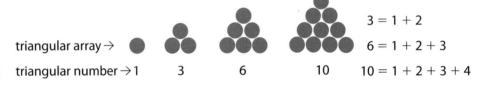

This sequence shows the pattern in triangular numbers.

sequence → 1   3   6   10
$+2$ $+3$ $+4$ $+5$

Since $10 + 5 = 15$, the next pyramid that the pep squad could build would have 15 members.

A sequence may have a pattern of repeated addition, subtraction, multiplication, division, or combined operations. The specific number sequence generated depends on the starting number as well as the rule.

Write a rule for the sequence $1, 3\frac{2}{3}, 6\frac{1}{3}, 9, \ldots$

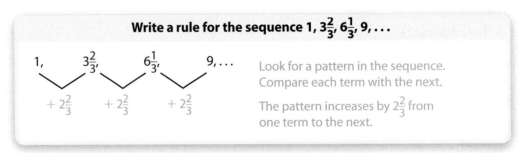

Look for a pattern in the sequence. Compare each term with the next.

The pattern increases by $2\frac{2}{3}$ from one term to the next.

So, a rule is to add $2\frac{2}{3}$ to each term to get the next possible term.

258

Extend a sequence.

Write a rule and use the rule to find the next three possible terms for the sequence 18,750; 3,750; 750; 150; . . .

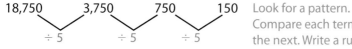

Look for a pattern. Compare each term with the next. Write a rule.

Rule: Divide each term by 5 to get the next term.

$150 \div 5 = 30$

$30 \div 5 = 6$ 18,750; 3,750; 750; 150; 30; 6; $1\frac{1}{5}$; . . .

$6 \div 5 = 1\frac{1}{5}$

Math Idea

From one term to the next in a sequence, the terms can change using addition, subtraction, multiplication, division, or a combination of operations.

So, the next three possible terms are 30, 6, and $1\frac{1}{5}$.

Use a variable.

Find the sixteenth term in the sequence 20, 40, 60, 80, . . .

1st	2nd	3rd	4th	nth
20	40	60	80	n
↓	↓	↓	↓	↓

20×1 20×2 20×3 20×4 $20 \times n$

Look for a pattern. Compare each term with the next.

Write a rule using words. Then write the rule as an algebraic expression.
Let n = 16 to find the 16th term.

Rule: Multiply the number of the term by 20.

The nth term is $20n$.

$20 \times 16 = 320$

So, the sixteenth term of the sequence is 320.

▶ Share and Show

1. Write a rule for the sequence.   100, 85, 70, 55, . . .

First, look for a pattern. Does the pattern increase or decrease? Then, compare each term with the next. Finally, write a rule.

Write a rule for the sequence, using words. Use the rule to find the next four possible terms in the sequence.

2. 17,500; 3,500; 700; 140, . . .   **3.** 5.64, 6, 6.36, 6.72, . . .   ✓**4.** 20, 31, 44, 59, . . .

Write a rule for the sequence, using a variable. Use the rule to find the sixteenth term.

5. 5, 10, 15, 20, . . .   **6.** 30, 60, 90, 120, . . .   ✓**7.** 240, 120, 80, 60, . . .

8. **Math Talk** **Explain** how to write two different rules for the sequence $3, 1, \frac{1}{3}, \frac{1}{9}, \ldots$

Write a rule for the sequence, using words. Use the rule to find the next four possible terms.

9. 2.5, 10, 40, 160, . . .

10. 15, 23, 33, 45, . . .

11. 343, 49, 7, 1, . . .

Write a rule for the sequence, using a variable. Use the rule to find the twelfth term.

12. 13, 26, 39, 52, . . .

13. 0.75, 1.5, 2.25, 3, . . .

14. $\frac{1}{6}, \frac{1}{3}, \frac{1}{2}, \frac{2}{3}, \ldots$

Write a rule for the sequence. Use the rule to find the unknown term.

15. 4, 2, 1, _, $\frac{1}{4}, \frac{1}{8}, \ldots$

16. 5, 15, _, 135, 405, . . .

17. 2, 3, 6, 11, _, 27, . . .

18. Write a rule for the pattern in the sequence of arrays on the right. Then draw the next 2 terms in the sequence.

19. In January, the pep squad practiced for a total of 4 hr. During February, they practiced for 8 hr. In March, they practiced for 12 hr, and in April, a total of 16 hr. If the pattern continues, how many hours will they practice in June?

20. The pep squad does a routine where one member performs a jump, and then another member jumps. After that 2 members jump, then 3 members jump, then 5 jump, and then 8 jump. Write a rule for the sequence. How many would jump next?

21. Reasoning Mr. Suarez wrote these two sequences on the board.

8, 16, 24, 32, . . .   64, 72, 80, 88, . . .

Do both sequences have the same rule? **Explain** your answer.

22. **Write Math** ▶ **What's the Error?** Mara says that a rule for the sequence below is to subtract 40.

80, 40, 20, 10, . . .

Explain Mara's error and give a possible rule.

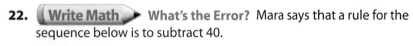

OCCT Test Prep Math Board

23. Which could be a rule for the sequence 0.02, 0.2, 2, 20, . . . ?

A add 0.18   **C** divide by 10

B add 1.8   **D** multiply by 10

24. Which could be a rule for the sequence 7.5, 15, 22.5, 30, . . . ?

A $n + 7.5$ **C** $7.5n$

B $n \div 7.5$ **D** $n - 7.5$

⭐ Standards Quick Check

Write a rule for the sequence. Use the rule to find the unknown term.

1. 50, ___, 42, 38, . . .

2. 11.2, 22.4, ___, 44.8 . . .

3. $\frac{1}{12}, \frac{1}{6}, \frac{1}{3}$, ___, . . .

4. 1,500, 300, 60, 12, ___, . . .

5. 21, ___, 63, 84 . . .

6. 100, 50, 25, ___, . . .

Challenge H.O.T.

Making a Pattern

You can use what you know about patterns to make your own.
The one at the right is a famous pattern called Pascal's Triangle.
Each number, other than the first and last in each row, is the sum
of the two numbers above. The red triangle shows that 3 is the sum of 1 and 2.

Pascal's Triangle

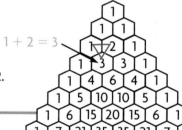

$1 + 2 = 3$

1 **Make a pattern like Pascal's Triangle.**
Replace each 1 with a 2. Use the rule of
adding two numbers next to each other
to find the number below them.

$2 + 2 = 4$

2 **Make a pattern using addition.**
Choose a number for the first term
and a number to add.

First Term: 8   Number to add: 5
Pattern: 8, 13, 18, 23, 28, . . .

1. Make a pattern using addition.

2. Make a pattern using multiplication.

3. Make a pattern similar to the pattern in Pascal's Triangle.

4. Another famous pattern is the Fibonacci sequence. This pattern is formed
by adding two successive numbers to get the next number.

Fibonacci sequence: 1, 1, 2, 3, 5, 8, 13, 21, . . . $1 + 1 = 2,\ 1 + 2 = 3, 2 + 3 = 5, . . .$
Make a pattern like the Fibonacci sequence.

LESSON 2

★ **1.1.** Generalize and extend patterns and functions using tables, graphs, and number properties (e.g., number sequences, prime and composite numbers, recursive patterns like the Fibonacci numbers.)

1.2. Write algebraic expressions and simple equations that correspond to a given situation.

Vocabulary

function

Materials

• MathBoard

Number Patterns and Functions

Essential Question How do you write an equation as a function for a pattern?

PROBLEM The drama club is making costumes for the school musical. The fabric the students want costs $5.50 per yard. They need 37 yd of fabric. If there is $209 in the costume budget, does the drama club have enough money to buy all the fabric it needs?

A **function** is a relationship between two quantities in which one quantity depends uniquely on the other. For every input, there is exactly one output.

Write an equation to represent a function.

Look for a pattern in the input/output table. The pattern is that as the number of yards of fabric increases by 1, the cost increases by $5.50. The drama club can use the rule for this pattern to write an equation. Then the students can determine if they have enough money to buy the fabric they need.

Rule: 5.5n

Let n equal the number of yards of fabric.

$5.5n = c$

$5.5n = 209$ Write an equation. Let c equal the total cost.

$\dfrac{5.5n}{5.5} = \dfrac{209}{5.5}$ Replace c with 209.

$n = 38$

Input	Output
Yards of Fabric	**Cost**
1	$5.50
2	$11.00
3	$16.50
4	$22.00
5	$27.50

So, the drama club has enough money to buy 38 yd of fabric which is 1 yd more than the 37 yd needed.

Write an equation to represent a function.

At a local skating rink, you pay $1.75 to rent skates, plus $3.00 for each hour you skate. Use the input/output table to find a pattern.

Input	hour, h	1	2	3	4
Rule	$3h + 1.75$	$3 \times 1 + 1.75$	$3 \times 2 + 1.75$	$3 \times 3 + 1.75$	$3 \times 4 + 1.75$
Output	total cost, c	$4.75	$7.75	$10.75	$13.75

The pattern is to multiply the number of hours you skate by 3, and then add 1.75.

Rule: $3h + 1.75$ Let h = hours.

So, an equation is $c = 3h + 1.75$ where c is total cost and h is number of hours.

Examples

Write an equation to represent the function. Use the equation to find the misszing term.`

x	1	2	3	4	5
y	1	8	27	64	■

Think: Each y-value is greater than or equal to the corresponding x-value. Since the patterns is increasing, the rule could use either multiplication or addition.

Pattern: Each x-value is cubed to find the y-value.

Rule: x^3

Equation: $y = x^3$ Use the rule to write an equation.

$y = 5^3$ Let $x = 5$.

$y = 125$ Solve for y.

ERROR ALERT

Be sure to look at all of the given x- and y- values before writing an equation to represent a function.

So, an equation is $y = x^3$, and the missing term is 125.

Write an equation to represent the two-step function. Use the equation to find the missing term.

x	1	2	3	4	5
y	2.65	4.65	6.65	■	10.65

Think: Compare x and y. The y-value is 0.65 more than twice the x-value.

Pattern: Multiply each x-value by 2. Then add 0.65.

Rule: $2x + 0.65$

Equation: $y = 2x + 0.65$ Use the rule to write an equation.

$y = 2 \times 4 + 0.65$ Let $x = 4$.

$y = 8.65$ Solve for y.

So, an equation is $y = 2x + 0.65$, and the missing term is 8.65.

▶ Share and Show   Math Board

Write an equation to represent the function.

1. Compare d and r in the table at the right. The variable r is always 7 less than d.

d	20	19	18	17	16
r	13	12	11	10	9

✓ **2.**

w	30	35	40	45	50
t	6	7	8	9	10

✓ **3.**

x	5	4	3	2	1
y	11	9	7	5	3

4. **Explain** how to wvrite an equation to describe a function shown by an input/output table.

Write an equation to represent the function.

5.

a	5	7	9	11	13
b	8.5	10.5	12.5	14.5	16.5

6.

c	65	50	35	20	5
d	50	35	20	5	⁻10

7.

p	1	2	3	4	5
w	3	6	9	12	15

8.

m	10	11	12	13	14
t	31	34	37	40	43

Write an equation to represent the function. Then use the equation to find the missing term.

9.

r	10	12	14	16	18
d	5	6	7	■	9

10.

x	20	25	30	35	40
y	5	■	15	20	25

11.

k	3	6	9	12	15
g	8	14	■	26	32

12.

m	180	160	140	120	100
h	167	147	■	107	87

Real World Data

For 13–14, use the chart.

13. Describe in words what the pattern shows for the first 5 costumes. Then write an equation to represent the function. Let *c* equal the number of costumes and *y* equal the amount of fabric.

14. How much do 5 costumes cost if fabric is $5.50 per yard? Write an equation to represent the function. Let *c* equal the amount of fabric and *t* equal the total cost.

Fabric for Costumes	
Number of Costumes	Amount of Fabric (in yards)
1	3.5
2	7.0
3	10.5
4	14.0
5	17.5

15. **Write Math** ▶ **Reasoning** Look at Problem 14. Suppose that each costume needs a zipper that costs $0.75. Write an equation to represent the new function. **Explain** how a change in one quantity affects a change in the other quantity.

 Math Board

16. The equation $b = 2a + 1$ represents the function in the table. What is the missing term?

a	3	5	7	9	15
b	7	11	15	■	31

A 4 **C** 23

B 19 **D** 82

17. The equation $y = x^2$ represents the function in the table. What is the missing term?

x	7	8	9	10	11
y	49	64	■	100	121

A 9 **C** 81

B 18 **D** 729

GO Technology
ONLINE Use HMH Mega Math, The Number Games, *Tiny's Think Tank*, Level K.

★ Standards Quick Check

Write an equation for the function. Use the equation to find the missing term.

1.

a	15	17	19	21	23	25
b	10	12	14	16	18	▪

2.

m	69	57	45	33	21	9
n	124	▪	100	88	76	64

3.

s	2.2	3.2	4.2	5.2	6.2	7.2
t	4.4	6.4	8.4	▪	12.4	14.4

4.

x	8	10	12	14	16	18
y	25	31	37	43	▪	55

Challenge H.O.T.

The Binary Number System

The binary, or base-two, number system uses only the digits 0 and 1. In the decimal system, each place value is ten times the place value to the right. In the binary system, each place value is twice the place value to the right. You can use powers of 2 to find the decimal equivalent of a binary number.

Find the decimal equivalent of 10101_{two}.

1	0	1	0	1
1×2^4	0×2^3	1×2^2	0×2^1	1×2^0
1×16	0×8	1×4	0×2	1×1
16	+ 0	+ 4	+ 0	+ 1

So, $10101_{two} = 16 + 4 + 1 = 21$.

Find the decimal equivalent for each binary number.

1. 1100_{two}

2. 1111_{two}

3. 10110_{two}

4. 11101_{two}

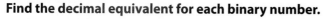

★ **1.1.** Generalize and extend patterns and functions using tables, graphs, and number properties (e.g., number sequences, prime and composite numbers, recursive patterns like the Fibonacci numbers.)

Materials
• MathBoard

Geometric Patterns

Essential Question How can you extend a geometric pattern?

 **Learn** REAL WORLD

PROBLEM Lin is working on a quilt. The first six square patches she has made are shown below. Look for a possible pattern. Draw the next three possible square patches.

Finding patterns in geometric figures is like solving a visual puzzle. Patterns can be based on shape, size, position, color, or number of figures.

Examples

Give a rule and draw the next three possible square patches.

Look for visual clues.

Position: The squares with the triangles inside are rotating 90° clockwise.
Color: The color of the triangles is changing from blue to red to green and back to blue.

So, the next three possible square patches are shown below:

You can also find patterns in three-dimensional figures.

Remember

Count cubes that might be hidden underneath other cubes.

Give a rule and draw the next two possible figures.

Look for visual clues.

Size: A bottom layer is being added to each successive figure.
Number: The number of cubes in the bottom layer increases by consecutive integers starting with 2.
A possible pattern for the number of cubes in the bottom layers of successive figures is 1, 3, 6, . . .

So, the next two possible figures are shown.

1. Draw the next two possible figures in the pattern. The figure rotates 90° clockwise. The small square remains shaded.

2. Draw the next two possible figures in the pattern. The arrow rotates 180°. The number of dots increases by one at each step.

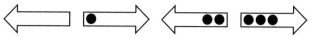

Give a rule and draw the next two possible figures.

3.

4.

5. Math Talk **Explain** how you would describe a geometric pattern to someone who cannot see it. Draw your own geometric pattern.

Practice and Problem Solving REAL WORLD

Give a rule and draw the next two possible figures.

6.

7.

For 8-9, use the blue and orange pattern.

8. Maria is drawing a pattern for an art project. The first four figures she drew are shown. Give a rule and draw the next two possible figures.

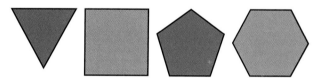

9. Write a rule different from the one you wrote in Problem 8. Then draw the next two figures using your new rule.

10. Write Math ▶ Write a rule for your own geometric pattern. Then draw the first 4 figures of the pattern.

★ OCCT Test Prep

11. How many cubes could be in the fourth figure?

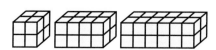

A 20   **C** 32
B 24   **D** 36

12. How many cubes could be in the fifth figure?

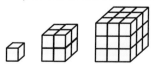

A 55   **C** 100
B 80   **D** 125

★ **1.1.** Generalize and extend patterns and functions using tables, graphs, and number properties (e.g., number sequences, prime and composite numbers, recursive patterns like the Fibonacci numbers.)

Problem Solving Workshop
Strategy: Solve a Simpler Problem

Essential Question How can you use patterns to solve simpler problems?

 Learn the Strategy REAL WORLD

You can use the strategy *solve a simpler problem* to solve problems that might, at first, seem too difficult to solve.

A simpler problem helps solve a difficult word problem.

Materials
• MathBoard

Sylvia follows a 6-week, fast-track training program to prepare for track tryouts. She begins each track workout with a 15-min slow jog. Then she runs around the track as fast as she can. In week 1, she runs $\frac{1}{8}$ mi. During week 2, she runs $\frac{1}{4}$ mi. In week 3, she runs $\frac{1}{2}$ mi, and in week 4, she runs 1 mi. If the pattern continues, how many miles does Sylvia run in week 10?

First organize the information. Then look for a pattern.

Week	1	$\frac{1}{8}$ mile	
Week	2	$\frac{1}{4}$ mile	$\frac{1}{4} = 2 \times \frac{1}{8}$
Week	3	$\frac{1}{2}$ mile	$\frac{1}{2} = 2 \times \frac{1}{4}$
Week	4	1 mile	$1 = 2 \times \frac{1}{2}$

Once you find a pattern, you can write a rule to help find the answer.

Math Talk

How does solving a simpler problem help you solve the original problem?

A simpler problem helps find the area of a complex figure.

Find the area of the figure below.

Break the complex figure into smaller figures, find the areas of the figures, and then find the sum of the areas to find the area of the complex figure.

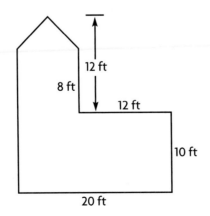

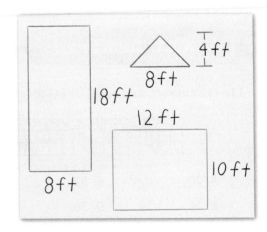

🔑 UNLOCK the Problem ▸ REAL WORLD

PROBLEM To celebrate Earth Week, the Math Club is planting a flower garden in a large area behind the school. The club members plan to plant ten rows of flowers. The first five rows will have the following number of flowers planted in each row: 1st—4 flowers, 2nd—7 flowers, 3rd—10 flowers, 4th—13 flowers, 5th—16 flowers. If the pattern continues, how many flowers will be in the tenth row?

Read the Problem

What do I need to find?

I need to find the number of flowers in the tenth row.

What information do I need to use?

I know that the first five rows will have the following number of flowers planted in each row: 1st—4 flowers, 2nd—7 flowers, 3rd—10 flowers, 4th—13 flowers, 5th—16 flowers.

How will I use the information?

I can organize the information in a table to look for a pattern.

Solve the Problem

Organize the information you were given in a table. Look for a pattern. Write an equation to describe the pattern.

Row	1	2	3	4	5
Number of Flowers	4	7	10	13	16

The number of flowers is one more than three times the row number. An equation describing this pattern is $f = 3r + 1$, where f is the number of flowers and r is the row number. To find the number of flowers in the tenth row, let r equal 10 and solve for f.

$$f = 3r + 1$$
$$= 3 \times 10 + 1$$
$$= 30 + 1$$
$$= 31$$

So, if the pattern continues, there will be 31 flowers in the tenth row.

1. The Green Club has designed a flower garden. The diagram shows the number of plants in the first eight sections of the garden. The gray lines divide each section. How many total plants will there be in the flower garden if there are fifteen sections?

   First, organize the information.

   Then, look for patterns.

   Finally, find the total number of plants in the flower garden.

☑ 2. **What if** there were only ten sections in the garden? How many plants would there be in the garden? How many plants would there be in the tenth section?

☑ 3. Tara and Randy designed a plant display. The first shelf holds 17 plants. The second shelf holds 13 plants. The third shelf holds 9 plants. If the pattern continues, how many plants could be on the fourth shelf and the fifth shelf?

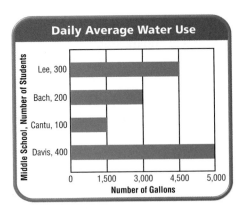

1 3 5 7 9 11 13 15

Section Number	Number of Plants	Total Plants in Garden	Pattern
1	1	1	1^2
2	3	$1 + 3 = 4$	2^2
3	5	$1 + 3 + 5 = 9$	3^2
4	7	$1 + 3 + 5 + 7 = 16$	4^2

▶ **On Your Own**

Solve by solving a simpler problem.

4. **Reasoning** Ridge Middle School has 600 students. Based on the graph at the right, about how many total gallons of water do you think the Ridge students use each day? **Explain** how you found your answer.

Daily Average Water Use

Middle School, Number of Students

Lee, 300
Bach, 200
Cantu, 100
Davis, 400

0   1,500   3,000   4,500   5,000
Number of Gallons

📊 **Real World Data**

For 5–6, use the Cart Weight table.

5. Carlos drives a tractor at the greenhouse. He pulls a cart to move bags of fertilizer. The table shows how the total weight of the cart is related to the number of bags of fertilizer on it. How much does the cart weigh if it is loaded with 48 bags of fertilizer?

6. **Write Math** ▶ **What's the Question?** Carlos also moves larger bags of fertilizer that weigh 25 pounds each. The answer is 500 pounds.

Cart Weight	
Number of Bags of Fertilizer	Total Weight (in pounds)
10	175
15	225
20	275
25	325

7. The Green Club started a drive to reuse old comic books. Members collected 25 lb of comic books in week 1 and 30 lb in week 2. In week 3, they collected 35 lb. If this pattern continues, how many pounds would they collect in week 5?

8. A wind farm needs 17 acres of land to produce one megawatt of electricity. That supplies enough energy for 250 homes. If a wind farm needs to produce enough megawatts for 125,000 homes, how many acres of land does it need?

Real World Data

For 9–11, use the circle graph on the right.

9. Two of the categories combine to be $\frac{3}{10}$ of average home energy consumption. Two other categories combine to be $\frac{13}{20}$ of average home energy consumption. Of these two combinations, name the combination that consumes the least energy.

10. About how many times as great is heating consumption as refrigeration and cooling consumption combined?

11. About how many times as great are heating and hot water combined as refrigeration and cooling combined?

12. **Open-Ended** Suppose you have 100 square feet in which to plant a garden. Make a plan for the garden. Have at least 5 different kinds of plants. Have the placement of all of the plants follow some kind of pattern. Explain your reasoning and draw a diagram of the garden.

13. **Pose a Problem** Look back at Problem 8. Write a similar problem by changing the number of homes that the wind farm needs to supply with energy.

Choose a Strategy

- Draw a Diagram
- Make a Model or Act It Out
- Make an Organized List
- Find a Pattern
- Make a Table or Graph
- Predict and Test
- Work Backward
- Solve a Simpler Problem
- Write an Equation
- Use Logical Reasoning

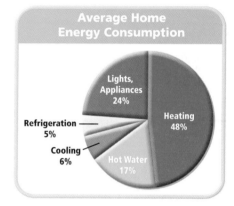

Average Home Energy Consumption

Lights, Appliances 24%
Heating 48%
Refrigeration 5%
Cooling 6%
Hot Water 17%

H.O.T. PROBLEM

The cost of electricity has increased over the last few years. In 2007, a family's average yearly electric bill was about $1,650.

14. During summer and winter months, families spend about 3 times as much on electricity as during spring or fall months. If a family spends $2 a day in April, about how much would the family spend for the month of August?

15. In 2004, the average yearly electric bill was about $200 more than one-half the average yearly bill in 2007. Find the average yearly bill in 2004.

⭐ Extra Practice

Set A

Write a rule for the sequence using words. Use the rule to find the next four possible terms. (pp. 258–261)

1. 16, 33, 50, 67, . . .

2. 2,400; 1,200; 600; 300, . . .

3. $\frac{1}{8}, \frac{1}{4}, \frac{3}{8}, \frac{1}{2}, \ldots$

4. 2, 4, 16, 96, . .

Write a rule for the sequence using a variable. Use the rule to find the tenth term.

5. 14, 28, 42, 56, . . .

6. $\frac{1}{9}, \frac{2}{9}, \frac{1}{3}, \frac{4}{9}, \ldots$

7. 3.4, 6.8, 10.2, 13.6, . . .

8. $\frac{3}{2}, 3, 4\frac{1}{2}, 6, \ldots$

9. 50, 46, 42, 38, . . .

10. 1,500, 300, 60, 12, . . .

11. 7, 14, 28, 56, . . .

12. 0.25, 1, 1.75, 2.5, . . .

13. $\frac{1}{2}, \frac{1}{6}, \frac{1}{4}, \frac{1}{3}, \ldots$

14. 21, 42, 63, 84, . . .

15. 11.2, 22.4, 33.6, 44.8, . . .

16. $\frac{3}{4}, 1\frac{1}{4}, 1\frac{3}{4}, 2\frac{1}{4}, \ldots$

17. 7.4, 12.6, 17.8, 23, . . .

18. 158, 131, 104, 77, . . .

19. 34.1, 53.6, 73.1, 92.6, . . .

20. $\frac{3}{6}, \frac{6}{12}, \frac{12}{24}, \frac{24}{48}, \ldots$

21. Madison trained for a bike marathon. In week 1, she rode 12 mi; in week 2, 24 mi; and in week 3, 36 mi. If the pattern continues, how many miles did she ride in week 6?

22. The cost of renting a large party tent is $12.75 for 1 hr, $25.50 for 2 hr, $38.25 for 3 hr, and $51.00 for 4 hr. Write a rule for the pattern. How much would it cost to rent this tent for 24 hr?

Set B

Write an equation to represent the function. (pp. 262–265)

1.

x	5	10	15	20	25	30
y	9	14	19	24	29	34

2.

a	3	5	7	9	11	13
b	9	15	21	27	33	39

3.

x	40	50	60	70	80	90
y	20	25	30	35	40	45

4.

a	3	5	7	9	11	13
b	10	16	22	28	34	40

5.

x	9	11	15	27	34	41
y	36	44	60	108	136	164

6.

a	6	7.5	9.25	12	15.75	20.2
b	9	11.25	13.875	18	23.625	30.3

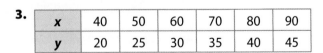

Technology

Use HMH Mega Math, The Numbers Game, *Tiny's Think Tank*, Levels J and U.

Set B (continued)

Write an equation to represent the function. Then use the equation to find the missing term.

7.

r	100	90	80	70	60	50
d	74	64	54	44	■	24

8.

c	6	8	10	12	14	16
d	24	■	40	48	56	64

9.

r	8	18	28	38	48	54
s	16	36	■	76	96	108

10.

v	16	26	36	46	56	70
t	8	■	18	23	28	35

11.

c	2	6	10	14	18	27
d	0	4	8	■	16	25

12.

a	100	80	60	40	20	10
c	25	20	■	10	5	2.5

13.

x	6	8	14	16	24	28
y	⁻36	⁻48	⁻84	■	⁻144	⁻168

14.

a	120	110	80	66	48	42
b	64	■	44	37	28	25

15. The prices of paint in a hardware store are listed at the right. Jona is buying paint for the backdrops of a school play. Write an equation that describes the function. What would be the price of 6 gal of paint?

Paint Prices	
Paint (in gal)	**Price**
1	$22.95
2	$45.90
3	$68.85
4	$91.80

Set C

Give a rule and draw the next two possible figures. (pp. 266–267)

1.

2.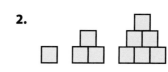

3. Draw a geometric pattern using a polygon or more than one polygon. Describe your pattern in words.

4. Draw a geometric pattern using cubes. Describe your pattern in words.

Vocabulary

There are patterns all around us, in words, shapes, designs, and numbers. Once you find a pattern, you can use it to predict what comes next. Sometimes you can find a pattern by saying the numbers aloud.

Find each pattern and use it to tell what comes next.

1. What number is next?

1, 3, 5, 7, 9, 11

($^+2, ^+2, ^+2$)

> Sometimes you can figure out a pattern by saying the numbers aloud.

2. What number is next?

4, 8, 6, 10, 8, 12, 10, 14, 12, 16, 14

($^+4, ^-2, ^+4, ^-2, ^+4, \ldots$)

> For number patterns, sometimes you need to look at all the numbers you are given to figure out the pattern.

3. What number is next?

24, 21, 18, 15, 12, 9

($^-3, ^-3, ^-3$)

> Some number patterns are made by adding the same number. Some are made by subtracting the same number.

Solve the problem.

Daria created some number patterns. In each pattern, she put one number that is not reasonable. Look at each pattern. Find the number that is not reasonable.

4. 1, 2, 4, 8, 6, 16, 32

5. 50, 43, 36, 39, 29, 22, 15

Writing Write a problem that can be solved by a pattern. Include a drawing.

Reading Look for this book in the library. *Alexander, Who Used to Be Rich Last Sunday* by Judith Viorst

#

H.O.T. Multistep Problems

1 Brett is helping his brother to build towers with blocks for a math project. ▬ 1.1.

• First they make six towers. The table shows the number of blocks used in each tower.

Tower	1	2	3	4	5	6
Number of blocks	3	11	19	27	35	43

• Write a rule that explains the number pattern Brett and his brother are using to build the towers. Show how you can test the rule using two of the numbers from the table. Then tell how many blocks would be in a seventh tower if Brett and his brother continued using the same rule. Show your work.

• Brett and his brother are going to build five new towers. They want to use a different number pattern to build these towers. Create a number pattern for the new towers and then write a rule.

Tower	1	2	3	4	5
Number of blocks					

• Brett's brother wants to decorate the towers. He makes a pattern to draw on the towers. Write a rule for the pattern. What is the next figure in the pattern? Show your work.

2 James wants to save some of his lunch money to buy a new bike. His mom gives him $20.00 at the beginning of each week for lunch. School lunch costs $2.20 a day. ▬ 1.1.; 1.2.

• If James buys lunch for the first three days of the week, how much money does James have left? Write a sequence to show how James will spend his $20.00.

• How much money would James spend if he buys lunch each day of the week. How much money is James able to save each week after buying his lunches?

• At James' school, every other week the school lunch costs half of what it does normally. What is the new rule that James should apply to figure out how much money he has to spend on lunch for the week where lunch is half price? How much money will James spend on lunch that week? How much money will James be able to save that week?

• Following the pattern of school lunch prices, how much will James spend on lunch a month and how much money will James save a month?

Practice for the OCCT

1 The table shows the relationship between the number of telephone books in a box, *x*, and the weight of the box in pounds, *y*. Which equation describes the relationship shown in the table? ◖ 1.2.

x	3	5	7	9
y	7	11	15	19

A $y = x + 4$

B $y = x + 7$

C $y = 2x + 1$

D $y = 2x$

2 If you walk at a constant rate of 3 miles per hour, which method can you use to find the number of hours it will take you to walk 10 miles? ◖ 1.1.

A add 3 and 12

B subtract 3 from 12

C multiply 10 by 3

D divide 10 by 3

3 Which rule can be used to find the next number in the pattern below? ◖ 1.1.

$$^-29, \; ^-18, \; ^-7, \; 4, \; ...$$

A add 11

B multiply by 2

C subtract 11

D divide by 0.5

4 The table shows the amount of money in dollars, *y*, that Taylor earns for each pair of sandals, *x*, that she decorates at the craft fair.

x	2	4	6	8
y	7	14	21	28

How many pairs of sandals must Taylor decorate to earn $42? ◖ 1.1.

A 9 pairs

B 10 pairs

C 12 pairs

D 14 pairs

5 A dance team makes a group pattern by adding dancers every 2 minutes. The table shows how the dancers join the group.

Time	1	3	5	7
Dancers added	1	3	5	7
Total Dancers	1	4	9	16

How many dancers are need if the pattern continues for 11 minutes? ◖ 1.1.

A 24   **C** 36

B 28   **D** 54

6 Gina was playing a game with her friend. She wrote down this sequence of numbers and told her friend to write the next 3 terms in the sequence.

6.5, 12.5, 24.5, 48.5, ...

What are the next three terms in the sequence? ◖ 1.1.

A 96, 192, 384

B 96.5, 192.5, 384.5

C 96.25, 192.25, 384.25

D 97, 193, 385

7 Which equation shows the relationship in the function table? 🔲 1.2.

x	1	2	3	4	5
y	2	4	6	8	10

A $y = x + 2$

B $2y = x$

C $y = 2x - 2$

D $y = 2x$

8 Steve used tiles to make this pattern:

How many tiles will Steve use along each side when the figure he makes has 64 tiles? 🔲 1.1.

A 8

B 12

C 16

D 18

9 Students followed a pattern to stack books. There is 1 book in the first stack, there are 4 books in the second stack, 9 books in the third stack, 16 books in the fourth stack, and so on for seven stacks of books. How many books are in the seventh stack? 🔲 1.1.

A 16

B 28

C 36

D 49

Problem Solving

10 Juan is displaying his coin collection in 8 rows. The numbers of coins in the first 4 rows are shown in the table. If the pattern continues, how many coins will be in the eighth row? 🔲 1.1.

Row	1	2	3	4
Number of Coins	3	6	9	12

11 A search plane uses a square pattern to narrow its search area. During the first hour, the plane searches 36 square miles. During the second hour, the plane searches 25 square miles. During the third hour, the plane searches 16 square miles. How many square miles will the plane search in the fifth hour? **Explain** how you know. 🔲 1.1.

12 Each hour, the number of people visiting a museum is 5 times the number of people visiting the previous hour. There are 5 people visiting in the first hour. During what hour will there be 625 people visiting the museum? **Explain** you answer. 🔲 1.1.

Performance Assessment

Writing Math When would you a use variable when writing an equation?

The First Superhighway

The Pennsylvania Turnpike was the first highway designed for modern high-speed long-distance travel. Completed in 1940, the turnpike crossed the Allegheny Mountains between Harrisburg and Pittsburg, Pennsylvania. It shortened travel time between those two cities by 3 hr.

1. The turnpike is 132 ft wide on the section called the Southwestern Expansion. That is $1\frac{5}{6}$ times the road's width on the portion called the Northeastern Extension. Write an equation you can use to find the width of the Northeastern Extension. Then solve the equation.

2. Originally 160 mi long, the Pennsylvania Turnpike has since been lengthened to 514 mi. Write and equation you can use to find how much longer the highway is today than it was in 1940. Then solve the equation.

For 3-5, use the figure, which shows distance on a section of the Pennsylvania Turnpike.

It is 100 mi farther from Blue Mountain to Valley Forge than it is from Valley Forge to Philadelphia. (Note: Diagram not drawn to scale.)

3. Use the variable m to write an expression for the distance from Blue Mountain to Valley Forge.

4. Write and simplify an expression for the distance from Pittsburg to Philadelphia.

5. It is 24 miles from Valley Forge to Philadelphia. How far is it from Pittsburg to Philadelphia?

Unit Learning Task

Aircraft and Submarines

Objective: To use integers to compare data.

1. Select an aircraft and a submarine to research. Aircraft may include jets, gliders, or helicopters.

2. How high can your aircraft fly? How deep can your submarine dive?

3. What is the difference in how high your aircraft can fly and your submarine can dive? **Show your work.**

4. Why are there limits to how high an aircraft can fly and to how deep a submarine can dive? **Explain**.

THE WORLD ALMANAC FOR KIDS

The Sound of Speed

Chuck Yeager and the X-1 research aircraft.

The Speed of Sound

Sound travels fast—very fast! It travels about 760 mi per hr through the air if you are measuring under dry conditions at sea level. For years, many people believed that it was not possible to fly an airplane faster than the speed of sound. But in 1947, Chuck Yeager fired up the rockets on his plane, the X-1, and became the first person to break the "sound barrier."

Scientists use a ratio called a Mach number to compare the speed of an airplane to the speed of sound. For example, an airplane traveling at Mach 3 is traveling at 3 times the speed of sound. The fastest known speed for a winged aircraft flown by a pilot is Mach 6.7. This record was set in 1967.

FACT·ACTIVITY

Use the table to help answer the questions.

Mach Number	1	2	3	4	5	6
Speed	760	■	■	■	■	■

1 The first Mach number, Mach 1, is approximately 760 mi per hr. Copy and complete the table showing the first six Mach numbers. Then make a graph of the data.

2 **Write Math** ▸ What does the shape and direction of the line in your graph tell you about the relationship between Mach number and speed?

3 The Concorde jet, which operated between 1976 and 2003, had a cruising speed of 1,350 mi per hr. Find the point for that speed on your graph. What was the approximate Mach number of the Concorde jet?

4 An F-15 military jet has a top speed of Mach 2.5. Find the point for that speed on your graph. What is the approximate speed of an F-15 in miles per hour?

5 How much faster, in miles per hour, can an F-15 travel than the speed of sound?

Sonic Boom!

A sonic boom is sound made by an object traveling faster than the speed of sound. The boom is caused by the compression of sound waves in front of the object. If a plane causes a sonic boom, the people on the ground can hear it, but the pilot cannot.

The X-43A is an unmanned experimental aircraft that flew at Mach 7 for 10 seconds. The X-43A was launched by a rocket but then its supersonic-combustion ramjet engine powered it to Mach 7.

FACT·ACTIVITY

1 The sound barrier has been broken by vehicles other than aircraft. The first land vehicle to break the sound barrier was driven by Andy Green, a British pilot, at Black Rock Desert in Nevada. On October 15, 1997, Green reached a world-record land speed of 763.035 mi per hr. At what Mach number was Green traveling?

2 Mach numbers can also be used to describe objects traveling slower than the speed of sound. For example, an object traveling 570 mi per hr is traveling at Mach 0.75.

This equation can be used to calculate the Mach number for any speed in miles per hour:

$y = \frac{x}{760}$ where y is the Mach number and x is the speed in miles per hour.

▶ Do some research to identify three fast animals, three fast humans, and three fast vehicles.

▶ Find their speeds in miles per hour, and convert their speeds into Mach numbers. How many times as fast would each have to travel in order to break the sound barrier?

▶ Calculate your own top running speed and convert it to a Mach number. How many times as fast would you have to travel to break the sound barrier?

▶ Decide how to best display all the data you have collected. Present your findings to the class.

Geometry and Measurement

BIG IDEAS!

- Three-dimensional figures can be classified according to their geometric properties.

- Attributes of two-dimensional fgures can be measured and computed using appropriate formulas.

- Measurement involves a comparison of an attribute of an object or situations with a unit that has the same attribute.

Math On Location
Online Videos

Landscape architects create beautiful spaces near buildings, using sculptures, water, and plants.

Parallel lines and congruent angles form views of pleasing and restful patterns.

Beautiful spaces surrounding tall buildings in a city form an amazing contrast.

Game
Capture the Corners

Object of the Game Practice moving along a coordinate grid.

Materials
- One Capture the Corners game board
- One deck of Capture the Corners cards
- Six game pieces, three in each of two colors

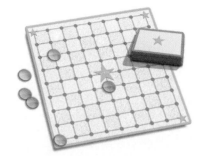

How to Play Play in pairs. Choose which color pieces each player will use. Shuffle the cards and place them face down in a pile. Players take turns using the following steps

1 Draw the top card from the pile. On your first turn, place a game piece on Start. After the first turn, either apply the card's instructions to a piece already on the board or to a piece you place on Start.

2 Solvethe equation on your card. A negative solution on a horizontal card means move left. A negative solution on a vertical card means move down. Move one of your game pieces the number and direction of the solution of the equation. Pieces must be on points or stars. No two pieces may occupy the same point.

How to Win Be the first player to have game pieces on two corners of the board.

Draw Conclusions
Complete these exercises after playing the game.

1. **WRITING** Describe a situation in which you would choose to place your third game piece on Start.

2. **REASONING** Suppose all of the cards read either "vertical x + 4 when x = 22" or "horizontal x + 2 when x = 1." What is the fewest number of turns you would need to win the game? Explain your answer.

Reading Vocabulary is important in everyday language. Mathematics also has its own set of words that you need to learn.

1. **Math words have specific meanings.** Many words have one meaning in everyday language and a different meaning in mathematics For example, in everyday language, an *axis* is an imaginary line through the center of the Earth, around which it rotates. In mathematics, an axis is a number line.

axis

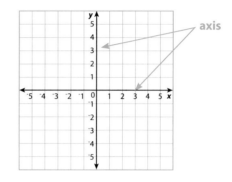
axis

I keep a log of all the math words I learn.

2. **You need to know the language of math in order to keep learning.** In mathematics, you learn something new in every grade. You learn something new in every chapter and lesson. In mathematics, you build on what you know.

Writing Preview Chapter 8. Make a list of words that are highlighted or in boldface type. Write "Yes" next to each word you know. Write "No" next to those that are new. Keep the list handy as you work on the lessons. Turn every "No" into a "Yes"!

WORD LOG—Chapter 8

	Word	Already Know	Meaning
Lesson 1	coordinate plane	No	

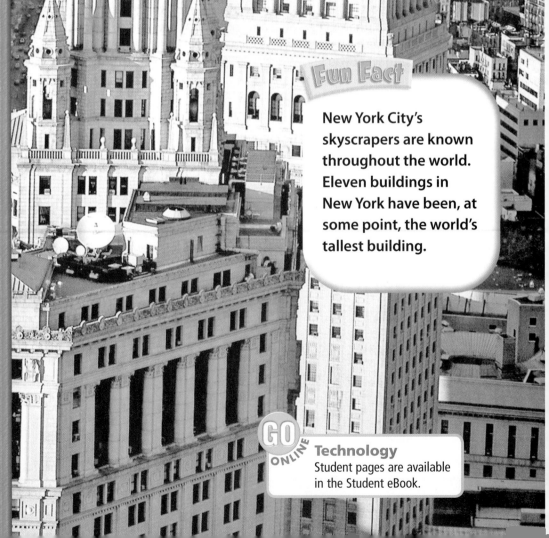

Geometry

Investigate

The city has commissioned you to design a new building to be built downtown. Choose at least two figures shown below and use them to create your new building. Draw your building. Then sketch the top, front, and side views.

Solid Figures	
Triangular pyramid	
Square pyramid	
Rectangular prism	
Triangular prism	

Fun Fact

New York City's skyscrapers are known throughout the world. Eleven buildings in New York have been, at some point, the world's tallest building.

GO ONLINE

Technology
Student pages are available in the Student eBook.

Show What You Know

Check your understanding of important skills needed for success in Chapter 8.

 ASSESSMENT
Soar To Success: Math.

▶ Identify Solid Figures

Name the figure.

1.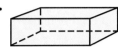

2.

3.

4.

5.

6.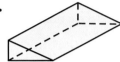

7.

8.

▶ Faces, Vertices, and Edges

Write the number of faces, vertices, and edges for each figure..

9.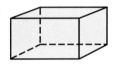

10.

11.

12.

Vocabulary

Visualize It!

Net of a
Rectangular Prism

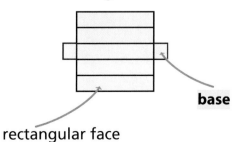

base

rectangular face

Language Tips

Words that look alike in English and Spanish often have the same meaning.

English	Spanish
lateral faces	cara lateral
polyhedron	poliedro

See English-Spanish Glossary.

3.3. Identify the characteristics of the rectangular coordinate system and use them to locate points and describe shapes drawn in all four quadrants.

Vocabulary

axes

coordinate plane

ordered pair

origin

quadrants

x-axis

y-axis

Materials
• MathBoard

Graph on a Coordinate Plane

Essential Question On the grid, what are the coordinates of the point?

PROBLEM Chelsea wants to research the remains of a sunken ship. She has a map that shows a grid of a nearby section of ocean, and she is told that the sunken ship rests at the point (4,D). How can Chelsea locate the sunken ship on the map?

Find the sunken ship on the map.

Locate points on a map by using pairs of coordinates.

According to Chelsea's information, the coordinates of the sunken ship are 4 and D. Place a point where line 4 and line D intersect.

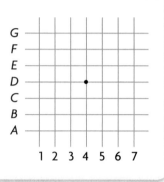

So, the point on the map that is both on line 4 and line D is the location of the sunken ship.

Use the same method to locate points on a **coordinate plane** like the one at the right.

Two number lines divide the coordinate plane. The horizontal number line is called the **x-axis**. The vertical number line is called the **y-axis**. These two **axes** divide the coordinate plane into four regions called **quadrants**. The two axes intersect at point (0,0), also known as the **origin**.

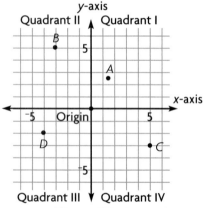

Point A: (1.5,2.5)
Point B: (⁻3,5)
Point C: (5,⁻3)
Point D: (⁻4,⁻2)

Using an **ordered pair** of coordinates like (⁻5,3), you can locate any point on the coordinate plane. The first number of an ordered pair tells you how far to move right or left from the origin. The second number tells you how far to move up or down.

On the coordinate plane above, the coordinates of point A are (1.5,2.5), of point B are (⁻3,5), of point C are (5,⁻3), and of point D are (⁻4,⁻2).

A point may be located at the origin, on the x-axis, on the y-axis, or in one of the four quadrants.

Examples

Write the ordered pair and the quadrant where each point is located on the coordinate plane.

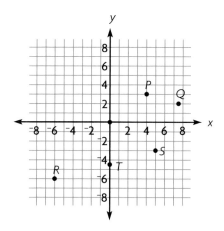

Start at the orgin. To find the *x*-coordinate, move right or left along the *x*-axis.

Then to find the *y*-coordinate, move up or down.

Point *P* is located at (4,3), in Quadrant I.

Point *Q* is located at about (7.5,2), in Quadrant I.

Point *R* is located at ($^-$6, $^-$6), in Quadrant III.

Point *S* is located at (5,$^-$3), in Quadrant IV.

Point *T* is located at about (0,$^-$4.5), in no quadrant. It is on the *y*-axis.

- In which quadrant would you find the point ($^-$3,0)?

Sketch a coordinate plane, and plot the points *A* (3,2.5) and *B* ($^-$4,3).

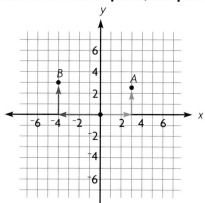

To locate point *A*, start at the origin and move 3 units to the right and 2.5 units up.

To locate point *B*, start at the origin and move 4 units to the left and 3 units up.

ERROR ALERT

The distance between two points should always be a positive number. When you subtract the coordinates, make sure to use absolute value.

Find the distance between points *C* and *E*.

To find the vertical distance between points, find the absolute value of the difference between their *y*-coordinates. To find horizontal distance, find the absolute value of the difference between *x*-coordinates.

Since points *C* and *E* are separated by a vertical distance, subtract the absolute value of their *y*-coordinates.

$$|2 - (^-1)| = |3| = 3$$

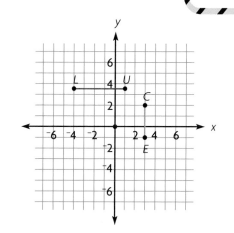

So, the distance between *C* and *E* is 3.

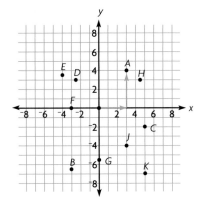

1. Write the ordered pair for point A. Name the quadrant where it is located.

Follow the green line from the origin to the right. Record the number.
Follow the green line up to point A. Record the number.

ordered pair: __?__   quadrant: __?__

Write the ordered pair for each point and the quadrant where it is located.

2. point B   **3.** point C   **4.** point D

5. point H   ✅ **6.** point J   ✅ **7.** point K

8. **Explain** what all the points in Quadrant III have in common.

▶ **Practice and Problem Solving** REAL WORLD

Write the ordered pair for each point and the quadrant where it is located.

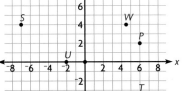

9. point P   **10.** point Q   **11.** point R

12. point V   **13.** point W   **14.** point Z

Using the coordinate plane at the right, find the distance between the two points.

15. P and T   **16.** R and V

17. S and W   **18.** U and Z

Sketch and label a coordinate plane, and plot the points.

19. S ($^-$4,6)   **20.** W (3.5,2)   **21.** A (5,$^-$3.5)

22. N ($^-$6,$^-$2.5)   **23.** D (0,1.5)   **24.** U ($^-$6,0)

25. Of the points you plotted above, find the distance between points N and U. Does a line connecting the two points show vertical distance or horizontal distance?

★ **OCCT Test Prep**

26. Which ordered pair is located in Quadrant II?

A ($^-$3,$^-$3)   **C** (7,8)

B ($^-$3, 9)   **D** ($^-$1,$^-$4)

27. Which ordered pair is located in Quadrant IV?

A ($^-$6,1)   **C** (2,$^-$3)

B ($^-$4,$^-$3)   **D** (5,4)

GO ONLINE — **Technology**
Use HMH Mega Math, The Number
Games, *ArachnaGraph,* Level H.

⭐ Standards Quick Check

Sketch and label a coordinate plane, and plot the points.

1. $N\,(^-7, ^-1.5)$

2. $D\,(4, 6.5)$

3. $U\,(^-3, ^-3)$

4. $J\,(5, 7)$

5. $W\,(^-4, 5.5)$

6. $T\,(^-3, ^-8)$

H.O.T.

Scatterplots

To interpret unfamiliar graphs, you can use visual thinking and what you see between *x*- and *y*-values. A scatterplot shows the relationship between two variables.

Positive

When the values of the two variables increase or decrease together, there is a **positive correlation.**

Negative

When the values of one variable increase while the others decrease, there is a **negative correlation.**

None

When the data points show no pattern of increase or decrease, there is **no correlation.**

Sketch a scatterplot that could represent the situation. Then identify the type of correlation between the variables.

1. amount of time walking *and* total distance that you walk

2. number of rooms in house *and* street address of house

Write *positive correlation, negative correlation,* or *no correlation* to describe the relationship shown in the scatterplot.

3.

4.

LESSON 2

3.3. Identify the characteristics of the rectangular coordinate system and use them to locate points and describe shapes drawn in all four quadrants.

Vocabulary

linear equation

Materials
• MathBoard

Graph Linear Equations

Essential Question How do you graph a linear equation from a table of values?

PROBLEM Patricio is exchanging euros, the currency in Spain, and U.S. dollars. On one day, the exchange rate is 1 euro equals about 1.29 U.S. dollars. An equation for this day relating euros, x, to U.S. dollars, y, is $y = 1.29x$. Graph this equation.

Graph the equation.

Use the equation to find values for x and y to form ordered pairs. Replace values for x and find the corresponding values for y.

$y = 1.29(1) = 1.29$ Replace x with 1, 2, and 3 in the equation.
$y = 1.29(2) = 2.58$ Find the corresponding values for y.
$y = 1.29(3) = 3.87$ Record your findings in a table.

Make a function table and write ordered pairs.

Euros (x)	0	1	2	3
U.S. Dollars (y)	0	1.29	2.58	3.87

Euros (x):   (0,0)   (2,2.58)
U.S. Dollars (y):   (1,1.29)   (3,3.87)

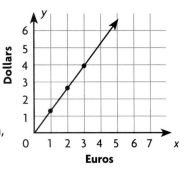

Plot the ordered pairs. Since this is a linear equation, draw a line through the points. The line represents all possible solutions to the equation.

The graph of some functions form a straight line. Equations that are straight lines when graphed are called **linear equations**.

Graph the linear equation $y = x + 4$.

Find values for x and y so you can write ordered pairs.
Replace values for x and find the corresponding values for y.

$y = {}^-2 + 4 = 2$ Replace x with $^-2$, 0, and 2 in the equation.
$y = 0 + 4 = 4$ Find the corresponding values for y.
$y = 2 + 4 = 6$ Record your findings in a function table.

Make a function table and write ordered pairs.

x	$^-2$	0	2
y	2	4	6

$(^-2,2)$, $(0,4)$, $(2,6)$

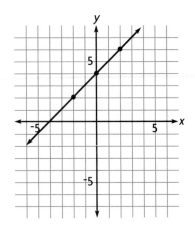

Plot the ordered pairs. Since this a linear equation, draw a line through the points. The line represents all possible solutions to the equation.

Example

Which function table corresponds to the graph?

Table A

x	y
⁻2	⁻6
0	0
2	6

Table B

x	y
⁻2	⁻5
0	⁻1
2	3

Table C

x	y
⁻2	⁻5
0	1
2	7

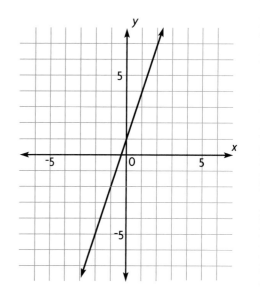

Check the ordered pairs from each table to see if they are on the line. If at least one of the ordered pairs is not on the line, then the table does not correspond to the graph. If all of the ordered pairs are on the line, then the table does correspond to the graph.

Table A: Check (⁻2, ⁻6). (⁻2, ⁻6) is not on the line, so Table A does not correspond to the graph.

Table B: Check (⁻2, ⁻5). (⁻2, ⁻5) is on the line. Check (0, ⁻1). (0, ⁻1) is not on the line, so Table B does not correspond to the graph.

Table C: Check (⁻2, ⁻5). (⁻2, ⁻5) is on the line. Check (0,1). (0,1) is on the line. Check (2,7). (2,7) is on the line.

So, Table C corresponds to the graph.

- Why are there arrows on the ends of the line?

- Explain how tables, graphs, and patterns relate to each other.

▶ Share and Show

1. Graph the equation $y = 2x + 5$ on a coordinate plane. Find values for x and y so you can form ordered pairs. Replace x with different values and find the corresponding values for y. Write ordered pairs, plot them, and draw a line through the points.

x	⁻3	0	2
y	⁻1	5	9

Tell which function table corresponds to the graph.

2. A

x	y
⁻1	⁻2
0	4
1	5

B

x	y
⁻2	⁻4
0	0
3	6

C

x	y
⁻1	⁻4
0	⁻3
2	⁻1

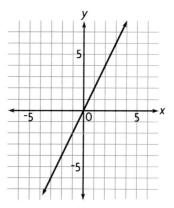

Graph the equation on a coordinate plane.

3. $y = x - 2$

4. $y = x + 6$

☑ 5. $y = 2x + 1$

☑ 6. $y = 3x - 2$

7. **Math Talk** **Explain** how you use the data in a function table to identify the graph of a linear equation.

Tell which function table corresponds to the graph on the coordinate plane.

8.

A
x	⁻2	0	2
y	⁻7	⁻3	1

B
x	⁻3	0	1
y	⁻5	⁻2	⁻1

C
x	⁻1	0	2
y	⁻1	1	5

9.

Q
x	⁻3	0	2
y	5	0	⁻4

R
x	⁻2	⁻1	1
y	3	1	⁻3

S
x	⁻2	0	5
y	7	5	0

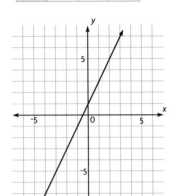

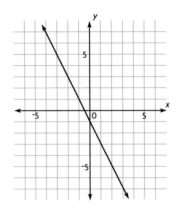

Graph the equation on a coordinate plane.

10. $y = 2x$

11. $y = x - 5$

12. $y = x + 2$

13. $y = 3x$

14. $y = {}^-3x$

15. $y = 2x - 1$

16. $y = 3x - 2$

17. $y = {}^-4x + 5$

18. On the day Amanda travels to Canada, the currency exchange rate is 1 U.S. dollar equals about 1.12 Canadian dollars. An equation relating U.S. dollars, x, to Canadian dollars, y, is $y = 1.12x$. Graph this equation. About how many Canadian dollars can Amanda get for 6 U.S. dollars?

19. While in Canada, Amanda goes hiking. She hikes at an average rate of 4 mi per hr. An equation relating the distance she travels, y, to the time in hours she hikes, x, is $y = 4x$. Graph this equation. About how far will Amanda hike in $2\frac{3}{4}$ hr?

20. **Write Math** Look back at Problems 18 and 19. **Explain** how the graph helped you answer the questions.

OCCT Test Prep

21. Which equation does the graph show?

A $y = x - 4$

B $y = x - 2$

C $y = x - 1$

D $y = x + 2$

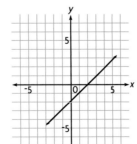

22. Which is the best estimate of the distance that could be traveled in 3.5 hours?

Driving at 50 Miles Per Hour

A 175 mi **B** 190 mi **C** 200 mi **D** 225 mi

Graph the equation on a coordinate grid.

1. Graph the equation $y = 5x$ for values of x from $^-3$ to 3.

2. Graph the equation $y = 2x - 2$ for values of x from $^-3$ to 3.

H.O.T.

Function Tables And Linear Equations

You know how to determine if a table of values corresponds to a graph of a linear equation. It is also important to know how to determine if a table of values corresponds to a linear equation. If a table of values does correspond to a linear equation, we say that it satisfies the linear equation.

Tell which table satisfies the linear equation $y = x + 1$.

Replace x and y with the corresponding values in the function tables. Then see if the resulting equation is true.

Table A

x	y
$^-2$	$^-1$
0	2
2	3

Try $(^-2, ^-1)$.

$y = x + 1$
$^-1 \stackrel{?}{=} {^-2} + 1$
$^-1 = {^-1}$

Try $(0, 2)$.

$y = x + 1$
$2 \stackrel{?}{=} 0 + 1$
$2 \neq 1$

$(^-2, ^-1)$ satisfies $y = x + 1$. $(0, 2)$ does not satisfy $y = x + 1$. There is no need to check $(2, 3)$.

Table B

x	y
$^-2$	$^-1$
0	1
2	3

Try $(^-2, ^-1)$.

$y = x + 1$
$^-1 \stackrel{?}{=} {^-2} + 1$
$^-1 = {^-1}$

Try $(0, 1)$.

$y = x + 1$
$1 \stackrel{?}{=} 0 + 1$
$1 = 1$

Try $(2, 3)$.

$y = x + 1$
$3 \stackrel{?}{=} 2 + 1$
$3 = 3$

$(^-2, ^-1)$, $(0, 1)$, and $(2, 3)$ satisfy $y = x + 1$.

So, Table B satisfies $y = x + 1$.

Tell which table satisfies the linear equation. Then graph the linear equation.

1. $y = x - 5$

2. $y = 3x$

3. $y = 2x + 1$

P

x	y
$^-2$	$^-3$
0	1
2	5

Q

x	y
$^-2$	$^-7$
0	$^-5$
2	$^-3$

R

x	y
$^-2$	$^-6$
0	0
2	6

★ **3.2.** Compare and contrast congruent and similar figures.

Vocabulary

corresponding angles

corresponding sides

similar figures

Materials
• MathBoard

Similar and Congruent Figures

Essential Question How can you identify and construct congruent figures?

Corresponding sides are sides that are in the same position in different plane figures. **Corresponding angles** are angles that are in the same position in different plane figures. When both the corresponding sides and angles are congruent, two figures are congruent.

Corresponding Sides	**Corresponding Angles**
$\overline{KL}$ corresponds to $\overline{RS}$, and $\overline{KL} \cong \overline{RS}$	$\angle K$ corresponds to $\angle R$, and $\angle K \cong \angle R$
$\overline{LM}$ corresponds to $\overline{ST}$, and $\overline{LM} \cong \overline{ST}$	$\angle L$ corresponds to $\angle S$, and $\angle L \cong \angle S$
$\overline{MN}$ corresponds to $\overline{TU}$, and $\overline{MN} \cong \overline{TU}$	$\angle M$ corresponds to $\angle T$, and $\angle M \cong \angle T$
$\overline{NK}$ corresponds to $\overline{UR}$, and $\overline{NK} \cong \overline{UR}$	$\angle N$ corresponds to $\angle U$, and $\angle N \cong \angle U$

Both the corresponding angles and sides of the figures are congruent, so $KLMN \cong RSTU$.

Figures with the same shape but not necessarily the same size are called **similar figures**. The symbol ~ is used to show that figures are similar.

Congruent figures have the same shape as well as the same size, so they are also similar. When two figures are similar, only their corresponding angles need to be congruent.

Corresponding Angles

$\angle A$ corresponds to $\angle F$, and $\angle A \cong \angle F$
$\angle B$ corresponds to $\angle G$, and $\angle B \cong \angle G$
$\angle C$ corresponds to $\angle H$, and $\angle C \cong \angle H$

The corresponding angles of the figure are congruent, so $\triangle ABC \sim \triangle FGH$.

Use ~ or ≅ to tell if the figures are similar or congruent. If the figures are not similar or congruent, write neither.

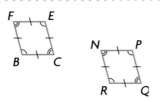

Both the corresponding angles and sides are congruent. So, $FECB \cong NPQR$.

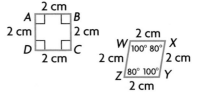

The corresponding angles are not congruent. So, the figures are neither similar nor congruent.

Find Similar Figures

If you multiply or divide the side lengths of a figure by the same value, you can find the corresponding side lengths of a similar figure.

Find the side lengths of △RST so it is similar to △JKL.

△JKL has side lengths of 20 in., 16 in., and 16 in. One way to find the side lengths of similar △RST is to divide the side lengths of △JKL by the same number. Here is what happens when that number is 2.

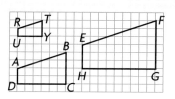

$\overline{RS}$: 16 in. ÷ 2 = 8 in. $\overline{ST}$: 16 in. ÷ 2 = 8 in. $\overline{RT}$: 20 in. ÷ 2 = 10 in.

So, using 2 as the divisor, △RST has sides with lengths 8 in., 8 in., and 10 in.

• What if you were to draw a similar figure by doubling the side lengths of △JKL? What would the new side lengths be?

Use graph paper to draw the similar figures.

Draw a figure similar to *RTYU* by doubling each side length of *RTYU*.

RTYU ≅ ABCD

Draw another figure similar to *RTYU* by tripling each side length of *RTYU*.

RTYU ≅ EFGH

• Is *ABCD* similar to *EFGH*? Explain.

Share and Show

1. Tell whether the figures are similar, congruent, or neither.

   Check whether the corresponding angles are congruent. Then check whether the corresponding sides are congruent.

Use ~ or ≅ to tell if the figures are similar or congruent. If the figures are not similar or congruent, write neither.

2.

3.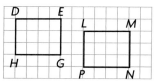

✓ 4.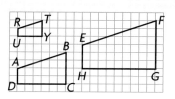

Draw the figures on graph paper. Mark any corresponding congruent sides and angles.

5. two similar isosceles triangles

6. two congruent rectangles

7. two similar squares

✓ 8. two congruent equilateral triangles

9. **Math Talk** **Explain** why two congruent figures must be similar, but two similar figures may or may not be congruent.

Practice and Problem Solving REAL WORLD

Use ~ or ≅ to tell if the figures are similar or congruent. If the figures are not similar or congruent, write neither.

10.

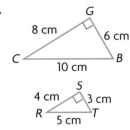

11.

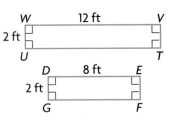

12.

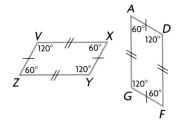

Draw the figures on graph paper. Mark any corresponding congruent sides and angles.

13. two congruent squares

14. two similar rectangles

15. two congruent isosceles triangles

16. two similar scalene triangles

 **Real World Data**

For 17–18, use the table.

17. Suppose you want to order a custom frame that is similar to the medium frame. Name two possible sets of dimensions for your frame.

18. **Reasoning** Are any two of the listed frame sizes similar? If so, state the sizes. If not, explain why.

19. **≡FAST FACT** *The Big Picture*, by Ando, is the world's largest rectangular canvas painting painted by a single artist. It measures 100 m by 12 m. How big would a reduced but similar version of the painting be if the dimensions were $\frac{1}{10}$ those of the original?

Most Popular Picture Frame Sizes	
Size	**Dimensions**
Small	4 in. × 6 in.
Medium	8 in. × 10 in.
Large	14 in. × 18 in.

20. **Write Math** **Explain** how the method of estimation used can affect how close an estimate is to the exact answer. Use examples to support your reasoning.

★ OCCT Test Prep

21. △UVW has side lengths of 6 in., 10 in., and 14 in. If △BDE ≅ △UVW and two sides of △BDE measure 18 in. and 30 in., how long is the third side of △BDE?

    A 12 in.   **C** 24 in.

    B 20 in.   **D** 42 in.

22. △ABC ≅ △LMN. If m∠B = 48° and m∠N = 92°, what is m∠A?

    A 40°   **C** 48°

    B 42°   **D** 88°

 Technology
Use HMH Mega Math, Ice Station Exploration, *Polar Planes*, Levels H and I.

★ Standards Quick Check

Draw the figure on graph paper. Mark any corresponding congruent sides and angles.

1. Draw a square similar to *ABCD* by dividing each side length by 2.

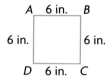

2. Draw a triangle similar to △*FGH* by tripling each side length.

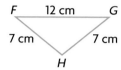

Challenge H.O.T.

A copy of a painting may be larger or smaller than the original painting, but it will be similar to it. *A Sunday Afternoon on the Island of La Grande Jatte*, a famous painting by Georges Seurat, hangs in the Art Institute of Chicago. The painting measures 120 in. by 81 in. An art student made a copy of the painting by dividing each side length by 3. What were the side lengths of the copy?

120 in. ÷ 3 = 40 in.   81 in. ÷ 3 = 27 in.

So, the dimensions of the copy were 40 in. by 27 in.

Find the side lengths of the painting or the copy of the painting.

1. painting measurements: 84 cm by 64 cm
copy side lengths: half those of painting

2. copy measurements: 12 in. by 16 in.
painting side lengths: twice those of copy

3. painting measurements: 60 cm. by 48 cm
copy side lengths: one-quarter those of painting

4. copy measurements: 9 in. by 14 in.
painting side lengths: 6 times those of copy

★ **3.1.** Compare and contrast the basic characteristics of three-dimensional figures (pyramids, prisms, cones, and cylinders).

Vocabulary

bases

lateral faces

polyhedron

right prism

vertex

Materials
• MathBoard
• colored pencils
• isometric dot paper

Math Idea

Solid figures can be identified by the shape of their bases, the number of their bases, and the shapes of their lateral faces or surfaces.

Types of Solid Figures

Essential Question How are prisms, pyramids, cylinders, and cones alike? Different?

 **Learn**

All solid figures have three dimensions–length, width, and height. In the following activity, you will explore ways in which solid figures are alike and ways in which they are different.

HANDS ON

Drawing solid figures.

❶ Copy the rectangular prism on isometric dot paper. Use three different colors: one for length, one for width, and one for height. Draw a rectangular prism with different dimensions.

❷ Copy the rectangular pyramid. Then draw a rectangular pyramid with different dimensions.

A **polyhedron** is a solid figure with faces that are polygons. The faces meet at the edges of the polyhedron. The edges meet at a point called a **vertex**.

A prism is a polyhedron with two congruent, parallel bases. A face is one of the polygons of a solid figure. A prism's **lateral faces** connect the two **bases**. In a **right prism**, the lateral faces are rectangles that are perpendicular to the bases.

A prism is named for the shape of its bases. Any polygon can be used as a base.

Rectangular Prism

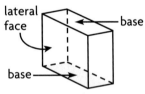
Pentagonal Prism

Name the figure.

All the faces are polygons, so the figure is a polyhedron.

The lateral faces are rectangles that are perpendicular to the bases, so the figure is a right prism.

The bases are parallel, congruent hexagons.

So, the figure is a right hexagonal prism.

More Solid Figures

A figure with a curved surface is not a polyhedron. An example is a sphere, which is a round object whose curved surface is the same distance from the center to all its points.

A cylinder is also not a polyhedron. It has two parallel, congruent circular bases and a curved lateral surface.

If you use line segments to connect a single point on one base of a cylinder to all of the points around the other base, you form a cone.

A cone is not a polyhedron. It has one flat circular base and a curved lateral surface. The point opposite the base is the vertex.

A pyramid is related to a prism in the same way a cone is related to a cylinder.

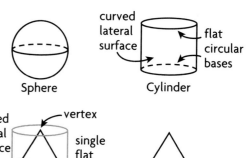
Sphere   Cylinder

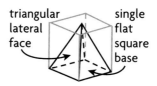
Cone

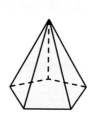
Square Pyramid

Name the figure.

All the faces are polygons, so the figure is a polyhedron.

The lateral faces are triangles with a common vertex, so the figure is a pyramid.

The base is a pentagon.

So, the figure is a pentagonal pyramid.

- How are a cylinder and a prism alike? How are they different? Explain.

- How are a cone and a cylinder alike? How are they different? Explain.

Remember

A pyramid is a solid figure whose one base is a polygon and whose other faces are triangles that meet at a common vertex.

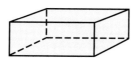

Name the figure at the right.

1. Its faces are polygons.

   Its lateral faces are rectangles.

   It has two congruent rectangular bases.

2. It has a flat circular base.

   It has a curved lateral surface.

   It has a vertex opposite the base.

Name the figure. Tell if it is a polyhedron. Write *yes* or *no*.

3.   ✓**4.**   **5.**   ✓**6.**

7. Math Talk **Explain** the difference between a prism and a pyramid.

▶ Practice and Problem Solving REAL WORLD

Name the figure. Tell if it is a polyhedron. Write *yes* or *no*.

8.  **9.**   **10.**   **11.**

Write *true* or *false* for each statement. Rewrite each false statement as a true statement.

12. A cone has no flat surfaces.

13. A triangular pyramid has six edges.

14. All pyramids have triangular bases.

15. An octagonal prism has eight faces.

Write *true* or *false* for each statement. Rewrite each false statement as a true statement.

16. a square pyramid   **17.** a cylinder   **18.** a cone   **19.** a pentagonal prism

Copy and complete the table.

Solid Figures	Number of Bases	Number of Faces	Number of Edges	Number of Vertices
20. triangular prism	▪	▪	▪	▪
21. rectangular pyramid	▪	▪	▪	▪
22. pentagonal prism	▪	▪	▪	▪

23. Name a solid figure that has the same number of faces as a rectangular prism, but not the same number of edges.

24. Write Math ▶ **What's the error?** Dominique said that the figure pictured at the right is a rectangular pyramid. What was her error? What is the correct name of the figure?

 ★ **OCCT Test Prep** Math Board

25. Mark is making a storage container in the shape of a cylinder. How many bases will the container have?

    A 0   **C** 4

    B 2   **D** 8

26. Gianna is making a jewelry box in the shape of a pentagonal prism. How many faces will the box have?

    A 5   **C** 7

    B 6   **D** 10

⭐ Standards Quick Check

Draw each figure.

1. hexagonal prism   **2.** pentagonal prism   **3.** sphere

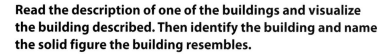

Geometry in Architecture

If asked to draw a picture of a building, you probably would not draw a complex building like the Louvre.

The Pentagon, Washington, D.C.

What would you draw? What solid figure would your building resemble? Architects use visualization to help them design buildings. You can use visualization and your knowledge of solid figures to solve problems by developing a mental picture based on given information.

Read the description of one of the buildings and visualize the building described. Then identify the building and name the solid figure the building resembles.

• This building has a square foundation.

• It has four exterior sides that are triangles.

• The sides meet at a common point at the top of the structure.

Entrance to the Louvre, Paris, France

Visualize the shape of the building by asking yourself the following questions:

• How many faces does the shape have?

• What are the shapes of the faces?

• How many bases does the shape have?

• What is the shape of the base?

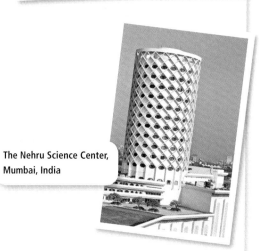

The Nehru Science Center, Mumbai, India

Read the description of one of the buildings and visualize the building described. Then identify the building and name the solid figure the building resembles.

1. Solve the problem in the Example.

2. Choose one of the other buildings pictured and write a description. What solid figure does the building resemble?

 **3.1.** Compare and contrast the basic characteristics of three-dimensional figures (pyramids, prisms, cones, and cylinders).

Materials
• MathBoard
• cereal box
• centimeter cubes
• centimeter graph paper

Views of Solid Figures

Essential Question What solid figures are a cereal box, a canister, the top of a building, and the roof of a rectangular house?

▶ **Learn**

The world around you is filled with objects that are shaped like geometric solid figures. A cereal box can model a rectangular prism. An oatmeal canister can model a cylinder. The roof of a house can model a triangular prism. The tops of some buildings can model a pyramid.

You may see these objects from different viewpoints, but you can determine their shapes from your knowledge of solid figures.

You can draw different views of solid figures.

HANDS ON

Drawing different views of a solid figure.

1 Look at the top of the box. Draw the top view. ▭

2 Look at the front of the box. Draw the front view.

3 Look at the side of the box. Draw the side view.

You can use different views of a solid figure to identify the figure.

Name the solid figure that has the given views.

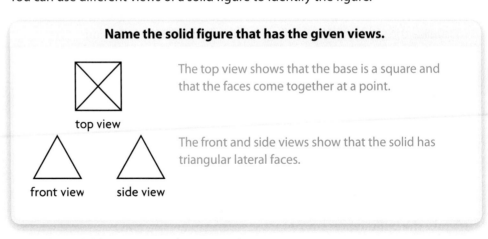

The top view shows that the base is a square and that the faces come together at a point.

The front and side views show that the solid has triangular lateral faces.

So, this solid figure is a square pyramid.

Using Models

You can build a model to find out what a solid figure would look like from the top, the front, and the side.

Build a model.

Use centimeter cubes to build the solid at the right.

The top view of the solid is shown below:

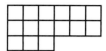

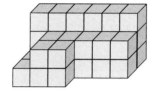

Draw the front view and the side view on graph paper.

- How many cubes do you see in the top view? the front view? the side view?

- Which views show how long the solid is?

Draw the front view of the solid figure formed by the cubes.

Think of the front view of each numbered cube.

In your drawing, show only the numbered faces, placing them in the correct relationship to one another.

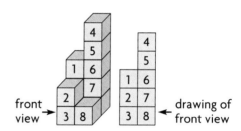

- Which of the numbered cubes could be removed from the stack without affecting the front view? Explain.

For 1–3, use the prism.

1. The yellow face is the top. Draw the top view of the prism.

2. The green face is the front. Draw the front view of the prism.

3. The blue face is the side. Draw the side view of the prism.

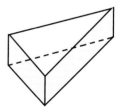

Name the solid figure that has the given views.

4.
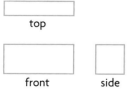

5.

6.
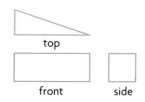

Draw the front, top, and side views of each solid.

7.

8.

✓**9.**

10. **Math Talk** **Explain** the similarities and differences between the top view of a prism and the top view of a pyramid.

▶ **Practice and Problem Solving** REAL WORLD

Name the solid figure that has the given views.

11.

12.

13.

Draw the front, top, and side views of each solid.

14.

15.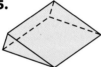

16.

17.

18. **Write Math** ▶ **What's the Question?** David compared the front, side, and top views of two different types of solid figures. The answer is "The top views are both circles."

★ **OCCT Test Prep** Math Board

19. Which of the following shows the top view of the pyramid below?

A

C

B

D

20. Which solid figure has the views below?

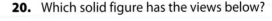
front   top   side

A cone

C hexagonal pyramid

B cube

D pentagonal prism

GO **Technology**
ONLINE Use HMH Mega Math, Ice Station Exploration, *Frozen Solids,* Level M.

⭐ Standards Quick Check

Each solid is made with 10 cubes. On graph paper, draw a top view, a front view, and a side view for each solid.

1.

2.

3.

4.

Challenge H.O.T.

Mat Plans

One way to visually represent a solid figure is by using a mat plan. A mat plan is a top view of a solid figure. Each box contains a number representing the number of cubes that are in the vertical column.

Use the mat plan to identify the correct isometric representation.

Mat Plan

1	2
	1

The squares with a 1 represent one cube in the column.

The square with a 2 represents two cubes in the column.

A.   **B.**

So, Figure A is the correct isometric representation.

Use the mat plan to identify the correct isometric representation.

1. | 1 | 3 | 4 | 2 |

A.   **B.**   **C.**   **D.**

2.

1	2	4
	1	3
		2

★ **3.1.** Compare and contrast the basic characteristics of three-dimensional figures (pyramids, prisms, cones, and cylinders).

Vocabulary

net

Materials
• MathBoard
• 5 in. × 8 in. index cards
• graph paper
• ruler
• scissors
• tape

Hands On
Models of Solid Figures

Essential Question How do you create a new view of a solid figure?

▶ **Investigate**

A net is a pattern of polygons that can be folded to form a polyhedron. You can make a net using paper, scissors, tape, and a ruler.

You can use a 5 in. × 8 in. index card to make a rectangular prism.

1 Use a ruler to measure and draw the faces on the index card.

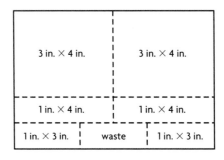

3 in. × 4 in.	3 in. × 4 in.
1 in. × 4 in.	1 in. × 4 in.
1 in. × 3 in.	waste	1 in. × 3 in.

2 Cut out the six faces.

3 Tape the pieces together to form the prism.

4 Remove the tape from some of the edges so that the pattern lies flat. The pattern is a **net** for the prism. The net may look like the one at the right.

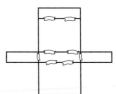

1. Explain how you can tell that the net will form a rectangular prism.

2. Compare your net with those of other classmates. How are they alike? How are they different?

3. **Evaluation** Do you think any pattern formed using the same six pieces would form a net for this rectangular prism? **Explain**.

▶ **Connect**

Making a net.

Look at the square pyramid on the right. You can use graph paper to make a net for a similar pyramid.

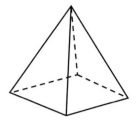

1 Make a list of the shapes you will need for the net. Make a sketch of what the net will look like.

2 Use a ruler to draw the net on a piece of graph paper. Use dashed lines to show where you will fold your net, and use solid lines to show where you will cut it.

3 Cut out your net.

Math Talk

What characteristics of prisms and pyramids should you consider when making a net?

4 Fold the net along the dashed lines and tape it together to form the pyramid.

• How could you change your net to make a different net for the pyramid?

▶ **Share and Show**

Use graph paper to draw a net for the given solid figure.

1. triangular prism

2. triangular pyramid

3. hexagonal prism

✓**4.** pentagonal pyramid

Identify the solid figure from its net.

5.

6.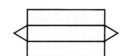

7.

✓**8.**

Copy the pattern and draw the missing portion so that the result is a net for the solid figure.

9. square prism

10. rectangular pryamid

11. pentagonal prism

12. **Write Math** ▶ **Explain** how you can use visualization to make a net for a hexagonal prism.

★ 3.1. Compare and contrast the basic characteristics of three-dimensional figures (pyramids, prisms, cones, and cylinders). *also* 3.2.; 3.3.

Materials
• MathBoard

Problem Solving Workshop
Skill: Make Generalizations

Essential Question How are the number of sides of the base of a solid figure related to the number of vertices and edges of the figure?

▶ **Use the Skill** REAL WORLD

PROBLEM Sarah is making models of prisms. She is using straws for the edges and balls of clay for the vertices. She has made three prisms and recorded the number of balls of clay and straws that she used. How many of each will she need to make a prism with a decagon base?

You can use known information to make generalizations that can then be applied to other situations.

	Triangular Prism	Rectangular Prism	Pentagonal prism
Number of Sides on Base	3	4	5
Number of Balls of Clay (vertices)	6 $6 = 2 \times 3$	8 $8 = 2 \times 4$	10 $10 = 2 \times 5$
Number of Straws (edges)	9 $9 = 3 \times 3$	12 $12 = 3 \times 4$	15 $15 = 3 \times 5$

Use the data in the table to make generalizations.

Generalization 1: The number of vertices is twice the number of sides on the base.

Generalization 2: The number of edges is three times the number of sides on the base.

Since a decagon has 10 sides, a prism whose base is a decagon must have 2×10, or 20 vertices, and 3×10, or 30 edges. So, Sarah will need 20 balls of clay and 30 straws to make a prism with a decagon base.

Solve.

a. What generalization can you make about the relationship between the number of balls of clay and the number of straws needed to make a prism?

b. What type of prism could be built using exactly 24 straws? How many balls of clay would be needed?

c. Add a row to the table showing the number of faces of each solid figure. What generalization can you make about the relationship between the number of sides on the base and the number of faces?

1. Marilyn is making 10 different pyramids with straws and balls of clay. She has already made the three pyramids pictured in the table. What rule can she use to determine the number of straws and balls of clay that she will need for each of the other pyramids?

   First, copy and complete the table.

   Then, compare the number of sides on the base to the number of balls of clay and the number of straws needed to make each pyramid.

   Finally, write generalizations and use them to help solve the problem.

   The number of balls of clay is _?_ the number of sides on the base.

   The number of straws is _?_ the number of sides on the base.

	Triangular Pyramid	Rectangular Pyramid	Pentagonal Pyramid
Number of Sides on Base			
Number of Balls of Clay (vertices)			
Number of Straws (edges)			

2. **What if** Marilyn wanted to write a generalization that shows the relationship between the number of vertices and the number of edges of a pyramid? What generalization could she make?

3. George is connecting cubes. The figure at the right shows 3 of the cubes that he connected. What generalizations can George make about the number of balls of clay and the number of straws needed to connect any number of cubes?

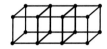

 Real World Data

4. Cameron is making string art. One of his designs contains polygons with string connecting every vertex with every other vertex. He is using red string for the sides of the polygons and blue string for the segments inside the polygons. How many segments of blue string will he need for a nonagon?

5. Hannah and 3 of her friends rented a rowboat for 2 hr. If the rental cost $45 and the friends shared the cost equally, how much did each person pay?

6. Mrs. Guerrero is a seamstress. It takes her 18 min to make a soccer jersey. How many soccer jerseys can she make in 2 hr?

7. Mr. Harrington has 196 boxes of nails to ship. Each carton holds 16 boxes. To see how many cartons he will need, he uses his calculator to divide 196 by 16 and gets a quotient of 12.25. How many boxes of nails will be left over once he has filled as many cartons as possible?

8. Phil, Jack, and Eduardo divided a bag of apples among themselves. Phil took half of the apples. Jack took half of those that remained. Eduardo took the remaining 6 apples. How many apples were there originally in the bag?

☆ Extra Practice

Set A

Write the ordered pair for each point and the quadrant where it is located. (pp. 288–291)

1. point A
2. point B
3. point C

4. point D
5. point E
6. point F

7. Find the distance between points A and F.

8. Find the distance between points A and B.

9. Find the distance between points C and D.

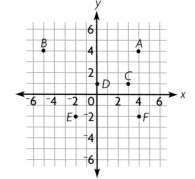

Write the ordered pair for each point and the quadrant where it is located.

10. point C
11. point D
12. point E

13. point F
14. point G
15. point I

16. Find the distance between points A and C.

17. Find the distance between points N and F.

18. Find the distance between points B and M.

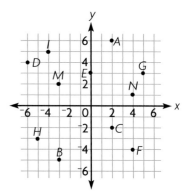

Set B

Graph the equation on a coordinate plane. (pp. 292–295)

1. $y = 3x$
2. $y = x - 4$
3. $y = 0.5x$
4. $y = {}^-2x$

5. $y = {}^-6 + x$
6. $y = {}^-4x - 2$
7. $y = {}^-0.5x + 4$
8. $y = 3x + 1$

9. $y = x$
10. $y = x + 1$
11. $y = x - 2$
12. $y = {}^-4x$

Set C

Use ~ or ≈ to tell if the figures are similar or congruent.
If the figures are not similar or congruent, write neither. (pp. 296–299)

1.
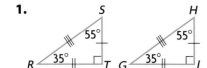

2.
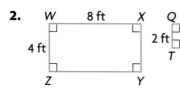

3.
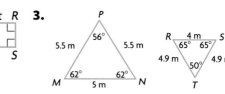

GO ONLINE **Technology**
Use HMH Mega Math, The Number
Games, *ArachnaGraph,* Levels H and L.

Set D

Name the figure. Tell if it is a polyhedron.
Write *yes* or *no*. (pp. 300–304)

1.

2.

3.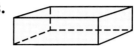

4.

Write *true* or *false* for each statement. Rewrite each false statement as a true statement.

5. A pentagonal prism has exactly five faces.

6. An octagonal prism has 24 edges.

7. A triangular pyramid has four vertices.

8. All rectangular prisms are cubes.

Draw each figure.

9. a hexagonal prism

10. a pentagonal pyramid

11. a triangular prism

12. a square prism

13. Name a solid figure that has double the number of faces of a rectangular pyramid.

14. Name a solid figure that has the same number of faces as a triangular prism, but a different number of vertices.

Set E

Name the solid figure that has the given views. (pp. 304–307)

1.

2.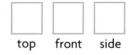

3.

4. The top view of a solid shows all 10 of the solid's edges. What shape is the solid?

5. Name a solid figure that has the same side view as a triangular pyramid but is not a prism.

Draw the front, top, and side views of each solid.

6.

7.

8.

9.

10.

11.

12.

13.

Vocabulary

You can graph a **linear equation** by finding **ordered pairs** that make the equation true and drawing a line through the points.

Use grid paper. Complete the steps to graph the linear equation $y = x + 5$.

    a. Make a function table.

    b. Write the ordered pairs.

    c. Graph the equation.

    d. Find two other points on the line and check to see if the coordinates make the equation true.

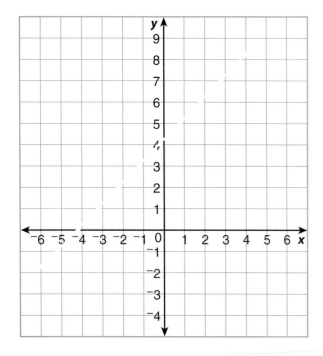

Writing Which is easier for you: generating a function from a line or generating a line from a function? Explain your answer.

Reading Look for this book in your library. *The Ancient Civilizations of Greece and Rome: Solving Algebraic Equations* by Kerri O'Donnell

☀ H.O.T. ☀ Multistep Problems

1 The Blake family is going on a three-day hiking and camping trip to see their favorite waterfall. The function $y = 2x$ shows the number of miles, y, that the Blakes hike in x hours. ▄ 3.3.

- Complete the function table below. Use the function table to sketch the graph of $y = 2x$.

hours, x	0	1	2	3	4
miles, y	0	2			

- **Explain** how to use the graph to predict how long it will take the Blakes to hike 11 miles. About how long will it take?

- The Blakes hiked for 3 hours the first day, 5 hours the second day, and 6 hours the third day. Sketch a graph that shows their progress each hour for the third day.

- Do the graphs show linear relationships or nonlinear relationships? **Explain**.

2 Usha wants to join a video store. The store closest to her house charges $7 as a one time fee and $2 to rent each video. ▄ 3.3.

- If Usha rents two videos on the day she opens the account, how much will she pay?

- Let c represent the total cost and let v represent the number of videos rented. Write a rule for the function that shows the relationship between c and v.

- Use the rule to write 3 ordered pairs. Create a coordinate grid and plot the 3 ordered pairs.

- What is the value of c if $v = 6$?

Practice for the OCCT

1 The top view of a solid shows all six of the solid's edges. What shape is the solid? 🔲 **3.1.**

    A hexagonal pyramid

    B triangular pyramid

    C cylinder

    D pentagonal prism

2 Which ordered pair is in Quadrant III? 🔲 **3.3.**

    A $(3,6)$

    B $(9,^-10)$

    C $(^-2,^-4)$

    D $(^-3,3)$

3 Which list of ordered pairs corresponds to the triangle on the grid? 🔲 **3.3.**

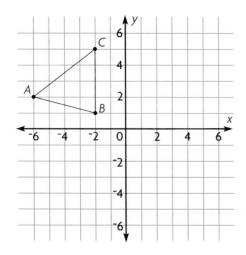

    A $A(^-6,2), B(^-2,2), C(^-5,^-5)$

    B $A(6,4), B(5,^-2), C(2,5)$

    C $A(6,^-2), B(2,^-2), C(5,5)$

    D $A(^-6,2), B(^-2,1), C(^-2,5)$

4 On the map grid shown, Yancey's house is 2 units to the left of point T. Which ordered pair represents the location of Yancey's house on the grid? 🔲 **3.3.**

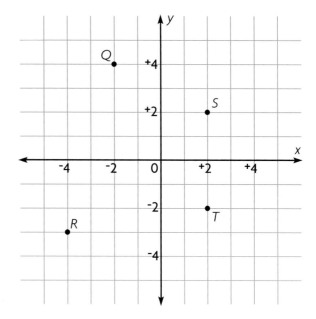

    A $(0,^-2)$

    B $(^-2,0)$

    C $(2,^-2)$

    D $(4,^-2)$

5 How many faces does a hexagonal prism have? 🔲 **3.1.**

    A 5   **C** 9

    B 8   **D** 12

6 What is the distance between point T $(^-6,4)$ and point W $(7,4)$ on a coordinate grid? 🔲 **3.3.**

    A 4 units   **C** 13 units

    B 9 units   **D** 15 units

7 Tom has a weekend job delivering pizzas. He is paid at the rate shown on the graph. Which equation shows the relationship between the number of pizzas delivered to how much Tom earns? 🔲 **3.3.**

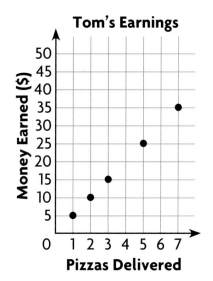

Tom's Earnings

A $y = x + 5$ **C** $10x$

B $y = 5x$ **D** $y = 15x$

8 Which ordered pair is located in Quadrant IV? 🔲 **3.3.**

A $(^-7, ^-9)$

B $(5,3)$

C $(6, ^-1)$

D $(^-4,7)$

9 Noah constructed a polyhedron using a pentagon and five isosceles triangles. What solid figure did he construct? 🔲 **3.1.**

`

A cylinder   **C** pentagonal pyramid

B cone   **D** hexagonal prism

Problem Solving

10 What is the distance between point Q (6, $^-$5) and point H (6,8) on a coordinate grid? 🔲 **3.3.**

11 A prism has 27 edges. How many vertices does it have? 🔲 **3.1.**

12 A point is located 3 units to the left of the origin and 3 units up. What ordered pair describes the location of the point? **Explain** how you found your answer. 🔲 **3.3.**

13 During a blizzard, the snow depth increased steadily by 2 inches each hour for 5 hours. Write an equation to represent the snow depth as a function of time. Then graph the function. 🔲 **3.3.**

14 Describe what generalization you can make to describe the relationship between the number of faces and the number of vertices of a rectangular prism. 🔲 **3.1.**

Chapter 9

Circumference and Measurement

Investigate

Suppose you are in charge of transporting several of each animal in the graph from one wildlife refuge to another. There are 5 cars on the trains and each car can hold 15 tons. Find three different combinations of animals that you could transport. Each combination must include all four kinds of animals.

Fun Fact

The African elephant is the largest land animal. It can weigh as much as 7 tons and can stand 11 ft tall. It can also eat up to 350 lb of food and drink between 30 and 50 gal of water per day.

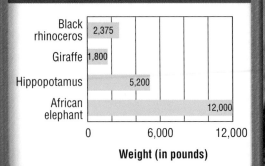

Average Weight of Large African Animals

Animal	Weight (in pounds)
Black rhinoceros	2,375
Giraffe	1,800
Hippopotamus	5,200
African elephant	12,000

Weight (in pounds) — 0, 6,000, 12,000

GO ONLINE

Technology
Student pages are available in the Student eBook.

Show What You Know

Check your understanding of important skills needed for success in Chapter 9.

▶ **Area of Circles**

Find the area to the nearest whole number. Use 3.14 for π.

1. 12 in.

2. 4.3 cm

3. $5\frac{1}{2}$ ft

4. 60 mm

▶ **Convert Units**

Complete

5. 6 ft = m in.   **6.** 6 ft = r yd   **7.** 120 min = v sec   **8.** 5 lb = h oz

9. 180 min = t hr   **10.** 24 in. = a ft   **11.** 6 yd = x ft   **12.** 120 hr = y days

Vocabulary

Visualize It!

Circumference of a circle.

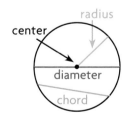

Circumference = π × *d*

***d* = 98 cm; π = 3.14**

C = πd

C ≈ 3.14 × 98

C ≈ 307.72

C = 308

Language Tips

Words that look alike in English and Spanish often have the same meaning.

English	Spanish
central angle	ángulo central
chord	cuerda

See **English-Spanish Glossary.**

★ **4.1.** Use formulas to find the circumference and area of circles in terms of pi.

Circles

Essential Question What are the components of a circle?

PROBLEM Stonehenge is a group of earth and stone circles constructed in southern England thousands of years ago. The best known circle is the outer circle of sarsen stones, or the Sarsen Circle. If the distance from the center of the Sarsen Circle to one of the sarsen stones is 16.5 m, what is the length of the diameter of the Sarsen Circle?

A circle is a plane figure that consists of all of the points that are equidistant from a point called the center. Circles are named by their centers. For example, the circle on the right is circle *C*.

Certain line segments in circles have special names.

> **chord:** a line segment with its endpoints on the circle
> radius: a line segment with one endpoint at the center and the other endpoint on the circle
> diameter: a line segment that passes through the center and has both endpoints on the circle

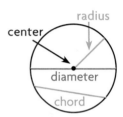

Vocabulary

central angle

chord

semicircle

Materials
• MathBoard
• compass
• straightedge

Use a formula to find the diameter.

The length of the diameter (*d*) is twice the length of the radius (*r*). You can write the formulas $d = 2r$, and $r = \frac{1}{2}d$. To find the diameter of the Sarsen Circle, you can use the formula $d = 2r$.

$d = 2r$ Write the formula.

$d = 2 \times 16.5$ Replace *r* with 16.5.

$d = 33$ Multiply.

So, the length of the diameter of the Sarsen Circle is 33 m.

HANDS ON

Construct a circle.

• Open the compass to 2 in. Use the compass to draw circle *P*.
• Use your ruler to draw and label radius $\overline{PT}$ and diameter $\overline{RS}$.
• Draw and label a line segment with two endpoints, *C* and *D*, on the circle so that the segment does not pass through *P*.
• What type of line segment is $\overline{CD}$?
• How long is the diameter of circle *P*?

Central Angle of a Circle

A **central angle** of a circle is an angle with its vertex at the center of the circle.

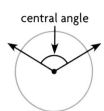

central angle

A complete rotation at the center of a circle equals 360°. You can use this fact to help find the measure of a central angle.

Use mental math to find the unknown angle measure.

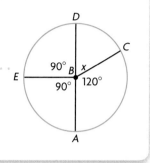

1 Find the sum of the angle measures you know.

$90° + 90° + 120° = 300°$

- -

2 Subtract the sum from 360°.

$360° - 300° = 60°$

So, the unknown angle measure is 60°.

Use algebra to find the unknown angle measure.

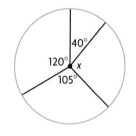

$x + 105 + 120 + 40 = 360$	The sum of the central angles is 360°.
$x + 265 = 360$	Add.
$x + 265 - 265 = 360 - 265$	Use the Subtraction Property of Equality.
$x + 0 = 95$	Use the Identity Property.
$x = 95$	

So, the unknown angle measure is 95°.

▶ **Share and Show** Math Board

1. Find the length of the diameter.

$d = 2r$

$d = 2 \times 21$

$d = \blacksquare$

2. Find the length of the radius.

$r = \frac{1}{2}d$

$r = \frac{1}{2} \times \blacksquare$

$r = \blacksquare$

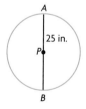

Use the given measure to find the diameter or radius.

3. $d = 12$ cm, $r = \blacksquare$ **4.** $r = 23$ in., $d = \blacksquare$ **5.** $d = 31$ ft, $r = \blacksquare$ ✓**6.** $r = 4.6$ m, $d = \blacksquare$

For 7–12, use the circle at the right. Name the given parts of the circle. Write *center*, *radius*, *diameter*, or *chord*.

7. B

8. $\overline{AC}$

9. $\overline{AD}$

10. $\overline{BE}$

11. $\overline{BD}$

12. $\overline{ED}$

Find the unknown angle measure.

13.

14.

✓**15.**

16. Math Talk **Explain** how the measures of a circle's radius and diameter are related.

Use the given measure to find the diameter or radius.

17. $d = 18$ in., $r = $ ▨

18. $r = 38$ mm, $d = $ ▨

19. $d = 7$ yd, $r = $ ▨

20. $r = 19.9$ m, $d = $ ▨

21. $d = 15$ cm, $r = $ ▨

22. $r = 9\frac{1}{2}$ ft, $d = $ ▨

23. $d = 4\frac{1}{4}$ in., $r = $ ▨

24. $r = 2.6$ m, $d = $ ▨

For 25–30, use the circle at the right. Name the given parts of the circle. Write *center*, *radius*, *diameter*, or *chord*.

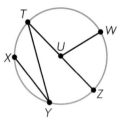

25. $\overline{UW}$

26. $\overline{TY}$

27. U

28. $\overline{XY}$

29. $\overline{TZ}$

30. $\overline{UZ}$

Find the unknown angle measure.

31.

32.

33.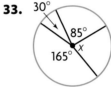

 Real World Data

For 34, use the table at the right.

34. Find the radius of the Aubrey Holes circle and the radius of the Z Holes circle. How far away is a point on the Aubrey Holes circle from the nearest point on the Z Holes circle?

35. Write Math ▶ The radius of circle P is 10 centimeters in length. Chord $\overline{ST}$ is 15 centimeters in length. Can $\overline{ST}$ be a diameter of the circle? **Explain.**

Stonehenge Circles	
Ring	**Diameter**
Aubrey Holes	100 meters
Y Holes	54 meters
Z Holes	40 meters
Sarsen Circle	33 meters

 ★ **OCCT Test Prep** | Math Board

36. A circle has a diameter of 18 in. What is the measure of the radius?

    A 9 in.   **C** 24 in.

    B 18 in.   **D** 36 in.

37. The central angles of a circle measure 132°, 78°, 67°, and $x°$. What is the value of x?

    A $x = 7$ **C** $x = 83$

    B $x = 77$ **D** $x = 360$

★ Standards Quick Check

Draw a circle with the given measurements.

1. radius = 3 in.

2. diameter = 4 cm

3. radius = 5 cm

4. diameter = 3.5 in.

5. radius = 7 cm

6. diameter = 6 in.

Challenge H.O.T.

Constructing Semicircles

A **semicircle** is one-half of a circle. You can construct a semicircle with a compass and a straight edge.

Construct a semicircle with a diameter of 2 in.		
1 Use a ruler to draw a line segment that is 2 in. long. Label the midpoint of the line *O*.	**2** Place the point of a compass on the midpoint, *O*, and open the compass so that the pencil is on an endpoint of the line segment.	**3** Draw an arc from one endpoint to the other endpoint forming a semicircle with a diameter of 2 in. 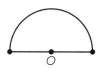

Draw a semicircle with the given measurement.

1. Construct a semicircle with a diameter of 5 cm.

2. Construct a semicircle with a diameter of 2 in.

3. Construct a semicircle with a radius of 3 cm.

LESSON 2

★ **4.1.** Use formulas to find the circumference and area of circles in terms of pi.

Vocabulary

circumference

Materials
• MathBoard
• calculator
• compass
• ruler
• string

Hands On
Estimate Circumference

Essential Question How does the diameter of a cirlce relate to the circumference?

▶ **Investigate**

Circumference is the distance around a circle. You can use string and a ruler to estimate the circumference of a circle.

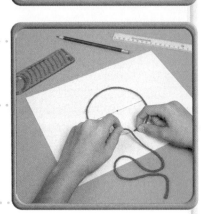

1 Use a compass to draw a circle. Mark the center of the circle. Use a ruler to draw a diameter of the circle. Remember that the diameter passes through the center of the circle.

2 Measure the diameter of the circle to the nearest tenth of a centimeter. Record your measurement.

3 Lay the string around the circle. Mark the string where it meets itself.

4 Use the ruler to measure the string from its end to the mark you made. Measure to the nearest tenth of a centimeter. Record your measurement.

5 Use a calculator to divide the circumference of your circle by the diameter. Record your result.

6 Display your results on the chalkboard with those of other students in the class by making a table like the one below.

Student Name	Circumference (C)	Diameter (d)	C ÷ d
▦	▦	▦	▦
▦	▦	▦	▦
▦	▦	▦	▦

1. About how many times as long as the diameter is the circumference of your circle?

2. Synthesis About how many times as long as the diameter is the circumference of the circles drawn by other students? What approximate value is $C \div d$, or $\frac{C}{d}$, for any circle?

► **Connect**

You can use the relationship between the diameter and the circumference of a circle to estimate the circumference of a circle when you know its diameter.

1 Find the diameter of the circle.

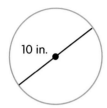

The diameter is 10 in.

2 Multiply the diameter of the circle by 3.

$3 \times 10 = 30$

3 Estimate the circumference of the circle.

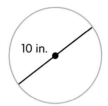

So, the circumference is approximately 30 in.

It is important to understand that since the circumference of a circle is a little more than 3 times its diameter, multiplying by 3 is only an estimate and also is an underestimate.

So, as the length of the diameter increases, the estimate becomes less accurate.

Math Talk

Describe the relationship between the diameter and the circumference of a circle.

► **Share and Show**

Use a compass and a ruler to draw a circle with the given radius. Estimate the circumference of the circle by using a string and ruler.

1. radius = 4 cm

2. radius = 10 cm

3. radius = 8 cm

4. radius = 5 cm

5. radius = 6.2 cm

✓**6.** radius = 7.3 cm

Estimate the circumference of the circle.

7.

6 yd

8.

5.4 m

9.

$9\frac{1}{2}$ ft

10.

18 mm

11.

25 in.

✓**12.**

$\frac{1}{2}$ in.

13. **Write Math** ▶ **Explain** how you could estimate the circumference of a circle using only a ruler.

Chapter 9 Lesson 2 325

LESSON 3

★ **4.1.** Use formulas to find the circumference and area of circles in terms of pi.

Vocabulary

pi

Materials
• MathBoard

ALGEBRA:
Find Circumference

Essential Question How do you use formulas to find the circumference of a circle?

PROBLEM The View is a circular revolving restaurant that overlooks Times Square in New York City. It is 47 stories high, providing views in every direction. The restaurant has a diameter of 112 ft. To the nearest foot, about how far does a person seated at the edge of the restaurant travel in one revolution?

In the previous lesson, you found that the value of the circumference divided by the diameter is a little more than 3 for any circle. For any circle, the circumference divided by the diameter is the same. This number is called **pi**, or π. The value of π is usually approximated as 3.14 or $\frac{22}{7}$. The relationship among circumference, diameter, and π can be written as $\frac{C}{d} = \pi$, where C is the circumference of the circle and d is the diameter of the circle.

Since $\frac{C}{d} = \pi$, you can get the formula $C = \pi d$ by multiplying both sides of the equation by d. Since the diameter of a circle is twice the length of the radius, or $d = 2r$, you can also write $C = \pi \times 2r$, or $C = 2\pi r$.

So, you can find the circumference of any circle by using the formula $C = \pi d$ or $C = 2\pi r$.

Find the circumference to the nearest foot. Use 3.14 for π.

Use the formula $C = \pi d$.

112 ft

$C = \pi d$ Write the formula.

$C \approx 3.14 \times 112$ Replace π with 3.14 and d with 112.

$C \approx 351.68$

$C \approx 352$ Round to the nearest foot.

Remember
You can use 3.14 or $\frac{22}{7}$ for π. These are common estimates of π.

So, a person seated at the edge of the restaurant travels about 352 ft in one revolution.

• **What if** a person were seated 5 ft in from the edge of the restaurant? About how far would that person travel in one revolution? HINT: The diameter decreases by $2 \times 5 = 10$, or 10 ft.

Use the Radius

When the radius of a circle is given, use $C = 2\pi r$ to find circumference.

Examples

Jeanette has a circular tablecloth with a radius of $3\frac{1}{2}$ ft. She wants to trim the tablecloth with fringe. How many feet of fringe will she need? Use $\frac{22}{7}$ for π.

$C = 2\pi r$ Write the formula.

$C \approx 2 \times \frac{22}{7} \times 3\frac{1}{2}$ Replace π with $\frac{22}{7}$ and r with $3\frac{1}{2}$.

$C \approx \frac{2}{1} \times \frac{\overset{11}{\cancel{22}}}{\underset{1}{\cancel{7}}} \times \frac{\overset{1}{\cancel{7}}}{\underset{1}{\cancel{2}}}$ Write 2 and $3\frac{1}{2}$ as fractions. Simplify. Multiply.

$C \approx \frac{22}{1}$ or 22

ERROR ALERT

Be sure you are using the correct circumference formula, depending on whether you know the diameter or the radius.

So, she will need about 22 ft of fringe.

You can find the diameter or radius of a circle when the circumference is known.

The circumference of a basketball hoop is 141.3 cm. What is the diameter of the hoop? Use 3.14 for π.

$C = \pi d$ Write the formula.

$141.3 \approx 3.14d$ Replace C with 141.3 and π with 3.14.

$\frac{141.3}{3.14} \approx \frac{3.14d}{3.14}$ Solve.

$45 \approx d$

So, the diameter of the basketball hoop is about 45 cm.

Share and Show Math Board

Find the circumference to the nearest whole number. Use 3.14 for π.

1.

8 cm

$C = \pi d$
$C \approx 3.14 \times 8$
$C \approx \blacksquare$

2.

3 ft

$C = 2\pi r$
$C \approx 2 \times 3.14 \times 3$
$C \approx \blacksquare$

Find the circumference to the nearest whole number. Use 3.14 or $\frac{22}{7}$ for π.

3.
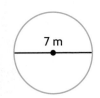
7 m

✓ **4.**

$17\frac{1}{2}$ yd

5.

2.8 cm

✓ **6.**

$5\frac{1}{2}$ in.

7. [Math Talk] **Explain** how you can find the circumference of a circle if you know its radius.

▶ **Practice and Problem Solving** REAL WORLD

Find the circumference to the nearest whole number. Use 3.14 or $\frac{22}{7}$ for π.

8.

20 in.

9.

$10\frac{1}{2}$ ft

10.

6.7 mm

11.

4.5 km

12.

6.4 m

13.

$14\frac{1}{4}$ yd

14.

10.52 cm

15.

$62\frac{1}{2}$ in.

16. diameter = 23 yd

17. radius = 40 mm

18. radius = 1.8 m

19. diameter = $4\frac{5}{11}$ mi

Find the diameter to the nearest whole number. Use 3.14 or $\frac{22}{7}$ for π.

20. circumference = 39.25 m

21. circumference = $13\frac{2}{7}$ yd

22. circumference = 19.625 km

23. ☰**FAST FACT** George W. G. Ferris built the first Ferris wheel in 1892. This wheel was 250 ft in diameter. About how far would a person sitting in one of the cars travel in 3 revolutions?

24. [Write Math] ▶ **What's the Error?** Lin said the circumference of a circle with an 11 ft radius was about 35 ft. Find and correct her error.

★ **OCCT Test Prep** Math Board

25. What is the circumference of a circle with a radius of 5.5 mm? Use 3.14 for π.

    A about 17 mm   **C** about 95 mm

    B about 35 mm   **D** about 190 mm

26. A band is being placed around a circular hat with a diameter of 8 inches. Which measure is closest to the length of the band that will go around the hat?

    A 10 inches   **C** 25 inches

    B 15 inches   **D** 50 inches

⬛★ Standards Quick Check

Find the circumference to the nearest whole number. Use 3.14 for π.

1. $10\frac{1}{2}$ yd

2. 2.5 km

3. 8.4 cm

Challenge H.O.T.

Write to Describe an Error

Finding and describing an error in another student's work or in your own work helps you avoid making errors on similar types of problems.

Will and Devon's class is assigned this problem to solve.

Bev's dog Riley has a leash that is 9 ft long. When Riley is outside, his leash is attached to a stake in the ground. To the nearest tenth of a foot, what is the length of the longest circular path that Riley can run when leashed to the stake?

This is Will's solution:

$C = \pi d$
$C \approx 3.14 \times 9$
$C \approx 28.26$

So, the longest circular path is about 28.3 ft.

Devon identified and described Will's error and showed her solution to the problem.

> Will did not understand that the length of the leash represented the radius of the circle, not the diameter. So, he should have used the formula $C = 2\pi r$.
>
> $$C = 2 \times 3.14 \times 9$$
> $$C = 56.52$$
>
> So, the longest circular path is about 56.5 ft.

Find and describe the error that led to the given incorrect solution. Then find the correct answer.

1. The circumference of the center circle on a basketball court is 11.492 m. To the nearest tenth of a meter, what is the radius of the circle? Claire's incorrect solution is about 3.7 m.

2. The diameter of Tamika's circular garden is 12 ft. What is the circumference of Tamika's garden? Jimmy's incorrect solution is about 75.4 ft.

★ **4.1.** Use formulas to find the circumference and area of circles in terms of pi.

Materials
- MathBoard
- calculator
- compass
- construction paper
- graph paper
- scissors

Hands On
Area of Circles

Essential Question What methods can you use to estimate the area of a circle?

▶ **Investigate**

You can use graph paper to help see the relationship between the area of a circle and its radius. This will also help you begin to write a formula for the area of a circle.

1 Draw a circle on graph paper. Make the radius of your circle a whole number.

2 Draw line segments to divide the circle into four equal sections. Shade one of the sections.

3 Estimate the area of $\frac{1}{4}$ of the circle by counting squares and partial squares in the shaded section.

4 Multiply your estimate for the area of $\frac{1}{4}$ of the circle by 4 in order to estimate the area of the entire circle.

5 Divide the estimated area of the circle by the square of the radius, or r^2.

6 Repeat the activity using a different-sized circle.

1. What was your result when you divided the estimated areas of your circles by the square of their radii?

2. Check with another student to see his or her results. Are his or her results close to yours?

3. Did the other student's circles have the same radii as yours? If so, check with another student.

4. **Analysis** What conclusions can you draw?

The relationship between the area and the square of the radius of any circle can be written as the area divided by the square of the radius, or $\frac{A}{r^2}$. The value of the area divided by the square of the radius is the same, or a "constant," for any circle. This constant is pi, or π. In the activity, $\frac{A}{r^2}$ was a little more than 3, or π. Because $\frac{A}{r^2} = \pi$, you get the formula $A = \pi r^2$ by multiplying each side of the equation by r^2. So, $A = \pi r^2$ is a formula for the area of a circle.

▶ **Connect**

Another way to write a formula for the area of a circle is to rearrange cut-up parts of a circle to approximate a parallelogram.

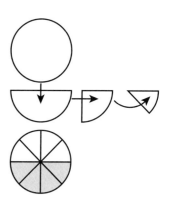

1 Use a compass to construct a circle on a sheet of construction paper.

2 Cut out the circle and fold it three times as shown.

3 Unfold the circle and trace the folds. Shade one half of the circle as shown.

4 Cut along the folds. Fit the pieces together to make a figure that approximates a parallelogram as shown.

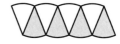

The figure has a height that is equal to the radius of the circle. Recall that a formula for the circumference of a circle is $C = 2\pi r$. The base of the figure is equal to one half the circumference of the circle, or $\frac{1}{2} \times 2\pi r$, or πr.

You can use the formula for the area of a parallelogram to help write a formula for the area of the figure, or a formula for the area of the circle.

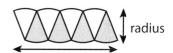

half the circumference

$A = bh$ Write the formula for the area of a parallelogram.
$A = \pi r \times r$ Replace b with πr and h with r.
$A = \pi r^2$ Simplify. ($r \times r = r^2$)

Math Talk

How can you find the area of a circle if you know the radius of the circle?

▶ **Share and Show**

Find the area of a circle with the given radius to the nearest whole number. Use 3.14 for π.

1. $r = 2$ ft   **2.** $r = 4$ m   **3.** $r = 6$ in.   **4.** $r = 8$ mm

5. $r = 9$ cm   **6.** $r = 10$ yd   **7.** $r = 0.5$ m   **8.** $r = \frac{4}{5}$ in.

Find the area of a circle with the given radius to the nearest whole number. Use $\frac{22}{7}$ for π.

9. $r = 14$ in.   **10.** $r = 28$ cm   **11.** $r = 49$ m   **12.** $r = 42$ ft

13. $r = 7$ ft   **14.** $r = 21$ m   **15.** $r = 70$ mm   **16.** $r = 5\frac{8}{11}$ in.

17. Write Math ▶ **Explain** how the area of a circle is related to the radius of the circle squared.

★ **4.1.** Use formulas to find the circumference and area of circles in terms of pi.

Materials
• MathBoard

ALGEBRA:

Area of Circles

Essential Question How do you find the area of a circle if you know the radius and a value for π? How do you find the area of a circle if you know the diameter and π?

PROBLEM The irrigation system on Mr. Martin's farm consists of 10 rotating sprinklers, each of which waters a circular area that has a radius of 9.3 m. What is the area of the plot watered by each sprinkler?

The diameter of a circle is a line segment that passes through the center and has its endpoints on the circle. If you know the radius or diameter of a circle, you can find the area by using the formula $A = \pi r^2$.

Find the area to the nearest whole number. Use 3.14 for π.

$A = \pi r^2$ — Write the formula.
$A \approx 3.14 \times (9.3)^2$ — Replace π with 3.14 and r with 9.3.
$A \approx 3.14 \times 86.49$ — Multiply.
$A \approx 271.5786$

9.3 m

So, the area of the plot watered by each sprinkler is about 272 m².

You can also find the area by using a calculator.

 271.7163486

The result from the calculator is slightly different since it uses more digits as an approximation for π.

A semicircle is one-half of a circle. Because of that, you can use the formula $A = \frac{1}{2}\pi r^2$ to find its area.

Math Idea
Use $\frac{22}{7}$ for π when it can be simplified by using the square of the radius.

Find the area of the semicircle. Use $\frac{22}{7}$ for π.

Divide the diameter by 2 to find the length of the radius.

28 ÷ 2 = 14, or 14 in.

$A = \frac{1}{2}\pi r^2$ — Write the formula.

$A \approx \frac{1}{2} \times \frac{22}{7} \times (14)^2$ — Replace π with $\frac{22}{7}$ and r with 14.

$A \approx \frac{1}{2} \times \frac{22}{7} \times 196$ — Multiply.

$A \approx \frac{1}{\overset{}{2}} \times \frac{\overset{11}{22}}{\overset{}{7}} \times \frac{\overset{28}{196}}{1}$ — Simplify and multiply.

$A \approx 308$

28 in.

So, the area of the semicircle is about 308 in.²

Find the area to the nearest whole number. Use 3.14 or $\frac{22}{7}$ for π.

1.
3 in.

$A = \pi r^2$
$A \approx 3.14 \times (3)^2$
$A \approx$ ▇

2.
16 cm

$A = \pi r^2$
$A \approx 3.14 \times 8^2$
$A \approx$ ▇

3.
7 yd

4.
10 cm

✅ **5.**
10 in.

✅ **6.**
12.2 m

7. Math Talk **Explain** how to find the area of a circle if you know the diameter.

Find the area to the nearest whole number. Use 3.14 or $\frac{22}{7}$ for π.

8.
15 m

9.
21 ft

10.
40 mm

11.
8.6 yd

12.
semicircle
16 cm

13.
$\frac{1}{4}$ circle
2 cm

14.
$\frac{1}{3}$ circle
6 in.

15.
$\frac{2}{3}$ circle
8 ft

16. Write Math ▶ **What's the Error?** Mike said the area of a circle with a radius of 6 cm was about 18.84 cm². Describe his error and find the correct area. Use 3.14 for π.

17. Mrs. Brown also uses rotating sprinklers to water her farm. If a sprinkler that can water a circular plot with a diameter of 15 m is placed in the center of a square plot of land that measures 15 m on a side, how much of the plot will not be watered?

A about 23 m² **C** about 48 m²

B about 38 m² **D** about 54 m²

18. Tammy has a square piece of cardboard that measures 18 in. by 18 in. What is the area of the largest circle she can cut from the piece of cardboard? Round your answer to the nearest whole number.

A about 254 in² **C** about 213 in²

B about 245 in² **D** about 165 in²

★ **4.2.** Convert, add or subtract measurements within the same system (e.g., 9'8" + 3'6", 150 minutes = ___ hours and ___ minutes, 6 square inches = ___ square feet).

Vocabulary

elapsed time

Materials

• MathBoard

Elapsed Time

Essential Question How is finding elapsed time like subtracting mixed numbers?

Learn REAL WORLD

PROBLEM Historic streetcars transport passengers along city streets and the waterfront in Seattle, Washington. Ana and her mother got off a streetcar at 9:45 a.m., shopped, and got back on a streetcar at 2:15 P.M. How much time elapsed while Ana and her mother were shopping?

Elapsed time is the time that passes from the start to the end of an activity or a period. Sometimes it is helpful to estimate the amount of time it will take you to complete a task.

When you know a start time and an end time, you can subtract to find elapsed time.

Subtract to find the exact elapsed time.

1 To subtract A.M. time from P.M. time, rename 2 hr 15 min.

```
  14 hr   15 min
   2 hr   15 min
 − 9 hr   45 min
```

- - - - - - - - - -

2 To subtract 45 min, rename 14 hr 15 min.

```
  13 hr   75 min
  14 hr   15 min
 − 9 hr   45 min
```

- - - - - - - - - -

3 Subtract the minutes.

```
  13 hr   75 min
 − 9 hr   45 min
          30 min
```

- - - - - - - - - -

4 Subtract the hours.

```
  13 hr   75 min
 − 9 hr   45 min
   4 hr   30 min
```

So, 4 hr and 30 min, or $4\frac{1}{2}$ hr, elapsed while Ana and her mother were shopping.

Find the elapsed time.

1. start: 4:20 P.M.   9 hr 50 min
end: 9:50 P.M.   − 4 hr 20 min

2. start: 8:17 A.M.   14 hr 35 min
end: 2:35 P.M.   − 8 hr 17 min

3. start: 6:21 A.M.
end: 7:37 A.M.

✓**4.** start: 8:26 A.M.
end: 11:58 A.M.

5. start: 9:37 A.M.
end: 3:45 P.M.

✓**6.** start: 10:24 A.M.
end: 1:07 P.M.

7. **Math Talk** **Explain** how to find the elapsed time when the start time
is A.M. and the end time is P.M.

► **Practice and Problem Solving** REAL WORLD

Find the elapsed time.

8. start: 9:37 A.M.
end: 10:50 A.M.

9. start: 3:58 P.M.
end: 4:01 P.M.

10. start: 7:21 A.M.
end: 3:55 P.M.

11. start: 8:48 A.M.
end: 11:26 P.M.

Find the end time.

12. start: 7.05 A.M.
work for 2 hr 20 min

13. start: 11:25 A.M.
drive for $2\frac{1}{2}$ hr

14. start: 10:44 A.M.
jog for $\frac{1}{4}$ hr

15. start: 11:43 A.M.
hike for $4\frac{1}{2}$ hr

Real World Data

For 16–18, use the Streetcar Schedule.

16. Carlos missed the streetcar that is scheduled for
a 20-min ride to Jackson Street. What time does
the streetcar depart from the Broad Street Station?

17. Sarah took a streetcar from Broad Street to Jackson Street.
Then she walked for 15 min to the stadium. The game lasted
3 hr and 10 min, ending at 2:47 P.M. What time did the streetcar
depart from Broad Street Station?

Seattle Streetcar Schedule	
Depart Broad Street Station	Arrive Jackson Street Station
7:27 A.M.	7:43 A.M.
11:04 A.M.	11:22 A.M.
12:24 P.M.	12:42 P.M.
6:04 P.M.	6:24 P.M.

18. **Write Math** ▶ Chris says a streetcar ride from Broad Street Station to Jackson Street
takes an average of 18 min. Check Chris' work. Explain how you found the average.

★ **OCCT Test Prep**

19. Marty's baseball game starts at 8:45 A.M. and
ends at 11:31 A.M. How long was Marty's
baseball game?

A 1 hr 42 min   **C** 2 hr 46 min

B 1 hr 58 min   **D** 2 hr 51 min

20. Boris' train leaves Seattle at 7:45 A.M. and
arrives in Everett at 8:37 A.M. How long is
Boris's train ride?

A 52 min   **C** 1 hr 8 min

B 92 min   **D** 1 hr 52 min

LESSON 7

★ 4.2. Convert, add or subtract measurements within the same system (e.g., 9'8" + 3'6", 150 minutes = ___ hours and ___ minutes, 6 square inches = ___ square feet).

Materials
• MathBoard

Square Units of Measure
1 sq ft = 144 sq in.
1 sq yd = 9 sq ft
1 sq mi = 27,878,400 sq ft
1 sq mi = 3,097,600 sq yd

ALGEBRA:

Customary Measurements

Essential Question How do you convert among customary units?

 **Learn** REAL WORLD

PROBLEM Kerrie scored a goal in her soccer game. Kerrie was 33 ft from the goal. How many yards from the goal was she?

To convert from a larger unit to a smaller unit, multiply. To convert from a smaller unit to a larger unit, divide.

Divide to convert to a larger unit.

number of feet	÷	number of feet in 1 yd	=	number of yards
↓		↓		↓
33	÷	3	=	11 yd

So, Kerrie was 11 yd from the goal.

Multiply to convert to a smaller unit.

How many inches from the goal was Kerrie?

number of feet	×	inches in 1 ft	=	number of inches
↓		↓		↓
33	×	12	=	396

So, Kerrie was 399 in. from the goal.

Examples

How many gallons and quarts are equal to 17 quarts?

number of quarts	÷	number of quarts in a gallon	=	number of gallons and quarts
↓		↓		↓
17	÷	4	=	4 gal 1 qt

So, there are 4 gal in qt in 17 quarts.

How many square feet are equal to 120 square yards?

square yards	×	number of sq feet in 1 sq yard	=	square feet
↓		↓		↓
120	×	9	=	1,080

So, there are 1,080 sq ft in 120 sq yd.

336

Share and Show

Convert to the given unit.

1. 4 lb = *x* oz

    4 × ■ = *x* oz

2. 60 in. = *y* ft

    60 ÷ ■ = *y* ft

3. 10 min = *z* sec

✔ **4.** 10 qt = *k* pt

5. 32 oz = *x* lb

✔ **6.** 13 c = *x* pt *y* c

7. [Math Talk] **Explain** how to convert from gallons to quarts and from quarts to gallons.

Practice and Problem Solving REAL WORLD

Convert to the given unit.

8. 3 T = *n* lb

9. 21 ft = *n* yd

10. 260 sec = *x* min *y* sec

11. 8 pt 1 c = *x* qt *y* c

12. 1,350 sq yd = *r* sq ft

13. 3 lb 5 oz = *b* oz

Compare. Write <, >, or = for each ⬭ .

14. 30 oz ⬭ 2 lb

15. 3 min ⬭ 160 sec.

16. 6 pt ⬭ 3 qt

17. 360 min ⬭ 5 hr

18. 6 gal ⬭ 30 qt

19. 19 sq ft ⬭ 2,592 sq in.

Real World Data

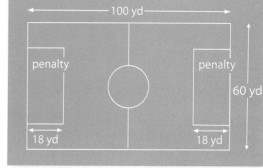

For 20–21, use the diagram at the right.

20. The long side of the town soccer field is next to a road. For safety, the town built a fence along the long side of the field. The fencing comes in 6-ft sections. How many sections were used to build the fence?

21. An American football field is 160 ft wide. Gina claims this is wider than the soccer field shown at the right. Is her claim correct? **Explain**.

22. [Write Math] ▶ The area of the soccer field is 600 sq yd. **Explain** how to calculate the area of the soccer field in square inches.

★ OCCT Test Prep

23. Cleo is $4\frac{1}{2}$ ft tall. What is her height in inches?

  A 1.5 in.   **C** 54 in.

  B 48 in.   **D** 60 in.

24. Cleo rode her bike for 7,392 ft. How many miles did Cleo ride her bike?

  A 0.8 mi   **C** 1.4 mi

  B 1.2 mi   **D** 2.3 mi

4.2. Convert, add or subtract measurements within the same system (e.g., 9'8" + 3'6", 150 minutes = ___ hours and ___ minutes, 6 square inches = ___ square feet).

Materials
• MathBoard

ALGEBRA:
Metric Measurements

Essential Question How do you convert among metric units?

PROBLEM During the 1840s, American pioneers traveled along the Oregon Trail in prairie schooners. Prairie schooners were slow-moving wagons, traveling about 3.2 km per hr. About how many meters did a prairie schooner travel in one hour?

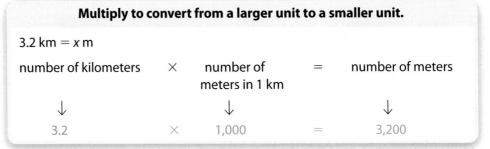

Multiply to convert from a larger unit to a smaller unit.

3.2 km = x m

number of kilometers	×	number of meters in 1 km	=	number of meters
↓		↓		↓
3.2	×	1,000	=	3,200

So, a prairie schooner traveled about 3,200 m in an hour.

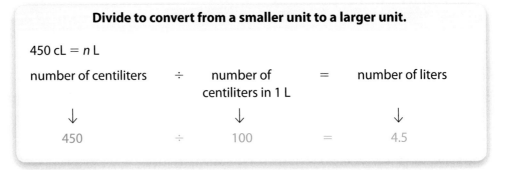

Divide to convert from a smaller unit to a larger unit.

450 cL = n L

number of centiliters	÷	number of centiliters in 1 L	=	number of liters
↓		↓		↓
450	÷	100	=	4.5

So, 450 cL = 4.5 L .

You can see the relationship among metric units to quickly convert among the units. Use the chart.

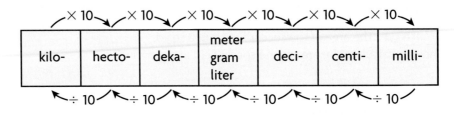

62 g = y kg

62 g = 0.062. kg   Kilograms are 3 places to the left of grams in the chart above. Move the decimal point 3 places to the left. This is the same as dividing by 1,000.

So, 62 g = 0.062 kg.

Convert to the given unit.

1. 25 cm = *b* mm
25 × ▓ = *b* mm

2. 4.3 cL = *y* L
4.3 ÷ ▓ = *y* L

3. 64 dm = *z* m

4. 7.13 g = *n* cg

◆ 5. 5.3 kL = *p* L

◆ 6. 5,000 ml = *n* cL

7. **Explain** the similarities and differences between converting meters to kilometers and converting kilograms to grams.

▶ **Practice and Problem Solving** REAL WORLD

Convert to the given unit.

8. 345 mm = *n* cm

9. 0.6 g = *k* cg

10. 3.5 L = *b* mL

11. 589 dm = *b* m

12. 1,200 km = *x* m

13. 0.75 kg = *z* mg

Compare. Write <, >, or = for each ◯ .

14. 500mL ◯ 50 L

15. 90.2 mm ◯ 9.02 cm

16. 5.6 m ◯ 56 cm

17. 40 g ◯ 4,000 mg

18. 540,000 dL ◯ 54 kL

19. 560 cg ◯ 5,600 dg

 **Real World Data**

For 20–22, use the diagram at the right.

20. A prairie schooner can make sharp turns because the front wheels are smaller than the back wheels. What is the difference in centimeters between the diameters of the wheels?

21. The neck yoke and tongue of a prairie schooner are 406 cm long in all. How does this length compare with the length of the wagon?

22. **Write Math** ▶ **What's the Error?** Erin says the width of the prairie schooner is 0.122 dm. Describe her error. Find the width of the prairie schooner in decimeters.

Tongue
Neck Yoke

front wheel diameter: 1.12 m
back wheel diameter: 1.27 m
wagon width: 1.22 m
wagon length: 3.05 m

 OCCT Test Prep

23. Lin drank 3.5 L of water and Connie drank 3,750 mL of water. How much more did Connie drink than Lin?

   A 3,725 mL more   **C** 250 mL more

   B 2,500 mL more   **D** 2.5 L more

24. How many dm are in 1,500 m?

   A 1,500   **C** 150,000

   B 15,000   **D** 1,500,000

LESSON 9

★ **4.2.** Convert, add or subtract measurements within the same system (e.g., 9'8" + 3'6", 150 minutes = ___ hours and ___ minutes, 6 square inches = ___ square feet).

Materials

- MathBoard
- bag of rice
- balance
- customary and metric measuring cup
- customary and metric ruler
- customary and metric tape measure
- eraser
- small containers
- small notebook
- spring scale

Hands On
Compare Measurements

Essential Question How does an estimate compare to an actual measurement?

▶ **Investigate**

Use what you know about customary and metric units of measure to estimate length, capacity, and weight or mass. Work with a partner.

1 Copy the table.

Measurement					
Object/Description	Type of Measure	Customary (Estimate)	Customary (Measured)	Metric (Estimate)	Metric (Measured)
Pencil	Length	■	■	■	■
Edge of desk	Length	■	■	■	■
1st container	Capacity	■	■	■	■
2nd container	Capacity	■	■	■	■
Eraser	Weight/Mass	■	■	■	■
Small notebook	Weight/Mass	■	■	■	■
Your desk to a wall	Distance	■	■	■	■
Width of your classroom	Distance	■	■	■	■

2 Estimate the measurement in customary units of each object in the table. Record your estimates in the table. Repeat for metric units. Use the following for reference.

A paper clip is about 1 in. long.	A needle is about 1 mm wide.
A slice of bread weighs about 1 oz.	A raisin's mass is about 1 g.
The capacity of a drinking glass is about 1 c.	The capacity of an eyedropper is about 1 mL.

1. Compare your estimates to those of your classmates. Are any of your estimates much greater or much less than your classmates' estimates? **Explain.**

2. Evaluation Which type of measure is easiest to estimate? **Explain.**

▶ **Connect**

Measuring objects.

Now measure each object that is listed in the table. Record the measurements in the table.

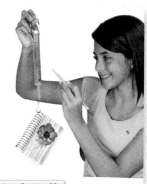

1 Measure length to the nearest sixteenth inch and to the nearest millimeter.

2 Measure capacity to the nearest quarter cup and to the nearest milliliter.

3 Measure weight and mass to the nearest ounce and to the nearest gram.

4 Measure distance to the most appropriate unit.

Math Talk

Explain how making actual measurements could improve your estimating skills.

5 Use <, >, or = to compare the measurements of the two lengths, two capacities, two weights/masses, and two distances. Use <, >, or = to compare your estimates to the actual measurements. Record your findings.

▶ **Share and Show**

Solve.

1. a. Find two objects in your classroom for which you can measure lengths. Estimate the lengths of both objects. Record your estimates.

  b. Measure the lengths of the objects to the nearest sixteenth inch. Record your measurements. What instrument did you use?

  c. Use <, >, or = to compare the two lengths. Then use <, >, or = to compare your estimates to the actual measurements. Record your findings.

2. a. Find two objects in your classroom for which you can measure capacities. Estimate the capacities of both objects. Record your estimates.

  b. Measure the capacities of the objects to the nearest milliliter. Record your measurements. What instrument did you use?

  c. Use <, >, or = to compare the two capacities. Then use <, >, or = to compare your estimates to the actual measurements. Record your findings.

3. a. Find two objects in your classroom for which you can measure weights. Estimate the weights of both objects. Record your estimates. What instrument did you use?

  b. Measure the weights of the objects to the nearest ounce. Record your measurements.

  c. Use <, >, or = to compare the two weights. Then use <, >, or = to compare your estimates to the actual measurements. Record your findings.

4. Write Math ▶ Describe a situation where you might use an estimate that is greater than the exact measurement instead of an estimate that is less than the actual measurement.

4.2. Convert, add or subtract measurements within the same system (e.g., 9′8″ + 3′6″, 150 minutes = ___ hours and ___ minutes, 6 square inches = ___ square feet).

Materials
• MathBoard

Problem Solving Workshop
Strategy: Compare Strategies

Essential Question How do models and tables differ?

> **UNLOCK the Problem** REAL WORLD

PROBLEM Pablo is making one pitcher of Aunt Maria's fruit punch for seven people. He mixes 2 pt of cranberry juice and 3 qt of orange juice. Does he have enough for each person to have 2 c of punch?

Read the Problem

What do I need to find?

I need to find if Pablo has enough of Aunt Maria's fruit punch for each person to have 2 cups of punch.

What information do I need to use?

I know that Pablo has 2 pints of cranberry juice and 3 quarts of orange juice and that each person will need 2 cups of punch.

How will I use the information?

I will make a model and a table to see if there is enough punch for everyone to have 2 cups.

Solve the Problem

Make a Model

Use counters to model the total number of cups in one pitcher of fruit punch.

Cranberry Juice 1 pt = 2 c

2 pt = 4 c

Orange Juice 1 qt = 2 pt and 1 pt = 2 c, so 1 qt = 4 c

3 qt = 12 c

Add: 4 c + 12 c = 16 c

Make a Table

Show the relationship among the units.

Cranberry Juice		
Pints	1	2
Cups	2	4

Orange Juice			
Quarts	1	2	3
Pints	2	4	6
Cups	4	8	12

So, 2 pt of cranberry juice makes 4 c, and 3 qt of orange juice makes 12 c.

Add: 4 c + 12 c = 16 c

So, Pablo has enough fruit punch for everyone to have 2 c.

► **Share and Show**

Choose a Strategy

- Draw a Diagram
- Predict and Test
- Make a Model or Act It Out
- Make an Organized List
- Find a Pattern
- Make a Table or Graph
- Work Backward
- Solve a Simpler Problem
- Write an Equation
- Use Logical Reasoning

Predict and test or draw a diagram to solve.

1. Laura wants to make 1-c strawberry fruit plates for 35 party guests. She has four 2-qt packages of strawberries. Does she have enough to make a 1-c strawberry fruit plate for each guest?

   First, find the total number of quarts Laura has.

   $$4 \times 2 \text{ qt} = 8 \text{ qt}$$

   Then, make a table.

   Strawberries

Quarts	1	2	3	4	5	6	7	8
Pints	2	4	6	8	10	12	14	16
Cups	4	8	12	16	20	24	28	32

   Finally, compare the total cups of strawberries that Laura has with the number of 1-c fruit plates that are needed.

   $$(460 - 10) \div 5$$

2. **What if** Laura used four 2-qt packages and two 1-pt packages of strawberries? Would she have enough to make a 1-c strawberry fruit plate for each guest?

3. Julio needs four streamers to use for decorations. He uses a tape measure to cut three streamers that have lengths of 7 ft, 10 ft, and 12 ft. He also needs a streamer with a length of 15 ft. Julio's tape measure is only 12 ft long. How can he use the first three streamers to measure a length of 15 ft?

► **On Your Own**

For 4–5, use the information from the advertisement.

4. It takes about 720 peanuts to make 1 lb of peanut butter. About how many peanuts were used to make the $2.19 jar of peanut butter?

5. **Reasoning** Alvin bought a total of 4 lb 8 oz of peanut butter. What combination of jars did he buy to get the best deal?

6. Janice is making sandwiches on white, wheat, and rye bread with either crunchy or creamy peanut butter. Each sandwich is topped with sliced banana, honey, or granola. How many different types of sandwiches can Janice make?

7. **Write Math** Both Jim and Tamika have savings accounts. Tamika has saved $35 more than 4 times what Jim has saved. Together they have saved a total of $535. How much has Jim saved? **Explain** how to use the problem solving strategy *predict and test* to solve this problem.

⭐ Extra Practice

Set A

Find the unknown angle measure. (pp. 320–323)

1.

2.

3.

4. A circle has central angles that measure 41°, 107°, 155°, and *n*. Find *n*.

5. A circle has a radius of 24.9 cm. What is the diameter of the circle?

6. A circle has a diameter of 24.9 cm. What is the radius of the circle?

Set B

Find the circumference to the nearest whole number.
Use 3.14 or $\frac{22}{7}$ for π. (pp. 326–329)

1.

2.

3.

4.

5. radius = 9.7 in.

6. diameter = $8\frac{1}{4}$ ft

7. radius = 25 cm

8. diameter = 250 m

9. In her backyard, Jessica has a circular pool with a diameter of 15 ft. How many linear feet of bricks does she need to line the edge of the pool?

10. For their state testing, students must run around a circle with a 4 m radius five times. What is the total distance that the students must run?

Find the diameter to the nearest whole number.
Use 3.14 or $\frac{22}{7}$ for π.

11. circumference = 67.51 m

12. circumference = 44 ft

13. circumference = 392.5 cm

Set C

Find the area to the nearest whole number. Use 3.14 or $\frac{22}{7}$ for π. (pp. 332–333)

1.

2.

3.

4.

5.

semicircle

6.

$\frac{3}{4}$ circle

7.

$\frac{2}{3}$ circle

8.

$\frac{2}{5}$ circle

9. What is the area of a circular tabletop with a radius of 40 inches?

10. A circular dartboard has a diameter of 50 cm. What is the area of the dartboard?

Technology
Use HMH Mega Math, Ice Station Exploration, *Arctic Algebra*, Level CC.

Set D

Find the elapsed time. (pp. 334–335)

1. start: 2:15 A.M.
end: 4:39 A.M.

2. start: 1:57 P.M.
end: 9:05 P.M.

3. start: 11:10 P.M.
end: 3:52 A.M.

4. start: 6:43 A.M.
end: 12:30 P.M.

5. A baseball game began at 7:31 P.M. and lasted 2 hr and 47 min. What time did the game end?

6. A train leaves the 5th Street station at 4:48 P.M. and arrives at the 101st Street station $1\frac{1}{4}$ hr later. What time does it arrive?

Set E

Find the unknown length. (pp. 336–337)

1. 15 ft = b in.

2. 21 ft = n yd

3. 480 min = x hr

4. 4 lb 8 oz = b oz

5. 3 pt 1 c = m c

6. 780 sec = p min

7. 21 gal 3 qt = a qt

8. 200 oz = s lb r oz

9. A homemade sailboat is 120 in. long. is the length of the sailboat in feet?

10. The sail of the homemade sailboat uses approximately 42 square yards of canvas. How many square feet would this be?

Compare. Write <, >, or = for each .

11. 48 ft ⬭ 17 yd

12. 24 hr ⬭ 1,380 min

13. 19c ⬭ 9 pt 1 c

14. 3,500 lb ⬭ 7 T

Set F

Convert to the given unit. (pp. 338-339)

1. 215 mm = n cm

2. 0.9 m = a cm

3. 12 dg = y mg

4. 8.2 L = b mL

5. 71 g = x kg

6. 10.1 cL = n L

7. 8 km = t cm

8. 240 mg = h g

9. A full box of cake mix is 517 g. What is the weight of the full box of cake mix in centigrams?

10. A container holds 2 L. What is the capacity of the container in kiloliters?

Compare. Write <, >, or = for each ⬭.

11. 300 g ⬭ 30 kg

12. 8.1 mm ⬭ 810 cm

13. 4 kL ⬭ 400 L

14. 0.7 dm ⬭ 70 mm

Vocabulary

Use an information wheel to organize ideas related to a vocabulary term such as circle.

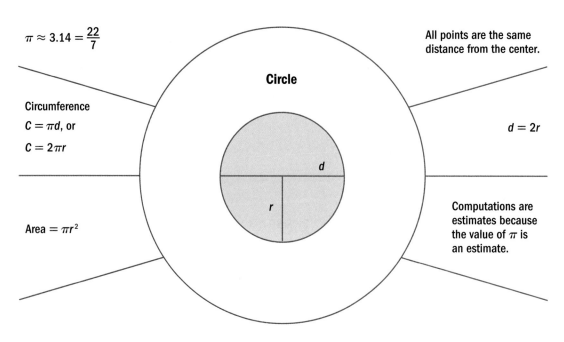

$\pi \approx 3.14 = \frac{22}{7}$

All points are the same distance from the center.

Circle

Circumference

$C = \pi d$, or

$C = 2\pi r$

$d = 2r$

d

r

Area $= \pi r^2$

Computations are estimates because the value of π is an estimate.

Writing

1. Describe how the circumference of a circle is like the perimeter of a polygon.

2. If you drew a circle on grid paper, how could you estimate its area by counting?

3. When you use the formula for the area of a circle, explain why it is important to remember the order of operations.

Reading Check out *Sir Cumference and the Dragon of Pi* by Cindy Neuschwander in your library

H.O.T. Multistep Problems

1 The gravitational pull of the moon and the sun cause the high and low tides of the oceans on earth. Because the moon is closer to the earth, its gravitational pull has more than twice the effect of the pull of the sun on the tides. In most places, two high tides and two low tides occur in a 24 hour and 50 minute period. The table below shows the times of high tides for 5 days at a beach. Use the table to answer the questions. ▬4.2.

- How much time is there between high tides each day?

- How much time is there between high tides from one day to the next (Sunday evening to Monday morning, for example)?

- Is the amount of time between high tides each day always the same?

- About what times would you predict for high tides on Friday of this same week?

2 The Museum of Anthropology at the University of California, Berkeley, was founded in 1901 by Phoebe Apperson Hearst. Visitors to the Hearst Museum can learn about the people of the world through artifacts from nearly all geographical regoins and cultures throughtout history. The museum has a large collection of ancient Greek coins, pottery, and art. ▬4.2.

- In about 600 B.C., the people of Athens, Greece, began producing silver coins weighing approximately 0.15 ounces each. About how many pounds would a bag of 1,000 silver coins weigh?

- The Parthenon in Athens is the most famous surviving building of ancient Greece. Construction records of the Parthenon show that some of the stones were brought from Pentelicus, which is more than 9 miles away. Suppose the stones were moved at a rate of 30 feet per minute. About how many hours would it take to carry the stones from Pentelicus to Athens? **Explain**.

- Write a word problem that can be solved using the information on this page. Solve the problem.

Practice for the OCCT

1 The Astrodome in Houston, Texas, is circular and has a diameter of 710 feet. What is its approximate circumference? ◄ 4.1.

  A about 1,110 ft

  B about 2,230 ft

  C about 4,460 ft

  D about 15,600 ft

2 Which equation could be used to find the area A, in square centimeters, of a circle with a diameter of 10 centimeters? ◄ 4.1.

  A $A = 5 \times \pi$

  B $A = 5^2 \times \pi$

  C $A = 10 \times \pi$

  D $A = 10^2 \times \pi$

3 A baseball player may stand in the on-deck circle while waiting for a turn at bat. The circle has a radius of 2.5 feet. What is the area of the circle? ◄ 4.1.

  A about 6.3 ft^2

  B about 15.7 ft^2

  C about 19.6 ft^2

  D about 78.5 ft^2

4 Mario had baseball practice from 3:45 P.M. until 5:12 P.M. How long was Mario's baseball practice? ◄ 4.2.

  A 1 hour 17 minutes

  B 1 hour 27 minutes

  C 2 hours 17 minutes

  D 2 hours 27 minuts

5 A penny has a diameter of 19.05 millimeters. What is the area of one side of the penny? ◄ 4.1.

  A 19.05π mm^2

  B 38.1π mm^2

  C 90.7π mm^2

  D 362.9π mm^2

6 Nancy practiced the clafinet for 47 minutes. If Nancy ended her practice at 1:10 P.M., at which time did Nancy start practicing? ◄ 4.2.

  A 12:23 P.M.

  B 12:23 A.M.

  C 11:33 P.M.

  D 11:33 A.M.

7 Which of the following is a measure greater than 2 meters? ◄ 4.2.

  A 0.2 kilometer

  B 2,000 millimeters

  C 20 decimeters

  D 20 centimeters

8 The number π represents the relationship between the circumference of a circle and its diameter. Which method could you use to find π? ◄ 4.1.

  A Divide the circumference by the diameter, and then divide by 2.

  B Divide the circumference by the diameter.

  C Multiply the circumference by the diameter, and then divide by 2.

  D Multiply the circumference by the diameter.

9 The radius of a circle is 40 feet. Which equation can be used to find the circumference C? 🔲 4.1.

A $C = 20 \times \pi$

B $C = 40 \times \pi$

C $C = 402 \times \pi$

D $C = 2 \times 40 \times \pi$

10 A circles diameter is 24 in. Which is the radius of the circle? 🔲 4.2.

A 6 in.

B 12 in.

C 36 in.

D 48 in.

11 Melinda needs to know how long it was going to take her to get to her aunt's house. Her aunt said that if she left at 7:30 A.M., Melinda would be able to get to her aunt's house at 1:15 P.M. How long will it take Melinda to get to her aunt's house? 🔲 4.2

A 4 hours 25 minutes

B 4 hours 55 minutes

C 5 hours 35 minutes

D 5 hours 45 minutes

12 Mario is $4\frac{3}{4}$ feet tall. What is his height in inches? 🔲 4.2.

A 4.3 inches

B 43 inches

C 48 inches

D 57 inches

Problem Solving

13 Adam purchased fertilizer for his rose bushed. The directions say to use half a cup for a 9 square foot region. How much is needed for 27ft^2? 🔲 4.2.

14 Ming has 400 mL of pineapple juice and 600 mL of apple juice. Does she have enough for a drink recipe that calls for 1 L of juice? 🔲 4.2.

15 **Explain** how to find the area of a circle if you know its circumference. 🔲 4.1.

16 To block off a street 20 yd across, a construction worker is using 3 ropes, each of which is 16 ft long. Does he have enough rope for the job? 🔲 4.2.

17 Explain how to find the elapsed time from 4:35 P.M. to 9:05 P.M. 🔲 4.2.

Performance Assessment

Writing Math Describe the difference between intersecting lines and perpendicular lines.

The Lake Pontchartrain Causeway

Lake Pontchartrain is the largest lake in Louisiana. The bridge above Lake Pontchartrain, named the Lake Pontchartrain Causeway, is about 24 miles long, making it the world's longest bridge over water. The Causeway actually consists of two bridges, also called spans. One span is for northbound traffic and the other is for southbound traffic. The spans are connected by seven "crossovers" which allow drivers moving in each direction to change direction.

For 1-4, use the drawing below, which shows a small section of the Lake Pontchartrain Causeway including two of its crossovers.

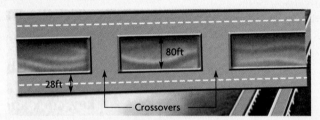

1. Describe the relationship between the two spans of the Causeway as parallel, perpendicular, intersecting, or skew.

2. Describe the relationship between a crossover and each span.

3. What types of angles are shown in the drawing?

4. Each span of the Lake Pontchartrain Causeway is 28 feet wide, and the spans are 80 feet apart. What is the total width of the Causeway?

5. Measurements taken at the north end of the Lake Pontchartrain show that the water level has been rising about 0.45 cm per year since 1931. By about how much did the water level rise from 1950 to 2000?

6. **Write About It** Find a photo of a bridge in your state. Identify and describe any lines, angles, and other plane figures that you see in the photo.

Unit Learning Task

Famous Buildings

Objective: To identify, describe, and classify solid figures.

1. Make a list of some famous buildings.

2. What building are you going to research? Prepare a presentation about the building.

3. What are the dimensions of the building you selected?

4. What solid figures do you see in the building you researched?

5. Select two other buildings. Compare and contrast these building with your building.

6. What can you use the dimensions of the building to find?

Quite a Hike!

Hiking the Appalachian Trail

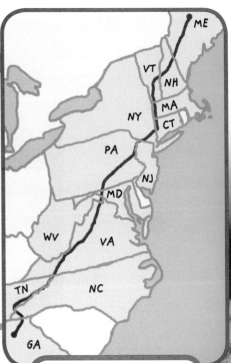

The Appalachian Trail

The United States Appalachian Trail runs approximately 2,174 mi from Springer Mountain in Georgia to Mount Katahdin in Maine. Each year, people from all over the United States come to hike the trail.

About 9,000 people have reported hiking the entire length of the Appalachian Trail. Some of these people hike the trail from beginning to end without stopping, but most hike parts of the trail at different times.

FACT · ACTIVITY

Keiko and her hiking club plan to hike the trail one state at a time. Keiko made a table to help her calculate some of the distances.

Appalachian Trail Distances				
State	Miles	Yards	Feet	Footsteps
Maryland	41	▪	▪	▪
Pennsylvania	229	▪	▪	▪
Massachusetts	90	▪	▪	▪
Vermont	150	▪	▪	▪
West Virginia	4	▪	▪	▪
Tennessee	293	▪	▪	▪

1 Keiko wants to find about how many footsteps she will take on the trail. She calculated that one of her footsteps is about 2 ft long. Copy and complete her table.

2 Someday Keiko hopes to walk the entire U.S. Appalachian Trail. About how many inches should she expect to walk in all?

3 **Write Math** ▸ **Explain** how you found the number of footsteps for each distance in Problem 1.

The International Trail

The first Saturday in June is the American Hiking Society's National Trails Day. Across the country, people get together to clean up and improve trails and learn more about the outdoors.

Although the U.S. Appalachian Trail ends at Mount Katahdin in Maine, that is not the end of the entire trail. Beginning at Mount Katahdin and crossing the border into Canada is the International Appalachian Trail. The total length of the International Appalachian Trail is 1,079 km.

FACT·ACTIVITY

Canada and many other countries use metric units such as meters and kilometers to measure distance. The United States uses customary units such as yards and miles.

Use the conversion chart to solve.

1 About how long is the International Appalachian Trail in miles? in meters? in yards?

2 **Write Math** ▶ Compare your answers for meters and yards. What does this tell you about the relationship between meters and yards?

3 Plan a hiking trip along the Appalachian Trails. Use the chart, the maps, and an atlas for help.

▶ Where will you begin and end your trip? How many miles will you hike in all?

▶ How many stops will you make? Where will you stop? For how many days will you hike?

▶ What is the average distance you will hike each day? Find the answer in meters or yards.

▶ How many steps will you take on your trip?

Quebec

New Brunswick

Maine

Appalacian Trail
International Appalacian Trail

Exact conversion: 1 km = 1,000 m

Approximate conversion: 1 mi ≈ 1.6 km

Unit 5

Ratio, Proportion, Percent, Data, and Probability

BIG IDEAS!

- A ratio is a comparison of part to whole, part to part, or whole to part; a proportion expresses an equivalent relationship between two ratios; percents can be expressed as fractions and decimals.

- Data can be collected in various formats and analyzed; data can be analyzed and displayed in various graphical formats.

- Probability measures the likelihood of simple and compound events and provides the basis for making predictions.

Math On Location
Online Videos

1

Ratios and statistics are used to understand the target market of a product before work on a commercial begins.

2

Storyboards that define the actors movements, expressions, and messages are drawn before filming begins.

3

When background, acting, voice, and music are combined, the specifications of message, time, and cost are reviewed.

Get Ready Game

Rapid Ratios

Materials
- One deck of number cards
- One deck of ratio cards

How to Play Play in pairs. Shuffle the number cards and deal three cards to each player. Place the rest of the cards face down in a pile. Turn over the top card and place it face up to form the discard pile. Place five ratio cards face up. Players take turns using these steps.

1 **Draw** the top card from either the face down pile or the discard pile. Decide whether you can use two of your cards to form a ratio that is equivalent to one of the face up ratios. If you can, place that ratio card and your pair of number cards face up in front of you.

2 **Finish** your turn by either drawing a card or discarding a card, so you have exactly three number cards in your hand again.

How to Win Be the first player to form three pairs of equivalent ratios.

Draw Conclusions
Complete these exercises after playing the game.

1. **WRITING** Explain how you decided which cards to discard at the end of your turn.

2. **REASONING** Based on playing the game, is it easier to form $\frac{8}{9}$ or $\frac{1}{2}$ during the game? Explain your reasoning.

Reading
You use strategies to help you in reading. You also use strategies to help you solve word problems.

In this unit you will solve problems involving fractions, decimals, and percents. You can use strategies to help you solve problems in this unit.

Read this problem:

Andrew rode his bike $2\frac{3}{10}$ miles to get to Ernie's Game Store.

His friend Xavier rode 2.25 miles. Who rode farther?

Before he solves the problem, Juan writes down problem-solving strategies that he knows.

Hmmm. I need to compare $2\frac{3}{10}$ with 2.25.

Problem Solving Strategies

Write an expression.

Work backward.

Use a simpler problem.

Draw a picture or diagram.

Use a model.

Writing
Copy the strategies Juan wrote down and add other strategies you know. Then use one of the strategies to solve the problem.

Ratio, Proportion, and Percent

Fun Fact

At a recent auction, a Beach Bomb, a 1:64-scale model of a Volkswagen van that has surfboards loaded in the rear, sold for $72,000.

Investigate

Choose a length from 8 in. to 12 in. for the total length of a scale model of the luxury sedan. Using the same scale, show the proportions you would solve to find the scale model length of three of the other cars. Then find the length of each model.

Vehicle Lengths	
Type of Vehicle	**Actual Length (in.)**
Mini sports car	143
Economy 2-door	160
Luxury convertible	175
Sport-utility vehicle	189
Luxury sedan, 4-door	222
Extended-cab truck, 4-door	231

Technology
Student pages are available in the Student eBook.

Show What You Know

Check your understanding of important skills needed for success in Chapter 10.

▶ Relate Decimals and Percents

Write the corresponding decimal or percent.

1. 0.12	**2.** 4%	**3.** 0.992	**4.** 30%	**5.** 15%
6. 62%	**7.** 0.333	**8.** 56%	**9.** 0.125	**10.** 0.11
11. 0.4	**12.** 98%	**13.** 0.68	**14.** 55%	**15.** 7%

▶ Write Decimals as Fractions

Write each decimal as a fraction.

16. 0.125	**17.** 0.25	**18.** 0.6	**19.** 0.4	**20.** 0.75
21. 0.45	**22.** 0.625	**23.** 0.12	**24.** 0.95	**25.** 0.06
26. 0.01	**27.** 0.05	**28.** 0.65	**29.** 0.42	**30.** 0.98

Vocabulary

Visualize It!

sixty-eight percent

Model	Percent	Fraction
	68%	$\frac{68}{100}$

Language Tips

Words that look alike in English and Spanish often have the same meaning.

English	Spanish
proportion	proporción
scale drawing	dibujo a escala

See English-Spanish Glossary.

LESSON 1

⭐ **2.1.** Convert compare, and order decimals, fractions, and percents using a variety of methods.

Vocabulary

equivalent ratio

rate

unit rate

Materials
• MathBoard

Ratios and Rates

Essential Question How do you use unit rates to solve problems?

PROBLEM A ruby-throated hummingbird is very small. A model of a ruby-throated hummingbird is in a conservatory display. The ratio of the size of the actual hummingbird to the model is 1 to 12. This means that each measure of the actual bird is 1 __ 12 as long as the corresponding measure of the model. Write this ratio in three ways.

A ratio is a comparison of two numbers. A ratio can be written in three ways.

using words	as a fraction	with a colon
1 to 12	$\dfrac{1}{12}$ ← first term / ← second term	1:12

Ratio Comparisons
Ratios can compare two amounts: a part to a part, a part to the whole, or the whole to a part.

Example

During the 2006 Great Backyard Bird Count, there were 5 ruby-throated hummingbirds spotted in Georgia and 9 spotted in Louisiana. Write the following ratios.

a. Georgia birds to Louisiana birds → $\dfrac{5}{9}$ part to part

b. Georgia birds to total number of birds → $\dfrac{5}{14}$ part to whole

c. total number of birds to Louisiana birds → $\dfrac{14}{9}$ whole to part

Equivalent ratios are ratios that name the same comparison. You can find equivalent ratios by multiplying both terms by the same number or dividing both terms by a common factor.

Write two equivalent ratios for $\frac{2}{4}$.

Divide.	**Multiply.**
$\dfrac{2 \div 2}{4 \div 2} = \dfrac{1}{2}$	$\dfrac{2 \times 3}{4 \times 3} = \dfrac{6}{12}$

So, $\dfrac{1}{2}$ and $\dfrac{6}{12}$ are equivalent ratios.

360

Rate and Unit Rate

A **rate** is a ratio that compares two quantities that have different units of measure.

$$\frac{\text{price} \rightarrow}{\text{weight} \rightarrow} \frac{\$12.70}{2 \text{ lb}}, \$12.70 \text{ for } 2 \text{ lb}$$

A **unit rate** is a rate that has a second term of 1.

$$\frac{\$12.70}{2} = \frac{\$12.70 \div 2}{2 \div 2} = \frac{\$6.35}{1}, \$6.35 \text{ per lb}$$

Write the ratio in fraction form. Then find the unit rate.

Certain hummingbirds can beat their wings 420 times every 6 sec.

① Write a ratio that compares beats to seconds.

rate: $\dfrac{\text{beats} \rightarrow}{\text{seconds} \rightarrow} \dfrac{420}{6}$

② Divide both terms by the second term

unit rate: $\dfrac{420 \div 6}{6 \div 6} = \dfrac{70}{1}$

So, certain hummingbirds beat their wings at a unit rate of 70 beats per sec.

You can use unit rates to make comparisons.

Compare unit rates.

During migration, a hummingbird can fly 210 mi in 7 hr, and a goose can fly 165 mi in 3 hr. Which bird flies at a faster rate?

① Write the rates for both birds.

hummingbird: $\dfrac{\text{miles} \rightarrow}{\text{hours} \rightarrow} \dfrac{210}{7}$

goose: $\dfrac{\text{miles} \rightarrow}{\text{hours} \rightarrow} \dfrac{165}{3}$

② Divide both terms by the second term

hummingbird: $\dfrac{210 \div 7}{7 \div 7} = \dfrac{30}{1}$

goose: $\dfrac{165 \div 3}{3 \div 3} = \dfrac{55}{1}$

③ Compare the unit rates.

$$\frac{30 \text{ mi}}{1 \text{ hr}} < \frac{55 \text{ mi}}{1 \text{ hr}}$$

55 mi per hr is faster than 30 mi per hr.

So, the goose flies at a faster rate.

• What if a goose flew 160 mi in 4 hr? Would the goose still fly at a faster rate?

Share and Show

1. Write the ratio of the number of stars to the number of stripes on the American flag. $\frac{\blacksquare}{13}$

2. Write the ratio of the number of stripes to stars on the American flag. $\frac{13}{\blacksquare}$

Write two equivalent ratios for each fraction.

3. $\frac{8}{16}$ 4. $\frac{4}{24}$ 5. $\frac{1}{3}$ ✓ 6. $\frac{3}{4}$

Write a ratio in fraction form. Then find the unit rate.

7. 16 servings for 8 people   8. 280 calories in 4 hr   9. $20.88 for 9 gal

10. 45 volunteers for 15 booths   11. 54 revolutions in 12 min   ✓ 12. $32.20 for 7 lb

13. **Math Talk** Explain the difference between a ratio and a rate.

Write two equivalent ratios for each fraction.

14. $\frac{15}{35}$ **15.** $\frac{16}{40}$ **16.** $\frac{8}{12}$ **17.** $\frac{22}{20}$ **18.** $\frac{3}{5}$ **19.** $\frac{2}{9}$

20. $\frac{5}{7}$ **21.** $\frac{4}{11}$ **22.** $\frac{5}{12}$ **23.** $\frac{9}{8}$ **24.** $\frac{6}{27}$ **25.** $\frac{2}{13}$

Write a ratio in fraction form. Then find the unit rate.

26. 288 pages in 12 days   **27.** 72 mi on 4 gal   **28.** $14.28 for 4 tickets

29. 108 items in 12 boxes   **30.** 112 students for 14 teachers   **31.** 90 cards in 6 packs

Determine whether the ratios are equivalent.

32. $\frac{6 \text{ in.}}{9 \text{ in.}}$ and $\frac{12 \text{ in.}}{18 \text{ in.}}$ **33.** $\frac{8 \text{ cm}}{10 \text{ cm}}$ and $\frac{6 \text{ cm}}{10 \text{ cm}}$ **34.** $\frac{16 \text{ ft}}{60 \text{ ft}}$ and $\frac{4 \text{ ft}}{15 \text{ ft}}$ **35.** $\frac{3 \text{ mi}}{14 \text{ mi}}$ and $\frac{9 \text{ mi}}{28 \text{ mi}}$

 **Algebra** **Find the missing term, *m*, that makes the ratios equivalent.**

36. 5 to 3; *m* to 9   **37.** 3:10; 21:*m*   **38.** $\frac{5}{m}, \frac{15}{21}$ **39.** 3:8; *m*:32

For 40–42, use the birdhouse at the right.

40. Write the ratio of *AB* to *BC*. Then write three equivalent ratios.

41. Write the ratio of the shortest length of the side of the triangle to the perimeter of the triangle. Then write three equivalent ratios.

42. Write the ratio of the perimeter of the triangle to the longest side of the triangle. Then write three equivalent ratios.

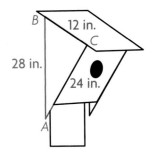

Real World Data

For 43–44, use the table.

43. Ryan wants to buy treats for the birds he feeds each day. He wants to buy either Honey Nut Sticks or Nutri-Biscuits. If Ryan wants to buy the treat that costs less per pack, which treat should he buy?

44. Which is the better buy per pack, the Fruit Bites or the Veggie Treats?

Cost of Bird Treats		
Name	Cost	Number of Packs
Fruit Bites	$5.76	4
Veggie Treats	$7.38	6
Honey Nut Sticks	$7.86	6
Nutri-Biscuits	$9.44	8

45. **Write Math** ▶ **What's the Question?** A veterinarian records a hummingbird's resting heart rate at 2,500 beats over a period of 10 min. The answer is 250 beats per minute.

★ OCCT Test Prep   Math Board

46. There are usually 2 boys for every 3 girls in a school drama club. If 21 girls sign up for drama club this year, how many boys would you expect to sign up?

     A 21   **C** 14

     B 18   **D** 12

47. A 32-oz box of cereal costs $3.84. Which is the unit rate for the box of cereal?

     A $3.84 for 32 oz   **C** $1.92 for 16 oz

     B $0.24 for 1 oz   **D** $0.12 for 1 oz

★ Standards Quick Check

Write two equivalent ratios for each fraction.

1. $\frac{7}{15}$

2. $\frac{24}{30}$

3. $\frac{10}{6}$

Write a ratio in fraction form. Then find the unit rate.

4. 390 mi in 6.5 hr

5. 1800° in 5 revolutions

6. $179.80 for 20 lb

H.O.T.

Economists use ratios and rates to study price increases and decreases. You can express an increase or decrease as a rate of change.

Using the table of costs recorded by the Consumer Price Index, what was the rate of change in the average cost of electricity from 2000 to 2005?

Average Cost of Products

	2000	2005
Electricity	$46.25	$52.97
Gas	$35.58	$55.42
Bread	$0.93	$1.04
Bananas	$0.50	$0.49

Find the rate of change per year.

$52.97 − $46.25 = $6.72   Find the change in price from 2000 to 2005.

2005 − 2000 = 5 yr   Subtract the years to find the change in time.

$\frac{price}{years} \rightarrow \frac{\$6.72}{5} = \frac{\$6.72 \div 5}{5 \div 5} \xrightarrow{round} \frac{\$1.344}{1} \approx \frac{\$1.34}{1\ yr}$ Write a ratio of the change in price to the change in price. Use this rate to find a unit rate.

So, the rate of change in the average cost of electricity from 2000 to 2005 was about $1.34 per yr.

For 1–3, use the table. Find the rate of change per year.

1. Gas

2. Bread

3. Bananas

★ **2.1.** Convert compare, and order decimals, fractions, and percents using a variety of methods. *also* **1.4.**

Materials
• MathBoard

ALGEBRA:
Write and Solve Proportions

Essential Question What ways can you solve proportion problems?

▶ **Learn** REAL WORLD

PROBLEM When the temperature is warm, the Anderson family likes to take rides on the family boat. The boat uses 2 gal of gasoline to travel 12 mi on a lake. How many gallons will the boat use if the Andersons travel 18 mi?

Write a proportion. Let *g* represent the unknown number of gallons.

$$\frac{\text{gallons used}}{\text{distance}} \rightarrow \frac{2}{12} = \frac{g}{18} \leftarrow \frac{\text{gallons}}{\text{distance}}$$

Solve the proportion by using cross products or equivalent fractions.

Use cross products and check.

$\frac{2}{12} = \frac{g}{18}$ Find the cross products.

$2 \times 18 = 12 \times g$ Multiply.

$36 = 12g$

$\frac{36}{12} = \frac{12g}{12}$ Divide.

$3 = g$

$\frac{2}{12} = \frac{g}{18}$ Check your solution.

$\frac{2}{12} \overset{?}{=} \frac{3}{18}$ Replace *g* with 3.

Find the cross products.

$2 \times 18 \overset{?}{=} 12 \times 3$ Multiply.

$36 = 36$ The solution

Remember

A proportion is an equation that shows two equivalent ratios.

So, the boat will use 3 gal if the Andersons travel 18 mi.

• Is your answer reasonable? Explain.

Use equivalent fractions.

When solving a proportion, you can also use a common denominator to form equivalent fractions.

$\frac{3}{4} = \frac{n}{8}$ Find a common denominator.

$\frac{3 \times 2}{4 \times 2} = \frac{n}{8}$

$\frac{6}{8} = \frac{n}{8}$ The denominators are the same, so the numerators are equal to each other.

$n = 6$

$\frac{3}{4} = \frac{n}{8}$ Check your solution.

$\frac{3}{4} \overset{?}{=} \frac{6}{8}$ Replace *n* with 6. Find the cross products.

$3 \times 8 \overset{?}{=} 4 \times 6$ Multiply.

$24 = 24$ The solution checks.

So, *n* = 6.

Convert Units of Measure

You can use proportions to convert units of measure.

Example

Felicia and Irma stand 5 yd apart on a dock, about to jump in a lake.

How many feet apart are the girls?

$$\frac{\text{yards} \to 1}{\text{feet} \to 3} = \frac{5}{x} \frac{\leftarrow \text{yards}}{\leftarrow \text{feet}}$$

Write a proportion using the conversion 1 yd = 3 ft. Let x represent the number of feet apart Felicia and Irma are standing.

$$\frac{1}{3} = \frac{5}{x}$$

Find the cross products.

$$1 \times x = 3 \times 5$$

Multiply.

$$x = 15$$

$$\frac{1}{3} = \frac{5}{x}$$

Check your solution.

$$\frac{1}{3} \overset{?}{=} \frac{5}{15}$$

Replace x with 15.
Find the cross products.

$$1 \times 15 \overset{?}{=} 3 \times 5$$

Multiply.

$$15 = 15$$

The solution checks.

So, Felicia and Irma are 15 ft apart.

▶ **Share and Show**

Solve the proportion.

1. $\frac{a}{10} = \frac{4}{8}$

$a \times 8 = 10 \times 4$

$8a = 40$

$\frac{8a}{8} = \frac{40}{8}$

$a = $ ▨

2. $\frac{6}{8} = \frac{a}{20}$ THINK: The LCM of 8 and 20 is 40.

$\frac{6 \times 5}{8 \times 5} = \frac{a \times 2}{20 \times 2}$

$\frac{30}{40} = \frac{2a}{40}$

$30 = 2a$

▨ $= a$

Solve the proportion.

3. $\frac{3}{6} = \frac{x}{4}$

4. $\frac{4}{5} = \frac{8}{b}$

5. $\frac{w}{7} = \frac{8}{14}$

6. $\frac{3}{15} = \frac{5}{c}$

✅ **7.** $\frac{6}{12} = \frac{g}{16}$

Use a proportion to convert to the given unit.

8. 3 ft = x in.

9. 15 cm = x mm

10. 12 ft = x yd

✅ **11.** 6 m = x cm

12. **Math Talk** Explain how to solve a proportion by using cross products.

Solve the proportion.

13. $\frac{2}{6} = \frac{z}{30}$

14. $\frac{5}{10} = \frac{55}{n}$

15. $\frac{k}{6} = \frac{25}{10}$

16. $\frac{d}{27} = \frac{3}{9}$

17. $\frac{v}{18} = \frac{7}{21}$

18. $\frac{16}{24} = \frac{w}{6}$

19. $\frac{18}{15} = \frac{6}{t}$

20. $\frac{6}{b} = \frac{36}{27}$

21. $\frac{14}{d} = \frac{6.25}{9}$

22. $\frac{40}{12.5} = \frac{8}{k}$

Use two of the given ratios to write a proportion.

23. $\frac{4}{8}, \frac{8}{16}, \frac{14}{8}$

24. $\frac{5}{9}, \frac{6}{15}, \frac{8}{20}$

25. $\frac{2}{12}, \frac{4}{16}, \frac{3}{18}$

26. $\frac{10}{14}, \frac{12}{15}, \frac{15}{21}$

27. $\frac{10}{16}, \frac{15}{24}, \frac{25}{32}$

Write a proportion and solve.

28. It takes 8 min for Wes to water-ski 2 laps around the lake. How many laps can he complete in 20 min?

29. Miriam and Vera spent a day out on a sailboat that is 22 ft long. What is the length of this boat in inches?

 **Real World Data**

For 31–32, use the table and the diagram.

30. At the family cookout, the Patels pass out T-shirts. Look at the ratio of length to width for each size. For which two sizes can you write a proportion?

31. Uncle David needs an extra-large T-shirt so that the ratio of length to width is the same as it is for the medium T-shirt. If his shirt is 40 in. long, how wide is it?

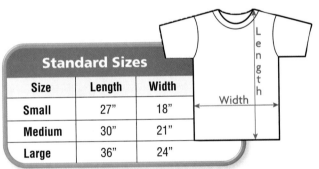

Standard Sizes		
Size	Length	Width
Small	27"	18"
Medium	30"	21"
Large	36"	24"

32. Jay is making rectangular buttons to pin on the T-shirts. He is making the buttons so the ratio of length to width is the same as that for the medium T-shirt. If the button has a length of 3 in., how wide is it?

33. **Write Math** ▶ **What's the Error?** Greg used these steps to solve a proportion. Describe his error and give the correct solution.

$$\frac{2}{6} = \frac{y}{9}$$
$$2y = 54$$
$$y = 27$$

 OCCT Test Prep Math Board

34. A speedboat can travel 24 mi on 3 gal of gas. How many miles could it travel on 5 gal of gas?

   A 30 mi   **C** 50 mi

   B 40 mi   **D** 60 mi

35. The mass of an egg is 58 g. Which proportion could be used to find the mass of this egg in milligrams?

   A $\frac{1}{1,000} = \frac{m}{58}$ **C** $\frac{1}{1,000} = \frac{58}{m}$

   B $\frac{58}{1,000} = \frac{1}{m}$ **D** $\frac{1,000}{58} = \frac{1}{m}$

★ Standards Quick Check

Solve the proportion.

1. $\frac{7}{10} = \frac{21}{x}$

2. $\frac{k}{5} = \frac{12}{30}$

3. $\frac{3}{11} = \frac{m}{33}$

4. $\frac{48}{x} = \frac{16}{5}$

5. $\frac{3}{18} = \frac{5}{x}$

6. $\frac{15}{20} = \frac{9}{x}$

Challenge H.O.T.

Unit Rates

A family is traveling from Lexington, Kentucky, to Chicago, Illinois. On the first day, the family drives 390 mi in 6 hr. Find the unit rate.

You can use a proportion to find the unit rate, or the distance the family is traveling each hour.

Use a proportion to find the unit rate.

$\frac{\text{miles}}{\text{hours}} \rightarrow \frac{390}{6} = \frac{m}{1}$ Write a proportion. The second term of the second ratio is 1 since you are finding a unit rate.

$\frac{390}{6} = \frac{m}{1}$ Find the cross products.

$390 \times 1 = 6 \times m$ Multiply.

$390 = 6m$

$\frac{390}{6} = \frac{6m}{6}$ Divide.

$65 = m$

So, the unit rate is $\frac{65\,\text{mi}}{1\,\text{hr}}$, or 65 mi per hr.

Use a proportion to find the unit rate.

1. 128 km in 8 hr

2. $4 for 10 apples

3. 144 students for 6 teachers

4. Randy and his family go to the town carnival. Tickets for the rides are $10 for 25 tickets. Explain how you can use the unit rate of the tickets to determine the cost of a ride that requires 5 tickets.

LESSON 3

2.1. Convert compare, and order decimals, fractions, and percents using a variety of methods.

3.2. Compare and contrast congruent and similar figures.

Materials
• MathBoard

ALGEBRA:
Ratios and Similar Figures

Essential Question How can you determine if two figures are similar?

 **Learn**

Some common objects, like wrenches, are similar. That is, they have the same shape. The corresponding angles and corresponding sides of similar geometric figures have special relationships.

Triangles *ABC* and *XYZ* are similar. Their corresponding angles and sides are listed below:

Corresponding Angles	Corresponding Sides
$\angle A$ and $\angle X$	$\overline{AB}$ and $\overline{XY}$
$\angle B$ and $\angle Y$	$\overline{BC}$ and $\overline{YZ}$
$\angle C$ and $\angle Z$	$\overline{CA}$ and $\overline{ZX}$

Example

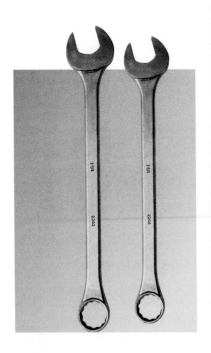

HJKL and VWXY are similar. Find the measures of $\angle V$, $\angle W$, $\angle X$, and $\angle Y$. Then find the ratio of the lengths of the corresponding sides.

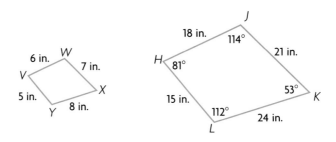

Corresponding angles are equal.

$m\angle H = m\angle V = 81°$ $m\angle J = m\angle W = 114°$

$m\angle K = m\angle X = 53°$ $m\angle L = m\angle Y = 112°$

$\dfrac{HJ}{VW} = \dfrac{18}{6} = \dfrac{3}{1}$ $\dfrac{JK}{WX} = \dfrac{21}{7} = \dfrac{3}{1}$

$\dfrac{KL}{XY} = \dfrac{24}{8} = \dfrac{3}{1}$ $\dfrac{LH}{YV} = \dfrac{15}{5} = \dfrac{3}{1}$

So, the ratio of the lengths of the corresponding sides is 3 to 1.

Polygons with four or more sides are similar only if their corresponding angles are congruent *and* the ratios of the lengths of their corresponding sides are equal.

Triangles are similar if their corresponding angles are congruent *or* if the ratios of the lengths of their corresponding sides are equal.

Tell whether *ABCD* is similar to *JKLM*.

Since these are quadrilaterals, check the measures of the corresponding angles and the ratio of the corresponding sides.

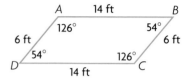

$m\angle A = m\angle J = 126°$ $m\angle B = m\angle K = 54°$

$m\angle C = m\angle L = 126°$ $m\angle D = m\angle M = 54°$

The corresponding angles are congruent.

$\dfrac{AB}{JK} = \dfrac{14}{7} = \dfrac{2}{1}$ $\dfrac{BC}{KL} = \dfrac{6}{3} = \dfrac{2}{1}$ $\dfrac{DC}{ML} = \dfrac{14}{7} = \dfrac{2}{1}$ $\dfrac{AD}{JM} = \dfrac{6}{3} = \dfrac{2}{1}$

The corresponding sides have the same ratio.

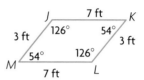

So, *ABCD* is similar to *JKLM*.

Tell if △*EFG* is similar to △*BCD*.

Since these are triangles, check either the measures of the corresponding angles or the ratios of the corresponding sides.

$m\angle E = 72°$ $m\angle B = 72°$

$m\angle F = 67°$ $m\angle C = 67°$

$m\angle G = 41°$ $m\angle D = 41°$

The corresponding angles are congruent.

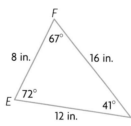
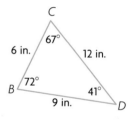

So, △*EFG* is similar to △*BCD*.

► **Share and Show**

1. △*GHJ* and △*MNP* are similar. Find the measures of $\angle M$, $\angle N$, and $\angle P$. Write the ratio of the lengths of the corresponding sides in simplest form.

   $m\angle G = m\angle M = 46°$ $\dfrac{GH}{MN} = \dfrac{14}{28} = \dfrac{1}{2}$

   $m\angle H = m\angle N = \blacksquare$

   $m\angle J = m\angle P = \blacksquare$ $\dfrac{HJ}{NP} = \dfrac{15}{30} = \dfrac{\blacksquare}{\blacksquare}$ $\dfrac{JG}{PM} = \dfrac{21}{42} = \dfrac{\blacksquare}{\blacksquare}$

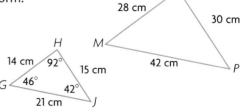

Tell whether the two figures are similar. Explain why or why not.

2.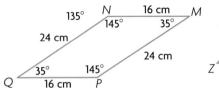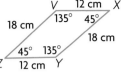

3.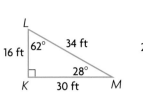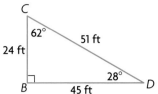

4. Math Talk **Explain** how to use ratios to tell whether two triangles are similar.

Practice and Problem Solving REAL WORLD

Tell whether the two figures are similar. Explain why or why not.

5.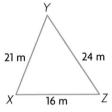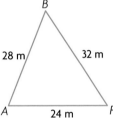

6.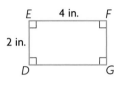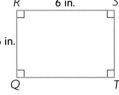

7.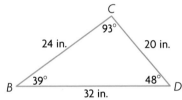

8.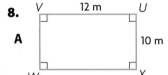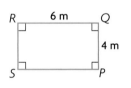

The figures in each pair are similar. Find the unknown measures.

9.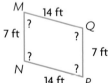

10.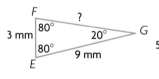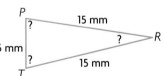

11. △*HJK* has side lengths of 24 m, 32 m, and 36 m. △*NMP* is similar to △*HJK*. Which could be the side lengths of △*NMP*?

   A 6 m, 8 m, 10 m   **C** 20 m, 24 m, 30 m

   B 8 m, 40 m, 45 m   **D** 36 m, 48 m, 54 m

12. The rectangles are similar. Which is the unknown length?

   A 12 ft   **C** 72 ft

   B 24 ft   **D** 96 ft

⬟★ Standards Quick Check

Tell whether the two figures are similar. Explain why or why not.

1.

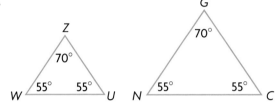

2.

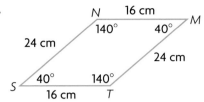

Challenge H.O.T.

Drawing Similar Figures

You can use grid paper to draw similar figures.

Rectangle *ABCD* is similar to rectangle *EFGH*. The ratio of the lengths of corresponding sides is $\frac{1}{2}$.

Since the ratio of the lengths of the corresponding sides is $\frac{1}{2}$, the sides of *EFGH* are drawn twice as long as the sides of *ABCD*.

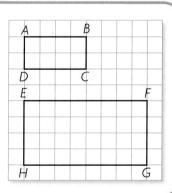

Use grid paper to draw the figures.

1. Draw rectangle *PQRS* with length 10 and width 6.
Draw rectangle *WXYZ* similar to *PQRS*. Use a ratio of $\frac{2}{1}$.

2. Draw rectangle *MNOP* with length 9 and width 6.
Draw rectangle *EFGH* similar to *MNOP*. Use a ratio of $\frac{1}{3}$.

★ **1.2.** Write algebraic expressions and simple equations that correspond to a given situation.

1.4. Write and solve one-step equations with one variable using number sense, the properties or operations, and the properties of inequalities (e.g., 1/3x + 9).

3.2. Compare and contrast congruent and similar figures.

Materials
• MathBoard

Problem Solving Workshop
Strategy: Write an Equation

Essential Question What kinds of equations can be used to solve problems?

Learn the Strategy REAL WORLD

Writing an equation can help you organize the information in a problem. You can use different kinds of equations to represent a variety of situations.

You can write a proportion.

Three magnesium atoms have a total of 36 electrons. A group of magnesium atoms has 84 electrons. How many magnesium atoms are there in the group?

$$\frac{3}{36} = \frac{n}{84}$$

You can write a one-step equation.

The ushers at the Saturday night show seated 354 people. This is 48 more people than the ushers seated at the Friday night show. How many people attended the Friday night show?

$$48 + f = 354$$

Math Talk

Tell what the variable represents in each equation.

You can write a multistep equation.

Four friends purchase 8 packs of bagel chips for $3.00 a pack and 12 containers of cream cheese for $2.00 a container. They decide to divide the total cost evenly among themselves. How much does each friend pay?

$$C = \frac{8 \times 3 + 12 \times 2}{4}$$

To write an equation, choose a variable to represent the unknown quantity. Then translate the words and numbers into an equation.

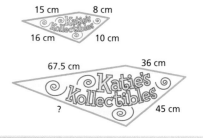

UNLOCK the Problem — REAL WORLD

PROBLEM Katie is starting her own business. She has a logo that she has enlarged so that the enlarged logo is similar to the original logo. Find the measurement of the longest side of the enlarged logo.

Read the Problem

What do I need to find?

I need to find the measure of the longest side of the enlarged logo.

What information do I need to use?

I know that the two logos are similar to each other. I need to use the ratio of the corresponding sides to determine the missing length.

How will I use the information?

I can write an equation to help me solve the problem.

Solve the Problem

Recall that in similar figures, the lengths of corresponding sides have the same ratio. Find the ratio of the corresponding side lengths. Choose a variable to represent the unknown measurement.

$$\frac{\text{shortest side of logo} \rightarrow}{\text{shortest side of enlargment} \rightarrow} = \frac{8}{36}$$

$$\frac{\text{longest side of logo} \rightarrow}{\text{longest side of enlargement} \rightarrow} = \frac{16}{s}$$

$\frac{8}{36} = \frac{16}{s}$ Write a proportion. Find the cross products.

$8 \times s = 36 \times 16$ Multiply.

$\frac{8s}{8} = \frac{76}{8}$ Divide.

$s = 72$

So, the measurement of the longest side of the enlarged logo is 72 cm.

---

1. Jonas decides to redecorate his coffee shop. He plans to paint one large shape on each wall to add variety and color to his sitting room. He sketches a small triangle that he will enlarge for the back wall of the room. Find the unknown measure of the enlarged triangle shown at the right.

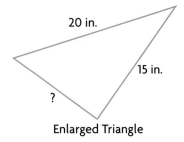

20 in.

15 in.

8 in.

6 in.

4 in.

Sketch

?

Enlarged Triangle

First, find equivalent ratios. Write a proportion.

$$\frac{\text{sketched side} \rightarrow 8}{\text{enlarged side} \rightarrow 20} = \frac{4}{s}$$

Then, find the cross products.

$8 \times s = 20 \times 4$

Finally solve the proportion.

2. **What if** the longest side of the enlarged triangle was 160 in.? What would be the length of the shortest side?

3. Beverly owns a frame shop. While framing a diploma, she notes that the frame and the diploma are similar. If the diploma has a length of 12 in. and a width of 10 in. and the length of the frame is 18 in., what is the width of the frame?

Write an equation to solve.

4. Raymond works as a part-time cashier at a rate of $8.00 per hour. If he makes $52.00 for each shift, how long is one of Raymond's shifts?

5. Evelyn looks at a monthly sales report. She wants to buy 55 more bath sets for November than she sold in October, so she buys 135 bath sets. How many bath sets did Evelyn sell in October?

110 mm

125 mm

6. Pete distributes a certain number of packages of note cards evenly among display hooks. If there are 16 packages on each of 8 hooks, how many packages are there in all?

7. Gabrielle decides to reduce the price of a $350 desk. The discounted price is $275. What is the amount of the discount?

8. Tom's company makes small plastic items. A new request comes in for small puzzles that can be attached to a keychain. He takes the design of a handheld puzzle and reduces its width as shown at the right. What is the height of the new puzzle in the diagram?

50 mm

9. Bob's discount store can fit 10 figurines on a 5-ft-long shelf. How many figurines can the store fit on a shelf that is 66 in. long?

10. **Write Math** ▶ **Explain** what type of problems can be solved by using a proportion.

Real World Data

For 11–14, use the diagram.

11. Suppose the area of square *A* is 4 sq. in. If the area of square *A* is one-ninth the area of square *D*, what is the length of one side of square *D*?

12. Amy is drawing a design with squares the same size as square *B*. She begins with 1 square in the first row, 3 squares in the second, 5 squares in the third, and continues this pattern for a total of 6 rows. Square A has an area of 4 sq. in., which is $\frac{9}{4}$ the area of square *B*. What is the total area of Amy's 6-row design?

13. Use the following clues to find the areas and perimeters of squares *C* and *E*.

    • The area of square *A* is 4 sq. in.
    • The perimeter of square *C* is twice the perimeter of square *A*.
    • The area of square *E* is nine-sixteenths the area of square *C*.

14. **Pose a Problem** Look back at Problem 12. Write a similar problem by changing the area of square A and the number of rows in Amy's design.

15. **Open-Ended** On one piece of graph paper, draw 5 different-sized rectangles. Label all sides and heights of each rectangle. Write 5 different problems using the rectangles. Make sure that the problems take at least two steps to solve. Two of the problems should involve two or more rectangles.

Choose a Strategy

• Write an Equation
• Draw a Diagram or Picture
• Make a Model or Act It Out
• Make an Organized List
• Find a Pattern
• Make a Table or Graph
• Predict and Test
• Work Backward
• Solve a Simpler Problem
• Use Logical Reasoning

 PROBLEM

Claude is drawing rows of two similar rectangles. For each row, he alternates between the two rectangles, and he leaves no space between them. The first rectangle is 12 mm high and 24 mm wide.

16. The ratio of the width of Claude's second rectangle to that of the first is $\frac{3}{4}$, and he is drawing his design on a piece of paper 23 cm wide. If he continues to alternate between the two rectangles, how many rectangles can he draw in each row?

17. Claude changes the width and the height of the second rectangle, keeping it similar to the first. The height is now 15 mm. Claude draws 8 rectangles per row. He mounts his design on a piece of construction paper 4 cm wider than the design itself. How wide is the piece of construction paper?

LESSON 5

★ **2.1.** Convert compare, and order decimals, fractions, and percents using a variety of methods.

3.2. Compare and contrast congruent and similar figures. *also* **1.2.**

Vocabulary

scale

scale drawing

Materials
• MathBoard
• inch graph paper
• tape

ALGEBRA:

Scale Drawings

Essential Question How can you use proportions to make scale drawings?

▶ Learn

Floor plans and maps are examples of scale drawings. A **scale drawing** is a drawing that is either smaller than (a reduction of) or larger than (an enlargement of) the real object it represents. The measurements on a scale drawing are proportional to the measurements of the real object.

Suppose Kelsey wants to design a floor plan for a rectangular terrarium where she will keep her pet mouse. The terrarium will have a length of 9 in. and a width of 6 in. The floor plan is to be a scale drawing of the terrarium.

Scale drawing.

1 On graph paper, make a scale drawing with measurements that are two-thirds of those of the bottom of the terrarium.

2 Write the ratio of the length of your scale drawing to the length of the terrarium.

3 Write the ratio of the width of your scale drawing to the width of the terrarium.

• Are the two ratios equal? Is your drawing similar to the bottom of the terrarium? Explain.

Make a scale drawing.

1 Tape 4 sheets of graph paper together in a 2-by-2 array.

2 Make a drawing with measurements that are twice those of the bottom of the terrarium.

3 Write the ratio of the length of your drawing to the length of the terrarium.

4 Write the ratio of the width of your drawing to the width of the terrarium.

• Are the ratios equal? Is your drawing similar to the width of the terrarium? Explain.

Scale

The ratio of two sets of measurements is called a scale. You can use a **scale** to find the unknown measurements of an actual object or a scale drawing of it. The drawing at the right is a scale drawing of a ladybug.

Scale
2cm=3mm

Find the length of the actual ladybug.

Measure the length of the scale drawing in centimeters.

$\dfrac{\text{drawing (cm)}}{\text{actual (mm)}} \rightarrow \dfrac{2}{3} = \dfrac{4}{b}$ Write a proportion. Let b represent the actual length of the ladybug.

$2 \times b = 3 \times 4$ Find the cross products and solve.

$2b = 12$

$b = 6$

So, the actual ladybug has a length of 6 mm.

A map is another kind of scale drawing. You can use a map to find the actual straight-line distance between two locations.

Example

Use the New Jersey map to find the actual straight-line distance between Toms River and Atlantic City.

Use a ruler to measure the straight-line distance on the map from Toms River to Atlantic City.

$$\text{map distance} \rightarrow 1\tfrac{3}{4} \text{ in., or } 1.75 \text{ in.}$$

$\dfrac{\text{drawing (in.)}}{\text{actual (mi)}} \rightarrow \dfrac{1}{24} = \dfrac{1.75}{d}$ Write a proportion. Let d represent the actual distance.

$1 \times d = 24 \times 1.75$ Find the cross products and solve.

$d = 42$

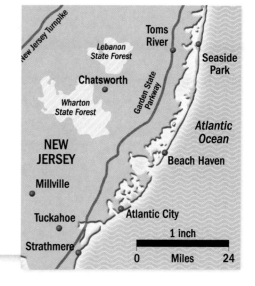

So, it is 42 mi from Toms River to Atlantic City.

- Is the map a reduction or an enlargement?

- Why do you need to measure the distance on the map before you write the proportion?

Find the straight-line distance between the cities.

Atlantic City to Chatsworth	Millville to Beach Haven
$\dfrac{1}{24} = \dfrac{1.25}{d}$	$\dfrac{1}{24} = \dfrac{1.5}{d}$
$1 \times d = 24 \times 1.25$	$1 \times d = 24 \times 1.5$
$d = 30$	$d = 36$
So, it is 30 mi from Atlantic City to Chatsworth.	So, it is 36 mi from Millville to Beach Haven.

Share and Show

Math Board

Find the unknown measurement. Include the unit.

1. scale: 3 cm = 1 cm
drawing length : 6 cm
actual length: ▨

$$\frac{\text{drawing (cm)}}{\text{actual (cm)}} \rightarrow \frac{3}{1} = \frac{6}{l}$$

2. scale: 4 cm = 6 ft
drawing length: ▨
actual length: 9 ft

✓ **3.** map scale: 4 cm = 15 m
drawing length: ▨
actual length: 37.5 m

✓ **4.** map scale: 3 in. = 82 yd
distance on map: 10.5 in.
actual length: ▨

5. **Math Talk** **Explain** how you can make a scale drawing of an object if you know the object's dimensions.

Practice and Problem Solving REAL WORLD

Find the unknown measurement. Include the unit.

6. scale: 6 cm = 18 m
drawing length: 15 cm
actual length: ▨

7. scale: 2 in. = 11 yd
drawing length: ▨
actual length: 27.5 yd

8. map scale: 8 mm = 24 km
measured distance: 35 mm
actual distance: ▨

9. scale: 2 ft = 21 in.
drawing length: ▨
actual length: 63 in.

10. map scale: 15 mm = 48 m
measured length: 72 mm
actual length: ▨

11. map scale: 1 in. = 52 mi
measured length: 1.75 in.
actual length: ▨

 Real World Data

For 12–14, use the map of Illinois. The scale is 1 cm = 50 mi.

12. Find the straight-line distance from Decatur to Chicago.

13. Find the straight-line distance from Decatur to Springfield.

14. A teacher decides to take his students on a field trip to a city in Illinois that is about 130 mi away. If the school is located in Carbondale, which city might be the destination?

 OCCT Test Prep

Math Board

15. Pamela uses a scale of 4 in. = 9 ft to draw a diagram of her backyard. The yard is 49.5 ft wide. How wide will the backyard be in her drawing?

A 22 in.
B 36 in.
C 49.5 in
D 99 in.

16. A tourist map with a scale of 1 cm = 4 km shows a theme park located 7 cm from a petting zoo. How far apart are the theme park and the petting zoo?

A 1.75 km
B 11 km
C 28 km
D 42 km

378 **Extra Practice** See page 398, Set D.

★ Standards Quick Check

Find the unknown measurement. Include the unit.

1. scale: 2 in. = 15 mi

drawing length: 13 in.

actual length: ▓

2. scale: 5 mm = 10 m

drawing length: ▓

actual length: 5 m

3. scale: 3 in. = 75 ft

drawing length: 7 in.

actual length: ▓

Challenge H.O.T.

When you learn about ancient civilizations, your social studies teacher might provide you with a map that shows the locations of various cities.

Find the actual distance between Athmonum and Araphen.

Use a ruler to measure the distance from Athmonum to Araphen. The map distance is 3.2 cm.

$\frac{cm}{mi} \rightarrow \frac{1}{3.3} = \frac{3.2}{d}$

The scale on the map is 1 cm = 3.3 mi. Write a proportion. Let d represent the actual distance.

$1 \times d = 3.2 \times 3.3$

$d = 10.56$

Find the cross products and solve.

So, it was 10.6 mi from Athmonum to Araphen.

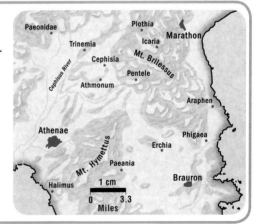

Find the actual distance between the two cities.

1. Trinemia to Plothia

2. Paeania to Phigaea

3. Paeonidae to Pentele

★ 2.1. Convert compare, and order decimals, fractions, and percents using a variety of methods.

Materials
• MathBoard

Proportional Reasoning

Essential Question How can you set up proportions to solve problems?

PROBLEM It takes Mr. Adams 45 min to pick 1 bushel of strawberries. He tells Mrs. Adams he plans to pick 2 bushels. Mrs. Adams expects that he will return within 75 min. Is her expectation reasonable?

Instead of solving proportions, you can sometimes use proportional reasoning to solve problems.

Determine the reasonableness of the solution.

Make a table that relates the time spent picking strawberries to the number of bushels.

Time	Bushels
45 min	1
90 min	2

Think: Since the number of bushels doubles, the time picking strawberries should also double.

So, Mrs. Adams' expectation is not reasonable because it does not allow Mr. Adams enough time to pick 2 bushels.

• Would Mrs. Adams' expectation be reasonable if it took Mr. Adams 30 min to pick 1 bushel of strawberries? Explain.

Example

If 18 marigolds cost $7.38, find the cost of 42 marigolds.

Make a table to organize the information. THINK: How can I get from 18 to 42?

Multiply

Marigolds	Cost
18	$7.38
36	$14.76
6	$2.46
42	$17.22

Think: Multiply by 2 to get the cost of 36 marigolds. Then because 36 + 6 = 42, divide the cost of 36 by 6 to get the cost of 6 marigolds. Add the cost of 36 marigolds to the cost of 6 marigolds.

Divide

Marigolds	Cost
18	$7.38
6	$2.46
42	$17.22

Think: $18 \div 3 = 6$ and $6 \times 7 = 42$, so divide the cost of 18 marigolds by 3 and multiply the result by 7.

So, the cost of 42 marigolds is $17.22.

Share and Show

Sidney's Earnings	
Time	Earnings
2 hr	$12.50
6 hr	

1. Find how much Sidney earns in 6 hr.

Use proportional reasoning to solve.

2. For $4, you can buy 6 tickets. How many tickets can you buy with $10?

3. Mrs. Bell grades 12 tests in 15 min. How long will it take her to grade 28 tests?

4. You spend $3.14 for 5 apples. How much will 20 apples cost?

5. **Math Talk** **Explain** how you could use proportional reasoning to determine whether the price for 36 eggs is reasonable if you know that 18 eggs cost $3.12.

Practice and Problem Solving REAL WORLD

Use proportional reasoning to solve.

6. Ken runs 2 mi in 16 min. At that rate, how far could he run in 40 min?

7. You buy 24 seed packs for $5.04. How much would 9 seed packs cost?

8. Dave walks 472 yd in 4 min. How long will it take him to walk 1,652 yds?

9. Garden space rents for $48 for $1\frac{1}{2}$ months. How much can a customer expect to pay for $\frac{1}{2}$ month?

10. The Meyers' grass grows 0.25 in. in 2 days. At this rate, how much does it grow in 3 days?

11. Maurice can read 50 pages of his book in 55 min. If he reads 33 pages, how long will it take him?

12. **Reasoning** On Thursday, a produce stand sells 8 peaches for $1.12. Over the weekend, this sign at the right is placed next to the peaches. Is this an increase or a decrease in the price of the peaches? **Explain.**

Produce Market
PRICE CHANGE
$2.12 for 12 peaches

13. Mr. Matthews is planning his garden for this year. He knows that he can grow 270 peanut plants in 6 rows. This year he will grow 15 rows of peanut plants. How many peanut plants can Mr. Matthews expect to grow in all?

14. **Write Math** Compare and contrast proportional reasoning with writing and solving a proportion.

OCCT Test Prep

15. Marty walks 5,280 feet in 10 minutes. How far will Marty walk in 25 minutes?

    A 1,120 ft   **C** 12,500 ft

    B 7,570 ft   **D** 13,200 ft

16. Warren needs a special spice for his restaurant. In the past, he ordered 5 lb of the spice for $55. How much would it cost Warren to order 12 lb of the spice?

    A $75   **C** $132

    B $98   **D** $254

LESSON 7

★ **2.1.** Convert compare, and order decimals, fractions, and percents using a variety of methods. *also* **2.2.c.**

Materials
• MathBoard

Percent

Essential Question What methods can you use to compare and order percents?

PROBLEM Sean has designed a mosaic wall mural. Twenty-five of the 100 tiles are blue. Write this relationship as a percent.

The ratio 25 out of 100 can be expressed as a percent. A percent is the ratio of a number to 100. Percent, %, means "per hundred."

$$\frac{\text{blue tiles}}{100} \rightarrow \frac{25}{100} = 25\%$$

So, 25% of Sean's mural is blue.

A percent can be between 0% and 100% or greater than 100%.

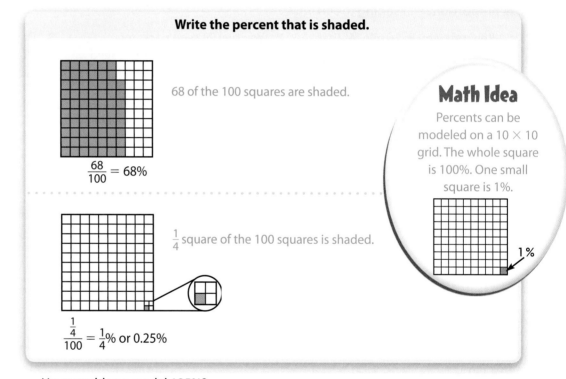

Write the percent that is shaded.

68 of the 100 squares are shaded.

$$\frac{68}{100} = 68\%$$

$\frac{1}{4}$ square of the 100 squares is shaded.

$$\frac{\frac{1}{4}}{100} = \frac{1}{4}\% \text{ or } 0.25\%$$

Math Idea

Percents can be modeled on a 10 × 10 grid. The whole square is 100%. One small square is 1%.

1 %

• How would you model 125%?

Ordering percents

Order 0.2%, 40%, 6%, and 300% from least to greatest.

Compare every possible pair of percents.

0.2% < 40%	0.2% < 6%	0.2% < 300%
40% > 6%	40% < 300%	6% < 300%

So, from least to greatest, the percents are 0.2%, 6%, 40%, and 300%.

► **Share and Show**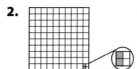

Write the percent that is shaded.

1. $26 \text{ out of } 100 = \frac{26}{100} = \blacksquare$

2. 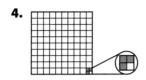 $\frac{1}{2}$ square of the 100 squares

$$\frac{\frac{1}{2}}{100} = \blacksquare$$

3.

4.

✓**5.**

✓**6.**

7. [Math Talk] **Explain** how $\frac{39}{100}$ can be written as a percent.

► **Practice and Problem Solving** REAL WORLD

Write the percent that is shaded.

8.

9.

10.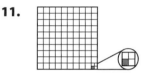

11.

Order from least to greatest.

12. 14%, 16%, 11%, 13%

13. 16%, 25%, 21%, 20%

14. 0.5%, 50%, 5%, 55%

15. 37%, 3.7%, 77%, 0.37%

16. 0.4%, 140%, 14%, 4.3%

17. 217%, 0.72%, 72%, 17%

For 18–20, use the mural.

18. Kendra used 100 tiles to design the mural shown. What percent of the mural is white?

19. Compare the percent of the mural that is red to the percent that is yellow. Use $<$, $>$, or $=$.

20. [Write Math] ► What must all the percents of the various colors of tile total? **Explain**.

★ **OCCT Test Prep** [Math Board]

21. Which is the percent that is shaded?

A 0.6%   **C** 16%

B 6%   **D** 60%

22. Which is the percent that is shaded?

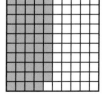

A 0.49%   **C** 49%

B 4.9%   **D** 490%

★ **2.1.** Convert compare, and order decimals, fractions, and percents using a variety of methods. *also* **2.2.c.**

Materials
• MathBoard

Percent, Decimals, and Fractions

Essential Question How do you write a value as a fraction, decimal, and percent?

PROBLEM In a survey of sixth graders in an after-school theater program, $\frac{3}{5}$ of the students said they attend a theater class and $\frac{5}{8}$ said they attend a dance class. What percent of students surveyed attend a theater class? What percent attend a dance class?

Examples

Write $\frac{3}{5}$ as an equivalent fraction with a denominator of 100.

$$\frac{3}{5} = \frac{3 \times 20}{5 \times 20} = \frac{60}{100}$$

Write an equivalent fraction with a denominator of 100.

$$= 60\%$$

Since percent is the ratio of a number to 100, write the ratio as a percent.

> **Remember**
>
> When you multiply decimal numbers by powers of 10, you move the decimal point one place to the right for each factor of 10.

Use division to write $\frac{5}{8}$ as a decimal.

$$8)\overline{5.000} \quad \begin{array}{c} 0.625 \end{array}$$

Divide the numerator, 5, by the denominator, 8.

$0.625 = 62.5\%$ Multiply by 100 by moving the decimal point two places to the right.

So, 60% of students are enrolled in a theater class and 62.5% in a dance class.

Write 0.7 as a percent. Use place value.

$$0.7 = \frac{7}{10}$$

Use place value to express the decimal as a ratio in fraction form.

$$= \frac{7 \times 10}{10 \times 10} = \frac{70}{100}$$

Write an equivalent fraction with a denominator of 100.

$$= 70\%$$

Since percent is the ratio of a number to 100, write the ratio as a percent.

Write 0.7 as a percent. Multiply by 100.

$0.7 = 0.70$ Multiply by 100 by moving the decimal point two places to the right.

$= 70\%$ Add a percent sign.

Percents to Fractions and Decimals

Examples

About 35% of the students in acting signed up for voice and speech during the next session. Write 35% as a fraction.

$35\% = \dfrac{35}{100}$ Write the percent as a fraction with a denominator of 100.

$\dfrac{35}{100} = \dfrac{35 \div 5}{100 \div 5} = \dfrac{7}{20}$ Write the fraction in simplest form.

So, 35% written as a fraction is $\dfrac{7}{20}$.

ERROR ALERT

When writing a decimal greater than 1 as a percent, remember to multiply by 100. Recall that 100% is equal to 1.00, or 1. So, any number greater than 1 will convert to a percent greater than 100%.

You can also convert percents to decimals.

Compared to last year, the number of students who said they took singing increased 228%. Write 228% as a decimal.

$228\% = \dfrac{228}{100}$ Write the percent as a fraction with a denominator of 100.

$= 2.28$ Write the fraction as a decimal.

So, 228% written as a decimal is 2.28.

• How can you write 28% as a decimal?

Sometimes it takes several steps to convert a percent less than 1% to a fraction or a decimal.

About 0.5% of middle school students said they had never seen a local theater production. Write 0.5% as a fraction and as a decimal.

To write 0.5% as a fraction, recall that percent means "per hundred."

$0.5\% = \dfrac{0.5}{100}$ Write the percent as a fraction with a denominator of 100.

$\dfrac{0.5}{100} = \dfrac{0.5 \times 10}{100 \times 10} = \dfrac{5}{1,000}$ Multiply the numerator and denominator by 10 to remove the decimal from the fraction.

$\dfrac{5}{1,000} = \dfrac{5 \div 5}{1,000 \div 5} = \dfrac{1}{200}$ Write the fraction in simplest form.

To write 0.5% as a decimal, divide by 100.

When you divide decimal numbers by powers of 10, you move the decimal point one place to the left for each factor of 10.

$0.5\% = 00.5\%$ Divide by 100. Move the decimal point two places to the left.

$= 0.005$ Remove the percent sign.

So, 0.5% can be written as $\dfrac{1}{200}$, or 0.005.

• How can you write 5.8% as a fraction and as a decimal? Explain.

▶ **Share and Show** | Math Board

1. Write 0.4 as a percent. $0.4 = \frac{4}{10} = \frac{4 \times 10}{10 \times 10} = \blacksquare\%$

Write each decimal or fraction as a percent.

2. 0.1   3. 0.25   4. 3.4   5. $\frac{4}{5}$ ✓6. $\frac{1}{4}$

Write each percent as a decimal and as a fraction in simplest form.

7. 20%   8. 50%   9. 24%   10. 0.6%   ✓11. 140%

12. Math Talk **Explain** how to write 1.0 as a percent.

 ▶ **Practice and Problem Solving** REAL WORLD

Write each decimal or fraction as a percent.

13. 0.04   14. 0.9   15. 1.6   16. $\frac{3}{10}$ 17. $\frac{1}{2}$

18. 0.625   19. $\frac{2}{5}$ 20. $\frac{7}{8}$ 21. 2.08   22. $1\frac{1}{5}$

Write each percent as a decimal and as a fraction in simplest form.

23. 1%   24. 10%   25. 76%   26. 355%   27. 0.5%

Write each percent as a decimal.

28. 89%   29. 30%   30. 9%   31. 0.2%   32. 150%

 Real World Data

For 33–35, use the table.

33. What fraction of class offerings are for students in middle school?

34. For which group are $\frac{3}{25}$ of the classes offered?

35. What percent of classes are not for high school students? Write that percent as a decimal.

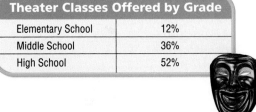

Theater Classes Offered by Grade	
Elementary School	12%
Middle School	36%
High School	52%

36. Write Math ▶ **What's the Error?** About 8.4% of the students enrolled are new to the theater program this season. Joe says 0.84 of the students were new this season. Is he correct? **Explain**.

★ **OCCT Test Prep** | Math Board

37. Which is $\frac{4}{5}$ written as a decimal and a percent?

   A 0.2, 40%   C 0.8, 80%

   B 0.6, 60%   D 0.08, 20%

38. Morton made 36 out of 48 free throws last season. What percent of his free throws did Morton make?

   A 36%   C 48%

   B 40%   D 75%

 Technology
Use HMH Mega Math, The Number
Games, *Buggy Bargains,* Level Q.

⭐ Standards Quick Check

Write each decimal or fraction as a percent.

1. $\frac{7}{10}$

2. 0.14

3. $1\frac{3}{4}$

4. $\frac{3}{6}$

5. 0.87

6. 2.5

Challenge H.O.T.

Nearly 2,500 years ago, the city of Athens experienced its Golden Age of drama. Twice a year, Athens held the *Dionysia,* which was a competition among three playwrights. Each submitted 3 tragedies, 1 mythological comedy, and 1 other comedy. Most plays had only 2 actors, along with 4 to 8 people who made up the chorus.

The table above shows the numbers of performers that three playwrights might have used in their plays. For which playwright was the percent of actors the greatest?

Dionysia Performers		
Playwright	**Actors**	**Chorus**
A	10	30
B	26%	74%
C	0.24	0.76

Convert to percents as needed. Then order *from greatest to least.*

Playwright A	$\frac{10}{10 + 30} = \frac{10}{40} = 0.25 = 25\%$
Playwright B	26%
Playwright C	$0.24 = \frac{24}{100} = 24\%$

26% > 25% > 24%

So, Playwright B used the greatest percent of actors.

Solve.

1. For which playwright was the percent of chorus performers the least?

2. Playwright D joins the competition with 20 performers, 6 of whom are actors. How does Playwright D's percent of actors compare to those of the other playwrights?

LESSON 9

★ **2.2.c.** Estimate and find solutions to single and multi-step problems using whole numbers, decimals, fractions, and percents (e.g., $\frac{7}{8} + \frac{8}{9}$ is about 2, 3.9 + 5.3 is about 9). *also* **2.1., 2.2.b.**

Materials
• MathBoard

Percent of a Number

Essential Question When finding a percent of a number, as for a tip, when would you use a fraction, a decimal, a proportion, or an estimate?

PROBLEM Betty's Breakfast Diner served 24 omelets yesterday. Of these omelets, 75% contained cheese. How many omelets contained cheese?

Find 75% of 24.

Use a fraction.

$75\% = \frac{75}{100}$	Write the percent as a ratio in fraction form.
$= \frac{3}{4}$	Write the ratio in simplest form.
$\frac{3}{4} \times \frac{24}{1} = \frac{72}{4} = 18$	Multiply the ratio by the number.

Use a decimal.

$75\% = 0.75$	Write the percent as a decimal.
$0.75 \times 24 = 18$	Multiply the decimal by the number.

So, 18 omelets contained cheese.

Math Idea

When finding the percent of a number, you can multiply the number by the percent using a fraction or a decimal.

• What percent of the omelets did not contain cheese? Explain.

Examples

Luke's breakfast bill came to $11.89. He wants to leave a 15% tip. About how much should he leave?

You can estimate to find the amount of the tip.

1 Estimate.
$11.89 is about $12.

2 Think: 15% = 10% + 5%
10% of $12 = 0.1 × 12 = $1.20
5% of $12 is half of $1.20,
or $0.60.

3 Add:
$1.20 + $0.60 = $1.80

So, Luke should leave $1.80.

Examples

Andrea and Mike spent $14.16 on two orders of waffles. They want to leave a 15% tip. What is the amount of the tip to the nearest cent?

Use a proportion.

$$15\% = \frac{15}{100}$$ Write the percent as a ratio.

$\dfrac{\text{amount of tip}}{\text{total amount}}$ $\dfrac{t}{14.16} = \dfrac{15}{100}$ Write a proportion. Let t represent the amount of the tip.

$$14.16 \times 15 = 100 \times t$$

$$212.4 = 100t$$ Find, cross products.

$$\frac{212.4}{100} = \frac{100t}{100}$$ Divide.

$$t = 2.124$$ Round the answer to the nearest cent.

$$t = 2.12$$

ERROR ALERT

When writing percents as decimals, you might forget to write a zero in the decimal. Remember that *percent* means "per hundred," so the number is divided by 100, which is the same as moving the decimal two places to the left.

Use an equation.

$$15\% = 0.15$$ Write the percent as a decimal.

$$t = 0.15 \times 14.16$$ Write an equation. Let t represent the tip.

$$t = 2.124, \text{ or about } 2.12$$ Multiply. Round to the nearest cent.

So, to the nearest cent, a 15% tip would be $2.12.

- How could you estimate to check if your answer is reasonable?

You can use a calculator to find the percent of a number.

Find 15% of 63.79.

 63 . 79 × 0.15 = 9.5685

So, 9.5685 is 15% of 63.79.

▶ Share and Show

1. Find 40% of 35.

$$40\% = 0.40$$

$$0.40 \times 35 = \blacksquare$$

2. Find 65% of 75.

$$65\% = \frac{65}{100}$$

$$\frac{65}{100} \times 75 = \blacksquare$$

Find the percent of the number.

3. 50% of 70   **4.** 15% of 40   **5.** 20% of 50   **6.** 175% of 24   ✓ **7.** 0.9% of 30

Estimate a 15% tip for each amount. Then find the tip to the nearest cent.

8. $4.95   **9.** $16.20   **10.** $22.15   **11.** $11.85   ✓ **12.** $39.50

13. [Math Talk] **Explain** two ways to find a percent of a number.

▶ Practice and Problem Solving > REAL WORLD

Find the percent of the number.

14. 25% of 36   **15.** 30% of 90   **16.** 1% of 60   **17.** 210% of 85   **18.** $\frac{1}{4}$% of 90

19. 75% of 52   **20.** 20% of 60   **21.** 3% of 24   **22.** 150% of 42   **23.** $\frac{1}{2}$% of 200

Estimate a 15% tip for each amount. Then find the tip to the nearest cent.

24. $12.00   **25.** $4.76   **26.** $7.89   **27.** $25.35   **28.** $48.90

29. $5.13   **30.** $58.98   **31.** $32.06   **32.** $2.80   **33.** $17.66

Use a proportion or write an equation to find a 20% tip. Round to the nearest cent.

34. $4.40   **35.** $14.20   **36.** $50.00   **37.** $23.80   **38.** $9.60

39. $20.20   **40.** $6.85   **41.** $33.75   **42.** $82.40   **43.** $53.55

44. A bakery made 72 muffins. By noon, 75% of the muffins were sold. How many muffins were sold by noon?

45. Maria works at the local electronics store. She saves her pay for a month and buys an MP3 player for $230. Sales tax of 8% of the price of the player was added to the cost. What was the amount of the sales tax on Maria's purchase?

46. There are 90 students in Grade 5. Ten percent of them were absent today. Fifteen percent of the 80 students in Grade 6 were absent today. What was the total number of students in the two grades who were absent today?

47. [Write Math] ▶ A diner ordered 144 bagels from a bakery. The order was for 80% plain and 20% sesame bagels. The bakery delivered 43 sesame bagels. **Explain** how you could use estimation to check if the delivery was correct.

 OCCT Test Prep

48. Which is a 15% tip on a bill of $36.54?

     A $4.84   **C** $5.48

     B $5.24   **D** $5.76

49. At basketball practice, Tony took 60 foul shots and made 70% of them. He had hoped to make 50 shots. By how many shots did he fall short of his goal?

     A 8 shots   **C** 12 shots

     B 10 shots   **D** 15 shots

⭐ Standards Quick Check

Estimate a 15% tip for each amount. Then find the tip to the nearest cent.

1. $11.00

2. $6.45

3. $28.13

You're Getting Warmer

Jeremy found a ski jacket with a regular price of $75.95 on sale at two stores. In the first store, the jacket price had been discounted twice. For last month's Early Winter sale, the price was discounted 20% off the regular price. Now the price is being discounted 40% off the Early Winter sale price. At the second store, the price has been discounted 50% off the regular price. Which store has the better sale price?

You can use the facts of the problem to draw conclusions.

You know that the regular price was $75.95. In the first store, the price was discounted twice, first by 20%, then by 40%. In the second store, it was discounted once, by 50%. One way to solve the problem is to find which store had the greater discount.

Estimate the price discount.

First store
First sale: $75.95 is about $76.
20% of $76 = about $15
First sale price: $76 − $15 = $61
40% of $61 = about $24
Estimated discount: $15 + $24 = $39

Second store
$75.95 is about $76.
50% of $76 = $38
Estimated discount: $38

The estimates are too close to allow you to draw firm conclusions.

Solve the problem using exact figures. Use these questions to decide whether your conclusions are reasonable and accurate:

• Does your solution answer the question?
• Is the answer reasonable?
• How does the answer compare to your estimates?

Draw conclusions to solve.

1. Solve the problem above.

2. Both White Mountain and Baxter Creek ski resorts had 220 in. of snow two years ago. White Mountain's total snowfall increased 10% last year and 15% more this year. Baxter Creek's increased 25% over the two years. Which resort had more snow this year?

★ **5.1.** Organize, construct displays, and interpret data to solve problems (e.g., data from student experiments, tables, diagrams, charts, graphs). *also* **2.1.; 2.2.c.**

Materials
• MathBoard

Problem Solving Workshop
Skill: Use a Graph

Essential Question From reading a graph, what general comparisons can be made?

▶ **Use the Skill** REAL WORLD

PROBLEM A geologist plans to visit 80 volcanoes in the United States. The circle graph represents the locations of the volcanoes. Use the circle graph to find how many of the volcanoes to be visited are in Alaska.

Graphs represent data visually. You can use the information in a graph to understand and solve problems. A circle graph shows data that represent parts of a whole. You can compare parts to the other parts or parts to the whole in a circle graph.

The whole circle represents 100% of the volcanoes to be visited, or 80 volcanoes.

Each sector represents part of the whole, or a percent of the total volcanoes to be visited.

The sector that represents Alaska shows that 60% of the volcanoes to be visited are in Alaska.

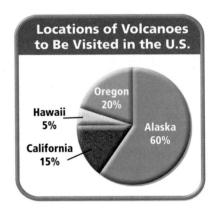

Locations of Volcanoes to Be Visited in the U.S.

Oregon 20%
Hawaii 5%
Alaska 60%
California 15%

To find the number of volcanoes to be visited in Alaska, find 60% of 80.

$$60\% = 0.6$$
$$0.6 \times 80 = 48$$

So, 48 of the volcanoes to be visited are in Alaska.

Use the circle graph to solve the problems.

a. How many of the volcanoes to be visited are in California?

b. How many of the volcanoes to be visited are in Oregon?

c. How many more volcanoes to be visited are in Alaska than in the other three states combined?

d. How can you use the fact that *48 volcanoes are to be visited in Alaska* to find the number to be visited in Hawaii?

1. The circle graph represents the locations of 20 volcanoes that the geologist plans to visit in other parts of the world. How many of the volcanoes are in Africa?

   First, find the sector of the graph that represents the percent of volcanoes in Africa.

   Then, find the fraction or decimal equivalent to the percent.

   Finally, multiply the fraction or decimal by the total number of volcanoes to be visited on the trip.

2. **What if** 40% of the volcanoes to be visited were in Africa? How many of the volcanoes would be in Africa?

3. Can you tell the total number of volcanoes to be visited in Antarctica, Europe, and Africa just by looking at the graph and using mental math? **Explain**.

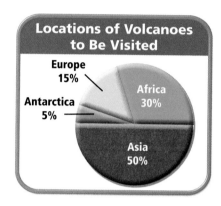

Real World Data

For 4–6, use the bar graph.

4. Which volcano has a height that is about 16% the height of Mount Spurr?

5. The average height of three of the volcanoes is 5,507 ft. Which three volcanoes are these?

6. Sam can hike up a mountain at an average rate of 25 ft per minute. Rounding to the nearest minute, how long would it take him to hike up Atka from sea level?

7. A teacher has 10 students going on a mountain trek. She is making a bag of trail mix for each student. How many ounces of trail mix will she have left over if she makes 8-ounce bags from 105 oz of trail mix?

8. Juice drinks are sold in packs of 6. Forty-three students are expected at the mountaineering club party. How many juice-drink packs should the planning committee purchase so that each student receives 1 juice drink?

9. Tickets for an extinct-volcano tour cost $79 each. Nine students have a total of $718 among them to take the tour. Do they have enough money to buy 9 tickets?

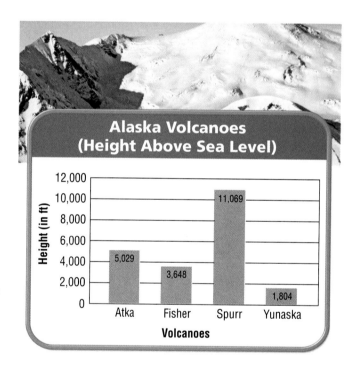

10. **Write Math** ▸ The 57 volcanoes of Alaska's Aleutian Islands extend 1,200 mi. A map has a scale of 1 in. = 75 mi. Which operation should you use to find the length of the Aleutians on the map? **Explain**. What is the map length?

LESSON 11

★ **2.2.c.** Estimate and find solutions to single and multi-step problems using whole numbers, decimals, fractions, and percents (e.g., $\frac{7}{8} + \frac{8}{9}$ is about 2, 3.9 + 5.3 is about 9). *also* **2.1., 2.2.b.**

Vocabulary

discount

sales tax

Materials
• MathBoard

Discount and Sales Tax

Essential Question After finding the discount on a sale item, how do you find the sale price? After finding the sales tax on an item, how do you find the total cost?

PROBLEM Tim wants to buy a snowboard for his winter vacation. He sees the newspaper ad shown at the right. What is the sale price of the snowboard with a 25% discount?

A **discount** is an amount that is subtracted from the regular price of an item.

Regular Price
Discount
Sale Price

Find the sale price.

❶ Find the discount.

discount = regular price × discount rate
     = \$120 × 25%
     = \$120 × 0.25
     = \$30.00

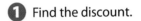

❷ Find the sale price.

sale price = regular price − discount
     = \$120.00 − \$30.0
     = \$90.00

So, the sale price of the snowboard is \$90.00.

Find the discount rate for the helmet.

❶ Find the amount of the discount.

discount = regular price − sale price
     = \$60 − \$51
     = \$9

❷ Find the discount rate.

discount rate = discount ÷ regular price
     = \$9 ÷ \$60
     = 0.15, or 15%

So, the discount rate is 15%.

Find the regular price of the ice skates.

The regular price has been discounted 40%. That means the sale price must be 60% of the regular price, since 100% − 40% = 60%.

THINK: sale price = 60% × regular price

Let n = the regular price.

$48	=	60% × n Write an equation relating the sale price and the regular price.
$48	=	0.6 × n Write the percent as a decimal.
$\frac{\$48}{0.6}$	=	$\frac{0.6n}{0.6}$ Divide both sides of the equation by 0.6.
$80	=	n

So, the regular price of the ice skates is $80.

Sales Tax

Most states charge a sales tax on purchases. A **sales tax** is calculated as a percent of the cost of an item. To find the amount of the sales tax, multiply the amount of the purchase by the sales tax rate.

Examples

Kate is buying a sled for $62. The sales tax rate is 5%. How much will she pay in sales tax?

Estimate. Think: 10% of $62 is about $6.00, so 5% of $62 is about $3.00.

sales tax = amount of purchase × sales tax rate

$= \$62 \times 5\%$

$= \$62 \times 0.05$

$= \$3.10$

The estimate of $3.00 is close to the answer $3.10, so the answer is reasonable. So, she will pay $3.10 in sales tax.

You can find the total cost of a purchase that includes sales tax.

Dennis is buying a pair of skis for $425. The sales tax rate is 6%. What is the total cost of the purchase?

Add the sales tax to the price.

$\$425 \times 6\% = \$425 \times 0.06$

$= \$25.50$

$\$425 + \$25.50 = \$450.50$

Multiply the price by 106% since 6% is added to the cost.

$\$425 \times 106\% = \$425 \times 1.06$

$= \$450.50$

So, the total cost of the purchase is $450.50.

▶ Share and Show

1. Find the discount.

$20\% \times \$45 = 0.2 \times \$45$

$\quad\quad = \blacksquare$

REGULARLY $45.00

NOW 20% OFF

2. Find the discount rate.

$\$100 - \$80 = \$20$

$\$20 \div \$100 = \blacksquare$, or $\blacksquare\%$

$100.00 $80.00

Find the sale price.

3. regular price: $44

25% OFF

4. regular price: $150

30% OFF

5. regular price: $27

10% DISCOUNT

✓**6.** regular price: $65

20% SAVINGS

Find the discount rate.

7. regular price: $90
sale price: $45

8. regular price: $35
sale price: $31.50

9. regular price: $60
sale price: $42

✓**10.** regular price: $110
sale price: $88

11. **Math Talk** **Explain** how you can find the total cost of a ski jacket with a price of $87.50 and a 6% sales tax rate.

▶ Practice and Problem Solving REAL WORLD

Find the sale price.

12. regular price: $30

15% OFF

13. regular price: $215

20% OFF

14. regular price: $75

50% DISCOUNT

15. regular price: $342

25% OFF

Find the discount rate.

16. regular price: $120
sale price: $84

17. regular price: $15
sale price: $13.50

18. regular price: $84
sale price: $63

19. regular price: $750
sale price: $600

⭐ Algebra Find the regular price.

20. sale price: $120
discount rate: 25%

21. sale price: $99
discount rate: 10%

22. sale price: $78.50
discount rate: 50%

23. sale price: $231
discount rate: 30%

Find the total cost of the purchase. Round to the nearest cent.

24. price: $129
sales tax: 6%

25. price: $14.95
sales tax: 4.5%

26. price: $1,029
sales tax: 5%

27. price: $89.95
sales tax: 6.25%

★ OCCT Test Prep

28. Which is the amount of discount of a sweater that is on sale for 40% off the regular price of $65?

A $26

C $34

B $31

D $39

29. Tom buys paint for $24.95. The sales tax rate is 5%. Which is the total cost?

A $3.75

C $26.20

B $12.47

D $37.46

⭐ Standards Quick Check

Find the discount rate.

1. regular price: $70

    sale price: $49

2. regular price: $160

    sale price: $152

3. regular price: $350

    sale price: $294

4. regular price: $18

    sale price: $13.50

5. regular price: $68

    sale price: $34

6. regular price: $45

    sale price: $36.90

Challenge H.O.T.

Different states have different sales tax rates. The table shows state sales tax rates for four states.

If you buy a computer for $1,595, how much will you pay in state sales tax in New York, Ohio, West Virginia, and Rhode Island?

sales tax = amount of purchase × sales tax rate

State Sales Tax Rates	
State	**Rate**
New York	4%
Ohio	5.5%
West Virginia	6%
Rhode Island	7%

Multiply the price by the percent. Round to the nearest cent.

New York	Ohio	West Virginia	Rhode Island
Sales tax	Sales tax	Sales tax	Sales tax
= $1,595 × 4%	= $1,595 × 5.5%	= $1,595 × 6%	= $1,595 × 7%
= $1,595 × 0.04	= $1,595 × 0.055	= $1,595 × 0.06	= $1,595 × 0.07
= $63.80	= $87.725	= $95.70	= $111.65
	= $87.73		

So, the state sales tax is $63.80 in New York, $87.73 in Ohio, $95.70 in West Virginia, and $111.65 in Rhode Island.

Find the state sales tax for each item in New York, Ohio, West Virginia, and Rhode Island.

1. a backpack that costs $25

2. a radio that costs $58.89

3. a stove that costs $750

☆ Extra Practice

Set A

Write two equivalent ratios for each fraction. (pp. 360–363)

1. $\frac{5}{6}$ **2.** $\frac{16}{20}$ **3.** $\frac{2}{3}$ **4.** $\frac{8}{26}$ **5.** $\frac{30}{12}$ **6.** $\frac{7}{8}$

7. $\frac{15}{25}$ **8.** $\frac{1}{9}$ **9.** $\frac{2}{7}$ **10.** $\frac{28}{16}$ **11.** $\frac{12}{18}$ **12.** $\frac{7}{35}$

13. Emily is making sun tea for a club picnic. She uses 3 large tea bags for every 4 quarts of water. How many tea bags will she need to make 20 quarts of tea?

Set B

Solve the proportion. (pp. 364–367)

1. $\frac{3}{5} = \frac{12}{x}$ **2.** $\frac{k}{14} = \frac{6}{7}$ **3.** $\frac{8}{r} = \frac{12}{24}$ **4.** $\frac{10}{20} = \frac{p}{24}$ **5.** $\frac{y}{15} = \frac{3}{18}$ **6.** $\frac{8}{20} = \frac{t}{15}$

7. $\frac{10}{16} = \frac{15}{z}$ **8.** $\frac{8}{m} = \frac{20}{25}$ **9.** $\frac{12}{32} = \frac{a}{16}$ **10.** $\frac{b}{21} = \frac{6}{42}$ **11.** $\frac{10}{h} = \frac{16}{80}$ **12.** $\frac{8}{36} = \frac{t}{54}$

13. A long-distance telephone company charges $3 for an 8-minute call to Germany. If Mr. Hagen makes a 24-minute call to Germany, how much will the phone call cost?

Set C

Tell whether the two figures are similar. Explain why or why not. (pp. 368–371)

1.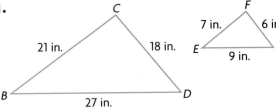

2.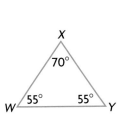

Set D

Find the unknown measurement. Include the unit. (pp. 376–379)

1. scale: 2 cm = 10 m
drawing length: 13 cm
actual length: ■

2. scale: 4 in. = 18 ft
drawing length: ■
actual length: 90 ft

3. scale: 5 cm = 1 m
drawing length: ■
actual length: 17.5 m

4. map scale: 2.5 in. = 30 mi
measured distance: ■
actual distance: 180 mi

5. map scale: 16 mm = 30 km
measured distance: ■
actual distance: 210 km

6. map scale: 1 in. = 58 mi
measured distance: 3 in. actual
distance: ■

go ONLINE Technology
Use HMH Mega Math, Ice Station
Exploration, *Arctic Algebra,* Level F.

Set E

Use proportional reasoning to solve. (pp. 380–381)

1. Jodee runs 3 mi in 24 min. If she continues her pace, how far could she run in 60 min?

2. You buy 12 hot dog buns for $4.92. How much would 3 hot dog buns cost?

3. Jeffery pays $5.98 to play for 20 min in the football experience tent. How much would it cost to play for 2 hr?

4. The print shop can make 18 shirts in 3 hr. How many shirts can the shop make in 7 hr?

5. A cake mix that serves 8 costs $2.75. Katie needs to serve cake to 48 people at a party. She says she expects to spend $16.50. Is the statement reasonable? **Explain** your answer.

6. Petra can inspect 80 shirts in 20 min. She says she can inspect 200 shirts in an hour. Is the statement reasonable? **Explain** your answer.

Set F

Write the percent that is shaded. (pp. 382–383)

1.

2.

3.

4.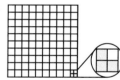

5.

6.

7.

8.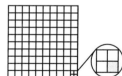

Set G

Write each decimal or fraction as a percent. (pp. 384–387)

1. 0.20 **2.** $\frac{5}{8}$ **3.** 1.4 **4.** $\frac{9}{10}$ **5.** 3.05 **6.** $1\frac{1}{2}$

7. $\frac{1}{5}$ **8.** 0.75 **9.** $2\frac{1}{4}$ **10.** 0.07 **11.** $\frac{3}{5}$ **12.** 0.875

13. Joaquin earned $\frac{11}{20}$ of his yearly income in the first quarter of the year. Write the fraction as a percent.

14. Mr. Walters calculated that 88% of the time, he has delivered all of the mail on his postal route before 2:00 P.M. Write this percent as a decimal and a fraction in lowest form.

Set H

Find the discount rate. (pp. 394–397)

1. regular price: $112
sale price: $84

2. regular price: $18
sale price: $9

3. regular price: $90
sale price: $72

4. regular price: $44
sale price: $39.60

Vocabulary

A **percent** compares a number to 100. Percents can also be written in fraction or decimal form.

10 × 10 Grid

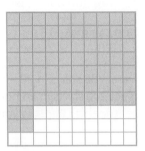

Harriet is painting her room. The model above shows how much of the room she has painted so far.

1. What percent of the room has been painted?

2. How much of the room has not yet been painted?
Show your work.

3. Draw a new model that shows how much of the room has not been painted.

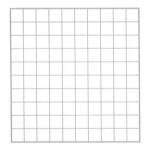

Writing Harriet wants to show the percent of the room she has painted as a fraction. Write a paragraph that tells her how.

Reading Look for this book in your library.
Piece = Part = Portion, by Scott Gifford

HOT Multistep Problems

1 A store sells a sweater that cost $80. It advertises a sale of 40% off plus an additional 10% off the sale price. Another store sells the same sweater for $80 and advertises a sale of 50% off. ⌐ 2.2.b.; 2.2.c.

- What is 40% off of the price of the sweater? How much is the sweater after the 40% off? **Explain** how you found the answer.

- Use the answer from the first question and find the new price of the sweater with an additional 10% off the sale price. **Explain.**

- What is 50% off of the original cost of the sweater? **Explain** how you got the answer.

- Is 40% off plus an additional 10% off the sale price the same as 50% off? **Explain.**

- Which is a better sale?

2 Nicky is saving his money to buy a new mountain bike. He puts $75 in a simple interest savings account, earning 4% per year for 2 years. ⌐ 2.2.b.; 2.2.c.

- How much will be in the account after 2 years? **Explain** how you found the answer.

- He decides to go shopping with the money from the account. He sees a pair of pants that has an original price of $30. It is on sale for 25% off. How much do the pants cost after the discount? **Explain.**

- Nicky's friend Andrew bought a shirt that has an original price of $20. It is on sale for $14. What percent is the discount on the shirt? **Explain.**

- The tax rate is 3%. How much tax will be paid on the $14 shirt? **Explain.**

Practice for the OCCT

1 Brenda goes to a computer store in Marion to buy a new computer. When she gets to the store, she sees that the computer she wants is discounted by 20%. The original cost of the computer was $840. How much was the computer after the 20% discount? 2.2.c.

  A $640

  B $672

  C $762

  D $782

2 Which ratio is *not* equivalent to 6 to 10? 2.1.

  A 6:10

  B 3:5

  C $\frac{18}{30}$

  D $\frac{5}{3}$

3 What is the value of *n* in the proportion $\frac{4}{7} = \frac{n}{21}$? 2.1.

  A 12

  B 18

  C 28

  D 37

4 Evan collects 24 shells at the beach. Kyla collects 12 more shells than Evan does. What is the ratio of Evan's shells to Kyla's shells? 2.1.

  A 1:2

  B 2:3

  C 3:2

  D 2:1

5 A recipe that makes 12 pints of salsa uses 35 tomatoes. Which proportion can *not* be used to find the number *t* of tomatoes needed to make 2 pints of salsa? 2.1.

  A $\frac{1}{6} = \frac{t}{35}$

  B $\frac{t}{35} = \frac{12}{2}$

  C $\frac{35}{12} = \frac{t}{2}$

  D $\frac{t}{35} = \frac{2}{12}$

6 Don and his friend had dinner at their favorite restaurant. The total bill, including tip, was $91.58. Don agreed to pay 60% of this bill. How much money did Don agree to pay? 2.2.c.

  A $36.63

  B $45.79

  C $54.95

  D $60.26

7 What is the value of *d* in the proportion $\frac{36}{42} = \frac{d}{28}$? 2.1.

  A 22

  B 24

  C 33

  D 50

8 LCD TV sales represented about 0.676% of the total sales of electronics in 2003. Which value is equal to 0.676%? 2.2.c.

  A 0.00676

  B $\frac{676}{1,000}$

  C $\frac{676}{100,000}$

  D $\frac{169}{25,000}$

9 Roberto paid $132 for a desk. The desk was discounted 20%. How much was the desk before the 20% discount? 🔖 2.2.c.

   A $160

   B $165

   C $170

   D $175

10 Ben works at the local computer store. He saved his money for two months to buy a portable music player for $270. Sales tax on the portable music player was 8%. How much sales tax did Ben pay for the portable music player? 🔖 2.2.c.

   A $12.45

   B $19.80

   C $21.60

   D $22.40

11 Tim used 12 feet of fleece to make a blanket and 2 feet of fleece to make a vest. What is the ratio of fleece for the blanket to fleece for the vest? 🔖 2.1.

   A $\frac{1}{10}$

   B $\frac{1}{6}$

   C $\frac{6}{1}$

   D $\frac{10}{1}$

12 A business made a $5,650 profit in May. In June, the business made about 92% of the profit for May. How much was the profit for June for the business? 🔖 2.2.c.

   A $1,628

   B $5,198

   C $5,558

   D $6,141

Problem Solving

13 A bake sale for a school trip raised $300. If 20% of the money was for bake sale expenses, how much went toward the trip? 🔖 2.2.c.

14 You have $200, and you would like to rent a sailboat for 4 hours. It costs $45 per hour or $130 per day. What percent of your total money will you save by choosing the better rate? 🔖 2.2.c.

15 Eve has 10 CDs in her collection and Mieko has 16 CDs. Eve adds x CDs to her collection and Mieko adds y CDs. Find two possible values for x and y so that the ratio of Eve's CDs to Mieko's CDs remains the same. **Explain** how you found your answer. 🔖 2.1.

16 In the United States, 21 out of every 100 people are under the age of 15. In a town of 20,000 people, how many people would you expect to be under the age of 15? 15 and over? **Explain** your reasoning. 🔖 2.1.

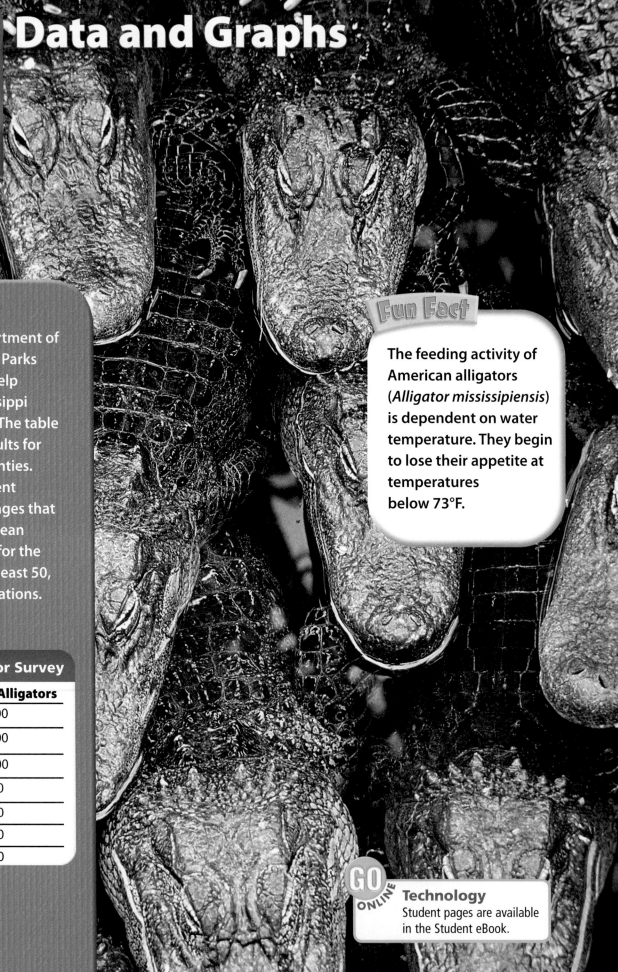

Data and Graphs

Investigate

The Mississippi Department of Wildlife Fisheries and Parks uses night-lights to help determine the Mississippi alligator population. The table shows the survey results for some Mississippi counties. Describe three different combinations of changes that would increase the mean number of alligators for the seven counties by at least 50, and show your calculations.

Mississippi Alligator Survey

County	Number of Alligators
Jackson	7,500
Hancock	3,900
Rankin	2,400
Harrison	850
Green	850
Marion	800
Madison	750

Fun Fact

The feeding activity of American alligators (*Alligator mississipiensis*) is dependent on water temperature. They begin to lose their appetite at temperatures below 73°F.

GO ONLINE

Technology
Student pages are available in the Student eBook.

Show What You Know

Check your understanding of important skills needed for success in Chapter 11.

ASSESSMENT
Soar To Success: Math.

▶ Mean

Find the mean for each set of data.

1. 2, 2, 3, 4, 5, 6, 8, 10

2. 17, 25, 26, 27, 28, 30, 32, 32, 35

▶ Median and Mode

Find the median and mode for each set of data.

3. 1, 1, 1, 1, 2, 2, 2, 3, 4, 7

4. 6, 0, 4, 6, 7, 4, 3, 1, 5, 2, 8

▶ Read and Interpret a Table

For 5–6, use the table at the right.

5. How many girls chose fish as their favorite pet?

6. How many boys chose a hamster as their favorite pet?

Students' Favorite Pet				
	Dog	**Cat**	**Fish**	**Hamster**
Girls	7	11	3	1
Boys	9	4	6	5

Vocabulary

Visualize It!

mean: 10.1

The average of a set of data. It is the sum of all of the numbers divided by the number of addends.

5.4, 6.3, 7.7, 7.7, 9.1, 10.1, 11.7, 13.3, 19.6

mode: 7.7

the number that occurs most often

median: 9.1

the middle number

Language Tips

Words that look alike in English and Spanish often have the same meaning.

English	Spanish
frequency table	tabla de frecuencia
population	población
sample	muestra

See **English-Spanish Glossary.**

Mean, Median, Mode, and Range

Essential Question What questions should you ask to determine the best type of sampling for a set of data?

★ **5.3.** Find the measures of central tendency (mean, median, mode, and range) of a set of data with and without outliers) and understand why a specific measure provides the most useful information in a given context. *also* **5.1.**

Materials
• MathBoard

PROBLEM Francisco is entering a paper airplane in a competition. During 6 test flights, his plane flew distances of 281 in., 275 in., 296 in., 280 in., 288 in., and 296 in. What are the mean, median, mode, and range of the data?

Certain types of measures can be used to describe a set of data.

You can use measures to describe data sets. The mean and median are measures that describe the center.

Example

> **ERROR ALERT**
> If no data values repeat, there are not several modes. There is no mode.

The mean is the average of a data set.

$(281 + 275 + 296 + 280 + 288 + 296) \div 6$

$1{,}716 \div 6 = 286$ Mean: 286

The median is the middle number or the average of the two middle numbers in an ordered data set.

275   280   281   288   296   296

$(281 + 288) \div 2 = 284.5$ Median: 284.5

The mode describes the most common value or values in a data set.

275   280   281   288   296   296   Mode: 296

The range is the difference between the greatest and least number in the data set.

275   280   281   288   296   296   Range: 21

$296 - 275 = 21$

So, the mean of the distances flown is 286 in., the median is 284.5 in., the mode is 296 in.

• If Francisco's paper airplane flew 281 inches instead of 280 inches in the first test flight, would the mode be the same? Explain.

• If Francisco conducted 5 test flights instead of 6, how would you find the median?

Examples

Beth is entering 5 paper airplanes in the competition. The table shows the maximum distance flown by each of her planes. When Beth retests Panther and Racer, both planes fly a distance of 350 in. What effects do the changed data have on the mean, median, mode, and range of the original airplane distances?

1 Find the mean, median, mode, and range of Beth's original airplane distances in the table.

Beth's Paper Airplanes	
Paper Airplanes	**Maximum Distance Flown (in.)**
Streamer	348
Spike	319
Panther	342
Dart	319
Racer	331

Mean: $(348 + 319 + 342 + 319 + 331) \div 5 = 331.8$

Median: 319   319   331   342   348; 331

Mode: 348   319   342   319   331; 319

Range: $348 - 319 = 29$

The mean is 331.8 in., the median is 331 in., and the mode is 319 in., and the range is 29.

2 Find the mean, median, mode, and range of the airplane distances using the new, changed data instead of the original.

Mean: $(348 + 319 + 350 + 319 + 350) \div 5 = 337.2$

Median: 319   319   348   350   350; 348

Mode: 348   319   350   319   350; 319 and 350

Range: $350 - 319 = 31$

The mean is 337.2 in., the median is 348 in., the modes are 319 in. and 350 in., and the range is 31 in.

3 Compare the new measures to the original measures.

Mean: 337.2 > 331.8   Median: 348 > 331

Mode: 2 modes > 1 mode   Range: 31 > 29

So, when the data are changed, the mean and median increase and the number of modes increases.

Remember

Each X in a line plot represents one data value.

The line plot shows the wingspans of paper airplanes in a competition. What are the mean, median, mode, and range of the data?

Mean: $(6 + 6.5 + 6.5 + 6.5 + 6.5 + 7.5 + 7.5 + 8 + 8 + 8) \div 10 = 7.1$

Median: 6, 6.5, 6.5, 6.5, 6.5, 7.5, 7.5, 8, 8, 8; $(6.5 + 7.5) \div 2 = 7$

Mode: 6.5   Range: $8 - 6 = 2$

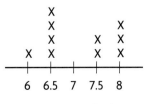

Wingspan (in.)

So, the mean is 7.1 in., the median is 7 in., and the mode is 6.5 in., and the range is 2 in.

1. Order the data below from least to greatest and find the mean, median, mode, and range.

$$25, 12, 33, 23, 25, 17$$

Find the mean, median, mode, and range.

2. 2.8, 4.1, 2.6, 1.4, 4.1   ✓ **3.** 80, 74, 82, 77, 86, 75   ✓ **4.** $\frac{1}{2}, \frac{3}{4}, \frac{1}{4}, \frac{3}{4}, \frac{1}{4}$

5. Math Talk **Explain** why not all sets of data have a mode. Give an example.

► **Practice and Problem Solving** REAL WORLD

Find the mean, median, mode, and range.

6. 140, 183, 85, 93, 97, 101, 85

7. $\frac{5}{6}, \frac{1}{4}, \frac{5}{12}, \frac{1}{4}, \frac{1}{2}, \frac{3}{4}$

8. 450, 325, 500, 450, 325, 50, 450, 450

9. 32.5, 41.9, 30.5, 32.6, 37.3, 39.8, 40.6, 41.2

 **Algebra** Use the given mean to find the value of *n* in each set of data.

10. 9, 6, 12, 3, *n*; mean: 9

11. 36, 42, 18, *n*; mean: 36

Real World Data

For 12–13, use the bar graph.

12. One of the paper airplanes in the competition was disqualified. The median time in the air of the remaining planes is 8 sec. Which paper airplane was disqualified?

13. **Reasoning** The 5 paper airplanes are thrown again for a second round. In this round, the mean, median, and mode of the times in the air are all 6 sec. What is one set of possible times for each plane?

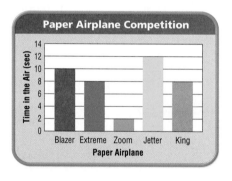

14. Write Math ► **What's the Question?** The 11 oldest competitors qualify for another event. The answer is that both measures are 13.

15. Which is the median of the data set?
9.6, 8.4, 6, 9, 7.8, 6

   A 3.6   **C** 7.8

   B 6   **D** 8.1

16. What is the mean of the data set?
84, 94, 84, 95, 99, 80, 84, 82

   A 75.2   **C** 87.75

   B 79.70   **D** 91.50

⬛ Standards Quick Check

Find the mean, median, mode, and range.

1. 67, 42, 90, 102, 37, 42, 67, 50, 46

2. 2.3, 4.6, 60.2, 11.2, 22.7, 31

3. $2\frac{1}{2}, \frac{1}{8}, 1\frac{5}{6}, \frac{3}{4}$

Comparing Data

Judges for a paper airplane competition award points for airplane design, distance flown, and time aloft. The table shows the results of a recent competition. Which category has the lowest mean score?

Paper Airplane Competition			
Airplane	**Design**	**Distance**	**Time**
Panther	5	1	6
Zoom	7	2	6
Blazer	7	8	9
Spike	3	4	5
King	9	6	9
Whiz	8	6	7

Design: (5 + 7 + 7 + 3 + 9 + 8) ÷ 6 = 6.5

Distance: (1 + 2 + 8 + 4 + 6 + 6) ÷ 6 = 4.5

Time: (6 + 6 + 9 + 5 + 9 + 7) ÷ 6 = 7

So, the distance category has the lowest mean score.

Solve.

1. In which category are the median and mode scores the same?

2. Which two airplanes have the greatest mean score?

3. How could you make the number of modes the same in each category by changing only one number in the table?

4. Change one score in each category. Predict how the change will affect the mean, median, mode, and range of the scores in each category. Test your predictions. Round each measure to the nearest tenth.

★ **5.3.** Find the measures of central tendency (mean, median, mode, and range) of a set of data with and without outliers) and understand why a specific measure provides the most useful information in a given context. *also* **5.1.**

Vocabulary

outlier

Materials
• MathBoard

Outliers

Essential Question How do outliers affect the mean, median, and mode of a set of data?

PROBLEM Hannah is researching the number of animals that students in her class have at their homes. Her results are shown on the line plot. Find the mean, median, and mode of the data with the outliers included and excluded. Then, compare the values and explain how the outliers affect the mean, median, and mode.

A value that is very small or very large compared to the majority of the values in a data set is called an **outlier**.

Example

> **Math Idea**
> You can quickly find the mode in a line plot by finding the tallest stack on the number line.

❶ Find the mean, median, and mode with the outliers included.

  Mean: $90 \div 12 = 7.5$

  Median: 0, 1, 2, 2, 2, 2, 3, 3, 3, 4, 33, 35; $(2 + 3) \div 2 = 2.5$

  Mode: 2

  With the outliers included, the mean is 7.5, the median is 2.5, and the mode is 2.

. . . .

❷ Find the mean, median, and mode with the outliers excluded. The outliers are 33 and 35, so exclude 33 and 35 from the data set.

  Mean: $22 \div 10 = 2.2$

  Median: 0, 1, 2, 2, 2, 2, 3, 3, 3, 4; $(2 + 2) \div 2 = 2$

  Mode: 2

  With the outliers excluded, the mean is 2.2, the median is 2, and the mode is 2.

. . . .

❸ Compare the mean, median, and mode with the outliers included to the mean, median, and mode with the outliers excluded.

  Mean: $7.5 > 2.2$ **Median:** $2.5 > 2$ **Mode:** $2 = 2$

So, when the outliers are excluded the mean and median decrease. Since 2 still occurs four times, the mode remains the same.

Example

Jim wants to move to California. The table shows the population, in thousands, of each of the counties he is considering. Find the mean, median, and mode of the data with the outlier included and excluded. Then compare the values and explain how the outlier affects the mean, median, and mode.

County Population (in thousands)	
250	185
18	242
317	255
214	247

1 Order the data from least to greatest and identify the outlier.

18, 185, 214, 242, 247, 250, 255, 317; outlier: 18

2 Find the mean, median, and mode with the outlier included.

Mean: 1,728 ÷ 8 = 216

Median: 18, 185, 214, 242, 247, 250, 255, 317; (242 + 247) ÷ 2 = 244.5

Mode: no mode

With the outlier included, the mean is 216, the median is 244.5, and the data does not contain a mode.

3 Find the mean, median, and mode with the outlier excluded. The outlier is 18, so exclude 18 from the data set.

Mean: 1,710 ÷ 7 ≈ 244.3

Median: 185, 214, 242, 247, 250, 255, 317; 247   **Mode:** no mode

With the outlier excluded, the mean is about 244.3, the median is 247, and the data does not contain a mode.

4 Compare the mean, median, and mode with the outliers included to the mean, median, and mode with the outliers excluded.

Mean: 216 < 244.3 **Median:** 244.5 < 247 **Mode:** no mode

So, when the outlier is excluded, the mean and median increase. However, there is no mode in the data set.

 ▶ **Share and Show** **Math Board**

1. The line plot shows the numbers of kilometers sixteen different people hiked. The outliers are 0.9 and 1. Find the mean, median, and mode of the data with the outliers included and excluded.

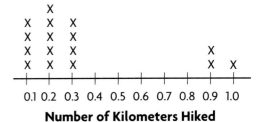

Number of Kilometers Hiked

Find the mean, median, and mode with the outliers included and excluded.
Explain how the outliers affect the mean, median, and mode.

2. 55, 52, 55, 50, 17, 47

3. 36, 42, 52, 42, 38, 40, 52, 42, 34, 42, 218

☑ **4.** 24, 34, 56, 25, 58, 26, 32, 27

☑ **5.** 0.1, 0.9, 1.3, 1.2, 0.9, 0.1, 1.1

6. | Math Talk | **Explain** when it is possible for a data set to have a mean that is less with the outliers included than with the outliers excluded. Give an example.

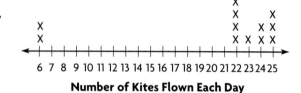

Find the mean, median, and mode with the outliers included and excluded.
Explain how the outliers affect the mean, median, and mode.

7. 81, 72, 79, 12, 86, 79, 80, 11

8. 5, 21, 4.6, 5.3, 5, 4.8, 5.3, 5, 5.2

9. 125, 158, 135, 166, 31, 166, 31

10. $1\frac{1}{2}, 1\frac{2}{5}, 3, 26\frac{2}{5}, 1\frac{1}{2}, 2\frac{3}{5}$

11.

```
                                    X
                          X       X
          X               X   X X
          X               X X X X
    +-+-+-+-+-+-+-+-+-+-+-+-+-+-+-+-+-+-+-+->
    6  7  8  9 10 11 12 13 14 15 16 17 18 19 20 21 22 23 24 25
```
Number of Kites Flown Each Day

12.

Number of Miles Biked					
2.5	2.2	0.2	2.5	3.0	2.4
3.0	2.5	2.2	3.0	0.4	2.5

 Real World Data

For 13–14, use the table.

13. What is the difference between the mean growth with and without the outlier included?

14. During July, each plant grows half of what it grew in June. Find the mean, median and mode, with the outlier included and excluded, of the total plant growth in June and July for all plants.

Plant Growth for June	
Plant	Growth (cm)
A	8
B	10
C	32
D	12

15. | Write Math | **What's the Question?** The answer is the mean of the data set decreases.

OCCT Test Prep | Math Board |

16. Which is the outlier in the set of data?

14, 13.7, 19.4, 37.2, 12, 11.9

A 11.9

B 13.7

C 19.4

D 37.2

17. How does the outlier affect the mean, median, and mode?

1.5, 0.75, 1.5, 3.75, 0.5, 1.5, 1

A The mean, median, and mode increase.

B The mean and mode increase.

C The mean and median increase.

D The mean and median decrease.

⭐ Standards Quick Check

Find the mean, median, and mode with the outliers included and excluded. Explain how the outliers affect the mean, median, and mode.

1. 25, 22, 25, 20, 42, 28

2. 85, 82, 86, 82, 16, 88, 93

3. 205, 203, 213, 204, 44, 208

Redwood Biking Trails

Biking and hiking are forms of exercise enjoyed by people of all ages. Bike trails across the country weave through a variety of scenic environments that enhance the biking experience. The trails at Redwood National Park lead bikers through prairies, old-growth redwood forests, and along beaches. The table shows the length of some randomly chosen trails at the park.

Redwood National Park	
Trails	**Approx. Length (mi)**
Lost Man Creek Trail	11
Coastal Trail	6
Little Bald Hill Trail	8
Ossagan Trail Loop	19
Davison Road	8
Davison Trail	8

Use the information to solve the problems.

1. What is the mean length of the trails with and without the outlier included?

2. Is the mode useful to describe the data? Why or why not?

3. **Reasoning** The median length of three trails that Rick biked on is 11 miles. Which two trails must Rick have biked on?

4. **Explain** how to find the range of the trail lengths. What is the range?

LESSON 3

5.1. Organize, construct displays, and interpret data to solve problems (e.g., data from student experiments, tables, diagrams, charts, graphs).

Vocabulary

cumulative frequency

frequency table

Materials
• MathBoard

Frequency Tables and Line Plots

Essential Question How do mean, median, mode, and range describe a set a data?

PROBLEM Hannah is training for a walkathon. The table shows the number of miles she walked each day. Use the data to predict how many miles Hannah will walk each day during the rest of her training.

Distance Hannah Walked (mi)				
4	2	9	3	3
5	5	1	4	2
5	2	5	4	5
4	9	3	2	4

Examples

Record each data value in a line plot.

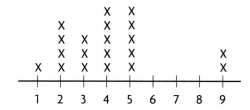

Distance Walked (mi)

A line plot helps you see where data cluster. On most days, Hannah walked 2–5 mi.

So, if she continues this pace, Hannah will probably walk 2–5 mi each day for the rest of her training.

A value separated from the rest of the data values is called an outlier. On a line plot, outliers appear next to the gaps created by groups of points without any data values.

What other information about the spread of the data do you see on the line plot?

Outliers	Gaps
The data value 9 is separate from the other data values.	There are no X's above 6, 7, or 8 on the number line.

So, there is an outlier of 9 mi.   So, there is a gap between 5 and 9 mi.

• When is a line plot an appropriate display of data?

414

Frequency Tables

A **frequency table** shows the total for each category or group. **Cumulative frequency** is a running total of frequencies. You can add a cumulative frequency column to a frequency table to answer questions about the data.

Example

Jill kept a record of her workout times in a tally chart. How many of Jill's workouts lasted 3 hr or less?

Jills' Workout Times	
1 Hour	ЖН II
2 Hours	ЖН ЖН I
3 Hours	IIII
4 Hours	ЖН I

Use the data to make a cumulative frequency table.

1 List the workout hours in the first column.

2 Record the frequency of workout hours in the frequency column.

3 Record the running total in the cumulative frequency column.

Jills' Workout Times		
Hours	**Frequency**	**Cumulative Frequency**
1	7	7
2	11	18
3	4	22
4	6	28

← 7 + 11 = 18
← 18 + 4 = 22
← 22 + 6 = 28

So, Jill worked out for 3 hr or less 22 times.

Math Idea

Interpreting a frequency table with a cumulative frequency column keeps you from having to perform tedious calculations.

The table shows the number of consecutive laps Ricardo swam each day. On how many days did Ricardo swim fewer than 18 consecutive laps?

Ricardo's Lap Swimming				
10	10	15	5	12
12	5	19	3	19
16	14	17	18	13
6	17	16	11	8

Make a cumulative frequency table with 4 intervals to solve the problem.

1 Find the range of the data. $19 - 3 = 16$

2 Use the range to determine the intervals.

Round 16 up to a number that is more than the greatest data value and divisible by the number of intervals.

Round 16 to 20. $20 > 19$ $20 \div 4 = 5$

Each interval will have 5 consecutive numbers.

Ricardo's Lap Swimming		
Number of Laps	**Frequency**	**Cumulative Frequency**
3–7	4	4
8–12	6	10
13–17	7	17
18–22	3	20

3 Start the first interval with the smallest data value, use intervals of 4, and **complete** the cumulative frequency table.

For 1–3, use the data in the tally chart.

1. Complete the cumulative frequency table.

Daily Distance Lionel Biked	
1–10 km	ЖЖ ЖЖ II
11–20 km	ЖЖ ЖЖ ЖЖ III
21–30 km	ЖЖ ЖЖ ЖЖ ЖЖ I
31–40 km	IIII

Daily Distance Lionel Biked		
Distance	Frequency	Cumulative Frequency
1–10 km	12	12
11–20 km	18	30
21–30 km		
31–40 km		

☑ **2.** On how many days did Lionel bike 30 km or less?   ☑ **3.** On how many days did Lionel bike less than 21 km?

4. [Math Talk] Explain how cumulative frequency tables help you interpret data.

► **Practice and Problem Solving** REAL WORLD

 Real World Data

For 5–10, use the data in the table.

Gloria's Daily Sit-ups				
13	3	14	13	12
12	13	4	15	12
15	13	14	3	11
13	13	12	14	15
11	14	13	15	11

5. Make a line plot of the data.

6. What gaps and outliers in the data do you see on the line plot?

7. Use the line plot to predict how many sit-ups Gloria will do each day if she continues her exercise program.

8. Make a cumulative frequency table of the data with 3 intervals.

9. **Explain** how you decided on the intervals.

★ **OCCT Test Prep**

10. How many students at summer camp are less than 16 yr old?

Students at Summer Camp		
Age	Frequency	Cumulative Frequency
7–9	13	13
10–12	40	53
13–15	21	74
16–18	20	94

A 21 students   **C** 53 students

B 40 students   **D** 74 students

11. How many hours of homework do you predict Jessie will do next week?

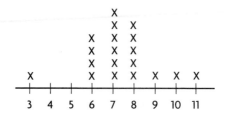

Jessie's Weekly Homework (hr)

A 3 hours   **C** 6–8 hours

B 4–5 hours   **D** 9–11 hours

GO ONLINE **Technology**
Use HMH Mega Math, The Numbers Games, *Arachna Graph*, Levels E and F.

☆ Standards Quick Check

For 1-2, use the data in the tables.

1. Complete the cumulative frequency table.

Calls	Frequency	Cumulative Frequency
0–4	13	13
5–9	11	
10–14		

Number of Calls Made per Day	
0–4	ⅢⅢ ⅢⅢ Ⅲ
5–9	ⅢⅢ ⅢⅢ Ⅰ
10–14	ⅢⅢ Ⅲ

2. How many days were the number of calls greater than 4?

Relative Frequency

What percent of the people in the survey rated the fitness center as excellent?

Solve the problem by finding the relative frequency of the excellent rating. **Relative frequency** is the frequency of the category divided by the sum of the frequencies.

Fitness Center Survey	
Excellent	ⅢⅢ ⅢⅢ ⅢⅢ Ⅲ
Good	ⅢⅢ ⅢⅢ ⅢⅢ
Fair	ⅢⅢ ⅢⅢ ⅢⅢ ⅢⅢ Ⅰ
Poor	ⅢⅢ Ⅰ

The frequency of the excellent rating is 18. The sum of the frequencies is 60. $18 \div 60 = 0.3 = 30\%$

So, 30% of the people in the survey rated the fitness center as excellent.

Fitness Center Survey		
Quality	Frequency	Relative Frequency
Excellent	18	
Good	15	
Fair	21	
Poor	6	

Solve.

1. What percent of the people in the survey rated the fitness center as fair?

2. What rating did $\frac{1}{4}$ of the people in the survey give the fitness center?

3. Which rating has a relative frequency of 10%?

4. What percent of the people rated the fitness center as fair or better?

LESSON 4

★ **5.1.** Organize, construct displays, and interpret data to solve problems (e.g., data from student experiments, tables, diagrams, charts, graphs).

Vocabulary

convenience sampling

population

random sampling

sample

sampling method

survey

systematic sampling

Materials
• MathBoard

Samples and Surveys

Essential Question How do frequency tables and line graphs display data?

A **survey** is a method of gathering information about a group. Surveys are usually made up of questions or other items that require responses. You can survey a **population**, the entire group of individuals or objects. Or, if the population is large, you can survey a part of the group, or a **sample**.

There are many types of **sampling methods**. The sampling method is the way in which a sample of a population is selected. The table below shows three different methods.

Sampling Method	Definition	Example
Random Sampling	Every individual or object in the population has an equal chance of being selected for the survey.	Assign a number to each student in the school. Then randomly select numbers using a computer.
Convenience Sampling	The most available individuals or objects in the population are selected to obtain results quickly.	Choose a convenient location, such as the library or cafeteria, and survey students as they walk in.
Systematic Sampling	An individual or object is randomly selected and then others are selected using a pattern.	Randomly choose a student from a list of students and then choose every fourth student.

Tell the best sampling method to use.

Ron has a week to conduct a survey of the preferred type of communication of students at his school. Which sampling method should Ron use so every student has an equal chance of being selected?

He should use random sampling. Random sampling would ensure that every student has an equal chance of being selected.

....

Meg takes a similar survey. She has a complete list of the students in fourth grade. Which sampling method should she use so that every third student from fourth grade is surveyed?

She should use systematic sampling. Systematic sampling uses a pattern to select students to survey.

• What type of sampling should Ron use if the assignment is due in 2 hr and he needs results quickly? Explain your reasoning.

► Share and Show

1. Anita wants to know if sixth-grade students prefer to use e-mail or text messaging, so she plans to make a survey. She needs the results quickly. Which sampling method should Anita use?

Tell the best sampling method to use.

2. Meg wants to find out how people in her neighborhood rate their cell phone reception. She wants responses from **every other household**.

3. Trey is taking a survey about the new school colors. Trey needs to take the survey on the bus ride home from school.

4. Belynda wants to know which theme middle school students at her school would like for the spring dance. She wants each student to have an equal chance of being selected.

5. **Math Talk** **Explain** why different sampling methods are used in surveys.

Tell the best sampling method to use.

6. A cable company employee wants to know which television channels people like best. She wants to survey people at the grocery store while she is shopping.

7. The owner of an Internet service provider wants to find out why customers chose his service. He wants each customer to have an equal chance of being surveyed.

For 8–9, use the data at the right.

8. Pat used a systematic sample for a survey about favorite sports. Which shows a systematic sample?

9. Juanita used a random sample for a survey about favorite colors. Which shows a random sample?

10. **Write Math** ► Suppose you are conducting a survey. Tell how you would choose a random sample.

Method A	1. James	2. Earl ✔
	3. Susie	4. Tim ✔	5. Jill
	6. Alex ✔	7. Mary	8. Carol ✔
Method B	1. Sam ✔	2. Matt
	3. Jane ✔	4. Paul ✔	5. Carly
	6. Zack	7. Sarah	8. Ryan ✔

✔ = selected for survey

 OCCT Test Prep

11. Mike wants to know the favorite website of students at his school. He asks students in the library. Which sampling method is Mike using?

    A convenience   **C** systematic

    B random   **D** another method

12. Brenda wants to know the favorite TV shows of her classmates. She choses the pieces of paper from a hat to get the information she is looking for. Which sampling method is Brenda using?

    A systematic   **C** random

    B another method   **D** convenience

LESSON 5

★ **5.1.** Organize, construct displays, and interpret data to solve problems (e.g., data from student experiments, tables, diagrams, charts, graphs).

Materials
• MathBoard

Math Talk

What is a question that could be answered by using each of the diagrams shown?

Problem Solving Workshop
Strategy: Draw a Diagram

Essential Question What types of diagrams can be used to solve problems?

▶ **Learn the Strategy** REAL WORLD

Drawing a diagram helps you to easily see the solution to a problem. You can use diagrams to solve different types of problems.

A Venn diagram shows relationships between groups.

The results of a survey show that 200 drivers sit in traffic driving to work, 350 sit in traffic driving home, and 50 sit in traffic driving both ways.

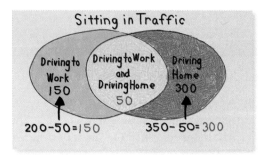

Some diagrams show direction and distance.

A bus driver leaves a bus station and travels 5 miles north, 10 miles east, 12 miles south, 6 miles west, and 7 miles north.

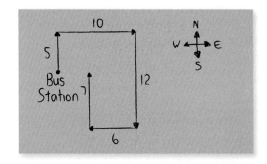

Other diagrams show size.

Jim and Sarah park their cars next to a curb that is 47 ft long. Each car is 16 ft long. Sarah parks 5 ft behind one end of the curb. Jim parks 2 ft behind Sarah.

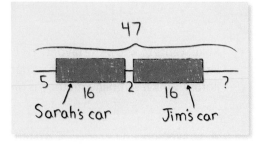

UNLOCK the Problem · REAL WORLD

PROBLEM Ben conducted a survey about the methods of transportation used by a group of commuters. The results show that 25 people commute by subway, 35 by bus, and 40 by car. Six people use both subway and bus, 10 use both bus and car, and 9 use both subway and car. Four people use all three methods of transportation. How many people were in the survey?

Read the Problem	Solve the Problem
What do I need to find? I need to find how many total people were surveyed.	Draw a Venn diagram with three overlapping circles. Label each circle with the form of transportation. Four people use the subway, bus, and car. 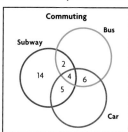
What information do I need to use? I know that the results showed that 25 people commute by subway, 35 by bus, and 40 by car. Six people use both subway and bus, 10 use both bus and car, and 9 use both subway and car. Four people use all three methods of transportation.	Since 6 people use the subway and bus in commuting, subtract $6 - 4 = 2$. So, 2 people use only the subway and the bus. Since 10 people use the bus and car in commuting, subtract $10 - 4 = 6$. So, 6 people use only the bus and a car. Since 9 people use the subway and car in commuting, subtract $9 - 4 = 5$. So, 5 people use only the subway and a car. Twenty-five people use the subway in commuting. Since $4 + 2 + 5 = 11$ and $25 - 11 = 14$, 14 people use only the subway.
How will I use the information? I can draw a Venn diagram with three overlapping circles to find out how many poeple were surveyed.	Use the same process to complete the other parts of the diagram. Then add all the numbers in the diagram 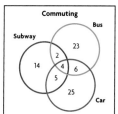 $14 + 2 + 23 + 5 +$ $4 + 6 + 25 = 79$ So, 79 people were in the survey.

Commuters were asked in a survey what types of roads they travel on to work. The results of the survey show that 90 commuters use side streets, 75 use expressways, and 85 use the interstate. Fifteen commuters use both side streets and expressways. Twenty-one use both expressways and the interstate. Eleven use both side streets and the interstate. Nine commuters use all three types of roads.

1. How many commuters are in the survey?

   First, draw a Venn diagram.

   Then, complete all the parts of the diagram.

   Finally, add all the numbers in the diagram.

☑ 2. **What if** 80 commuters use side streets, 65 use expressways, and 75 use the interstate? All the other conditions remain the same. How many commuters would be in the survey?

☑ 3. Bob, Fran, Pat, and Nino all take the same bus to work. Bob's office is 12 blocks north of Fran's office. Pat's office is 4 blocks south of Fran's office. Nino's office is north of Pat's office and halfway between Bob and Pat's offices. How far is Nino's office from Bob's office?

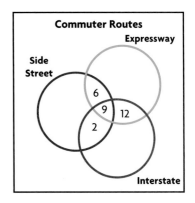

On Your Own

Draw a diagram to solve.

4. Bev and Denny live the same distance from work. They both leave home at 7:45 A.M. and walk to work at the same speed. Denny arrives at work at 8:15 A.M. Bev realizes halfway to work that she forgot something. She goes back home at the same speed and then walks to work again. If she spends 3 minutes at home, what time does Bev arrive at work?

5. Santiago asked a random sample of commuters the following question in a survey: When is rush hour traffic the worst, Monday, Wednesday, or Friday? Twenty-four commuters voted for Monday, 27 for Wednesday, and 30 for Friday. Seven commuters voted for Monday and Wednesday. Nine voted for Wednesday and Friday. Ten voted for Monday and Friday. Three voted for Monday, Wednesday, and Friday. How many total commuters were surveyed?

6. Linda is in a car pool. She leaves her house and drives $2\frac{1}{2}$ mi south to pick up Pedro. Then she drives $1\frac{1}{4}$ mi east and $2\frac{3}{4}$ mi north to pick up Donna. From Donna's house, she drives $\frac{1}{4}$ mi south. How far is Linda from her house now?

7. **Write Math** What's the Error? There are 5 posters of equal size on the wall of a train station, side by side. The wall is 120 in. wide. There are 3 in. between posters and 4 in. at each end of the wall. Kendall claims that each poster must be 100 in. wide. Describe her error and find the actual width.

Real World Data

For 8–12, use the Commuter Rail Survey.

8. Karen commutes to and from work 20 days each month. She votes for the train pass that is least expensive for her commute. Which pass does Karen vote for? How much does she save in 1 month by using that pass instead of the next least expensive pass?

9. Larry votes for the ten-ride train pass. When he buys the pass, he hands the clerk 3 bills and she gives him $5.25 in change. What 3 bills does Larry hand the clerk?

10. Three-fourths of the commuters in the survey voted for the monthly pass. One-third of the other commuters in the survey voted for the ten-ride pass. The remaining votes were evenly split between one-way passes and one-day passes. Thirty commuters voted for one-day passes. How many commuters were in the survey?

11. **Pose a Problem** Rewrite Problem 8 with Karen commuting a different number of days per month. Solve the problem.

12. **Open-Ended Problem** Suppose you are using the commuter rail to go to work. Decide how many days you are going to use the commuter rail each month. Then decide which pass makes the most sense for you to purchase.

Choose a Strategy
- Use Logical Reasoning
- Draw a Diagram or Picture
- Make a Model or Act It Out
- Make an Organized List
- Find a Pattern
- Make a Table or Graph
- Predict and Test
- Work Backward
- Solve a Simpler Problem
- Write an Equation

Commuter Rail Survey

Which train pass do you buy most often? Check 1 box.

☐ One-Way Pass	$5.25
☐ One-Day Pass	$10.50
☐ Ten-Ride Pass	$44.75
☐ Monthly Pass	$139.25

 **H.O.T. PROBLEM**

Students from Samuel's grade traveled to the beach, mountains, or amusement park for their summer vacation. Some went to more than one of these places.

13. Half of Samuel's class traveled to the mountains for summer vacation. There were more students who traveled only to the beach than only to an amusement park. Six students traveled to both the beach and an amusement park. If there are 24 students in Samuel's class, how many students could there be who traveled only to the beach?

14. Sixty students in Samuel's grade traveled only to the beach for summer vacation. Two-thirds of that number traveled either to the mountains or to an amusement park. Of those two-thirds, one-fourth traveled to both the mountains and an amusement park. If 19 students traveled to the mountains, how many more students traveled to an amusement park than to the mountains?

★ **5.1.** Organize, construct displays, and interpret data to solve problems (e.g., data from student experiments, tables, diagrams, charts, graphs).

Vocabulary

double-bar graph

Materials

• MathBoard

ERROR ALERT

Be sure to

• include a title.

• label the scales.

• provide a key.

Bar Graphs

Essential Question What components are necessary for a bar graph?

▶ **Learn** REAL WORLD

PROBLEM Many schools sponsor activities focused on the arts. The table shows the percents of elementary schools that offer extracurricular arts programs in two different regions of the country. Which region has a greater percent of schools offering field trips to art museums?

A bar graph is a useful way to display and analyze data that is grouped in categories. A **double-bar graph** helps to compare two sets of data.

Use the data in the table to make a double-bar graph.

Elementary Schools with Arts Programs			
Region	Field trips to performances	Field trips to art museums	Visiting artists
Southeast	82%	38%	37%
West	77%	67%	34%

❶ Determine an appropriate scale. Numbers vary from 34% to 82%. So, use a scale from 0 to 100%.

❷ Use the data to determine the length of the bars. Make the bars of equal width.

❸ Use different colors to represent the different sets of data.

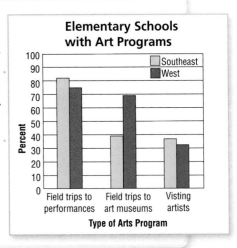

In comparing the field trips to art museums, the West region has the taller bar. So, the West region offers a greater percent of trips to art museums.

▶ **Share and Show** Math Board

1. Suppose you added the data at the right to the graph above. Would the bars be longer than some of the bars shown? If so, which bars?

Region	After-school Arts Program
Southeast	42%
West	55%

For 2–5, use the table.

✔ **2.** Make a double-bar graph using the data in the table.

3. Compare the matching bars for men and women. Which shows the greatest difference?

✔ **4.** What type of entertainment should Mr. and Mrs. Jones choose so that they will most likely enjoy it equally?

5. `Math Talk` **Explain** the steps you should follow when making a bar graph. In your explanation, refer to the graph you made in Exercise 2.

Favorite Types of Entertainment		
	Men	Women
Movies	19%	40%
Television	46%	31%
Live Shows	35%	29%

▶ Practice and Problem Solving REAL WORLD

For 6–8, use the table.

6. Use the data in the table to make a double-bar graph.

7. Which type of financial support has declined from ten years ago to this season?

8. Compare the total financial support from ten years ago with the total for this season. Which type of support shows the greatest difference?

Financial Support for Symphony (in millions of dollars)			
	Income from Concerts	Private Contributions	Government Grants
Ten years ago	470	350	60
This season	520	570	50

For 9–11, use the bar graph.

9. Which two types of movies, when combined, are about as popular as action movies?

10. Each percent represents the number of people out of 100 who chose each type of movie. If the graph shows the results for 400 people, how many people favored each type of movie?

11. `Write Math` **What's the Error?** Stephanie claims that if 5,000 people took the survey, then 65 people chose science fiction. Find her error and correct it.

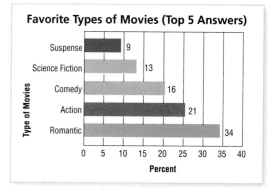

Favorite Types of Movies (Top 5 Answers)

★ OCCT Test Prep

Math Board

12. Look at the bar graph for Exercises 9–11. How many people voted for their favorite type of movie?

   A 350   **C** 395

   B 365   **D** 400

13. Look at the bar graph for Exercises 9–11. Which type of movie is about half as popular as romantic movies?

   A suspense   **C** science fiction

   B comedy   **D** action

5.1. Organize, construct displays, and interpret data to solve problems (e.g., data from student experiments, tables, diagrams, charts, graphs).

Vocabulary

double-line graph

Materials
• MathBoard

Remember

The jagged line on the scale shows a break in the scale. Some numbers are left out.

Line Graphs

Essential Question What components are necessary for a line graph?

PROBLEM Over 80% of consumers buy music CDs from stores. The table shows the type of stores where people have bought music. Analyze the data. How have people's CD-buying habits changed during the time shown?

A **double-line graph** helps to compare two sets of data that change over time.

Use the data in the table to make a double-line graph.

Music CDs Sold				
Store Type	2000	2001	2002	2003
Music Store	54%	43%	37%	33%
Department Store	41%	42%	51%	53%

1 Determine an appropriate scale. Numbers vary from 33% to 54%. So, use a scale from 0% to 60%.

2 Mark a point in one color for each year's percent sold at music stores, and connect the points.

3 Mark a point in another color for each year's percent sold at department stores. Connect the points.

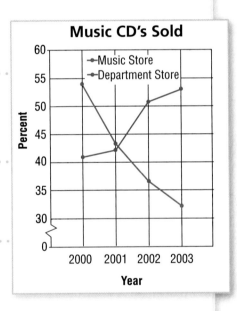

The red line shows that the trend from one year to the next in percent purchased at music stores has gone down, while the blue line shows the percent purchased at department stores has gone up.

So, people are buying fewer of their music CDs at music stores and more at department stores.

• Look at the double-line graph above. What conclusion could you make about music CD sales in 2001? Explain.

▶ Share and Show

1. Suppose you added the data at the right to the graph above. Would the trends for each type of store remain the same?

Department	2004
Music Store	32%
Department Store	54%

For 2–5, use the table.

✓ **2.** Use the data in the table at the right to make a double-line graph.

✓ **3.** Between which years did the percent of hip-hop music sales increase the most?

4. Find the difference in percent of sales between the two types of music for each year. Order the differences from least to greatest.

5. [Math Talk] **Explain** how you can use the double-line graph in Exercise 2 to make predictions about the future percents of sales of the two types of music.

Percent of Music by Type Sold		
Type of music	Hip-Hop	Rhythm and Blues
1955	7%	11%
1998	8%	13%
2001	11%	11%
2004	12%	11%

▶ ## Practice and Problem Solving REAL WORLD

For 6–7, use the table.

6. Use the data in the table to make a double-bar graph.

7. **Reasoning** Describe the trend of listening time from age 8 to age 18. **Explain** your reasoning.

Minutes Per Day Listening to Audio Media			
Listening Device	8-10 year-olds	11-14 year-olds	15-18 year-olds
Radio	29	57	75
CD/Tapes/MP3s	30	45	69

For 8–10, use the line graph.

8. Which two years show the same percent of music sales for jazz music?

9. Find the difference in the percent of jazz music sales between each pair of years. Between which two years was the greatest increase?

10. [Write Math] ▶ Melissa says that the trend for purchases of jazz music have been declining in recent years. Do you agree or disagree? **Explain**

★ ## OCCT Test Prep [Math Board]

11. Use the line graph about jazz music above. Between which two years is there the greatest decrease in sales of jazz music?

  A 1999–2000   **C** 2001–2002

  B 2000–2001   **D** 2002–2003

12. Use the line graph about jazz music above. What was the largest increase in sales during any two years?

  A 0.1%   **C** 0.8%

  B 0.5%   **D** 1.3%

★ 5.1. Organize, construct displays, and interpret data to solve problems (e.g., data from student experiments, tables, diagrams, charts, graphs).

Vocabulary

circle graph

Materials
• MathBoard

Circle Graphs

Essential Question What components are need for a circle graph?

PROBLEM Almost everyone has a favorite color. Many people also have colors they favor the least. How does the percent of people who choose purple as their least favorite color compare with the percent of people who choose yellow? The circle graph below, which shows the results of a survey, can help you answer that question.

A **circle graph** helps you compare parts of the data with the whole and with other parts.

Examples

Find the parts that represent purple and yellow. Compare the percents of people choosing purple and yellow as their least favorite color.

Purple was chosen by 26% of the people, and yellow was chosen by 13%.

$26 \div 13 = 2$

So, twice as many people chose purple as their least favorite color as chose yellow.

Of all girls surveyed, what fraction chose blue?

Find the part that represents the number of girls who chose blue as their favorite color.

105 girls chose blue as their favorite color.

Find the total number of girls who participated in the survey by adding the number of girls who chose each color.

$105 + 18 + 9 + 60 + 69 + 27 + 12 = 300$

Write as a fraction in simplest form. $\frac{105}{300} = \frac{7}{20}$

So, $\frac{7}{20}$ of all girls surveyed chose blue as their favorite color.

• What percent of girls chose blue as their favorite color?

▶ **Share and Show**

1. In the Least Favorite Color example, 4% of the people surveyed chose red as their least favorite color and 12% chose gray. How does the percent who chose gray compare with the percent who chose red?

For 2–4, use the circle graph at the right.

✓ **2.** Write a fraction in simplest form to represent the number of boys who chose purple or gray as their least favorite color.

3. What percent of boys chose yellow as their least favorite color?

✓ **4.** How does the number of boys who chose gray as their least favorite color compare with the number who chose green?

5. **Math Talk** **Explain** why you would use a circle graph to compare the results of a survey.

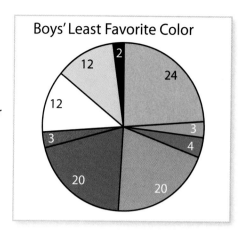

Boys' Least Favorite Color

▶ **Practice and Problem Solving** REAL WORLD

For 6–9, use the circle graph at the right.

6. Write a fraction in simplest form that represents the cost of the paint thinner compared to the total cost of the painting supplies.

7. Which three items combine to make up $\frac{3}{4}$ of the total cost?

8. What conclusion could you make about the cost of paint? Is your conclusion valid? **Explain.**

9. How does the cost of a drop cloth compare with the cost of white paint and a brush/roller combined?

Cost of Painting Supplies

For 10–12, use the circle graph at the right.

10. What two types of books make up $\frac{2}{5}$ of the books in the arts and crafts section? **Explain.**

11. **Reasoning** Clay counted 120 knitting or sewing books in the central library. Based on the data given, how many woodworking books does the library have? **Explain.**

12. **Write Math** ▶ **What's the Question?** The answer is that when combined, they are almost double the percent of painting books.

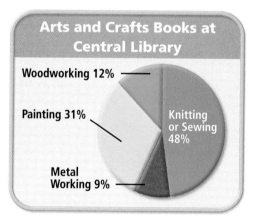

Arts and Crafts Books at Central Library

★ **OCCT Test Prep**

13. A circle graph shows the results of 320 people surveyed. What fraction of the graph would represent the 100 people who answered yes?

   A $\frac{4}{15}$ **C** $\frac{5}{16}$

   B $\frac{3}{10}$ **D** $\frac{3}{8}$

14. A circle graph shows the results of 580 people surveyed. What fraction of the graph would represent the 145 people who answered maybe?

   A $\frac{1}{4}$ **C** $\frac{9}{15}$

   B $\frac{8}{10}$ **D** $\frac{10}{15}$

Extra Practice See page 451, Set E.

★ **5.1.** Organize, construct displays, and interpret data to solve problems (e.g., data from student experiments, tables, diagrams, charts, graphs).

Materials
• MathBoard

Make and Analyze Graphs

Essential Question How can you use bar graphs, line graphs, and circle graphs to display data?

PROBLEM The music CDs in Vanessa's home were mixed up. Vanessa organized the CDs by music type and by who owns them, as shown in the table. How many more jazz CDs do her parents own than Vanessa owns?

Number of CDs In Vanessa's Family						
	Oldies	**Rock**	**Country**	**Pop**	**Jazz**	**Classical**
Vanessa	1	12	14	9	3	4
Parents	10	6	2	5	7	5

A bar graph is a useful way to display data that is grouped in categories. A double-bar graph helps compare two sets of data.

Make a double-bar graph.

1 Determine an appropriate scale. Numbers vary from 1 to 14. Use a scale from 0 to 20.

2 Use bars of equal width. Use the data to determine the lengths of the bars.

3 Use different colors or patterns to represent the different sets of data. Be sure to title the graph, label both axes, and include a key that identifies the data sets.

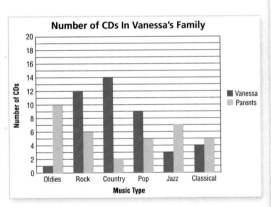

The green bar shows that Vanessa's parents have 7 jazz CDs.

The purple bar shows that Vanessa has 3 jazz CDs.

So, her parents own 7 − 3, or 4, more jazz CDs than Vanessa owns.

• Explain the relationship between the table and the double-bar graph.

Double-Line Graphs and Circle Graphs

A double-line graph helps you compare two sets of data that change over time.

Over 80% of consumers buy music CDs from stores. The table from the Recording Industry Association of America shows the types of stores where people have bought music for several years. Analyze the data. How has the trend in people's music-buying habits changed?

Make a double-line graph.

❶ Determine an appropriate scale. Numbers vary from 32% to 54%. So, use a scale from 0% to 60%.

Source of Music Sales					
	2000	**2001**	**2002**	**2003**	**2004**
Music Store	42%	43%	37%	33%	32%
Other Store	41%	42%	51%	53%	54%

❷ Mark a point for each percent sold at music stores. Connect the points.

❸ Mark a point for each percent sold at other stores. Use a different color to connect the points.

❹ Title the graph and both axes. Include a key.

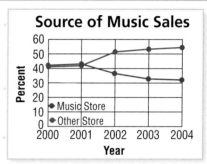

The blue line shows that from 2000 to 2004, the trend for percent of music purchases at music stores went down, while the red line shows that the trend for percent of music purchases at other stores went up.

So, people are buying less music at music stores than at other stores.

- Between which two years did the greatest change in the percent of music sales occur in each of the types of stores?

ERROR ALERT

Read the key carefully. Trace your finger on the appropriate line for each label.

A circle graph helps you compare parts of data to other parts of the whole.

Vanessa compares the types of CDs she owns, using a circle graph. How many rock CDs does she have for every jazz CD?

Make a double-line graph.

The percents in a circle graph have a sum of 100%, or one whole.

Find the parts that represent rock and jazz CDs.

Rock CDs make up 28% of her total, while jazz CDs make up 7%.

$28 \div 7 = 4$

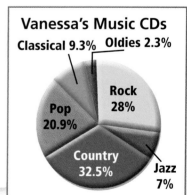

So, Vanessa has 4 rock CDs for every jazz CD.

For 1–5, use the table below.

Types of Music Sold (percent of total)				
	1995	1998	2001	2004
Rock	34	26	24	24
Country	17	14	11	13

Percent of Music Sold

[graph: Percent on y-axis (0 to 50), Year on x-axis (1995, 1998, 2001, 2004), Rock line shown]

✓ **1.** Copy and complete the double-line graph at the right by graphing the data for country music.

2. For the years shown in the graph, when was rock music most popular?

3. Between which two years did the greatest decline occur in the percent of rock music sold?

✓ **4.** What is the relationship between the sales of country music and the sales of rock music over the years?

5. **Math Talk** **Explain** why it is most appropriate to use a double-line graph to display the data in the table for Exercise 1.

▶ **Practice and Problem Solving** REAL WORLD

For 6–9, use the table at the right.

6. Make a double-bar graph using the data in the table.

7. Describe how sources of financial support of symphony orchestras have changed over the last ten years.

8. If the data for orchestra support this season were represented in a circle graph, which section of the circle would be the largest?

Sources of Support for Orchestras (in millions)			
	Income from Concerts	Private Contributions	Government Grants
10 Years Ago	$470	$350	$70
This Season	$530	$580	$50

9. **Reasoning** If concert income increases by about the same amount in the next 10 years as it increased in the last 10 years, will it reach $600 million? **Explain**.

★ **OCCT Test Prep**

10. Maria gathered information from students at her high school on what they want their jobs to be when they are an adult. Which type of graph should Maria use to show this type of data?

A double-line graph   C circle graph

B line graph   D bar graph

11. Jessica is doing an experiment for her science class. She is growing two plants under different conditions. What type of graph should Jessica use to display the height of each plant over a 3-week time span?

A double-bar graph   C circle graph

B double-line graph   D histogram

 Technology
Use HMH Mega Math, The Number
Games, *Arachna Graph,* Level L.

⭐ Standards Quick Check

Use the circle graph.

1. In 2004, what percent of music was purchased by people over 19?

2. What fraction of music was purchased by people aged 20–39?

3. **What's the Question?** The fraction of music purchased is $\frac{11}{50}$.

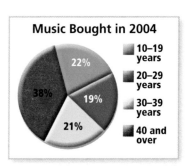

Music Bought in 2004

■ 10–19 years
■ 20–29 years
□ 30–39 years
■ 40 and over

Challenge 🌟 H.O.T.

Circle Graphs And Diagrams

You may be able to show the information in a circle graph using a diagram.

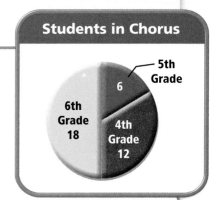

Students in Chorus

The circle graph shows the number of 4th, 5th, and 6th graders in the school chorus. Make a diagram showing the information in the graph.

$12 + 6 + 18 = 36$ Find the total of the data.

$4^{th}: \frac{12}{36} = \frac{1}{3}; \quad 5^{th}: \frac{6}{36} = \frac{1}{6}; \quad 6^{th}: \frac{18}{36} = \frac{1}{2}$ Write a fraction in simplest form representing each grade.

$\frac{1}{3} = \frac{4}{12}; \quad \frac{1}{6} = \frac{2}{12}; \quad \frac{1}{2} = \frac{6}{12}$ Write equivalent fractions.

Students in Chorus

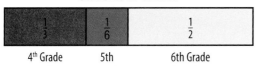

| $\frac{1}{3}$ | $\frac{1}{6}$ | $\frac{1}{2}$ |

4ᵗʰ Grade   5th   6th Grade
12 students   6 students   18 students

Draw a diagram representing the 36 students. Use the fractions $\frac{1}{3}, \frac{1}{6}$, and $\frac{1}{2}$ to complete the diagram.

Draw a diagram showing the information in the circle graph.

1. **Soccer Record**

   Ties 2
   Losses 6
   Wins 12

2. **6th Grade Pets**

   Others 4
   Birds 4
   Cats 12
   Dogs 28

3. **Survey Results**

   Maybe 10%
   Yes 40%
   No 50%

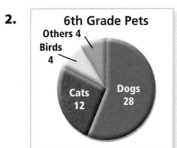

⭐ **5.1.** Organize, construct displays, and interpret data to solve problems (e.g., data from student experiments, tables, diagrams, charts, graphs).

Stem-and-Leaf Plots and Histograms

Essential Question How can you use a stem-and-leaf plot to help make a histogram?

▶ **Learn** REAL WORLD

PROBLEM Health experts say that you should exercise 30 min per day. Tyler's classmates monitored the exact number of minutes they exercised one day. Their results are recorded below. How do the mode and median for this data compare to the goal of 30 min per day?

Vocabulary

histogram

stem-and-leaf plot

Materials
• MathBoard

Number of Minutes Exercised								
21	52	35	25	55	10	35	39	48
44	10	30	18	25	22	25	40	15

You can use a **stem-and-leaf plot** to organize data when you want to see each item in the data.

Make a stem-and-leaf plot.

1 Group the data by the tens digits. Then order the data from least to greatest.

10, 10, 15, 18
21, 22, 25, 25, 25
30, 35, 35, 39
40, 44, 48
52, 55

2 Use the tens digits as stems. Use the ones digits as leaves. Write the leaves in increasing order. The row 4 | 0 4 8 means 40, 44, and 48.

Number of Minutes Exercised

Stem	Leaves				
1	0	0	5	8	
2	1	2	5	5	5
3	0	5	5	9	
4	0	4	8		
5	2	5			

3 Use the stem-and-leaf plot to help find the mode and the median.

Mode: The mode is 25, because 25 occurs most often.
Median: There are 18 scores. The number halfway between the ninth and tenth scores is the median.

$$\frac{25 + 30}{2} = 27.5,\text{ so } 27.5 \text{ is the median.}$$

So, both the mode and median are less than the goal of 30 min per day.

• Find the range. Explain how the stem-and-leaf plot makes it easy to find the range of the data.

• Explain the relationship between the table of values and the stem-and-leaf plot.

Histograms

A health organization collected the data below from 30 people in a mall. How many people can do 30 or more sit-ups in a minute?

Sit-Ups Per Minute														
45	18	37	20	30	55	45	10	8	45	39	14	22	14	52
35	25	49	37	42	15	18	5	25	10	8	20	28	45	50

A bar graph can show information for individuals. With this much data, it is more effective to group the data into intervals. A **histogram** is a bar graph that shows the frequency, or number of occurrences, of data within intervals. The bars in a histogram are connected rather than separated.

Make a histogram for the data above.

1 Make a frequency table using intervals of 10.

Interval	0–9	10–19	20–29	30–39	40–49	50–59
Frequency	3	7	6	5	6	3

2 Title the graph, and label the scales and axes.

3 Graph the number of people who performed the number of sit-ups within each interval.

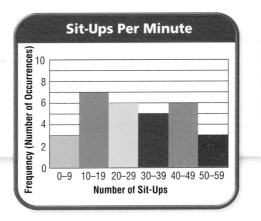

Remember

The interval 0–9 represents 10 different values.

 ▶ **Share and Show** · Math Board

For 1, use the data at the right.

1. a. Copy and complete the stem-and-leaf plot shown below to organize the ages of people at the health club.

Stem	Leaves
1	
2	
3	

Ages of People at the Health Club				
30	26	38	22	33
31	34	19	29	26
21	18	28	25	22

b. Use your stem-and-leaf plot to help find the median age of the people at the health club.

2. a. Copy and complete the frequency table below, using the data to the right. Then make a histogram.

Hours of TV/week	0–4	5–9	10–14	15–19	20–24
Frequency					

Number of Hours of TV Watching per Week				
4	14	24	17	10
21	21	15	20	23
5	22	19	18	8
24	19	20	22	24

b. How many people watch TV at least 5 hours but fewer than 20 hours in one week?

3. **Math Talk** **Explain** how you can use the histogram in Exercise 2 to find the number of people who did 19 or fewer sit-ups in a minute.

▶ Practice and Problem Solving REAL WORLD

For 4–6, use the Travel Time data table.

4. a. Make a stem-and-leaf plot of the data.

   b. Use the stem-and-leaf plot to help find the mean, median, mode, and range of the travel times.

5. How many of the states listed have a longer average travel time than California?

6. **Explain** how the stem-and-leaf plot would change if the average travel times for the states listed each increased by 5 minutes.

Average Travel Time to Work	
State	**Minutes**
Arizona	23
California	27
Illinois	28
Kansas	18
Massachusetts	26
Michigan	23
Ohio	22
New York	31
Pennsylvania	25
Texas	24

For 7–8, use the Ages of People data table.

7. a. Make a histogram of the ages of people in the park.

   b. Use the histogram to find the number of people in the park who are under the age of 10.

Ages of People in the Park							
3	34	5	36	55	58	7	11
12	8	6	2	44	31	22	26
29	30	32	10	5	4	6	18

8. Let m be the number of people in their 20s and 30s, and let n be the number of people in their 40s and 50s. What is the value of $m - n$? What does this tell you?

 OCCT Test Prep

9. There are 5 bars on a histogram of a data set with a range of 29 and a minimum value of 18. Which is the first interval on the histogram?

    A 0–5   **C** 18–23

    B 18–22   **D** 30–35

10. What is the mode of the data set?

Stem	Leaves							
1	2	5	7	9	9			
2	0	1	1	1	2	3	4	8
3	2							

    A 1   **C** 19

    B 9   **D** 21

⭐ Standards Quick Check

Tell whether a bar graph or a histogram is more appropriate. Explain your reasoning.

1. number of votes for five different actors in an awards ceremony

2. amount of money spent by 50 different customers at a convenience store

3. **Explain** how a bar graph and a histogram are similar and how they are different.

Shapes Of Data Displays

When you look at a histogram, its shape can tell you how the data are spread out among different intervals. This histogram shows the number of people in different age groups who said they use the Internet at least once a week.

Think about the shape the bars form. Then answer the questions.

1. Does the overall shape look almost the same on both sides of the tallest bar? What does the shape tell you about the number of people below age 30 and above age 39 who use the Internet?

2. Which data values are represented by the middle of the histogram?

3. Are there any outliers? If so, what data values do they represent?

4. Which data values occur most frequently?

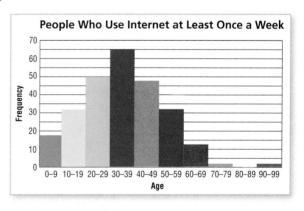

People Who Use Internet at Least Once a Week

★ 5.1. Organize, construct displays, and interpret data to solve problems (e.g., data from student experiments, tables, diagrams, charts, graphs).

Materials
• MathBoard

Compare Graphs

Essential Question How can you use graphs to compare data?

PROBLEM The city of Chicago has many interesting and entertaining museums. Using data given in the table below, Gabriella and Tom each made a graph showing attendance at two of the museums.

Average Daily Attendance					
	2000	**2001**	**2002**	**2003**	**2004**
Children's Museum	1,192	1,890	1,876	1,827	1,699
Museum of Contemporary Art	855	699	665	663	584

Compare the graphs.

Gabriella's graph shows upward and downward trends in the data and helps compare a museum's rising or falling attendance over time.

So, line graphs are good for showing changes over time.

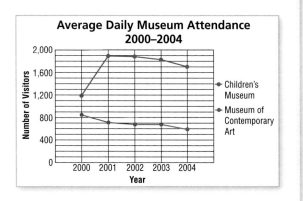

Tom's graph is similar to Gabriella's graph because it shows two sets of data and uses the same scale, labels, and title. However, the double-bar graph allows him to look at a year and make a side-by-side comparison. This way he can easily see the difference between the attendances of each category or year.

So, bar graphs are good for comparing categories.

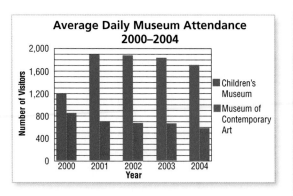

For 1–4, use the graphs below.

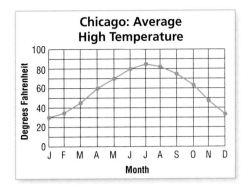

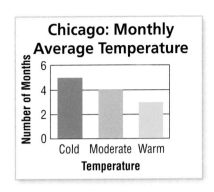

1. Ashley wants to visit Chicago during a month when the average temperature is above 60°F and likely to increase. The line graph shows the average monthly temperature data and the bar graph shows the number of cold, moderate, and warm months. Which graph should Ashley use to choose a month for her trip?

2. Which graph makes it easier to decide if Chicago is a "cold" or "warm" city?

3. How might the temperature data in the bar graph be used?

4. **Math Talk** Explain which graph is better suited for the data.

Practice and Problem Solving REAL WORLD

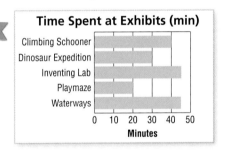

For 5–6, use the bar and circle graph at the right.

5. Which graph better compares the time spent at the dinosaur exhibit to the total time spent at the museum?

6. Which graph makes it easier to find the difference between the longest and shortest lengths of time spent viewing exhibits?

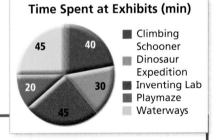

OCCT Test Prep

7. Which type of graph would be best to help compare the favorite museum activities of boys and of girls?

   A double-bar graph
   B circle graph
   C pictograph
   D histogram

8. Which type of graph would be best to help compare the stock price of a company over 2 years?

   A circle graph
   B stem-and-leaf plot
   C double-line graph
   D double-bar graph

★ **5.1.** Organize, construct displays, and interpret data to solve problems (e.g., data from student experiments, tables, diagrams, charts, graphs).

Materials
• MathBoard

Choose an Appropriate Graph

Essential Question What types of data would you use for each type of graph?

PROBLEM Baseball statistics provide many opportunities for making graphs, but what kind of graph is appropriate? The answer depends on the type of data and what you need to show.

Examples

Bar or double-bar graph

The data displayed in the graph shows runs scored at home games and away games for three teams.

Bar or double-bar graphs are best for data that are grouped in categories.

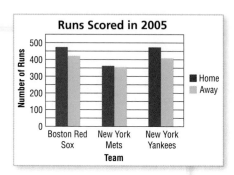

Line or double-line graph

The graph displays data about the average number of fans who attended Chicago Cubs games and Chicago White Sox games from 2001 to 2005.

Line or double-line graphs are best to show data that changes over time.

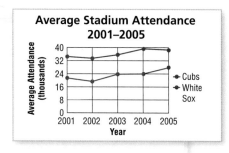

Circle graph

The data displayed shows the percent of first-place votes each of five players received in the voting for the League Rookie of the Year.

Circle graphs are best to show data that compare parts to the whole or to other parts.

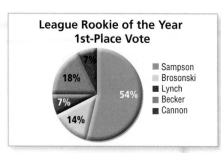

Pictograph

Number of Triples by Seven Pittsburgh Pirates Players

Sanchez   ⚾
Mackowiak   ⚾ ⚾ ⚾
Duffy   ⚾ ⚾
Bautista   ⚾ ⚾
Bay   ⚾ ⚾
Redman   ⚾ ⚾
Giles   ⚾ ⚾ ⚾ ⚾

Key: ⚾ = 2 triples

The data shows the number of triples hit by seven Pittsburgh Pirates players.

Pictographs are best to show data that is countable.

Histogram

The data displayed in the graph shows attendance at Jacobs Field for all 81 home games of the 2005 season. The data is grouped into intervals of 5,000.

Histograms are best for showing data that is grouped in intervals.

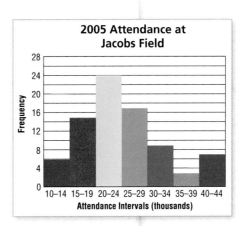

- Would more or less information about attendance be displayed if the intervals were 10,000 instead of 5,000? Explain.

▶ Share and Show

1. Alonso records the number of sixth graders who played on baseball teams in 2003, 2004, 2005, and 2006. Since the data changes over time, what graph would be most appropriate for the set of data?

For 2–4, name the best graph to display the data.

2. A research company counts the number of hot dogs sold by 3 different hot dog stands around the stadium.

✓ 3. A school board determines how much the total school sports budget allows for baseball, basketball, soccer, and tennis.

✓ 4. Jason groups the ages of 50 people whose favorite sport is baseball into intervals of 10.

5. **Math Talk** **Explain** when a pictograph would be best to display a set of data.

For 6–11, name the best graph to display the data.

6. the amount of the total practice time spent on each type of drill in soccer practice

7. the number of hits David and Joseph made each baseball season for the last 4 years

8. the height of every member of the basketball team

9. the number of wins and losses for 5 volleyball teams

10. the number of hours practiced in one week by 6 football teams

11. changes in the total number of students on sports teams over the past 10 years

For 12–13, use the tables.

12. Make a bar graph and a pictograph showing the number of bottles of water consumed by 5 players.

13. The table shows the number of points Mike and Julio scored each week during their club basketball season. What graph would be best to compare the points scored by Mike and Julio each week? **Explain**.

Bottles of Water Consumed				
Ann	John	Kayla	Grace	Jacob
15	20	10	15	5

Points Scored				
	Week 1	Week 2	Week 3	Week 4
Mike	39	28	25	26
Julio	32	30	28	35

14. ☰**FAST FACT** Wayne Gretzky holds the record for the most hockey goals scored in a career, 894. What graph would be best to display the numbers of goals scored by the top ten all-time scorers?

15. The data to the right shows the number of games that 17 different New York Yankees pitchers appeared in for the 2005 season. How many more pitchers appeared in 10–19 games than in 30–39 games? Make the most appropriate graph to help answer the question.

PITCHER APPEARANCES
71 79 14 15 34 18 30 64 17
34 16 29 13 13 13 19 67

16. Write Math ▶ Describe a set of data that would best be displayed using a line graph. **Explain** why a line graph would be best.

 OCCT Test Prep 🖊 Math Board

17. Which is the best graph to display the data in the chart?

A double-bar graph

B circle graph

C pictograph

D histogram

Chicago Cubs June Record		
	Wins	Losses
2005	14	13
2004	15	12
2003	12	15
2002	12	12

18. What kind of graph is best to display data about the percent of students who voted for their favorite lunch sandwich?

A double-bar graph

B circle graph

C pictograph

D histogram

⭐ Standards Quick Check

Name the best graph to display the data.

1. the number of students who play the following instruments: piano, violin, saxaphone

2. the number of absences that students have during a particular school year

Challenge H.O.T.

Population Pyramid

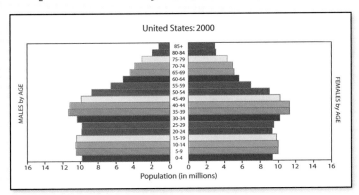

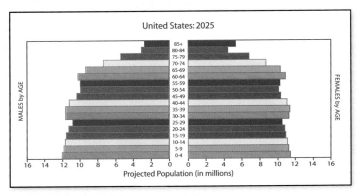

A population pyramid is a special type of histogram. It is a graph that shows the distribution of population by age and gender. The intervals are written vertically, and the bars appear to the left and right of the vertical scale. Like a double-bar graph, a population pyramid displays data about two groups.

Use the information in the population pyramids to solve the problems.

1. About how many more 10- to 14-year-old females than 70- to 74-year-old males were there in 2000?

2. Compare the number of 0- to 4-year-old males and females in 2000. Is the relationship the same or different than that shown in 2025?

3. Compare the number of 40- to 44-year-olds in 2000 and 2025. What generalization can you make about the age group?

4. **Write Math** ▶ Describe the general shape of both population pyramids. **Explain** what the change in shape tells you about the two populations.

Materials
• MathBoard

Problem Solving Workshop
Skill: Draw Conclusions

Essential Question What conclusions can be drawn from graphs?

PROBLEM Suppose you are playing a computer game and have to find an object on the screen in the middle of other shapes or objects, called distracters. Will it take longer to find the object among few or many distracters? Scientists perform experiments to determine answers to questions like this.

The table and the graph below display data about how different numbers of distracters affect reaction time using two different-shaped objects. Analyze the data to draw conclusions.

	Shape of Distracter	Number of Distracters
Condition 1	squares	5
Condition 2	squares	10
Condition 3	squares	15
Condition 4	cubes	5
Condition 5	cubes	10
Condition 6	cubes	15

Conditions 1, 2, and 3 use a square. The reaction times increase as the number of distracters increases.

Conditions 4, 5, and 6 use a cube. Again, the reaction times increase as the number of distracters increases.

So, the more distracters there are, the longer the reaction time is.

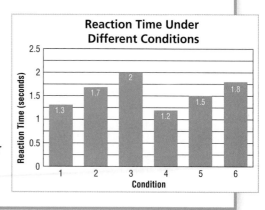

Draw conclusions from the data.

a. In the experiment above, which had the greater effect on reaction time, the shape of the distracters or the number of distracters?

b. Suppose the experiment were repeated using 20 distracter cubes. Based on the data, estimate the reaction time. Explain your reasoning.

c. When 50 distracter cubes were used, the reaction time was 4 seconds. Based on the data, if 50 distracter squares were used, would you expect the reaction time to be less than or greater than 4 seconds? Explain.

Share and Show Math Board

1. Luis tested the reaction times of seven students who had varying years of experience playing video games. Look at the data in the table and the graph. What conclusion can you draw about the reaction times of students A, B, and C? of students D, E, F, and G? of all the students?

Video Game Experience

Student	A	B	C	D	E	F	G
Number of Years	0	1	4	6	6	7	8

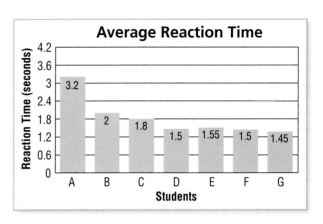

2. **What if** a student was added to the test that has been playing video games for 3 years? Based on the data, predict the reaction time of the student.

3. Peter predicted that as the day gets later, peoples' reaction times slow down. So, he tested his classmates' reaction times throughout the day. Look at the data in the graph at the right. Was Peter's prediction accurate? What conclusions can you draw about the reaction times at different hours of the day?

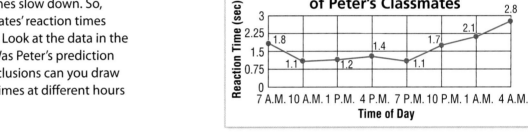

Mixed Applications

For 4–7, use the table and the double-bar graph.

4. Write the percent of teens who answered *yes* to using the Internet to get news and current events information in 2004 as a fraction and a decimal.

5. From 2000 to 2004, the percent of teens that read about health, fitness, and diet information online increased. Suppose this activity increases by the same amount between 2004 and 2008. About what percent will a new graph show for that category?

6. Suppose a sample of 100 teenagers were surveyed in 2004. Based on the results shown in the graph, estimate how many students said they bought items like music, books, and clothing online.

7. **Write Math** Make a generalization about how teen online activities have changed. **Explain** how you came to that conclusion.

What Teens Do Online

A	Play games online
B	Get news and current events information
C	Buy items like music, books, and clothing
D	Read about health, fitness, or diet information
E	Read about movies, TV, music groups, or sports stars

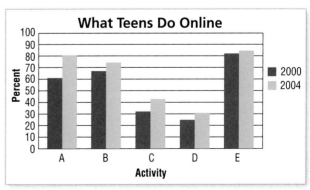

★ **5.1.** Organize, construct displays, and interpret data to solve problems (e.g., data from student experiments, tables, diagrams, charts, graphs).

Materials
• MathBoard

Find Unknown Values

Essential Question What ways can you find unknown values?

PROBLEM Brittany is training for a triathlon, which is a swimming, biking, and running race. The following table shows how long it takes Brittany to swim different distances. How many yards can Brittany swim in 3.5 min?

Brittany's Swimming Rate					
Time (min)	1	2	3	4	5
Distance (yd)	40	80	120	160	200

You can use a line graph to display the data and find the unknown data.

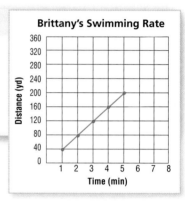

Use a line graph.

Make a line graph for the given data. Locate the point on the line for 3.5 min on the horizontal scale. The vertical scale for that point shows 140 yd.

So, Brittany can swim 140 yd in 3.5 min.

• How would you use the line graph to predict how many yards Brittany can swim in 6 min?

Use logical reasoning and arithmetic.

How many yards can Brittany swim in 8 min if she continues to swim at a constant rate?

Look at the data in the table. Since the rate is constant, you can logically find how far she swims in 8 min by using what you already know about the times she has recorded. You know how far she swims in 5 min, how far she swims in 3 min, and that $5 + 3 = 8$.

$200 + 120 = 320$ Add the yards she swims in 5 min to the yards she swims in 3 min.

So, Brittany can swim 320 yd in 8 min.

• Use logical reasoning and arithmetic to find out how many yards she can swim in 10 min. Explain.

Example

If Brittany continues to swim at a constant rate, how many minutes will it take her to swim 240 yd?

> Look at the data in the table on the previous page. As Brittany's time increases by 1 min, the distance increases 40 yd.
>
> $240 \div 40 = 6$ Divide the total distance by 40.
>
> Because each 40-yd distance takes 1 minute to swim and because $240 \div 40 = 6$, it takes Brittany 6 min to swim 240 yd.

ERROR ALERT

Be sure the units are the same. Since the rate is per minute, the time must be minutes as well.

- If Brittany swims at the same rate, how many seconds will it take her to swim 320 yd?

▶ Share and Show

For 1–3, use the graph.

1. The graph at the right shows the speed Brittany can run. Look between 1 hr and 2 hr on the horizontal axis of the graph. How far will Brittany run in $1\frac{1}{2}$ hr?

2. Brittany can run 15 mi in 3 hr. At the same rate, how many miles can she run in twice the time?

3. What if Brittany can run at a rate of 5 miles per hour? Use the formula $d = rt$ to find how much time it will take her to run 25 mi.

Brittany's Running Rate

(line graph: Distance (mi) on vertical axis from 0 to 25; Time (hr) on horizontal axis from 1 to 4; points at (1,5), (2,10), (3,15), (4,20))

For 4–8, use the table.

4. Make a line graph to display Marco's swimming speed.

5. At this rate, how far does Marco swim in $1\frac{1}{2}$ min?

6. Marco has been swimming at the same rate for 8 min. How many yards has Marco gone?

7. If Marco swam at the same rate to the buoy 600 yd from the start, how long did it take?

8. **Math Talk** **Explain** how you can use a line graph of the data in the table to determine how far Marco can swim in $3\frac{1}{2}$ min.

Marco's Swimming Rate				
Time (min)	1	2	3	4
Distance (yd)	50	100	150	200

For 9–11, use the table.

9. Make a line graph using the data in the table. How long does it take Janine to walk 5 mi?

10. If Janine continues walking at the same rate for 6 hr, how far will she go?

11. Find how many miles Janine goes if she walks at the same rate for 90 min.

Janine's Walking Rate				
Time (hr)	1	2	3	4
Distance (mi)	2	4	6	8

12. **≣FAST FACT** In the 2002 International Association of Athletics Federations Grand Prix, Tim Montgomery ran at an average rate of 23 mi per hr, breaking the previous world record. If he could keep up this incredible pace for 30 min, how far would he run?

For 13–15, use the graph.

13. Mike bicycles 1 mi in 4 min, or 15 mi per hr. If he continues this rate, how far will Mike travel in 7 hr?

14. Mike has been biking for 1 hr 15 min. Is it more likely that Mike has traveled more than or less than 20 mi?

15. **Pose a Problem** Look back at Problem 13. Write a similar question by changing the amount of time Mike bikes.

Mike's Biking Rate

For 16–18, use the table.

16. The table shows how Katie's average swim times changed with practice. Make a line graph. Use the graph to estimate what Katie's average swim time could be after $2\frac{1}{2}$ months of practice.

17. Find what Katie's time could be in month 7.

Katie's Average Swim Time for 200 yd					
Month	1	2	3	4	5
Time (min)	6	5.7	5.4	5.1	4.8

18. **Write Math** ▶ **Explain** how you can use logical reasoning to find your answer for Exercise 17.

★ **OCCT Test Prep** Math Board

19. In approximately how many hours can John run 48 mi?

John's Running Speed				
Time (hours)	1	2	3	4
Distance (miles)	4	8	12	15

A 7 hr   C 10 hr

B 9 hr   D 12 hr

20. In approximately how many hours can Nick ride 100 mi?

Nick's Biking Speed				
Time (hours)	1	2	3	4
Distance (miles)	19	38	57	76

A 2 hr   C 6 hr

B 5 hr   D 8 hr

★ Standards Quick Check

Use the table.

1. If Pam types at a rate of 52 words per minute, how many words will she type in $2\frac{1}{2}$ minutes?

Pam's Typing Speed				
Time (minutes)	1	2	3	4
Words	52	104	156	208

Challenge H.O.T.

Write Questions

Students in Mr. James's class learned that a population pyramid is a special kind of histogram. It is a graph that shows the distribution of population by age and gender. Age intervals are written on the vertical scale, and the bars appear to the left and right of that scale. The bars compare the population in millions of males and females in different age intervals. The population pyramid is like a double-bar graph because it displays data about two groups. Students wrote the following questions and answers about the 2000 population pyramid:

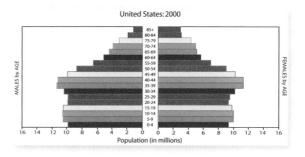

United States: 2000

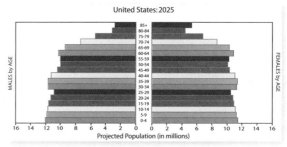

United States: 2025

- About how many males 20–24 years old were there in 2000?
  Look at the red bar to the left. There were about 10 million males.

- Were there more males or more females who were 75–79?
  Compare the left and right yellow bars. There were more females.

- About how many more males than females were there who were 10–14 years old?
  Estimate the numbers for the left and right green bars. There were about 1 million more males.

Use the data in the population pyramids to write questions. Answer your questions.

1. Write a question about people 5–9 years old in 2000.

2. Write a comparison question about people 60–64 years old in 2000.

3. Write a subtraction question and an addition question about the 2025 graph.

4. Write two questions that compare data on the 2000 and 2025 graphs.

⭐ Extra Practice

Set A

Find the mean, median, and mode. (pp. 406–409)

1. 1,1,1,1,1,1,1

2. 12, 25, 14, 31, 27, 18, 9, 13

3. $\frac{1}{3}, \frac{2}{3}, \frac{2}{3}, \frac{1}{4}, \frac{3}{4}, \frac{1}{2}$

4. $3\frac{2}{3}, 3\frac{5}{6}, 6\frac{1}{4}, \frac{1}{4}$

5. 4.1, 6.2, 4.3, 8.4, 9.5, 6.6, 8.7, 7.8, 3.9, 2

6.

Cocoon Discoveries							
Biologist	A	B	C	D	E	F	G
Cocoon	77	96	96	115	108	104	104

Set B

For 1–8, use the data in the table. (pp. 414–417)

1. Make a line plot of the data.

2. What gaps and outliers do you see in the data?

3. Make a cumulative frequency table of the data using 4 intervals.

4. Explain how you found the intervals.

5. Use the line plot to find the number of days that only 3 butterflies were sighted.

6. Can you use the cumulative frequency table to find the mean, median, and mode for the number of butterflies sighted? Explain.

7. Use the cumulative frequency table to find the number of days that at least 8 butterflies were sighted.

8. Use the cumulative frequency table to find the number of days that fewer than 4 butterflies were sighted.

Butterflies Sighted				
5	7	3	0	1
3	5	4	3	3
0	14	7	6	0
2	0	3	3	1

Set C

Use the table at the right. (pp. 424–425)

1. Use the data in the table to make a double-bar graph.

2. On which day was there the greatest difference between the number of bottles of water and sports drink sold?

Concession Stand Sales			
	Friday	Saturday	Sunday
Bottled Water	19	25	21
Sports Drink	13	26	14

Set D

Use the table at the right. (pp. 426–427)

1. Use the data in the table to make a double-bar graph.

2. Between which years did science increase the most as the favorite subject?

Favorite Subject (in Percent)			
	2000	2002	2004
Math	23	18	10
Science	9	11	29

GO ONLINE —Technology—
Use HMH Mega Math, The Number Games, *Arachnagraph,* Levels E & F.

Set E

Use the circle graph at the right. (pp. 428–429)

1. Which item makes up the largest percent of the student's expenditures?

2. Which 3 items combine to make up just over one quarter of the student's expenditures?

3. Which 3 items combined make up half of the students expenditures?

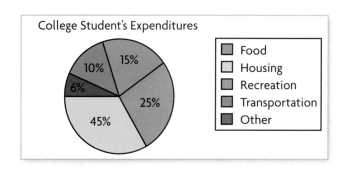

College Student's Expenditures

15% · 10% · 6% · 25% · 45%

☐ Food
☐ Housing
☐ Recreation
☐ Transportation
☐ Other

Set F

Use the table at the right. (pp. 430–433)

1. Make a double-line graph of the data in the table.

2. For the subjects shown in the graph, what is the least preferred subject for boys?

3. Make a generalization about the preference of subjects between males and females.

Subject Preferred (Percent of Total)			
	Math	**Science**	**English**
Boys	23	18	10
Girls	9	11	29

Set G

Use the table at the right. (pp. 434–437)

1. Make a histogram for the number of pizzas sold at baseball games.

Interval	6–10	11–15	16–20	21–25	26–30	31–35	36–40
Frequency							

Number of Pizzas Sold				
21	6	12	16	27
31	15	28	20	40
37	9	26	29	30
12	24	25	24	18

2. Make a frequency table using intervals of 5. At how many games were from 21 to 35 pizzas sold?

3. Make a stem-and-leaf plot for the data and use it to find the median number of pizzas sold during a baseball game.

Set H

For 1–3, use the graphs at the right. (pp. 438–439)

1. To find out in which month ice cream sales are lowest, which graph should you use?

2. During which month are ice cream sales the highest?

3. About how many days (May–September) are ice cream sales in the low category?

Daily Sales for May Through September

Number of Days: 120, 80, 40, 0 — Low, Medium, High — Sales

Ice Cream Sales

Number sold: 400, 300, 200, 100, 0 — May Jun Jul Aug Sep — Month

Reading & Writing Math

Vocabulary

In this chapter you made and read graphs and **frequency tables**. You also learned how to find **mean**, **median**, and **mode**. Each provides different information about the same data set.

Mr. Jackson surveyed his fifth-grade students. He asked, "How much do you spend for lunch each day?" The tally chart shows his data.

Lunch	
Amount	**Number of Students**
$1.00	卌 卌 II
$1.25	II
$1.50	卌 II
$1.75	卌 III
$2.00	III
$2.25	I
$2.50	II

Use the information in the tally chart to answer the questions.

1. What is the mode of this data?

2. What is the median of this data?

Writing Jessica arrived late to class. She told Mr. Jackson she spent $2.25 each day for lunch. Does this change the median or mode? Tell why or why not.

Reading Check out this book in your library.
Tiger Math: Learning to Graph from a Baby Tiger
by Ann Whitehead Nagda

H.O.T. Multistep Problems

1 Alice would like to know what the favorite lunch foods are of the students in her school. Her school has 3 grades: fourth, fifth, and sixth. There are about 5 classes per grade and about 25 students per class. ⚑ 5.1.

- Should Alice survey the population or use a sample? **Explain** why.

- Write a question that Alice could ask in order to gather data for her survey.

- Suppose Alice gathers the following data for her survey.

Food	Frequency
Hamburger	10
Salad	8
Sandwich	3
Pizza	12
Other	7

- How many students answered her question?

- Organize the data in a bar graph.

- Write a conclusion based upon Alice's data.

2 Jeremy surveyed 400 students: 200 girls and 200 boys, at Jones Valley Elementary School. He asked them what types of things they like to read. The circle graph shows the results of the survey. ⚑ 5.1.

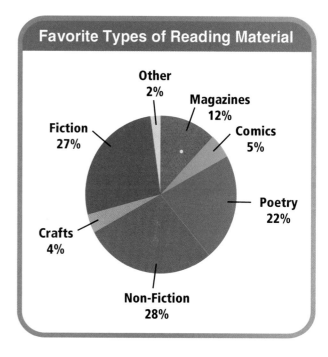

Favorite Types of Reading Material

Other 2%
Magazines 12%
Comics 5%
Fiction 27%
Poetry 22%
Crafts 4%
Non-Fiction 28%

- Which two categories together include more than half of the students?

- How many students surveyed like reading comics best?

- Maria says that 48 students like magazines best. Does the data support her conclusion? **Explain**.

- Joseph says that more boys like comics than girls do. Does the data support his conclusion? **Explain**.

Practice for the OCCT

1 What is the mode of the data set 81, 72, 46, 68, 91, 54, 83, 94, 41, 91? ⬛ **5.3.**

- **A** 46
- **B** 81
- **C** 83
- **D** 91

2 Which data display would be most appropriate to represent data as parts of a whole? ⬛ **5.1.**

- **A** line plot
- **B** line graph
- **C** box-and-whisker plot
- **D** circle graph

3 A survey was conducted in which the participants were asked, "How many TVs are in your home?" The results of this survey are shown in the line plot.

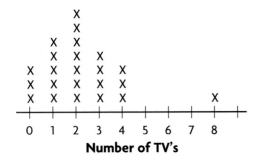

What is the most frequent response? ⬛ **5.1.**

- **A** 1
- **B** 2
- **C** 3
- **D** 8

4 The price of DVD players at a store are listed below. What is the median? ⬛ **5.3.**

$58, $70, $150, $95, $140, $68, $56, $130, $130, $66, $60, $95, $150, $142, $85, $125

- **A** $95
- **B** $95.50
- **C** $130
- **D** $150

5 The number of years that the first 10 Presidents lived is shown by the stem-and-leaf plot. Which set of data does the stem-and-leaf plot show? ⬛ **5.1.**

Stem	Leaves
6	7 8
7	1 3 8 9
8	0 3 5
9	0

- **A** 84, 94, 74, 58, 79, 84, 83, 81, 90, 77
- **B** 67, 91, 82, 87, 73, 84, 78, 79, 68, 71
- **C** 67, 90, 83, 85, 73, 80, 78, 79, 68, 71
- **D** 67, 83, 90, 85, 73, 88, 78, 79, 68, 71

6 What part of the whole bouquet are tulips? ⬛ **5.1.**

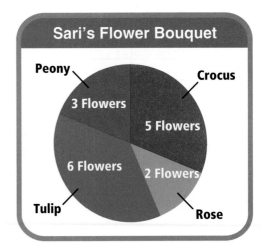

- **A** $\frac{3}{8}$
- **B** $\frac{1}{5}$
- **C** $\frac{1}{6}$
- **D** $\frac{1}{15}$

7 What is the mean of the data set 81, 72, 46, 68, 91, 54, 83, 94, and 41? ⬛ **5.3.**

- **A** 40
- **B** 60
- **C** 70
- **D** 83

8 The double-line graph shows the price of two stocks over several months.

Stock Prices

Which correctly identifies the trends in stock prices from March to July? 🔹 **5.1.**

A stock A increased, stock B increased

B stock A increased, stock B decreased

C stock A decreased, stock B increased

D stock A decreased, stock B decreased

9 The stem-and-leaf plot shows the high temperatures recorded over 7 days in Carmel.

High Temperatures

Stem	Leaves
8	0 2 6
7	1 1 3
6	8

Which set of data does the plot represent? 🔹 **5.1.**

A 86, 82, 80, 73, 71, 71, 68

B 86, 82, 80, 73, 71, 68, 68

C 86, 82, 80, 73, 73, 71, 68

D 88, 73, 71, 71, 66, 62, 60

Problem Solving

10 What is the mode of the following data set? 🔹 **5.3.**

45.1, 5.6, 84.5, 5.6, 45.1,
84.9, 91.8, 74.4, 5.6, 45.4, 19.7

11 On her last seven English tests, Bertha scored 89, 90, 89, 91, 91, 90, and 51. **Explain** why the mean is not a good measure to represent her last seven scores. 🔹 **5.3.**

12 A real estate agent says that the median cost of a home in the area is $115,000. Does $115,000 describe the price well for one house? Why or why not? 🔹 **5.3.**

13 In a survey asking students the number of hours spent on homework last night, the most frequent response was 0.5 hour. The typical response was 1 hour. Which response represents the mode? Does the other response represent the mean or the median? **Explain.** 🔹 **5.3.**

Probability

Investigate

Suppose you are in line with two customers ahead of you in a school cafeteria. Each of you must choose one item from the hot case and one from the cold case for your meal. Think of the choices you will make. The customer two places ahead of you in line chooses a roast beef sandwich and a house salad. If the customer immediately in front of you makes choices randomly, find the probability that he or she will make the same choices as you.

Number of Items Remaining

Hot Case		Cold Case	
Roast beef sandwich	2	Caesar salad	5
Grilled cheese	4	House salad	2
Chicken soup bowl	5	Fruit bowl	4
Vegetable soupbowl	3	Yogurt	3

Fun Fact

John Montagu (1718–1792), the fourth Earl of Sandwich, was not the inventor of the sandwich, but many people mistakenly credit him with the discovery.

Sandwich Menu

Breads: wheat
white
rye

Meats:
ham, turkey
roast beef, chicken salad
tuna salad

Cheeses:
provolone
monterey jack
cheddar, swiss

GO ONLINE

Technology
Student pages are available in the Student eBook.

Show What You Know

ASSESSMENT
Soar To Success: Math.

▶ ## Simplest Form of Fractions

Write each fraction in simplest form.

1. $\frac{3}{12}$ 2. $\frac{6}{9}$ 3. $\frac{14}{40}$ 4. $\frac{15}{40}$ 5. $\frac{42}{56}$

6. $\frac{36}{78}$ 7. $\frac{18}{75}$ 8. $\frac{33}{55}$ 9. $\frac{72}{120}$ 10. $\frac{200}{600}$

▶ ## Fractions, Decimals, and Percents

Write each fraction as a decimal and percent.

11. $\frac{3}{5}$ 12. $\frac{1}{8}$ 13. $\frac{9}{10}$ 14. $\frac{3}{4}$ 15. $\frac{7}{20}$

16. $\frac{14}{25}$ 17. $\frac{1}{4}$ 18. $\frac{7}{25}$ 19. $\frac{4}{5}$ 20. $\frac{9}{25}$

▶ ## Solve Proportions

Solve for n.

21. $\frac{3}{n} = \frac{9}{24}$ 22. $\frac{n}{5} = \frac{4}{20}$ 23. $\frac{4}{7} = \frac{12}{n}$ 24. $\frac{3}{4} = \frac{n}{28}$ 25. $\frac{n}{20} = \frac{1}{2}$

26. $\frac{9}{n} = \frac{3}{5}$ 27. $\frac{5}{15} = \frac{n}{3}$ 28. $\frac{n}{100} = \frac{7}{20}$ 29. $\frac{14}{15} = \frac{28}{n}$ 30. $\frac{9}{n} = \frac{3}{14}$

Vocabulary

Visualize It!

Dependent Event

Events of which the outcome of the first event affects the possible outcomes of the second event.

Compound events

Independent Event

Events of which the outcome of the first event does not affect the possible outcomes of the second event.

Language Tips

Words that look alike in English and Spanish often have the same meaning.

English	Spanish
outcome probability	resultado probabilidad
experimental probability	probabilidad experimental
theoretical probability	probabilidad teórico

See **English-Spanish Glossary.**

★ **5.0.** The student will use data analysis, probability, and statistics to interpret data in a variety of contexts.

complementary events

outcome

probability

sample space

theoretical probability

Materials
• MathBoard

Theoretical Probability

Essential Question How does knowing the number of favorable outcomes of an experiment help you find the theoretical probability of an event occurring?

PROBLEM Brenda and 11 other students in the art club each write his or her name on equally-sized cards and place their cards in a bag. The student whose name is randomly drawn will lead the next club meeting. What is the probability that Brenda's name will be drawn?

A possible result of an experiment is called an **outcome**. The **sample space** of an experiment is the set of all possible outcomes. The **probability** of an event is a measure of the likelihood that the event will occur. This measure ranges from 0, or impossible, to 1, or certain. As shown below, the closer the probability is to 1, the more likely the event is to occur.

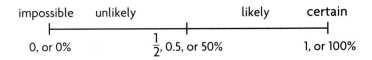

impossible   unlikely   likely   certain

0, or 0% $\frac{1}{2}$, 0.5, or 50%   1, or 100%

The **theoretical probability** of an event, written P(event), is the ratio of the number of favorable outcomes to the number of possible, equally likely outcomes. This ratio can be written as a fraction.

$$P(\text{event}) = \frac{\text{number of favorable outcomes}}{\text{number of possible, equally likely outcomes}}$$

Find the probability of randomly drawing Brenda's name from the bag.

1 favorable outcome: Brenda   Count the favorable outcomes.

12 possible outcomes: 12 different names in   Count the possible outcomes.
the bag

$P(\text{Brenda}) = \frac{1}{12} \begin{array}{l} \leftarrow \text{favorable} \\ \leftarrow \text{possible} \end{array}$ Write the ratio of favorable outcomes to possible outcomes.

So, the probability of drawing Brenda's name is $\frac{1}{12}$.

Find each probability.

Each letter of the word CHALLENGES is written on cards that are equally-sized and placed in a bag. One card is selected at random. Find each probability. Write each as a fraction, a decimal, and a percent.

P(consonant) =   P(E or L) = $\frac{2}{10} + \frac{2}{10} = \frac{4}{10} =$

$\frac{7}{10}$, 0.7, or 70% $\frac{2}{5}$, 0.4, or 40%

Complementary Events

Complementary events are two events whose probabilities add up to 1. If you roll a number cube labeled 1–6, the events "rolling a 3" and "rolling any number other than 3" are complementary events. The probabilities of these events are written P(3) and P(not 3).

> Since the probabilities of complementary events add up to 1, P(A) + P(not A) = 1. So, P(not A) = 1 − P(A).

Examples

One afternoon in the game club, Fischer rolls a number cube labeled 1–6. Find the probability that he does not roll a 4. Write the answer as a fraction, a decimal, and a percent.

Write the ratio of favorable outcomes to possible outcomes.

5 favorable outcomes: 1, 2, 3, 5, or 6

6 possible outcomes: 6 numbers on cube

$P(\text{not } 4) = \frac{5}{6}$ $\frac{\text{favorable outcomes}}{\text{possible outcomes}}$

Use the complementary event.

$P(\text{not } 4) = 1 - P(4)$

$P(\text{not } 4) = 1 - \frac{1}{6}$

$P(\text{not } 4) = \frac{5}{6}$

So, the probability of Fischer's not rolling a 4 is $\frac{5}{6}$, 0.83, or $83\frac{1}{3}\%$.

Raul and Lois use the spinner at the right. Find each probability. Write each answer as a fraction, a decimal, and a percent.

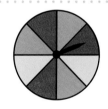

$P(\text{not blue}) = 1 - P(\text{blue})$

$= 1 - \frac{3}{8}$

$= \frac{5}{8}$

$P(\text{not yellow}) = 1 - P(\text{yellow})$

$= 1 - \frac{2}{8}$

$= \frac{6}{8}, \text{or } \frac{3}{4}$

So, P(not blue) is $\frac{5}{8}$, 0.625, or $62\frac{1}{2}\%$.

So, P(not yellow) is $\frac{3}{4}$, 0.75, or 75%.

- **What if** the spinner had 4 red sections, 2 blue sections, and 2 yellow sections, all equal in size? What would P(not red) be?

Use the spinner at the right to find each probability. Write each answer as a fraction, a decimal, and a percent.

1. P(green) $\frac{\text{favorable outcomes}}{\text{Possible outcomes}} = \frac{\blacksquare}{8} = \frac{\blacksquare}{\blacksquare}$, $\blacksquare$, $\blacksquare\%$

2. P(brown)   3. P(not red)

4. P(brown or red)   ✅ 5. P(not brown)

A number cube is labeled 1–6. Find each probability. Write each answer as a fraction, a decimal, and a percent.

6. P(5)

7. P(odd)

8. P(8)

9. P(not divisible by 2)

10. P(1 or 4)

 11. P(3 or even)

12. **Math Talk** **Explain** how to find the probability of randomly choosing a D or a W from a bag containing 26 different letters written on equally-sized cards.

Practice and Problem Solving REAL WORLD

Use the spinner at the right to find each probability. Write each answer as a fraction, a decimal, and a percent.

13. P(purple)

14. P(orange)

15. P(blue or green)

16. P(not orange)

17. P(white)

18. P(green or red)

19. P(not yellow)

20. P(purple or orange)

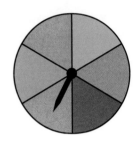

A number cube is labeled 1–6. Find each probability. Write each answer as a fraction, a decimal, and a percent.

21. P(1)

22. P(not 4)

23. P(not even)

24. P(not divisible by 3)

25. P(12)

26. P(2 or 8)

27. P(5 or 6)

28. P(less than 3)

29. P(not greater than 5)

Algebra **Julia solves the equations $2 = x - 1$, $6x = 12$, and $4 + x = 2$. One of her solutions is selected at random. Find each probability.**

30. $P(x = 2)$

31. $P(x > 23)$

32. $P(x < 0)$

33. $P(x = 22)$

34. **Write Math** **What's the Question?** Equally-sized cards numbered 2, 2, 2, 4, 4, and 5 are placed in a bag. The answer is 50%.

OCCT Test Prep

35. The numbers 1–10 are written on equally-sized cards and put in a bag. Which is the probability of randomly drawing a 7 or a 9?

   A $\frac{1}{8}$ **C** 25%

   B 0.2   **D** 0.35

36. Duncan rolls a number cube labeled 1–6. What is the likelihood that he will roll a number less than 6?

   A impossible   **C** likely

   B not likely   **D** certain

★ Standards Quick Check

Use the table to answer the questions.

1. Is it impossible, unlikely, likely, or certain that a club member chosen at random is 12 years old?

2. A member is chosen at random. Which has a greater probability choosing a member whose first name begins with T or choosing a member whose last name begins with T? **Explain** your answer.

Chess Club	
Member	**Age**
Tony Deveaux	12
Kim Habib	11
Travis O'Conner	12
Andrea Taylor	13
Ned Taylor	13
Guy Vanatta	12
Trent Williams	12
Nathan Wood	12

Challenge H.O.T.

Using Area Models for Probability

Elaina has a bag that contains 5 blue, 5 red, 4 green, and 6 yellow marbles that are all the same size. You can show the sample space by drawing an area model like the one at the right. Elaina's bag contains 20 marbles, so the model is drawn on a 4 × 5 grid with 20 squares. Each square represents 1 possible outcome when randomly choosing a marble from the bag. You can use this model to find P(green).

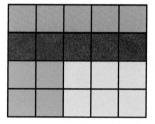

4 favorable outcomes: green squares	Count the favorable outcomes.
20 possible outcomes: total squares	Count the possible outcomes in the sample space.
$P(\text{green}) = \dfrac{4}{20} \overset{\leftarrow \text{favorable}}{\leftarrow \text{possible}}$	Write the ratio of favorable outcomes to possible outcomes.
$= \dfrac{1}{5}$	Simplify.

Use the area model above to find each probability.

1. P(yellow)   **2.** P(red or blue)   **3.** P(not green)   **4.** P(not black)   **5.** P(purple)

Suppose Keri has a bag that contains 4 orange, 2 green, 6 white, 3 purple, and 3 brown marbles that are all the same size. Make an area model to illustrate the sample space. Then find each probability.

6. P(brown)   **7.** P(white or orange)   **8.** P(not red)   **9.** P(not green)   **10.** P(white)

LESSON 2

⭐ **5.0.** The student will use data analysis, probability, and statistics to interpret data in a variety of contexts.

Vocabulary

experimental probability

Materials
• MathBoard
• number cubes labeled 1-6

Experimental Probability

Essential Question How do you determine experimental probability and compare it to theoretical probability?

PROBLEM A spinner has 16 equal sections that are either red, orange, yellow, or green. Cara spun the pointer 20 times and recorded her results in the table shown below. What is the experimental probability of spinning each color?

The **experimental probability** of an event is the ratio of the number of times a favorable outcome actually occurs to the total number of trials, or the total number of times you do the activity. This ratio can be written as a fraction.

$$P(\text{event}) = \frac{\text{number of favorable outcomes that occur}}{\text{total number of trials}}$$

Examples

Look at Cara's results in the table. Find the experimental probability of spinning each color. Write it as a fraction, a decimal, and a percent.

Color	Red	Orange	Yellow	Green
Spins	2	11	4	3

$P(\text{red}) = \frac{2}{20} = \frac{1}{10}, 0.1, 10\%$ $P(\text{orange}) = \frac{11}{20}, 0.55, 55\%$

$P(\text{yellow}) = \frac{4}{20} = \frac{1}{5}, 0.2, 20\%$ $P(\text{green}) = \frac{3}{20}, 0.15, 15\%$

• Based on the results, which color do you think appears most often on the spinner? Which occurs least often? Explain your reasoning.

You can use experimental probabilities to estimate the probability of future events.

A game spinner has equal sections. Each section is marked 2, 4, or 8. During the game, Jenny records her first 30 spins. Her results are shown in the table. Based on these experimental results, estimate how many times Jenny can expect the pointer to land on 4 in her next 10 spins.

Number	2	4	8
Spins	18	9	3

$P(4) = \frac{9}{30} = \frac{3}{10}, 0.3, 30\%$ Find the experimental probability of spinning a 4.

$\frac{3}{10} \times 10 = 3$ Multiply 10 spins by the experimental probability, $\frac{3}{10}$.

So, Jenny can expect the pointer to land on 4 about three times in her next 10 spins.

Compare Experimental and Theoretical Probability
Example

Suppose the spinner in the first example on the page 552 has 2 red sections, 8 orange sections, 3 yellow sections, and 3 green sections. Make a table to compare the experimental and theoretical probabilities of spinning each color.

Color	Experimental Probability	Theoretical Probability	Compare
Red	10%	$\frac{2}{16} = 12.5\%$	10% < 12.5%
Orange	55%	$\frac{8}{16} = 50\%$	55% > 50%
Yellow	20%	$\frac{3}{16} = 18.75\%$	20% > 18.75%
Green	15%	$\frac{3}{16} = 18.75\%$	15% < 18.75%

So, the experimental probabilities of spinning red and green are less than the theoretical probabilities. The experimental probabilities of spinning orange and yellow are greater than the theoretical probabilities.

 HANDS ON

Finding theoretical probability.

- Find the theoretical probability of rolling each number on a number cube.

- Roll the cube at least 25 times. Record the outcome of each roll.

- Use your results to find the experimental probability of rolling each number on the number cube.

- Make a table to compare the theoretical probabilities with your experimental probabilities.

- Based on your experimental results, how many times can you expect to roll a 4 in your next 50 trials?

- Roll the cube 50 times, and record each outcome of 4. Compare your result to your estimate.

- Are your experimental probabilities close to the theoretical probabilities? Explain.

▶ **Share and Show** Math Board

1. Lydia tosses a coin 40 times and records her results in the table. Find the experimental probability of tossing heads and tails.

Heads	Tails
25	15

$P(\text{heads}) = \frac{\blacksquare}{40}$, or $\frac{\blacksquare}{8}$, 0.625, 62.5% $P(\text{tails}) = \frac{\blacksquare}{40}$, or $\frac{\blacksquare}{8}$, 0.375, 37.5%

Ed randomly selects a marble from a bag of equally-sized marbles and then replaces it. He does this 45 times. For 2–4, use his results shown in the table to find each experimental probability. Write each answer as a fraction, a decimal, and a percent.

Color	Red	Blue	Green
Times Selected	18	15	12

2. P(red)   **3.** P(blue)   ✓ **4.** P(green)

The cards at the right are placed in a bag. Jill randomly chooses and replaces a card 20 times. For 5–6, use her results shown in the table.

Letter	M	A	T	H
Times chosen	2	6	8	4

5. Based on the experimental results, estimate how many times Jill can expect to choose the letter M in her next 10 tries.

 6. Based on the experimental results, estimate how many times Jill can expect to choose the letter T in her next 30 tries.

7. **Math Talk** Look back at Problem 5. Find the theoretical probability of choosing M. How does this compare to Jill's experimental probability?

▶ **Practice and Problem Solving** REAL WORLD

A spinner is divided into equal sections that are marked with letters. Tyrone spins the pointer 40 times. For 8–13, use his results shown in the table to find each experimental probability. Write each answer as a fraction, a decimal, and a percent.

8. P(A)

9. P(C)

10. P(E)

11. P(G)

12. P(J)

13. P(vowel)

Letter	A	C	E	G	J
Spins	12	5	9	6	8

For 14–15, look back at the data for 8–13.

14. Based on the experimental results, estimate how many times Tyrone can expect the pointer to land on A in his next 10 spins.

15. Based on the experimental results, estimate how many times Tyrone can expect the pointer to land on J in his next 20 spins.

 Real World Data

For 16, use the table at the right.

16. Colleen and Bill each flip a coin at the same time and record their results in the table. Find the experimental probability that Colleen's coin comes up tails and Bill's coin comes up heads. Compare this with the theoretical probability, which is 25%.

17. Compare and contrast the methods for finding experimental and theoretical probabilities.

Outcome	Times Recorded
Both toss heads	19
Colleen—heads, Bill—tails	16
Colleen—tails, Bill—heads	16
Both toss tails	21

★ **OCCT Test Prep** Math Board

18. Mark tosses a coin 45 times and records 15 heads and 30 tails. Which is the experimental probability of tossing tails?

A 25% C 66%

B 42.5% D 75%

19. Cagle tosses a coin 80 times and records 34 heads and 46 tails. Which is the experimental probability of tossing tails?

A 25% C 57.5%

B 32.4% D 67%

⬤★ Standards Quick Check

A spinner divided into equal sections that are marked with letters is spun 40 times. Use the results in the table to find each experimental probability. Write each answer as a fraction, a decimal, and a percent.

1. P(M)   **2.** P(K)

3. P(L)   **4.** P(X)

Benjamin's Spins					
Letter	X	M	K	L	P
Spins	8	7	6	9	10

Challenge H.O.T.

Designing and Conducting an Experiment

One way to solve a probability problem is to perform an experiment that reflects the problem itself. The results can be analyzed to give a probable solution.

Think of a simple activity that can be performed that has two possible outcomes. Let one outcome represent "dolphin show" and the other outcome represent "whale show."

Thirty students are going on a field trip to Ocean Park. Each student will randomly choose to attend either the dolphin show or the whale show. How can you find the experimental probability of any one student choosing the whale show?

❶ Decide how many times the activity should be repeated and what results to record.

❷ Use theoretical probability to predict how many students will choose the whale show.

❸ Conduct the experiment. Use your experimental results to predict how many students will choose the whale show.

Use the steps above to conduct an experiment and answer the questions.

1. Describe how you conducted your experiment.   **2.** What are the results of your experiment?

★ **5.0.** The student will use data analysis, probability, and statistics to interpret data in a variety of contexts.

Materials
• MathBoard

Estimate Probability

Essential Question How can we predict the probability of an event occurring in the future?

PROBLEM John made 12 baskets out of his last 30 attempts of shooting a basketball. Based on that record, estimate the probability that John will make a basket on his next attempt.

You can use experimental probabilities to estimate the probability of a future event.

Examples

Based on John's performance, estimate how many baskets he will make on his next 40 attempts.

$P(\text{basket}) = \frac{12}{30} = \frac{2}{5}, 0.4, 40\%$ Find the experimental probability of making a basket.

$0.4 \times 40 = 16$ Multiply 0.4 by 40.

So, John will make about 16 baskets out of his next 40 attempts.

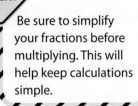

ERROR ALERT

Be sure to simplify your fractions before multiplying. This will help keep calculations simple.

John is shooting 3-point baskets and makes 3 baskets out of 30 attempts. Based on his performance so far, about how many baskets can John expect to make on his next 40 attempts at shooting a 3-point basket?

$P(\text{3-point basket}) = \frac{3}{30} = \frac{1}{10}, 0.1, 10\%$ Find the experimental probability of making a 3-point basket.

$\frac{1}{10} \times 40 = \frac{40}{10} = 4$ Multiply $\frac{1}{10}$ by 40.

So, John will make about four 3-point baskets out of his next 40 attempts.

• **What if** John made 6 out of 30 3-point baskets? About how many 3-point baskets can John expect to make on his next 40 attempts?

Share and Show

1. Danielle made 3 soccer goals in 8 tries.

Based on her experience, estimate how many goals she can expect to make in her next 24 tries.

$P(\text{goal}) = \frac{3}{8}, 0.375, 37.5\%$

$\frac{3}{8} \times 24 = \blacksquare$

A box contains equally-sized colored buttons. Meg randomly selects a button and replaces it. She does this 40 times. For 2–3, use her table of results.

Color	Red	Yellow	Orange	White
Times Selected	6	4	14	16

✓ **2.** Estimate how many times Meg can expect to select a yellow button on her next 50 tries.

✓ **3.** Estimate how many times Meg can expect to select a white button on her next 30 tries.

4. **Math Talk** **Explain** how you can use experimental results to estimate the number of times a future event will take place.

Practice and Problem Solving REAL WORLD

A bag contains equally-sized colored tiles. Logan randomly selects a tile and replaces it. He does this 25 times. For 5–8, use his table of results.

Color	Purple	Black	Green	Blue
Times Selected	5	3	8	9

5. Estimate how many times Logan can expect to select a black tile on his next 50 tries.

6. Estimate how many times Logan can expect to select a blue tile on his next 50 tries.

7. Estimate how many times Logan can expect to select a green or purple tile on his next 75 attempts.

8. Estimate how many times Logan can expect to select a black or blue tile on his next 75 tries.

Brian spins a pointer on a spinner with 6 equally-sized regions 50 times. For 9–10, use his table of results.

Section	A	B	C	D	E	F
Spin	5	6	9	12	10	8

9. Estimate how many times Brian can expect the pointer to land on C or D in the next 64 spins.

10. Estimate how many times Brian can expect the pointer to land on a vowel in the next 200 spins.

Real World Data

For 11–12, use the table.

11. Estimate the number of hits William can expect to get in his next 120 times at bat.

12. **Write Math** **What's the Error?** Bryce multiplies $\frac{12}{25}$ by 100 and says Aaron can expect to make about 60 hits in his next 100 times at bat. Describe and correct his error.

Baseball Statistics

	Hits	Times at Bat
Charlie	65	150
Aaron	84	175
William	100	200

 OCCT Test Prep

13. Ron makes 11 free throws out of 24 attempts. About how many free throws can Ron expect in his next 72 attempts?

   A about 11   **C** about 33

   B about 26   **D** about 40

14. Tim completes 9 football passes in 15 attempts. About how many completed passes he can expect in his next 25 attempts?

   A about 4   **C** about 9

   B about 6   **D** about 15

⭐ **5.0.** The student will use data analysis, probability, and statistics to interpret data in a variety of contexts.

Materials
• MathBoard

Make Predictions

Essential Question How can you use probability to make predictions?

PROBLEM A southwestern company creates polished gems from rocks. In a random sample of 200 rocks, 30 were properly shaped to be cut and polished. Predict the number of rocks that could be cut and polished from a truckload of 800 rocks.

You can use the results from a sample and write a proportion to make predictions about outcomes.

Examples

Use the sample to find the probability that a randomly selected rock is shaped properly to be cut and polished.

$\frac{3}{20} = \frac{n}{800}$ Write a proportion. $\frac{30}{200}$ simplifies to $\frac{3}{20}$. Find the cross-products.

$3 \times 800 = 20 \times n$ Multiply.

$2{,}400 = 20n$

$\frac{2{,}400}{20} = \frac{20n}{20}$ Divide.

$120 = n$

So, about 120 rocks from a truckload of 800 would be properly shaped.

You can also use a table or graph to make predictions about outcomes.

The graph shows the favorite gemstone of 210 randomly selected students from Woodruff Middle School. If there are 1,800 students at the school, about how many of them prefer emeralds?

P(prefers emeralds) $= \frac{28}{210} = \frac{2}{15}$ Find the probability that a randomly selected student prefers emeralds.

$\frac{2}{15} = \frac{n}{1{,}800}$ Write a proportion. Find the cross products.

$2 \times 1{,}800 = 15 \times n$ Multiply.

$\frac{3{,}600}{15} = \frac{15n}{15}$ Divide.

$240 = n$

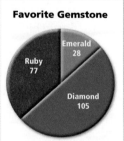

Favorite Gemstone

Ruby 77
Emerald 28
Diamond 105

So, about 240 students would prefer emeralds.

1. A jewelry vendor showcases 750 rings. Sandy browses through a random sample of 25 rings and finds that 8 of them are made with diamonds. Predict the number of rings in the showcase that are made with diamonds.

$$\frac{8}{25} = \frac{n}{750}$$

   ▨ = n

The table shows the results of a survey of 240 randomly selected students at a middle school. For 2–7, predict how many of the school's 2,100 students have the indicated preference.

Preferred Necklace Length						
Length (in inches)	15	16	18	20	22	24
Number of Students	64	52	44	36	25	19

2. 15 in.   **3.** 16 in.   **4.** 18 in.   **5.** 20 in.   ✓ **6.** 22 in.   ✓ **7.** 24 in.

8. 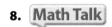 **Explain** why you need to round to the nearest whole number when you are making predictions about student preferences.

► **Practice and Problem Solving** REAL WORLD

The graph shows the results of a random survey of 320 students at a middle school. For 9–14, predict how many of the school's 2,000 students have the indicated favorite.

9. Oval   **10.** Square   **11.** Other

12. Raindrop   **13.** Circle   **14.** Rectangle

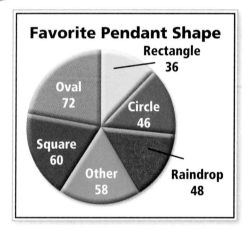

Favorite Pendant Shape
Rectangle 36
Oval 72
Circle 46
Square 60
Other 58
Raindrop 48

There are 600 gems of 5 types in a bag. In a random sample of 25 gems from the bag, there are 2 sapphires, 3 opals, 5 garnets, 7 jades, and 8 peridots. For 15–19, predict the number of each type of gem in the bag.

15. sapphires   **16.** opals   **17.** garnets
18. jades   **19.** peridots

For 20, use the survey results of the 200 students surveyed.

20. **Sense or Nonsense** Owen uses the survey to predict that about 40 of the 120 students in his after-school science club would collect rocks. Does his prediction make sense? **Explain.**

What Students Collect	
Rocks	60
Coins	?
Pins	?
Other	20

★ **OCCT Test Prep**

21. In a random sample of 20 steel beams, 3 were found to be defective. How many steel beams in 1,000 would you predict to be defective?

   A about 50   **C** about 1,000

   B about 150   **D** about 1,950

22. In a random sample of 80 rings, 4 were found to be defective. How many rings in 5,000 would you predict to be defective?

   A about 16   **C** about 1,250

   B about 250   **D** about 4,750

5.1. Organize, construct displays, and interpret data to solve problems (e.g., data from student experiments, tables, diagrams, charts, graphs). *also* **5.0.**

Materials
• MathBoard

Problem Solving Workshop
Strategy: Make an Organized List

Essential Question When making an organized list to solve problems, how do you make sure to include all information?

> **UNLOCK the Problem** REAL WORLD

PROBLEM Hailey and her mom are shopping for a new pair of shoes. Hailey wants either running shoes or walking shoes. She can wear either size $5\frac{1}{2}$ or size 6. The available colors are white, blue, black, and gray. How many choices does she have?

Read the Problem	Solve the Problem
What do I need to find?	List all possible combinations of shoe type, size, and color that are available to Hailey.
I need to find the number of choices Hailey has for shoes.	running, $5\frac{1}{2}$, white walking, $5\frac{1}{2}$, white
	running, $5\frac{1}{2}$, blue walking, $5\frac{1}{2}$, blue
What information do I need to use?	running, $5\frac{1}{2}$, black walking, $5\frac{1}{2}$, black
	running, $5\frac{1}{2}$, gray walking, $5\frac{1}{2}$, gray
I know that there are 2 types of shoes, 2 sizes of shoes and 4 colors of shoes for Hailey to choose from.	running, 6, white walking, 6, white
	running, 6, blue walking, 6, blue
	running, 6, black walking, 6, black
How will I use the information?	running, 6, gray walking, 6, gray
I will list all the possible combinations of shoes, sizes, and colors to determine how many choices Hailey has.	So, there are 16 possible choices for Hailey's shoes.

Make an organized list to solve.

1. Warren is looking for a new hat. He would like a baseball cap, a western hat, or a visor. Each hat is available in brown, black, or gray. Warren can wear hat size $7\frac{1}{8}$ or $7\frac{1}{4}$. How many choices does he have?

   First, list all possible combinations of baseball caps.

   Then, write similar lists for all the possible combinations of western hats and visors.

   Finally, count the total number of hat combinations.

✓ 2. **What if** Warren considers an additional color of blue? How many choices would he have then?

✓ 3. Christian manages a grocery store. On late evenings, he needs to make sure that of the 4 cash registers, 2 are open. How many different combinations of 2 open registers are there?

Choose a Strategy

- Make an Organized List
- Draw a Diagram or Picture
- Make a Model or Act It Out
- Find a Pattern
- Make a Table or Graph
- Predict and Test
- Work Backward
- Solve a Simpler Problem
- Write an Equation
- Use Logical Reasoning

baseball, brown, $7\frac{1}{8}$

baseball, brown, $7\frac{1}{4}$

baseball, black, $7\frac{1}{8}$

baseball, black, $7\frac{1}{4}$

baseball, gray, $7\frac{1}{8}$

baseball, gray, $7\frac{1}{4}$

Register 1 Register 2 Register 3 Register 4

On Your Own

A sporting goods store sells 5 different types of running shoes at an average price of $39.95 per pair. Use this information for 4–5.

4. Three of the pairs of running shoes sell at prices of $44.85, $29.95, and $36.99. If one of the remaining pairs sells for $6.00 more than the other remaining pair, what are the prices of the remaining two pairs?

5. The store recorded running shoe sales of about $25,935 during a 3-week period in the spring. If the store was open every day, what was the average number of pairs of running shoes that the store sold per day during that period?

6. Kelly and Dean want to walk through a hobby store, an antiques store, and a bookstore, but they have time to go to only 2 stores. Dean writes the names of the stores on index cards, shuffles them, and asks Kelly to choose 2 of them. How many different combinations of choices do they have?

7. Each retail supervisor will take turns going for a 45-minute lunch break. Suzie will go first and then Jess. Rick and Matthew will go next. Matthew will finish his break at 2:00 P.M. At what time will Jess leave for her break?

8. **Write Math** ▶ Look at the table. **Explain** how you can predict the cost of shipping a 12-lb package.

Shipping Cost at ABC Express				
Weight	2 lb	4 lb	6 lb	8 lb
Cost	$2.04	$4.08	$6.12	$8.16

★ **5.2.** Use the fundamental counting principle on sets with up to five items to determine the number of possible outcomes.

Vocabulary

compound event

Fundamental Counting Principle

tree diagram

Materials
• MathBoard

Outcomes of Compound Events

Essential Question What are some methods you can use to find outcomes of compound events?

PROBLEM At camp, each camper gets one sandwich for lunch. The meat choices are turkey, roast beef, and ham. The bread choices are white, wheat, or multi-grain bread. If one of each type of sandwich is on every table, how many sandwich choices are on each table?

A **compound event** occurs when you combine two or more simple events in an outcome. You can make a list or use a grid to make a table to find the sample space of compound events.

Make a list.

Meats	Breads
Turkey	White
Roast Beef	Wheat
Ham	Multigrain

List each meat with each type of bread. Then count the items in the list.

turkey, white	roast beef, white	ham, white
turkey, wheat	roast beef, wheat	ham, wheat
turkey, multigrain	roast beef, multigrain	ham, multigrain

Use a grid to make a table.

	Bread		
	White (A)	**Wheat (B)**	**Multigrain (C)**
Turkey (T)	T, A	T, B	T, C
Roast Beef (R)	R, A	R, B	R, C
Ham (H)	H, A	H, B	H, C

(Meat)

List the types of bread in a row and the types of meat in a column.

Count the number of choices.

ERROR ALERT

Check your list to be sure that all outcomes have been listed and there are no duplicates.

So, there are 9 sandwich choices on each table.

• **What if** pumpernickel is added to the bread choices? How many sandwich choices would there be?

Tomás chooses a sandwich at random. What is the probability that he chooses ham on wheat bread?

Look at the table above.

$P(ham, wheat) = \frac{1}{9}$

There is 1 favorable outcome and 9 possible outcomes in the sample space.

So, the probability of choosing ham on wheat bread is $\frac{1}{9}$.

Compound Events

A **tree diagram** is an organized diagram that lists all possible outcomes for compound events.

Find the number of possible outcomes when tossing 3 coins.

Draw a tree diagram.

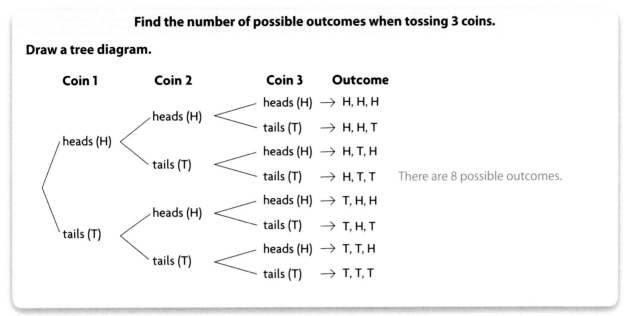

There are 8 possible outcomes.

So, there are 8 possible outcomes when tossing 3 coins.

You can also use the Fundamental Counting Principle to find the number of possible outcomes of compound events.

The **Fundamental Counting Principle** states that if one event has *m* possible outcomes and a second event has *n* possible outcomes, then there are $m \times n$ possible outcomes for the two events together.

Use the Fundamental Counting Principle.

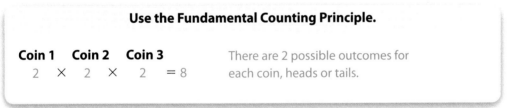

Coin 1   Coin 2   Coin 3
  2   ×   2   ×   2   = 8

There are 2 possible outcomes for each coin, heads or tails.

So, there are 8 possible outcomes when tossing 3 coins.

- You have a choice of 4 pizza crusts and 6 toppings. Use the Fundamental Counting Principle to find the number of possible outcomes.

Find the probability that all 3 coins land heads up.

There is 1 possible outcome for all 3 coins landing heads up. There are 8 possible outcomes when tossing 3 coins.

Look at all the outcomes on the tree diagram.

$P(\text{heads, heads, heads}) = \frac{1}{8}$

Write the probability.

So, the probability of tossing 3 heads when tossing 3 coins is $\frac{1}{8}$.

- What is the probability that all 3 coins land tails up?

▶ Share and Show   Math Board

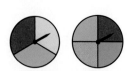

1. Copy and complete the table to find the number of possible outcomes when spinning the pointers on these 2 spinners.

		Spinner 2			
		Red (R)	Green (G)	Blue (B)	Pink (P)
Spinner 1	Red (R)	R, R	R, G		
	Yellow (Y)	Y, R	Y, G		
	Green (G)	G, R	G,G		

Use a grid to make a table, make a list, or draw a tree diagram to show the number of possible outcomes for each situation.

2. a red, blue, or green shirt with jeans or shorts

✓3. a dance pairing of Ron, Paul, Jason, or Zack with Jill, Kara, Breanna, or Susie

Use the Fundamental Counting Principle to find the number of possible outcomes for each situation.

4. selecting from three colored marbles and from three colored tiles

✓5. a choice of 2 bagels, 3 fruits, and 2 drinks

6. [Math Talk] **Explain** how to use the Fundamental Counting Principle to find the number of possible outcomes when rolling 4 number cubes labeled 1 to 6.

▶ Practice and Problem Solving REAL WORLD

Use a grid to make a table, make a list, or draw a tree diagram to show the number of possible outcomes for each situation.

7. a choice of yellow gold, white gold, or silver for a 16 in., 18 in., 20 in., or 22 in. chain

8. rolling a number cube labeled 1 to 6 and spinning the pointer of a spinner with 3 sections

9. a choice of 5 salads and 4 dressings

10. rolling a number cube labeled 1 to 6 and tossing a coin

Use the Fundamental Counting Principle to find the number of possible outcomes for each situation.

11. typing a letter to Tiera, Gwen, or Alice with a font size of 12 or 14 points

12. having a beach party or pool party this weekend or next weekend and inviting 8 or 10 guests

★ OCCT Test Prep   Math Board

13. Jim's team is voting for a captain and co-captain from the players listed. How many possible combinations are there?

 A 5

 B 6

 C 9

 D 12

Captain	Co-Captain
Chad	James
Jason	Doug
	Kevin

14. What is the probability of spinning red, red, and green when spinning the pointers of the three spinners?

 A $\frac{1}{36}$ **C** $\frac{1}{4}$

 B $\frac{1}{12}$ **D** $\frac{1}{3}$

⭐ Standards Quick Check

For 1–3, use the breakfast menu. A breakfast plate consists of 1 main dish, 1 side item, and 1 fruit.

1. Use the Fundamental Counting Principle to find the number of possible breakfast plates.

2. Draw a tree diagram of all possible breakfast plates. Find the probability of randomly choosing French toast, pineapple, and sausage.

3. **What's the Error?** Describe the error Jan made at the right in listing all possible outcomes of choosing vanilla, chocolate, or strawberry ice cream in a cup, sugar cone, or waffle cone.

Bailey's Breakfast Bar		
Main Dish	**Side Items**	**Fruit**
Eggs	Hash Browns	Pineapple
Pancakes	Grits	Bananas
French Toast	Sausage	

vanilla, cup	vanilla, sugar cone
chocolate, cup	chocolate, sugar cone
strawberry, cup	strawberry, sugar cone

Challenge H.O.T.

Senet is the oldest known board game. Ancient Egyptians used a 3 × 10 playing board and four 2-sided sticks to play. The sticks were tossed to find how many spaces to move, similar to rolling number cubes in popular board games today. Each stick was painted on one side and unpainted on the other side.

Answer each question about tossing 4 Senet sticks.

1. Draw a tree diagram to show all the possible outcomes when tossing four 2-sided sticks. Use P for painted and U for unpainted.

2. Compare the probability of tossing 4 painted sticks with the probability of tossing a 2 on a number cube labeled 1 to 6.

3. What is the probability of tossing 3 painted sticks and 1 unpainted stick or 2 painted sticks and 2 unpainted sticks?

⭐ **5.0.** The student will use data analysis, probability, and statistics to interpret data in a variety of contexts.

Vocabulary

dependent events

independent events

Materials

- MathBoard
- 10 index cards
- box
- 5-section spinner
- 5 blue and 5 red marbles

Hands On
Explore Independent and Dependent Events

Essential Question How do independent events differ from dependent events?

▶ **Investigate**

Events for which the outcome of the first event does not affect the outcomes of the second event are **independent events.** Events for which the outcome of the first event does affect the outcomes of the second event are **dependent events.**

1 **Start the first experiment.** Number the index cards from 1 to 10 and place them in the box. Draw a card from the box without looking and record its number. Set the card aside.

2 What are the possible numbers that you can still draw from the box? Draw a second card without looking and record its number.

3 **Start the second experiment.** Replace all the cards in the box. Draw a card from the box without looking and record its number. Then replace this card in the box.

4 What are the possible numbers that you can still draw from the box? Draw a second card without looking and record its number.

1. In the first experiment, how did drawing the first number without replacing it affect the choices for drawing the second number? Are the events independent or dependent? Explain.

2. In the second experiment, how did drawing the first number and replacing it affect the choices for drawing the second number? Explain.

3. **Synthesis** What is the difference between independent and dependent events?

▶ Connect

You can compare the possible outcomes of two events to determine if the events are independent or dependent.

① Color one section of the spinner red, one blue, one green, one yellow, and one purple. Spin the pointer of the 5-section spinner twice and determine whether the events are independent or dependent.

There are 5 possible outcomes, red, blue, green, yellow, and purple, for the second spin regardless of the outcome of the first spin. The choices remain unchanged. The first spin does not affect the possible outcomes of the second spin.

So, the events are independent.

- -

② Select a marble from a bag containing 5 blue and 5 red marbles, do not replace it, and then select a second marble from the same bag. Determine whether the selections are independent or dependent.

Only 9 of the 10 choices are available for the second selection since one marble was removed on the first selection. So the first choice does affect the possible choices on the second selection.

So, the events are dependent.

Math Talk

Describe a situation that models independent events and another situation that models dependent events.

▶ Share and Show

Write *independent* or *dependent* to describe the events. Then explain your choice.

1. Draw a marble from a bag of 20 marbles, don't replace it, and draw a second marble.

✓ **2.** Select a card from a box containing cards, labeled 1 to 10, do not replace it, and select a second card from the same box.

3. Toss a coin and then roll a number cube labeled 1 to 6.

✓ **4.** Spin the pointers on two spinners each divided equally into yellow, red, and blue.

5. A number cube labeled 1 to 6 is rolled twice.

6. Toss a coin three times.

7. **Write Math** ▶ A jar contains cards labeled 1, 2, 2, 3, 4. **Explain** whether it is possible to select 2, do not replace it, and select 2 again.

LESSON 8

★ **5.0.** The student will use data analysis, probability, and statistics to interpret data in a variety of contexts.

Materials
• MathBoard

Independent Events

Essential Question How do you find the probability of an independent event?

Learn REAL WORLD

PROBLEM Roger writes 4 science words and definitions on index cards and shuffles the cards. He randomly draws a card, studies its definition, and then replaces the card and reshuffles the stack. He then randomly draws a card again. What is the probability that he will draw the definition for *mass* twice in a row?

To find the probability of two independent events, use the formula below to multiply their probabilities.

If A and B are independent events, then $P(A, B) = P(A) \times P(B)$.

Find P(mass, mass).

$P(mass) = \frac{1}{4}$

$P(mass, mass) = P(mass) \times P(mass)$

$\qquad = \frac{1}{4} \times \frac{1}{4} = \frac{1}{16}$

Find the probability of drawing the card for *mass*.

Multiply the probabilities.

So, the probability is $\frac{1}{16}$, 0.0625, or 6.25%.

Example

Bev spins the pointers on the spinners, one time each. Find P(yellow, not red).

$P(yellow, not red) = P(yellow) \times P(not red)$

$\qquad = \frac{1}{5} \times \frac{3}{4} = \frac{3}{20}$

So, the probability is $\frac{3}{20}$, 0.15, or 15%.

Share and Show

1. Maddie rolls a number cube labeled 1 to 6 twice. Find the probability that she rolls an even number on the first roll and an odd number on the second roll.   First roll: Second roll:

$\qquad P(even) = \frac{3}{6} = \frac{1}{2}$ $\qquad\qquad P(odd) = \frac{3}{6} = \frac{1}{2}$

$\qquad\qquad P(even, odd) = \frac{1}{2} \times \frac{1}{2} = \frac{\blacksquare}{\blacksquare}$

Delilah spins the pointers, one time each, on the spinners at the right.
For 2–4, find the probability of each event.

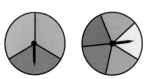

2. P(green, blue)   ✓**3.** P(orange, not red)   ✓**4.** P(green, blue or red)

5. **Math Talk** **Explain** how to find the probability of two independent events.

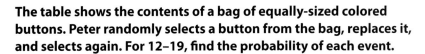

Juan spins the pointers, one time each, on the spinners at the right.
For 6–11, find the probability of each event.

6. P(purple, green)   **7.** P(yellow, not orange)   **8.** P(not red, not green)

9. P(not purple, orange)   **10.** P(red or purple, green)   **11.** P(yellow or red, not green)

The table shows the contents of a bag of equally-sized colored buttons. Peter randomly selects a button from the bag, replaces it, and selects again. For 12–19, find the probability of each event.

Red	Blue	Green	White
4	3	2	3

12. P(red, blue)   **13.** P(red, not blue)   **14.** P(not green, not white)   **15.** P(white, white)

16. P(not red, red)   **17.** P(white, blue, red)   **18.** P(green, not red, blue)   **19.** P(blue, blue, blue)

For 20–23, use the table. Ashton has to study facts about people, plants, and animals for her test. She writes each fact on an index card and shuffles the cards.

People	Plants	Animals
8	2	10

20. If Ashton removes the animals from her stack of cards, what is the probability that she will randomly draw a plant, replace it, and then draw a person? Is this event more likely with, or without, the animals included? **Explain.**

21. Ashton randomly draws a person, replaces the card, and randomly draws another card. What is the probability that the second card she drew was the same person?

22. What is the probability that Ashton randomly draws 3 animals in a row if she replaces each card that she draws?

23. **Reasoning** Suppose Ashton draws a card, replaces it, and draws another card. Are P(people, plants) and P(plants, people) equal? **Explain.**

24. **Write Math** ▶ **What's the Question?** Mia has a quarter and a nickel. She flips each coin. The answer is 25%.

 OCCT Test Prep

25. What is the probability of tossing a coin that lands heads up and then rolling an odd number on a cube labeled 1 to 6?

A 10%.   C 20%

B 15%   D 25%

26. What is the probability of tossing a coin that lands tails up and then rolling a 1 or 3 on a cube labeled 1 to 6?

A $\frac{1}{9}$ C $\frac{2}{5}$

B $\frac{1}{6}$ D $\frac{3}{4}$

LESSON 9

★ **5.0.** The student will use data analysis, probability, and statistics to interpret data in a variety of contexts.

Materials
• MathBoard

Dependent Events

Essential Question How do you find the probability of dependent events?

PROBLEM Michelle is selecting music for a dance recital. She has a collection of 16 CDs in a case. She randomly selects a CD from the case, does not replace it, and then randomly selects another. The contents of the case are shown in the table. What is the probability that Michelle will select a soft rock CD and then a classical CD?

Soft Rock	Classical	Movie Soundtrack	Hip Hop
4	3	3	6

To find the probability of two dependent events, use the formula below.

> If A and B are dependent events, then
> $P(A, B) = P(A) \times P(B \text{ after } A)$.

Find P(soft rock, classical).

$P(\text{soft rock, classical}) = P(\text{soft rock}) \times P(\text{classical after soft rock})$

Michelle's first selection:

$P(\text{soft rock}) = \frac{4}{16} = \frac{1}{4}$ There are 4 soft rock CDs in a case of 16 CDs.

Michelle's second selection:

$P(\text{classical after soft rock}) = \frac{3}{15} = \frac{1}{5}$ There are 3 classical CDs in a case that now has 15 CDs.

$P(\text{soft rock, classical}) = \frac{1}{4} \times \frac{1}{5} = \frac{1}{20}$ Multiply the probabilities.

Math Idea

When 2 events are dependent, calculate the probability of the second event after the first event has taken place.

So, the probability that Michelle will select a soft rock CD and then a classical CD is $\frac{1}{20}$.

• Find P(hip hop, movie soundtrack).

▶ Share and Show

1. Twelve index cards labeled 1–12 are placed in a jar. Find the probability of randomly drawing an even number and then an odd number if the first card is not replaced.

First draw: Second draw:

$P(\text{even}) = \frac{6}{12} = \frac{1}{2}$ $P(\text{odd after even}) = \frac{6}{11}$

$P(\text{even, odd}) = \frac{1}{2} \times \frac{6}{11} = \frac{\blacksquare}{\blacksquare}$

Without looking, Sid draws a card from the jar, does not replace it, and selects another card. For 2–7, find the probability of each event.

2. P(S, S) **3.** P(R, L or A) **4.** P(not O, O)

5. P(not C, not C) **6.** P(M, O, O) ✔**7.** P(L, M)

8. **Math Talk** **Explain** how to find the probability of dependent events.

CLASSROOM

▶ **Practice and Problem Solving** REAL WORLD

Without looking, Linda draws a card from the jar, does not replace it, and selects another card. For 9–17, find the probability of each event.

9. P(H, E) **10.** P(C, R) **11.** P(not C, C)

12. P(E, not H) **13.** P(not E, not E) **14.** P(C or R, H)

15. P(R, C or E) **16.** P(H, C or R) **17.** P(E, E, C)

CHEER

⭐**Algebra** **A bag contains 100 equally-sized tiles. There are x red tiles and y blue tiles. If tiles are chosen without replacement, write an algebraic expression for each probability.**

18. P(red, blue) **19.** P(blue, red) **20.** P(blue, blue)

Real World Data

For 21–23, use the table. For a dance recital, students at a dance school randomly draw dance styles written on index cards from a bag until the bag is empty.

Ballet	Swing	Tap	Ballroom
3	6	9	6

21. Suppose 1 of each dance type is selected. For the next 2 selections, find P(ballroom, tap).

22. **Reasoning** For the first 2 selections, show how P(swing, not swing) and P(not swing, swing) are calculated differently.

23. **Write Math** **What's the Error?** Wanda uses $\frac{3}{24} \times \frac{6}{24}$ to find P(ballet, swing) for the two cards selected. Describe and correct her error.

★ **OCCT Test Prep** Math Board

24. A bag contains equally-sized tiles that have the letters A, P, P, L, E, S. Bob randomly selects 2 tiles, one at a time without replacement. What is P(A, P)?

 A $\frac{4}{5}$ **C** $\frac{1}{15}$

 B $\frac{2}{3}$ **D** $\frac{1}{20}$

25. A bag contains 4 red, 3 blue, and 2 green equally-sized marbles. Jim randomly selects 3 marbles, one at a time without replacement. What is P(red, green, blue)?

 A $\frac{1}{21}$ **C** $\frac{1}{4}$

 B $\frac{1}{6}$ **D** $\frac{1}{3}$

Extra Practice See page 487, Set E.

LESSON 10

★ **5.2.** Use the fundamental counting principle on sets with up to five items to determine the number of possible outcomes.

Vocabulary

combination

permutation

Materials
• MathBoard

Remember

You can use the Fundamental Counting Principle to find the total number of possible outcomes for two or more events by multiplying the possible number of outcomes for each event.

Permutations and Combinations

Essential Question How does the concept of order affect whether the selection of different items is a permutation or combination?

PROBLEM Iva, Rick, Jane, and Elliot are chosen to perform in the school talent show. In how many ways can they be arranged to be the first and second acts in the show?

The order of the first two acts is important, so you need to find the number of permutations. A **permutation** is a selection of different items in which the order of the items is important.

To find the number of permutations, you can either make a list or use the Fundamental Counting Principle.

Find the number of permutations. Make a list.

Since the order of the first two acts is important, list the four students in all the possible ways that they can appear first or second.	I, R	I, J	I, E
	R, I	R, J	R, E
Check to make sure that each permutation is listed and that no permutation appears more than once. Then count the permutations in the list.	J, I	J, R	J, E
	E, I	E, R	E, J

There are 12 permutations.

Use the Fundamental Counting Principle.

There are 4 possible students for the acts. Once the first student has been chosen, there are 3 choices left for the second act. Since the order is only important for the first two acts, multiply the number of choices for the first two acts.

Choices for first act		Choices for second act	
4	×	3	= 12 permutations

So, they can be arranged in 12 ways to be the first and second acts.

• Make a tree diagram to show the number of ways to arrange the students.

• Lexi, Bailey, Hogan, and Mikel are warming up to bat. Use the Fundamental Counting Principle to find the number of permutations for the first 4 batters.

Combinations

A **combination** is a selection of different items in which the order of the items is not important.

Tomás is selecting volunteers for his skit in the school talent show. For his skit, he needs 3 volunteers from the audience. Stacy, Eva, Gail, and Pete raise their hands. How many combinations of 3 of these 4 audience members are possible?

Start by choosing an audience member. Combine that person with all the possible pairs of other audience members. Then list all the remaining combinations.

Count the total combinations in your list.

Check your answer by reading your list. Do not use any combinations that simply change the order of a combination already listed. For example, "Eva, Gail, Stacy" should not be counted since the same choice of these 3 has already been listed.

Stacy, Eva, Gail

Stacy, Eva, Pete

Stacy, Gail, Pete

Eva, Gail, Pete

So, there are 4 possible combinations of audience members.

- **What if** Tomás needs only 2 volunteers from the same group of 4? How many combinations of audience members would be possible?

Math Idea

Two selections of the same items placed in different orders are both the same combination, but they are considered 2 different *permutations*.

Share and Show

1. Use the Fundamental Counting Principle to find the number of possible permutations when Gabrielle awards first, second, third, and fourth prizes to the top 4 of the 5 finalists in a competition.

   1st   2nd   3rd   4th

   5   ×   4   ×   3   ×   2 = ▩

2. Complete the list to find the number of combinations when Gabrielle awards 4 equal prizes to the top 4 of the 5 finalists in a competition.

   1, 2, 3, and 4   1, 2, 3, and 5

   1, 2, 4, and 5   1, 3, 4, and 5

   2, 3, ▩, and ▩

Find the number of permutations for the situation.

3. Harry, Jenn, Melissa, Leah, and Connor are running for president and vice president of the school art club.

✅ 4. Donna is making a beaded necklace with 6 different colors of beads. She lines up the beads from left to right.

Find the number of combinations for the situation.

5. Kerri sees 3 DVDs that she wants at the store. She buys 2 of them.

✅ 6. Ansley chooses 4 sandwich toppings from lettuce, tomatoes, onions, cucumbers, pickles, and olives.

7. **Math Talk** **Explain** the difference between permutations and combinations.

Find the number of permutations for the situation.

8. Mrs. Kio's drama class has 22 students. She needs to cast 3 students as main characters for an upcoming play.

9. Reni is using the digits 5, 6, 7, 8, and 9 to make a 5-digit number.

10. A canoe race has 7 participating teams. The sponsors of the race are giving different awards for the first-, second-, and third-place finishers.

11. Fernanda and Alex each select a game piece for a board game. There are 4 different game pieces.

12. Justin has 8 different pictures from his class field trip. He plans to display 3 of them in a row.

13. Alexandria is arranging a collection of 10 mystery novels on a bookshelf.

Find the number of combinations for the situation.

14. Mr. Martin chooses 3 hall monitors from 4 responsible students.

15. Rory has 5 music CDs. He is selecting 2 of them to take on a trip.

16. Juan is making a flower arrangement with 2 types of flowers. He chooses from red roses, white roses, tulips, and orchids.

17. Mrs. Brooks has 6 photos of kids involved in science labs. She gives 5 to the yearbook committee.

18. Nicky selects 3 fruit drinks from a cooler of 6 assorted fruit drinks.

19. Kristen is picking 6 letters from her name to use for a code.

For 20–25, tell whether the selection is a permutation or a combination.

20. the number of handshakes among 8 people if everyone shakes each person's hand once

21. a committee of 5 chosen from a student club with 40 members

22. Aimee selects 2 shirts from a total of 5 shirts

23. the first, second, and third students in a lunch line made up of 14 students

24. a selection of 10 songs for a CD mix chosen from a collection of 300 songs

25. a group of 4 students from a class of 24 students to work together on a science project

26. In a middle-school science competition, cash prizes are awarded to the first-, second-, and third-place winners. Use the Fundamental Counting Principle to find the number of possible ways the 45 students in the competition could be arranged in these 3 prize categories.

27. Seven students from Ms. Dixon's science class are eligible to participate in the county science fair competition. If each school can send 4 students, how many combinations of students from Ms. Dixon's class could there be?

OCCT Test Prep Math Board

28. Bobbi collects souvenir bells from the places she visits. She has 5 bells on the bottom shelf of a display case. In how many different ways can she arrange them from left to right?

    A 5   **C** 50

    B 25   **D** 120

29. The local theater is showing 6 different movies. Hank and Deb are going to choose 2 movies to see this weekend. How many different combinations are possible?

    A 6   **C** 30

    B 15   **D** 36

★ Standards Quick Check

Use the sign-up sheet for a school talent show.

1. Ms. Elrod thinks the final 2 acts of the show should be singing acts. Make a tree diagram that shows all possible selections for these acts. How many times is each pair of students listed in the outcomes?

2. In how many different ways can the instrument acts be arranged so that one performs at the beginning of the show, one in the middle, and one at the end?

3. **Reasoning** Why is selecting one dancer for the fourth act and a different dancer for the fifth act of the show different from selecting 2 dancers to perform a duet?

Sign-up Sheet

Name	Act
Miyah	sing
Vic	play an instrument
Parker	sing
Allyssa	dance
Cole	dance
Kayleigh	sing
Claire	sing
Ted	play an instrument
Delaney	dance
Madeline	dance
Trevor	play an instrument

In music, the C major scale consists of 8 notes. A chord has 3 or more different notes that are played at the same time. The table lists types of chords that are named by the number of notes the chords contain.

Find the number of permutations or combinations for the situation.

1. Manni is selecting notes from the C major scale for a hexachord. How many combinations are there?

2. Charlie listens to a tetrachord and lists the notes it contains. In how many ways can Charlie list each individual note of this tetrachord from left to right?

Notes	Chord
3	Trichord
4	Tetrachord
5	Pentachord
6	Hexachord

Extra Practice

Set A

A number cube is labeled 1–6. Find each probability. Write each answer as a fraction, a decimal, and a percent. (pp. 458–461)

1. P(4) **2.** P(not 5) **3.** P(not odd) **4.** P(odd)

5. P(even) **6.** P(greater than 3) **7.** P(1 or 2) **8.** P(3 or 8)

9. P(divisible by 3) **10.** P(10) **11.** P(4 or not 4) **12.** P(less than 5)

13. Suppose Carmelita has a bag that contains 5 red, 6 orange, 2 blue, 3 white, and 4 purple marbles that are all the same size. Find the probability that she will randomly choose a marble that is not orange.

14. Suppose Jeffery has a box that contains same-sized slips of paper. On each slip of paper is written a letter. There are 8 L's, 4 E's, 9 T's, and 3 S's. Is it impossible, unlikely, likely, or certain that Jeffery will randomly choose a J?

Set B

A spinner is divided into equal sections that are marked with letters. Shiloh spins the pointer 40 times. Use her results, shown in the table, to find each experimental probability. Write each answer as a fraction, a decimal, and a percent. (pp. 462–465)

1. P(A) **2.** P(M) **3.** P(I)

4. P(O) **5.** P(K) **6.** P(W)

Shiloh's Spins						
Letter	A	M	I	O	K	W
Spins	10	5	7	8	4	6

7. Based on the experiment results, how many times can Shiloh expect the spinner to land on the A in her next 20 spins?

8. Based on the experiment results, how many times can Shiloh expect the spinner to land on the K in her next 20 spins?

Set C

The graph shows the result of a random survey of 400 students at a middle school. Predict how many of the school's 2,200 students have the indicated preference. (pp. 468–469)

1. Country **2.** Classical **3.** Rock

4. Inspirational **5.** Blues **6.** Jazz

7. In a box of clearance CDs, Jane randomly selects 40 CDs, 16 of which are rock CDs. How many of the 200 CDs in the box would you predict to be rock?

8. In a random survey of 120 warehouse shoppers, 75 preferred using a cart over a wagon. Predict how many out of 2,000 shoppers would prefer carts.

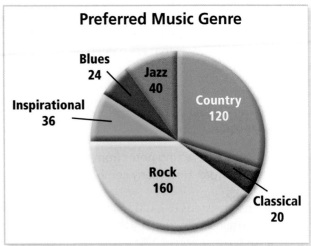

Preferred Music Genre

Blues 24
Jazz 40
Inspirational 36
Country 120
Rock 160
Classical 20

Set D

Use a grid to make a table, make a list, or draw a tree diagram to show the number of possible outcomes for each situation. (pp. 472–475)

1. a choice of cheddar, Swiss, or American cheese with white, wheat, or rye bread

2. rolling a number cube labeled 1–6 and spinning a spinner with 2 sections

3. a choice of a white, navy, or yellow shirt with khaki or brown pants

4. tossing a coin and spinning a spinner with 3 sections

Use the Fundamental Counting Principle to find the number of possible outcomes for each situation.

5. having lemonade or orangeade with pretzels, popcorn, or wheat crackers

6. taking a bus, a car, or a train to an exhibition; then having a video guide, a tour guide, or a self-guided tour to see an exhibit

7. a choice of white, wheat, rye, or sourdough bread with ham, turkey, or roast beef and swiss or cheddar cheese

8. watching a comedy, a drama, or an action film at 12:00 P.M., 2:00 P.M., 4:00 P.M., or 6:00 P.M.

Set E

Without looking, Sidney draws a card from the jar, does not replace it, and then selects another card. Find the probability of each event. (pp. 480–481)

1. P(P, N)

2. P(E, E)

3. P(A, N)

4. P(L, P)

5. P(E, N)

6. P(E, P)

7. P(L, not E)

8. P(A, P or N)

9. Helen has a bag of equally-sized marbles containing 5 blue marbles and 5 white marbles. What is the probability that she will randomly choose 3 white marbles in a row without replacing any of the marbles?

10. Dimetrus has a jar with equally-sized slips of paper in it. Each slip of paper has a letter of his name written on it. He draws a letter and replaces it. What is the probability that the next letter he draws is the same letter?

Set F

Find the number of combinations for the situation. (pp. 482–485)

1. Elizabeth chooses 4 flowers from a bunch of 5 flowers.

2. Rhianna has 6 DVDs. She is selecting 2 to bring to a friend's house.

3. Corinne buys 3 pieces of fruit out of a basket of 7 pieces of assorted fruit.

4. Paulo is picking 4 numbers from his 7-digit phone number for a code.

5. James is picking 2 colors of tile out of 6 colors for an art project.

6. Carmen has 5 dogs. She is selecting 2 to go on a walk.

Reading & Writing Math

Vocabulary

The total number of possible outcomes affects the probability of an event. Use what you know about outcomes and probability to answer these questions.

Problem 1

- You will put 10 tiles in the bag.
- You want the probability of picking a green tile to be $\frac{3}{10}$.
- It has to be equally likely that you will pick a yellow tile or a red tile.
- It has to be possible to pick a blue tile.

  1. How many red tiles will you use?

  2. How many yellow tiles?

  3. How many blue tiles?

  4. How many green tiles?

  5. Explain your reasoning.

. . . .

Problem 2

- You put 2 tiles each of four different colors in the bag.
- You will take turns picking tiles with a friend.
- After each of you has picked a tile, you return both tiles to the bag.

  6. Make a tree diagram to show all the possible combinations of picks.

  7. How many combinations of picks are there?

Writing Write how knowing all the combinations you can make with clothing is useful in everyday life.

Reading You might enjoy reading *Jumanji* by Chris Van Allsburg

H.O.T. Multistep Problems

1 Jane plays baseball in her local little league. During her last few games, Jane made a base hit 8 times for her 20 attempts at bat. ◄ 5.0.

- Estimate the probability that Jane will make a base hit during her next attempt. **Explain** how you got the answer.

- During a later game, Jane makes 2 base hits. Estimate how many attempts she made. **Explain** your answer.

- Throughout the entire season, Jane makes 48 attempts for a base hit. Estimate how many times she does **not** make a base hit.

- Charlie makes about half as many base hits as Jane. If Charlie makes 50 attempts, estimate the number of base hits he makes.

2 Marc is playing a game with his brother John. Marc flips a penny 40 times. The penny lands on heads 18 times. It lands on tails 22 times. ◄ 5.0.; 5.2.

- What is the fraction that represents the experimental probability of the penny coming up heads? Tails? **Explain**.

- Write the experimental probability as a fraction in simplest form for the penny to land on heads or tails.

- Predict the outcome of future trials for the penny to land on heads out of 120 more tosses. Then do the same for the penny landing on tails out of 80 more tosses. **Explain**.

Practice for the OCCT

1. A bag contains 26 tiles, each labeled with a different letter of the alphabet. To the nearest percent, what is the probability that a tile chosen at random is a consonant? (include *y*) 📱 5.0.

   A 19%

   B 23%

   C 77%

   D 81%

2. The table shows the results of tossing a coin 30 times. What is the experimental probability that the coin lands on tails? 📱 5.0.

Result	heads	tails
Times tossed	18	12

   A $\frac{2}{5}$

   B $\frac{1}{2}$

   C $\frac{3}{5}$

   D $2\frac{1}{2}$

3. In a middle school, 70 students take French, 144 students take Spanish, and the remaining 166 students do not take a language. No student takes both. What is the probability, round to the nearest percent, that a student chosen at random takes Spanish? 📱 5.0.

   A 18%   **C** 48%

   B 38%   **D** 61%

4. You have two state quarters and one quarter that is not a state quarter. You randomly choose two quarters. What is the probability that both coins are state quarters? 📱 5.0.

   A $\frac{1}{9}$

   B $\frac{1}{6}$

   C $\frac{1}{3}$

   D $\frac{2}{3}$

5. A spinner is divided into five sections, labeled from 1 to 5. The table shows the results of several spins. In 100 spins, how many times would you expect to land on section 5? 📱 5.0.

Section	1	2	3	4	5
Times landed	1	3	5	5	6

   A 20

   B 30

   C 43

   D 60

6. The integers from 1 through 10 are written on separate pieces of paper. You randomly choose two numbers, one at a time, but you do not replace them. What is the probability that both numbers are odd? 📱 5.0.

   A $\frac{2}{9}$

   B $\frac{1}{4}$

   C $\frac{1}{2}$

   D $\frac{17}{18}$

7. Events A and B are independent. The probability of A is 0.25 and the probability of B is 0.3. What is the probability of A and B? 📱 5.0.

   A 5%

   B 7.5%

   C 45%

   D 55%

8. At a school, 53% of the students are boys. What is the probability that a randomly selected student is a girl? 📱 5.0.

   A 0.47

   B 0.53

   C 0.57

   D 0.63

9. Events A and B are dependent with $P(A) = \frac{2}{5}$ and $P(B$ given $A) = \frac{1}{5}$. What is $P(A$ and $B)$? 📖 5.0.

A $\frac{2}{25}$

B $\frac{1}{5}$

C $\frac{3}{10}$

D $\frac{3}{5}$

10. Tanya decides to listen to a CD with 12 songs. Three of these are her favorites. If the songs play in random order, what is the probability that the first song played is one of her favorites? 📖 5.0.

A $\frac{1}{12}$

B $\frac{1}{4}$

C $\frac{1}{3}$

D $\frac{3}{4}$

11. You randomly choose answers A, B, C, and D for each of 3 multiple choice questions. How many outcomes are possible? 📖 5.2.

A 3

B 4

C 12

D 64

12. Mandy has 2 navy, 10 white, and 8 black pairs of socks in a drawer. If Mandy grabs a pair of socks without looking, what is the probability that she will grab a navy pair from the drawer? 📖 5.0.

A 10%

B 40%

C 50%

D 80%

Problem Solving

13. Sam is making a tomato sauce. For each sauce, he will choose 2 additional ingredients from among cheese, garlic, basil, and oregano. How many choices does he have? 📖 5.2.

14. You roll two number cubes. What is the probability that the sum of the numbers is less than 5? **Explain** your reasoning. 📖 5.0.

15. In a random sample of 90 bolts, 5 were found to be defective. **Explain** how you could predict the number of defective bolts in a sample of 2,000. 📖 5.0.

16. A bus stops at the end of your street every 30 minutes. You arrive at the bus stop at a randomly chosen time. What is the probability that you wait less than 10 minutes? **Explain** your reasoning. 📖 5.0.

Performance Assessment

Write Math With what type of data would you use a double-line graph?
a circle graph?

Martinsburg Weather

Martinsburg, located in West Virginia's second largest county, Berkeley, was founded in 1778.
Martinsburg is located along the Cumberland Trail, which was an early passage to the west.

For 1–3, use the double-line graph.

1. What does the graph show about the difference between the average high temperature and the average low temperature in Martinsburg from January through December?

2. By about how many degrees does the average low temperature change from January to March?

3. **Stretch Your Thinking** Find average high temperatures and average low temperatures of your city from January to December. Make a double-line graph to display your data.

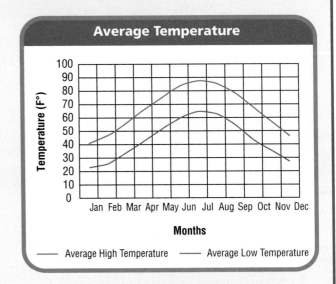

For 4–5, use the circle graph. The circle graph shows the average percents of clear, cloudy, and partly cloudy days in Martinsburg each year.

4. The number of cloudy and partly cloudy days per year is about how many times the number of clear days?

5. Would you say that clear days and partly cloudy days account for a little less than half or more than half of the days per year? Explain your thinking.

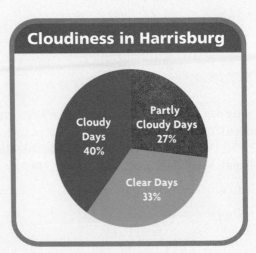

Unit Learning Task

Board Games

Objective: To solve problems using probability skills.

1. List your favorite board games. **Discuss** how players move around the board in the game.

2. **Discuss** what considerations game-makers may have when developing a board game.

3. Create your own fair board game that uses a spinner or number cube to move around the board.

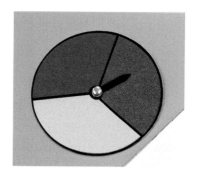

4. How do you know if the game is fair? **Explain**.

Money Around the World

When Is a Dollar Not a Dollar?

Find a book that shows its price on the back cover. Does it actually show two prices, one for the United States and one for Canada? Does the Canadian price seem higher? Why do you think that is?

Both Canada and the United States use dollars as their currency, but a Canadian dollar is not the same as a U.S. dollar. They have different values. On one date, the U.S. dollar was worth $1.14 in Canadian dollars.

FACT·ACTIVITY

Currency Conversions**

Country	1 U.S. Dollar is Worth:
Canada	1.14 Canadian dollars
Mexico	10.44 pesos
Czech Republic	23.77 crowns
Japan	115.88 yen
European Union	0.84 euro
Singapore	1.62 Singapore dollars
Lebanon	1,507.5 pounds
Kuwait	0.29 dinar
Colombia	2,247 pesos
Russia	28.03 rubles

conversions

Use the currency conversion table.

Value of United States Dollars in Some Countries

U.S. dollars	$1	$2	$3	$4	$5
Mexican pesos	10.44	20.88	▢	▢	▢
Kuwaiti dinars	0.29	▢	0.87	▢	▢
Japanese yen	115.88	▢	▢		▢

1. Copy and complete the table above.

2. Write and solve a proportion to find how many Singapore dollars would be exchanged for 8 U.S. dollars.

3. **Write Math** If an item's price is 8.4 euros, is that greater than, less than, or equal to 10 U.S. dollars? **Explain** your answer.

From Dollars to Dinars

Knowing the value of the U.S. dollar is really important when you travel to other countries. You need to know whether a sweatshirt costs $20 or $200! Currency values change every day. Most daily newspapers report the values of various currencies and whether or not the value of the dollar rose or fell.

Whale tooth

FACT·ACTIVITY

Suppose that you are in charge of the treasury department of a new country. Think of a name for your country's currency. Decide how many U.S. dollars will initially equal one of your currency (look at the table on the previous page for ideas).

1 A visitor to your country brings 200 U.S. dollars with her. How much of your currency should she receive?

2 Choose three other countries shown in the conversion table. What is the exchange rate between your currency and each of those currencies?

3 Suppose you have 50 units of each of the currencies you chose. How much is each amount worth in your own currency?

4 **Write Math** ▸ Write the ratio of your currency to U.S. dollars. Compare your currency to a classmate's. Whose currency has a higher exchange rate with U.S. dollars? **Explain** how you would calculate an exchange rate between your two currencies.

Rob's currency: the robbie

1 robbie = 8.5 U.S. dollars

Canadian dollars:

1 U.S. dollar = 1.14 Canadian dollars

1 robbie = 8.5 × 1.14 = 9.69 Canadian dollars

So, 1 robbie = 9.69 Canadian dollars.

After the OCCT

Review the Priority Academic Student Skills

Compare and Order Rational Numbers H2
Fractions, Decimals, and Percents H3
Compare and Order Fractions, Decimals, and Mixed Numbers H4
Exponents H5
Greatest Common Factor H6
Least Common Multiple H7
Add and Subtract Integers H8
Multiply and Divide Integers H9
Multiply Decimals H10
Divide Decimals H11
Multiply Fractions and Mixed Numbers H12
Divide Fractions and Mixed Numbers H13
Solve Equations H14
Write and Solve Proportions H15
Evaluate Algebraic Expressions H16
Percent of a Number H17
Inequalities H18
Number Patterns and Functions H19
Congruent Figures H20
Ordered Pairs H21
Circumference H22
Area of Circles H23
Analyze Data H24
Stem-and-Leaf Plots H26
Frequency Tables H27
Circle Graphs H28
Double-Bar Graphs H29
Mean, Median, Mode, and Range H30
Combinations H31

Review the Priority Academic Student Skills H2

These pages are used after the Oklahoma Core Curriculum Test (OCCT) as a learning check-up to make sure you are on track in meeting the Priority Academic Student Skills. Mastering these mathematical skills will assist in you being prepared for the next grade.

OCCT Test-Taking Strategies H32

Review these strategies before the Oklahoma Core Curriculum Test (OCCT) to improve your test-taking skills. There are tips for reading and understanding problems and understanding and answering the question.

Practice Facts BF1

These pages will help you improve your memory of basic facts. Review addition, subtraction, multiplication, and division facts by using these sets of exercises throughout the year.

Table of Measures TM1

This table will help you remember the relationship of important measures you have learned.

Glossary GL1

The mathematics vocabulary words and phrases you will learn and use are defined in this glossary. Following each entry is the Spanish translation.

Index I1

When you want to review a topic look in the index for a list of the pages where the topic is taught.

Review the Priority Academic Student Skills

Compare and Order Rational Numbers

📕 **2.1.** Convert compare, and order decimals, fractions, and percents using a variety of methods.

On a number line, each number is greater than any other number to its left and less than any number to its right.

Examples

Compare ⁻3 and 4. Use <, >, or =.

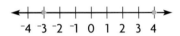
-4 -3 -2 -1 0 1 2 3 4

⁻3 is to the left of 4 on a number line.

So, −3 < 4 and 4 > ⁻3.

Order 8, ⁻8, and 6 from least to greatest.

Since −8 is the only negative number, it is the least.

6 < 8

⁻8 < 6 < 8

So, from least to greatest, the numbers are ⁻8, 6, and 8.

ERROR ALERT

When comparing negative and positive numbers, the smallest negative number is the number furthest to the left on a number line.

 On Your Own

Compare. Write <, >, or = for each ⬭.

1. 25 ⬭> ⁻14

2. −5 ⬭> ⁻16

3. ⁻157 ⬭< ⁻187

4. −17 ⬭< 17

5. ⁻132 ⬭= ⁻132

6. ⁻1,781 ⬭> ⁻1,782

7. ⁻874 ⬭< ⁻847

8. ⁻2,574 ⬭= ⁻2,574

9. 17,815 ⬭< 17,851

10. ⁻507 ⬭> ⁻578

Order the numbers from least to greatest.

11. 15, ⁻45, 84, ⁻19

12. ⁻75, 184, ⁻458, 98

13. 1,574, ⁻1,574, 157

14. ⁻69, ⁻4,748, , ⁻584, 687

15. 87, ⁻748, 748, ⁻87

16. 874, ⁻554, 19, ⁻1,487

17. 29, 48, ⁻48, ⁻84, 5

18. ⁻654, ⁻674, ⁻564, ⁻746

19. Read the problem below. **Explain** why B cannot be the correct answer. **COMMON ERROR** Then choose the correct answer.

Which shows the numbers 16, ⁻54, 54, ⁻76 ordered from least to greatest?

A 54, 16, ⁻54, ⁻76

B ⁻54, ⁻76, 16, 54

C ⁻76, ⁻54, 16, 54

D 76, 54, 16, 54

⭐ Review the Priority Academic Student Skills

Fractions, Decimals, and Percents

⬛ **2.1.** Convert compare, and order decimals, fractions, and percents using a variety of methods.

Percent means "per hundred" or "hundredths." The symbol used to write a percent is %. You can use place value and equivalent fractions to write a fraction or a decimal as a percent.

Examples

Write 0.39 as a fraction and as a percent.

Use place value to write the decimal as a fraction.

0.39   THINK: 0.39 is 39 hundredths.

$0.39 = \frac{39}{100}$ Percent means "per 100."

$\frac{39}{100} = 39\%$

So, $0.39 = \frac{39}{100} = 39\%$.

Write $\frac{2}{5}$ as a decimal and as a percent.

Write an equivalent fraction with 100 as the denominator.

$\frac{2}{5} = \frac{2 \times 20}{5 \times 20} = \frac{40}{100}$ THINK: $\frac{40}{100}$ is 40 hundredths.

Use place value and the meaning of percent.

$\frac{40}{100} = 0.40 = 40\%$

So, $\frac{2}{5} = 0.40 = 40\%$.

ERROR ALERT

Be sure to use the correct place value when writing a decimal as a fraction or a fraction as a decimal.

▶ On Your Own

Copy and complete the table. Write each fraction in simplest form.

	Fraction	Decimal	Percent
1.	$\frac{9}{10}$	⬛	⬛
2.	⬛	0.15	⬛
3.	⬛	⬛	55%
4.	$\frac{1}{5}$	⬛	⬛
5.	⬛	0.82	⬛
6.	⬛	⬛	42%
7.	$\frac{11}{50}$	⬛	⬛
8.	⬛	0.87	⬛
9.	⬛	⬛	25%
10.	$\frac{6}{100}$	⬛	⬛

11. Leah got 20 out of 25 questions correct on a math test. What percent of the questions did she answer correctly?

12. Over $\frac{3}{5}$ of the students in Dan's class like to eat seafood. Write $\frac{3}{5}$ as a decimal and as a percent.

13. Read the problem below. **Explain** why B cannot be the correct answer. Then choose the correct answer.

COMMON ERROR

Which shows 0.3 written as a fraction?

A $\frac{1}{3}$ **C** $\frac{3}{10}$

B $\frac{3}{100}$ **D** $\frac{3}{1,000}$

★ Review the Priority Academic Student Skills

Compare and Order Fractions, Decimals, and Mixed Numbers

⬛ **2.1.** Convert compare, and order decimals, fractions, and percents using a variety of methods.

Examples

Compare $^-2\frac{2}{5}$ and $^-2\frac{4}{5}$ by using a number line.

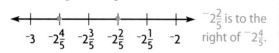

$-3 \quad -2\frac{4}{5} \quad -2\frac{3}{5} \quad -2\frac{2}{5} \quad -2\frac{1}{5} \quad -2$

$^-2\frac{2}{5}$ is to the right of $^-2\frac{4}{5}$.

So, $^-2\frac{2}{5} > {}^-2\frac{4}{5}$.

Compare $\frac{^-3}{4}$ and $\frac{^-1}{5}$.

$\frac{^-3}{4} = \frac{^-15}{20} \qquad \frac{^-1}{5} = \frac{^-4}{20}$

Write equivalent fractions by using the least common denominator, 20.

$^-15 < {}^-4$

Compare the numerators.

So, $\frac{^-3}{4} < \frac{^-1}{5}$.

Order $\frac{^-1}{5}, {}^-1\frac{1}{5}, {}^-0.50, {}^-0.05$ from least to greatest.

The only positive number is $1\frac{1}{5}$, so it is the greatest.

$^-0.50 = \frac{^-50}{100} \qquad {}^-0.05 = \frac{^-5}{100}$

Use place value to write the decimals as fractions.

Write equivalent fractions with a denominator of 100.

$\frac{^-1 \times 20}{5 \times 20} = \frac{^-20}{100} \qquad \frac{^-50}{100} = \frac{^-50}{100} \qquad \frac{^-5}{100} = \frac{^-5}{100}$

$^-50 < {}^-20 < {}^-5$

Compare the numerators.

ERROR ALERT

When comparing fractions and mixed numbers be sure the denominators are the same before comparing numerators.

So, from least to greatest, the numbers are $^-0.50, \frac{^-1}{5}, {}^-0.05,$ and $1\frac{1}{5}$.

▶ **On Your Own**

Compare. Write <, >, or =.

1. $^-1\frac{1}{8}$ ⬤ $\frac{7}{8}$

2. $\frac{5}{9}$ ⬤ $\frac{5}{6}$

3. $\frac{11}{16}$ ⬤ $\frac{9}{16}$

4. 0.5 ⬤ $\frac{1}{2}$

5. 0.3 ⬤ 0.25

6. $12\frac{4}{5}$ ⬤ $12\frac{2}{5}$

Order the numbers from least to greatest.

7. $^-4.0, {}^-0.004, {}^-0.04, {}^-0.4$

8. $\frac{1}{8}, \frac{^-1}{8}, \frac{^-5}{8}, \frac{5}{8}$

9. $\frac{77}{100}, 0.7, 7.7, \frac{7}{100}$

10. Read the problem below. **Explain** why A cannot be the correct answer choice. Then choose the correct answer. **COMMON ERROR**

Which numbers are ordered from least to greatest?

A $0.3, 0.03, 3\frac{1}{10}, \frac{1}{10}$

B $0.03, \frac{1}{10}, 0.3, 3\frac{1}{10}$

C $0.3, 0.03, \frac{1}{10}, 3\frac{1}{10}$

D $3\frac{1}{10}, 0.3, 0.03, \frac{1}{10}$

Review the Priority Academic Student Skills

Exponents

2.2.e. Build and recognize models of multiples to develop the concept of exponents and simplify numerical expressions with exponents and parentheses using order of operations.

Numbers may be written in different ways. For example, $10,000 = 10 \times 10 \times 10 \times 10 = 10^4$. 10^4 is the exponential form. For 10^4, the exponent is 4 and the base is 10. An exponent tells how many times the base is used as a factor, or multiplied by itself.

Examples

Change the expression to exponential form.

7×7

7^2 (read as 7 squared)

$2 \times 2 \times 2$

2^3 (read as 2 cubed)

$3 \times 3 \times 3 \times 3$

3^4

$15 \times 15 \times 15 \times 15 \times 15$

15^5

Identify the exponent and the base. Then find the value of the number.

Base $= 10$
Exponent $= 5$ 10^5
$10 \times 10 \times 10 \times 10 \times 10 = 100,000$

Base $= 8$
Exponent $= 4$ 8^4
$8 \times 8 \times 8 \times 8 = 4,096$

Base $= 25$
Exponent $= 3$ 25^3
$25 \times 25 \times 25 = 15,625$

ERROR ALERT

The exponent is never used as one of the factors in multiplication. It simply shows how often the base is multiplied by itself.

▶ On Your Own

Write in exponential form.

1. $60 \times 60 \times 60$

2. $7 \times 7 \times 7 \times 7 \times 7 \times 7 \times 7$

3. 4×4

4. $12 \times 12 \times 12 \times 12 \times 12$

Identify the exponent and the base, then find the value.

5. 1^{100}

6. 3^6

7. 4^3

8. 100^2

9. 9^4

10. 0^{12}

11. Read the problem below. **Explain** why A cannot be the correct answer choice. Then choose the correct answer.

    COMMON ERROR

    Find the value of 2^3.

    A 6

    B 8

    C 9

    D 16

⬠ Review the Priority Academic Student Skills

Greatest Common Factor

⬠ **2.2.a.** Multiply and divide fractions and mixed numbers to solve problems using a variety of methods.

The **greatest common factor,** or **GCF**, is the greatest factor that two or more numbers have in common. Since a number is divisible by its factors, the greatest common factor is sometimes called the greatest common divisor, or GCD.

You can use a list, prime factorization, or a ladder diagram to find the GCF of two or more numbers.

Examples

Use prime factorization to find the GCF of 9, 18, and 63.

$$9 = 3 \times 3$$
$$18 = 3 \times 3 \times 2$$
$$63 = 3 \times 3 \times 7$$
↓ ↓
$$3 \times 3 = 9$$

Write the prime factorization of each number.

Find the product of the common prime factors.

So, the GCF of 9, 18, and 63 is 9.

Use a ladder diagram to find the GCF of 84 and 66.

```
2 | 84 | 66
3 | 42 | 33
     14   11
```

$$2 \times 3 = 6$$

Divide each number by a common factor of the numbers. Keep dividing until the quotients have no common factors.

Find the product of the divisors.

So, the GCF of 84 and 66 is 6.

ERROR ALERT

The factors for the GCF are the digits along the left side of the ladder diagram, not the digits along the bottom.

▶ On Your Own

Find the GCF.

1. 20, 12

2. 32, 48

3. 100, 200

4. 350, 210

4. 87, 39

6. 95, 45

5. 18, 44

8. 66, 165

9. 6, 15, 24

10. 72, 114, 120

11. 35, 45, 65

12. 70, 105, 140

13. 15, 25, 35

14. 14, 28, 42

15. 12, 16, 36

16. 8, 12, 30

17. Read the problem below. **Explain** why C cannot be the correct answer. Then choose the correct answer.

COMMON ERROR

Find the GCF of 45 and 55.

A 495

B 165

C 99

D 5

Review the Priority Academic Student Skills

Least Common Multiple

▸ **2.2.a.** Multiply and divide fractions and mixed numbers to solve problems using a variety of methods.

The **least common multiple**, or **LCM**, is the smallest number, other than 0, that is a common multiple of two or more given numbers.

Examples

Find the LCM of 6 and 9.

Use a list.

Multiples of 6: 6, 12, 18, 24, 30, 36, 42, 48, 54, …

Multiples of 9: 9, 18, 27, 36, 45, 54, 63, 72, 81, …

The first three common multiples of 6 and 9 are 18, 36, and 54.

Find the LCM of 20 and 18.

Use prime factorization.

$20 = 2 \times 2 \times 5$, or $2^2 \times 5$

$18 = 3 \times 3 \times 2$, or $3^2 \times 2$

Write each factor the greatest number of times it appears in any prime factorization. Use exponents if possible. Multiply.

$2^2 \times 3^2 \times 5 = 180$

ERROR ALERT

Be sure to use each factor only once when using prime factorization, but use the greatest exponent given for that factor.

So, the least common multiple, or LCM, of 6 and 9 is 18.

So, the least common multiple, or LCM, of 20 and 18 is 180.

▸ On Your Own

Find the LCM.

1. 10, 6

2. 8, 15

3. 32, 45

4. 20, 9

5. 14, 22

6. 10, 50

7. 12, 18

8. 40, 60

9. 8, 42

10. 15, 50

11. 18, 30

12. 48, 96

13. 4, 9, 12

14. 3, 6, 14

15. 25, 30, 40

16. 9, 10, 15

17. 8, 12, 15

18. 9, 14, 63

19. 12, 16, 45

20. 21, 25, 35

21. What are two common multiples of 4, 10, and 12?

22. Read the problem below. **Explain** why C cannot be the correct answer. Then choose the correct answer.

COMMON ERROR

What is the least common multiple of 33 and 15?

A 495

B 165

C 55

D 3

★ Review the
Priority Academic Student Skills

Add and Subtract Integers

▬ **2.2.d.** Use the basic operations on integers to solve problems.

Integer rules

When adding integers with like signs, add the absolute values of the addends. Use the sign of the addends for the sum.

When adding integers with unlike signs, subtract the lesser absolute value from the greater absolute value. Use the sign of the addend with the greater absolute value for the sum.

When finding the difference between two integers, write the expression as an addition expression. Then use the rules for the addition of integers.

Examples

Add integers with like signs.

$13 + 5 = 18$

$^-4 + \,^-6 = \,^-10$

Add the absolute values of the integers.
Use the sign of the addends for the sum.

Add integers with unlike signs.

$^-9 + 3 = \,^-6$

$7 + \,^-2 = 5$

Subtract the lesser absolute value from the greater absolute value. Use the sign of the addend with the greater absolute value for the sum.

To subtract integers, write the expression as an addition expression and then add.

$8 - 11 = 8 + \,^-11$

$\quad\quad = \,^-3$

$1 - (^-3) = 1 + 3$

$\quad\quad\quad = 4$

ERROR ALERT

Work from left to right when adding and subtracting integers.

▶ On Your Own

Find the value of the expression.

1. $^-7 + (^-6)$

2. $2 - 5$

3. $^-8 + 10$

4. $1 - (^-2)$

5. $^-4 - (^-22)$

6. $^-50 - 55$

7. At 8 P.M., the temperature was 4°F. By midnight, the temperature dropped 12°F and then rose 7°F by morning. What was the morning temperature?

8. Read the problem below. **Explain** why C cannot be the correct answer choice. Then choose the correct answer. **COMMON ERROR**

Find the value of $6 - \,^-3 + 1$

A 2

B 4

C 8

D 10

⭐ Review the Priority Academic Student Skills

Multiply and Divide Integers

⭐ **2.2.d.** Use the basic operations on integers to solve problems.

Integer rules:

The product of two integers with like signs is positive.
The product of two integers with unlike signs is negative.
The quotient of two integers with like signs is positive.
The quotient of two integers with unlike signs is negatiwve.

Examples

Find the product or quotient.

$^-11 \times {}^-5$
$^-11 \times {}^-5 = 55$
The product is positive since the integers have like signs.

$4 \times {}^-6$
$4 \times {}^-6 = {}^-24$
The product is negative since the integers have unlike signs.

$^-18 \div {}^-6$
$^-18 \div {}^-6 = 3$
The quotient is positive since the integers have like signs.

$^-27 \div 9$
$^-27 \div 9 = {}^-3$
The quotient is negative since the integers have unlike signs.

Find $24 \div (3 \times 4)$.

$24 \div (3 \times 4) = 24 \div 12$
$= 2$

First multiply 3×4.
Then divide $24 \div 12$.

ERROR ALERT

Be sure to show the product or quotient of two negative integers as positive.

▶ On Your Own

Find the value of the expression.

1. $^-9 \times 5$

2. $7 \times {}^-12$

3. $44 \div {}^-11$

4. $^-6 \times {}^-8$

5. $^-24 \div {}^-3$

6. $80 \div {}^-10$

7. $8 \div {}^-2 \times {}^-4$

8. $^-6 \times 6 \div {}^-3$

9. Angela typed 90 words. If the words are evenly divided into 5 columns, how many words are in each column?

10. Read the problem below. **Explain** why D cannot be the correct answer. Then choose the correct answer. **COMMON ERROR**

Find the value of $^-15 \div {}^-5$.

A 10

B 3

C $\frac{-1}{3}$

D $^-3$

Review the Priority Academic Student Skills

Multiply Decimals

2.2.b. Multiply and divide decimals by one- or two-digit multipliers or divisors to solve problems.

When performing operations with decimals, it is important to understand where the decimal point should be placed in the answer.

ERROR ALERT

When multiplying decimals, be sure to count the number of decimals points in the two factors and use that many decimals points in the product.

Examples

Multiply. $9.65 × 38.5

Estimate. $10 × 40 = $400

```
   $9.65      ← 2 decimal places
  ×38.5       ← 1 decimal place
   4825
  77200
 +289500
 $371.525     ← 3 decimal places
```

Multiply. 3.78 × 4.52

Estimate. 4 × 5 = 20

```
    3.78      ← 2 decimal places
   ×4.52      ← 2 decimal place
    756
  18900
 +151200
  17.0856     ← 4 decimal places
```

▶ On Your Own

Estimate. Then solve.

1. 1.27 × 5.63

1. 75.2 × 93.1

3. 4.8 × 6.4

4. 14.21 × 5.2

5. 101.4 × 6.9

6. 7.9 × 85.17

7. 34 × 2.5

8. 40.528 × 3.4

9. 9.45 × 143.02

10. 15.36 × 15.36

11. 8.61 × 1.8

12. 4.5 × 62.71

13. 100.8 ×70.9

14. 51.89 × 74.3

15. 36.5 × 28.34

16. 854.2 × 65.31

17. Read the problem below. **Explain** why C cannot be the correct answer. Then choose the correct answer.

What is 36.8 × 3.2?

A 100.48

B 104.67

C 117.7

D 117.76

COMMON ERROR

Review the Priority Academic Student Skills

Divide Decimals

2.2.b. Multiply and divide decimals by one- or two-digit multipliers or divisors to solve problems.

When performing operations with decimals, it is important to understand where the decimal point should be placed in the answer.

Examples

Divide. 163.68 ÷ 4.4

Estimate. 160 ÷ 4 = 40

$$
4.4\overline{)163.68} \quad \rightarrow \quad
\begin{array}{r}
37.2 \\
44\overline{)1636.8} \\
-132 \\
\hline
316 \\
-308 \\
\hline
88 \\
-88 \\
\hline
0
\end{array}
$$

Divide. 281.14 ÷ 6.9

Estimate. 280 ÷ 7 = 40

$$
6.9\overline{)281.14} \quad \rightarrow \quad
\begin{array}{r}
40.7r31 \\
6.9\overline{)281.14} \\
-276 \\
\hline
514 \\
-483 \\
\hline
31
\end{array}
$$

ERROR ALERT

When dividing decimals, be sure to move the decimal point in the dividend only the number of places that you moved the decimal point in the divisor.

On Your Own

Estimate. Then solve.

1. 501.84 ÷ 10.2

2. 4,058.09 ÷ 77.15

3. 1,968.796 ÷ 35.14

4. 924.882 ÷ 36.1

5. 244.692 ÷ 19.42

6. 462.25 ÷ 21.5

7. 706.88 ÷ 9.4

8. 572.265 ÷ 36.45

9. 71.175 ÷ 6.5

10. 888.38 ÷ 41.32

11. 4,802.5 ÷ 106.25

12. 169.778 ÷ 6.7

13. Read the problem below. **Explain** why C cannot be the correct answer. Then choose the correct answer.

    COMMON ERROR

    What is 36.8 ÷ 3.2?

    A 1.15

    B 11.5

    C 115

    D 1,150

⬡★ Review the Priority Academic Student Skills

Multiply Fractions and Mixed Numbers

📖 **2.2.a.** Multiply and divide fractions and mixed numbers to solve problems using a variety of methods.

A **mixed number** consists of a whole number and a fraction. Before multiplying mixed numbers, rewrite them as fractions.

A fraction is in **simplest form** when the only common factor of the numerator and denominator is 1.

Fractions do not have to have common denominators when multiplying. Simply multiply across the numerators and across the denominators.

Examples

Find the product of $\frac{3}{4} \times \frac{5}{9}$. Write in simplest form.

$\frac{3}{4} \times \frac{5}{9} = \frac{3}{4} \times \frac{5}{9} = \frac{1}{4} \times \frac{5}{3}$

$\frac{1}{4} \times \frac{5}{3} = 1 \times \frac{5}{4} \times 3 = \frac{5}{12}$

Look at diagonal numerators and denominators. Simplify if they have a common factor. 3 and 9 can each be divided by 3.

Multiply the numerators. Multiply the denominators. The answer is in simplest form.

ERROR ALERT

Mixed numbers must be rewritten as fractions before multiplying.

$1\frac{1}{2} \times 2\frac{1}{2} \neq 2\frac{1}{4}$; the correct answer is $\frac{15}{4}$ or $3\frac{3}{4}$.

Find the product of $1\frac{2}{5} \times 2\frac{1}{6}$. Write in simplest form.

$1\frac{2}{5} = \frac{7}{5}$ AND $2\frac{1}{6} = \frac{13}{6}$

To multiply, write each mixed number as a fraction.

$\frac{7}{5} \times \frac{13}{6} = \frac{91}{30}$ or $3\frac{1}{30}$

Multiply the numerators. Multiply the denominators. Write the number as a mixed number or fraction in simplest form.

▶ On Your Own

Write each mixed number as a fraction.

1. $3\frac{7}{8}$ 2. $1\frac{2}{5}$ 3. $8\frac{3}{4}$

Write each mixed number as a fraction.

4. $\frac{2}{3} \times \frac{5}{6}$ 5. $\frac{1}{4} \times \frac{3}{7}$ 6. $\frac{1}{2} \times \frac{8}{16}$

7. $5\frac{1}{2} \times 1\frac{1}{2}$ 8. $1\frac{2}{7} \times 1\frac{1}{7}$ 9. $3\frac{1}{3} \times 1\frac{4}{5}$

10. Read the problem below. **Explain** why A cannot be the correct answer. Then choose the correct answer.

COMMON ERROR

Find the product of $4\frac{4}{5} \times 1\frac{1}{4}$.

A $4\frac{4}{20}$ **B** 5   **C** $5\frac{4}{20}$ **D** 6

★ Review the Priority Academic Student Skills

Divide Fractions and Mixed Numbers

★ **2.2.a.** Multiply and divide fractions and mixed numbers to solve problems using a variety of methods.

Two numbers are reciprocals or multiplicative inverses if their product is 1. For example, dividing by $\frac{2}{3}$ is the same as multiplying by $\frac{3}{2}$. Fractions do NOT have to have common denominators when dividing. Change fraction division problems into fraction multiplication problems using the reciprocal of the divisor.

Examples

Find the quotient of $\frac{3}{4} \div \frac{2}{3}$. Write in simplest form.

$\frac{3}{4} \div \frac{2}{3} = \frac{3}{4} \times \frac{3}{2}$

$\frac{3}{4} \times \frac{3}{2} = 3 \times \frac{3}{4} \times 2 = \frac{9}{8}$ or $1\frac{1}{8}$

Step 1: Do NOT change the first fraction.

Step 2: Change the division sign to multiplication.

Step 3: Change the second fraction (which is the divisor) to its reciprocal.

Multiply the numerators. Multiply the denominators. Write the answer as a fraction or mixed number in simplest form.

ERROR ALERT

Use the reciprocal of the divisor ONLY when changing a division problem into a multiplication problem.

$\frac{1}{2} \div \frac{3}{5} = \frac{1}{2} \times \frac{5}{3}$,

NOT $\frac{2}{1} \times \frac{5}{3}$

Find the quotient of $2\frac{2}{5} \div 3\frac{1}{4}$. Write in simplest form.

$2\frac{2}{5} = \frac{12}{5}$ AND $3\frac{1}{4} = \frac{13}{4}$

$\frac{12}{5} \div \frac{13}{4} = \frac{12}{5} \times \frac{4}{13}$

$\frac{12}{5} \times \frac{4}{13} = 12 \times \frac{4}{5} \times 13 = \frac{48}{65}$

Step 1: Write each mixed number as a fraction. Do NOT change the first fraction.

Step 2: Change the division sign to multiplication. Change the second fraction to its reciprocal.

Step 3: Multiply the numerators. Multiply the denominators. Write the number in simplest form.

▶ On Your Own

Write the reciprocal of each number.

1. $\frac{12}{17}$ **2.** $\frac{9}{4}$ **3.** 5

Find the quotient. Write in simplest form.

4. $\frac{2}{3} \div \frac{5}{6}$ **5.** $1\frac{2}{7} \div 1\frac{1}{7}$ **6.** $1\frac{1}{2} \div 1\frac{2}{9}$

COMMON ERROR

7. Read the problem below. **Explain** why C cannot be the correct answer. Then choose the correct answer.

Find the quotient of $\frac{4}{5} \div 4$.

A $\frac{1}{5}$ **B** $\frac{16}{5}$ **C** $\frac{5}{16}$ **D** 5

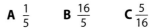

★ Review the Priority Academic Student Skills

Solve Equations

🔖 **1.4.** Write and solve one-step equations with one variable using number sense, the properties or operations, and the properties of inequalities (e.g., 1/3x + 9).

The **Addition**, **Subtraction**, **Multiplication**, and **Division Properties of Equality** can be used when solving equations.

The Addition and Subtraction Properties of Equality state that when you add or subtract both sides of an equation by the same number, the two sides of the equation remain equal. The Multiplication Property of Equality states that when you multiply both sides of an equation by the same number, the two sides of the equation remain equal. The Division Property of Equality states that when you divide both sides of an equation by the same nonzero number, the two sides remain equal.

ERROR ALERT

Be sure to use the inverse operation to get the variable alone on one side of the equation.

Examples

$x + 12 = 27$

$x + 12 = 27$	Write the equation.
$x + 12 - 12 = 27 - 12$	Use the Subtraction Property of Equality.
$x + 0 = 15$	
$x = 15$	Check your solution.
$x + 12 = 27$	
$15 + 12 \overset{?}{=} 27$	The solution checks.
$27 = 27 ✓$	

So, $x = 15$.

$6x = 180$

$6x = 180$	Write the equation.
$\dfrac{6x}{6} = \dfrac{180}{6}$	Use the Division Property of Equality,
$1 \times x = 30$	
$x = 30$	Check your solution.
$6x = 180$	
$6 \times 30 \overset{?}{=} 180$	The solution checks.
$180 = 180 ✓$	

So, $x = 30$.

▶ On Your Own

Solve and check.

1. $x + 14 = 20$

2. $5x = 65$

3. $5x = 45$

4. $\dfrac{c}{2} = 31$

5. $h - 32 = 15$

6. $10x = 57$

7. $\dfrac{3}{4}r = 9$

8. $p + 62 = 100$

9. $17 = k - 12$

10. $\dfrac{m}{7} = 4$

11. $60 = 12n$

12. $x + 7 = 28$

13. Read the problem below. **Explain** why A cannot be the correct answer. Then choose the correct answer.

COMMON ERROR

Solve. $\dfrac{m}{4} = 8$

A $m = 2$ **C** $m = 32$

B $m = 12$ **D** $m = 64$

Review the Priority Academic Student Skills

Write and Solve Proportions

▰ **2.1.** Convert compare, and order decimals, fractions, and percents using a variety of methods.

A **proportion** is an equation that shows two equivalent ratios. A proportion can be solved by using cross products or equivalent fractions.

ERROR ALERT
> When using equivalent fractions, be sure to multiply the numerator and denominator by the same number.

Examples

Solve using cross products.

$$\frac{n}{12} = \frac{5}{6}$$

$\frac{n}{12} \overset{\longleftarrow}{=} \overset{\longrightarrow}{\frac{5}{6}}$ Find the cross products.

$n \times 6 = 12 \times 5$ Multiply.

$6n = 60$

$\frac{6n}{6} = \frac{60}{6}$ Divide.

$n = 10$

So, $n = 10$.

Solve using equivalent fractions.

$$\frac{2}{5} = \frac{x}{20}$$

$\frac{2}{5} = \frac{x}{20}$ Find a common

$\frac{2 \times 4}{5 \times 4} = \frac{x}{20}$ denominator.

$\frac{8}{20} = \frac{x}{20}$ The denominators are the

$x = 8$ same, so set the numerators equal to each other.

So, $x = 8$.

Marcus is making bag lunches for the students in the summer camp program. He places an apple in each bag. If 5 cases of apples will fill 75 bags, find how many cases of apples are needed to fill 180 bags.

$\frac{\text{cases of apples}}{\text{lunch bags}} \longrightarrow \frac{5}{75} = \frac{c}{180}$

$5 \times 180 = 75 \times c$ Write a proportion.

$\frac{900}{75} = \frac{75c}{75}$

$12 = c$

So, 12 cases of apples are needed.

▶ On Your Own

Solve the proportion.

1. $\frac{9}{10} = \frac{p}{30}$

2. $\frac{7}{25} = \frac{21}{y}$

3. $\frac{6}{11} = \frac{x}{55}$

4. $\frac{12}{17} = \frac{d}{51}$

5. $\frac{30}{c} = \frac{5}{9}$

6. $\frac{8}{32} = \frac{j}{25}$

7. Sara is walking to the local park. It takes her 28 min to walk 7 mi. If she continued at this pace, how long would it take her to walk 10 mi to the ice cream shop?

8. Read the problem below. **Explain** why A cannot be the correct answer. Then choose the correct answer.

COMMON ERROR

Solve. $\frac{y}{32} = \frac{5}{8}$

A 5   **C** 20

B 29   **D** 160

⬤ Review the
Priority Academic Student Skills

Evaluate Algebraic Expressions

⬤ **1.3.** Use substitution to simplify and evaluate algebraic expressions (e.g., if x = 5 evaluate 3 - 5x).

A variable is a letter that stands for a value in an algebraic expression. To evaluate an algebraic expression, first replace the variables with known values. Then solve using order of operations.

Examples

Evaluate. $4 \div y + 3 \times 5$
where $y = 2$.

$4 \div y + 3 \times 5$	Replace y with 2.
$4 \div 2 + 3 \times 5$	Divide.
$2 + 3 \times 5$	Multiply.
$2 + 15 = 17$	Add.

So, for $y = 2$, $4 \div y + 3 \times 5 = 17$

Evaluate. $4z + 5t$
where $z = 4$ and $t = 2$.

$4z + 5t$	Replace z with 4 and t with 2.
$4(4) + 5(2)$	Multiply.
$16 + 10 = 26$	Add.

So, for $z = 4$ and $t = 2$, $4z + 5t = 26$

ERROR ALERT

Be sure to replace the correct variable with its given value. For example, when $a = 6$ and $c = 3$,
$c^2 + 5a - 2$ is equal to
$3^2 + 5(6) - 2$. It is not equal to
$6^2 + 5(3) - 2$.

Evaluate. $b^2 + 2b - 6$ where $b = {}^-7$.

$b^2 + 2b - 6$	Replace b with ⁻7.
$({}^-7)^2 + 2({}^-7) - 6$	Clear the exponents.
$49 + 2({}^-7) - 6$	Multiply.
$49 - 14 - 6$	Subtract.

So, for $b = {}^-7$, $b^2 + 2b - 6 = 29$

▶ On Your Own

Write in exponential form.

1. $x + 10$
where $x = 6$

2. $x + 10$
where $x = {}^-5$

3. ${}^-2y \div 7$
where $y = 28$

4. $13z + 13$
where $z = 3$

5. $t^2 - 2t + 5$
where $t = 2$

6. $4g + 2 - f$
where $g = 4, f = 12$

7. Read the problem below. **Explain** why B cannot be the correct answer choice. Then choose the correct answer.

COMMON ERROR

If $x = {}^-6$ and $y = 3$, what is $x^2 - 2y + 10$?

A $6^2 - 2({}^-3) + 10 = 52$

B $3^2 - 2({}^-6) + 10 = 31$

C ${}^-6 - 2(3) + 10 = 2$

D $({}^-6)^2 - 2(3) + 10 = 40$

★ Review the Priority Academic Student Skills

Percent of a Number

🔖 **2.2.c.** Estimate and find solutions to single and multi-step problems using whole numbers, decimals, fractions, and percents (e.g., $\frac{7}{8}$ 1 $\frac{8}{9}$ is about 2, 3.9 1 5.3 is about 9).

Percent, %, means "per hundred." Percents can be estimated by using numbers such as 5% or 10%, which are easier to compute. To find the percent of a number, first change the percent to a fraction or a decimal, and then multiply. Problems can also be solved by writing and solving an equation.

Examples

Find 52% of 240.

Use a decimal.

$52\% = 0.52$ Change the percent to a decimal.

$0.52 \times 240 = 124.8$ Multiply the decimal by the number.

So, 52% of 240 is 124.8.

Estimate a 15% tip for $35.26. Then find the tip to the nearest cent.

Estimate.

$35.26 is about $35.

Think: $15\% = 10\% + 5\%$
     10% of $35 = $3.50
       5% of $35 is half of $3.50, or $1.75.

Add: $3.50 + $1.75 = $5.25

Solve.

Let t = amount of tip.
   $t = 0.15 \times 35.26$
   $t = 5.289$, or about 5.29

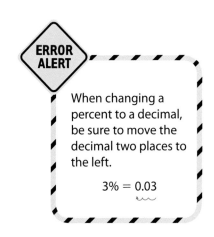

ERROR ALERT

When changing a percent to a decimal, be sure to move the decimal two places to the left.

$3\% = 0.03$

So, a 15% tip would be estimated as $5.25; and the tip to the nearest cent is $5.29.

▶ On Your Own

Find the percent of the number.

1. 25% of 48

2. 69% of 150

3. 8% of 365

4. 82% of 70

Estimate a 15% tip for each amount. Then find the tip to the nearest cent.

5. $15.00

6. $46.20

7. $6.44

8. $27.35

9. Read the problem below. **Explain** why A cannot be the correct answer. Then choose the correct answer.

COMMON ERROR

Find 36% of $150.

A $540   C $5.40

B $54   D $0.54

★ Review the Priority Academic Student Skills

Inequalities

📖 **1.4.** Write and solve one-step equations with one variable using number sense, the properties or operations, and the properties of inequalities (e.g., $1/3x + 9$).

An equation shows that two quantities are equal in value. Solve an equation by adding or subtracting the same number from both sides, or by multiplying or dividing both sides by the same number.

An inequality shows that two quantities are not equal in value. Solve an inequality by adding or subtracting the same number from both sides. Or, multiply or divide both sides of the inequality by the same positive number.

ERROR ALERT

If an operation is performed on one side of an equation or inequality, the same operation must be performed on the other side.

Examples

Write and solve an equation.

Jay has $200 in his back account. He made a deposit, and now has $265. How much did Jay deposit?

$$\$200 \quad + \quad d \quad = \quad \$265$$

↓   ↓   ↓

original amount   deposit   new amount

Subtract $200 from each side.

The deposit was $65.

$$\$200 + d = \$265$$
$$\underline{-\$200 \quad -\$200}$$
$$d = \$65$$

Solve the equation for y.

$2y = 6$ Divide each side by 2.

         Check.

$\dfrac{2y}{2} = \dfrac{6}{2}$

$y = 3$ $2 \times 3 = 6$

So, $y = 3$.

Solve the inequality for t.

$t - 5 > 9$

$t - 5 > 9$ Add 5 to each side.
$\underline{+5 \;+5}$ Check with a number
$t > 14$ greater than 14.
          $15 - 5 = 10, 10 > 9$

So, $t > 14$.

▶ On Your Own

Solve for x.

1. $x + 13 > 3$

2. $x + 10 = 33$

3. $3x = 4$

4. $5x = 15$

5. $\dfrac{x}{6} = 5$

6. $x + 5 < 16$

7. $9x = 36$

8. $7x > 49$

9. Read the problem below. **Explain** why C cannot be the correct answer choice. Then choose the correct answer.

COMMON ERROR

Solve $x + 20 > 30$ for x.

A $x > 10$

B $x > 210$

C $x > 50$

D $x > 600$

 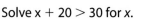

⭐ Review the Priority Academic Student Skills

Number Patterns and Functions

1.1. Generalize and extend patterns and functions using tables, graphs, and number properties (e.g., number sequences, prime and composite numbers, recursive patterns like the Fibonacci numbers.)

A function is a relationship between two quantities in which one quantity depends uniquely on the other. For every input, there is exactly one output.

You can write an equation to represent a function and use the equation to find a missing term.

Example

Write an equation to represent the function. Use the equation to find the missing term.

x	1	2	3	4	5
y	3	5	7	9	■

Think: Each y-value is greater than the corresponding x-value. Since the pattern is increasing, the rule could use either multiplication, addition, or both.

ERROR ALERT

Be sure that the rule shows a relationship between every input and its corresponding output.

Pattern: Each y-value is one more than twice the x-value.

Rule: $2x + 1$

Equation: $y = 2x + 1$ Write an equation.

$y = 2 \times 5 + 1$ Replace x with 5.

$y = 11$ Solve for y.

So, an equation is $y = 2x + 1$, and the missing term is 11.

▶ On Your Own

Write an equation to represent the function. Then use the equation to find the missing term.

1.

x	1	2	3	4	5
y	11	12	■	14	15

2.

x	25	30	35	40	45
y	10	15	20	25	■

3.

x	11	15	19	23	27
y	33	■	57	69	81

4.

x	2	4	6	8	10
y	1	2	■	4	5

5.

x	1	2	3	4	5
y	5	9	13	17	■

6. Juanita sells souvenirs for $3.00 each plus a $1.00 service charge. Write an equation to describe the function relating the total cost, t, to the number of souvenirs purchased, s. What is the total cost of 12 souvenirs?

7. Read the problem below. **Explain** why A cannot be the correct answer. Then choose the correct answer. Which equation represents the function?

COMMON ERROR

x	1	2	3	4	5
y	4	8	12	16	20

A $y = x + 3$ **C** $y = x + 6$

B $y = 4x$ **D** $y = 2x + 2$

Review the Priority Academic Student Skills

Student Handbook

Congruent Figures

⬛ **3.2.** Compare and contrast congruent and similar figures.

Sides that are in the same position in different figures are corresponding sides. Angles that are in the same position in different figures are corresponding angles. If the corresponding sides and corresponding angles in two figures are congruent, then the figures are congruent figures.

ERROR ALERT

For two figures to be congruent, all corresponding sides must be the same length, and all corresponding angles must have the same measure.

Examples

These two figures are congruent.

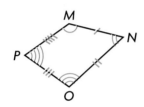

$\overline{MN}$ corresponds to $\overline{WX}$

$\angle L$ corresponds to $\angle Z$

$\angle O$ corresponds to $\angle Y$

All corresponding sides and corresponding angles are congruent.

Find the corresponding side length and the corresponding angle measure.

$\overline{MN}$ is 3 cm long. $\angle O$ is 89°.

So, $\overline{WX}$ is 3 cm long.   So, $\angle Y$ is 89°.

The corresponding side is $\overline{WX}$.   The corresponding angle is $\angle Y$.

▶ On Your Own

Solve.

  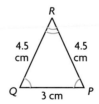

1. Which side of △ABC corresponds to $\overline{EF}$?

2. Which two triangles are congruent?

3. Which angle on corresponds to $\angle F$?

4. Which $\angle F$ is 63°, what is the measure of $\angle E$?

5. Read the problem below. **COMMON ERROR** **Explain** why B cannot be the correct answer choice. Then choose the correct answer. A quadrilateral has angle measures of 33°, 147°, 33°, and 147°.

What are the angle measures of a congruent figure?

A 30°, 150°, 30°, and 150°

B 33°, 147°, 39°, and 141°

C 33°, 147°, 90°, and 90°

D 33°, 147°, 33°, and 147°

★ Review the Priority Academic Student Skills

Ordered Pairs

▆ **3.3.** Identify the characteristics of the rectangular coordinate system and use them to locate points and describe shapes drawn in all four quadrants.

An ordered pair identifies an exact position on a coordinate grid. The x-coordinate is given first and shows how far left or right to move, and the y-coordinate is given second, and shows how far up or down to move. The origin is at (0,0) and is where the x-axis and y-axis intersect.

Examples

Graph points on a coordinate grid:
Point A (1,5); Point B (9,8)

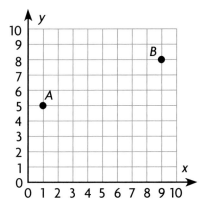

For Point A, find 1 by moving right one from the origin on the x-axis. Follow the grid line up 4 on the y-axis. Draw Point A.

For Point B, find 9 on the x-axis. Find 8 on the y-axis. Point B is at the intersection of these grid lines. Draw Point B.

Describe the location of points C and D on a coordinate grid.

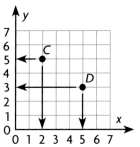

ERROR ALERT

The x-coordinate is always given first in an ordered pair. The y-coordinate is always given second.

The x-coordinate for Point C is 2.
The y-coordinate for Point C is 5.

Point C is at (2,5).
The x-coordinate for Point D is 5.
The y-coordinate for Point D is 3.

Point D is at (5,3).

▶ On Your Own

Graph and label the points of the ordered pairs.

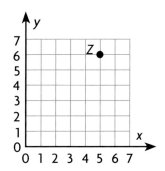

1. Point V (4,4)
2. Point W (2,1)
3. Point X (2,7)
4. Point Y (7,4)

5. Read the problem below. **Explain** why B cannot be the correct answer choice. Then choose the correct answer. **COMMON ERROR**

   Which ordered pair describes the location of Point Z?

   A (4,6)   **C** (7,3)

   B (6,5)   **D** (5,6)

Review the Priority Academic Student Skills

Circumference

🔖 **4.1.** Use formulas to find the circumference and area of circles in terms of pi.

For any circle, the **circumference** divided by the diameter is the same. This number is called **pi,** or π. The value of π is usually approximated as 3.14 or $\frac{22}{7}$. The relationship among circumference, diameter, and π can be written as $\frac{C}{d} = \pi$.

Since $\frac{C}{d} = \pi$, you can get the formula $C = \pi d$ by multiplying both sides of the equation by d. Since the diameter is twice the length of the radius, or $d = 2r$, you can also write $C = \pi \times 2r$, or $C = 2\pi r$.

So, you can find the circumference of any circle by using the formula $C = \pi d$ or $C = 2\pi r$.

ERROR ALERT

Be sure to determine whether the diameter or radius is given when finding circumference. Then use the appropriate formula.

Examples

Find the circumference of the circle to the nearest whole number. Use 3.14 or $\frac{22}{7}$ for π.

12.3 cm

$C = \pi d$	Write the formula.
$C \approx 3.14 \times 12.3$	Replace π with 3.14 and d with 12.3. Multiply.
$C \approx 38.622$	Round to the nearest whole number.
$C \approx 39$	

$1\frac{1}{4}$ in.

$C = 2\pi r$	Write the formula.
$C \approx 2 \times \frac{22}{7} \times 1\frac{1}{4}$	Replace π with $\frac{22}{7}$ and r with $1\frac{1}{4}$.
$C \approx \frac{2}{1} \times \frac{22}{7} \times \frac{5}{4}$	Write 2 and $1\frac{1}{4}$ as fractions. Simplify.
$C \approx \frac{55}{7} = 7\frac{6}{7}$	Multiply.

So, the circumference is about 39 cm.

So, the circumference is about 8 in.

▶ On Your Own

Find the circumference to the nearest whole number. Use 3.14 or $\frac{22}{7}$ for π.

1.

9 ft

2.

22 mm

3.

$2\frac{4}{5}$ in.

4.

3.9 cm

5. Read the problem below. **Explain** why B cannot be the correct answer. Then choose the correct answer.   **COMMON ERROR**

Find the circumference to the nearest whole number of a circle with a diameter of 14 m.

A about 44 m   **C** about 100 m

B about 88 m   **D** about 154 m

Review the Priority Academic Student Skills

Area of Circles

⬛ **4.1.** Use formulas to find the circumference and area of circles in terms of pi.

ERROR ALERT

If you know the radius or diameter of a circle, you can find its area using the formula $A = \pi r^2$. You can also find the area of a semicircle, or one-half of a circle, by using the formula $A = \frac{1}{2}\pi r^2$. To find the area of other partial circles, multiply the area of the entire circle by the fractional part of the circle.

When finding the area of a partial circle, you must multiply by the fractional part of the entire circle.

Examples

Find the area to the nearest whole number. Use 3.14 for π.

22 mm

$A = \pi r^2$ — Write the formula.

$A \approx 3.14 \times 11^2$ — Replace π with 3.14 and r with 11.

$A \approx 3.14 \times 121$ — Multiply.

$A \approx 379.94$

So, the area of the circle is about 380 mm².

Find the area of the partial circle to the nearest whole number. Use 3.14 for π.

9 in.

$A = \frac{3}{4}\pi r^2$ — Write the formula.

$A \approx 0.75 \times 3.14 \times 9^2$ — Rewrite $\frac{3}{4}$ as 0.75. Replace π with 3.14 and r with 9.

$A \approx 0.75 \times 3.14 \times 81$ — Multiply.

$A \approx 190.755$

So, the area of the partial circle is about 191 in.²

▶ On Your Own

Find the area to the nearest whole number. Use 3.14 or $\frac{22}{7}$ for π.

1. 4 ft

2. 126 mm

3. 1.8 km

4. 36 yd

Find the area. Use 3.14 or $\frac{22}{7}$ for π.

5.  semicircle
46 in.

6. ◹ $\frac{1}{4}$ circle
9.2 cm

7. Find the difference to the nearest whole number between the areas of a circle with a radius of 12 m and a circle with a diameter of 23 m.

8. Read the problem below. **Explain** why D cannot be the correct answer. Then choose the correct answer.

COMMON ERROR

Find the area of the semicircle to the nearest whole number.

32.8 m

A about 52 m² **C** about 422 m²

B about 103 m² **D** about 845 m²

★ Review the Priority Academic Student Skills

Analyze Data

🔊 **5.1.** Organize, construct displays, and interpret data to solve problems (e.g., data from student experiments, tables, diagrams, charts, graphs).

A **biased question** suggests or leads to a specific response, or excludes a certain group.

When a specific response is not suggested in a question, it is an **unbiased question**.

Biased: Is delicous pizza your favorite food?

Unbiased: What is your favorite food?

Examples

Sam asked his classmates, "Which color should we use for the school banner: the red, the green, or the beautiful blue?" The graph shows the results of his survey. Is the graph misleading? Explain.

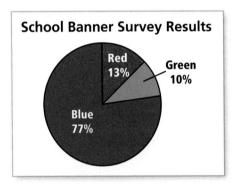

Sam's question is biased since it singles out one color as better than the others. Because of this, more students probably chose blue instead of red or green.

So, Sam's graph is misleading because his question is biased.

Maggie made a graph to display the number of concert tickets she and two classmates sold. Maggie concluded that she sold twice as many tickets as Philip and Neil. Is her conclusion valid? Explain.

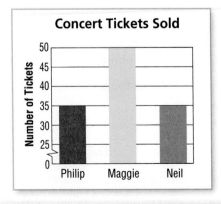

The bar for Maggie's ticket sales appears to be twice the length of Philip's bar and Neil's bar. The numbers show that this is misleading since she sold 50 tickets, while Philip and Neil sold 35 tickets each. The graph is misleading because of the broken scale between 0 and 25.

⬦ ERROR ALERT

Be sure to evaluate the questions used in a survey to gather data. Data obtained from a survey with a biased question may result in a misleading graph.

So, Maggie's conclusion is not valid.

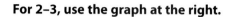
On Your Own

1. Ellen surveys 50 randomly selected students about shopping. She asks, "Would you rather enjoy catalog shopping or waste your time at a mall or flea market?" The results are shown in the graph at the right. Ellen concludes that most students prefer shopping by catalog. Is her conclusion valid? Explain.

For 2–3, use the graph at the right.

2. The graph shows the bank account balances of Carla and her brothers, Mark, Bob, and Ned. Is the graph misleading? Explain.

3. When looking at the graph, Carla concludes that she has twice as much money as her brother Ned. Is her conclusion valid? Explain.

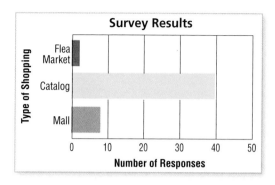

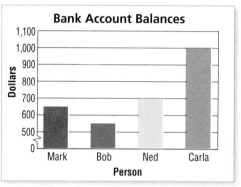

Solve.

4. Read the problem below. **Explain** why D cannot be the correct answer choice. Then choose the correct answer.

 COMMON ERROR

Which statement is true about the data shown in the graph below?

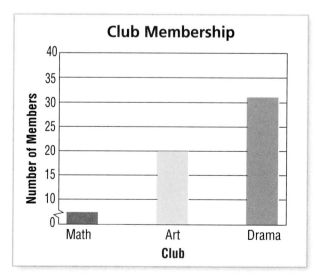

A Less than 10 students are in the math club.

B The art club has fewer than 20 members.

C The drama club has twice as many members as the art club.

D The math club has about one-sixth the number of members as the art club.

5. Read the problem below. **Explain** why A cannot be the correct answer choice. Then choose the correct answer. COMMON ERROR

Which question is *not* biased?

A Isn't summer the best season?

B Do you like apples more than pears?

C What is your favorite sport?

D Do you prefer classical music, or loud, annoying rock music?

⭐ Review the Priority Academic Student Skills

Stem-and-Leaf Plots

🔖 **5.1.** Organize, construct displays, and interpret data to solve problems (e.g., data from student experiments, tables, diagrams, charts, graphs).

A stem-and-leaf plot is a way to organize data. Every number from a set of data is represented in a stem-and-leaf plot. Each number is split into a stem (the left digit or digits) and a leaf (the right digit).

Examples

This stem-and-leaf plot shows the number of minutes students spent eating lunch.

The stems column shows the tens digits of the numbers.

Each tens digit is only listed once.

The leaves column shows every ones digit, even if the same number appears many times.

Number of Minutes Eating Lunch	
Stem	**Leaves**
1	1 1 1 4 5 5
2	0 1 3
3	3 4
4	0 1

A stem of 1 and a leaf of 4 represent 14 minutes.

A stem of 3 and a leaf of 3 represent 33 minutes.

The longest time spent eating was 41 minutes.

The time that occurred most often was 11 minutes.

Interpret the stem-and-leaf plot. How many students spent 20 to 29 minutes eating lunch?

Find the 2 in the stem column. Count the number of digits in the leaves column.

So, 3 students spent between 20 to 29 minutes eating lunch.

ERROR ALERT

When a set of data has two-digit numbers, the tens digits are used as stems in a stem-and-leaf plot. The ones digits are the leaves.

 **On Your Own**

The plot shows the average number of breaths a swim team's members take per minute.

1. What is the smallest number of breaths per minute?

2. What is the largest number of breaths per minute?

3. How many people take 11 breaths per minute?

4. Which number of breaths per minute occurs most often?

Breaths Per Minute	
Stem	**Leaves**
1	1 1 3 4 5
2	0 1 2 2 2
3	4
4	0 2 7

5. Read the problem below. **Explain** why D cannot be the correct answer choice. Then choose the correct answer.

COMMON ERROR

A swimmer takes 48 breaths per minute. How would this be shown on the stem and leaf plot?

A Stem, 0; leaf 8

B Stem, 4; leaf 8

C Stem, 0; leaf 48

D Stem, 8; leaf 4

Review the Priority Academic Student Skills

Frequency Tables

5.1. Organize, construct displays, and interpret data to solve problems (e.g., data from student experiments, tables, diagrams, charts, graphs).

A frequency table is a way to organize data. The table is divided into several categories or groups, and gives the total for each group.

Examples

Identify a frequency table's parts.

The title tells the type of information the table contains.

Steps Juno climbed each day.

Daily Steps Juno Climbed

Step Number	Frequency
100 – 200	2
201 – 300	14
301 – 400	6
401 – 500	9

How many groups are there? 4

What does the *frequency* column show? The number of times Juno completed each group.

Interpret the frequency table.

How many times did Juno climb between 100 and 200 steps? 2

How many times did Juno climb more than 300 steps? 6 + 9 = 15

Which number of steps did she climb most often? 201–300 steps

How many more times did Juno climb 201–300 steps than 301–400 steps? 14 − 6 = 8

How many total days did Juno climb steps? 2 + 14 + 6 + 9 = 31

ERROR ALERT

Adding up the numbers in each group will give you the total number. For example, in the frequency table to the left, adding the number of days in each group gives the total number of days that Juno climbed steps.

On Your Own

Favorite Weekend Activity Survey Results

Activity	Frequency
Hiking	22
Reading	34
Computer Time	21
Volunteering	22

1. For how many people is hiking the favorite activity?

2. How many people chose hiking or reading as a favorite?

3. Which activity do the most people have as a favorite?

4. How many more people are there that like to read than like to volunteer?

5. Read the problem below. **Explain** why D cannot be the correct answer choice. Then choose the correct answer.

COMMON ERROR

What is the total number of people that were surveyed about their favorite weekend activity?

A 99   **C** 21

B 77   **D** 34

★ Review the Priority Academic Student Skills

Circle Graphs

☛ **5.1.** Organize, construct displays, and interpret data to solve problems (e.g., data from student experiments, tables, diagrams, charts, graphs).

Circle graphs show how parts of the data are related to the whole and to each other.

The circle graph on the right shows the different types of instruments played by students in a school band.

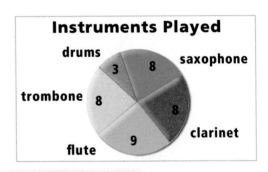

Instruments Played

Examples

Interpret the circle graph.

How many different types of instruments are played? 5—drums, saxophone, trombone, clarinet, flute
How many total instruments are played? $3 + 8 + 8 + 8 + 9 = 36$
Which instrument do most of the students play? Flute
How many students play the trombone? 8

ERROR ALERT

Each section of a circle graph represents a part of the whole data set. The whole data set is all of the sections added together.

What fraction or portion of the instruments played are clarinets?

Identify the number of clarinets played. 8
Identify the total number of instruments played. 36
Write a fraction in simplest form representing clarinets played. $\frac{8}{36} = \frac{2}{9}$
So, $\frac{2}{9}$ of the instruments played are clarinets.

▶ On Your Own

Use the circle graph to answer 1–5.

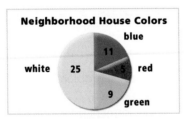

Neighborhood House Colors

1. How many houses are there in there neighborhood?

2. How many houses are blue?

3. How many different house colors are there?

4. How many more houses are painted white than are painted green?

5. Read the problem below. **COMMON ERROR** **Explain** why B cannot be the correct answer choice. Then choose the correct answer.

   What fraction of the houses are painted red?

   A $\frac{11}{25}$

   B $\frac{5}{25}$

   C $\frac{1}{10}$

   D $\frac{9}{40}$

☆ Review the Priority Academic Student Skills

Double-Bar Graphs

📎 **5.1.** Organize, construct displays, and interpret data to solve problems (e.g., data from student experiments, tables, diagrams, charts, graphs).

A bar graph is a way to display data that is grouped in categories.

A **double-bar graph** helps to compare two or more sets of data.

This double bar graph uses red bars to show the books Megan owns. It uses blue bars to show the books Tasha owns.

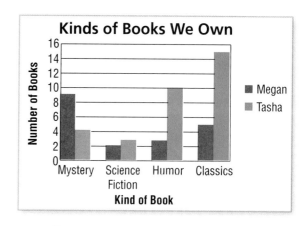

Example

How many more mysteries does Megan own than Tasha?

Find the category called "Mystery."
Megan's bar reaches to 9. Tasha's bar reaches to 4.
Subtract: 9 − 4 = 5.

Megan owns 5 more mysteries than Tasha.

ERROR ALERT

Pay attention to the scale. If a bar reaches between two numbers, it has a value that is between those two numbers.

▶ On Your Own

Use the double-bar graph to answer the questions.

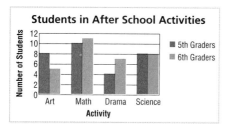

1. Which activity has more 5th graders than 6th graders?

2. How many more 6th graders than 5th graders are in Drama?

3. Which after school activity has the same number of 5th and 6th graders?

4. Which after school activity has the least number of 6th graders?

5. Read the problem below. **Explain** why C cannot be the correct answer. Then choose the correct answer. **COMMON ERROR**

   Use the double bar graph on the left. How many students in all are in Art after school?

   A 5

   B 8

   C 12

   D 13

★ Review the Priority Academic Student Skills

Mean, Median, Mode, and Range

⬛ **5.3.** Find the measures of central tendency (mean, median, mode, and range) of a set of data 9with and without outliers) and understand why a specific measure provides the most useful information in a given context.

ERROR ALERT

The data set must be ordered to find the median. If there is no middle value, the median is the average of the two middle values.

You can use measures to describe data sets. Mean and median are measures that describe the center. **Mean** is the average of a data set. **Median** is the middle value or the average of the two middle values in an ordered data set. **Mode** is a measure that describes the most common value or values in a data set. **Range** is the difference between the greatest and least values in the data set.

Examples
Find the mean, median, mode, and range.

```
            X
      X   X       X
  X   X   X   X   X
  +---+---+---+---+---
  10  11  12  13  14
```

Mean: $\dfrac{10 + 11 + 11 + 11 + 12 + 12 + 13 + 14 + 14}{9}$

$= \dfrac{108}{9} = 12$

Median: 10, 11, 11, 11, 12, 12, 13, 14, 14

Mode: 11

Range: $14 - 10 = 4$

Type of Kite	Number of Kites
Diamond	80
Sled	95
Stunt	67
Japanese Edo	90

Mean: $\dfrac{80 + 95 + 67 + 90}{4} = \dfrac{332}{4} = 83$

Median: 67, 80, 90, 95
$\qquad (80 + 90) \div 2 = 85$

Mode: none

Range: $95 - 67 = 28$

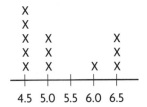

▶ On Your Own

Find the mean, median, mode, and range.

1. 49, 53, 44, 42, 59, 50, 44, 50, 41, 50, 50

2.
```
  X
  X
  X   X           X
  X   X           X
  X   X       X   X
  +---+---+---+---+---
 4.5 5.0 5.5 6.0 6.5
```

3. 110, 104, 102, 106, 110, 110

4. 64.1, 64.9, 64.7, 64.7, 64.3, 64.6

5. Read the problem below. **Explain** why A cannot be the correct answer. Then choose the correct answer.

COMMON ERROR

Find the median of the data set.
   24, 22, 21, 21, 29, 25, 26, 24, 2

A 29   C 24

B 23.6   D 21

⭐ Review the Priority Academic Student Skills

Combinations

📋 **5.2.** Use the fundamental counting principle on sets with up to five items to determine the number of possible outcomes.

A combination is a selection of items from a group of choices.

ERROR ALERT

Remember to include all of the choices when determining how many combinations are possible.

Examples

Marc's dad is going to go buy a new car. How many possible combinations does Marc's dad have to choose from? *Use a tree diagram to find possible combinations.*

Color	Type	Combination
Blue	Car	Blue Car
	Truck	Blue Truck
Red	Car	Red Car
	Truck	Red Truck
Black	Car	Black Car
	Truck	Black Truck
Green	Car	Green Car
	Truck	Green Truck

There are 8 possible combinations:
Blue Car
Blue Truck
Red Car
Red Truck
Black Car
Black Truck
Green Car
Green Truck

▶ On Your Own

Find the number of combinations for each situation.

1. Josie has 3 choices of ice cream flavors; strawberry, vanilla, chocolate, and 3 different toppings; hot fudge, pineapple, caramel.

2. Melvin has 4 pairs of pants; grey, black, khaki, white, 3 shirts; red, blue, orange, and 3 pairs of shoes; sandels, sneakers, dress shoes.

3. Keisha has 3 types of deli meats; turkey, tuna, roast beef, 3 types of bread; wheat, white, kaiser roll, and 5 types of cheese; american, swiss, cheddar, provolone, muenster.

4. Read the problem below. **Explain** why A cannot be the correct answer choice. Then choose the correct answer.

   COMMON ERROR

   Camren has several combinations to choose from as to where to go on vacation. She could go to England, Ireland, or Germany. She could go with her mom, her dad, or her brother. She could go for 5 days, 7 days, or ten days. How many combinations does Camren have?

   A 6   **C** 21

   B 9   **D** 27

OCCT Test-Taking Strategies
Tips For Taking Math Tests

Being a good test-taker is like being a good problem solver. When you answer test questions, you are solving problems. Remember to **Read to Understand**, **Plan**, **Solve**, and **Check**.

Read to Understand

Read the problem.

- Look for math terms and recall their meanings.

- Reread the problem and think about the question.

- Use the details in the problem and the question.

---

1. Bob took some friends to dinner. If the dinner cost $52 and he left a 20% tip, what is the total he spent on dinner including tip?

   A $10.40

   B $41.60

   C $52.20

   D $62.40

Test Tip

Understand the problem.
The problem is multistep and requires you to find the total amount Bob spent on dinner. Reread the problem to compare the details to the answer choices. You can use estimation instead of calculating the amount of the tip and then adding the tip to the cost. The answer is **D**.

- Each word is important. Missing a word or reading it incorrectly could cause you to get the wrong answer.

- Pay attention to words that are in *italics* and words and phrases like *round*, *best*, and *least to greatest*.

---

2. One morning, the temperature was 8° Fahrenheit (F) below zero. The temperature *rose* 18°F by 1:00 P.M. and then *dropped* 12°F by evening. What was the evening temperature?

   A 2°F below zero

   B 10°F below zero

   C 12°F above zero

   D 38°F above zero

Test Tip

Look for important words.
The words *below*, *rose*, and *dropped* are important. The temperature 8° Fahrenheit *below* zero indicates $-8°F$. *Rose* indicates an increase or addition. *Dropped* indicates a decrease or subtraction. Carefully perform the operations to find the correct solution. The answer is **A**.

Plan

Think about how you can solve the problem.

• See if you can solve the problem with the information given.

• Pictures, charts, tables, and graphs may have the information you need.

• Sometimes the answer choices have information to help solve the problem.

---

3. Pablo is going to choose one sandwich from the meats and breads listed below. Which set shows all his possible choices?

> Meat: Tuna, Turkey
>
> Bread: White, Wheat, Oat

A {(white, tuna), (white, turkey)}

B {(wheat, tuna), (wheat, turkey)}

C {(oat, tuna), (oat, turkey), (white, tuna), (white, turkey)}

D {(white, tuna), (white, turkey), (wheat, tuna), (wheat, turkey), (oat, tuna), (oat, turkey)}

Test Tip

Get the information you need.
The answer choices give four different sets. Think about each one and the number of choices in each. The problem asks for all the choices, so be sure all the breads and all the meats are paired together. The answer is **D**.

• You may need to write a number sentence and solve it to answer the question.

• Some problems have two or more steps.

• In some problems, you need to look at relationships instead of computing an answer.

• If the path to the solution isn't clear, choose a problem solving strategy and use it to solve the problem.

---

4. Sue found the mean and median of the set {9, 9, 12}. If 7 were added to the set, then

A the mean would decrease.

B the mean would increase.

C the median would increase.

D the median would decrease.

Test Tip

Decide on a plan.
From the choices given, you must think of how a number that is less than the others will affect the mean and the median. If you use *logical reasoning,* you can see that the median will remain the same and the mean will decrease. The answer is **A**.

Solve

Follow your plan, working logically and carefully.

- Estimate the answer. Compare it to the answer choices.

- Use reasoning to find the most likely choices.

- Make sure you complete all the steps needed to answer the problem.

- If your answer does not match any of the answer choices, check the numbers you used. Then check your computation.

---

5. A cell-phone company charges $0.06 per minute for local calls and $0.08 per minute for long-distance calls. Which expression gives the total cost in dollars for x minutes of local calls and y minutes of long-distance calls?

   A 0.14xy

   B 0.14(x + y)

   C 0.06x + 0.08y

   D 0.06x − 0.08y

Test Tip

Eliminate choices.
It is important to understand that x represents minutes of local calls and y represents minutes of long-distance calls. You can eliminate choices A and B, since you would not add $0.06 and $0.08 because they are separate charges. Choice D shows subtraction, so it can be eliminated. The answer is **C**.

- If your answer still does not match one of the choices, look for another form of the number, such as a decimal instead of a fraction.

- If answer choices are given as pictures, look at each one by itself while you cover the other three.

- Read answer choices that are statements and relate them to the information in the problem one by one.

---

6. Lamar paid $35.10 for a skateboard. The amount included an 8% sales tax. What was the cost of the skateboard before the tax?

   A $37.91

   B $32.50

   C $8.00

   D $2.81

Test Tip

Choose the answer.
Since the question asks for the cost of the skateboard before the tax, you need to subtract the tax to find the answer. So, choose the answer that is less than and close to $35.10. The answer is **B**.

Take time to catch your mistakes.

- Be sure you answered the question asked.

- Check for important words you might have missed.

- Be sure you used all the information you needed.

- Check your computation by using a different method.

Test Tip

Check your work.
You need to write and solve a proportion to find the length of $\overline{PQ}$. Check to be sure you have set up the proportion correctly. Then review your computation for any errors. The answer is **A**.

7. $\triangle MNO$ is similar to $\triangle PQR$. What is the length of $\overline{PQ}$?

A 7.5 feet

B 9 feet

C 10 feet

D 12 feet

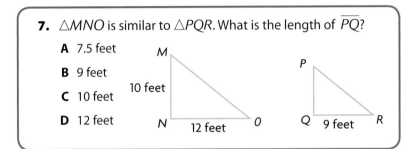

Tips for Short-Answer and Extended-Response Items

- Plan to spend 5 to 10 minutes on each question.

- Read the question carefully and think about what you are asked to do. You may be asked to explain your answer with sentences and/or pictures.

- Plan how to organize your response.

- As you write your answer, look back at the question. Make sure you understand the question.

- Leave time to reread your answer and correct any mistakes.

Photo Credits

Credits

Practice Addition

	L	M	N	O	P
A	70 + 8	43 + 5	58 + 7	29 + 6	85 + 8
B	69 + 4	67 +18	24 +36	19 +22	57 +49
C	264 + 58	836 + 54	329 + 92	747 + 21	1,641 + 385
D	3,231 + 578	5,822 + 927	8,534 + 299	4,605 +2,493	5,619 +2,537
E	3,229 +6,008	7,924 +1,437	84,520 + 3,864	91,234 + 6	274,051 + 40,318
F	0.4 +0.9	0.8 +0.7	2.6 +8.1	3.5 +7.7	0.31 +2.04
G	5.92 +3.15	2.79 +5.88	8.64 +5.23	2.55 +4.77	5.62 +3.25
H	4.98 +1.99	7.98 +8.47	0.218 +2.143	8.360 +5.216	5.816 +3.215
I	7.992 +3.582	4.557 +3.685	7.364 +7.859	22.78 +37.46	17.31 +12.89
J	8.26 +26.15	4.68 +48.37	6.37 +44.83	31.18 +125.50	29.54 +737.29
K	19.75 +321.63	2.01 +96.99	198.79 + 66.74	936.77 +245.83	9.80 +236.75

Practice Subtraction

	L	M	N	O	P
A	68 − 5	82 − 7	74 −43	81 −56	50 −38
B	87 −68	148 − 17	562 − 79	394 −145	560 −217
C	750 −192	827 −792	423 −358	578 −396	1,460 − 316
D	4,960 − 681	7,234 − 997	6,857 − 868	7,500 − 244	8,000 − 562
E	35,120 − 6,299	24,665 − 7,759	74,772 − 4,804	36,009 −19,148	68,200 −49,361
F	11.4 − 6.2	26.8 − 4.3	54.3 − 9.5	77.6 − 8.8	17.3 −16.5
G	58.2 −24.9	76.8 −44.9	91.3 −74.8	13.20 − 8.17	45.40 − 9.65
H	35.51 −23.17	47.26 −34.37	8.026 −7.317	3.004 −2.995	9.327 −6.438
I	6.518 −4.629	36.234 − 8.884	19.408 − 1.582	13.601 −10.311	45.008 −32.471
J	50.093 −42.999	98.765 −56.789	630.71 −527.21	942.31 −429.57	4,300.02 − 189.57
K	657.2 − 8.9	3,941.87 − 649.99	98.213 − 7.608	8,922.64 − 365.77	2,123.45 − 6.67

Practice Multiplication

	L	M	N	O	P
A	20 × 4	30 × 2	30 + 3	24 × 2	31 × 3
B	46 × 2	37 × 4	74 × 4	63 × 8	58 × 9
C	61 ×20	84 ×40	76 ×30	68 ×50	92 ×60
D	26 ×14	93 −15	50 ×38	81 ×54	79 ×43
E	680 × 35	710 × 52	825 ×173	522 ×286	463 ×836
F	0.5 ×0.9	3.6 ×1.7	1.3 ×2.5	5.9 ×3.1	4.2 ×8.7
G	3.14 ×6.8	7.24 ×0.8	9.65 ×0.4	7.25 ×1.8	9.97 ×0.9
H	17.31 × 2.06	8.26 ×0.87	31.82 ×15.5	15.4 × 6.27	12.8 × 4.16
I	17.3 × 2.06	165.4 × 7.4	139.2 × 8.17	935.5 × 3.25	987.2 × 7.8
J	246.28 × 25.55	950.8 × 52.4	825.2 × 9.63	440.7 ×425.2	2,145.2 × 527.5
K	128.7 ×513.9	1,414.8 × 673.5	294.8 × 63.2	6,352.4 × 23.56	1,427.3 × 631.2

Practice Division

	N	O	P	Q	R
A	$8\overline{)72}$	$27\overline{)108}$	$6\overline{)138}$	$4\overline{)816}$	$5\overline{)525}$
B	$6\overline{)624}$	$7\overline{)763}$	$4\overline{)836}$	$5\overline{)205}$	$2\overline{)164}$
C	$7\overline{)642}$	$9\overline{)700}$	$2\overline{)785}$	$5\overline{)277}$	$3\overline{)343}$
D	$90 \div 30$	$40 \div 20$	$160 \div 40$	$360 \div 40$	$540 \div 90$
E	$630 \div 70$	$3,000 \div 60$	$100 \div 20$	$560 \div 70$	$3,500 \div 50$
F	$630 \div 58$	$4,801 \div 37$	$100 \div 21$	$560 \div 82$	$1,875 \div 19$
G	$900 \div 300$	$480 \div 240$	$840 \div 105$	$1,500 \div 300$	$9,800 \div 800$
H	$1.2 \div 4$	$0.12 \div 4$	$3.5 \div 5$	$3.2 \div 4$	$0.18 \div 9$
I	$3.69 \div 3$	$83.7 \div 9$	$44.8 \div 4$	$6.4 \div 8$	$19.75 \div 5$
J	$2.24 \div 4$	$4.48 \div 2.8$	$3.78 \div 3$	$12.1 \div 1.1$	$229.6 \div 8.2$
K	$0.38\overline{)13.3}$	$0.55\overline{)2.42}$	$2.48\overline{)1.3392}$	$6.41\overline{)135.892}$	$15\overline{)10.8}$
L	$9\overline{)43.65}$	$18.2\overline{)378.56}$	$49.3\overline{)201.144}$	$29.1\overline{)186.24}$	$18.2\overline{)378.56}$
M	$4.9\overline{)303.8}$	$6.1\overline{)408.7}$	$9.96\overline{)92.628}$	$0.84\overline{)0.336}$	$0.42\overline{)4.788}$

Table of Measures

METRIC

Length

1 millimeter (mm) = 0.001 meter (m)
1 centimeter (cm) = 0.01 meter
1 decimeter (dm) = 0.1 meter
1 kilometer (km) = 1,000 meters

CUSTOMARY

Length

1 foot (ft) = 12 inches (in.)
1 yard (yd) = 36 inches
1 yard = 3 feet
1 mile (mi) = 5,280 feet
1 mile = 1,760 yards

Volume/Capacity/Mass for Water

1 cubic centimeter (cm^3) $\longrightarrow$ 1 milliliter $\longrightarrow$ 1 gram
1,000 cubic centimeters $\longrightarrow$ 1 liter $\longrightarrow$ 1 kilogram

SYMBOLS

$<$	is less than	1:2	ratio of 1 to 2
$>$	is greater than	%	percent
$\leq$	is less than or equal to	$\cong$	is congruent to
$\geq$	is greater than or equal to	$\approx$	is approximately equal to
$=$	is equal to	$\perp$	is perpendicular to
$\neq$	is not equal to	$\parallel$	is parallel to
10^2	ten squared	$\overleftrightarrow{AB}$	line AB
10^3	ten cubed	$\overrightarrow{AB}$	ray AB
10^4	the fourth power of 10	$\overline{AB}$	line segment AB
2^3	the third power of 2, or two cubed	$\angle ABC$	angle ABC
$^+7$	positive 7	$m\angle A$	measure of $\angle A$
$^-7$	negative 7	$\triangle ABC$	triangle ABC
$|{-}4|$	the absolute value of negative 4	$\circ$	degree
(4,7)	ordered pair (x,y)	π	pi (about 3.14, or $\frac{22}{7}$)
$5/hr	the rate $5 per hour	P(4)	the probability of the event 4

FORMULAS

Perimeter

Polygon	$P =$ sum of the lengths of the sides
Rectangle	$P = 2(l + w)$, or $P = 2l + 2w$
Square	$P = 4s$

Circumference

Circle	$C = 2\pi r$, or $C = \pi d$

Area

Circle	$A = \pi r^2$	Square	$A = s^2$
Parallelogram	$A = bh$	Trapezoid	$A = \frac{1}{2}h(b_1 + b_2)$
Rectangle	$A = lw$	Triangle	$A = \frac{1}{2}bh$

Surface Area

Cylinder	$S = 2\pi rh + 2\pi r^2$

Volume

Cylinder	$V = Bh$, or $V = \pi r^2 h$	Triangular Prism	$V = Bh$
Rectangular Prism	$V = Bh$, or $V = lwh$		

Consumer

Distance traveled	$d = rt$	Interest (simple)	$I = prt$

Other

Celsius (°C)	$C = \frac{5}{9} \times (F - 32)$	Diameter	$d = 2r$
Fahrenheit (°F)	$F = (\frac{9}{5} \times C) + 32$	Radius	$r = \frac{1}{2}d$

★ Glossary

absolute value [abʹsə•lo͞ot valʹyo͞o] **valor absoluto** The distance of an integer from zero on a number line

abundant number [ə•bunʹdent numʹber] **número abundante** A natural number whose proper divisors have a sum that is greater than the number

acute angle [ə•kyo͞otʹ angʹgəl] **ángulo agudo** An angle whose measure is greater than 0° and less than 90°

acute triangle [ə•kyo͞otʹ trīʹangʹgəl] **triángulo acutángulo** A triangle with all angles less than 90°

addends [adʹendz] **sumandos** Numbers that are added in an addition problem

Addition Property of Equality [ə•diʹshən präʹpər•tē əv i•kwolʹə•tē] **propiedad de suma de la igualdad** The property that states that if you add the same number to both sides of an equation, the sides remain equal

additive inverse [aʹdə•tiv inʹvərs] **inverso aditivo** The number which, when added to the given number, equals zero

adjacent angles [ə•jāʹsənt angʹgəlz] **ángulos adyacentes** Side-by-side pairs of angles that have a common vertex and a common ray

Example:

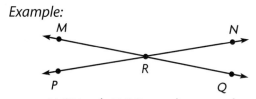

∠MRN and ∠NRQ are adjacent angles.

algebraic expression [al•jə•brāʹik ik•spreʹshən] **expresión algebraica** An expression that includes at least one variable
Examples: x + 5, 3a − 4

alternate exterior angles [ôl′tər•nət ek•stir′ē•ər ang′gəlz] **ángulos alternos externos** A pair of exterior angles on opposite sides of the transversal
Example:

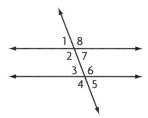

Angles 1 and 5 and angles 4 and 8 are pairs of alternate exterior angles.

alternate interior angles [ôl′tər•nət in•tir′ē•ər ang′gəlz] **ángulos alternos internos** A pair of interior angles on opposite sides of the transversal
Example:

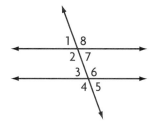

Angles 2 and 6 and angles 3 and 7 are pairs of alternate interior angles.

altitude [al′te tood] **altitud** A line segment between a vertex of a triangle and the side not containing the given vertex, perpendicular to that side; a line segment showing the height of a figure

angle [ang′gəl] **ángulo** A figure formed by two rays with a common endpoint
Example:

angle bisector [ang′gəl bī•sek′tər] **bisectriz de un ángulo** A ray that divides an angle into two congruent angles

area [âr′ē•ə] **área** The number of square units needed to cover a given surface

Associative Property [ə•sō′shē•ə•tiv prä′pər•tē] **propiedad asociativa** The property that states that whatever way addends are grouped or factors are grouped does not change the sum or the product

Examples: 12 + (5 + 9) = (12 + 5) + 9
(9 × 8) × 3 = 9 × (8 × 3)

axes [ak′sēz] **ejes** The horizontal number line (x-axis) and the vertical number line (y-axis) on the coordinate plane

bar graph [bär′ graf] **gráfica de barras** A graph that displays countable data with horizontal or vertical bars

base (arithmetic) [bās] **base (aritmética)** A number used as a repeated factor
Example: 83 = 8 × 8 × 8; 8 is the base.

base (geometry) [bās] **base (geometria)** In two dimensions, one side of a triangle or parallelogram which is used to help find the area. In three dimensions, a plane figure, usually a polygon or circle, which is used to partially describe a solid figure
Examples:

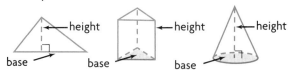

benchmark [bench′märk] **punto de referencia** A reference point on a number line that is useful for rounding fractions

bisect [bǐ′sekt] **bisecar** To divide into two congruent parts

box-and-whisker graph [bäks•ənd•hwis′kər graf] **diagrama de caja y brazos** A graph that shows how far apart and how evenly data are distributed
Example:

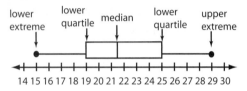

Celsius [səl′sē•əs] **Celsius** A metric scale for measuring temperature

central angle [sen′trəl an′gəl] **ángulo central** An angle in a circle with its vertex at the center of the circle

certain [sûr′tən] **seguro** Sure to happen

chord [kord] **cuerda** A line segment with endpoints on a circle
Example:

circle [sûr′kəl] **círculo** The set of all points a given distance from a point called the center
Example:

circle graph [sûr′kəl graf] **gráfica circular** A graph that lets you compare parts to the whole and to other parts
Example:

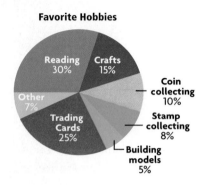

Favorite Hobbies

circumference [sûr•kum′fər•əns] **Circunferencia** The distance around a circle

Word History

Circumference comes from the combination of the Latin prefix *circum-*, which means "around," and the Latin word *ferre,* which means "to carry." Together, the parts mean "to carry around."

clustering [klus′tər•ing] **agrupamiento** A method used to estimate a sum when all addends are about the same

combination [kom′bə•nā′shən] **combinación** A selection of different items in which the order is not important

Commutative Property [kə•myoo′tə•tiv prä′pər•tē] **propiedad conmutativa** The property that states that if the order of addends or factors is changed, the sum or product stays the same
Examples: $6 + 7 = 7 + 6$
$7 \times 3 = 3 \times 7$

compatible numbers [kəm•pat′ə•bəl num′bərz] **números compatibles** Pairs of numbers that are easy to compute mentally

compensation [kom•pen•sā′shən] **compensación** An estimation strategy in which you change one addend to a multiple of ten and then adjust the other addend to keep the balance

complement [kom•plə•mənt] **complemento** In probability, the complement of an event is a new event consisting of all outcomes in the sample space that are not outcomes of the original event. The sum of the probability of an event and its complement is 1.

complementary angles [kom•plə•men′tər•ē ang′gəlz] **ángulos complementarios** Two angles whose measures have a sum of 90°

Example:

complementary events [kom•plə•men′tər•ē i•vənts′] **sucesos complementarios** Two separate events that together include all possible outcomes of an experiment and for which the sum of the two corresponding probabilities is always exactly 1

composite number [käm•pä′zət num′bər] **número compuesto** A whole number greater than 1 that has more than two whole-number factors

compound event [kom′pound i•vent′] **evento compuesto** An event made of two or more simple events

congruent [kən•grōō′ənt] **congruente** Having the same size and shape

conjecture [kən•jek′chər] **conjetura** A statement, based on limited observations, that has been proposed to be true in all cases, but has not yet been proven true or false

convenience sample [kən•vēn′yən(t)s sam′pəl] **muestra conveniente** The most available individuals or objects in the population that are selected to obtain results quickly

coordinate plane [kō•ôr′də•nət plān] **plano de coordenadas** A plane formed by a horizontal line (*x*-axis) that intersects a vertical line (*y*-axis)

corresponding angles [kôr•ə•spän′ding ang′gəlz] **ángulos correspondientes** Angles that appear in the same positions in relation to a transversal and two lines crossed by the transversal
Example:

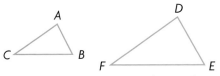

Pairs of Corresponding Angles

∠1 and ∠3	∠2 and ∠4
∠5 and ∠7	∠6 and ∠8

corresponding angles [kôr•ə•spän′ding ang′gəlz] **ángulos correspondientes** Angles that are in the same position in different plane figures
Example:

∠*A* and ∠*D* are corresponding angles.

corresponding sides [kôr•ə•spän′ding sīdz] **lados correspondientes** Sides that are in the same position in different plane figures

Example:

$\overline{CA}$ and $\overline{FD}$ are corresponding sides.

cube [kyo͞ob] **cubo** A rectangular solid with six congruent square faces
Example:

cumulative frequency [kyo͞o′myə•lə•tiv frēk′wən(t)•sē] **frecuencia acumulativa** A running total of the number of subjects surveyed

cylinder [si′lən•dər] **cilindro** A solid figure that has two flat parallel, congruent circular bases
Example:

D

decagon [de′kə•gän] **decágono** A polygon with 10 sides
Examples:

decimal [de′sə•məl] **decimal** A number with one or more digits to the right of the decimal point

deficient number [di•fish′ənt num′ber] **número deficiente** A natural number whose proper divisors have a sum that is less than the number

denominator [di•nä′mə•nā•tər] **denominador** The part of a fraction that tells how many equal parts are in the whole

Example: $\frac{3}{4}$ denominator

dependent events [di•pen′dənt i•vənts′] **sucesos dependientes** Events for which the outcome of the first event affects the possible outcomes of the second event

diagonal [dī•a′gə•nəl] **diagonal** A line segment that connects two nonadjacent vertices of a polygon

Example:

diameter [dī•am′ə•tər] **diámetro** A line segment that passes through the center of a circle and has its endpoints on the circle

Example:

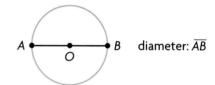

dilation [dī•lā′shən] **dilatación** A transformation that enlarges or reduces a figure
Example:

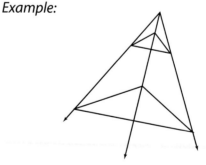

dimension [di•men′shən] **dimensión** The length, width, or height of a figure

discount [dis′kount] **descuento** An amount that is subtracted from the regular price of an item

Distributive Property [di•stri'byoo•tiv prä'pər•tē] **propiedad distributiva** The property that states that multiplying a sum by a number is the same as multiplying each addend by the number and then adding the products. The property also holds for subtraction.
Example:
$14 \times 21 = 14 \times (20 + 1) = (14 \times 20) + (14 \times 1)$
$15 \times 18 = 15 \times (20 + 2) = (15 \times 20) - (15 \times 2)$

dividend [di'və•dend] **dividendo** The number that is to be divided in a division problem

Example: In $5.6 \div 8$, 5.6 is the dividend.

divisible [də•vi'zəbəl] **divisible** A number is divisible by another number if the quotient is a natural number and the remainder is zero.

Example: 18 is divisible by 3.

Division Property of Equality [di•vi'zhən prä'pər•tē əv i•kwä'lə•tē] **propiedad de división de la igualdad** The property that states that if you divide both sides of an equation by the same nonzero number, the sides remain equal

divisor [di•vī'zər] **divisor** The number that divides the dividend
Example: In $4.5 \div 0.9$, 0.9 is the divisor.

double-bar graph [də' bəl bar graf] **gráfica de doble barra** A graph that helps to compare two sets of data

double-line graph [də' bəl līn graf] **gráfica lineal doble** A graph that helps to compare two sets of data that change over time

edge [ej] **arista** The line segment where two faces of a solid figure meet
Example:

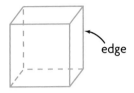
edge

edge [ej] **nodo** A connection between vertices in a network

elapsed time [i•lapst' tīme] **tiempo transcurrido** The time that passes from the start to the end of an activity or period

Egyptian fraction [i•jip'shən frak'shən] **fracción egipcia** A fraction written as a sum of distinct unit fractions

endpoint [end'point] **extremo** Either of two points of a line segment such that all other points of the line segment are between them; the point from which a ray begins
Examples:

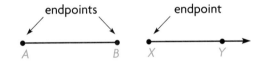

equally likely [ē'kwə•lē lī'klē] **igualmente probable** Having the same chance of occurring

equation [i•kwā'zhən] **ecuación** A statement that shows that two quantities are equal

equilateral triangle [ē•kwə•la'tə•rəl trī'ang•gəl] **triángulo equilátero** A triangle with three congruent sides
Example:

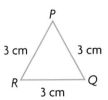

equivalent decimals [ē•kwiv′ə•lənt desemelz] **decimales equivalentes** Two or more decimals that name the same number or amount

equivalent fractions [ē•kwiv′ə•lənt frak′shənz] **fracciones equivalentes** Fractions that name the same amount or part

equivalent ratios [ē•kwiv′ə•lənt rā′shē•ōz] **razones equivalentes** Ratios that name the same comparison

estimate [es′tə•mət] **estimación** A number close to an exact amount

evaluate [i•val′yo͞o•āt] **evaluar** To find the value of a numerical or algebraic expression

event [i•vent′] **suceso** A set of outcomes

even vertex [ē′vən vûr′teks] **vértice par** In a network, a point where an even number of edges meet

experimental probability [ik•sper•ə•men′təl prä•bə•bil′ə•tē] **probabilidad experimental** The ratio of the number of favorable outcomes that occur to the total number of trials, or times, the activity is performed

exponent [ik•spō′nənt] **exponente** A number that tells how many times a base is used as a factor
Example: $2^3 = 2 \times 2 \times 2 = 8$; 3 is the exponent.

expression [ik•spre′shən] **expresión** A mathematical phrase that combines operations, numerals, and sometimes variables to name a number

exterior angles [ik•stir′ē•ər ang′gəlz] **ángulos externos** Angles on the outside of two lines intersected by a transversal

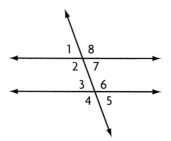

∠1, ∠4, ∠5, and ∠8 are exterior angles.

face [fās] **cara** One of the polygons of a solid figure
Example:

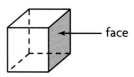

face

factor [fak′tər] **factor** A number that is multiplied by another number to find a product

Fahrenheit [fâr′ən•hīt] **Fahrenheit** A customary scale for measuring temperature

formula [fôr′myə•lə] **fórmula** A rule that is expressed with symbols
Example: $A = lw$

fractal [frak′təl] **fractal** A figure with repeating patterns containing shapes that are like the whole but of different sizes throughout

fraction [frak′shən] **fracción** A number that names a part of a whole or part of a group

frequency table [frē′kwən•sē tā′bəl] **tabla de frecuencia** A table representing totals for individual categories or groups

function [funk'shən] **función** A relationship between two quantities in which one quantity depends uniquely on the other

Word History

The word *function* comes from the Latin word *fungi* which means "perform." A mathematical function can be thought of as "performing" an operation or operations on a set of values.

Fundamental Counting Principle
[fun•də•men'təl koun'ting prin'sə•pəl] **principio fundamental de conteo** If one event has m possible outcomes and a second event has n possible outcomes, then there are $m \times n$ total possible outcomes.

greatest common divisor (GCD) [grā'təst ko'mən də•vī'zər] **máximo común divisor (MCD)** The greatest divisor that two or more numbers have in common

greatest common factor (GCF) [grā'təst ko'mən fak'tər] **máximo factor común (MFC)** The greatest factor that two or more numbers have in common

height [hīt] **altura** A measure of a polygon or solid figure, taken as the length of a perpendicular from the base of the figure

Example:

heptagon [həp'tə•gän] **heptágono** A polygon with 7 sides
Example:

hexagon [hek'sə•gän] **hexágono** A six-sided polygon
Examples:

histogram [his'tə•gram] **histograma** A bar graph that shows the number of times data occur in certain ranges or intervals

Identity Property of Addition [ī•den'tə•tē prä'pər•tē əv ə•di'shən] **propiedad de identidad de la suma** The property that states that the sum of zero and any number is that number
Example: $25 + 0 = 25$

Identity Property of Multiplication [ī•den'tə•tē prä'pər•tē əv mul•tə•plə•kā'shən] **propiedad de identidad de la multiplicación** The property that states that the product of any number and 1 is that number
Example: $12 \times 1 = 12$

image [i'mij] **imagen** The result of a transformation

impossible [im•po'sə•bəl] **imposible** Never able to happen

independent events [in•də•pen'dənt i•vents'] **sucesos independientes** Events for which the outcome of the first event does not affect the possible outcomes of the second event

inequality [in•i•kwä'le•tē] **desigualdad** An algebraic or numerical sentence that contains the symbol $<$, $>$, $\leq$, $\geq$, or $\neq$
Example: $x + 3 > 5$

integers [in′ti•jərz] **enteros** The set of whole numbers and their opposites

interior angles [in•tir′ē•ər ang′gəlz] **ángulos interiores** Angles between two lines intersected by a transversal

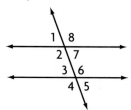

∠2, ∠3, ∠6, and ∠7 are interior angles.

intersecting planes [in•tər•sekt′ing plānz] **planos secantes** If two distinct planes have a point in common, the planes are intersecting and their intersection is a line.

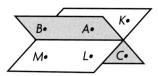

inverse operations [in•vərs′ ä•pə•rā′shənz] **operaciones inversas** Operations that undo each other, like addition and subtraction or multiplication and division

irrational number [i•ra′shə•nəl num′bər] **número irracional** A number that cannot be expressed as a repeating or terminating decimal

isosceles triangle [ī•sä′sə•lēz tri′ang•gəl] **triángulo isósceles** A triangle with exactly two congruent sides
Example:

7 in.   7 in.

5 in.

iteration [i•te•ra′shən] **iteración** A step in the process of repeating something over and over again

lateral face [lat′ər•əl fās] **cara lateral** Any surface of a polyhedron other than a base

lateral surface [la′tə•rəl sûr′fəs] **superficie lateral** For pyramids and cones, the lateral surface consists of all the surfaces except the base. For prisms and cylinders, the lateral surface consists of all the surfaces except the bases.

least common denominator (LCD) [lēst ko′mən di•nä′mə•nā•tər] **mínimo común denominador (m.c.d.)** The least common multiple of two or more denominators

least common multiple (LCM) [lēst ko′mən mul′tə•pəl] **mínimo común múltiplo (m.c.m.)** The smallest number, other than zero, that is a common multiple of two or more numbers

like terms [līk tûrmz] **términos semejantes** Expressions that have the same variable with the same exponent

linear equation [li′nē•ər i•kwā′zhen] **ecuación lineal** An equation that, when graphed, forms a straight line

line graph [līn graf] **gráfica lineal** A graph that uses line segments to show how data change over time

line plot [līn plot] **diagrama de puntos** A graph that shows frequency of data along a number line
Example:

```
        x
        x         x
x   x   x   x   x
+---+---+---+---+---+---+
1   2   3   4   5   6   7
```
Miles Jogged

line segment [līn seg′mənt] **segmento** A part of a line with two endpoints
Example:

line of symmetry [līn əv si′mə•trē] **eje de simetria** A line across which a figure is symmetric

line symmetry [līn si′mə•trē] **simetria axial** A figure has line symmetry if a line can separate the figure into two congruent parts

lower extreme [lo′er ik•strēm′] **extremo inferior** The least number in a set of data

lower quartile [lo′er kwôr′tīl] **primer cuartil** The median of the lower half of a set of data

mean [mēn] **media** The sum of a group of numbers divided by the number of addends

measure of central tendency [me′zhər əv sen′trəl ten′dən(t)•sē] **medida de tendencia central** Measure of the location of the center of a data set

median [mē′dē•ən] **mediana** The middle value in a group of numbers arranged in order

midpoint [mid′point] **punto medio** The point that divides a line segment into two congruent line segments

mixed number [mikst num′bər] **número mixto** A number represented by a whole number and a fraction

mode [mōd] **moda** The number or item that occurs most often in a set of data

multiple [mul′tə•pəl] **múltiplo** The product of two natural numbers is a multiple of each of those numbers.

Multiplication Property of Equality [mul•tə•plə•kā′shən prä′pər•tē əv i•kwä′lə•tē] **propiedad de multiplicación de la igualdad** The property that states that if you multiply both sides of an equation by the same number, the sides remain equal

multiplicative inverse [mul•tə•pli′kə•tiv in′vərs] **inverso multiplicativo** A reciprocal of a number that is multiplied by that number resulting in a product of 1

natural numbers [na′chə•rəl num′bərz] **números naturales** The set of counting numbers: 1, 2, 3, 4, . . .

negative correlation [ne′gə•tiv kôr•e•lā′•shən] **correlación negativa** In a scatterplot, a possible pattern formed from data points that show that the values of one variable increase as the values of the other variable decrease

negative integers [ne′gə•tiv in′ti•jərz] **enteros negativos** Integers to the left of zero on the number line)

net [net] **plantilla** An arrangement of two-dimensional figures that folds to form a polyhedron
Example:

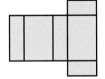

network [net′wûrk] **gráfica de red** A graph with vertices and edges. In a network, a vertex is a point that represents an object. An edge is a connection between vertices.

no correlation [no kôr•e•lā′•shən] **no correlación** In a scatterplot, data points are scattered and no pattern can be formed from the points.

nonagon [no′nə•gän′] **eneágono** A closed plane figure bounded by nine straight lines that form nine interior angles

numerator [nōō′mə•rā•tər] **numerador** The part of a fraction that tells how many parts are being used

numerical expression [nōō•mâr′i•kəl ik•spre′shən] **expresión numérica** A mathematical phrase that uses only numbers and operation symbols

obtuse angle [äb•tōōs′ ang′gəl] **ángulo obtuso** An angle whose measure is greater than 90° and less than 180°

obtuse triangle [äb•tōōs′ trī′ang•gəl] **triángulo obtusángulo** A triangle with one angle greater than 90°
Example:

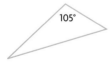

105°

octagon [ok′ta•gän] **octágono** A polygon with 8 sides and 8 angles
Examples:

odds against an event [odz ə•genst′ ən i•vent′] **probabilidades en contra de un suceso** A comparison of the number of unfavorable outcomes to the number of favorable outcomes when all outcomes are equally likely

odds in favor of an event [odz in fā′vər uv ən i•vent′] **probabilidades a favor de un suceso** A comparison of the number of favorable outcomes to the number of unfavorable outcomes when all outcomes are equally likely

odd vertex [od vûr′teks] **vértice impar** In a network, a point where an odd number of edges meet

opposites [ä′pə•zəts] **opuestos** Two numbers that are an equal distance from zero on the number line

ordered pair [ôr′dərd pâr] **par ordenado** A pair of numbers that can be used to locate a point on the coordinate plane
Examples: (0,2), (3,4), (⁻4,5)

order of operations [ôr′dər əv ä•pə•rā′shənz] **orden de las operaciones** The process for evaluating expressions: first perform the operations in parentheses, clear the exponents, perform all multiplication and division, and then perform all addition and subtraction.

origin [ôr′ə•jən] **origen** The point where the x-axis and the y-axis in the coordinate plane intersect, (0,0)

outcome [out′kəm] **resultado** A possible result of a probability experiment

outlier [out′lī•ər] **valor atípico** A value that is very small or very large compared to the majority of the values in a data set

overestimate [ō•vər•es′tə•mət] **sobrestimación** An estimate that is greater than the exact answer

parallel lines [pârʹə•lel līnz] **líneas paralelas**
Lines in a plane that are always the same
distance apart
Example:

parallelogram [pârʹə•le•lə•gram]
paralelogramo A quadrilateral where
opposite sides are parallel and congruent

Example:

parallel planes [pârʹə•lel planz] **planos
paralelos** Planes that are always the same
distance apart

pattern [patʹərn] **patrón** An ordered set of
numbers or objects. The order helps you
predict what will come next.
Examples: 2, 4, 6, 8, 10

pentagon [penʹtə•gän] **pentágono** A polygon
with five sides and five angles
Examples:

percent (%) [pər•sentʹ] **porcentaje** The ratio
of a number to 100; percent means "per
hundred."

perfect number [pûrʹfikt numʹbər] **número
perfecto** A number that is equal to the sum
of its proper divisors

perimeter [pə•riʹmə•tər] **perímetro** The
distance around a figure

permutation [pər•myü•tāʹshən] **permutación** A
selection of different items in which the order
is important

perpendicular bisector [pûr•pen•dikʹyə•lər
bī•sekʹtər] **bisectriz perpendicular** A line that
intersects a line segment at its midpoint and
forms a 90° angle
Example:

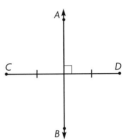

$\overleftrightarrow{AB}$ is a perpendicular bisector of $\overline{CD}$

perpendicular lines [pûr•pen•diʹkyə•lər līnz]
líneas perpendiculares Two lines that
intersect to form right, or 90°, angles
Example:

perpendicular planes [pər•pen•dikʹyə•lər plānz]
planos perpendiculares Two planes that
intersect to form right, or 90°, angles

perspective [pər•spekʹtiv] **perspectiva** A
technique used to make objects that are
drawn on a flat surface appear to be three-
dimensional

pi (ī) [pī] **pi (π)** The area of a unit circle; the ratio
of the circumference of a circle to its diameter;
ī ≈ 3.14 or $\frac{22}{7}$

plane [plān] **plano** A flat surface that extends
without end in all directions

point of rotation [point əv rō•tāʹshən] **punto de
rotación** The central point around which a
figure is rotated

polygon [pä′lē•gän] **polígono** A closed plane figure formed by three or more straight sides that are line segments
Examples:

polygons   not polygons

polyhedron [pä•lē•hē′drən] **poliedro** A solid figure with flat faces that are polygons

population [pä•pyə•lā′shən] **población** The entire group of objects or individuals considered for a survey

positive correlation [pä′zə•tiv kôr•ə•lā′shən] **correlación positiva** When values of two sets of data increase or decrease together

positive integers [pä′zə•tiv in′ti•jərz] **enteros positivos** Integers to the right of zero on the number line

precision [pri•sizh′ən] **precisión** A property of measurement that is related to the unit of measure used; the smaller the unit of measure used, the more precise the measurement. (p. 530)

preimage [prē′i•mij] **preimagen** The original figure in a transformation (p. 492)

prime factorization [prīm fak•tə•ri•zā′shən] **descomposición en factores primos** A number written as the product of all of its prime factors (p. 92)
Example: $24 = 2^3 \times 3$

prime number [prīm num′bər] **número primo** A whole number greater than 1 that has exactly two factors, 1 and itself

principal [prin′sə•pəl] **capital** The amount of money borrowed or saved

prism [priz′əm] **prisma** A solid figure that has two congruent, polygon-shaped bases, and other faces that are all rectangles
Example:

probability [prä•bə•bil′ə•tē] **probabilidad** A measure of the likelihood that an event will occur

product [prä′dəkt] **producto** The answer in a multiplication problem

proper divisors [pro′pər di•vī′zərz] **divisores propios** The divisors of a number except for the number itself

Property of Zero [prä′pər•tē əv zē′rō] **propiedad del cero** The property that states that the product of any number and zero is zero

proportion [prə•pôr′shən] **proporción** An equation that shows that two ratios are equal
Example: $\frac{1}{3} = \frac{3}{9}$

Word History

Proportion comes from the Latin word *proportio,* a translation from the Greek word for *analogy.* Like a proportion in mathematics, an analogy refers to things that share a similar relation.

quadrants [kwäd′rənts] **cuadrantes** The four regions of the coordinate plane

quadrilateral [kwä•drə•lat′ə•rəl] **cuadrilátero** A closed plane figure formed by four straight sides that are connected line segments and has four angles (p. 440)

quotient [kwō′shənt] **cociente** The number, not including the remainder, that results from dividing

radius [rā′dē•əs] **radio** A line segment with one endpoint at the center of a circle and the other endpoint on the circle
Example:

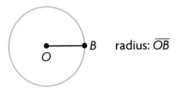

radius: $\overline{OB}$

random sample [ran′dəm sam′pəl] **muestra al azar** A sample in which each subject in the overall population has an equal chance of being selected

range [rānj] **rango** The difference between the greatest and least numbers in a group

rate [rāt] **tasa** A ratio that compares two quantities having different units of measure

ratio [rā′shē•ō] **razón** A comparison of two numbers, a and b, that can be written as a fraction $\frac{a}{b}$ (pp. 110, 620)

rational number [ra′shə•nəl num′bər] **número racional** Any number that can be written as $\frac{a}{b}$ where a and b are integers and $b \neq 0$

ray [rā] **rayo** A part of a line with a single endpoint
Example:

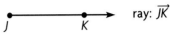

ray: $\overrightarrow{JK}$

reciprocal [ri•sip′rə•kəl] **recíproco** Two numbers are reciprocals of each other if their product equals 1.

rectangle [rek′tan•gəl] **rectángulo** A parallelogram with 4 right angles
Example:

reflection [ri•flek′shən] **reflexión** A movement of a figure by flipping it over a line

regular polygon [reg′yə•lər pä′lē•gän] **polígono regular** A polygon in which all sides are congruent and all angles are congruent

Example:

relative frequency [rel′ə•tiv frē′kwən•sē] **frecuencia relativa** The number of observations in a category divided by the total number of observations

repeating decimal [ri•pēt′ing de′sə•məl] **decimal periódico** A decimal representation of a number that eventually has a repeating pattern that continues forever

rhombus [räm′bəs] **rombo** A parallelogram with four congruent sides
Example:

right angle [rīt ang′gəl] **ángulo recto** An angle which is half of a straight angle with its measurement being 90°
Example:

right prism [rīt priz′əm] **prisma recto** A prism with rectangular lateral faces that are perpendicular to the base

right triangle [rīt trī′ang•gəl] **triángulo rectángulo** A triangle with one right angle

rotation [rō•tā′shən] **rotación** A movement of a figure by turning it around a fixed point

rotational symmetry [rō•tā′shən•əl si′mə•trē] **simetria rotacional** The property of a figure that can be rotated less than 3608 around its center point and still look exactly the same as the original figure

sales tax [sālz taks] **impuesto a las ventas** A percent of the cost of an item, added onto the item's cost

sample [sam′pəl] **muestra** A representative part of a population

sample space [sam′pəl spās] **espacio de muestra** The set of all possible outcomes

sampling method [săm′plĭng mĕth′əd] **método de muestreo** The way in which a sample of a population is selected

scale [skal] **escala** A ratio between two sets of measurements

scale drawing [skal drô′ing] **dibujo a escala** A drawing that shows a real object smaller than (a reduction) or larger than (an enlargement) the real object

scalene triangle [skā′lēn trī′ang•gəl] **triángulo escaleno** A triangle with no congruent sides

Example:

scatterplot [skat′ər•plät] **diagrama de dispersión** A graph with points plotted to show a relationship between two variables

scientific notation [sī′ən•tif ′ik nō•tā′shən] **notación científica** A method of writing very large or very small numbers by using powers of 10 (p. 76)
Examples: $1{,}200{,}000 = 1.2 \times 10^6$
$0.023 = 2.3 \times 10^{-2}$

semicircle [se′mē•sər•kəl] **semicírculo** One-half of a circle

sequence [sē′kwəns] **secuencia** An ordered set of numbers

similar figures [si′mə•lər fig′yərz] **figuras semejantes** Figures with the same shape but not necessarily the same size

simple interest [sim′pəl in′trəst] **interés simple** A fixed percent of the principal, paid yearly

simplest form [sim′pləst fôrm] **mínima expresión** The form in which the numerator and denominator of a fraction have no common factors other than 1

simulation [sim•yə′lā•shən] **simulación** A model of an experiment that would be too difficult or too time-consuming to actually perform

skew lines [skyōo līnz] **rectas alabeadas** Lines that are not in the same plane, are not parallel, and do not intersect

solution [sə•lōō′shən] **solución** A value that, when substituted for a variable in an equation, makes the equation true

square [skwâr] **cuadrado** A rectangle with four congruent sides
Example:

square [skwâr] **cuadrado** The product of a number and itself; a number with an exponent of 2

stem-and-leaf plot [stem ənd lēf plät] **diagrama de tallo y hojas** A type of graph that shows groups of data arranged by place value

straight angle [strāt ang′gəl] **ángulo llano** An angle whose measure is 180°
Example:

Subtraction Property of Equality [sub•trak′shən prä′pər•tē əv i•kwol′ə•tē] **propiedad de resta de la igualdad** The property that states that if you subtract the same number from both sides of an equation, the sides remain equal

sum [sum] **suma o total** The answer to an addition problem

Word History

The ancient Greeks and Romans added columns of numbers from the bottom to the top. They wrote the answer or **sum** at the top. The words **sum** and *summit* are from the Latin root *summus,* which means "highest."

supplementary angles [sup•lə•men′tə•rē ang′gəlz] **ángulos suplementarios** Two angles whose measures have a sum of 180°

Example:

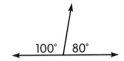

surface area [sûr′fəs âr′ē•ə] **área total** The sum of the areas of the separate surfaces of a solid figure

survey [sûr′vā] **encuesta** A method of gathering information about a population

systematic sample [sis•tem′ik sam′pəl] **muestra sistemática** A sample of a population that has been selected using a pattern (p. 208)
Example:

Systematic Sample	
23d: Bill	53d: Chelsea
33d: Joyce	63d: Mary
43d: Atkin	73d: Brad

term [tûrm] **término** Each number in a sequence

terminating decimal [tûr′mə•nāt•ing de′sə•məl] **decimal exacto** A decimal representation of a number that eventually ends

terms [tûrmz] **términos** The parts of an expression that are separated by an addition or subtraction sign

theoretical probability [thē•ə•re′ti•kəl prä•bə•bil′ə•tē] **probabilidad teórica** A comparison of the number of favorable outcomes to the number of possible equally likely outcomes

transformation [trans•fər′mā′shən] **transformación** The moving of a figure by a translation, reflection, or rotation

translation [trans•lā′shən] **traslación** A movement of a figure along a straight line

transversal [trans•vûr′səl] **línea transversal** A line that crosses two or more lines

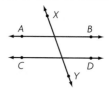

$\overleftrightarrow{XY}$ **is a transversal.**

trapezoid [tra′pə•zoid] **trapecio** A quadrilateral with exactly two parallel sides
Examples:

tree diagram [trē dī′ə•gram] **diagrama de árbol** A diagram that shows all possible outcomes of an event

triangle inequality [tri′ang•gəl in′i•kwä′lə•tē] **desigualdad triangular** The sum of the lengths of any two sides of a triangle is greater than the length of the third side (p. 442)

triangular number [tri′ang′gyə•lər num′bər] **número triangular** A number that can be represented by a triangular array
Example:

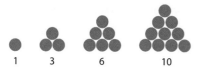

1   3   6   10

underestimate [un•dər•es′tə•mət] **subestimación** An estimate that is less than the exact answer

unit fraction [yōō′nət frak′shən] **fracción unitaria** A fraction with 1 in the numerator

unit rate [yōō′nət rāt] **tasa por unidad** A rate expressed so that the second term in the ratio is one unit
Example: 55 mi per hr

unlike fractions [un′līk frak′shənz] **fracciones no semejantes** Fractions with different denominators

upper extreme [up′ər ik•strēm′] **extremo superior** The greatest number in a set of data

upper quartile [up′ər kwôr′tīl] **tercer cuartil** The median of the upper half of a set of data

variable [vâr′ē•ə•bəl] **variable** A letter or symbol that stands for one or more numbers

Venn diagram [ven dī′ə•gram] **diagrama de Venn** A diagram that shows relationships

vertex [vûr′teks] **vértice** The point where two or more rays meet; the point of intersection of two sides of a polygon; the point of intersection of three or more edges of a solid figure; the top point of a cone

Examples:

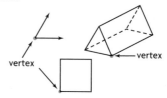

vertex   vertex

vertex [vûr′teks] **nodo** In a network, a point that represents a location

vertical angles [vûr′ti•kəl ang•gəlz] **ángulos verticales** A pair of opposite congruent angles formed where two lines intersect

Example:

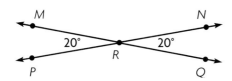

∠MRP and ∠NRQ are vertical angles.

volume [väl′yəm] **volumen** The number of cubic units needed to occupy a given space

whole number [hōl num′bər] **número entero** One of the numbers 0, 1, 2, 3, 4, ... The set of whole numbers goes on without end.

x*-axis** [eks′ak•səs] **eje de la *x The horizontal number line on a coordinate plane

x*-coordinate** [eks•kō•ôrd′ə•nət] **coordenada *x The first number in an ordered pair. It tells the distance to move right or left from (0,0).

y*-axis** [wī′ak•səs] **eje de la *y The vertical number line on a coordinate plane

y*-coordinate** [wī•kō•ôrd′ə•nət] **coordenada *y The second number in an ordered pair. It tells the distance to move up or down from (0,0).

Zero Property of Multiplication [zē′rō prä′pər•tē əv mul•tə•plə•kā′shən] **propiedad del cero de la multiplicación** The property that states that the product of any number and zero is zero

Index

A

Activities. *See also* Practice
Get Ready Game, 2, 76, 176, 284, 376
Hands On
  add and subtract fractions, 124–127
  algebra
    find circumference, 326–329
    ratios and similar figures, 368–371
    scale drawings, 376–379
    write and solve proportions, 364–367
  area of circles, 330–331
  circles, 320–323
  compare measurements, 340–341
  divide fractions and mixed numbers, 158–161
  divisibility, 80–83
  division of fractions, 146–149
  division with decimals, 56–57, 58–61
  equivalent fractions and simplest form, 94–97
  estimate area, 330–331
  estimate circumference, 324–325
  explore division of fractions, 148–151
  explore division with decimals, 56–57
  fractions, decimals, and percents, 104–105
  models of solid figures, 308–309
  multiply fractions, 142–145
  understand fractions, 92–93
  views of solid figures, 304–307
Math on Location, 1, 75, 175, 283, 375
Solve Multistep Problems, 27, 67, 115, 167, 219, 253, 275, 315, 347, 401, 453, 489
Unit Projects, 71, 171, 279, 351, 493
World Almanac, 72–73, 172–173, 280–281, 352–353, 494–495
Addition
decimals, 40–43, H8

equations, 234–235
  solving, 240–241
estimating sums, 120–123
fractions, 124–127
integers, 184–187
mixed numbers, 128–131
practice, 136–139
sums
  estimating, 120–123
whole numbers, 8–9
Algebra. *See also* Equations
algebraic expressions, 224–227, 228–231, H16
area
  of circles, 332–333
circumference, find, 326–329
customary measurements, 336–337
exponents, 16–19
metric measurement, 338–339
number properties, 22–23
order of operations, 20–21
ratios and similar figures, 368–371
scale drawings, 376–379
write and solve proportions, 364–367
Analyze data, H24–H25
Approximation. *See* Estimation
Area
circles, 330–331, 332–333, H23
Assessment
Performance Assessment, 70, 170, 278, 350, 492
Show What You Know, 5, 31, 79, 119, 179, 223, 257, 287, 319, 359, 405, 457

B

Bar graphs, 424–425
Basic Facts, H36–H39

C

Choose a Method, 62–63
Choose an Appropriate Graph, 440–443
Choose the Operation, 162–163
Circle graphs, 428–429, H28
Circles. *See also* Circumference
area, 330–331, 332–333, H23
understanding, 320–323
Circumference
estimating, 324–325
finding, 326–329, H22
Combinations
probability, 482–485, H31
Compare and order fractions
decimals and mixed numbers, H4
Compare Strategies, 238–239, 342–343
Comparison
Compare Strategies, 238–239, 342–343
decimals, 106–109
fractions, 106–109
graphs, 438–439
percents, 106–109
rational numbers, 210–211, H2
Complementary angles, 320–321
Compound event outcomes, 472–475
Congruent figures, H20
Coordinate plane
graph on, 288–291
Customary measurement, 336–337

D

Data, analyze, H24–H25
Data and statistics
Draw Conclusions, 444–445
frequency tables, 414–417, H27
line plots, 414–417
make and analyze, in graphs, 430–433
mean, 406–409, H30

median, 406–409, H30
mode, 406–409, H30
outliers, 410–413
range, 406–409, H30
samples, 418–419
surveys, 418–419
unknown values, finding, 446–449

Decimals
addition, 40–43
comparing, 106–109, H4
division, 56–57, 58–61, H11
by whole numbers, 52–55
estimating with, 32–35
fractions, relationship to, 100–103,
104–107, 106–109, 384–387, H3
multiplication, 40–43, H10
multiply, 40–43
ordering, H4
percents, relationship to, 104–105,
106–109, 384–387, H3
renaming
fractions as, 100–103, 104–105
subtraction, 36–39

Dependent events, 476–477,
478–479

Diagrams
Draw a Diagram, 420–423

Difference
estimating, 120–123

Differentiated Instruction
Get Ready Game, 2, 76, 176, 284,
376
Show What You Know, 5, 31, 79,
119, 179, 223, 257, 387, 319, 359,
405, 457

Discount, as percent, 460–463

Divisibility, 80–83

Division
with decimals, 56–57, 58–61, H11
by whole numbers, 52–55
Distributive Property in, 22–23,
212–215
equations, solving, 246–249
estimating, quotients, 140–141
fractions, 148–151, 158–161, H13
integers, 196–197, H9
mixed numbers, 158–161, H13
quotients, estimating, 140–141
remainders, 14–15
whole numbers, 10–13

Double-bar graphs, H29

Draw a Diagram, 420–423

Draw Conclusions, 444–445

Drawing
Draw a Diagram, 420–423
scale drawings, 376–379

Elapsed time, 334–335

Equations
addition, 234–235, 240–241
division, 246–247
graphing linear equations,
292–295
linear, 292–295
multiplication, 242–245
order of operations, 20–21
solving equations
addition, 234–235
division, 246–247
multiplication, 242–245
practice, 248–249
Student Handbook, H14
subtraction, 236–237
subtraction, 236–237, 240–241
words in, 232–233
Write an Equation, 372–375

Equivalent fractions
simplest form, 94–97

Estimation
addition, 120–123
decimals, 32–35
differences, 120–123
discounts, 394–397
division, 140–141
predictions, 468–469
probability, 466–467
products, 140–141
quotients, in division, 140–141
sales tax, 394–397
subtraction, 120–123
sums, 120–123

Evaluation
of algebraic expressions, 228–231,
H16

Events and probability
compound event outcomes,
472–475
dependent, 476–477, 478–479
independent, 476–477, 478–479

Experimental Probability, 462–465

Explore
division
of decimals, 52–53
of fractions, 148–151
independent and dependent
events, 476–477

Exponents, 16–19, H5

Expressions, algebraic, 224–227,
228–231, H16

Experimental probability, 462–465

Extra Practice, 24–25, 64–65,
112–113, 164–165, 216–217,
250–251, 272–273, 312–313,
344–345, 398–399, 450–451,
486–487

Factorization, prime, 86–87

Factors
greatest common factor (GCF),
88–917, 94–97, H6

Figures. *See* Geometry and
geometric figures
congruent, similar and, 296–299,
H20
models of solid, 308–309
similar and congruent, 296–299,
H20
solid, types of, 300–303
solid, views of, 304–307
types of solid, 300–303
views of solid, 304–307

Fractions
addition, 124–127
comparing, 106–109
decimals, relationship to, 100–103
104–105, 106–109, 384–387, H3
divisibility, 80–83
division, 148–151, 158–161, H13
equivalent, and simplest form,
94–97
greatest common factor (GCF),
88–91, 94–97, H6
least common multiple (LCM),
88–91, 94–97, H7
in mixed numbers, 98–99
multiplication, 142–145, H12
percents, relationship to, 104–105,
106–109, H3

prime factorization, 86–87
reciprocals, 152–153, 154–157
remainders, 14–15
renaming
    decimals as, 100–103, 104–105
    mixed numbers, 98–99
subtraction, 124–127
understand, 92–93
Frequency tables, 414–417, H27
Functions
of numbers, 262–265

GCF (greatest common factor), 88–91, 94–97, H6
Geometric patterns, 266–267
Geometry and geometric figures.
    See also Three-dimensional figures;
    Two-dimensional figures
    area
        circles, 330–331, 332–333, H23
    polygons
        construct a scale, 376–379
Get Ready Games, 2, 76, 176, 284, 376
Glossary, GL1–GL18
Graphic organizers. *See* Diagrams; Tables
Graphs and graphing
    bar graphs, 424–425
    Choose an Appropriate Graph, 440–443
    circle graphs, 428–429, H28
    comparing, 438–439
    coordinate plane
        graphing on, 288–291
        transformation on, 374–377
    double-bar graphs, H29
    frequency tables, 414–417, H27
    functions of, 286–287
    histograms, 434–437
    line graphs, 426–427
    line plots, 414–417
    linear equations, 292–295
    Make a Graph, 294–297
    make and analyze, 430–433
    mean, 406–409, H30
    median, 406–409, H30
    mode, 406–409, H30
    outliers, 410–413

plotting ordered pairs, H21
range, H30
stem-and-leaf plots, 434–437, H26
Use a Graph, 392–393
Greatest common factor (GCF), 88–91, 94–97, H6

Handbook, Student. *See* Student Handbook
Hands On
    add and subtract fractions, 124–127
    algebra
        find circumference, 326–329
        ratios and similar figures, 368–371
        scale drawings, 376–379
        write and solve proportions, 364–367
    area of circles, 326–327
    circles, 390–393
    compare measurements, 340–341
    divide fractions and mixed numbers, 158–161
    divisibility, 80–83
    division of fractions, 148–151
    division with decimals, 56–57, 58–61
    equivalent fractions and simplest form, 94–97
    estimate circumference, 324–325
    explore
        division of fractions, 148–151
        division with decimals, 56–57
    fractions, decimals, and percents, 104–105
    model of solid figures, 308–309
    multiply fractions, 142–145
Histograms, 434–437, H27

Independent events, 467–468, 478–479
Inequalities
    on a number line, 278–281, H18

Integers
    add and subtract, H8
    addition, 184–187, H8
    division, 196–197, H9
    divide, multiply and, H9
    multiplication, 193–197, H9
    multiply, and divide, H9
    operations with, 198–201, H7
    subtraction, 188–191, H8
    understanding, 180–183
Intervention
    Show What You Know, 5, 31, 79, 119, 179, 223, 257, 287, 319, 359, 405, 457

Least common multiple (LCM), 88–91, 94–97, H7
Line graphs, 426–427
Line plots, 414–417
Linear equations, graphing, 292–295
Lists
    combinations and permutations, 482–485
    Make an Organized List, 470–471

Make a Generalization, 310–311
Make a Table, 44–47
Make an Organized List, 470–471
Make Predictions, 468–469
Math on Location, 1, 75, 175, 283, 375
Mean, 406–409, H30
Measurement
    area
        circles, 330–331, 332–333, H23
    customary, 336–337
    metric, 338–339
    Table of Measures, TM1–TM2
Median, 406–409, H30
Metric measurement, 338–339
Mixed numbers
    addition, 128–131
    compare, H4
    division, 158–161, H13

Index

fractions in, 98–99
multiplication, 146–147, H12
order, H4
subtraction, 128–131
Mode, 406–409, H30
Multiples
  least common multiple (LCM),
    88–91, 94–97, H7
Multiplication
  decimals, 40–43, H10
  equations, solving, 242–245
  estimating, products, 140–141
  exponents, 16–19, H5
  fractions, 142–145, H12
  integers, 191–193, H8
  mixed numbers, 142–145, H12
  products, estimating, 140–141
  whole numbers, 10–13
Multistep Problems, 27, 67, 115,
  167, 219, 253, 275, 315, 347, 401,
  453, 489

N

Number properties, 38–39
Numbers. *See also* specific numbers
  functions, 262–265, H19
  integers
    addition, 184–187
    division, 196–197
    multiplication, 192–195
    operations with, 198–201
    subtraction, 188–191
    understanding, 180–183
  mixed
    addition, 128–131
    fractions in, 98–99
    subtraction, 128–131
  patterns, 262–265, H19
  percent of, 388–391, H17
  prime, 84–85
  rational
    comparing and ordering, H2
    ordering, 210–211, H2
    properties, 212–215
    understanding, 206–209
  whole
    addition, 8–9
    division, 10–13
    of decimals by whole numbers,
      48–51

multiplication, 10–13
place value, 6–7
subtraction, 8–9
Number properties
  Associative, 22–23, 212–215
  Commutative (Order), 22–23,
    212–215
  Distributive Property, 22–23,
    212–215
  expressions, 22–23

  Identity Property, 22–23,
    212–215
  rational numbers, 212–215
Number theory. See also Algebra
  divisibility, 80–83
  exponents, 16–19, H5
  expressions, algebraic, 224–227,
    228–231, H16
  integers
    addition, 184–187
    division, 196–197
    multiplication, 192–195
    operations with, 198–201,
      H7
    subtraction, 188–191
    understanding, 180–183
  prime numbers, 84–85

O

OCCT
  Practice for the OCCT, 28–29,
    68–69, 116–117, 164–165,
    216–217, 250–251, 272–273,
    312–313, 344–345, 398–399,
    450–451, 486–487
  OCCT Taking Taking Strategies,
    H32–H35
Oklahoma
  Practice for the OCCT, 28–29,
    68–69, 116–117, 168–169,
    220–221, 254–255, 276–277,
    316–317, 348–349, 402–403,
    454–455, 490–491
  OCCT Taking Taking Strategies,
    H32–H35
Operations. *See also* specific
  operations
  Basic Facts, H36–H39
  Choose a Method, 62–63

with integers, 198–201, H7
order of operations, 20–21
Order of operations, 20–21
Ordered pairs, H21
Ordering
  fractions, decimals, and percents,
    106–109
  rational numbers, 210–211, H2
Organization
  Make an Organized List, 470–471
Outcome of compound events,
  472–475
Outliers, 410–413

P

Parentheses
  in order of operations, 20–21
Patterns
  extending, to nth term, 268–271
  geometric, 266–267
  in sequences, 258–261
Percents
  comparing, 106–109
  decimals, relationships to,
    104–105, 106–109, 384–387, H3
  discount, 394–397
  fractions, relationship to, 104–105,
    106–109, H3
  of a number, 388–391, H17
  sales tax, 394–397
  understanding, 382–383
Performance Assessment, 70, 170,
  278, 350, 492
Permutations in probability,
  482–485
Place value
  whole numbers, 6–7
  decimals, 32–35
Plane figures
  area
    circles, 330–331, 332–333, H23
  polygons
    construct a scale, 376–379
Polygons
  construct a scale, 376–379
Polyhedra. *See* Three-dimensional
  figures
Practice. *See also* Activities
  addition, 136–139
  Extra Practice, 24–25, 64–65,

112–113, 164–165, 216–217, 250–251, 272–273, 312–313, 344–345, 398–399, 450–451, 486–487

Get Ready Games, 2, 76, 176, 284, 376

Practice for the OCCT, 28–29, 68–69, 116–117, 168–169, 220–221, 254–255, 276–277, 316–317, 348–349, 402–403, 454–455, 490–491

solving equations, 248–249

subtraction, 136–139

Predict and Test, 202–205

Predictions

Make Predictions, 468–469

making, and probability, 468–469

Predict and Test, 202–205

Prime factorization, 86–87

Prime numbers, 84–85

Prior Knowledge

Show What You Know, 5, 31, 79, 119, 179, 223, 257, 287, 319, 359, 405, 457

Probability

combinations, 482–485

estimating, 466–467

events

compound event outcomes, 472–475

dependent, 476–477, 478–479

independent, 476–477, 478–479

experimental, 462–465

making predictions, 468–469

permutations, 482–485

theoretical, 458–461

Problem solving applications

Multistep Problems, 27, 67, 115, 167, 219, 253, 275, 315, 347, 401, 453, 489

Problem solving strategies

Choose a Method, 62–63

Choose an Appropriate Graph, 440–443

division, interpret the remainder, 14–15

Make a Table, 48–51

Solve a Simpler Problem, 268–271

Problem Solving Workshop Skill

Choose the Operation, 162–163

Draw Conclusions, 444–445

Interpret the Remainder, 14–15

make generalizations, 310–311

multistep problems, 134–135

Use a Graph, 392–393

Use a Table, 110–111

Problem Solving Workshop Strategy

Compare Strategies, 238–239, 342–343

Draw a Diagram, 420–423

Make a Table, 48–51

Make an Organized List, 470–471

Predict and Test, 202–205

Solve a Simpler Problem, 268–271

Write an Equation, 372–375

Products

estimating, 140–141

Properties

of numbers, in algebra, 22–23

of rational numbers, 212–215

Proportions

proportional reasoning, 380–381

write and solve, 364–367, H15

Quotients

estimating, 140–141

Radius, and area of circles, 330–331, 332–333, H23

Range, 406–409, H30

Rates

and ratios, 360–363

Rational numbers

comparing, 210–211, H2

ordering, 210–211, H2

properties, 212–215

understanding, 206–209

Ratios

proportions

proportional reasoning, 380–381

write and solve, 364–367, H15

and rates, 360–363

and similar figures, 368–371

Reading and reading skills

Draw a Diagram, 420–423

Draw Conclusions, 444–445

Reading and Writing Math, 3, 26, 66, 114, 166, 218, 252, 274, 314, 346, 400, 452, 488

Reading and Writing Math, 3, 26, 66, 114, 166, 218, 252, 274, 314, 346, 400, 452, 488

Reasoning

proportional reasoning, 380–381

Reciprocals, 152–153, 154–157

Recording

subtraction with renaming, 132–133

Relationships, mathematical

decimals

to fractions, 100–103, 104–105, 106–109, 384–387, H3

to percents, 104–105, 106–109, 384–387, H3

fractions

to decimals, 100–103, 104–105, 106–109, 384–387, H3

and mixed numbers, 98–99

to percents, 104–105, 106–109, H3

percent

to decimals, 104–105, 106–109, 384–387, H3

to fractions, 104–105, 106–109, H3

Remainders

interpreting, 14–15

Renaming

fractions

as decimals, 100–103, 104–105

as mixed numbers, 98–99

subtraction with, 132–133

Review and test

Practice for the OCCT, 28–29, 68–69, 116–117, 168–169, 220–221, 254–255, 276–277, 316–317, 348–349, 402–403, 454–455, 490–491

Predict and Test, 202–205

Show What You Know, 5, 31, 79, 119, 179, 223, 257, 287, 319, 359, 405, 457

OCCT Test-Taking Strategies, H32–H35

S

Sales tax, as percent, 394–397
Samples, 418–419
Scale drawings, 376–379
Sequences
    patterns in, 258–261
Shapes. *See* Geometry and
    geometric figures
Show What You Know, 5, 31, 79,
    119, 179, 223, 257, 287, 319, 359,
    405, 457

Simplest form, equivalent fractions,
    94–97
Solve a Simpler Problem, 268–271
Statistics. *See* Data and statistics
Stem-and-leaf plots, 434–437, H25
Strategies. *See* Problem solving
    strategies
Student Handbook, H1–H41
    add and subtract integers, H8
    analyze data, H24–H25
    area of circles, H23
    Basic Facts, BF1–BF4
    circle graphs, H28
    circumference, H22
    combinations, H31
    congruent figures, H20
    divide decimals, H11
    divide fractions and mixed
        numbers, H13
    double bar graphs, H29
    evaluate algebraic expressions,
        H16
    exponents, H5
    fractions, decimals, and percents,
        H3
    frequency tables, H27
    glossary, H42–H57
    greatest common factor (GCF), H6
    Handbook Review, H1
    inequalities, H18
    least common multiple (LCM), H7
    mean, median, mode, and range,
        H30
    multiply and divide integers, H9
    multiply decimals, H8
    multiply fractions and mixed
        numbers, H12
    number patterns and functions,
        H19

    OCCT Test-Taking Strategies,
        H32–H35
    ordered pairs, H21
    percent of a number, H17
    rational numbers, comparing and
        ordering, H2
    solve equations, H14
    stem-and-leaf plots, H26
    Table of Measures, TM1–TM2
    write and solve proportions, H15
Subtraction
    decimals, 36–39
    differences, estimating, 120–123
    equations, 240–241
        solving, 236–237
    estimating differences, 120–123
    fractions, 124–127
    integers, 188–191, H8
    mixed numbers, 128–131
    practice, 136–139
    with renaming, 132–133
    whole numbers, 8–9
Sums
    estimating, 120–123
Surveys, 418–419

Table of Measures, TM1–TM2
Tables
    frequency tables, 414–417, H27
    Make a Table, 44–47
    Table of Measures, H40–H41
    Use a Table, 110–111
Theoretical probability, 458–611
Time, elapsed 334–335
Two-dimensional figures
    polygons
        construct a scale, 376–379

Unknown values
    finding, 446–449
Use a Graph, 392–393
Use a Table, 110–111
Use Reciprocals, 154–157

Whole numbers
    addition, 8–9
    division, 10–13
    of decimals by whole numbers,
        52–55
    multiplication, 10–13
    place value, 6–7
    subtraction, 8–9
Words in equations, 232–233
World Almanac, 72–73, 172–173,
    280–281, 352–353, 494–495
Write an Equation, 372–375
Writing and writing skills
    algebraic expressions, 224–227
    proportions, 364–367, H15
    Reading and Writing Math, 3, 26,
        66, 114, 166, 218, 252, 274, 314,
        346, 400, 452
    Write an Equation, 372–375

Index